Looking at Movies

Second Edition

W. W. NORTON & COMPANY
NEW YORK • LONDON

RICHARD BARSAM

Looking at Movies
An Introduction to Film

Second Edition

W. W. Norton & Company has been independent since its founding in 1923, when William Warder Norton and Mary D. Herter Norton first published lectures delivered at the People's Institute, the adult education division of New York City's Cooper Union. The Nortons soon expanded their program beyond the Institute, publishing books by celebrated academics from America and abroad. By mid-century, the two major pillars of Norton's publishing program—trade books and college texts—were firmly established. In the 1950s, the Norton family transferred control of the company to its employees, and today with a staff of four hundred and a comparable number of trade, college, and professional titles published each year W. W. Norton & Company stands as the largest and oldest publishing house owned wholly by its employees.

Editor: Peter Simon
Project Editor: Thomas Foley
Production Manager: Benjamin Reynolds
Copy Editor: Stephanie Hiebert
Electronic Media Editor: Eileen Connell
Managing Editor, College: Marian Johnson
Assistant Editor: Birgit Larsson
Art Director: Rubina Yeh
Cover and Text Designer: Lissi Sigillo
Indexer: Cohen and Carruth, Inc.

Developmental Editor for the First Edition: Kurt Wildermuth
Contributing Consultant: Dave Monahan
Author photograph taken by Michael Schmelling

The text of this book is composed in Benton Modern Two.
Page layout by Carole Desnoes.
Composition by GGS Book Services.
Digital art file manipulation by Jay's Publishers Services.
Drawn art by ElectraGraphics, Inc.
Manufacturing by VonHoffmann.

Library of Congress Cataloging-in-Publication Data

Barsam, Richard Meran.
    Looking at movies : an introduction to film / Richard Barsam—2nd ed.
        p. cm.
    Includes bibliographical references and index.

    ISBN 13: 978-0-393-92865-5 (pbk.)
    ISBN 10: 0-393-92865-9 (pbk.)

    1. Motion pictures. 2. Cinematography. I. Title.
PN1994.B313 2006
791.42—dc22

                            2006046643

W. W. Norton & Company, Inc., 500 Fifth Avenue, New York, N.Y. 10110
                    www.wwnorton.com

W. W. Norton & Company Ltd., Castle House, 75/76 Wells Street, London W1T 3QT

2 3 4 5 6 7 8 9 0

About the Author

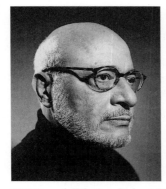

RICHARD BARSAM (Ph.D., University of Southern California) is Professor Emeritus of Film Studies at Hunter College. He is the author of *Nonfiction Film: A Critical History* (rev., exp. ed. 1992), *The Vision of Robert Flaherty: The Artist as Myth and Filmmaker* (1988), *In the Dark: A Primer for the Movies* (1977), and *Filmguide to "Triumph of the Will"* (1975); editor of *Nonfiction Film Theory and Criticism* (1976); and contributing author to Paul Monaco's *The Sixties: 1960–1969* (Vol. 8, *History of the American Cinema*, 2001) and *Filming Robert Flaherty's "Louisiana Story": The Helen Van Dongen Diary* (ed. Eva Orbanz, 1998). His articles and book reviews have appeared in *Cinema Journal*, *Quarterly Review of Film Studies*, *Film Comment*, *Studies in Visual Communication*, and *Harper's*. He has been a member of the Executive Council of the Society for Cinema and Media Studies, the Editorial Board of *Cinema Journal*, and the Board of Advisers of the *History of American Cinema* series, and he cofounded the journal *Persistence of Vision*.

Contents

CHAPTER 2 **Narrative** 53

CHAPTER 8 Thinking About Movies, Theory, and Meaning 315

To Students

In 1936, the art historian Erwin Panofsky had an insight into the movies as a form of popular art—an observation that is more true today than it was when he wrote it:

> If all the serious lyrical poets, composers, painters and sculptors were forced by law to stop their activities, a rather small fraction of the general public would become aware of the fact and a still smaller fraction would seriously regret it. If the same thing were to happen with the movies the social consequences would be catastrophic.[1]

Decades later, we would hardly know what to do without movies. They are a major presence in our lives and, like personal computers, perhaps one of the most influential products of our technological age. In fact, some commentators feel that movies are too popular, too influential, too much a part of our lives. Since their invention a little more than a hundred years ago, movies have become one of the world's largest industries and the most powerful art form of our time.

A source of entertainment that makes us see beyond the borders of our previous experience, movies have always possessed powers to amaze, frighten, and enlighten us. They challenge our senses, emotions, and intellects, pushing us to say, often passionately, that we *love* (or *hate*) them. Because they arouse our most public and private feelings—and can overwhelm us with their sights and sounds—it's easy to be excited by movies. The challenge is to join that enthusiasm with understanding, to say *why* we feel so strongly about particular movies. That's one reason why this book encourages you to go beyond movies' stories, to understand how those stories are told. Movies are not reality, after all—only illusions of reality—and (as with most works of art) their form and content work as an interrelated system, one that asks us to accept it as a given rather than as the product of a process. But as you read this book devoted to *looking* at movies—that is, not just passively watching them, but actively considering the relation of their form and their content—remember that there is no one way to look at any film, no one critical perspective that is inherently better than another, no one meaning that you can insist on after a single screening. Indeed, movies are so diverse in their nature that no single approach could ever do them justice.

This is not a book on film history, but it includes relevant historical information and covers a broad range of movies; not a book on theory, but it introduces some of the most essential approaches to interpreting movies; not a book about filmmaking, but one that explains production processes, equipment, and techniques; not a book of criticism, but one that shows you how to think and write about the films you study in your classes.

Everything we see on the movie screen—everything that engages our senses, emotions, and

[1] Erwin Panofsky, "Style and Medium in the Motion Pictures," in *Film Theory and Criticism: Introductory Readings*, 5th ed., ed. Leo Braudy and Marshall Cohen (New York: Oxford University Press, 1999), 280.

minds—results from hundreds of decisions affecting the interrelation of formal cinematic elements: narrative, composition, design, cinematography, acting, editing, and sound. Organized around chapters devoted to those formal elements, this book encourages you to look at movies with an understanding and appreciation of how filmmakers make the decisions that help them tell a story and create the foundation for its meaning. After all, in the real life of the movies, on the screen, it is not historians, theorists, or critics—important and valuable as their work is—but filmmakers who continually shape and revise our understanding and appreciation of film art.

The second century of movie history is well under way, and as I write, the entire process of making, exhibiting, and archiving movies is fast becoming a digital enterprise, especially outside of the mainstream industry. As the technology for making movies continues to evolve, however, the principles of film art covered in this book remain essentially the same. The things you learn about these principles and the analytic skills you hone as you read this book will help you look at motion pictures intelligently and perceptively throughout your life, no matter which medium delivers those pictures to you.

— Richard Barsam

Features of the Book

Students in an introductory film course who read *Looking at Movies* carefully and take full advantage of the support materials surrounding the text will finish the course with a solid grounding in the major principles of film form as well as a more perceptive and analytic eye. A short description of the book's main features follows.

A Focus on Analytic Skills

A good introductory film book needs to help students make the transition from the natural enjoyment of movies to a critical understanding—expressed in analytic writing—of the form, content, and meaning(s) of movies. *Looking at Movies* accomplishes the task by providing a variety of approaches and resources.

Model Analyses

Hundreds of illustrative examples and analytic readings of film form throughout the book provide students with concrete models for their own analytic work. In addition to providing dozens of new examples, the Second Edition has been revised to make sample analyses more concise and focused. Longer sample analyses are available on the *Looking at Movies* website, at wwnorton.com/movies.

New "Screening Checklists"

Each chapter ends with an "Analyzing" section that includes a new "Screening Checklist" feature. This series of leading questions prompts students to apply what they've learned in the chapter to their own critical viewing, in class or at home. Downloadable versions of these checklists are available on the *Looking at Movies* website, at wwnorton.com/movies.

New Chapter: "Thinking About Movies, Theory, and Meaning"

Chapter 8 expands on the previous edition's coverage of film theory, including more material on key theories, more "applied readings," more information on genre study and film history, and an end-of-chapter "Analyzing Movies" summary that helps students begin to apply theory to their own analytic work.

New DVD Tutorials

A special icon in the text— **⊙ DVD**—links to short tutorials on the supplemental DVD that elaborate on or illustrate key concepts in the text, thus *showing* students how to look at movies analytically. These DVD tutorials were specifically produced for, and are exclusive to, *Looking at Movies*, Second Edition.

New Supplement: "Writing About Movies"

Written by Karen Gocsik (Executive Director of the Writing Program at Dartmouth College) and Richard Barsam, "Writing About Movies" is a short, clear, and practical overview of the process of writing papers for film studies courses. This supplement is packaged free of charge with every new copy of *Looking at Movies*, Second Edition, and is also available on the *Looking at Movies* website, at wwnorton.com/movies.

The Most Visually Dynamic Text Available

Looking at Movies was written with one goal in mind: to prepare students for a lifetime of intelligent and perceptive viewing of motion pictures. Much of that preparation will happen through words, so *Looking at Movies* is clear, direct, and enjoyable to read. But in recognition of the central role played by visuals in the film studies classroom, *Looking at Movies* includes an illustration program that is both visually appealing and pedagogically focused, as well as accompanying moving-image media that are second to none.

Hundreds of In-Text Illustrations

The text is accompanied by over six hundred illustrations, in color and black and white. Nearly all the still pictures were captured from digital or analog sources, thus ensuring that the images directly reflect the textual discussions and the films from which they're taken. Unlike publicity stills, which are attractive as photographs but almost useless as teaching aids, the captured stills throughout this book provide visual information that will help students learn as they read and—because they are reproduced in the aspect ratio of the original source—will serve as accurate reference points for students' analysis.

Nearly Four Hours of Moving-Image Media

Two DVDs are packaged with every new copy of *Looking at Movies*, Second Edition. These DVDs offer nearly four hours of two different types of content:

1. On Disc 1 are twenty tutorials, totaling more than two hours altogether, that elaborate on or illustrate key concepts in the text. Produced, scripted, directed, and edited by Professor Dave Monahan at the University of North Carolina, Wilmington, with the extensive support and assistance of his colleagues and students, these DVD tutorials were specifically created to complement *Looking at Movies*, Second Edition, and they are exclusive to this text. The tutorials guide students' eyes to *see* what the text can only *describe*, and because they are presented in full-screen format, they are suitable for presentation in class as "lecture launchers," as well as for students' self-study.

2. On Disc 2, we offer a mini-anthology of twelve complete short films ranging from five minutes to half an hour in length. These short films are accomplished and entertaining examples of the form, as well as useful material for short in-class activities or for students' analysis. Most of the films are also accompanied by optional audio commentary from the directors. This commentary was recorded specifically for *Looking at Movies*, Second Edition.

Multimedia Essays Online

Throughout the text, opportunities for further exploration of various topics are signaled by a special icon— **WEB** —that points students to the *Looking at Movies* website, where they will find a short illustrated essay on the topic. These twenty-five essays extend the reach of *Looking at Movies* considerably, and they provide cinephiles with plenty of extra material to savor and learn from. The essays can be found on the *Looking at Movies* website at wwnorton.com/movies.

Streamlined Presentation; Improved Pedagogy

Looking at Movies, Second Edition, has been revised to be even clearer and more direct in its presentation of key terms and concepts than the first edition. Terms are defined earlier in each chapter, new pedagogical elements have been added, and several chapters have been reorganized and shortened to be as clear and direct in their presentation as possible. The following sections describe the highlights of the text's improved pedagogy.

New Learning Objectives

A checklist at the beginning of every chapter provides students with a brief summary of the core concepts to be covered in the chapter.

Extensive Captions

As in the previous edition, each illustration in *Looking at Movies*, Second Edition, is accompanied by a caption that elaborates on a key concept or that guides students to look at elements of the film more analytically. These captions expand on the in-text presentation and reinforce students' retention of key concepts.

Questions for Review

Review questions at the end of each chapter test students' knowledge of the concepts first mentioned in the "Learning Objectives" section at the beginning of the chapter.

New "Further Viewing" Features

At the end of each chapter, "Movies Described or Illustrated in This Chapter" provides students with a list that they can use as a guide for future viewing or as a source for class assignments. A new appendix, "For Further Viewing," offers several different "best of" lists—including a list of Academy Award "Best Picture" winners since 1927, the American Film Institute's list of "One Hundred Greatest American Movies of All Time," and others—for even more viewing options. Students looking for "good movie" recommendations won't be disappointed with what they find in *Looking at Movies*, Second Edition.

Chapter-by-Chapter Pedagogical Materials on the Website (wwnorton.com/movies)

> Chapter outlines provide students with short overviews of each chapter's presentation.
> The "Learning Objectives" section reviews core concepts for each chapter.
> More than 250 quiz questions test students' retention of core concepts.
> An extensive time line for each chapter highlights significant events in film history that intersect with the subject of the chapter.
> Printable versions of the end-of-chapter screening checklists allow students to take notes during screenings.

> A generous selection of sample analyses provides students with models for their own analytic writing.
> The entire "Writing About Movies" supplement is available in convenient searchable and downloadable PDF format.
> The full text of the glossary is available online for easy reference.

ebook

An ebook version of *Looking at Movies* will be available in time for the fall 2007 semester, offering students an alternative to the printed text. Students buying the ebook will also receive the two supplementary DVDs and access to the student website. Visit norton**ebooks**.com for more information.

Ancillaries for Instructors

Test Bank

Available in Microsoft Word–, ExamView-, Blackboard-, and WebCT-compatible formats, the test bank for *Looking at Movies* offers nearly five hundred multiple-choice questions.

Norton Resource Library

The test bank, a brief instructor's guide to the DVDs, and a sample syllabus are among the resources available at the online Norton Resource Library: wwnorton.com/nrl.

A Note About Textual Conventions

Boldface type is used to highlight terms that are defined in the glossary at the point where they are introduced in the text.

Italics are used in the "Learning Objectives" at the start of each chapter and in the "Questions for Review" at the end of each chapter to highlight key terms and concepts that students should learn in reading the chapter. Italics are also used to call attention to a term after the point at which the term was formally defined, or to introduce a term that holds lesser importance than the terms defined in the glossary do. Finally, italics are used occasionally for emphasis.

References to movies in the text include the year the movie was released and the director's name. Members of the crew who are particularly important to the main topic of the chapter are also identified. For example, in Chapter 4, on cinematography, a reference to *The Matrix* might look like this:

Andy and Larry Wachowski's *The Matrix* (1999: cinematographer: Bill Pope).

The movie lists provided at the end of each chapter identify films that are used as illustrations of examples in the chapter. In each case, only the movie title, year, and director are included. Other relevant information about the films listed can be found in the chapter itself.

Acknowledgments

Writing a book is most often a solitary experience, but writing one about movies seems very much, at times, like the collaborative effort involved in making a movie. In writing this Second Edition of *Looking at Movies*, I am, above all, grateful to two excellent partners: Pete Simon and Dave Monahan. Pete, my editor at W. W. Norton since the inception of this project in 1997, understood what students and instructors wanted in a new edition and guided me in preparing it. As in any undertaking of this scope, there was plenty of struggle and compromise, but I believe we have emerged from that with a much stronger book. Other collaborators at Norton were Stephanie Hiebert, copy editor; Eileen Connell, e-media editor and marketer; Benjamin Reynolds, production manager; Thom Foley, project editor; Marian Johnson, college managing editor; Lissi Sigillo, text and cover designer; Carol Desnoes, layout artist; Jack Lamb, media designer; Rubina Yeh, art director; Cohen Carruth, Inc., indexers; and Birgit Larsson, assistant editor. No author could ask for a more creative, supportive team.

Dave Monahan, Assistant Professor of Film Studies at the University of North Carolina, Wilmington, with whom I worked closely on the first edition, remained my primary contributing consultant in preparing this edition. He used the first edition in his classes and gave me the benefit of his commentaries on that experience. As a result, I implemented dozens of his suggestions throughout the new book. Dave also undertook major new responsibilities as the supplementary-materials author. In that role, he created the unique teaching tutorials on the DVDs and new materials for the website. My thanks also to Richard Wiebe, Dave's assistant, for his tireless efforts in the production of the DVD and also to Kodak for its generous contributions to that part of the project.

Special thanks are due to the friends and colleagues who contributed suggestions, material, and technical support for this edition: Luis-Antonio Bocchi, Richard Koss, Vinny LoBrutto, and Renato Tonelli.

Throughout this project, Edgar Munhall has supported me with his firm encouragement, support, and companionship. Once again, I dedicate this book to him.

Reviewers

I would like to join the publisher in thanking all of the professors and students who provided valuable guidance as I planned this revision. *Looking at Movies* is as much their book as mine, and I am grateful to both students and faculty who have cared enough about this text to offer a hand in making it better.

The following colleagues either read and critiqued chapters or responded to a lengthy questionnaire from the publisher in preparation for the second edition: Rebecca Alvin, Edwin Arnold, Antje Ascheid, Dyrk Ashton, Tony Avruch, Peter Bailey, Scott Baugh, Harry Benshoff, Mark Berrettini, Yifen Beus, Mike Birch, Robin Blaetz, Ellen Bland, Carroll Blue, James Bogan, Karen Budra, Don Bullens, Gerald Burgess, Jeremy Butler, Gary Byrd, Ed Cameron, Jose Cardenas, Jerry Carlson, Diane Carson, Robert Castaldo, Beth Clary, Darcy Cohn, Marie Connelly, Roger

Cook, Robert Coscarelli, Bob Cousins, Donna Davidson, Rebecca Dean, Marshall Deutelbaum, Kent DeYoung, Michael DiRaimo, Carol Dole, Dan Dootson, John Ernst, James Fairchild, Adam Fischer, Craig Fischer, Tay Fizdale, Karen Fulton, Christopher Gittings, Barry Goldfarb, Neil Goldstein, Daryl Gonder, Patrick Gonder, Cynthia Gottshall, Curtis Green, William Green, Tracy Greene, Michael Griffin, Peter Hadorn, William Hagerty, John Harrigan, Catherine Hastings, Sherri Hill, Glenn Hopp, Tamra Horton, Alan Hutchison, Mike Hypio, Tom Isbell, Delmar Jacobs, Mitchell Jarosz, John Lee Jellicorse, Matthew Judd, Charles Keil, Joyce Kessel, Mark Kessler, Garland Kimmer, Lynn Kirby, David Kranz, James Kreul, Mikael Kreuzriegler, Cory Lash, Leon Lewis, Vincent LoBrutto, Jane Long, John Long, Jay Loughrin, Daniel Machon, Travis Malone, Todd McGowan, Casey McKittrick, Maria Mendoza-Enright, Andrea Mensch, Sharon Mitchler, Mary Alice Molgard, John Moses, Sheila Nayar, Sarah Nilsen, Ian Olney, Hank Ottinger, Dan Pal, Gary Peterson, Klaus Phillips, Alexander Pitofsky, Lisa Plinski, Leland Poague, Walter Renaud, Patricia Roby, Carole Rodgers, Stuart Rosenberg, Ben Russell, Kevin Sandler, Bennet Schaber, Mike Schoenecke, Hertha Schulze, David Seitz, Timothy Shary, Robert Sheppard, Charles Silet, Eric Smoodin, Ken Stofferahn, Bill Swanson, Molly Swiger, Joe Tarantowski, Susan Tavernetti, Edwin Thompson, Frank Tomasulo, Deborah Tudor, Bill Vincent, Richard Vincent, Ken White, Mark Williams, Deborah Wilson, Elizabeth Wright, and Michael Zryd.

The following students participated in focus groups with the publisher or provided written critiques of the first edition in preparation for the second: Ashley Acosta, Dewitt Ray Austin, Kyle Austin, Erik Autenrieth, Jason Barnes, Elizabeth Bissette, Courtney Bowman, Kaitlyn Brasiskis, Luke Bruehlman, Bailey Carlberg, Brendan Carter, Jessie Clendenin, Ben Cohen, Jerrod Copeland, Kelly Copeland, Andrew Cranford, Jonathan Crow, Luke Dalecki, Matthew Draeger, William Eberhart, Margaret Finlayson, Sara Giarratana, Elizabeth Ivey, Gait Jordan, Ryan Kawamoto, Miller King, Cullen Kotzian, Kayla Leasure, Adam Lee, Will Lewis, Alexander Loops, Judson MacGregor, Joseph Mahan, Patrick McCarthy, Brian McGovern, Brandon Moors, Jonathan Muedder, Lanira Murphy, Tyler Nance, Brian Neal, Bethany Nuckolls, McKenna Oakes, Sarah Parker, Corey Penrod, Adam Price, Jake Pritchard, Bethany Qualls, Carrie Riley, Lauren Rinere, Kari Rosen, Sarah Rushing, Brittany Ryan, Kenneth Shufelt, Nathaniel Sloan, Will Sredzienski, Ben Stolte, Christina Theisen, Landon Watanabe, Alexandra Weinstein, Matthew Whaley, John Williamson, Chase Wrenn, and Travis Wrenn.

The following colleagues responded to questionnaires or offered substantive critiques of manuscript chapters in preparation for the first edition: Norma M. Alter, Roy Anker, Robert Baird, Robin Bates, Todd Berliner, Matthew Bernstein, Dennis Bingham, Michael Budd, Marcia Butzel, Jackie Byars, Sandra Camargo, William V. Costanzo, David Cook, Donna Davidson-Symonds, Charles Derry, John M. Desmond, Gerald Duchovnay, Dirk Eitzen, Eric Friedman, Anne Friedberg, Maureen Furniss, Krin Gabbard, Susan Glassow, William Gombash, Claudia L. Gorbman, Diana J. Grahn, Leger Grindon, Ina Rae Hark, Gary L. Harmon, Joan Hawkins, Thomas Hemmeter, Elizabeth Henry, Terence Hoagwood, Amelia S. Holberg, Theodore Hovet, Bryan Hull, Matthew Hurt, Christopher P. Jacobs, Joseph G. Kickasola, Jeffrey F. Klenotic, Arthur Knight, Joy Korinek, Walter Korte, Donald Larsson, Leonard Leff, George Lellis, Julia Lesage, Julie R. Levinson, Leon Lewis, Anthony Libby, Susan Linville, Paul Loukides, Charles J. Maland, Phillipe D. Mather, Melani McAlister, Mary A. McCay, Joan McGettigan, Toby Miller, Stuart Minnis, Gerard Molyneaux, Robert Barry Moore, Diane Negra, Kimberly Neuendorf, Richard Neupert, Robert A. Nowlan, Patrice Petro, Carl Plantinga, Dana Polan, David Popowski, Glenn Reed, Diana Reep, Jack Riggs, Karen Schneider, Robert Shelton, Craig Shurtleff, Don Staples, Lisa Sternlieb, George Toles, Gerry Veeder, William Vincent, Michael Walsh, Eugene Walz, Gretchen S. Watson, Steven J. Whitton, Clyde V. Williams, Tony Williams, and J. Emmett Winn.

Thank you all.

— Richard Barsam

What Is a Movie?

The Wizard of Oz (1939). Victor Fleming, director.

Learning Objectives

After reading this chapter, you should be able to

➤ Differentiate between *form* and *content* in a movie, and be able to explain how they're related.

➤ Understand how movies manipulate *space* and *time*.

➤ Explain how movies provide an *illusion of movement*.

➤ Distinguish between *realism* and *antirealism*, and explain how achieving *verisimilitude* is important to them both.

➤ Explain what is meant by *cinematic language* and why we identify with the *camera lens*.

➤ Differentiate *narrative*, *nonfiction*, *animated*, and *experimental* movies.

➤ Understand what *genre* is and why it is important.

➤ Explain the most significant (or defining) characteristics of a *movie*.

➤ Begin *looking at movies* more analytically and perceptively.

Looking at Movies

In just over a hundred years, movies have evolved into a complex form of artistic representation and communication: they are at once a hugely influential, wildly profitable, global industry and a modern art—the most popular art form today. Like so many aspects of contemporary culture—cars, computers, instant access to information and images—movies are so thoroughly integrated into our daily lives that we often simply take them for granted. For most of us most of the time, movies are a break from our daily obligations—a form of escape, entertainment, and pleasure. But underneath their surfaces, all movies, even the most blatantly commercial ones, contain layers of complexity and meaning that can be studied, analyzed, and appreciated. This book is devoted to that task—to *looking at* movies rather than just passively watching them. By the time you've fin-

ished reading *Looking at Movies*, you will have a thorough sense of the major components of film form, and a beginning understanding of the "language" of movies.

Although this chapter introduces in broad strokes the major principles of film and the various types of films, you already know some of this material. And given what you know, you might think that answering the question posed in the title of this chapter—*What Is a Movie?*—is not all that complicated, and at first you'd be right. After all, if you're like most of today's college students you have probably watched thousands of hours of motion picture content by now. But despite all that you have learned *from* those movies *about* the movies, what you've learned you know primarily on an instinctual level, somewhat as children are able to use language before they understand grammar. Thus, in all likelihood you don't know the names of the things you've learned about the movies or how to categorize and understand them within the system of cinematic language. As a result, you may find that learning what a movie is all about is more challenging than you thought. Let's start with a core principle of all art: the relationship between form and content.

Form and Content

If you've ever watched an unedited portion of surveillance tape—say, from a convenience store or a bank—you know that it's a boring, almost pointless activity. Even when you watch an important event occurring—when, for example, a robbery has been recorded on tape—your excitement comes almost completely from knowing that the event really happened, and not from the videotape's having been shot in an exciting way or even adequately recording the event and providing evidence for the police. The surveillance camera's vantage point is always above and away from the action; the lens provides a single, unchanging wide-angle view of the action; and the process of watching the robbery from beginning to end on the tape will (necessarily) take the same amount of time that it actually took to occur.

By contrast, consider a scene from David Mamet's *Heist* (2001), a smart, cool, twist-filled thriller that contains both simulated surveillance coverage and movie footage of a heist—both, of course, made specifically for the purpose of telling the story. Joe Moore (Gene Hackman) is the criminal's criminal behind the story. Although the main plot involves an elaborate gold heist that Moore has planned, before the heist occurs we see him and his crew in action as they bust into a jewelry store (where they've already had the employees drugged) and steal its valuable inventory. We see Don "Pinky" Pincus (Ricky Jay) smashing open showcase after showcase and loading the jewels into a bag. As he's doing this, Moore, who is meticulous in his planning, does not seem overly concerned that the video surveillance system is running. Has he forgotten to turn the system off? Is he so self-confident that he can ignore it? No, he knows, as we do, that none of these three cameras is going to reveal the identity of his men, who are wearing masks.

On a three-panel video monitor on the security guard's desk, footage from three cameras is displayed. Footage of Pincus at work, taken from a camera with a wide-angle lens that is positioned high on a wall in the rear of the shop, appears on the right-hand screen. With Pincus's back turned to the camera, which is probably 75 feet away, we understand why Moore is so coolly detached about the surveillance system, although he does eventually disable it. Unlike the vibrant color shots of Pincus smashing the showcases in this scene, the black-and-white surveillance tape has no visual interest for us whatsoever. And, as Moore knows, it will have no value to the police either.

The three shots from *Heist*—the first of one

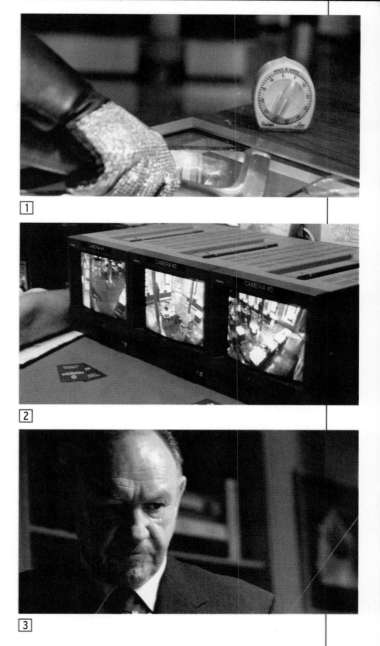

1

2

3

Movies Versus Surveillance Tapes We activate surveillance cameras and later view their tapes for a specific reason, unrelated to aesthetics. We want to know who did what at the scene of a crime, and the unscripted, relatively formless reality on the recording helps us solve a practical problem as quickly as possible. Works of art, such as movies, have deliberate forms that convey information beyond who did what. [1] Here, in a scene from David Mamet's *Heist* (2001), we see a color close-up of Don "Pinky" Pincus's (Ricky Jay) gloved hand smashing a showcase; this shot, and the others in the sequence in which it appears, reveal the ingenuity, skill, and determination with which this jewel heist is being carried out *and* being filmed. [2] Here we see the three-panel video monitor on the security guard's desk, and, although the shot is taken from a long distance away, if you look very closely at the right-hand screen, you just might see Pincus at work. He's the single figure behind the column in the background center of the image. [3] In this shot, however, Joe Moore (Gene Hackman), the cool ringleader of this crime team, seems unperturbed about the surveillance system because he knows that the tape recording of Pincus is without value.

thief, the second from a simulated surveillance tape of the robbery, the third of Joe Moore—are all recorded on motion picture media. And even though the second shot, which is in black and white, is different from the others, which are in color, the shots differ from each other in a more important way. Only the first and third reflect what goes into making a movie: writing, designing, acting, cinematography, editing, and sound—all elements of cinematic form. The key to understanding the difference between the surveillance tape and the overall movie is *form*.

The form of *Heist* has been deliberately manipulated by artists (director-screenwriter David Mamet and his collaborators) to shape and influence the viewer's experience of its *content*. In contrast, the form of the surveillance tape is constant and unchanging: the tape artlessly records (a limited) reality from a fixed point of view and with chronological continuity. If this were a real surveillance tape (not one made as part of a movie), no one, except the person who installed the camera on the ceiling and the employee who switched the recorder on for the day, would have made a conscious decision about how the action would be filmed. The meaning of the surveillance tape, to the extent that it has a meaning, is almost completely determined by *what* is recorded on video rather than by *how* it looks as we watch it. In the scene from *Heist* (or any other movie), however, our understanding of the action is continually influenced and adjusted by its deliberately crafted form. All the details that contribute to *Heist*'s look and feel—clothing, set design, blocking, acting, camera movement, editing of shots, accompanying music, and many other technical elements—together constitute the film's form and are crucially important to our sense of the film's meaning.

The relationship between form and content is a central concern in all art, and it underlies our study of movies, too. At the most basic level, we might see **content** as the subject of an artwork and **form** as the means through which that subject is expressed. Such a perspective might help us to distinguish one work of art from another, or to compare the styles and visions of different artists approaching the same subject. If we look at three sculptures of a male nude, for example—by Praxiteles, Alberto Giacometti, and Keith Haring, artists spanning history from ancient Greece to the present—we can see crucial differences in vision, style, and meaning (see the illustration on page 5). Each sculpture can be said to express the same subject, the male nude, but clearly they differ in form. Of the three, Praxiteles' sculpture, *Hermes Carrying the Infant Dionysus*, comes closest to resembling a flesh-and-blood body. Giacometti's *Walking Man* (1960) elongates and exaggerates anatomical features, but the figure remains recognizable as a male human. Haring's *Self Portrait* (1989) smooths out and simplifies the contours of the human body to create an even more abstract rendering.

Once we recognize the formal differences and similarities among these three sculptures, we can ask questions about how the respective forms shape our emotional and intellectual responses to the subject matter. Look again at the ancient Greek sculpture. Although there might once have been a living man whose body looked like this, very few bodies do. The sculpture is an idealization—less a matter of recording the way a particular man actually looked than of visually describing an ideal male form. As such, it is as much an interpretation of the subject matter as, and thus no more "real" than, the other two sculptures. Giacometti's version, because of its exaggerated form, conveys a sense of isolation, perhaps even anguish. Haring's sculpture, relying on stylized and almost cartoonlike form, seems more playful and mischievous than the other two. Suddenly, because of the different form each sculpture takes, we realize that the *content* of each has changed: they are no longer *about* the same subject. Praxiteles' sculpture is somehow about defining an ideal; Giacometti's seems to reach for something that lies beneath the surface of human life and the human form; and Haring's appears to celebrate the body as a source of joy. As we become more attentive to their formal differences, these sculptures become more unlike each other in their content too.

Thus, form and content—rather than being separate things that come together to produce art—are instead two aspects of the entire formal *system* of a work of art. They are interrelated, interdependent, and interactive. Sometimes, of course, we

[1]

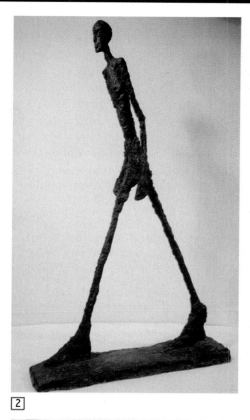

[2]

Form and Content   Compare these sculptures: [1] *Hermes Carrying the Infant Dionysus*, by Praxiteles, who lived in Greece during the fourth century BCE; [2] *Walking Man*, by Alberto Giacometti (1901–1966), a Swiss artist; and [3] *Self Portrait*, by Keith Haring (1958–1990), an American. Although all three works depict the male figure, their forms are so different that their meanings, too, must be different. What, then, is the relationship between the form of an artwork and its content?

might have good reasons, conceptually and critically, to isolate the content of a film from its form. It might be useful to do so when, say, comparing the rendition in Ridley Scott's *Black Hawk Down* (2001; screenwriter: Ken Nolan) of the 1993 U.S. military intervention in Somalia with a historical account of the same event. In such an analysis, issues of completeness, accuracy, and reliability would take precedence over formal qualities of the film, such as cinematography and editing. By focusing solely on content, however, we risk overlooking the aspects that make movies unique as an art form and interesting as individual works of art.

[3]

Focusing on Content   On October 3, 1993, nearly a hundred U.S. Army Rangers parachuted into Mogadishu, the capital of Somalia, to capture two men. Their mission was supposed to take about an hour, but they ended up in a fifteen-hour battle, the longest sustained ground attack involving American soldiers since the Vietnam War. Two U.S. Black Hawk helicopters were destroyed; eighteen Americans and hundreds of Somalis were killed; military and civilian casualties numbered in the thousands. Whereas its source, Mark Bowden's best-selling nonfiction book of the same title, was a minute-by-minute account of the firefight, Ridley Scott's narrative film *Black Hawk Down* (2001) re-creates events by dramatically condensing the action into 144 minutes. Clearly, the book and the movie differ in their form, and we might have interesting discussions about their differences. But for many viewers, the primary concern is the *content* of both book and movie. What relationship does each work bear to the facts? What would it mean, in this case, to say that the movie is better than the book, or vice versa?

Form and Expectations

Our decision to see a particular movie is almost always based on certain expectations. Perhaps we have enjoyed previous work by the director, the screenwriter, or the actors; or publicity, advertisements, friends, or reviews have attracted us; or the *genre* is appealing; or we're curious about the techniques used to make the movie.

Even if we have no such preconceptions before stepping into a movie theater, we will form impressions very quickly once the movie begins, sometimes even from the moment the opening credits roll. (In Hollywood, producers and screenwriters assume that audiences decide whether they like or dislike a movie within its first ten minutes.) As the movie continues, we experience a more complex web of expectations, many of which may be tied to the *narrative*—the formal component that connects the events within the world of the movie—and, specifically, to our sense that certain events follow others (related by cause and effect, logic, or something else).

Very often a movie starts with a (perhaps *the*) "normal" world, which is altered by a particular incident, or catalyst, that forces the characters to act in pursuit of a goal. And once the narrative begins, we ask questions about the story's outcome, questions we will be asking ourselves repeatedly and waiting to have answered over the course of the film. In a famous quotation, the nineteenth-century Russian playwright Anton Chekhov said that when a theater audience sees a character produce a gun in the first act, they expect that gun to be used before the play ends. Movie audiences feel similar expectations. When an explosion occurs at the beginning of Orson Welles's *Touch of Evil* (1958; screenwriter: Welles), we ask if "Mike" Vargas (Charlton Heston) will track down the killer. After the first attack in Steven Spielberg's *Jaws* (1975; screenwriters: Peter Benchley and Carl Gottlieb), we wonder if Chief Brody (Roy Scheider) or someone else will kill the shark.

In Sam Mendes's *American Beauty* (1999; screenwriter: Alan Ball), the very first scene introduces us to two of the film's central characters—Jane Burnham (Thora Birch), the daughter of Lester Burnham (Kevin Spacey); and Ricky Fitts (Wes Bentley), the charismatic marijuana dealer and video artist who lives next door—in a manner that plants the idea that Ricky will kill Lester. The scene opens with Jane onscreen being videotaped by Ricky, whom we can hear but not see. Jane complains about her father, calling him a "horny geek-boy" rather than a "role model," and she concludes that "someone really should put him out of his misery." Ricky, still offscreen, asks, "Want me to kill him for you?" After a moment's pause, Jane looks straight into the camera and replies, "Yeah, would you?" This scene (and the one that immediately follows, in which Lester tells us in a voice-over that "in less than a year, I'll be dead") shapes our expectations during the rest of the movie.

As we learn more about Ricky's rebellious and idiosyncratic nature, we wonder whether he may be capable of using a deadly weapon at some point.

Our suspense is heightened as we learn more about Ricky's father, Frank Fitts (Chris Cooper), a gung ho, physically abusive marine colonel who collects Nazi memorabilia. The complications mount as Ricky and Lester strike up a friendly rapport and as Jane's mother, Carolyn Burnham (Annette Bening), starts brandishing a gun, implying that she will use it to kill the husband she despises. At each point, we adjust our expectations about the final outcome, even as we know (because Lester has told us) what that outcome will be.

Director Alfred Hitchcock treated his audiences' expectations in ironic, even playful ways—sometimes using the gun, so to speak, and sometimes not—and this became one of his major stylistic traits. Hitchcock used the otherwise meaningless term *MacGuffin* to refer to an object, document, or secret within a story that is of vital importance to the characters and thus motivates their actions and the conflict, but that turns out to be less significant to the overall narrative than we might at first imagine.[1] In *Psycho* (1960; screenwriter: Joseph Stefano), for example, Marion Crane (Janet Leigh) believes that the $40,000 she steals from her employer will help her start a new life. Instead, her flight with the money leads to the Bates Motel, the psychopath Norman Bates (Anthony Perkins), and her murder. The money plays no role in motivating Bates's murderous actions; in fact, he doesn't seem to know it exists. Once the murder has occurred, the money—a classic MacGuffin—is of no real importance to the rest of the movie.

Even as the narrative form of a movie is shaping and sometimes confounding our expectations, other formal qualities may perform similar functions. Seemingly insignificant and abstract elements of film such as color schemes, sounds, the length of shots, and the movement of the camera often cooperate with dramatic elements to either heighten or confuse our expectations. One way they do this is by establishing *patterns*.

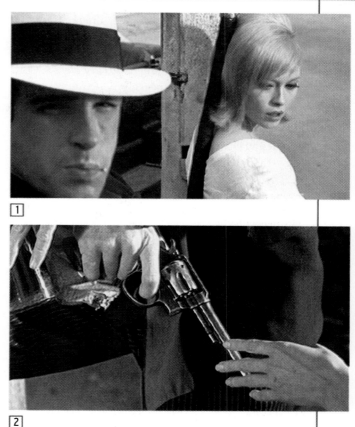

Expectations in *Bonnie and Clyde* Much of the development and ultimate impact of Arthur Penn's *Bonnie and Clyde* (1967) depends on the sexual chemistry between the title characters [1], established through physical expression, dialogue, and overt symbolism. Early in the film, Clyde (Warren Beatty), ruthless and handsome, brandishes his gun threateningly and phallically [2]. Attracted by this display and others, the beautiful Bonnie (Faye Dunaway) is as surprised as we are when Clyde later rebuffs her obvious sexual attraction to him (at one point, he demurs, "I ain't much of a lover boy"). We may not like this contradiction, but it is established early in the film and quickly teaches us that our expectations will not always be satisfied.

Patterns

Instinctively, we search for patterns and progressions in all art forms. The more these meet our expectations (or contradict them in interesting ways), the more likely we are to enjoy, analyze, and interpret the work. When we read a sonnet, for example, we expect it to follow a certain pattern

[1] Hitchcock discusses the MacGuffin in François Truffaut, *Hitchcock*, rev. ed. (New York: Simon & Schuster, 1985), 137–39.

that depends on its type. The Elizabethan, or Shakespearean, sonnet consists of fourteen lines, usually written in iambic pentameter: three quatrains and a couplet, rhyming *abab cdcd efef gg*. Consider Shakespeare's Sonnet 55:[2]

Not marble nor the gilded **monuments**	**a**
Of princes shall outlive this powerful **rhyme,**	**b**
But you shall shine more bright in these **contents**	**a**
Than unswept stone besmeared with sluttish **time.**	**b**
When wasteful war shall statues **overturn**	**c**
And broils root out the work of **masonry,**	**d**
Nor Mars his sword nor war's quick fire shall **burn**	**c**
The living record of your **memory.**	**d**
'Gainst death and all oblivious **enmity**	**e**
Shall you pace forth; your praise shall still find **room**	**f**
Even in the eyes of all **posterity**	**e**
That wear this world out to the ending **doom.**	**f**
So, till the judgement that yourself **arise,**	**g**
You live in this, and dwell in lovers' **eyes.**	**g**

Artistic form does not always follow the expectations with which we begin an analysis of it. If the context changes, so will our experiences and expectations. Faced with a contemporary poem titled "Sonnet," we would be surprised to find not, say, a fourteen-line love poem in iambic pentameter, but an epic prose poem about war. If we immediately adjust our understanding of the sonnet to include this form, we run the risk of widening the definition so much that it becomes meaningless. In other words, we come to the poem with certain expectations because of the title, but the form then defies those expectations. Our response to that defiance need not be acceptance. Instead, we must ask questions about the form. Has the poet applied this title because she really expects us to consider the poem a sonnet? If so, is she wrong? If the title doesn't fit, is the rest of the poem faulty? Is the poet simply being playful? Or is she ironically commenting on the sonnet form, the limitations of that form, literary history, and so on?

As we read a poem or watch a movie, we become aware that the poet or the director has organized the work according to certain structural principles. We respond to these and readjust our responses as the work moves forward. Consider as an analogy those critical-thinking tests that ask us to continue a series of which only the first few units are given. Perhaps we are given a series from the Roman alphabet, such as ABAB. Without any other information, our prediction about the next letter in the series would likely be *A*. But look again at the Shakespearean sonnet above. If we were told that the series ABAB is the beginning of a sonnet's rhyme scheme, then our sense of the form of ABAB would change completely, and we would confidently say that *C* comes next.

The penultimate scene in D. W. Griffith's *Way Down East* (1920; scenario: Anthony Paul Kelly), one of the most famous chase scenes in movie history, illustrates how the movies depend on our recognition of patterns. Banished from a "respectable" family's house because of her scandalous past, Anna Moore (Lillian Gish) tries to walk through a blizzard but quickly becomes disoriented and wanders onto a partially frozen river. She faints on an ice floe and, after much suspense, is rescued by David Bartlett (Richard Barthelmess) just as she is about to go over a huge waterfall to what clearly would have been her death.

To heighten the drama of his characters' predicament, Griffith employs *parallel editing*—a technique that makes different lines of action appear to be occurring simultaneously. Griffith shows us Anna on the ice (A), David jumping from one floe to another as he tries to catch up with her (B), and Niagara Falls (C). As we watch these three lines of action edited together (in a general pattern of ABCACBCABCACBC), they appear simultaneous. We assume that the river flows over Niagara Falls, and that the ice floe that Anna is on is heading down that river. It doesn't matter that the actors weren't literally in danger of going over a waterfall (although the filming—which took place on the Connecticut River in cold weather—was somewhat dangerous for the actors) or that David's

---

[2] This example is adapted from Barbara Herrnstein Smith, *Poetic Closure: A Study of How Poems End* (Chicago: University of Chicago Press, 1968), 1–27.

[1]

[2]

[3]

[4]

Parallel Editing in *Way Down East* Pioneering director D. W. Griffith risked the lives of actors Lillian Gish and Richard Barthelmess to film *Way Down East*'s now classic "ice break" scene—a scene that builds suspense by exposing us to a pattern of different shots called *parallel editing*. Griffith shot much of the blizzard and ice floe footage along the Connecticut River, then edited it together with studio shots and scenes of Niagara Falls. Gish, thinly dressed, was freezing on the ice and was periodically revived with hot tea. Although the dangers during filming were real enough, the "reality" portrayed in the final scene—a rescue from the certain death that would result from a plunge over Niagara Falls—is wholly the result of Griffith's use of a pattern of editing that has by now become a standard technique in narrative filmmaking.

actions did not occur simultaneously with Anna's progress downriver on the floe. The form of the scene, established by the pattern of parallel editing, has created an *illusion* of connections among these various shots—leaving us with an impression of a continuous, anxiety-producing drama.

The editing in one scene of Jonathan Demme's *The Silence of the Lambs* (1991; screenwriter: Ted Tally) takes advantage of our natural interpretation of parallel action to achieve a disorienting effect. Because earlier in the movie Demme has already shown us countless versions of a formal pattern in which two elements seen in separation are alternated and related (ABABAB), we expect that pattern to be repeated when shots of the serial killer Buffalo Bill (Ted Levine) arguing with his intended victim in his basement are intercut with shots of the FBI team preparing to storm a house. We naturally assume that the FBI has targeted the same house in which Buffalo Bill is going about his grisly business. When the FBI attacks a different house, the pattern is broken, thwarting our expectations and setting in motion the suspenseful scene that follows.

[1]

[2]

[3]

[4]

[5]

[6]

Patterns and Suspense Filmmakers can use patterns to catch us unawares. In *The Silence of the Lambs* (1991), Jonathan Demme exploits our sense that when shots are juxtaposed, they must share a logical connection. After FBI agents surround a house, an agent disguised as a delivery man (Lamont Arnold) rings the doorbell [1]; a bell rings in the serial killer Buffalo Bill's (Ted Levine) basement [2]; Bill reacts to that ring [3], leaves behind the prisoner he was about to harm, goes upstairs, and answers his front door [4], revealing not the delivery man we expect to see but Clarice Starling (Jodie Foster). As agents storm the house they've been staking out [5], Clarice and Bill continue to talk [6]. The agents have entered the wrong house, Clarice is now alone with a psychopath, and our anxiety rises as a result of the surprise.

Patterns in *Battleship Potemkin* Soviet filmmaker and theorist Sergei Eisenstein helped pioneer the expressive use of patterns in movies using a dynamic form of editing called *montage*. Eisenstein's montage during the "Odessa Steps" sequence of *Battleship Potemkin* (1925) brings violence to a climax in both what we see and how we see it. After Cossacks fire [1] on a young mother [2], she collapses [3], sending her baby's carriage rolling [4]; an older woman reacts [5] to the carriage's flight down a series of steps [6], and a student cries out [7] as the carriage hits bottom [8]. The pattern of movement from shot to shot accentuates the devastating energy of the content of this scene.

[1]

[2]

one of the two actors in that bar scene were to back away from the other and thus disappear from the screen, you would perceive her as moving to another part of the bar—that is, into a continuation of the space already established in the scene. You can easily imagine this movement because of the *fluidity* of movie space, more of which is necessarily suggested than is shown.

⟩WEB The "Staging" of Movies

The key to the unique power of movies to manipulate our sense of space is the motion picture camera, particularly its lens. We identify with this lens, for it determines our perception of cinematic space. Indeed, if we didn't automatically make this identification—assuming, for example, that the camera's point of view is a sort of roving, omniscient one with which we are supposed to identify—movies would be almost incomprehensible. The key to understanding our connection to the camera lens lies in the differences between *how* the human eye and the camera eye see. The camera eye perceives what's placed before it through a series of different pictures (*shots*), made with different lenses, from different camera positions and angles, using different movements, under different lighting, and so on. Although the camera eye and the human eye can both see the movements, colors, textures, sizes, and locations of people, places, and things, the camera eye is more selective in its view. The camera frames its image, for example, and can widen and foreshorten space. Through camera positioning, the lens can record a *close-up*, removing from our view the surrounding visual context that we see in real life, no matter how close we get to an object. In

Space and Time in *Henry V* The unique ability of movies to manipulate space and time becomes obvious when we compare a staged version of a play to a film adaptation of that same play. [1] A staging of Shakespeare's *Henry V* at the Alabama Shakespeare Festival shows the title character rousing his men to battle. As in many theatrical productions, the actor resorts to a stage convention—facing and addressing the theater audience rather than the other actors—to overcome a practical limitation of theatrical space (that is, the problem of not being heard by the audience if he speaks toward the backstage area). Similarly, the theater is not conducive to staging convincing battle scenes, so combat is usually just referred to in plays, rather than played out. In movies, however, these limitations of space and time don't apply. [2] Kenneth Branagh's 1989 film adaptation of Shakespeare's *Henry V* brings us close to the violent action of the famous Battle of Agincourt, transporting us from place to place within the cinematic space, and speeding up and slowing down our sense of time for heightened emotional effect.

short, the camera *mediates* between the exterior (the world) and the interior (our eyes and brains).

We use the term **mediation**, a key concept in film theory, literally to mean the process by which an agent, structure, or other formal element, whether human or technological, transfers something from one place to another. No matter how straightforward the mediation of the camera eye may seem, it always involves selection and manipulation of what is seen. This is what mediation as a concept implies. Unlike the video surveillance camera that we mentioned at the beginning of the chapter, the motion picture camera eye is not an artless recorder of "reality." It is instead one of a number of expressive tools that filmmakers use to influence our interpretation of the movie's meaning.

Cinema's ability to manipulate space is illustrated in Charles Chaplin's *The Gold Rush* (1925). This brilliant comedy portrays the adventures of two prospectors: the "Little Fellow" (Chaplin) and his nemesis, Big Jim McKay (Mack Swain). After many twists and turns of the plot, the two find themselves sharing an isolated cabin. At night, the winds of a fierce storm blow the cabin to the brink of a deep abyss. Waking and walking about, the Little Fellow slides toward the door (and almost certain death). The danger is established by our first seeing the sharp precipice on which the cabin is located and then by seeing the Little Fellow sliding toward the door that opens out over the abyss. Subsequently, we see him and Big Jim engaged in a struggle for survival, which requires that they maintain the balance of the cabin on the edge of the abyss.

The suspense exists because individual shots—one made outdoors, the other safely in a studio—have been edited together to create the illusion that they form part of a complete space. As we watch the cabin sway and teeter on the cliff's edge, we imagine the hapless adventurers inside; when the action cuts to the interior of the cabin and we see the floor pitching back and forth, we imagine the cabin perched precariously on the edge. The experience of these shots as a continuous record of action occurring in a complete (and realistic) space is an illusion that no other art form can convey as effectively as movies can.

The manipulation of time (as well as space), a

function of editing, is handled with great irony, cinematic power, and emotional impact in the "Baptism and Murder" **scene** in Francis Ford Coppola's *The Godfather* (1972). This five-minute **sequence** consists of thirty-six shots made at different locations. The primary location is a church where Michael Corleone (Al Pacino), the newly named godfather of the Corleone mob, and his wife, Kay (Diane Keaton), attend their nephew's baptism. Symbolically, Michael is also the child's godfather. Coppola cuts back and forth between the baptism; the preparations for five murders, which Michael has ordered, at five different locations; and the murders themselves.

Each time we return to the baptism, it continues where it left off for one of these cutaways to other actions. We know this from the continuity of the priest's actions, Latin incantations, and the Bach organ music. This continuity tells us not only that these actions are taking place simultaneously, but also that Michael is involved in all of them, either directly or indirectly. The simultaneity is further strengthened by the organ music, which underscores every scene in the sequence, not just those that take place in the cathedral—music that picks up in pitch and loudness as the sequence progresses, rising to particular climaxes as the murders are committed. As the priest says to Michael, "Go in peace, and may the Lord be with you," we are left to reconcile this meticulously timed, simultaneous occurrence of sacred and criminal acts.

Movies Depend on Light

One of the most powerful black-and-white films ever made, John Ford's *The Grapes of Wrath* (1940), tells the story of an Oklahoma farming family forced off their land by the violent dust storms that plagued the region during the Great Depression of the 1930s. The eldest son, Tom Joad (Henry Fonda), returns home after serving a prison sentence, only to find that his family has left their farm for the supposedly greener pastures of California. Tom and an itinerant preacher named Casy (John Carradine), whom he has met along the way, enter the Joad house, using a candle to help them see inside the pitch-black interior. Lurking in the dark, but illuminated

[1]

[4]

[2]

[5]

[3]

[6]

Manipulating Space in *The Gold Rush* Film editing can convince us that we're seeing a complete space and a continuous action, even though individual shots have been filmed in different places and at different times. In Charles Chaplin's *The Gold Rush* (1925), an exterior shot of the cabin

[1] establishes the danger that the main characters only slowly become aware of [2]. As the cabin hangs in the balance [3], alternating interior and exterior shots [4–6] accentuate our sense of suspense and amusement.

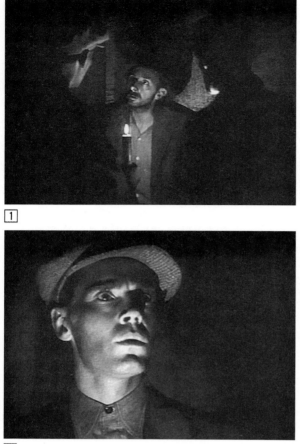

1

2

Expressive Use of Light in *The Grapes of Wrath*
Strong contrasts between light and dark (called *chiaroscuro*) make movies visually interesting and focus our attention on significant details. But that's not all that they accomplish. They can also evoke moods and meanings, and even symbolically complement the other formal elements of a movie, as in these frames from John Ford's *The Grapes of Wrath* (1940).

by the candlelight, is Muley Graves (John Qualen), a farmer who has refused to leave Oklahoma with his family. As Muley tells Tom and Casy what has happened in the area, Tom holds the candle so that he and Casy can see him better, and the contrasts between the dark background and Muley's haunted face, illuminated by the flickering candle, reveal their collective state of mind: despair. The story is told less through words than through the overtly symbolic light of a single candle. Such sharp

contrasts of light and dark occur throughout the film, thus providing a pattern of meaning.

Lighting is responsible for the image we see on the screen, whether photographed (*shot*) on film or video, caught on a disk, created with a computer, or, as in animation, drawn on pieces of celluloid known as **cels**. Lighting is also responsible for significant effects in each shot or scene. It enhances the texture, depth, emotions, and mood of a shot. It accents the rough texture of a cobblestoned street in Carol Reed's *The Third Man* (1949), helps to extend the illusion of depth in Orson Welles's *Citizen Kane* (1941), and emphasizes a character's subjective feelings of apprehension or suspense in such film noirs as Billy Wilder's *Double Indemnity* (1944). In fact, lighting often conveys these things by augmenting, complicating, or even contradicting other cinematic elements within the shot (e.g., dialogue, movement, or composition). Lighting also affects the ways in which we see and think about a movie's characters. It can make a character's face appear attractive or unattractive, make the viewer like a character or be afraid of her, and reveal a character's state of mind.

These are just a few of the basic ways that movies depend on light to achieve their effects (for a more complete discussion, see "Lighting" in Chapter 4). On one hand, this is a mundane technical reality—after all, the ability to see anything depends on light. On the other hand, it is a fundamental and unique characteristic of film art. Moviemaking technology, derived from still photography, makes it possible to capture light in seemingly infinite ways. To understand the optical effects in movies, we need to understand the technology behind them.

Photography   In one sense, movies are simply a natural progression in the history of photography. The word **photography** means, literally, "writing with light" and, technically, the static representation or reproduction of light. The concept has its beginnings in ancient Greece. In the fourth century BCE, the Greek philosopher Aristotle theorized about a device that later would be known as the **camera obscura** (Latin for "dark chamber"; Fig. 1.1). In the late fifteenth century, Leonardo da

FIGURE 1.1 **Camera Obscura**

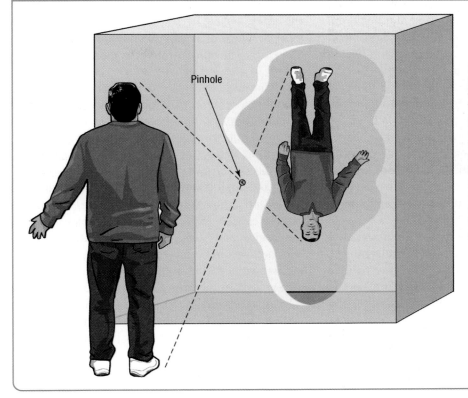

Pinhole

Before the advent of photosensitive film, the camera obscura was used to facilitate lifelike *drawing*. In this simple schematic, for example, the interior "wall" upon which the upside-down image is projected was usually whitened; an artist could place a piece of drawing paper on the wall and trace the image on to it.

Vinci's drawings gave tangible form to the idea. Both simple and ingenious, the camera obscura may be a box, or it may be a room large enough for a viewer to stand inside. Light entering through a tiny hole (later a lens) on one side of the box or room projects an image from the outside onto the opposite side or wall. An artist might then trace the image onto a piece of paper.

Photography was developed during the first four decades of the nineteenth century by Thomas Wedgwood, William Henry Fox Talbot, and Sir John Herschel in England; Joseph-Nicéphore Niepce and Louis-Jacques-Mandé Daguerre in France; and George Eastman in the United States. In 1802, Wedgwood made the first recorded attempt to produce photographs. However, these were not camera images as we know them, but basically silhouettes of objects placed on paper or leather sensitized with chemicals and exposed to light. These images faded quickly, for Wedgwood did not know how to fix (stabilize) them. Unaware of Wedgwood's work, Talbot devised a chemical method for recording the images he observed in his camera obscura. More important was the significant progress he made toward fixing the image, and he invented the **negative**, or negative photographic image on transparent material, which makes possible the reproduction of the image.

Niepce experimented with sunlight and the camera obscura to make photographic copies of engravings, as well as actual photographs from nature. The results of this heliographic (that is, sun-drawn) process—crude paper prints—were not particularly successful, but Niepce's discoveries influenced Daguerre, who, by 1837, was able to create a detailed image on a copper plate treated with chemicals—an image remarkable for its fidelity and detail. In 1839, Herschel perfected *hypo* (short for hyposulfite thiosulfate—that is, sodium thiosulfate), a compound that fixed the image on paper and thus arrested the effect of light on it. Herschel first used the word *photography* in 1839 in a lecture at the Royal Society of London for the Promotion of Natural Knowledge. What followed were primarily technological improvements on Herschel's discovery.

In 1851, glass-plate negatives replaced the paper plates. More durable but heavy, glass was replaced by gelatin-covered paper in 1881. The new gelatin process reduced, from fifteen minutes to one-thousandth of a second, the time necessary to make a photographic exposure and thus made it possible to record action spontaneously and simultaneously as it occurred. In 1887, George Eastman began the mass production of a paper "film" coated with a gelatin emulsion; in 1889, Eastman improved the process by substituting clear plastic (film) for the paper base. Though there have been subsequent technological improvements, this is the photographic film we know today.

This experimentation with optical principles and still photography in the nineteenth century made it possible to take and reproduce photographic images that could *simulate* action in the image. But simulation was not enough for the scientists, artists, and members of the general public who wanted to see images of life in motion. The intermediary step between still photography and cinematography came with the development of *series photography*.

Series Photography

Series photography records the phases of an action. In a series of still photographs, we see, for example, a man or a horse in changing positions that suggest movement, though the images themselves are static. Within a few years, three men—Pierre-Jules-César Janssen, Eadweard Muybridge, and Étienne-Jules Marey— contributed to its development.

In 1874, Janssen, a French astronomer, developed the **revolver photographique**, or *chrono-photographic gun*, a cylinder-shaped camera that creates exposures automatically, at short intervals, on different segments of a revolving plate. In 1877,

Muybridge, an English photographer working in California, used a group of electrically operated cameras (first twelve, then twenty-four) to produce the first series of photographs of continuous motion. On May 4, 1880, using an early projector known as the **magic lantern** and his **zoopraxi-scope** (a version of the magic lantern, with a revolving disk that had his photographs arranged around the center), Muybridge gave the first public demonstration of photographic images in motion— a cumbersome process, but a breakthrough.

In 1882, Marey, a French physiologist, made the first series of photographs of continuous motion using the **fusil photographique** (another form of the chrono-photographic gun), a single, portable camera capable of taking twelve continuous images. Muybridge and Marey later collaborated in Paris, but each was more interested in using the process for his own scientific studies than for making or projecting motion pictures as such. Marey's invention solved the problems created by Muybridge's use of a battery of cameras, but the series was limited to forty images—a total of three or four seconds.

Motion Picture Photography The experiments that Janssen, Muybridge, and Marey conducted with various kinds of moving pictures were limited in almost every way, but the technologies needed to make moving pictures on film were in place and awaited only a synthesis. In 1891, William Kennedy Laurie Dickson, working with associates in Thomas Edison's research laboratory, invented the **kinetograph** (the first motion picture camera) and the **kinetoscope** (a peephole viewer). The first motion picture made in the kinetograph—actually the earliest complete film on record at the Library of Congress—was Dickson's *Edison Kinetoscopic Record of a Sneeze* (1894), popularly known as *Fred Ott's Sneeze*, which represents, on Edison and Dickson's part, a brilliant choice of a single, self-contained action for a single, self-contained film of very limitedlength.

DVD *Fred Ott's Sneeze*

In 1893, Edison and his staff began making movies inside a crude, hot, cramped shack known as the **Black Maria**. This was really the first movie

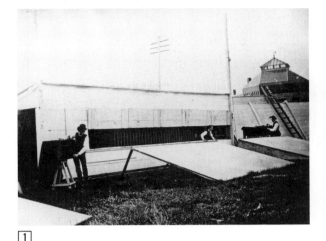

Series Photography Eadweard Muybridge's famous series of photographs documenting a horse in motion were made possible by a number of cameras placed side by side in the structure pictured here [1]. The cameras were tied to individual trip wires. As the horse broke each wire, a camera's shutter would be set off. The result of this experiment—a series of sixteen exposures [2]—proved that a trotting horse momentarily has all four feet off the ground at once (see the third frame). Series photography has been revived as a strategy for creating special effects in contemporary movies.

Edison's Kinetograph and the Black Maria These images show Thomas Edison's Black Maria—the first motion picture "studio"—pictured from the outside [1] and the inside [2]. The interior view shows how awkward and static the kinetograph was, because of both its bulk and its need to be tethered to a power source. In addition, the performers had very little room to move, and the environment was hot and airless. The makeshift quality of the studio, as well as its relatively modest size, is evident from the external view.

studio, for it contained the camera, technicians, and actors. The camera was limited in moving on a trolley closer to or away from the subject. Light was provided by the sun, which entered through an aperture in the roof, and the entire "studio" could be rotated to catch the light.

In 1889, George Eastman began mass-producing **celluloid roll film**, also known as **motion picture film** or *raw film stock*, which consists of long strips of perforated cellulose acetate on which a rapid succession of still photographs known as **frames** can be recorded. One side of the strip is layered

FIGURE 1.2 | The Motion Picture Camera

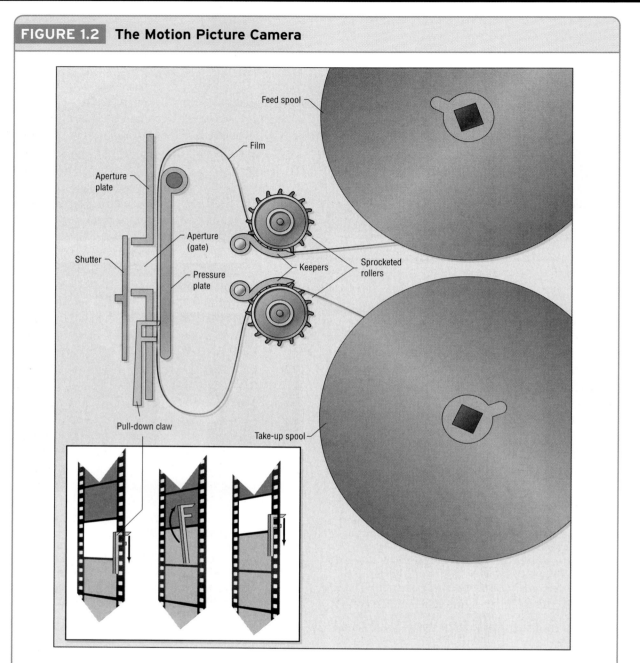

The motion picture camera moves unexposed film from one storage area, called the **feed spool** (or, in professional cameras today, the portion of the *magazine* that stores unexposed film), along the **sprocketed rollers**, which control the speed of that film as it moves through the camera and toward the lens, which focuses the image on the film as it is exposed. The **aperture** (or *gate*) is essentially the window through which each frame of film is exposed. The **shutter**—a mechanism that shields the film from light while each frame is moved into place—is synchronized with the motion of the **pull-down claw**, a mechanism used in both cameras and projectors to advance the film frame by frame. The pull-down claw holds each frame still for the fraction of a second that the shutter allows the aperture to be open so that the film can be exposed. The **take-up spool** (or, again, the portion of the magazine that stores exposed film) winds the film after it has been exposed.

with an emulsion consisting of light-sensitive crystals and dyes; the other side is covered with a backing that reduces reflections. One side of the strip is perforated with sprocket holes that facilitate the movement of the stock through the sprocket wheels of the *camera*, the *processor*, and the *projector*. These three machines bring images to the screen in three distinct stages, and light plays a vital role throughout.

→ WEB The Cinematographe and Other Movie Cameras

In the first stage, **shooting**, the camera exposes film to light, allowing that radiant energy to burn a negative image onto each frame. In the second stage, **processing**, the negative is developed into a positive print that the filmmaker can then screen in order to plan the editing, a process that produces the final print. In the third stage, **projecting**, the final print is run through a projector, which shoots through the film a beam of light intense enough to reverse the initial process and project a large image on the movie screen. (This account greatly condenses the entire process to emphasize, at this point, only the cycle of light common to all three stages.)

Projecting a strip of exposed frames at the same speed—generally 16 frames per second (fps) for silent film, 24 fps for sound—creates the illusion of movement. Silent cameras and projectors were often hand-cranked, and so the actual speed of the camera, which then had to be matched by the projectionist, could vary from 12 to 24 fps. Cameras and projectors used for making and exhibiting professional films are powered by electric motors that ensure a perfect movement of the film (Fig. 1.2). As digital technology replaces this mechanical process, it is changing the equipment and media on which the images are captured, processed, and projected, but the role of light remains the same essential component.

A movie film's **format** is the **gauge**, or width, of the film stock and its perforations, measured in millimeters, and the size and shape of the image frame as seen on the screen (Fig. 1.3). Formats extend from Super 8mm through 70mm, and beyond into such specialized formats as IMAX (ten times bigger than a conventional 35mm frame and three times bigger than a standard 70mm frame). The format chosen depends on the type of film being made, the financing available to support the project, and the overall visual look that the filmmaker wants to achieve. For example, a low-key, fairly low-budget, and intimate *narrative film* (such as Phil Morrison's *Junebug*, 2005) might be shot in 16mm or 35mm format, but an action-filled, broad, and expensive *nonfiction film* (such as Luc Jacquet's *March of the Penguins*, 2005) might require a 70mm or IMAX format. The **film stock length** is the number of feet (or meters) or the number of reels being used in a particular film. The **film stock speed** (or *exposure index*), the degree to which it is light-sensitive, ranges from very fast, at which it requires little light, to very slow, at which it requires a lot of light. As will be discussed further in Chapter 4, film is also categorized into black-and-white and color stock.

Today's digital technology (video or electronic photography) is transforming the making of motion pictures; nevertheless, just like conventional cinematographic technology, it uses a lens to capture light and record images. The primary difference between these technologies is that a film camera captures light on film stock, which, after processing, can be viewed on editing tables or through projectors; a video camera instead records images on magnetic tape, diskettes, or a computer hard disk, to be projected on a screen or viewed through a television receiver or monitor. It is too early to know if, when, and at what cost the entertainment industry will fully convert to digital production, but one of the dominant trends currently bridging the gap is to shoot a movie on film and edit it on video, using computers.

For the release of George Lucas's *Star Wars: Episode II—Attack of the Clones* (2002), which was shot entirely with digital cameras, a digital projection system was employed in selected theaters. For the first time in history, a feature movie was produced and exhibited without a strip of celluloid clicking through the camera, printer, and projector. Walter Murch, an editor whose name is synonymous with editing theory and practice, cut Anthony Minghella's *Cold Mountain* (2003) on Final Cut Pro, software that is available in consumer editions; and Jonathan Caouette's *Tarnation* (2003) was the first released feature film to be cut on iMovie, which is part of the standard software

FIGURE 1.3 Standard Film Gauges

sound track   sound track   sound track

70mm   35mm   16mm   Super 8mm 8mm

The most common variations on standard motion picture film gauges.

on Apple's personal computers. In short, digital technology is now widely used to make both professional and home movies.

Movies Provide an Illusion of Movement

Above all else, the movies *move* (the word *movies* is a shortened version of the phrase *moving pictures*, which literally captures the central importance of movement to film art). Or rather, they *seem* to move. As we sit in a movie theater, believing ourselves to be watching a continuously lit screen portraying fluid, uninterrupted movement, we are actually watching a quick succession of twenty-four individual still photographs per second. And as the projector moves one of these images out of the frame to bring the next one in, the screen goes dark. Although the movies are distinguished from other arts by their dependence on light and movement, we spend a good amount of our time in movie theaters sitting in complete darkness, facing a screen with nothing projected on it at all!

The movement we see on the movie screen is an illusion, made possible by two interacting optical and perceptual phenomena: persistence of vision and the phi phenomenon. **Persistence of vision** is the process by which the human brain retains an image for a fraction of a second longer than the eye records it. You can observe this phenomenon by quickly switching a light on and then off in a dark room. Doing this, you should see an afterimage of the objects in the room, or at least of whatever you were looking at directly when you switched the light on. Similarly, in the movie theater we see a smooth flow of images and not the darkness between frames. Thus the persistence of vision gives the *illusion of succession*, or one image following another without interruption. However, we must also experience the *illusion of movement*, or figures and objects within the image changing position simultaneously without actually moving.

The **phi phenomenon** is the illusion of movement created by events that succeed each other rapidly, as when two adjacent lights flash on and off alternately and we seem to see a single light shifting back and forth. The phi phenomenon is related to **critical flicker fusion**, which occurs when a single light flickers on and off with such speed that the individual pulses of light fuse together to give the illusion of continuous light. (Early movies were called *flicks* because the projectors that were used often ran at slower speeds than were necessary to sustain this illusion; the result was not continuous light, but a *flickering* image onscreen. The most acute human eye can discern no more than fifty pulses of light per second. Because the shutters of modern projectors "double-flash" each frame of film, we watch forty-eight pulses per second, close enough to the limit of perception to eliminate our awareness of the flicker effect.) The movie projector relies on such phenomena to trick us into perceiving separate images as one continuous image; and because each successive image differs only slightly from the one that precedes it, we perceive **apparent motion** rather than a series of jerky movements.

The most dazzling contemporary films, such as Andy and Larry Wachowski's *The Matrix* (1999), are full of kinetic excitement that makes the impossible look totally possible. How do they do this? Special effects, involving the most advanced computer technology in both hardware and software, play a large role in creating this virtual reality. Indeed, seamlessly integrated to create the film's virtual realm, special effects reportedly constitute 20 percent of *The Matrix*. But such sophisticated effects would not be possible without the simple illusions just discussed. Much of what we regard as the absolute cutting edge of moviemaking technology capitalizes on these illusions, especially the speeding up or slowing down of movement to achieve the desired effects.

In making *The Matrix*, the filmmakers initially discovered that a number of the required action sequences might not be possible, because they required that motion be captured at exceptionally high speeds. That is, to create the illusion of such slow motion, the camera would have had to speed up beyond its capacity. Working with engineers, the filmmakers developed new technology in a process that resembled Muybridge's experiments in the 1870s. For example, a scene in which Neo (Keanu Reeves) is fired at by another protagonist in the virtual world was shot not by one motion picture camera, but by 120 still cameras mounted in a rollercoaster-style arc. Fired by a computer-driven program, this system ensured accuracy to within one-thousandth of a second.

Realism and Antirealism

All of the unique features of film form described in the preceding discussion combine to make it possible for filmmakers to create vivid and believable worlds on the screen. Although not every film strives to be "realistic," nearly all films attempt to immerse us in a world that is depicted convincingly on its own terms. Moving picture technology arose primarily from attempts to record natural images through photography, but it also was shaped by similar attempts in painting and literature. That is, the realist impulse of the visual arts—recording the visible facts of people, places, and social life, for a working-class and growing middle-class audience—helped inspire the first motion pictures. However, it very soon became clear that movies could be used to create *anti*realist as well as realist worlds.

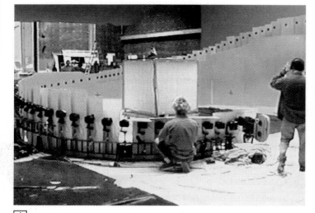

1

2

3

Movement in *The Matrix* For Andy and Larry Wachowski's *The Matrix* (1999), special-effects supervisors Steve Courtley and Brian Cox employed a setup much like that used by Eadweard Muybridge for his serial photography experiments (see pages 18 and 19): They placed 120 still cameras in an arc and coordinated their exposures using computers. The individual frames, shot from various angles but in much quicker succession than is possible with a motion picture camera, could then be edited together to create the slow camera-movement effect (sometimes called *bullet time*) for which *The Matrix* is famous. Despite its contemporary look, this special-effects technique is grounded in principles and methods established during the earliest years of motion picture history.

Between 1895 and 1905, the French filmmakers Auguste and Louis Lumière and Georges Méliès established the two basic directions that the cinema would follow: the Lumières' **realism** (an interest in or concern for the actual or real, a tendency to view or represent things as they really are) and Méliès's **antirealism** (an interest in or concern for the abstract, speculative, or fantastic). Although in the following years a notion evolved that a movie was either realistic or fantastic, in fact movies in general and any movie in particular can be both. Today, many movies mix the real and the fantastic— especially those in the *science fiction*, *action*, and *thriller* genres.

Realism is a complex concept, in part because it refers to several significant and related ideas. Most of us believe the world really exists, but we don't agree about the level on which it exists. Some

[1]

[2]

[3]

Mixing the Real and the Fantastic *Donnie Darko* (2001; director: Richard Kelly) shifts back and forth between showing a realistic depiction of the life of Donnie Darko (Jake Gyllenhaal) and his fantastic take on it. Darko is an intelligent, sensitive, and schizophrenic teenager who is seeing a therapist, and his normal suburban family blames his aberrant behavior on his failure to take his medication. [1] When he is in control, he seems to be the only student in the class who understands the reading assignment. When he is most troubled and loses control, he stares into a mirror, looking deranged [2], and then listens to the voice of a huge, demonic, imaginary rabbit [3] who encourages him to commit crimes. Donnie's motivating belief is in some kind of time travel, and just as the story ends, it curves back on itself to *before* the time it actually started. The movie asks more questions than it answers and leaves the viewer with a provocative vision of how close the line between the real and the fantastic can be.

people trust in their senses, experiences, thoughts, and feelings. Others trust in a variety of historical, political, sociological, economic, and philosophical theories to provide a framework for understanding. Still others rely on a combination of both approaches. Realism in the movies basically overrides these approaches and implies that the world it depicts looks, sounds, and moves like the real world. It is also a way of treating subject matter that reflects everyday life. Realistic characters are expected to do things that conform to our experiences and expectations of real people. Artists in every medium, however, make choices about what aspects of "reality" to depict and how to depict them. Realism, no matter how lifelike it might appear, always involves *mediation*, and thus interpretation. In the ways it is created and the ways it is perceived, realism is a kind of illusion.

If the characteristics listed here are one way to define realism in the movies, then we can define *antirealism* as a treatment that is against or the opposite of realism. We can illustrate the difference between realism and antirealism by contrasting two portrait paintings. The first, *The Hon. Frances Duncombe*, by the eighteenth-century English painter Thomas Gainsborough, realistically depicts a recognizable woman. Its form is *representational*, meaning that it represents its subject in a form that conforms to our experiences and expectations of *how* a woman looks. The overall composition of the painting and the placement of the figure emphasize unity, symmetry, and order. If you were to see the painting firsthand, you would notice that Gainsborough worked with light, rapid brush strokes and that he used delicate colors. Compare this with a second portrait, *Nude Descending a Staircase, No. 2*, by the twentieth-century French artist Marcel Duchamp, who worked in the styles of cubism, futurism, dadaism, and surrealism.

Even in the largest sense of portraiture, Duchamp's work may not represent, to most people, a recognizable woman. Duchamp has transformed a woman's natural appearance (which we know from life) into a radically altered form of sharp angles and fractured shapes. Clearly, the twentieth-century painting is less representational

[1]

[2]

Realism Versus Antirealism [1] *The Hon. Frances Duncombe* (1777), a realistic portrait painted by Thomas

Gainsborough. [2] *Nude Descending a Staircase, No. 2* (1912), the antirealistic work of Marcel Duchamp.

than its eighteenth-century predecessor. We say "less representational" because although its form is not completely recognizable, Duchamp's representation has sufficient form for us to at least identify it as a human being. If you were to see this painting firsthand, you would notice that the figure of the woman suggests an overall flatness, rather than the round, human quality of Gainsborough's figure, and that the brush strokes and the colors are bold, rather than delicate.

Verisimilitude

Whether a movie is realistic, antirealistic, or a combination of the two, it can achieve a convincing appearance of truth, a quality that we call **verisimilitude**. Movies are *verisimilar* when they convince you that the things on the screen—people, places, what have you, no matter how fantastic or antirealistic—are "really there." In other words, the movie's vision seems internally consistent, giving you a sense that in the world onscreen, *things could be just like that*. Of course, you can be convinced by the physical verisimilitude of the world being depicted and still be unconvinced by the "unreality" of the characters, their portrayal by the actors, the physical or logical implausibility of the action, and so on.

In addition, audiences' expectations concerning "reality" change over time and across cultures, of

[1]

[2]

Verisimilitude   Whether presenting a scene from everyday life, as in Louis Lumière's *Employees Leaving the Lumière Factory* (1895) [1], or showing a fantastical scenario, as in Georges Méliès's *A Trip to the Moon* (1902) [2], motion pictures were recognized from the very beginning for their ability to create a feeling of *being there*, of seeing something

that could actually happen. The Lumière brothers favored what they called *actualités*—minidocumentaries of scenes from everyday life; Méliès made movies directly inspired by his interest in magicians' illusions. Yet both the Lumières and Méliès wanted to portray their onscreen worlds convincingly—to achieve *verisimilitude* in their work.

⊙ DVD The Lumière Brothers' "Actualités"

course. A movie made in Germany in the 1930s may have been considered thoroughly verisimilar by those Germans who viewed it at the time but may seem utterly unfamiliar and perhaps even unbelievable to contemporary American viewers. Films that succeed in seeming verisimilar across cultures and times often enjoy the sort of critical and popular success that prompts people to call them *timeless*.

Some of the most popular and successful movies of all time convincingly depict imaginative or supernatural worlds and events that have little or nothing in common with our actual experiences. For example, Victor Fleming's *Gone With the Wind* (1939) treats the American South of the Civil War as a soap opera rather than important history; Steven Spielberg's *Jurassic Park* (1993) almost convinces us that the dinosaur amusement park of the title really exists, just as Andy and Larry Wachowski's *The Matrix* (1999) makes us believe in an imaginary place below the surface of our everyday lives where everything is as bad as it possibly can be; and John Lasseter's *Toy Story* (1995), a feature-length animation, brings us into the world of children's toys through a saturation of detail (when

Woody walks on Andy's bed, for example, we can even see his foot indentations on the comforter).

In Ridley Scott's *Gladiator* (2000), people, places, and things look, sound, and move in ways that are believable and even convincing, not because they are true to our experiences but because they conform to what common knowledge tells us about how life might have been lived and how things might have looked in the ancient world. More to the point, *Gladiator* adheres to the cinematic conventions established by previous movies about the ancient world—dozens of them, ranging from Fred Niblo's *Ben-Hur: A Tale of the Christ* (1925) to William Wyler's remake of *Ben-Hur* (1959) to Stanley Kubrick's *Spartacus* (1960)—and thus satisfies our individual experiences with the subject matter of the film.

Cinematic Language

By **cinematic language**, we mean the accepted systems, methods, or conventions by which the movies communicate with the viewer. The language

[1]

[2]

Believable Worlds In what sense are the worlds portrayed in Ridley Scott's *Gladiator* [1] and Steven Spielberg's *Jurassic Park* [2] believable? On what basis can we call these films *realistic*? After all, does anyone alive today know how gladiatorial combat in ancient Rome actually occurred? Who among us knows what dinosaurs looked like or how they acted during the Mesozoic era? A more useful and flexible concept that helps explain the movies' unique capacity to create believable worlds is *verisimilitude*—the quality of appearing true, probable, or likely.

we use when we speak or write is based, for the purpose of this explanation, on words. Each of those words has a generally accepted meaning, but when presented in a certain context, that word can take on a much wider range of meanings. Authors arrange words into a system (or *text*) of larger components (sentences, paragraphs, chapters, and so on) to create character, action, and the other elements that permit the viewer to reach conclusions about the text's meaning. Similarly, filmmakers have a language based on shots, each of which is arranged, combined into a system (or *movie*) of larger components (scenes, sequences, etc.) that

create characters and action, and also provide us with elements from which we determine meaning. Furthermore, within scenes and sequences a filmmaker can juxtapose shots to create a more complex meaning than is usually achieved in standard prose. As viewers, we analyze that language and its particular resources of expression and meaning. If your instructor refers to the *text* of a movie, or asks you to *read* a particular shot, scene, or movie, he is asking you to apply your understanding of cinematic language.

The conventions that make up cinematic language are flexible, not rules; they imply a practice that has evolved through film history, not an indisputable or "correct" way of doing things. In fact, cinematic conventions represent a degree of agreement between the filmmaker and the audience about the mediating element between them: the film itself. Although filmmakers frequently build upon conventions with their own innovations, they nonetheless understand and appreciate that these conventions were themselves the result of innovations. For example, a dissolve between two shots usually indicates the passing of time, but it does not indicate the extent of that duration, so in the hands of one filmmaker it might mean two minutes, and in the hands of another, several years. Thus, you will begin to understand and appreciate that the development of cinematic language, and thus the cinema itself, is founded on this tension between convention and innovation.

In all of this, we identify with the camera lens. The filmmaker (here in this introduction we use that generic term instead of the specific terms *screenwriter, director, cinematographer, editor,* etc., that we shall use as we proceed) uses the camera as a maker of meaning, just as the painter uses the brush or the writer uses the pen: the angles, heights, and movements of the camera function both as a set of techniques and as expressive material, the cinematic equivalent of brush strokes or of nouns, verbs, and adjectives. From years of looking at movies, you are already aware of how cinematic language creates meaning: how close-ups have the power to change our proximity to a character or low camera angles usually suggest that the subject of the shot is superior or threatening.

All of the following chapters of this book will expand on this introduction to the language of cinema, and although they will focus mainly on the conventional meanings and methods of that language, you will also see exceptions. Soon you will understand how these and other elements of cinematic language help set movies apart from the other arts. Even as the technology used to make and display movies continues to evolve, the principles of film art covered in this book will remain essentially the same, and the knowledge and skill you acquire by reading this book will help you look at motion pictures intelligently and perceptively throughout your life, no matter which medium delivers those pictures to you.

Using cinematic conventions, filmmakers transform experiences—their own, others', purely imaginary ones, or some combination of all three—into viewing experiences that can be understood and appreciated by audiences. In addition to bringing our acceptance and understanding of conventions to looking at movies, we bring our individual experiences. Obviously these experiences vary widely from person to person, not only in substance but also in the extent to which each of us trusts them. Personal observations of life may not be verifiable, quantifiable, or even believable, yet they are part of our perception of the world. They may reflect various influences, from intellectual substance to anti-intellectual prejudice; as a result, some people may regard gladiator movies as more meaningful than scholarly books on the subject. Thus, both cinematic conventions and individual experiences play significant roles in shaping the "reality" depicted by films.

Types of Movies

Just as soon as the movies were invented, people looking for ways to categorize them decided that a movie was either realistic or fantastic. Based on notions of realism, that distinction was sufficient for a few years, but as the making of movies began to evolve through a process of invention, convention, and innovation into an art form, so, too, did different types of movies emerge. Today we recognize four primary types of movies: *narrative films*, *nonfiction films*, *animated films*, and *experimental films*. And even though we can agree on a working definition for each type—just as we can agree on what a close-up is—we understand that the lines between these types are not hard-and-fast. Indeed, we celebrate that flexibility as being one of the principal attributes of the creative and performing arts.

Looking back on film history, we realize that this flexibility to cross transparent borders was there from the beginning. Nonetheless, we find usefulness as well as comfort in categories, and we recognize that once we understand the conventions of, say, the nonfiction film, we can better understand the filmmaker who deliberately blurs the line between narrative and nonfiction categories to create a hybrid work that has a vitality all its own. With that in mind, let's take a look at the four major categories of movies.

Narrative Films

Narrative films, or *fiction films*—the principal product of the worldwide movie industry—are the movies with which we are the most familiar (and thus the ones that are this book's primary concern). *Fiction* means that the stories these films tell—and the characters, places, and events they represent— were conceived in the minds of the films' creators. These stories may be wholly imaginary or based on true occurrences, realistic or unrealistic or both, but because their content has been selected and arranged in various ways (which we will examine throughout this book), we regard them as fiction. They are based on a script written by the screenwriter; staged and directed for the camera by the director on a studio setting or an actual location; and populated with actors.
WEB Film Genres

Genre **Genre** refers to the categorization of fiction films by the stories they tell or the ways they tell them. Genres are defined by sets of conventions— aspects of storytelling such as recurring themes and situations, and aspects of visual style such as décor, lighting, and sound. These conventions play a very

Action Genre In Quentin Tarantino's *Kill Bill: Vol. 1* (2003), the action genre combines with numerous other genres to create a genre all its own. For example, it reflects the influence of the Japanese samurai epic and the classic American western, but it transforms these in ways that make it unique. For one thing, its hero is not a man, but rather The Bride (Uma Thurman), a blond American woman, not a Japanese warrior or Texas cowboy, whose mastery of Japanese swordplay in the massacre at the "House of Blue Leaves" is one of the most stunningly conceived and realized fight scenes in movie history.

important part in how we look at movies for several reasons: they have provided a significant consistency to filmmaking since its beginnings, we readily identify with their familiar conditions, and they offer rich opportunities for analyzing both the movies themselves and the cultures in and for which they are made. From the outset, it is useful to remember that the concept of genre is a very flexible one; as you will see in this discussion, genres adapt as the result of various influences. Furthermore, because of this flexibility, there is little consensus about when a particular type of filmmaking deserves to be designated as a genre. In addition, genres frequently overlap. For our purposes, here is a list of some major genres of narrative films (with identifying characteristics and examples):

> *Action*. Action (or adventure) movies involve their characters in a series of fast-paced events and astonishing physical feats, fights, and chases; extensive violence; and exotic locales. Examples include the series featuring the characters James Bond and Indiana Jones, James Cameron's *The Terminator* (1984), John McTiernan's *Die Hard* (1988), and Andy and Larry Wachowski's *The Matrix* (1999). Action movies can overlap with other genres, ranging from westerns to thrillers.

> *Biography*. These movies, sometimes called *biopics*, tell the life stories of well-known people and are among the most popular of all movies. There are many approaches to making biographical films, and some outstanding achievements include William Dieterle's *The Life of Emile Zola* (1937), featuring celebrated actor Paul Muni in the role of the great French novelist; Michael Apted's *Coal Miner's Daughter* (1980), with Sissy Spacek as country-and-western singer Loretta Lynn; Spike Lee's *Malcolm X* (1992), with Denzel Washington as the Black Nationalist leader; and Taylor Hackford's *Ray* (2004), with Jamie Foxx as legendary singer Ray Charles.

> *Comedy*. One of the most complex genres, comedy can be simply defined as a story that

Biopic Genre In this shot from Bill Condon's *Kinsey* (2004), Dr. Alfred Kinsey (Liam Neeson), noted authority on human sexual behavior, is talking to reporters; his wife, Clara (Laura Linney), is at his side. In the movie, Kinsey, a pioneer in encouraging Americans to better understand human sexuality, gender, and reproduction, is depicted as a victim of his own unidentified sexuality, as well as of the society he was trying to educate.

makes us laugh and ends happily. Various techniques make us laugh, including satire, parody, ludicrous character behavior, irony, verbal wit, physical plot incidents, and obscenity for humorous effect. *Black comedy* makes us laugh at what, by standards of polite behavior, we shouldn't. Memorable comedies include Ernst Lubitsch's *Trouble in Paradise* (1932), Billy Wilder's *Some Like It Hot* (1959), and Woody Allen's *Annie Hall* (1977).

> *Fantasy.* Fantasy movies tell stories about highly improbable, sometimes impossible, characters and events. Because they take place in worlds we can know only through the imagination, the directors of these movies are challenged to make the unreal seem real. Fantastic elements, of course, play a role in many narrative films, but pure fantasy films are in a category all by themselves. One of the very first, Georges Méliès's *A Trip to the Moon* (1902) takes a delightfully comic look at its subject. Other fantasy films—some comic, others not—include Victor Fleming's *The Wizard of Oz* (1939), Peter Jackson's "Lord of the Rings" trilogy (2001–03), and the Harry Potter movies (the work of various directors). The fantasy and science fiction genres often overlap, as in George Lucas's "Star Wars" movies and Stanley Kubrick's *2001: A Space Odyssey* (1968). Many elaborate crime movies, like David Mamet's *Heist* (2001) or the James Bond series, border on fantasy.

> *Film noir.* French for "black film," the term *film noir* refers to highly stylized crime films, indebted to or based on detective stories, and generally characterized by their somber tones and pessimistic moods. Film noir stories concentrate on crime and corruption; on characters (heroes and villains alike) who tend to be cynical, disillusioned, and often insecure or impotent loners. The mood of the stories is enhanced by characteristic visual elements, including sleazy nighttime settings lit to emphasize contrasts between black and white, create deep shadows, and enhance the fatalistic mood; the oblique composition of images; and the use of exaggerated camera setups and angles.

Because of its easily identifiable cinematic style, film noir should be regarded both as a style and a genre. Among the classic Hollywood film noirs are John Huston's *The Maltese Falcon* (1941), Billy Wilder's *Double Indemnity* (1944), Alfred Hitchcock's *Spellbound* (1945), Tay Garnett's *The Postman Always Rings Twice* (1946), Orson Welles's *The Lady From Shanghai* (1947), Nicholas Ray's *They Live by Night* (1948), and Fritz Lang's *The Big Heat* (1953). The generic

Gross-out Comedy Today's comedy takes many forms, including the loony, audacious gross-out type found in Bobby and Peter Farrelly's *There's Something About Mary* (1998). Here, in a hilarious sequence, Mary Jensen (Cameron Diaz) has used some of Ted Stroehmann's (Ben Stiller, *left, back to camera*) "hair gel"—a ridiculous situation that they both manage to survive.

transformation, known as *neo-noir*, includes Orson Welles's *Touch of Evil* (1958), Roman Polanski's *Chinatown* (1974), Joel Coen's *Blood Simple* (1984), Stephen Frears's *The Grifters* (1990), and James Dearden's *A Kiss Before Dying* (1991).

> *Gangster.* Gangster movies, in which the emphasis is on the underworld, can overlap with action movies, biopics, film noirs, and mysteries. The original gangster movies, such as Mervyn LeRoy's *Little Caesar* (1931), told the story of the rise and fall of a fictitious gangster. In later variations on the genre—like Arthur Penn's *Bonnie and Clyde* (1967)—the stories were based on the lives of actual criminals or—in the case of Francis Ford Coppola's *The Godfather* (1972) and its sequels, or Martin Scorsese's *Goodfellas* (1990)—on fictional characters that seemed right out of news reports. Others, like Steven Soderbergh's *Ocean's Eleven* (2001) depict the crime as a cool, stylish romp. The gangster genre has been transformed to include inner-

Gangster Genre During the 1970s the gangster genre acknowledged the inner-city, teenage street gangs that were part of the culture of that time. Walter Hill's *The Warriors* (1979), the inspiration for today's video game of the same name, uses cartoon images that morph into live-action images. Here we see Swan (Michael Beck), one of the leaders of the Warriors gang, taking on members of the rival Furies gang in Central Park. These gangs and their dialogue at first suggest a very macho conflict, but the acting, costuming, and makeup, as well as such gang names as "Swan," provide distinctly homoerotic implications. Today, *The Warriors* seems more camp than anything else.

city, teenage street gangs such as those depicted in Walter Hill's *The Warriors* (1979).

> *Horror.* Horror films use any means necessary to make us cringe, scare us, or even terrify us. They tell stories based on suspense, surprise, or shock; feature characters with physical, psychological, or emotional deformities; and are usually photographed in settings that, however familiar, are frightening because of what we see and hear. Some horror films have psychological significance (Rouben Mamoulian's *Dr. Jekyll and Mr. Hyde*, 1931, for example); others show us the "human" face of horror (James Whale's *The Bride of Frankenstein*, 1935); some link sex and violence (Jacques Tourneur's *Cat People*, 1942, and Paul Schrader's remake, 1982); some introduce us to the occult (William Friedkin's *The Exorcist*, 1973); and still others cause revulsion and disgust by focusing on the depths of human psychopathology (Jonathan Demme's *The Silence of the Lambs*, 1991).

> *Melodrama.* A melodrama is a story incorporating real-life events that builds to powerful climaxes, contains stereotypical characters, and illustrates exaggerated physical and emotional behavior. Melodramas focus on personal, moral, social, family, racial, ethnic, cultural, or "women's" issues. They tug at our hearts, often deliberately provoking tears over situations of human crisis. We find melodramatic aspects in other genres where characters face intense issues. A few notable examples are D. W. Griffith's *Way Down East* (1920), King Vidor's *Stella Dallas* (1937; see Chapter 5), Kimberly Peirce's *Boys Don't Cry* (1999), and Todd Haynes's *Far From Heaven* (2002).

> *Musical.* Musicals tell their stories using characters that express themselves with song and dance, as well as spoken dialogue. Unless the singing and dancing are integrated seamlessly into the story (as in Jerome Robbins and Robert Wise's *West Side Story*, 1961), these elements often interrupt the development of the plot (as in any of the Fred Astaire and Ginger Rogers movies, where their singing and dancing are better than the

Melodrama Genre   The melodrama genre evolves with the times, but certain themes and treatments remain constant. Douglas Sirk's *Imitation of Life* (1959), a family story with an interracial theme, is a classic melodrama, the spirit of which inspired Todd Haynes's *Far From Heaven* (2002). Haynes's movie is set in the 1950s in suburban Connecticut. In this scene, Cathy Whitaker (Julianne Moore), accompanied by her housekeeper Sybil (Viola Davis), learns from the police that her husband has been arrested for loitering. Next, her husband admits his homosexuality and divorces her, and she falls in love with a widowed African American (played by Dennis Haysbert). But this new love affair further complicates her life, and she is eventually left alone. Although the story is sensitively told, it has soap opera at its heart.

Mystery Genre   Curtis Hanson's *L. A. Confidential* (1997), a very sophisticated crime movie, is rich in the atmosphere of a seedy Los Angeles in the 1950s. Everyone is corrupt, including the two characters we see here: Lynn Bracken (Kim Basinger), the femme fatale intentionally groomed to resemble the 1940s movie star Veronica Lake, and Officer Wendell "Bud" White (Russell Crowe). Lynn works for the prostitution ring that holds the clue to the crime that White is trying to solve.

plots). The first "talkie," Alan Crosland's *The Jazz Singer* (1927), was also the first musical. "Classic" musicals include Victor Fleming's *The Wizard of Oz* (1939), Vincente Minnelli's *An American in Paris* (1951), and Stanley Donen and Gene Kelly's *Singin' in the Rain* (1952). The musical genre was completely transformed in Baz Luhrmann's *Moulin Rouge!* (2001).

> *Mystery*. Mysteries tell stories that emphasize the sequential and sometimes suspenseful work of a detective (professional or amateur) who discovers the identity of a criminal (usually a murderer). Thus, mysteries are often called *crime* or *detective* movies, often overlap with film noir (see above), and sometimes include aspects of the thriller (see below). Classic mysteries featuring detectives include Edwin S. Porter's *The Great Train Robbery* (1903), the first movie to tell the story of a sheriff apprehending thieves; the seven films

in the Thin Man series (1934–47), with William Powell and Myrna Loy as amateur sleuths, Nick and Nora Charles; John Huston's *The Maltese Falcon* (1941), with Humphrey Bogart as private detective Sam Spade; and the many films featuring such characters as Miss Marple, Bulldog Drummond, Philip Marlowe, and Hercule Poirot.

> *Romance*. Although the original romance film featured a "boy meets girl" story, today there are "girl meets girl" and "boy meets boy" movie romances as well. Romantic movies emphasize the challenges to starting a love relationship, the emotional ups and downs that follow, and usually, but not always, a happy ending. A few notable titles in this very popular genre include such heterosexual romances as George Cukor's *Camille* (1936), Alfred Hitchcock's *Rebecca* (1940), Michael Curtiz's *Casablanca* (1942), George Stevens's *A Place in the Sun* (1951), Spike Lee's *Jungle Fever* (1991), Nora Ephron's *Sleepless in Seattle* (1993), as well as homosexual romances such as Rose Troche's *Go Fish* (1994) and Ang Lee's *Brokeback Mountain* (2005).

> *Science fiction*. Literally, science fiction films deal with the fortunes or misfortunes that

Romance Genre Charles Herman-Wurmfeld's *Kissing Jessica Stein* (2001) is a delightful romantic comedy about two women who fall in love but don't have much of a clue about where to go from there. Jessica Stein (Jennifer Westfeldt, *right*), a neurotic copy editor who has been single for a long time, meets Helen Cooper (Heather Juergensen, *left*), another professional woman who is experienced with men but has advertised for a girlfriend. In this scene, they are looking at a sex manual for lesbians. The contrast between Jennifer's touching awkwardness and Helen's equally touching astonishment at what she sees is depicted with a light comic touch. The movie has no message except that the only way to explain sexual attraction is that it happens.

result from using science in highly imaginative stories of exploration, discovery, experimentation, or extraterrestrial invasion. The first authentic science fiction film on a grand scale was William Cameron Menzies's *Things to Come* (1936), a movie that, in its scope and design, foreshadows George Lucas's "Star Wars" movies or Stanley Kubrick's *2001: A Space Odyssey* (1968; see "Fantasy" above). During the so-called Cold War that followed World War II, there were widespread fears of alien invasions and nuclear holocausts— subjects of two classic sci-fi movies: Christian Nyby's *The Thing From Another World* (1951) and Robert Wise's *The Day the Earth Stood Still* (1951), respectively. Other impressive examples include James Whale's *Frankenstein* (1931), George Lucas's *THX 1138* (1971), Robert Wise's *The Andromeda Strain* (1971), Steven Spielberg's *Close Encounters of the Third Kind* (1997) and *War of the Worlds* (2005); and Ridley Scott's *Alien* (1979) and *Blade Runner* (1982).

> *Thriller*. Thrillers generate excitement, nervous tension, and anxiety, primarily through *suspense* about what will happen next in a movie. Thrillers often overlap with other genres, and today, the term *thriller* is used quite loosely to describe a variety of movies, ranging from crime heists to spy movies. No matter what the story, a thriller is characterized more by the *effect* it has on us than anything else. A great thriller keeps us on the edge of our seats, at the very least, and sometimes puts us on the verge of hysteria as we watch characters slowly moving toward their fates. Classic thrillers include Robert Siodmak's *The Spiral Staircase* (1946), Alfred Hitchcock's *Psycho* (1960), Stanley Kubrick's *The Shining* (1980), Jonathan Demme's *The Silence of the Lambs* (1991), David Fincher's *Se7en* (1995), and Christopher Nolan's *Memento* (2000).

> *War*. War films usually take one of two approaches: either the war is the major action of the film, as in Steven Spielberg's *Saving Private Ryan* (1998), or it is the background for the action, as in William Wyler's *The Best Years of Our Lives* (1946). The genre includes such subgenres as the prisoner-of-war film (David Lean's *The Bridge on the River Kwai*, 1957), the resistance film (Robert Bres-

Thriller Genre In Alfred Hitchcock's absurd, comic thriller *North by Northwest* (1959), Eve Kendall (Eva Marie Saint) plays yet another of the director's two-faced femme fatales, here seducing Roger O. Thornhill (Cary Grant). We're not exactly sure whose side she's on, but after a series of daring escapes, including the famous sequence on the face of Mount Rushmore, the two eventually end up together.

War Genre Like many other war films, Terrence Malick's *The Thin Red Line* (1998) is about a major conflict—this one at Guadalcanal during World War II. True to the genre, this movie combines superb combat footage with beautifully etched portraits of the fighting men, here portrayed by a magnificent cast headed by Nick Nolte as Lieutenant Colonel Gordon Tall, a man so bitter about not being promoted, and so gung ho about winning, that he stands on the thin red line, the crossing point between sanity and madness.

1

2

Western Genre Howard Hawks's *Red River* (1948) is a classic western, noted for its relentlessly spare story, awesome outdoor beauty, and casting. Hawks took advantage of the viewers' expectations of a western, not in his casting of John Wayne [1, *left*] as Thomas Dunson, the indomitable, hardened cattle driver—a typical enough role for Wayne—but in his choice of Montgomery Clift [1 and 2, *right*] as Matthew "Matt" Garth, a physically beautiful man who seems gentle and soft in contrast to Wayne's character. *Red River* was the first western to deal seriously with the genre's male stereotypes, and, in the overall conflict between the two men, Garth proves to be the better one for the task at hand.

son's *A Man Escaped*, 1956, which is also a prisoner-of-war film), the antiwar film (Lewis Milestone's *All Quiet on the Western Front*, 1930), the "war is hell" film (Francis Ford Coppola's *Apocalypse Now*, 1979), the war-hero film (Sergei Eisenstein and Dmitri Vasilyev's *Alexander Nevsky*, 1938), the wartime romance (Michael Curtiz's *Casablanca*, 1942), and even the wartime suspense comedy (Billy Wilder's *Five Graves to Cairo*, 1943).

> *Western.* For the most part, westerns tell the story of the U.S. westward expansion after the Civil War. That history has sometimes been told as fact, but most often as myth. Westerns tell the stories of the American pioneers who struggled to cross the vast midwestern plains; fought off the Native Americans, whose land they claimed and settled; founded towns and established in them institutions of commerce, justice, education, religion, and culture. The settings are the mountains and wide-open spaces of the American West; the characters are the Native Americans and pioneers who become ranchers, cowboys, prospectors, sheriffs, opportunists of all kinds, and criminals.

In terms of straightforward storytelling and superior cinematic values, any list of the top westerns would include John Ford's *Stagecoach* (1939) and *The Searchers* (1956), Fred Zinnemann's *High Noon* (1952), Sam Peckinpah's *The Wild Bunch* (1969), Sergio

Leone's *Once Upon a Time in the West* (1968), and Clint Eastwood's *Unforgiven* (1992). Kevin Costner's *Dances With Wolves* (1990), as well as many of John Ford's movies, are among the most accurate westerns in their depiction of Native Americans. Lighthearted takes on the genre include Elliot Silverstein's *Cat Ballou* (1965), George Roy Hill's *Butch Cassidy and the Sundance Kid* (1969), and Mel Brooks's *Blazing Saddles* (1974).

Films belong to the same genre not because they tell the same story but because their stories share certain conventions in the way they are told (their *plots*), and in the handling of their characters, settings, and themes. Although the films may tell *similar* stories, the forms through which they tell the stories can vary considerably. The opening scenes of many westerns, for example, often present very similar exposition, but each director may present a different variation on the formula. (**Exposition**, which lays the foundation for the storytelling, includes the images, action, and dialogue necessary to give the audience the background of the characters and the nature of their situation.)

We like genre films because we are familiar with their conventions—their use of cinematic language—and because, when we go to see an action film, for instance, we know generally what to expect and enjoy having our expectations fulfilled. Once the movie industry realized the power of genre to attract audiences and sell tickets, it exploited that power by keeping most of the genres up-to-date with changing cultural conditions. Thus, it was once sufficient in a biographical film (or biopic) to have a straightforward account of a person's life, usually focusing on the positive aspects of the individual's career and achievements. Ironically, in the early years such movies were more concerned with the setting of the story than with the development of the character. Alfred E. Green's *Disraeli* (1929) is one example. Actor George Arliss, who played British Prime Minister Benjamin Disraeli, made a profession out of playing such historical figures as Cardinal Richelieu, the Duke of Wellington, and Voltaire. Costumes, makeup, and wigs helped him look like the charac-

ters he was portraying, but there was little character depth in his *characterization*.

Today that approach seems quaint in light of the many contemporary biopics of substance—films in which we see the main characters as fully rounded human beings. For example, Bill Condon's *Kinsey* (2004), based on the life of Dr. Alfred Kinsey, the first American specialist in human sexual behavior, reveals that Kinsey, played by Liam Neeson, had problems identifying his own sexual orientation. The same honesty about the ups and downs in a character's professional and personal lives is evident in James Mangold's *Walk the Line* (2005), an account of the legendary country music star Johnny Cash (played by Joaquin Phoenix).

Genre movies are successful because they appeal to our love of certain kinds of storytelling, our desire to be satisfied repeatedly with the same formula, and our habit of bonding with those who like the same movies (think of the "Star Wars" or "Lord of the Rings" groupies). The concept of genre has been essential to the development of the movie industry and movie audiences: give people what they want and they will buy it. This simple economic principle helps us understand the phenomenal growth of the movie industry from the 1930s on, as well as the mind-numbing mediocrity of so many of the movies it produced. Catering to the least thoughtful members of an audience often results in a formulaic approach to making movies that include stereotypes (often blatant) and run-of-the-mill situations in all aspects of the story, from setting and action to character and theme. This does not mean that a mediocre genre film is unworthy of your attention, for how many times have you gone to a movie fully acknowledging from the beginning that you wanted to see it no matter how "bad" it was? Hollywood exploits this behavior by ensuring that genre films appeal to a wide range of viewers. Today the classic genres continue to exist largely in terms of creative variations on their conventions.

Genres stay vital and interesting to audiences when filmmakers expand on and play with the genre's conventions, as when certain filmmakers (e.g., Antoine Fuqua in *Training Day*, 2001), bring the conventions of action films up to date by increasing the levels of violence. Where appropriate, two or more genres can be combined to form a hybrid genre. Sometimes the result takes the form of a pastiche, as in Quentin Tarantino's *Kill Bill: Vol. 1* (2003), a film that borrows not only from Japanese animation, but also from many genres—including the western, musical, drama, thriller, action, horror, comedy, and crime.

Although conventional genre films may strictly follow ideological conventions (regarding class, race, sex, gender, and so on), filmmakers also use genres to arouse and then adapt audiences' ideological expectations. Thus, when Mel Brooks's *Blazing Saddles* (1974), an outlandish comedy, presents an African American sheriff in the American West of the 1860s, the movie parodies the western genre and offers social criticism, calling attention to how genres can reinforce stereotypes. Dennis Hopper's *Easy Rider* (1969)—combining the road movie, the biker movie, and the male-buddy movie (all subgenres)—makes a statement about divisions between "straight" and "hippie" subcultures. And Ridley Scott's *Thelma & Louise* (1991)—combining the road movie and the female-buddy movie—creates a feminist parable.

To understand how complex a single genre can be, let's consider comedy. Movies are categorized as comedies because they make us laugh, but we quickly realize that each is unique because it is funny in its own way. Comedies, in fact, prove why movie genres exist. They give us what we expect, they make us laugh and ask for more, and they make money, often in spite of themselves. As a result, the comic genre in the movies has evolved into such a complex system that we rely on defined subgenres to keep track of its development.

The silent-movie comedies of the 1920s—featuring such legends as Max Linder, Charlie Chaplin, Buster Keaton, Roscoe "Fatty" Arbuckle, Harry Langdon, Harold Lloyd, many of whom worked for producer Mack Sennett—were known as *slapstick comedy* because aggression or violent behavior, not verbal humor, was the source of the laughs. (The term *slapstick* refers to the two pieces of wood, hinged together, that clowns used to produce a sharp sound that simulated the sound of one person striking another.)

After the arrival of sound, movie comedy continued the sight gags of the slapstick tradition (Laurel and Hardy, the Marx Brothers, W. C. Fields), but relied increasingly on verbal wit. Through the 1930s, a wide variety of subgenres developed: comedy of wit (Ernst Lubitsch's *Trouble in Paradise*, 1932); romantic comedy (Rouben Mamoulian's *Love Me Tonight*, 1932), screwball comedy (Frank Capra's *It Happened One Night*, 1934), farce (any Marx Brothers movie), and sentimental comedy, often with a political twist (Frank Capra's *Meet John Doe*, 1941).

By the 1940s, comedy was perhaps the most popular genre in American movies, and it remains that way today, although another group of subgenres has developed, most in response to our changing cultural expectations of what is funny and what is now permissible to laugh at. These include light sex comedies (Billy Wilder's *Some Like It Hot*, 1959), gross-out sex comedies (Bobby and Peter Farrelly's *Stuck on You*, 2003), and neurotic sex comedies (almost any Woody Allen movie), as well as satire laced with black comedy (Stanley Kubrick's *Dr. Strangelove or: How I Learned to Stop Worrying and Love the Bomb*, 1964), outrageous farce (Mel Brooks's *The Producers*, 1968, and Susan Stroman's musical remake, 2005), and a whole subgenre of comedy that is associated with the comedian's name: Alec Guinness, Jacques Tati, Jim Carrey, Whoopi Goldberg, and Will Ferrell, to name but a few.

On one hand, as a form of cinematic language, genres involve filmic realities—however stereotyped—that audiences can easily recognize and understand and that film distributors can market (e.g., "The Scariest Thriller Ever Made"). On the other hand, genres evolve, changing with the times and adapting to audience expectations, which are in turn influenced by a large range of factors—technological, cultural, social, political, economic, and so on. **Generic transformation** is the process by which a particular genre is adapted to meet the expectations of a changing society. Arguably, genres that don't evolve lose the audience's interest quickly and fade away.

The western, perhaps the most American of all genres, began to fade away in the 1960s. With certain exceptions—including Sergio Leone's *Once*

Upon a Time in the West (1968), Arthur Penn's *Little Big Man* (1970), Kevin Costner's *Dances With Wolves* (1990), and Clint Eastwood's *Unforgiven* (1992)—the western no longer had the same appeal that it had for previous generations of movie audiences. Part of the explanation was that most westerns were out of touch with reality, made by directors who ignored the roles played by Native Americans and women in the development of this country; that they relied instead on the fatigued nature of the good guys/bad guys conflict and equally tired myths about the West; and that they ended up creating a world that might as well have come from outer space.

Just when we thought that the western was dead—for all practical purposes, meaning severely diminished box-office appeal—it was transformed in an original way in Ang Lee's *Brokeback Mountain* (2005). The director remains true to Annie Proulx's short story, on which the screenplay is based, but what he transforms is our fixed idea of the conventions of the western. Gone is the conflict between the white man and the Native Americans on the frontier, the saloon, and the shootout on main street. Gone is the cowboy, with his apparently sexless existence, high moral purpose, and uncanny sense of nature. In place of these traditional western elements, against a background of spectacular western scenery (a staple of all westerns), Lee gives us the story of two ranch hands who fall in love with one another. In Ang Lee's process of generic transformation, he has revived some of the elements of the western to tell a story that is not about sex, but rather about loneliness, love, heartbreak, and, ultimately, sorrow—elements borrowed from yet other genres, notably the melodrama and romance.

Brokeback Mountain is set in the Wyoming of the 1960s, where and when its transformation of the traditional "boy meets girl" romance would have been even less acceptable than it would be in many parts of the country today. Even though some viewers recognized homoerotic longing in such classic westerns as Howard Hawks's *Red River* (1948) and George Roy Hill's *Butch Cassidy and the Sundance Kid* (1969), this was not a dominant theme in those movies. Today, in a culture where grappling with one's sexual identity is a staple of books and television talk shows, but very few movies, *Brokeback Mountain* demonstrates that generic transformation can work in very powerful ways not only to expand the original concept of the western genre, but also, in this case, to encourage the viewer to think more about the subject.

Nonfiction Films

Narrative film is not the only film type being transformed by audience expectations as well as the impact of the independent movie at the box office. The **nonfiction film** (often used synonymously with the term *documentary film*) is enjoying a renaissance that is unprecedented in its long history. Once it might have been possible to define the nonfiction film as Polish director Krzysztof Kieslowski did: a film "describing the world . . . life as it is, not how it might exist in the imagination."[5] Given recent developments in the handling of the established conventions of nonfiction filmmaking, however, this is no longer true (if it ever was). An Errol Morris, Werner Herzog, or Michael Moore nonfiction film is as imaginative as the individual filmmaker's talents can make it. Indeed, if we had no need for categories, we might say that the *narrative* and *nonfiction* approaches to making movies have, in some cases, overlapped so significantly that they have created a hybrid. Today, many narrative movies incorporate techniques that were once thought to be solely in the province of the nonfiction film, and vice versa.

Traditionally, nonfiction films have been made in four basic styles—*factual*, *instructional*, *documentary*, and *propaganda*. That these categories can overlap to create other hybrid forms demonstrates the versatility of the type and helps account for the production of thousands of nonfiction films each year. We do not assume that a nonfiction *film* tells the "truth" about its subject, because any act of filmmaking involves mediation between filmmaker and subject. As we will see in subsequent chapters,

[5] From "An Introduction to *The Decalogue*," in the special DVD edition released by Facets Multimedia, 2003.

every aspect of filmmaking, no matter what type of film is being made, uses formal elements and technical properties—such as narration, camera angles, editing, and music—that alter the material being filmed. Thus, strictly speaking, a nonfiction film, even though it is usually about real people, places, and events, is no more "true" than a fiction film.

Factual films usually present people, places, or processes in straightforward ways meant to entertain and instruct without unduly influencing audiences. Early examples include the Lumière brothers' *actualités*—films of trains arriving, boats leaving, soldiers marching off to the front, and the like—and the hundreds of films produced on all sides during World War I, when film became a weapon of information *and* disinformation (or *propaganda*, as we'll discuss shortly). Director Robert Flaherty insisted that his classic *Nanook of the North* (1922) was a factual account of Inuit life in the sub-Arctic, even though it clearly reflects Flaherty's staging for the camera of events and the Inuit perspective on them. Perhaps the best we can say for this captivating film is that it is true to human nature but not true to the life the Inuits were living when Flaherty made the film. Thus it has little factual or anthropological value.

Nanook of the North   Robert Flaherty's *Nanook of the North* (1922), a pioneering nonfiction film, gave general audiences their first visual encounter with Inuit culture. Its subject matter made it significant (and successful), and its use of narrative film techniques was pathbreaking. Flaherty edited together many different kinds of shots and angles, for example, and directed the Inuit through reenactments of life events, some of which—hunting with spears—were no longer part of their lives.

⊃WEB Factual and Dramatic Aspects of Nonfiction Film

The three other nonfiction film subtypes can be distinguished by their rising concern with influencing viewers. **Instructional films** seek to educate viewers about common interests rather than persuading them to accept particular ideas. During World War II, instructional films were used to teach members of the armed forces and civilians about the challenges of wartime, such as homeland security and food shortages. Today such films (on DVD for home consumption) are more likely to teach skills, such as cooking techniques or exercise routines. **Documentary films** were conceived and advocated by John Grierson, a British film producer who had his greatest influence in the 1930s. Their founding purpose was to address social injustice.

When documentaries are produced by governments and carry governments' messages, they overlap with **propaganda films**, which systematically disseminate deceptive or distorted information. For a brief period, the U.S. government directly and indirectly produced such films. A noteworthy example is Pare Lorentz's *The River* (1937), which proclaims the benefits of forest, land, and water conservation, particularly as carried out by President Franklin D. Roosevelt's Tennessee Valley Authority projects concerned with hydroelectric power. *The River* is particularly worth seeing today, not necessarily for its concern with conserving natural resources—an argument that has since been more powerfully voiced elsewhere—but rather for its eloquent cinematography, narration, and music.

Genuine documentaries—those concerned with social issues and particularly with corporate and governmental injustice of all kinds—continue to be made by independent filmmakers and network television producers. Many of them are controversial, such as Errol Morris's *The Fog of War* (2003), or Michael Moore's preachy *Fahrenheit 9/11* (2004), which attempts to show how the administration of

President George W. Bush used the 9/11 terrorist attacks to justify its agenda for waging wars in Afghanistan and Iraq.

Other films warn us of dangers at home: Kelly Anderson and Tami Gold's *Making a Killing: Philip Morris, Kraft and Global Tobacco Addiction* (2000) reveals the tactics of Philip Morris, warning viewers of how the company spreads tobacco addiction by abusing its size, promotional expertise, and political power. Liz Garbus's *Girlhood* (2003) records what happens when teenage girls who have spent time in prison for drug addiction or violence cope with moving back into a society that treats juvenile offenders like adult criminals.

The most famous propaganda film ever made, Leni Riefenstahl's *Triumph of the Will* (1935), records many events at the 1934 Nuremberg rally of the Nazi Party and thus might mistakenly be considered a "factual" film. But through its carefully planned cinematography and editing, it also presents a highly glorified image of Adolf Hitler, primarily for the consumption of non-German audiences before World War II.

Soon after that war began, the United States started production of all the above types of nonfiction films. The seven-part "Why We Fight" series (1943–45), made by Frank Capra, the legendary director of narrative comedies, constitutes the single most powerful nonfiction film achievement in the war effort.[6] Addressed to those in civilian and military audiences who doubted the need for another world war, these films depict Nazi aggression and brutality, the major battles of the war, and, finally, the impact of prewar and war efforts on American public opinion. Remarkable compilation films—lucid and fresh in their handling of many cinematic sources, historically balanced, and persuasively and dramatically presented—the "Why We Fight" films are also remarkable propaganda, made by film experts who had studied and restudied the best Nazi and British precedents. They are also, unfortunately, very racist in their

Controversial Nonfiction Films   Any honest attempt to discuss war in general and the Vietnam War in particular ends up being controversial, and Errol Morris's *The Fog of War: Eleven Lessons from the Life of Robert S. McNamara* (2003) is no exception. Given the passionate feelings on both sides about the war, and the fact that former Secretary of Defense McNamara was the United States' number one hawk, it is an understandably ambivalent portrait of him. Yet Morris is willing to listen to the powerful lessons that McNamara has learned from a lifetime of experience with war (including World War II), and he shows considerable empathy, but he lets McNamara make all the points and does not judge him. Near the end of this fascinating, important film, McNamara says, "What the 'fog of war' means is that war is so complex, it's beyond the ability of the human mind to comprehend all the variables. Our judgment and understanding are not adequate, and we kill people—unnecessarily." The "unnecessarily," spoken softly and haltingly, is as close to an expression of regret as he gets.

depiction of the military enemies of the United States at the time: the German, Italian, and Japanese people.

The continuing vitality of the nonfiction film is demonstrated not only in the variety of its content, but also in the imagination of its directors. Jeffrey Blitz's *Spellbound* (2002), not to be confused with Alfred Hitchcock's 1945 movie of the same title, seems at first to be only a likable, gentle, old-fashioned documentary about eight teenagers who seek to win the National Spelling Bee. However, Blitz also ridicules some of the young spellers and their families, so in the end it's not certain what his attitude toward the spelling bee is. Harry Alex Rubin and Dana Adam Shapiro's *Murderball* (2005) is about quadriplegic, wheelchair-bound rugby players. Jim Fields and Michael Gramaglia's *End of the Century* (2003) tells the story of the legendary

---

[6] Ironically, filmmaker Eugene Jarecki used the same title, *Why We Fight* (2005), for his equally well-researched and absorbing critique of U.S. militarism since the end of World War II.

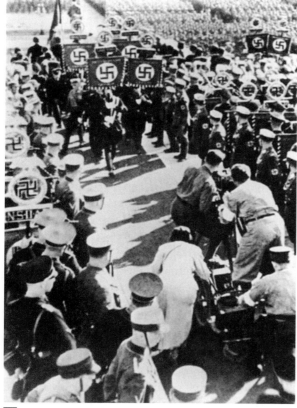

Triumph of the Will   The most accomplished (and notorious) propaganda film of all time, Leni Riefenstahl's *Triumph of the Will* (1935), is studied by both historians and scholars of film. Much of the blocking of the 1934 Nuremberg Nazi rally was crafted specifically with the camera in mind. [1] Riefenstahl, wearing a white dress and helping to push the camera, films a procession during the rally. [2] Taken from a distant perspective, this shot conveys many concepts that the filmmaker and the Nazis wanted the world to see: order, discipline, and magnitude.

punk rock band The Ramones. Each of these daring, idiosyncratic movies had successful runs in movie theaters.

Because of movies like these, we have begun to take notice of nonfiction films for their box-office potential. After Michael Moore's *Fahrenheit 9/11*, the second-highest-grossing nonfiction film is Luc Jacquet's *March of the Penguins* (2005), which recounts the harrowing age-old trek of emperor penguins to their traditional breeding grounds in Antarctica. As another significant indication of the increasing power and popularity of the nonfiction film, both of these titles were subject to intense public debate and controversy (the first because it challenged the Bush administration; the second because it was initially championed by cultural conservatives for its supposed celebration of "family values," a claim that was promptly and loudly criticized by experts of animal behavior).

Among other successful and controversial nonfiction films are Lauren Lazin's *Tupac: Resurrection* (2003), about the life of rap star Tupac Shakur. Rather than look into the circumstances surrounding his 1996 murder, including the rivalries between gangs as well as rap stars, Lazin has compiled a great deal of footage—including much of Shakur himself—to try to "resurrect" his life. Two notable documentary filmmakers take aim at the consumer culture: Robert Greenwald in *Wal-Mart: The High Cost of Low Price* (2005), an attack on Wal-Mart's policies and practices; and Morgan Spurlock in *Super Size Me* (2004), which pokes fun at fast-food culture while making serious points about the fat-laden content of McDonald's offerings. Finally, Werner Herzog, a filmmaker who has made some of the most mesmerizing nonfiction films in history, and who is also a cult figure for his fiction films, released *Grizzly Man* (2005), a film

A Documentary Takes on the Consumer Culture
Morgan Spurlock's *Super Size Me* (2004) is a day-by-day record of his ordeal in eating nothing but food from McDonald's for 30 days: his "Mac Attack." In good health when he starts, and monitored by three doctors throughout the month, he ends up depressed, exhausted, and weighing 24.5 pounds more. The film doesn't tell us anything that we didn't already know about the dangers of fast food, but it tells the story with originality and authority.

about Timothy Treadwell, a man who forsakes civilization, goes to live among the Alaskan grizzly bears, and videotapes his own death as he is torn apart and eaten by a bear. He's the classic Herzog subject, an obsessive person pursuing a singular passion in spite of logic, common sense, and terrifying odds.

⮕ WEB Nonfiction Films: Direct Cinema

Animated Films

Next to narrative films, animation is today the second most popular type of film with audiences. Before computer-generated imagery, which accounts for virtually all animated films today, **animated films** (or *cartoons*) were made by photographing drawings, other graphic images, silhouettes, or inanimate objects frame by frame with a special animation camera. Small changes were made in each drawing, and thus each frame showed a slight change in the subject and/or its movement. Making a traditional animated film is a very arduous effort, for, theoretically, twenty-four individual drawings or setups are necessary to make one second of film (or 14,400 for ten minutes). When these frames are projected on a screen at the standard speed of 24 fps, persistence of

vision creates the illusion of continuous movement. Such animated images have been made since the beginning of motion pictures and—if we include persistence-of-vision devices such as the thaumatrope, the phenakistoscope, and the praxinoscope—have existed since the early 1800s.

At the beginning of motion pictures, animated films of great creative originality and importance were made in France by Georges Méliès (*The Four Troublesome Heads*, 1898) and Émile Cohl (*Fantasmagorie*, 1908); and in the United States by J. Stuart Blackton (*The Enchanted Drawing*, 1900), Winsor McCay (*Gertie the Dinosaur*, 1914), and John Randolph Bray, whose *Colonel Heeza Liar's African Hunt* (1914) was both the first commercially released animated cartoon and the opening segment of the first animated cartoon series.

Of the several basic ways of making animated films—*drawing, puppet animation, clay animation, pixilation,* and *computer animation*—drawing has, until recently, been the most common, as well as the most tedious, technique. First, artists drew characters in different movements and objects in different places on individual pieces of celluloid known as *cels*. These cels were then layered and photographed one by one on top of a static painted background. Under the worldwide influence of the Walt Disney Studios, which released its first animated film, *Steamboat Willie*—featuring Mickey Mouse—in 1928, this process became the industry standard. Although other animators at this time—Max Fleischer, Paul Terry, Walter Lantz, Pat Sullivan, Ub Iwerks, and Otto Messmer—created enduring cartoon figures (Krazy Kat and Felix the Cat, for example), the diminutive Mickey Mouse made Walt Disney the giant of the American animation industry.

Following the success of *Steamboat Willie*, Disney explored the artistic relationship between visuals, music, and color in such cartoons as *The Skeleton Dance* (1929), *Flowers and Trees* (1932), and *Three Little Pigs* (1933). There soon followed such early classics as *Snow White and the Seven Dwarfs* (1937), the first American animated feature; *Pinocchio* (1940); and *Fantasia* (1940), which set varied animated scenes to classical music. In later years, Disney Studios produced more-elaborate full-length films such as *Beauty and the Beast* (1991), the first animated film to receive an Academy Award nomination for Best Picture; *The Lion King* (1994); and *Tarzan* (1999). Although Disney Studios ceased producing hand-drawn animated features in 2003, for decades the name *Disney* was virtually synonymous with animated movies.

Despite Walt Disney's dominance in the world of animation, there were many alternatives to his style in the work of such artists as Chuck Jones, Friz Freleng, and Tex Avery, which often poked fun at Disney stereotypes. Some of Disney's artists—Peter Burns, Robert Cannon, John Hubley, Gene Deitch, and Ernest Pintoff—broke away from Disney during a strike and formed United Productions of America, where they created such memorable characters as Mr. Magoo and Gerald McBoing-Boing. The advent of television brought a new group of animators—including Bill Hanna, Joe Barbera, and Jay Ward—and a surge of films (for an insatiable TV audience) featuring Yogi Bear, the Flintstones, Huckleberry Hound, Rocky and Bullwinkle, and other characters. At the same time, animation was flourishing in Canada, Yugoslavia, Czechoslovakia, and Russia.

Among the other forms of animation, *puppet animation*, long an indispensable element in the brilliant animated movies made in Eastern and Central Europe, uses three-dimensional figures or puppets that are moved incrementally for each frame of film. *Clay animation* starts with clay molds, from which dimensional plasticine figures are made; they depict action as they are changed in small increments through several frames. *Pixilation* photographs real people, animals, or objects, which move (or are moved) slightly between exposures and are then photographed again, creating the illusion that they are moving under their own power.

Animation (and special effects) has also been fused with live action. The use of three-dimensional models and stop-motion photography by special-effects expert Willis O'Brien contributed greatly to the success of Merian C. Cooper and Ernest B. Schoedsack's original version of *King Kong* (1933). O'Brien teamed with Ray Harryhausen, famous for his model and puppet animation, in a variation on the King Kong theme in Schoedsack's *Mighty Joe Young* (1949), and Harryhausen alone created some

very menacing dinosaurs for Don Chaffey's *One Million Years B.C.* (1966). This trend continued in such films as Robert Zemeckis's *Who Framed Roger Rabbit* (1988)—an enormously influential work—Henry Selick's *The Nightmare Before Christmas* (1993), and Nick Park's series of "Wallace and Gromit" films (begun in 1990), Steven Spielberg's *Jurassic Park* (1993), and Peter Jackson's "Lord of

Animation [1] Walt Disney's *Snow White and the Seven Dwarfs* (1937), the first American animated feature film, was produced by a painstaking process involving many levels of drawing (such as this preliminary sketch of Snow White gazing into the magic mirror). [2] A little less than sixty years later, John Lasseter's *Toy Story* (1995) took the emerging technologies of computer-generated imagery (CGI) to their logical extreme. It was the first animated film created entirely by computer.

New Wave Animation Hayao Miyazaki's richly imaginative *Spirited Away* (2001) represents a new wave of creativity in the animation industry while preserving some of the core stylistic traits that made the Walt Disney Studios the dominant force in cartoon production since 1928. These traits include exquisite hand-drawn images that depict plausible characters meeting daunting challenges in an enchanted world. Unlike Disney, though, Miyazaki uses soft, misty colors to depict this action. The hero of *Spirited Away* is a wide-eyed little girl, Chihiro/Sen, who wanders into an enormous bathhouse haunted by spirits. In this image, we see four major characters: Haku (disguised as a dragon; voice of Jason Marsden), Chihiro/Sen (Daveigh Chase), Zeniba (Suzanne Pleshette), and No-Face (Bob Bergen). While the term "magical" is much over-used, it's entirely appropriate here. Disney Studios released the English-language version of the movie, which won the 2003 Oscar for Best Animated Feature.

the Rings" trilogy (2001–03). The crossover from animation to special effects has contributed greatly to the dominance of special effects in the movies of the past fifty years.

Making animated movies is easily as complex and expensive as making narrative films. Because of its unique nature, the production of animated movies has been done in such professional animation studios as Pixar, DreamWorks Animation, Walt Disney Feature Animation, Sony Pictures Animation, and Studio Ghibli (Japan), among many others. Even though we refer to a *Disney* or *Miyazaki* animated movie (just as we do a *John Ford* or *Steven Spielberg* narrative movie), it is not just one illustrator but many creative artists who are involved in bringing any animated story to the screen.

Today, computer-generated imaging (CGI) has transformed animation, as well as the other types of moviemaking. The computer can easily handle the laborious, repetitive task of making the many similar images needed to create the illusion of movement. In the first decade of its widespread use, CGI has produced such favorite movies as John Lasseter's *Toy Story* (1995), the first animated film created entirely on the computer, Lasseter, Ash Brannon, and Lee Unkrich's *Toy Story 2* (1999), and Lasseter and Andrew Stanton's *A Bug's Life* (1998); Andrew Adamson and Vicky Jenson's *Shrek* (2001) and its sequels; Andrew Stanton and Lee Unkrich's *Finding Nemo* (2003); Brad Bird's *The Iron Giant* (1999) and *The Incredibles* (2004); and Sylvain Chomet's *The Triplets of Belleville* (2003).

Today's style of animation seems to take one of three forms: (1) images that strive for the three-dimensional realism of the narrative film (e.g., *The Incredibles*, 2004); (2) images that exploit the inherently unrealistic, two-dimensional limitations of experimental films or abstract art (e.g., *Finding Nemo*, 2003); and (3) images made in the Japanese style of animation known as *anime*, which is influenced by Japanese *manga* comic books and features graphics and characters straight out of Japanese pop culture. We are at a point where the world of Walt Disney has given way to that of Hayao Miyazaki, now considered the world's greatest living animator. His importance, indeed his influence, has less to do with the commercial mainstream of animation than with making a more sophisticated kind of animation art that appeals to both children and adults.

Like Disney, Miyazaki draws all of his characters and backgrounds by hand, although, as noted earlier, Disney Studios stopped producing hand-drawn films in 2003. Miyazaki rejects CGI and, like Disney, owns his own production facilities, the Studio Ghibli. Whereas Disney's world is loud, three-dimensional, and theatrical, Miyazaki's is quiet, flat, and contemplative. Although both Disney and Miyazaki make films that feature visual beauty and vibrant colors, Disney's films, especially the classic ones, are often based on fairy tales. Miyazaki's films, in contrast, are based on his own original stories or adaptations of lesser-known works, and his characters are often fantastical creatures. Disney divides his characters into clear-cut good guys and bad guys; Miyazaki identifies his characters not so much as black-and-white stereotypes as more fully rounded characters who have the freedom to redeem themselves. Miyazaki views the natural world with a sense of wonder and the modern world with distaste, and he often sets his films in futuristic cities. He pays meticulous attention to realistic detail. In the United States, his best-known films are *Howl's Moving Castle* (2004); *Spirited Away* (2001), which won the Oscar for Best Animated Feature Film; *Princess Mononoke* (1997); and *My Neighbor Totoro* (1988).

WEB Animation Techniques

Experimental Films

Experimental films are also known as *avant-garde films*, a term implying that they are in the vanguard, out in front of traditional films. Any film that cannot easily be classified as fiction, nonfiction, or animated—and thus pushes the boundaries of what most people think the movies are or should be— falls into this type. Experimental films are usually about unfamiliar, unorthodox, or obscure subject matter and are ordinarily made by independent (even underground) filmmakers, not studios, often with innovative techniques that call attention to, question, and even challenge their own artifice.

For example, Michael Snow's *Wavelength* (1967) is a forty-five-minute film that consists, in what we see, only of an exceedingly slow zoom lens shot through a loft. Although human figures wander in and out of the frame, departing at will from that frame or being excluded from it as the camera moves slowly past them, the film is almost totally devoid of any human significance. Snow's central concern is space: how to conceive it, film it, and encourage viewers to make meaning of it. *Wavelength* is replete with differing qualities of space, light, exposures, focal lengths, and printing techniques, all offering rich possibilities for how we perceive these elements and interpret their meaning. As we know, space is fundamental to cinema, particularly in how it is framed, lighted, and photographed, and usually in what that space contains. For those who believe that a movie must represent the human condition, *Wavelength* seems empty. But

Experimental Film: Style as Subject   Among many other random repetitions and animations, Fernand Léger and Dudley Murphy's *Ballet mécanique* (1924) repeatedly loops footage of a woman climbing stairs. This action lacks completion or narrative purpose and instead functions as a rhythmic counterpart to other sections of the film, in which more abstract objects are animated and choreographed in (as the title puts it) a "mechanical ballet."

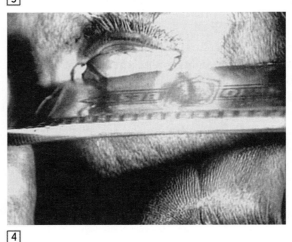

[1]

[3]

[2]

[4]

Experimental Film: Image as Shock   Luis Buñuel and Salvador Dalí collaborated to produce *An Andalusian Dog* (1929), one of the most famous experimental films. Through special effects, its notorious opening sequence can be summarized in four shots: [1] the title—"Once upon a time . . . ," which, under the circumstances is an absurd use of the classic beginning of a nursery story; [2] an image of a man (who has just finished sharpening his straight razor);

[3] an image of the hand of a differently dressed man holding a razor near a woman's eyeball with the implication that he will slit it; and [4] an image of a slit eyeball. There is no logic to this sequence, for the woman's eye is not slit; rather the slit eyeball appears to belong to an animal. The sequence is meant to shock the viewer, to surprise us, to make us "see" differently, but not to explain what we are seeing.

for those who believe, with D. W. Griffith, that a movie is meant, above all, *to make us see*, the work demonstrates the importance of utterly unconventional filmmaking.

Because most experimental films do not tell a story in the conventional sense, but rather use nonlinear patterns of development, abstract images, or images produced by means other than cinematography (e.g., drawing directly on film stock to create

an image, or re-editing fiction or nonfiction footage for graphic effect), they help us understand in yet another way why movies are an art form. Disregarding the traditional expectations of audiences, experimental films remind us that film—like painting, sculpture, music, or architecture—can be made in as many ways as there are artists.

In the 1920s, a truly experimental cinema movement was born in France, with its national climate of avant-garde artistic expression. Among the most notable works were films by painters: René Clair's *Entr'acte* (1924), Fernand Léger and Dudley Murphy's *Ballet mécanique* (1924), Marcel Duchamp's *Anémic cinéma* (1926), and Man Ray's *Emak-Bakia* (1926). These films are characterized uniformly by their surreal content, often dependent on dream impressions rather than objective observation; their abstract images, which tend to be shapes and patterns with no meaning other than the forms themselves; their absence of actors performing within a narrative context; and their desire to shock not only our sensibilities but also our morals. The most important of these films, the surrealist dreamscape *An Andalusian Dog* (1929), was made in France by the Spanish filmmaker Luis Buñuel and the Spanish painter Salvador Dalí. Re-creating the sexual nature of dreams, this film's images metamorphose continually, defy continuity, and even attack causality—as in one scene when a pair of breasts dissolves into buttocks.

Although an alternative cinema has existed in the United States since the 1920s—an achievement of substance and style that is all the more remarkable in a country where filmmaking is synonymous with Hollywood—the first experimental filmmakers here were either European-born or influenced by the French, Russians, and Germans. The first major American experimental filmmaker was Maya Deren, whose surreal films—*Meshes of the Afternoon* (1943), co-directed with her husband, Alexander Hammid, is the best known—virtually established alternative filmmaking in this country. Deren's work combines her interests in various fields, including film, philosophy, ethnography, and dance, and it remains the touchstone for those studying avant-garde movies.

Concerned with the manipulation of space and time, which, after all, is the essence of filmmaking, Deren experimented with defying continuity, erasing the line between dream and reality. She used the cinematic equivalent of **stream of consciousness**, a literary style that gained prominence in the 1920s in the hands of such writers as Marcel Proust, Virginia Woolf, James Joyce, and Dorothy Richardson, and that attempted to capture the unedited flow of experience through the mind. In *Meshes*, Deren is both the creative mind behind the film and the creative performer on the screen. She takes certain recognizable motifs—a key, a knife, a flower, a telephone receiver, and a shadowy figure walking down a garden path—and repeats them throughout the film, each time transfiguring them into something else. So, for example, the knife evolves into a key and the flower into a knife. These changing motifs are linked visually but also structurally. Deren's ideas and achievements bridge the gap between the surrealism of the French avant-garde films and such dream-related movies as Alain Resnais's *Last Year at Marienbad* (1961), Federico Fellini's $8\frac{1}{2}$ (1963), Ingmar Bergman's *Persona* (1966), and Luis Buñuel's *The Milky Way* (1969).

Greatly influenced by Deren's work, an American underground cinema emerged in the 1950s and has since favored four subgenres—the formal, the self-reflexive, the satirical, and the sexual—each of which tends to include aspects of the lyrical approach so typical of Deren. Works of pure form include John Whitney's early experiments with computer imagery in such films as *Matrix* (1971); Shirley Clarke's *Skyscraper* (1960), one of several lighthearted, abstract tributes to city life; Peter Kubelka's *Arnulf Rainer* (1960), which created its images through abstract dots; Jordan Belson's *Allures* (1961), using abstract color animation; Robert Breer's *Fist Fight* (1964), which combines animation, images of handwriting, and other material; and Ernie Gehr's *The Astronomer's Dream* (2003), in which he speeds up the images so much that they become vertical purple lines.

Self-reflexive films, meaning those that represent their own conditions of production (movies, in other words, about movies, moviemaking, moviemakers, and so on), include Hans Richter's *Dreams That Money Can Buy* (1947), in the spirit of surrealism; Stan Brakhage's five-part *Dog Star Man* (1962–64), whose lyricism is greatly influenced by Deren's work; Bruce Baillie's *Mass for the Dakota Sioux* (1964), which combines a lyrical vision and social commentary; Hollis Frampton's *Zorn's Lemma* (1970), a complex meditation on cinematic structure, space, and movement; and Michael Snow's *Wavelength* (1967), which we already discussed.

Films that take a satirical view of life include

James Broughton's *Mother's Day* (1948), on childhood; Stan van der Beek's *Death Breath* (1964), an apocalyptic vision using cartoons and other imagery; Bruce Conner's *Marilyn Times Five* (1973), which makes its comic points by compiling stock footage from other sources; and Mike Kuchar's *Sins of the Fleshapoids* (1965), an underground look at the horror genre. Satirical and sexual films often overlap, particularly in their portrayal of sexual activities that challenge conventional ideas of "normality." Examples of these include Kenneth Anger's *Scorpio Rising* (1964), an explicit homosexual fantasy that is tame by today's standards; Jack Smith's *Flaming Creatures* (1963), a major test case for pornography laws; and many of Andy Warhol's films, including *Lonesome Cowboys* (1969). The directors who made these films tended to be obsessed, as was Deren, with expressing themselves and their subconscious through cinematic forms and images.

Experimental filmmakers have traditionally expressed a highly personal and deeply felt vision in presenting their worlds. Although far fewer experimental films are made today than, say, in the period between the 1920s and the 1960s, the form continues to offer a wide-open field for cinematic creativity. Today, video artists such as Bill Viola have attracted great attention to their work, which is often shown in museums and art galleries. Ironically—considering their avant-garde origins—experimental cinema and video are influential on mainstream cinema. Since the collapse of the studio system, the growth of independent cinema has fostered a crossover and synthesis of conventional and experimental aesthetics and technique, and the growing use of computers in filmmaking has created a new wave of technological and aesthetic experimentation (see "Appendix: Hollywood Production Systems"). But, as has happened so often in film history, such revolutions in filmmaking may quickly enter the conventional cinematic language.

Summary: What Is a Movie?

As a summary effort to answer the question posed by the title of this chapter—*What Is a Movie?*—let's consider the elements that describe and thus help to define movies. Most definitions in reference books are not adequate for our purposes. Consider this definition of the term *motion picture* from the *Merriam-Webster Online Dictionary*: "a series of pictures projected on a screen in rapid succession with objects shown in successive positions slightly changed so as to produce the optical effect of a continuous picture in which the objects move"[7] or this one from the *Encyclopædia Britannica* online: "series of still photographs on film, projected in rapid succession onto a screen by means of light. Because of the optical phenomenon known as persistence of vision, this gives the illusion of actual, smooth, and continuous movement."[8] These definitions get some of the concept adequately, but not all that we need.

Rather than try to develop a precise dictionary definition that would meet the challenge of including both the art and science of the movies in one phrase, let's take a different approach. Although we know that there are several types of movies, narrative movies are the most familiar and are this book's primary concern. As we proceed with our study, keep in mind this short list of their most significant (or defining) characteristics:

> A movie is a story or event recorded by a camera; a sequence of these photographs is projected onto a screen with sufficient speed to create the illusion of motion and continuity.
> Movies depend on photography and, thus, on light.
> Movies manipulate space and time in ways that no other art form can.
> In a movie, the relationship of its form and content is central to its existence.
> A movie can create a sense of realism and/or antirealism, but it should also create verisimilitude.
> A movie creates its effects and meanings through a unique mode of expression that we call *cinematic language*.
> Making a movie usually involves a highly collaborative effort of many artists and technicians.

[7] From <www.m-w.com/dictionary/motion%20picture>.
[8] From <www.britannica.com/eb/article-9110698>.

→ Analyzing Movies

As we said at the beginning of the chapter, the primary goal of *Looking at Movies* is to help you graduate from being a spectator of movies—from merely *watching* them—to actively and analytically *looking at* them. The chapters that follow provide very specific information about each of the major formal components of film—information that you can use to write and talk intelligently about the films you view in class and at home. Once you've read the chapter on cinematography, for example, you will have at hand the basic vocabulary to describe accurately the camera work you see onscreen.

As you read the subsequent chapters of this book, you will acquire a specialized vocabulary for describing, analyzing, discussing, and writing about the movies you see. But now, as a beginning student of film, armed only with the general knowledge that you've acquired in this first chapter, you can begin looking at movies more analytically and perceptively. You can easily say more than "I liked" or "I didn't like" the movie, because you can enumerate and understand both its strengths and its weaknesses. In doing that, you can begin to understand that all movies, even the most blatantly commercial ones, express themselves through a complex cinematic language.

The following checklist provides a few ideas about how to start. As you follow these suggestions, be sure to provide at least one good example to support your interpretation.

Screening Checklist: What Is a Movie?

➤ Before and after you see a movie, think about the direct meanings, as well as the implications, of its *title*. The title of David Lynch's *Mulholland Drive* (2001) is a specific geographic reference, but once you've seen the movie, you'll understand that it functions as a metaphor for a larger body of meaning. Richard Kelly's *Donnie Darko* (2001) makes us wonder if Darko is a real name (it is), or if it is a not-so-subtle clue that Donnie has a dark side (he does). Try to explain the title's meaning if it isn't self-evident.

➤ Since most of the movies that you study in your introductory film class will be narrative films, you should ask whether a particular film can be linked with a specific *genre* and, if so, to what extent it does/does not fulfill your expectations of that genre.

➤ Do any narrative or visual *patterns* recur a sufficient number of times to suggest a struc-

tural element in themselves? If so, what are these patterns? Do they help you determine the meaning of the film?

➤ Do you notice anything particular about the movie's presentation of *cinematic space*—what you see on the screen? Lots of landscapes or close-ups? Moving or static camera?

➤ Does the director handle *cinematic time* in a way that calls attention to it?

➤ Does the director's use of *lighting* help to create meaning? If so, how?

➤ Do you identify with the camera lens? What does the director *compel* you to see? What is left to your imagination? What does the director leave out altogether? In the end, besides showing you the action, how does the director's use of the camera help to create the movie's meaning?

Questions for Review

1. How and why do we differentiate between *form* and *content* in a movie, and why are they relevant to one another?
2. How does a movie manipulate *space* and *time*?
3. How do the movies create an *illusion of movement*?
4. What is the difference between *realism* and *antirealism* in a movie, and why is *verisimilitude* important to them both?
5. What is meant by *cinematic language*? Why is it important to the ways that movies *communicate* with viewers?
6. Why do we identify with the *camera lens*?
7. What are the main differences between the four basic types of movies?
8. What is *genre*? Why is it important? What are five basic movie genres?
9. How would you define what a movie is?
10. At this point, would you say that learning what a movie is all about is more challenging than you first thought? If so, why?

DVD FEATURES: CHAPTER 1

The following tutorials on the DVD provide more information about topics covered in Chapter 1:

- "Fred Ott's Sneeze"
- The Lumière Brothers' "Actualités"

Movies Described or Illustrated in This Chapter

American Beauty (1999). Sam Mendes, director.

An Andalusian Dog (1929). Luis Buñuel, director.

Battleship Potemkin (1925). Sergei M. Eisenstein, director.

Black Hawk Down (2001). Ridley Scott, director.

Bonnie and Clyde (1967). Arthur Penn, director.

Brokeback Mountain (2005). Ang Lee, director.

A Bug's Life (1998). John Lasseter and Andrew Stanton, directors.

Citizen Kane (1941). Orson Welles, director.

Cold Mountain (2003). Anthony Minghella, director.

Donnie Darko (2001). Richard Kelly, director.

Double Indemnity (1944). Billy Wilder, director.

Dr. Strangelove or: How I Learned to Stop Worrying and Love the Bomb (1963). Stanley Kubrick, director.

Edison Kinetoscopic Record of a Sneeze (1894). William K. L. Dickson, director.

Employees Leaving the Lumière Factory (1895). Louis Lumière, director.

End of the Century (2003). Jim Fields and Michael Gramaglia, directors.

Fahrenheit 9/11 (2004). Michael Moore, director.

Far From Heaven (2002). Todd Haynes, director.

Finding Nemo (2003). Andrew Stanton and Lee Unkrich, directors.

The Fog of War: Eleven Lessons From the Life of Robert S. McNamara (2003). Errol Morris, director.

Girlhood (2003). Liz Garbus, director.

Gladiator (2000). Ridley Scott, director.

The Godfather (1972). Francis Ford Coppola, director.

The Gold Rush (1925). Charles Chaplin, director.

Gone With the Wind (1939). Victor Fleming, director.

The Grapes of Wrath (1940). John Ford, director.

Grizzly Man (2005). Werner Herzog, director.

Heist (2001). David Mamet, director.

Henry V (1989). Kenneth Branagh, director.

Howl's Moving Castle (2004). Hayao Miyazaki, director.

The Incredibles (2004). Brad Bird, director.

The Iron Giant (1999). Brad Bird, director.

Jaws (1975). Steven Spielberg, director.

Junebug (2005). Phil Morrison, director.

Jurassic Park (1993). Steven Spielberg, director.

Kill Bill: Vol. 1 (2003). Quentin Tarantino, director.

Kinsey (2004). Bill Condon, director.

Kissing Jessica Stein (2001). Charles Herman-Wurmfeld, director.

L. A. Confidential (1997). Curtis Hanson, director.

Making a Killing: Philip Morris, Kraft and Global Tobacco Addiction (2000). Kelly Anderson and Tami Gold, directors.

March of the Penguins (2005). Luc Jacquet, director.

The Matrix (1999). Andy and Larry Wachowski, directors.

Meshes of the Afternoon (1943). Maya Deren and Alexander Hammid, directors.

Murderball (2005). Harry Alex Rubin and Dana Adam Shapiro, directors.

My Neighbor Totoro (1988). Hayao Miyazaki, director.

Nanook of the North (1922). Robert Flaherty, director.

North by Northwest (1959). Alfred Hitchcock, director.

Princess Mononoke (1997). Hayao Miyazaki, director.

Psycho (1960). Alfred Hitchcock, director.

Red River (1948). Howard Hawks, director.

The River (1937). Pare Lorentz, director.

Shrek (2001). Andrew Adamson and Vicky Jenson, directors.

The Silence of the Lambs (1991). Jonathan Demme, director.

Snow White and the Seven Dwarfs (1937). Walt Disney, producer.

Spellbound (2002). Jeffrey Blitz, director.

Spirited Away (2001). Hayao Miyazaki, director.

Star Wars: Episode II—Attack of the Clones (2002). George Lucas, director.

Super Size Me (2004). Morgan Spurlock, director.

Tarnation (2003). Jonathan Caouette, director.

There's Something About Mary (1998). Bobby and Peter Farrelly, directors.

The Thin Red Line (1998). Terrence Malick, director.

The Third Man (1949). Carol Reed, director.

Touch of Evil (1958). Orson Welles, director.

Toy Story (1995). John Lasseter, director.

A Trip to the Moon (1902). George Méliès, director.

The Triplets of Belleville (2003). Sylvain Chomet, director.

Triumph of the Will (1935). Leni Riefenstahl, director.

Tupac: Resurrection (2003). Lauren Lazin, director.

Wal-Mart: The High Cost of Low Price (2005). Robert Greenwald, director.

The Warriors (1979). Walter Hill, director.

Wavelength (1967). Michael Snow, director.

Way Down East (1920). D. W. Griffith, director.

Why We Fight (2005). Eugene Jarecki, director.

"Why We Fight" series (1943–45). Frank Capra, director.

Pride & Prejudice (2005). Joe Wright, director; Deborah Moggach, screenwriter.

After reading this chapter, you should be able to

➤ Differentiate between the *story* and the *plot* of a movie.

➤ Know the responsibilities of the screenwriter.

➤ Know the difference between *diegetic* and *nondiegetic* elements of a movie's plot.

➤ Understand the importance of the *order* (chronological or nonchronological), *significance* (*hubs* versus *satellites*), and *duration* of plot events.

➤ Understand the three kinds of relationships between *screen duration* and *story duration*.

➤ Distinguish characters by their importance (*major* versus *minor* characters), their complexity (*round* versus *flat*), their motivation, and their role in the narrative (e.g., *protagonist*, *antagonist*).

➤ Explain the significance of *setting* to film narrative.

➤ Know the difference between *surprise* and *suspense*.

➤ Explain what comprises the *scope* of a story.

➤ Understand the difference between *narration* and *narrator*, as well as how they complement one another.

What Is Narrative?

At its simplest level, a movie's **narrative** is the telling of its story. As you learn more about movies generally, you will learn that narrative, an essential element of a movie's form, contains numerous elements. Overall, this book focuses on movies that tell a story, works that emphasize a fictional narrative. Narratives play an essential part in our lives, and we are naturally inclined to look for narrative structure in life and in art. Although our lives may seem like "one thing after another" while we're living them, we nonetheless continually attempt to make narrative sense of them and to translate the various "things"

(what we did over the weekend, the courses of our romantic relationships, our education up to this point, etc.) into stories that we can tell our friends, our families, and even ourselves. We do this by establishing connections among events, creating chains of cause and effect. This activity—inferring causal relationships among events that occur in sequence or close to one another—runs through our conscious lives, and it sometimes even finds its way into our unconscious lives as we dream. Is it any wonder, then, that we're drawn to stories?

The storytelling impulse runs through motion picture history, and telling the story is often what the most profitable movies are all about. When movies were first developed, they often limited themselves to documenting an action—a sneeze, a kiss, the swing of a bat, the gait of a horse. These early films were only briefly interesting to audiences, however, and they soon became mere curiosities in nickelodeons. Only after they began to tell stories did the movies reach a level of extraordinary popularity with audiences; and today, the movies discussed in the common culture, the movies most of us pay to see, the movies we commonly have in mind when we say the word *movies*, are those that tell stories.

WEB Evolution of Narrative Form

In telling a movie's story, filmmakers decide what (and what not) to show, how to dress characters and decorate sets, how to direct actors, how to use sound and music, and so on. As a result of these decisions, we receive information with which to interpret the unfolding narrative. When crucial information is missing, we fill in details based on our lived experiences, on our sense of what "normally" happens in movies, and on what has been shown to us already—on what, given the characters and events already portrayed, seems likely to occur within the world onscreen. The more we see of a movie, the more precise our predictions and interpretations become. Similarly, the more movies we have seen, the better able we are to creatively anticipate the many directions that a movie we're watching might take.

Obviously, too, our ability to anticipate is shaped by how much life we have lived. But narrative is so

[1]

[2]

Narrative Form and the Biopic A biographical movie, or *biopic*, provides particularly rich opportunities to ask why the filmmakers chose to tell the story the way they did. After all, the facts of the main character's life are objectively verifiable and follow a particular order. But storytellers' shaping of that material, the form those facts take, determines how compelling the movie is dramatically, how interesting it is cinematically, and what it means ultimately. [1] Graeme Clifford's *Frances* (1982; screenwriters: Eric Bergren, Christopher De Vore, Nicholas Kazan), starring Jessica Lange as Frances Farmer, is one type of biopic, relying on objective facts to guide the narrative and thus encouraging us to analyze other formal structures within the film, such as the acting. [2] Werner Herzog's *Aguirre: The Wrath of God* (1972; screenwriter: Herzog), starring Klaus Kinski as Don Lope de Aguirre, is another type, using biographical facts as raw material for a more subjective narrative and thus inviting us to compare the historical record with the artistic vision.

tightly woven into our experience of life and art, seemingly such a natural part of human existence, that we often can be unaware of its parts and its effects. This chapter will describe some of those parts and trace some of those effects. Because narrative is *form*, something made, the product of deliberate decisions concerning content, we need to look as closely at *how* movies tell their stories as we look at what happens within the stories. Let's begin by considering how the narratives of contemporary films fit into the overall production process.

The Screenwriter

Screenwriters are responsible for creating the movie's story—either from scratch or adapting it from another format (such as a short story, novel, television show, or play)—and (depending on their contract) for writing the screenplay in its various stages. During preproduction, the story is referred to as the *property* and may be an idea that a writer has "pitched" to the producer, an outline, or a completed script. No rules determine how an idea should be developed or an existing literary property should be adapted into a film script, but the process usually consists of several stages, involving many rewrites. Likewise, no rule dictates the number of people who are eventually involved in the process. One person may write all the stages of the screenplay or may collaborate from the beginning with other screenwriters; sometimes the director is the sole screenwriter or co-screenwriter.

Before the breakdown of the Hollywood studio system and the emergence of the independent film, each of the major studios maintained its own staff of writers, to whom ideas were assigned depending on the writers' specialty and experience. Each writer was responsible by contract to write a specified number of films each year. Today the majority of scripts are written in their entirety by independent screenwriters (either as write-for-hires or on spec) and submitted as polished revisions. Many other screenplays, especially for movies created for mass appeal, are written by committee, meaning a collaboration of director, producer, editor, and others, including *script doctors* (professional screenwriters who are hired to review a screenplay and improve it). Whether working alone or in collaboration with others, a screenwriter has significant influence over the screenplay and the completed movie, and, thus, its artistic, critical, and box-office success.

Despite the widespread existence of seminars, books, and software programs that promise to teach the essentials of screenwriting overnight, becoming a professional screenwriter requires the possession of innate talents and skills that can be enhanced by experience. Such skills include understanding the interaction of story, plot, and narrative; being able to write visually (meaning not only putting a world on the page, but also foreseeing it on the screen); and being able to create characters and dialogue. Screenwriters must understand the conventions and expectations of the various genres, work within deadlines that are often unreasonable, and be able to collaborate, particularly with the producer and director, and to anticipate that their original ideas may be extensively and even radically altered before the shooting starts. In addition to creating a compelling story, engaging plot, and fascinating characters, screenwriters must have a solid understanding of what is marketable. Finally, if they are presenting a finished screenplay, it must conform to industry expectations regarding format and style.

Although a screenwriter's particular responsibilities on any individual production are covered by contract, the process of getting a project completed invariably raises issues of screen credit—often a hotly contested matter—for which the Writers Guild of America, the screenwriters' union, provides services of arbitration and mediation. Many distinguished screenwriters have been involved in bitter contests over their credits, including Herman J. Mankiewicz on *Citizen Kane* and Robert Towne on *Chinatown*.

Evolution of a Typical Screenplay

Going from idea to finished movie is usually a long, complex process, involving not only the story idea itself, but also securing the financing necessary to permit the idea to evolve into a screenplay. But for most producers and directors, the most important starting point, in the words of director Pedro Almodóvar, is "the value of the script." That *value*—its worth in terms of the combined goals of the screenwriter, producer, and director—is what drives this process forward.

The earliest form of the screenplay may be a **treatment** or **synopsis**, an outline of the action that briefly describes the essential ideas and structure for the film. The treatment is discussed and developed in sessions known as **story conferences**, during which it is transformed from an outline into what is known as a **rough-draft screenplay** or **scenario**. At some point, these story conferences will be expanded to involve such key personnel as the production manager and the art director, as well as members of their individual teams.

Next, the director transforms the literal script images of each scene into visualizations of specific shots and setups. The result is a strategy for shooting each scene (and its component shots). Some directors keep all this information in their heads; others develop a storyboard before shooting. A **storyboard** is a shot-by-shot (sometimes a scene-by-scene) breakdown that combines sketches or photographs of how each shot is to look with written descriptions of the other elements that are to accompany each shot, including dialogue, sound, and music. These images are arranged in the order of the action and mounted on sturdy cardboard panels, but filmmakers today are increasingly turning to computerized storyboards that, much like a word processing program, offer greater flexibility in rearranging the images to visualize a shot before shooting and editing.

A storyboard serves several important functions. It is a graphical representation of the director's conception of the film and thus is vital in helping to explain the director's concepts to the production team. It serves as an organizational tool, enabling the production manager to organize the actual shooting to maximize all resources, especially the assignment of personnel. The production team uses this information to see if it has enough shots to cover the action in usable and effective sequences. Furthermore, a storyboard assists in maintaining the continuity of the movie. Because a movie is shot mostly out of sequence, it is essential to know in advance how edited shots in a sequence will relate to one another. The director must be concerned with the general continuity of space and time, as well as with the specific continuity of such elements as lighting, camera setups, action, props, costume, makeup, sound, and performance. Long after the shooting has stopped, the sets have been struck, and the actors have gone off to other work, a well-prepared storyboard will continue to provide backup for the work that remains to be done.

Before shooting, one of the director's final responsibilities is to prepare the **shooting script**, which lists the details of each shot and can thus be followed by the director and actors during filming. Even when relying on *improvisation* (that is, having the actors make up material on the spot), the director will also have a detailed shooting script. The costs of making traditional films are simply too great to permit even the best-funded director to work without this essential tool. The shooting script therefore serves as an invaluable guide and reference point for all members of the production unit, indicating where everything ought to be. It breaks down the individual shots by location (interior or exterior), setting (kitchen, football stadium, etc.), type (close-up, long shot, etc.), and the editing technique to be used between these shots (cut, wipe, dissolve, fade-out, etc.).

Once the shooting script has been developed, the director proceeds with the other key members of the team to determine *how* to shoot. Their decisions will cover everything from fully visualizing the film in setups, determining which shots will be made in the studio and which will be made on location, establishing a photographic strategy and determining the visual look for each shot, settling the film's color palette, determining the film's tempo with final editing in mind, and casting the actors. All of these decisions will be based on the story; if the story changes (during rewrites), then these elements will change also.

Now imagine you are a filmmaker who wants to adapt a novel for the screen. It's a complex work with interlocking major and minor themes,

Storyboard Three frames from the storyboard for Alfred Hitchcock's *The Birds* (1963; screenwriter: Evan Hunter).

numerous characters, settings in many different locations, and a time frame involving both past and present actions, but your budget will not permit you to include everything. Your first challenge is to determine how to tell this story in a way that will retain on the screen those aspects of the novel that attracted you in the first place without exceeding your financial and logistical resources. You will thus be making decisions that involve both the content and the form of your narrative: what aspects of the story to tell and how to tell them. In making these decisions, you will need to

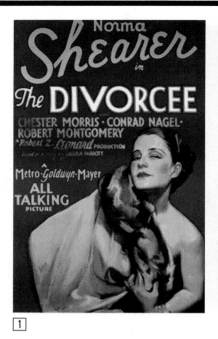

[1]

[2]

▶WEB Movies and Morality

Regulating Content Social mores, pressure from various organizations and authorities, and the desire to please a mass audience have helped regulate the content and distribution of movies, especially of mainstream Hollywood movies. During the early 1920s, after several years of relatively frank portrayals of sex and violence onscreen (a period in which the industry also suffered a wave of scandals), Hollywood faced a credible threat of censorship from state governments and of boycotts from Catholic and other religious groups. In 1922, in response to these pressures, Hollywood producers formed a regulatory agency called the Motion Picture Producers and Distributors of America (MPPDA, later the Motion Picture Association of America, or MPAA), headed by Will Hays, postmaster general under President Warren G. Harding. Originally conceived as a public relations entity to offset bad publicity and deflect negative attention away from Hollywood, the Hays Office (as the agency was commonly known) in 1930 adopted the Motion Picture Production Code, a detailed set of guidelines concerning acceptable and unacceptable subject matter. Nudity, adultery, homosexuality, gratuitous or unpunished violence, and religious blasphemy were among the many types of content that the code strongly discouraged. Perhaps even more significantly, the code explicitly stated that art can influence, for the worse, the morality of those who consume it (an idea that Hollywood has been reconsidering ever since).

Many movies made in 1930 or immediately thereafter illustrate the industry's awkward transition to the new standards. (To read the Motion Picture Production Code of 1930, see Gerald Mast [ed.], *The Movies in Our Midst: Documents in the Cultural History of Film in America* [Chicago: University of Chicago Press, 1982], 321–33.) [1] Directed by the uncredited Robert Z. Leonard, *The Divorcee* (1930; screenwriters: Nick Grinde and Zelda Sears),

one of the first movies released after the Motion Picture Production Code was announced, is about a woman who takes three lovers after discovering her husband's infidelity. Although the Hays Office warned MGM not to produce the movie, the studio's head of production, Irving Thalberg, pushed the project forward, casting his wife, Norma Shearer, in the lead role and encouraging many other Hollywood power brokers to award Shearer the Oscar for Best Actress. The fact that Shearer had played virtuous women in previous films helped the movie avoid serious scrutiny, but later *The Divorcee* would be cited by protectors of public morality as justifying strict enforcement of the code. [2] Shot in 1930, Howard Hawks's *Scarface* (screenwriter: Ben Hecht) was delayed for two years while Hawks battled with the Hays Office over its violent content. Although the movie was released as *Scarface, Shame of a Nation* and also simply as *The Shame of a Nation*, with a moralistic ending and many scenes removed, civic groups and politicians nonetheless cited it as evidence of Hollywood's amorality.

Adherence to the Motion Picture Production Code remained fundamentally voluntary until the summer of 1934, when Joseph Breen, a prominent Catholic layman, was appointed head of the Production Code Administration (PCA), the enforcement arm of the MPPDA. For at least twenty years, the PCA rigidly controlled the general character and the particular details of Hollywood storytelling. After a period of practical irrelevance, the code was officially replaced in 1968, when the MPAA adopted the rating system that remains in use today.

To read more about the code and the nature of Hollywood filmmaking from 1930 through the summer of 1934, see Thomas Doherty, *Pre-Code Hollywood: Sex, Immorality, and Insurrection in American Cinema, 1930–1934* (New York: Columbia University Press, 1999), and Jon Lewis, *Hollywood v. Hard Core: How the Struggle Over Censorship Created the Modern Film Industry* (New York: New York University Press, 2000).

understand, implicitly or explicitly, the major elements of narrative form.

Elements of Narrative

Narrative theory (sometimes called *narratology*) has a long history, starting with Aristotle and continuing with great vigor today. Aristotle said that a good story should have three sequential parts: a beginning, a middle, and an end—a concept that has had a profound effect on the history of playwriting and screenwriting. French New Wave director Jean-Luc Godard, who helped to revolutionize cinematic style in the 1950s, agreed that a story should have a beginning, a middle, and an end, but he added, "Not necessarily in that order." Given the extraordinary freedom and flexibility with which cinema can handle time (especially compared to the limited ways in which the theater handles time), the directors of some of the most challenging movies ever made—including many contemporary examples—would seem to agree with Godard. Today Aristotle's three-part structure has been expanded into five parts:

1. **Exposition.** Everything preceding and including the **inciting moment**—the event or situation that sets the rest of the narrative in motion.
2. **Rising action.** The development of the action of the narrative toward a climax.
3. **Climax.** The narrative's turning point.
4. **Falling action.** The events that follow the climax and bring the narrative from climax to conclusion.
5. **Denouement** (pronounced "day-new-mawn"). The resolution or conclusion of the narrative.

This pattern follows the familiar pyramidal pattern shown in Fig. 2.1.

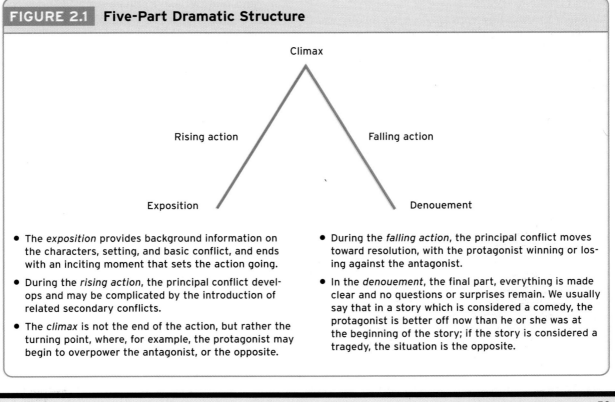

FIGURE 2.1 Five-Part Dramatic Structure

Climax

Rising action

Falling action

Exposition

Denouement

- The *exposition* provides background information on the characters, setting, and basic conflict, and ends with an inciting moment that sets the action going.
- During the *rising action*, the principal conflict develops and may be complicated by the introduction of related secondary conflicts.
- The *climax* is not the end of the action, but rather the turning point, where, for example, the protagonist may begin to overpower the antagonist, or the opposite.
- During the *falling action*, the principal conflict moves toward resolution, with the protagonist winning or losing against the antagonist.
- In the *denouement*, the final part, everything is made clear and no questions or surprises remain. We usually say that in a story which is considered a comedy, the protagonist is better off now than he or she was at the beginning of the story; if the story is considered a tragedy, the situation is the opposite.

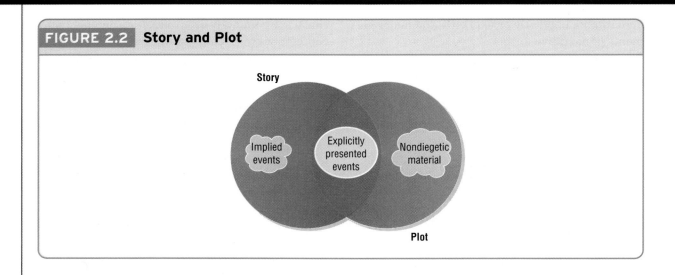

FIGURE 2.2 Story and Plot

Story

Implied events

Explicitly presented events

Nondiegetic material

Plot

The complexities of narratology are beyond the scope of this book,[1] but we can begin our study by distinguishing between two fundamental elements: story and plot.

Story and Plot

Although in everyday conversation we might use the words *story* and *plot* interchangeably, they mean different things when we write and speak about movies. A movie's **story** consists of (1) all the narrative events that are explicitly presented on the screen plus (2) all the events that are implicit or that we infer to have happened but are not explicitly presented. The total world of the story—the events, characters, objects, settings, and sounds that form the world in which the story occurs—is called its **diegesis**, and the elements that make up the diegesis are called **diegetic elements**. By contrast, the things that we see and hear on the screen but that come from outside the world of the story

are called **nondiegetic elements** (including background music, titles and credits, or voice-over comment from an omniscient narrator). A movie's **plot** is a structure for presenting everything that we see and hear in a film: (1) the diegetic events arranged in a certain order plus (2) nondiegetic material. Story and plot overlap because each includes the narrative events that we explicitly see and hear onscreen (Fig. 2.2).

One way to understand the difference between story and plot is to consider the story elements of a particular movie and determine which of them count as plot elements. Let's examine a very well-known movie, Michael Curtiz's *Casablanca* (1942; screenwriters: Julius J. Epstein, Philip G. Epstein, and Howard Koch):

1. The time is 1941, soon after the beginning of World War II. This background information counts as *story*, but it comes to us through *nondiegetic plot elements*:

    OPENING TITLE AND CREDITS: Film title and cast and production credits appear over a political map of Africa; music consists of "La Marseillaise" (the French national anthem) and Morrocan-sounding background music. Use of "La Marseillaise" at the beginning and end of the film signals a theme of solidarity with the Free French.

[1] This discussion of narrative theory adapts material from, and is indebted to, Seymour Chatman, *Story and Discourse: Narrative Structure in Fiction and Film* (Ithaca, N.Y.: Cornell University Press, 1978), and *Coming to Terms: The Rhetoric of Narrative in Fiction and Film* (Ithaca, N.Y.: Cornell University Press, 1990). Other works of contemporary narrative theory are recommended in the bibliography at the end of this book.

NARRATION: In the style of contemporary newsreels, a "voice of God" narrator explains how refugees try to reach Lisbon, Marseilles, Oran, or Casablanca in the wake of the Nazi takeover of Europe; a spinning globe appears with a zoom-in shot toward Western Europe—Allied powers in light tone, neutral nations in medium tone, and Axis powers in dark tone—with superimposed documentary footage of refugees.

2. Rick Blaine (Humphrey Bogart) is an American with a mysterious past. Apart from the fact that at some point he became an underground fighter in Europe, his life before we first see him is *story, not plot*. Characters comment on his past (suggesting, for instance, that he once killed a man), and we infer that certain romantic and political relationships between the past and the present form part of the story, but none of the events are illustrated.

3. Rick left Paris after the Germans occupied the city. Again, this information is *story, not plot*, because we hear about it after it has occurred.

4. Although Rick had planned to come to Casablanca with his lover, Ilsa Lund (Ingrid Bergman), she jilted him at the last minute. *Story, not plot*.

5. A man murdered Nazi couriers and took two exit visas from them. *Story, not plot*.

6. The man who murdered the couriers entrusts Rick with the exit visas. (When this occurs, we find out the information in item 5.) Because we *see* and don't just hear about the handoff of visas, this is our first *plot event*.

From here on, apart from one flashback, the plot is chronological and straightforward, holding together the story, which concerns the interaction of politics, personal ethics, and love:

7. Rick knows that he can sell the visas for a great deal of money, but he could be arrested for the sale and says that he will not risk his life for anyone.

8. Rick's former lover, Ilsa, and her husband, Victor Laszlo (Paul Henreid), wanted by the Nazis for being a Resistance leader, arrive in Casablanca needing exit visas to continue their flight to freedom, but Rick will not sell his to them.

9. Flashback to June 1940: Rick and Ilsa in Paris.

10. Rick also refuses Laszlo's suggestion that he use the visas to take Ilsa to safety. And so on.

If you have an assignment to analyze this (or any other) movie and write about it, consider identifying the five parts of the three-act structure and drawing a diagram (such as the one shown in Fig. 2.1) to illustrate them.

Of course, Rick was accompanied to Casablanca by his loyal friend Sam (Arthur "Dooley" Wilson), the pianist and singer at Rick's Café Américain. When played by Sam, "As Time Goes By" is diegetic music because it occurs within the world of the story, but the same musical theme is nondiegetic when played by an orchestra that we

Story or Plot?   "You played it for her, you can play it for me. Play it!" In Michael Curtiz's *Casablanca* (1942), Sam (Dooley Wilson) provides the sound track to Rick's (Humphrey Bogart) broken heart: "It's still the same old story, / A fight for love and glory, / A case of do or die. / The world will always welcome lovers, / As time goes by." Because it is not shown or explicitly described in the movie, the event that broke Rick's heart is part of the underlying *story* of the movie, not part of its *plot*.

never see and cannot infer to be somewhere in the surroundings.

The relationship between plot and story is important to filmmakers and to the audience. From the filmmaker's perspective, the story exists as a *precondition* for the plot, and the filmmaker must understand what story is being told before going through the difficult job of selecting events to show onscreen and determining the order in which they will be presented. For us as viewers, the story is an abstraction—a *construct*—that we piece together as the elements of the plot unfold before us onscreen, and our impressions about the story often shift and adjust throughout the movie as more of the plot is revealed. The plots of some movies—classic murder mysteries, for example—lead us to an unambiguous sense of the story by the time they are done. Other movies' plots reveal very little about the causal relationships among narrative events, thus leaving us to puzzle over those connections, to construct the story ourselves. As you view movies more critically and analytically, pay attention not only to the story as you have inferred it, but also to how it was conveyed through its plot. Understanding this basic distinction will help you appreciate and analyze the overall form of the movie more perceptively.

To picture the relationship between plot and story slightly differently, and to become more aware of the deliberate ways in which filmmakers construct plots from stories, you might watch a number of different movies that tell a story with which you are familiar—for example, Walt Disney's *Cinderella* (1950; screenwriters: Ken Anderson et al.), Frank Tashlin's *Cinderfella* (1960, starring Jerry Lewis; screenwriter: Tashlin), Garry Marshall's *Pretty Woman* (1990, starring Julia Roberts; screenwriter: J. F. Lawton), Andy Tennant's *Ever After* (1998, starring Drew Barrymore; screenwriters: Susannah Grant, Tennant, and Rick Parks), John Pasquin's *Miss Congeniality 2: Armed and Fabulous* (2005, starring Sandra Bullock; screenwriters: Marc Lawrence, Katie Ford, and Caryn Lucas)—all of which rely on the basic story structure of the well-known fairy tale. This sort of critical comparison will enable you to see more clearly how the plots differ, how the formal decisions made

by the filmmakers have shaped those differences, and how the overall form of each movie alters your perception of the underlying story. When James Cameron planned to make a movie about the sinking of the HMS *Titanic*, he had to contend with the fact that there were already three feature films on the subject, as well as numerous television movies and documentaries. Moreover, everyone knew the story. So he created a narrative structure that was based on a **backstory**, a fictional history behind the situation extant at the start of the main story: the story of Rose Calvert's diamond. That device, as well as a powerful romantic story and astonishing special effects, made his *Titanic* (1997) one of the greatest box-office hits in history.

Through plot, screenwriters and directors can provide structure to stories and guide (if not control) viewers' emotional responses. In fact, a particular plot may be little more than a sequence of devices for arousing predictable responses of concern and excitement in audiences. We accept such a plot because we know it will lead to the resolution of conflicts, mysteries, and frustrations in the story. Peter Jackson's "Lord of the Rings" trilogy (2001–03), while faithful to the spirit of J. R. R. Tolkien's novels, is very different from the books; movies are, by their nature, different from the books on which they are based. Jackson's trilogy is a lavish visual interpretation of Tolkien's literary vision, and thus its mythical world is different from the one each of us imagines as we read those books. Nevertheless, the movies tell the story of good versus evil and of Frodo's difficult journey from the idyllic shire to the chaotic larger world beyond. Because this journey is also from childhood to adulthood—and we have read it before in countless books and seen it before (in Victor Fleming's *The Wizard of Oz* [1939], among other movies)—we naturally have expectations about plot, story, and characters. With one exception (the scene in which the character Sméagol is transformed into the computer-generated Gollum), the plot events occur chronologically.

Jackson relies heavily on action scenes, which are exciting, and special effects, which are wondrous. And he had to eliminate or combine certain characters and details in order to manage the vast

Adaptation of Literary Sources [1] David Lean's *Great Expectations* (1946; screenwriters: Anthony Havelock-Allan, Lean, Cecil McGivern, Ronald Neame, and Kay Walsh) takes place, as Dickens's novel does, in nineteenth-century England. The young protagonist (John Mills), a student in London named Pip as in the novel, confronts his previously anonymous benefactor, Magwitch (Finlay Currie). [2] Fifty-two years later, Alfonso Cuarón's version of the same story (*Great Expectations*, 1998; screenwriter: Mitch Glazer) is set in contemporary America. Finn (Ethan Hawke), a painter in New York City, confronts his previously anonymous benefactor, Arthur Lustig (Robert De Niro). An analysis of the differences between these two adaptations of the same novel can lead you to a deeper appreciation of the power of filmmakers' decisions regarding plot specifically and film form more generally.

amount of source material. However, it is the ending—as happy a Hollywood ending as in *The Wizard of Oz*—that challenges us. You are no doubt familiar enough with quest movies to expect that, in the end, the good protagonist will defeat the evil antagonist and that the hero's quest will reach a satisfactory conclusion. In contrast to Tolkien's much darker and more pessimistic ending, that is exactly what happens in Jackson's version. In the movie's last segment, Frodo continues his journey as he boards a ship with his mentors and sails away, and Sam returns to find that the shire is almost exactly as he left it, just as Dorothy finds Kansas pretty much as she left it. We assume that Sam will live "happily ever after," the conclusion of all fairy tales.

Order

Bringing **order** to the plot events is one of the most fundamental decisions that filmmakers make about relaying story information through the plot. Unlike story order, which necessarily flows chronologically (as does life), plot order can be manipulated so that events are presented in nonchronological sequences that emphasize importance or meaning or that establish desired expectations in audiences. Many of the movies that puzzle but delight audiences—Danny Boyle's *Trainspotting* (1996; screenwriter: John Hodge), Christopher Nolan's *Memento* (2000; screenwriters: Christopher and Jonathan Nolan), or Michel Gondry's *Eternal Sunshine of the Spotless Mind* (2004; screenwriters: Charlie Kaufman, Gondry, and Pierre Bismuth)—are built on risky moves by the filmmakers to scramble plot order or play with it in such a way that discerning the underlying story can be one of the audience's chief sources of interest and enjoyment. If any of these movies' plots had presented the story information in strict chronological order, viewers might have found them much less challenging.

Like so many other aspects of filmmaking, conventions of plot order have been established and challenged over the course of film history. For example, Orson Welles and Herman J. Mankiewicz, the co-screenwriters of *Citizen Kane* (1941), adopted an approach to plot order so radical for its time that it actually bewildered many viewers with its unconventional narrative style and structure. The movie's plot consists of nine sequences, five of which are flashbacks. The second of these sequences, the "News on the March" newsreel, grounds us by presenting Kane's (Welles) life in a reasonably chronological line; but Mr. Thompson (William Alland), the newsreel reporter, does not conduct his search for the meaning of *Rosebud* chronologically. His investigation is a kind of detective story, and Welles and Mankiewicz incorporate ellipses (gaps and jumps) into the narrative to make the film's form another kind of detective story. That is, just as Thompson tries to assemble clues about Kane's life into a solution of that life's mystery, so we must, even as we watch, fill in plot details and give it order. *Citizen Kane* presented techniques, ideas, and demands on an audience that are now a standard part of film vocabulary, yet at the time audiences were unprepared for the challenge of taking in and working with so many audiovisual facts so quickly.

However challenging it was for its time, the plot structure of *Citizen Kane* has been so influential that it is now considered conventional. Among the many movies that it influenced is Quentin Tarantino's *Pulp Fiction* (1994; screenwriters: Tarantino and Roger Avary). The plot of *Pulp Fiction*, which is full of surprises, is constructed in a nonlinear way and fragments the passing of time. We might have to see the movie several times before being able to say at what point—in the plot and in the story—Vincent Vega (John Travolta) dies, for instance.

By contrast, Gaspar Noé's *Irréversible* (2002;

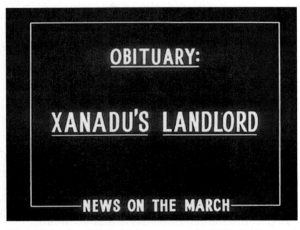

Plot Order in *Citizen Kane* To provide a straightforward account of Charles Foster Kane's life and help viewers get their bearings within a highly unconventional plot order, Orson Welles's *Citizen Kane* (1941) begins with a fictionalized mini-documentary. "News on the March" is a satire on the famous weekly newsreel series *The March of Time* (1935–51), which was shown in movie theaters and which mixed location footage with dramatic reenactments. Using this culturally familiar narrative device as an anchor for the rest of the movie, Welles tried to ensure that viewers wouldn't lose their way in the overall plot.

screenwriter: Noé), which takes place within the span of one day, begins with an appalling revenge murder, after which the plot order—much of the action is equally violent—unfolds in reverse. The movie's overall form is also aggressive. The spinning, swooping camera work is disorienting; the handheld camera gives it a documentary look that is nullified by the fact that it is an intensely subjective account of two men's vengeance; and each episode unfolds in an uninterrupted long take. We have to ask *why*, aside from the novelty and shock value, Noé has chosen to tell the story in reverse chronological order and to use these other techniques; why does he believe that these stylistic aspects are more suited to telling his story than conventional narrative techniques? Because the work stands on its own, he does not have to answer these questions. Nonetheless, there appears to be a disconnect between the story and plot of his movie.

Christopher Nolan's *Memento* (2000), a puzzle movie like M. Night Shyamalan's *The Sixth Sense* (1999) or Bryan Singer's *The Usual Suspects* (1995), is a far more successful experiment with plot order than either of these others. The story itself is fairly superficial; it's the telling that counts. Nolan alternates black-and-white sequences—which move forward in chronological order in telling the story—with color sequences that move backward in an order that confuses chronology. Like Gaspar Noé's *Irréversible*, *Memento* ends with the story's beginning—a structure that creates surprise and suspense and challenges the audience's expectations of movie narrative. And like *Citizen Kane*, *Memento* asks us to pay close attention to story and plot, challenges our basic assumptions of how we experience and remember what we have done, and, literally, requires us to put the pieces of the puzzle together. If you have the time and patience to do that, you'll find that the puzzle is remarkably well constructed.

WEB Story, Plot, and Time in Film

Despite these experiments with the chronological order of plot events, most narrative films follow a more or less chronological order. As we noted earlier in the "Story and Plot" section, *Casablanca*, one of the most popular movies of all time, follows

Plot Order in *Memento* In Christopher Nolan's *Memento* (2000), Leonard Shelby (Guy Pearce) suffers from a disorder that prevents him from forming short-term memories. To remember details of his life, he takes Polaroid snapshots, jots notes on scraps of paper, and even tattoos "The Facts" on his body. The movie's two-stranded plot order, both chronological and reverse chronological, likewise challenges us to recall what we've seen and how the parts fit together.

a relatively straightforward plot order, in which the flashback to Paris is the only event presented out of chronological sequence. In this wartime romance, the most important thing to the audience is the resolution of the dilemma that faces Rick and the Laszlos, and the plot is completely appropriate for telling their story.

In discussions of plot order, you will often hear the term *backstory*, the experiences of a character or the circumstances of an event that supposedly have occurred before the start of the movie's narrative. Movies like *Irréversible* and *Memento* utilize a variation on this narrative convention by telling the narrative in reverse chronological order, thus structuring the plot entirely of backstory.

Events: Hubs and Satellites

In any plot, some events are more important than others, and we infer their relative significance through the director's selection and arrangement of both major and minor details of action, character, or setting. We can distinguish between the events that seem crucial to the plot (and thus to the underlying story) and those that play a less crucial or even a supplementary role.

Hubs are major events or branching points in the plot structure that force characters to choose between or among alternate paths. Ridley Scott's

Gladiator (2000; screenwriters: David Franzoni, John Logan, and William Nicholson) recounts three stages in the life of Maximus (Russell Crowe) as he moves from general to slave, slave to gladiator, and gladiator to savior of the Roman people. Soon after the film opens, Emperor Marcus Aurelius (Richard Harris) dies, a hub event that forces the main character to escape the guards of the succeeding emperor, Commodus (Joaquin Phoenix), or be killed by them. Each succeeding stage in the plot turns on such hubs, which force Maximus to face similar choices.

Satellites, on the other hand, are minor plot events that add texture and complexity to characters and events but are not *essential* elements within the narrative. The love that Lucilla (Connie Nielsen), Commodus's sister, has long felt for Maximus—before he was married, during his mar-

Hubs and Satellites in *Gladiator* In Ridley Scott's *Gladiator* (2000), the death of Emperor Marcus Aurelius (Richard Harris) [1] instantly transforms the fortunes of General Maximus (Russell Crowe) for the worse, setting the plot in motion. Lucilla's (Connie Nielsen) love for Maximus [2] informs the plot through a series of satellites, then produces a hub event near the end.

riage, and after his wife was murdered by Commodus's guards—creates satellite events. Her love surfaces at key moments, troubling and tempting Maximus; but because other things are more important to him, he is not forced to make a decision based on his feelings for her. Satellites enrich and complicate the diegesis (the world of the story) in a narrative film, but no single satellite is indispensable to the story. When filmmakers make decisions about which scenes to cut from a film during the editing phase, they generally look for satellites that, for one reason or another, don't contribute enough to the overall movie. As a critical viewer of movies, you can use these two terms—*hubs* and *satellites*—both to diagram a plot (as a practical way to understand it) and to chart a course of the major and minor events confronting the characters.

Duration

Events, in life and in the movies, take time to occur. **Duration** is this length of time. When talking about narrative movies specifically, we can identify three specific kinds of duration: **story duration** is the amount of time that the implied story takes to occur; **plot duration** is the elapsed time of those events within the story that the film explicitly pres-

ents (in other words, the elapsed time of the plot); and **screen duration** is the movie's running time onscreen. In *Citizen Kane*, the plot duration is approximately one week (the duration of Thompson's search), the story duration is more than seventy years (the span of Kane's life) and the screen duration is one hour and fifty-nine minutes, the time it takes us to watch the film from beginning to end without interruption.

These distinctions are relatively simple in *Citizen Kane*, but the three-part relation of story, plot, and screen durations can become quite complex in some movies. Balancing the three elements is especially complex for a filmmaker because the screen duration is necessarily constrained by financial and other considerations. Movies may have become longer on average over the years, but filmmakers still must present their stories within a relatively short span of time. Because moviegoers generally regard films that run more than three hours as too long, such movies risk failure at the box office. Fig. 2.3 illustrates the relationship between story duration and plot duration in a hypothetical movie. The story duration in this illustration—one week—is depicted in a plot that covers four discrete but crucial days in that week.

The relationships among the three types of

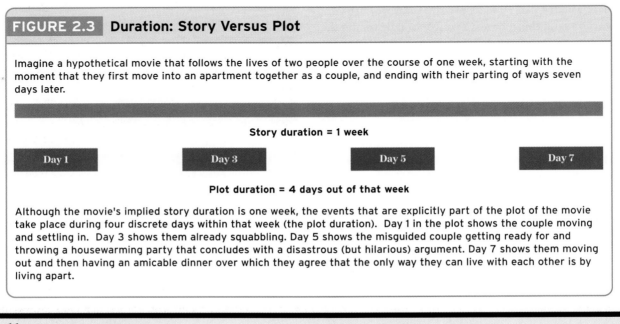

FIGURE 2.3 Duration: Story Versus Plot

Imagine a hypothetical movie that follows the lives of two people over the course of one week, starting with the moment that they first move into an apartment together as a couple, and ending with their parting of ways seven days later.

Story duration = 1 week

| Day 1 | Day 3 | Day 5 | Day 7 |

Plot duration = 4 days out of that week

Although the movie's implied story duration is one week, the events that are explicitly part of the plot of the movie take place during four discrete days within that week (the plot duration). Day 1 in the plot shows the couple moving and settling in. Day 3 shows them already squabbling. Day 5 shows the misguided couple getting ready for and throwing a housewarming party that concludes with a disastrous (but hilarious) argument. Day 7 shows them moving out and then having an amicable dinner over which they agree that the only way they can live with each other is by living apart.

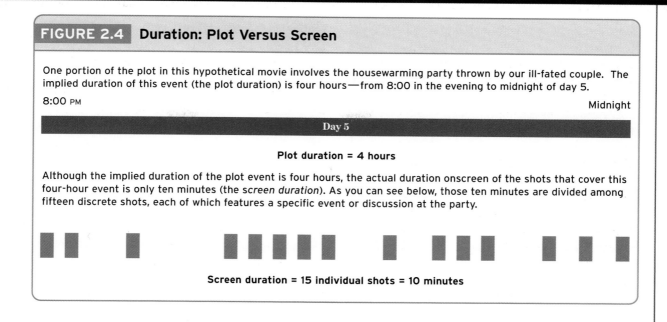

FIGURE 2.4 Duration: Plot Versus Screen

One portion of the plot in this hypothetical movie involves the housewarming party thrown by our ill-fated couple. The implied duration of this event (the plot duration) is four hours—from 8:00 in the evening to midnight of day 5.

8:00 PM   Midnight

Day 5

Plot duration = 4 hours

Although the implied duration of the plot event is four hours, the actual duration onscreen of the shots that cover this four-hour event is only ten minutes (the *screen duration*). As you can see below, those ten minutes are divided among fifteen discrete shots, each of which features a specific event or discussion at the party.

Screen duration = 15 individual shots = 10 minutes

duration can be isolated and analyzed not only in the context of the entire narrative of the film, but also within its constituent parts—in scenes and sequences. In these smaller parts, however, the relationship between plot duration and story duration generally remains stable; that is, in most mainstream Hollywood movies, the duration of a plot event is assumed to be equivalent to the duration of the story event that it implies. At the level of scenes (a sequence of related shots), the more interesting relationship is usually between screen duration and plot duration. We can generally characterize that relationship in one of three ways: (1) in a **summary relationship**, screen duration is shorter than plot duration; (2) in **real time**, screen duration corresponds directly to plot duration; and (3) in a **stretch relationship**, screen duration is longer than plot duration.

Both stretch and summary relationships are established primarily through editing techniques (discussed in detail in Chapter 6). The summary relationship is very familiar and occurs much more frequently in mainstream movies than do the other two. The summary relationship is depicted in Fig. 2.4, which illustrates one scene in our hypothetical movie; the screen duration of this scene is ten minutes, but the implied duration of the plot event is

four hours. In Terrence Malick's *Days of Heaven* (1978; screenwriter: Malick; see "Framing of the Shot" in Chapter 4), a thirty-second sequence of time-lapse cinematography shows the seeds of a wheat plant germinating under the soil, the wheat grass sprouting and its tips turning a golden color. This haunting shot, which is a metaphor for the more gradual changes that occur on farms in the cycle from planting to germination to harvest, depicts in a very short time on the screen a growth period that lasts much longer. In *Citizen Kane*, Welles depicts the steady disintegration of Kane's first marriage to Emily Norton (Ruth Warrick) through a rapid *montage* of six shots at the breakfast table that take two minutes on the screen but depict seven years of their life together. Through changes in dress, hairstyle, seating, and their preferences in newspapers, we see the couple's relationship go from amorous passion to sarcastic hostility. Summary relationships are essential to telling movie stories, especially long and complicated ones.

Because it is less common than summary, the stretch relationship is often used to highlight a plot event, stressing its importance to the overall narrative. A stretch relationship can be achieved by special effects such as slow motion, particularly when a graceful effect is needed, as in showing a reunited

Summary Relationship A sequence in Martin Scorsese's *Raging Bull* (1980; screenwriters: Paul Schrader and Mardik Martin) covers three years (story duration) in a few minutes (screen duration). Black-and-white shots of Jake La Motta's (Robert De Niro) most significant boxing matches from 1944 to 1947 are intercut with color shots from home movies that show La Motta and his second wife, Vickie (Cathy Moriarty), during the early years of their marriage.

couple running slowly toward one another. It can also be constructed by editing techniques. The "Odessa Steps" sequence in Sergei Eisenstein's *Battleship Potemkin* (1925; screenwriters: Nina Agadzhanova, Nikolai Aseyev, Eisenstein, and Sergei Tretyakov) uses editing to stretch out the plot duration of the massacre so that our experience of it onscreen lasts longer than it would have taken to occur in reality. Eisenstein does this

because he wants us to see the massacre as an important and meaningful event, as well as to increase our anxiety and empathy for the victims.

The real-time relationship is the least common of the three relationships between screen duration and plot duration, but its use has always interested and delighted film buffs. Many directors use real time within films to create uninterrupted "reality" on the screen, but directors rarely use it for entire

Real-Time Relationship Mike Figgis's *Timecode* (2000; screenwriter: Figgis) offers a dramatic and daring version of real time. Split into quarters, the screen displays four distinct but overlapping stories, each shot in one continuous ninety-three-minute take (the length of an ordinary digital videocassette), uninterrupted by editing.

films. Fred Zinnemann's *High Noon* (1952; screenwriter: Carl Foreman) and Alfred Hitchcock's *Rope* (1948; screenwriter: Arthur Laurents) are two outstanding films that present a real-time relationship between screen and plot duration. In *Rope*, Hitchcock used the *long take* (discussed further in Chapter 4)—an unedited, continuous shot—to preserve real time. One roll of motion picture film can record approximately eleven minutes of action, and thus Hitchcock made an eighty-minute film with ten shots that range in length from four minutes and forty seconds to ten minutes.[2] Six of the cuts between these shots are virtually unnoticeable because Hitchcock has the camera pass behind the backs of people or furniture and then makes the cut on a dark screen; four others are ordinary hard cuts from one person to another. Even these hard cuts do not break time or space, so the result is fluid storytelling in which the plot duration equals the screen duration of eighty minutes.

In most traditional narrative movies, cuts and other editing devices punctuate the flow of the narrative and graphically indicate that the images occur in human-made **cinematic time**, not seamless real time. As viewers, we think that movies pass before us in the present tense, but we also understand that cinematic time can be manipulated through editing, among other means. As we accept these manipulative conventions, we also recognize that classic Hollywood editing generally goes out of its way to avoid calling attention to itself. Furthermore, it attempts to reflect the natural mental processes by which human consciousness moves back and forth between reality and illusion, shifting between past, present, and future.

Abel Gance's masterpiece *Napoléon* (1927; screenwriter: Gance) not only exhibits each of the relationships between duration and plot that have just been described but also includes some of the most dazzling technical innovations in film history. The legendary French director's handling of time, speed, and movement builds dramatically on D. W. Griffith's earlier experiments in awakening us to the manifold possibilities of the cinematic medium for manipulating both time and space. With astonishing fluidity, Gance jumps forward and backward in time, so that a moment in the present is often related to events that preceded it and often foreshadows the events that will follow. For example, in the famous snowball sequence near the beginning

[2] Various critics have said that each shot in *Rope* lasts ten minutes, but the DVD release of the film shows the timings (rounded off) to be as follows: opening credits, 2:09; shot 1, 9:50; shot 2, 8:00; shot 3, 7:50; shot 4, 7:09; shot 5, 10:00; shot 6, 7:40; shot 7, 8:00; shot 8, 10:00; shot 9, 4:40; shot 10, 5:40; closing credits, 00:28.

of the film, Napoléon's participation in a schoolyard snowball fight becomes a genuine battle—on one hand to restore the young man's reputation among his stupid, class-conscious schoolmates, and on the other, to point toward his destiny as a military genius. To extend his control over *Napoléon*'s cinematic time, Gance introduced the Polyvision process, which used three synchronized cameras (and three synchronized projectors) to put three different actions on the screen simultaneously, as in a triptych, or to spread one vast composition across three screens. *Napoléon* concludes with not only such a triptych, but also, within each panel, a rapid recapitulation of footage seen previously in the film—again a fluid demonstration of the symbolic continuity of past, present, and future.

Suspense Versus Surprise

It is important to distinguish between *suspense*, which has been mentioned in the preceding discussions, and *surprise*. Although they are often confused, suspense and surprise are two fundamentally different elements in the development of many movie plots. Alfred Hitchcock mastered the unique properties of each, taking great care to ensure that they were integral to the internal logic of his plots. In a conversation with French director François Truffaut, Hitchcock explained the terms:

> We are now having a very innocent little chat. Let us suppose that there is a bomb underneath this table between us. Nothing happens, and then all of a sudden, "Boom!"
>
> There is an explosion. The public is *surprised*, but prior to this surprise, it has seen an absolutely ordinary scene of no special consequence. Now, let us take a *suspense* situation. The bomb is underneath the table and the public *knows* it, probably because they have seen the anarchist place it there. The public is *aware* that the bomb is going to explode at one o'clock and there is a clock in the decor. The public can see that it is a quarter to one. In these conditions this same innocuous conversation becomes fascinating because the public is participating in the scene. The audience is longing to warn the characters on the screen: "You shouldn't

be talking about such trivial matters. There's a bomb beneath you and it's about to explode!"

> In the first scene we have given the public fifteen seconds of *surprise* at the moment of the explosion. In the second we have provided them with fifteen minutes of *suspense*. The conclusion is that whenever possible the public must be informed. Except when the surprise is a twist, that is, when the unexpected ending is, in itself, the highlight of the story.[3]

Because there are no repeat surprises, we can be surprised in the same way only once. As a result, a **surprise**, a being taken unawares, can be shocking, and our emotional response to it is generally short-lived. By contrast, suspense is a more drawn-out (and some would say more enjoyable) experience—one that we may seek out even when we know what happens in a movie. **Suspense** is the anxiety brought on by a partial uncertainty: the end is certain, but the means is uncertain. Or, even more interestingly, we may know *both* the result and the means by which it's brought about, but we still feel suspense: we know what's going to happen and we want to warn and protect the characters, for we have grown to empathize with them (though we can intellectually acknowledge the fact that they aren't "real" people).

◎ DVD Suspense and Surprise

Repetition

The **repetition**, or number of times, with which a story element recurs in a plot is an important aspect of narrative form. If an event occurs once in a plot, we accept it as a functioning part of the narrative's progression. Its appearance more than once, however, suggests a pattern and thus a higher level of importance. Like order and duration, then, repetition serves not only as a means of relaying story information but also as a *signal* that a particular event has a meaning or significance that should be acknowledged in our interpretation and analysis.

[3] Alfred Hitchcock, qtd. in François Truffaut, *Hitchcock*, rev. ed. (New York: Simon & Schuster, 1984), 73.

[1]

[2]

Surprise Versus Suspense [1] Neil Jordan's *The Crying Game* (1992; screenwriter: Jordan) takes a very surprising turn when Fergus (Stephen Rea, *background*), an Irish terrorist, discovers that Dil (Jaye Davidson, *foreground*), the dark-skinned beauty he has fallen for, is a male transvestite. Knowing that this revelation (in addition to the movie's interracial romance) would shock many people, the filmmakers ran advertisements stating, "The movie everyone's talking about, but no one is giving away its secrets." This strategy achieved its aim, and the movie was very popular in part because of the surprise, but *The Crying Game* does not evoke suspense once we know the secret at its core. [2] Billy Wilder's *Some Like It Hot* (1959; screenwriters: Wilder and I. A. L. Diamond) concerns two musicians who witness a mob murder, disguise themselves as women, and leave town to work in an all-woman band.

Although their attempts to maintain this disguise are frustrated by their desires for the women who surround them, they persist through a series of hilarious turns that heighten the suspense. When will they be discovered? What will happen as a result? Eventually, a rich millionaire, Osgood Fielding III (Joe E. Brown, *left*) falls in love with Jerry/Daphne (Jack Lemmon, *right*), who frantically explains to Osgood that they can't marry because they are both men. As a surprise to cap the suspense, Osgood simply shrugs his shoulders and makes one of the greatest comebacks in movie history: "Well, nobody's perfect."

Story events can be repeated in various ways. A character may remember a key event at several times during the movie, indicating the psychological, intellectual, or physical importance of that event. The use of flashbacks or slow-motion sequences tends to give a mythical quality to memory, making the past seem more significant than it might actually have been. For example, in Atom Egoyan's *The Sweet Hereafter* (1997; screenwriter: Egoyan), Mitchell Stephens (Ian Holm) is so troubled by his teenage daughter's drug addiction that he tries to put it out of his mind by frequently visualizing more pleasant memories of her as a child. In another form of repetition, the director relies on editing to contrast past and present.

The **familiar image** is defined by film theorist Stefan Scharff as any image that a director periodically repeats in a movie (with or without variations) to help stabilize its narrative. By its repetition, the image calls attention to itself as a narrative (as well as visual) element. Theoretically, the composition and framing of such images should remain the same, although variations on these elements are frequently used as long as they preserve the integrity of the original image. An example of the rhythmic use of identical images occurs in Sergei Eisenstein's repetition of a set of images (steps, soldiers, mother holding baby, mother with baby in carriage, woman shot in stomach, woman with broken glasses, etc.) in the "Odessa Steps" sequence of *Battleship Potemkin*. Other movies rely on our familiarity with the original image to make variations in it that we will recognize. In Howard Hawks's *Red River* (1948; screenwriters: Borden Chase and Charles Schnee), the familiar image is that of "Groot" Nadine (Walter Brennan) in the driver's seat of a stagecoach, which is repeated many times in order to emphasize his importance to the journey, as well as to connect him to the actions of other characters.

Characters

Characters, another essential element of film narrative, play functional roles within the plot, either acting or being acted on. Stories can't exist if either plot or characters are missing. But at their best, characters don't have merely a technical function, as if they were mere pieces on a chessboard. After all, we go to movies in large part to witness stories about characters whom we can *imagine as real people*, with complex personalities and lives. When we infer a story from a plot, we employ our imaginations to enlarge our sense not only of what has happened, but also of the personalities within the world of that story. Thus, when we talk about characters in our analyses of movies, we should consider them both as beings who (much like living, breathing people) have discernible traits, habits, and dispositions and as formal elements that help develop the narrative.

One way to discuss characters, then, is in terms of the complexity of their traits. Making a very useful distinction, English novelist and literary theorist E. M. Forster said that there were two kinds of characters: *round* and *flat*.[4] **Round characters** are complex and three-dimensional, possessing several traits, sometimes even contradictory ones. Because they are lifelike and believable, round characters are unpredictable, capable of surprising us in a convincing way. Both Charlotte (Scarlett Johansson) and Bob Harris (Bill Murray) are round characters in Sofia Coppola's *Lost in Translation* (2003; screenwriter: Coppola). Although the typical cinematic portrayal of a young woman and an older man ends in a romantic relationship between them, Coppola avoids this approach to show the independent, unpredictable nature of her characters.

By contrast, **flat characters** are one-dimensional, possessing one or very few discernible traits, and their motivations and actions are generally predictable. Frodo (Elijah Wood) in Peter Jackson's "Lord of the Rings" trilogy (2001–03; screenwriters: Fran Walsh, Philippa Boyens, Stephen Sinclair, and Jackson) is a flat

character. For one thing, he is not a "real" human being, but a member of the imaginary race of hobbits, albeit the *ideal* hobbit for the quest. His motivations—dedication and the urgings of his pure heart—help him to resist temptation, but in the end, he gives in and is saved not by his own free will, but by the intervention of fate. All of the characters in Frank Miller and Robert Rodriguez's *Sin City* (2005; screenwriter: Miller) are as flat as the one-dimensional comic-book characters that inspired them.

We also distinguish between *major characters* and *minor characters*—categories that signal the relative importance of characters within the narrative. **Major characters**, the most important characters to the plot, make the most things happen or have the most things happen to them. Because plots depend on conflict, major characters—who, of course, can be either male or female—are often further described as **protagonists** and **antagonists**.

Although the protagonist is the central figure of a story and is often referred to as the *hero*, a protagonist is not necessarily a hero. Recognizing that the very idea of a hero has evolved significantly through time, we should consider the changing attitudes of different cultures about the notion of heroism when we use the term. We once saw the protagonist-as-hero as someone like Jefferson Smith (James Stewart) in Frank Capra's *Mr. Smith Goes to Washington* (1939; screenwriter: Sidney Buchman) or Sister Elizabeth Kenny (Rosalind Russell) in Dudley Nichols's *Sister Kenny* (1946; screenwriters: Alexander Knox, Mary McCarthy, and Nichols)—both characters who exemplified courage and good deeds. In the last two decades, however, the evolution and influence of the independent film has made it virtually impossible to draw a composite figure of the American movie hero. In the movies, today's hero can be a virtuous person—Captain Jack Aubrey (Russell Crowe) in Peter Weir's *Master and Commander: The Far Side of the World* (2003; screenwriters: Weir and John Collee), who commands his British ship in major naval victories over the Napoleonic fleet, or Lieutenant Ellen Ripley (Sigourney Weaver) in Ridley Scott's *Alien* (1979; screenwriter: Dan O'Bannon), who vanquishes man-eating creatures.

[4] E. M. Forster, *Aspects of the Novel* (New York: Harcourt, Brace, and World, 1927), 103–18.

[1]

[2]

Round and Flat Characters   [1] Charlotte (Scarlett Johansson) and Bob (Bill Murray) are round characters in Sofia Coppola's *Lost in Translation* (2003). We recognize them as "real" people by their natural appearance, contemporary clothing and overall look, fashionable lifestyle, and most of all, by the free will with which they make their own choices in life. Here, at a contentious dinner in a Japanese restaurant that is as foreign as their relationship, their friendship begins to unravel over the issue of their age differences. [2] By contrast, Frodo (Elijah Wood) in Peter Jackson's *The Return of the King* (2003; the final movie in the "Lord of the Rings" trilogy) is a flat character who is nonetheless the ideal hobbit in looks and manner. The character of Frodo is costumed and made up with slightly pointed ears and large furry feet; to this character, actor Elijah Wood brings his preternaturally sweet smile and large eyes (sometimes gray-blue as here, sometimes emerald green). This image is from the penultimate scene, in which Frodo says goodbye to his fellow hobbits. Sweet, dedicated, and adventurous as he is, Frodo is a one-dimensional character whose actions are controlled by the overall mythical tale in which he is caught.

There are also heroes who show a darker, more hostile nature, such as Travis Bickle (Robert De Niro) in Martin Scorsese's *Taxi Driver* (1976; screenwriter: Paul Schrader), who lashes out at the depravity he finds on New York's streets, or Aileen Wuornos (Charlize Theron) in Patty Jenkins's *Monster* (2003; screenwriter: Jenkins), a prostitute who becomes a serial killer. (Be careful not to confuse the actor's reputation with the role being played; actors can be cast in roles that conform with the audience's experience and expectations of them, as well as cast against type or audience expectation.)

In summary, a protagonist can be a hero, and those heroes can either be good guys or bad guys in their struggle with whatever they oppose or that opposes them. No matter what type of character the protagonist is, the story is ordinarily about this person, whose actions are essential to the action and programs of the plot. In any event, the protagonist should have clear convictions and well-motivated actions, and be able to change and evolve in response to events and other characters.

The antagonist is a character opposing the protagonist, and thus, in all likelihood, the one who provokes the protagonist's actions or reactions. The scenario can be as simple as the hero (protagonist) versus the villain (antagonist), but because we know that life is more complicated than that, we should be prepared to see the antagonist as not just one character but also as a group of characters (a political party, members of a street gang, residents of a neighborhood, etc.) such as the CIA versus Jason Bourne (Matt Damon) in Paul Greengrass's *The Bourne Supremacy* (2004; screenwriter: Tony Gilroy), or a force of nature such as the shark in Steven Spielberg's *Jaws* (1975; screenwriters: Peter Benchley and Carl Gottlieb) or the iceberg in James Cameron's *Titanic* (1997; screenwriter: Cameron). Notice how different the protagonists and antagonists are in these movies: Jason Bourne, a renegade CIA agent, evades the agency's evil attempts to kill him. The shark hunters differ in why they want to destroy the man-eater; shark-hunter Quint (Robert Shaw) wants revenge, while Police Chief Martin Brody (Roy Scheider) wants to make his town's beach safe. And in *Titanic*, the protagonist, Jack Dawson (Leonardo DiCaprio), who is a *victim* of the iceberg, hopes he'll survive the tragedy and be reunited with his love.

In contrast to major characters, **minor characters** play a less important role in the overall movie, functioning usually as a means of moving the plot forward or of fleshing out the motivations of the major characters. **Marginal characters** lack definition and are onscreen for very short periods of time. Although major characters are, generally speaking, also richer (rounder) than minor characters, they need not be. In this regard, Joel Cairo (Peter Lorre) in John Huston's *The Maltese Falcon* (1941; screenwriter: Huston) is a minor round character, and Indiana Jones (Harrison Ford) in Steven Spielberg's *Raiders of the Lost Ark* (1981; screenwriters: George Lucas and Phillip Kaufman) is a major flat character. Indiana Jones is a doubly flat character because he's almost a one-dimensional cartoon figure, which is the way Ford plays him.

A movie's characters—whether round, flat, major, minor, or marginal—do not necessarily arouse our sympathy. We develop our knowledge of all characters in several ways: from their traits, motivations, and actions; from the ways in which a narrator or other characters describe them; and from the style in which the actors who play them interpret them. Although characters can be motivated by many factors—social, economic, ethnic, racial, religious, sexual, or emotional, to name a few—the strongest motivation is usually psychological. Part of the challenge and enjoyment of interpreting a movie is figuring out characters' motivations, something we do all the time in our daily lives when interpreting other people's behavior. We cannot easily say that what characters do is *natural*, because naturalness, like eccentricity, is a cultural phenomenon; it varies from one society to another and from one era to another in the same society. Instead, we can ask whether or not the behavior is *probable* within the context of the film. If a character's action makes sense in the world of the movie, we won't need additional explanation to understand what motivated the action.

Here we must distinguish between character and **characterization**, the process of the actor's interpreting a character in a movie. Characterization differs according to the actor, the character, the screenplay, and the director (see Chapter 5). As narrative movies developed through their history, filmmakers increasingly left things out of their movies' characterization, or left them implicit, or left them to viewers to determine. Audiences learned to understand and accept these changing **cinematic conventions**, automatically filling in what was missing and thus themselves becoming responsible for the verisimilitude of the actions. Today we may feel that filmmakers who offer too much explanation actually insult our intelligence. As we watch movies from other eras, though, we should be aware (and forgiving) of the ways in which the *conventions* of explaining character or establishing motivation have changed over time. Consider, for example, Orson Welles's second movie, *The Magnificent Ambersons* (1942; screenwriter: Welles). Although Welles does not appear in the movie, he narrates it, and he chose to begin the movie by reading his own adaptation of the first chapter of the Booth Tarkington novel on which it is based. In *Citizen Kane*, co-screenwriters Herman J. Mankiewicz and Orson Welles revolutionized narrative conventions of American movies, but in *The Magnificent Ambersons*, Welles seems not to have trusted his skill at telling a story visually, and instead he returned to narrative conventions more typical of contemporary radio broadcasting, of which he was the undisputed master. For several

Character Motivation In Lars von Trier's *Breaking the Waves* (1996; screenwriters: von Trier and Peter Asmussen), simpleminded and good-hearted Bess McNeill (Emily Watson) receives instructions either from God or from a voice in her head. When Bess becomes erratic and self-destructive, we must decide if she is insane, masochistic, victimized, or saintly, and we don't have a clear sense of how to interpret her behavior until the very end.

Unmotivated Behavior   In David Lynch's *Blue Velvet* (1986), Frank Booth (Dennis Hopper), who represents the darkest side of life in a small Northwest town, inhales nitrous oxide to heighten his sexual excitement, repeats the word *mommy*, and says, "Baby wants blue velvet," before he assaults his sex slave, Dorothy (Isabella Rossellini). His behavior isn't motivated in a way that we can easily identify, so his character is a disturbing and vivid mystery.

years, week after week, he brought novels and plays to life for the listening audience. Although Welles introduces many of the characters in *Ambersons* by showing them, it is his voice and words that dominate the characterization. Today this approach seems as old-fashioned as Tarkington's novel in the way it reveals information about the characters. Welles gives us information about characters' actions and thoughts that we could have figured out ourselves from watching the action.

If a character behaves or speaks in a way that disrupts the verisimilitude (in its improbability or eccentricity), we generally expect some form of explanation that can help us redefine either the world of the movie or the character. If no explanation is forthcoming, we are faced with a puzzle: either the improbability has revealed a flaw in the movie's form (in its unity and balance), or it has been *intentionally* placed in the movie to serve some other formal purpose. Either way, we should be alert to such moments. In Curtis Hanson's *Wonder Boys* (2000; screenwriter: Steven Kloves), a novelist, Grady Tripp (Michael Douglas), displays assorted peculiarities, which we initially read in light of his appearing to have writer's block, his heavy use of marijuana, his extramarital affair, and his failing marriage. Ultimately, we understand both his peculiarities and the background characteristics as related to (even symptoms of) the larger question of the state of Tripp's life—that is, to his having reached a midlife crisis that affects his perceptions and actions.

By contrast, some movies leave extremely eccentric actions unmotivated, to be understood as representing very disturbed characters, people with whom none of us (let's hope) have any familiarity. Jonathan Demme's *The Silence of the Lambs* (1991; screenwriter: Ted Tally), for example, provides no explanation for why Hannibal Lecter (Anthony Hopkins) commits such unspeakable acts as eating human flesh. Lecter speaks candidly and humorously about his crimes, but the movie has more to do with how Lecter's sociopathology can assist in the apprehension of another sociopath than with Lecter's own motivation. Likewise, David Lynch's *Blue Velvet* (1986; screenwriter: Lynch) presents Frank Booth (Dennis Hopper) as a case study in abnormal, violent, even psychopathic behavior. Booth's fetishistically rubbing a piece of blue velvet and repeating the word *mommy* hint at Freudian explanations and past traumas, but do so without offering resolution, perhaps even in a tongue-in-cheek manner. In psychoanalytic terms, Booth seems more an eruption of the id—the unconscious source of needs and drives—than an actual human being with recognizable feelings.

Setting

The **setting** of a movie is the time and place in which the story occurs. It not only establishes the date, city, or country but also provides the characters' social, educational, and cultural backgrounds and other identifying factors vital for understanding them, such as what they wear, eat, and drink. Setting sometimes provides an implicit explanation for actions or traits that we might otherwise consider eccentric, because cultural norms vary from place to place and throughout time. Certain genres are associated with specific settings—for example, westerns with wide-open country, film noirs with dark city streets, and horror movies with creepy houses.

In addition to providing us with essential contextual information that helps us understand story events and character motivation, setting adds texture to the movie's diegesis, enriching our sense of the overall world of the movie. Terrence Malick's *Days of Heaven* (1978; screenwriter: Malick) features magnificent landscapes in the American West of the 1920s. At first, the extraordinary visual imagery seems to take precedence over the narrative. However, the settings—the vast wheat fields and the great solitary house against the sky—directly complement the depth and power of the narrative, which is concerned with the cycle of the seasons, the work connected with each season, and how fate, greed, sexual passion, and jealousy can lead to tragedy. Here, setting also helps to reveal

Setting in Science Fiction   Based on Philip K. Dick's science fiction novel *Do Androids Dream of Electric Sheep?* (1968), Ridley Scott's *Blade Runner* (1982) takes place in 2019, in an imaginary world where cities such as Los Angeles are ruled by technology and saturated with visual information. In most science fiction films, setting plays an important part in our understanding of the narrative, so sci-fi filmmakers spend considerable time, money, and effort to make the setting come to life.

the characters' states of mind. They are from the Chicago slums, and once they arrive in the pristine wheat fields of the West, they are lonely and alienated from themselves and their values. They cannot adapt, and thus end tragically. Here, setting is destiny.

Other films tell stories closely related to their international, national, or regional settings, such as the specific neighborhoods of New York City that form the backdrop of many Woody Allen films. But think of the many different ways in which Manhattan has been photographed, including the many film noirs with their harsh black-and-white contrasts; the sour colors of Martin Scorsese's *Taxi Driver* (1976; screenwriter: Paul Schrader); or the bright colors of Alfred Hitchcock's *North by Northwest* (1959; screenwriter: Ernest Lehman).

Settings are not always drawn from real-life locales; an opening title card tells us that F. W. Murnau's *Sunrise: A Song of Two Humans* (1927; screenwriter: Carl Mayer) takes place in "no place and every place." Stanley Kubrick's *2001: A Space Odyssey* (1968; screenwriters: Kubrick and Arthur C. Clarke) creates an entirely new space–time continuum, and Tim Burton's *Charlie and the Chocolate Factory* (2005; screenwriter: John August) creates the most fantastic chocolate factory in the world.

The attraction of science fiction films such as George Lucas's *Star Wars* (1977; screenwriter: Lucas) and Ridley Scott's *Blade Runner* (1982; director's cut released 1992; screenwriters: Hampton Fancher and David Webb Peoples) is often attributed to their almost totally unfamiliar settings. These stories about outer space and future cities have a mythical or symbolic significance beyond that of stories set on Earth. Their settings may be verisimilar and appropriate for the purpose of the story, whether or not we can verify them as "real."

Scope

Related to *duration* and *setting* is **scope**—the overall range, in time and place, of the movie's story. Stories can range from the distant past to the narrative present, or they can be narrowly focused on a short period, even a matter of moments. They can take us from one galaxy to another, or they can remain inside a single room. They can present a rather limited perspective on their world, or they can show us several alternative perspectives. Determining the general scope of a movie's story—understanding its relative expansiveness—can help you piece together and understand other aspects of the movie as a whole.

Scope Bernardo Bertolucci's *The Last Emperor* (1987; screenwriters: Mark Peploe and Bertolucci) recounts the comparatively small story of the title character, China's Pu Yi (John Lone), against the political changes enveloping China as it moved from monarchy to communism from 1908 to 1967. Even though the two stories occur simultaneously and are related causally, the expansive scope of the historical epic takes precedence over the story of the emperor's life.

For example, the *biopic*, a film about a person's life—whether historical or fictional—might tell the story in one of two ways: through one significant episode or period in the life of a person, or through a series of events in a single life, sometimes beginning with birth and ending in old age. Biopics remain one of the great staples of movie production. Think of the variety of subjects in these recent movies: opera diva Maria Callas in Franco Zeffirelli's *Callas Forever* (2002; screenwriters: Martin Sherman and Zeffirelli); sex researcher Dr. Alfred Kinsey in Bill Condon's *Kinsey* (2004; screenwriter: Condon); Ernesto "Che" Guevara, Latin American revolutionary, in Walter Salles's *The Motorcycle Diaries* (2004; screenwriter: Jose Rivera); Harvey Pekar, the eccentric comic-book artist, in Shari Springer Berman and Robert Pulcini's *American Splendor* (2003; screenwriters: Berman and Pulcini); tycoon Howard Hughes in Martin Scorsese's *The Aviator* (2004; screenwriter: John Logan); or singer Ray Charles in Taylor Hackford's *Ray* (2004; screenwriter: James L. White).

WEB The Biopic and the Historical Drama

Many war films have been limited in scope to the story of a single battle; others have treated an entire war. Steven Spielberg's *Saving Private Ryan* (1998; screenwriter: Robert Rodat) covers two stories happening simultaneously: the larger story is that of the June 1944 D-Day invasion of Normandy, involving the vast Allied army; the more intimate story, and the one that gives the film its title, presents what happens from the time the U.S. government orders that Private Ryan (Matt Damon) be removed from combat to the time it actually happens. Both stories are seen from the American point of view, perceptually and politically.

By contrast, Ken Annakin, Andrew Marton, and Bernhard Wicki's *The Longest Day* (1962; screenwriters: Romain Gary, James Jones, David Pursall, Jack Seddon, and Cornelius Ryan) relates the D-Day invasion to what was happening in four countries—the United States, France, England, and Germany—though also from the perspective of American politics. Thus its scope is broader, enhanced by the viewpoints of its large cast of characters. Although Terrence Malick's *The Thin*

Red Line (1998; screenwriter: Malick) focuses on the American invasion of the Japanese-held Pacific island of Guadalcanal, it ultimately uses the historical setting as a very personal backdrop for a meditation on war and its horrors.

Narration and Narrators

The word **narration**, which literally means telling a story, also implies that there will be a storyteller narrator. In a movie, although we *see* the action on the screen—who is making it happen, who is affected by it, and who reacts to it—we instinctively understand that the camera itself can be both a visual recorder and a narrator, showing us what the director wants us to see and in what conditions (setting, lighting, camera position and angle, etc.). This visual narration can take several forms. It can be **omniscient** (or unrestricted), giving us a third-person view of all aspects of the movie's action or characters; or **restricted**, a narration that reveals information to the audience only as a specific character learns of it. In terms of the depth with which the narration reveals action or character, it can be objective (we see and hear what the character is doing and saying); it can indicate the physical point of view from which the character sees things (see "Framing and Point of View" in Chapter 4); or it can take us into the character's

Breaking the "Fourth Wall"   Soon after his first fight with Tyler Durden (Brad Pitt), the unnamed Narrator (Edward Norton) in David Fincher's *Fight Club* (1999) not only changes the tone and speed of his narration, but breaks the "fourth wall" (the assumed barrier between the characters in the movie and the audience) to address us directly. In this image, where Tyler (background, dressed as a waiter) serves food at a fancy banquet, the Narrator describes Tyler's minor rebellions (the splicing of pornography into a family film at the cinema where he was a projectionist, the urinating into food service trays used at the banquet, etc.) and takes a certain delight in Tyler's anarchistic behaviors. Whatever reason the director had for breaking the fourth wall and having the Narrator's tone change, it clearly signals a shift in his outlook.

inner subjectivity, revealing such mental processes as thoughts, dreams, fantasies, or fears. Obviously, narration is one of the screenwriter's (and director's) most powerful and flexible tools.

We can readily understand how visual narration works by studying silent movies. Take, for example, F. W. Murnau's *The Last Laugh* (1924; screenwriter: Carl Mayer), a movie whose visual images communicate its action and meaning so clearly that it needs but a single intertitle (at the end) to help explain what is going to happen to the protagonist. To put it another way, words are not important to the telling of Murnau's story. Some movies use one or more **narrators** to help tell the story. The narrator's voice can be that of an actual character in the movie (**first-person narration**) or that of a person who is not a character (**voice-over narration**). In Amy Heckerling's *Clueless* (1995; screenwriter: Heckerling), a delightful contemporary parody of Jane Austen's novel *Emma* (1815), Cher Horowitz (Alicia Silverstone) is the major character and first-person narrator. Through her offscreen narration, she sets the cultural, moral,

Voice-over Narration   In Amy Heckerling's *Clueless* (1995), Alicia Silverstone plays the lovable but airheaded Cher Horowitz. She is also the offscreen narrator who keeps us up to speed in this satire of life among teenagers in Beverly Hills.

political, and aesthetic tone of the movie's world—Beverly Hills teenagers—from her unique perspective as a beautiful, rich, spoiled, and essentially likable character.

The tone taken by a movie's narrator reflects the screenwriter's and director's psychological, emotional, and intellectual attitudes toward their story. These attitudes are also vital to their shaping of the characters and action, as well as to how the director guides the actors' characterizations of their roles. Lars von Trier's *Dogville* (2003; screenwriter: von Trier) expresses his misanthropic vision of the United States, a view enhanced by the patronizing, upper-class British voice of the offscreen narrator (John Hurt). Such narration leaves little question about the director's view of his story.

Similarly, the offscreen Narrator (Edward Norton), one of the major characters in David Fincher's *Fight Club* (1999; screenwriter: Jim Uhls), describes his odyssey from a lonely thirty-something young professional, who gets actively involved in underground fight clubs, and eventually moves toward anarchy and the destruction of our materialistic civilization. The voice that Norton uses to narrate this journey indicates that his point of view changes from doubt to conviction to confusion. To introduce himself, he describes his nerdy way of life and meaningless existence, which we not only see in his miserable and pathetic attempts to alleviate his loneliness by attending support groups for people with conditions he does not have, but also *hear* in the tone of his weary voice. By the conclusion of the movie, however, we realize that this character may not be who he seems to be (or says he is) and thus is unreliable as a narrator.

These two provocative movies reflect not only their makers, but also their times, just as the narration of many films in the Cold War period—such as John Frankenheimer's *The Manchurian Candidate* (1962; screenwriter: George Axelrod; uncredited voice-over narrator: Paul Frees)—reflect a fear of Communism expressed in the "voice of God" tone of the narration, itself reminiscent of the tone of deep social concern expressed in such classic documentaries as Pare Lorentz's *The Plow That Broke the Plains* (1936) or Frank Capra's "Why We Fight" series (1943–45). Thus, narration, as well as narrator, not only extends the meaning of the screenplay, but can also reflect the historical period in which a movie was filmed.

Looking at Narrative: John Ford's *Stagecoach*

Let's examine John Ford's *Stagecoach* (1939; screenwriter: Dudley Nichols), perhaps *the* classic western, using the elements of narrative we've just discussed: story, plot, order, hubs and satellites, duration, suspense versus surprise, repetition, characters, settings, scope, and narration.

Story

The story of *Stagecoach* is based on a familiar convention (sometimes called the *ship of fools*) in which a diverse group of people—perhaps passengers traveling to a common destination, or residents of a hotel—must confront a common danger and, through that experience, confront themselves, both as individuals and as members of a group. Ford revitalized this convention and the often formulaic western genre by presenting sharp psychological portraits of vivid characters, magnificent imagery, and pointed social commentary and by emphasizing all three of these components more than the Indian fight, which was what audiences expected would be stressed.

Written by Dudley Nichols, the screenplay is based on Ernest Haycox's 1937 short story "Stage to Lordsburg."[5] The story concerns a diverse group of people (male and female; weak and strong; from different places, backgrounds, and professions; and with dissimilar temperaments) who have either been living in or are passing through the frontier town of Tonto. Despite a warning from the U.S. Cavalry that Apache warriors, under the command of the dreaded Geronimo, have cut the telegraph wires and threatened the settlers' safety, this group

[5] Both the story and the screenplay are in Dudley Nichols, *Stagecoach: A Film by John Ford and Dudley Nichols* (New York: Simon & Schuster, 1971). See also Edward Buscombe's excellent analysis of the film, *Stagecoach* (London: British Film Institute, 1992), to which I am indebted.

[1]

[4]

[2]

[5]

[3]

[6]

The Cast of Characters in *Stagecoach*   [1] Buck Rickabaugh (Andy Devine, *left*) and Marshal Curly Wilcox (George Bancroft); [2] Dallas (Claire Trevor) and Henry Gatewood (Berton Churchill); [3] the Ringo Kid (John Wayne);

[4] Gatewood and Lucy Mallory (Louise Platt); [5] Samuel Peacock (Donald Meek, *left*) and Dr. Josiah Boone (Thomas Mitchell); and [6] Mr. Hatfield (John Carradine).

boards a stagecoach to Lordsburg. In charge of the coach is Buck Rickabaugh (Andy Devine), the driver, and Marshal Curly Wilcox (George Bancroft), who is on the lookout for an escaped prisoner called the Ringo Kid (John Wayne). The seven passengers include (1) Lucy Mallory (Louise Platt), the aloof, Southern-born, and (as we later learn) pregnant wife of a cavalry officer whom she has come west to join; (2) Samuel Peacock (Donald Meek), a liquor salesman; (3) Dr. Josiah Boone (Thomas Mitchell), a doctor who still carries his bag of equipment, even though he has been kicked out of the profession for malpractice and now is being driven out of Tonto for drunkenness; (4) Mr. Hatfield (John Carradine), a Southern gambler, who is proud of the fact that he served in Lucy's father's regiment in the Civil War and leaves Tonto to serve as her protector on the trip; (5) Henry Gatewood (Berton Churchill), the Tonto bank president, who is leaving town with a mysterious satchel that we later learn contains money he stole from his bank; and (6) Dallas (Claire Trevor), a good-hearted prostitute, who has been driven out of town by a group of Tonto's righteous women. The seventh passenger, Ringo, has been heading for Lordsburg to avenge his father's murder, but when his horse becomes lame outside Tonto, he stops the stagecoach and is arrested by the marshal before he boards. Each passenger has personal reasons for leaving Tonto (or, in Ringo's case, prison) and making the perilous journey. Lucy, Hatfield, Gatewood, and Peacock all have specific purposes for traveling to Lordsburg; Dallas and Dr. Boone are being forced to leave town; and the Ringo Kid has a grudge to settle.

Plot

The plot of *Stagecoach* covers the two-day trip from Tonto to Lordsburg and is developed in a strictly chronological way without flashbacks or flashforwards. The events follow one another coherently and logically, and their relations of cause and effect are easy to discern. Balance, harmony, and unity are the principal keys to understanding the relationship between the story and the plot. Indeed, the eminent French film theorist and critic André Bazin notes that

Stagecoach (1939) is the ideal example of the maturity of a style brought to classic perfection. John Ford struck the ideal balance between social myth, historical reconstruction, psychological truth, and the traditional theme of the Western mise en scène. None of these elements dominated any other. *Stagecoach* is like a wheel, so perfectly made that it remains in equilibrium on its axis in any position.[6]

Order

As already noted, Ford maintains strict chronological order in using the journey to structure the story events. The journey provides both chronological and geographical markers for dividing the sequences. Furthermore, it reveals a clear pattern of cause and effect created primarily by each character's desire to go to Lordsburg on this particular day. That pattern proceeds to conflict (created both by internal character interaction and by the external Apache attack, which frustrates the characters' desires), reaches a turning point (the victory over the Apaches), and concludes with a resolution (Ringo's revenge on the Plummers, whose testimony had put him in prison, and his riding off a free man with the woman he loves). Otherwise, the plot order is not manipulated in any way.

Diegetic and Nondiegetic Elements

The diegetic elements are everything in the story except the opening and closing titles and credits and the background music, all of which are, of course, nondiegetic. One very important formal element in *Stagecoach* is American folk music, including the song "Bury Me Not on the Lone Prairie," most often heard in connection with Buck and representing his justifiable fears of dying on the range; a honky-tonk piano in the bar; and a symphonic score mixing many familiar folk tunes. The film's main theme is Stephen Foster's classic ballad "I Dream of Jeannie with the Light-Brown Hair." A

---

[6] André Bazin, "Evolution of the Western," in *What Is Cinema?* trans. Hugh Gray (Berkeley: University of California Press, 1967–71), 2:149.

song about remembering the past, perhaps with regret or loss, it is closely associated with the Old South and evokes the memories of Lucy Mallory and Hatfield: the devastating Civil War, the uncertain westward movement, the fragmented western territories, and, in all of this, a yearning for a simpler time and a woman with light brown hair.

Hubs and Satellites

The hubs in *Stagecoach*—those major events or branching points in the plot structure that force characters to choose between or among alternate paths—include (in the order of the plot)

1. The passengers' decision to leave Tonto in spite of the cavalry's warning about Geronimo and his troops
2. Marshal Wilcox's decision to let Ringo join the party
3. The passengers' vote to leave the Dry Fork station for Lordsburg, even though a relief unit of cavalry has not yet arrived
4. Dr. Boone's willingness to sober up and deliver the baby
5. Dallas's decision at the Apache Wells station to accept Ringo's proposal
6. The group's decision to delay departure from Apache Wells until Lucy has rested from childbirth and is ready to travel
7. Ringo's attempt to escape at Apache Wells
8. The passengers' decision at the burned-out ferry landing to try to reach Lordsburg, even though they realize that an Apache attack may be imminent
9. Ringo's willingness to risk his life to bring the coach under control

Hubs in *Stagecoach* These twelve images illustrate the plot hubs in John Ford's *Stagecoach* (characters are listed from left to right): [1] Peacock, Curly, Hatfield, Lucy; [2] Buck, Curly, Ringo, cavalry captain; [3] Dallas, Ringo, Lucy, Buck, Curly, Peacock, Gatewood, Hatfield; [4] Curly, Peacock, Ringo; [5] Ringo and Dallas; [6] Gatewood, Buck, Curly, Hatfield, Peacock; [7] Ringo; [8] Buck, Curly, Dallas, Ringo; [9] Ringo; [10] cavalry flag bearer and bugler; [11] Ringo and Curly; [12] Curly, Ringo, and Dallas.

1

2

3

4

5

9

6

10

7

11

8

12

10. The arrival of the cavalry soon after the Apache attack has begun

11. Marshal Wilcox's decision to reward Ringo's bravery by allowing him ten minutes of freedom in which to confront the Plummers

12. The marshal's decision to set Ringo free

The principal satellites—those minor plot events that add texture and complexity to characters and events but are not *essential* elements within the narrative—include (in plot order) the Apaches' cutting of the telephone wires; Gatewood's anxiety about getting to Lordsburg no matter what happens along the route; Peacock's anxiety over Dr. Boone's helping himself to his stock of liquor; Buck's wavering enthusiasm for driving the stagecoach against the odds; Lucy's, Hatfield's, and Gatewood's demonstrations of their self-perceived social superiority, especially at the lunch table at Dry Fork; Hatfield's attempt to defend Lucy from Apache attack, which results in his being shot; Marshal Wilcox's distribution of weapons to the travelers for their self-defense during the Apache attack; Wilcox's arrest of Gatewood for embezzlement; and Ringo's successful killing of the three Plummer brothers.

Duration

The story duration includes what we know and what we infer from the total lives of all the characters (e.g., Lucy's privileged upbringing in Virginia, marriage to a military officer, current pregnancy, and the route of her trip out west up until the moment the movie begins). The plot duration includes the time of those events within the story that the film chooses to tell—here the two days of the trip from Tonto to Lordsburg. The screen duration, or running time, is ninety-six minutes.

Suspense

In 1875, it took two days for a fast stagecoach to make the trip from Tonto to Lordsburg, and the plot follows this two-day trip chronologically. However, the pace also serves other functions. The fear

first expressed in the opening moments at mention of the name Geronimo intensifies the suspense of the imminent Indian attack, thus providing a decisive crisis during which the characters respond to the challenges and rigors of the trip and reveal their true selves. Will Lucy stop acting like a spoiled rich woman? Will Dr. Boone sober up in time to deliver her child? Will Dallas accept Ringo's proposal? Because we know little of their origins, we must trust in what we see of their current surroundings, as well as their interactions with each other and with the community (both the community of Tonto and the "community" that develops on the journey).

Repetition

Although no story events recur in *Stagecoach*, character traits both recur (e.g., Gatewood's insensitive desire to keep moving, no matter what, puts in danger both individuals and the group as a whole) and are transformed as a result of the journey (e.g., Lucy tenderly acknowledges Dallas's invaluable assistance during childbirth: "Dallas, if there's ever anything I can do for . . ."). Ford also repeats a three-part editing pattern some dozen times in the movie: (shot 1) *long shot* of the stagecoach rolling along the plain; (shot 2) a *two-shot* of Curly and Buck on the driver's seat; (shot 3) a *middle shot* or *close-up* of the passengers inside. We could broadly consider the recurrences of this series of shots as repetitions of familiar images.

Characters

All the characters inside the stagecoach—Dallas, Ringo, Hatfield, Peacock, Gatewood, Dr. Boone, and Lucy—are major, because they make the most things happen and have the most things happen to them. Dallas, Ringo, Dr. Boone, and Lucy are round characters: three-dimensional, possessing several traits, and unpredictable. The flat characters—one-dimensional, possessing one or very few discernible traits, and generally predictable—include Hatfield, Peacock, and Gatewood. Buck Rickabaugh and Marshal Wilcox, riding on the bench at the exterior front of the coach, are essentially minor (and flat) characters; they play less important roles and usually function as a means of moving the plot forward or of fleshing out the motivations of the major characters. Geronimo, the antagonist whose presence is crucial to the plot, is not developed at all. He's a menacing offscreen presence, about as flat a character as we can imagine.

Setting

The story takes place in settings constructed in Hollywood—the interiors and exteriors of two towns and the stagecoach—and on actual locations in the spectacular Monument Valley of northern Arizona. Beautiful and important as Monument Valley and other exterior shots are to the film, the shots made inside the stagecoach as it speeds through the valley are essential to developing other themes in the movie. As the war with the Apaches signifies the territorial changes taking place outside, another drama is taking place among the passengers. In journeying through changing scenery, they also change through their responses to the dangers they face and their relations with, and reactions to, one another. This may be a wilderness, but the settlers have brought from the East and the South their notions of social respectability and status. Thus, as the film begins in Tonto, they enter the stagecoach in the descending order of their apparent importance within the film's social scale:

1. Gatewood, the banker, is a highly respected social pillar of Tonto.
2. Lucy, the transient army wife, is a respected Southern aristocrat.
3. Hatfield, the transient gambler, seems to be a gentleman.
4. Peacock, the transient whisky salesman, is barely acceptable.

Settings in *Stagecoach* [1] Main street of Tonto, where the horses are being attached to the stagecoach before the journey begins. [2] The stagecoach, with its cavalry escort, entering the first phase of the journey. [3] Apache attack on the stagecoach. [4] Main street of Lordsburg, where residents watch the stagecoach arrive.

5. Dr. Boone has been run out of town by the Law and Order League.
6. Dallas, a prostitute, has also been run out of town.
7. Ringo, an escaped convict, has no social status.

However, after the challenges and conflicts of the two-day trip, Ford reverses this order of importance as the characters leave the coach in Lordsburg:

1. Ringo becomes the hero through his heroic defense of the stagecoach.
2. Dallas becomes the heroine by showing dignity in the face of humiliation and compassion in helping to deliver Lucy's baby.
3. Dr. Boone is redeemed when he sobers up and delivers Lucy's baby.
4. Peacock does not change.
5. Hatfield is redeemed by chivalrously dying to defend Lucy.
6. Lucy, still aloof, nonetheless acknowledges Dallas's kindness.
7. Gatewood is apprehended as a bank thief.

There is plenty of irony in these changes. At the end of the trip, the pretentious, overbearing Gatewood becomes the prisoner, while Ringo—who is guarded by the marshal and feared by some of the passengers because he is an escaped convict—becomes the hero. Dallas's compassion takes precedence over Lucy's cold, haughty manner, and so on.

Scope

The story's overall range in time and place is broad, extending from early events—Dallas orphaned by an Indian massacre and the comparatively more pleasant childhood that Lucy enjoyed in Virginia—to those we see onscreen. And although we look essentially at the events on the two days that it takes the stagecoach to go from Tonto to Lordsburg, we are also aware of the larger scope of American history, particularly the westward movement, Ford's favorite subject. Made right before the start of World War II in Europe, *Stagecoach* presents a historical, social, and mythical vision of American civilization in the 1870s. Ford looked back at the movement west because he saw that period as characterized by clear, simple virtues and values. He viewed the pioneers as establishing the traditions for which Americans would soon be fighting: freedom, democracy, justice, and individualism.

One of the social themes of the movie is *manifest destiny*, a term used by conservative nationalists to explain that the territorial expansion of the United States was not only inevitable but also ordained by God. In that effort, embodied in the westward movement, the struggle to expand would be waged against the Native Americans. In his handling of the story, Ford strives to make a realistic depiction of settlers' life in a frontier town and the dangers awaiting them in the wilderness. Although scholars differ in interpreting the politics of Ford's vision, particularly as it relates to his depictions of whites and Native Americans (depictions that vary throughout his many movies), here his Apaches, just like the white men, are both noble (in their struggle) and savage (in war). Whether this particular story actually happened is not the point. As we understand American history, it could have happened. Ford accurately depicts the Apaches as well as the settlers—the stakes are high for each group—and though the cavalry rather theatrically arrives to save the stagecoach party, both sides suffer casualties and neither side "wins." In fact, Ringo's heroism during the Indian attack permits the stagecoach party to reach Lordsburg safely and earns him the freedom to avenge the deaths of his father and brother. That, of course, is one of the movie's personal themes: Ringo's revenge.

However, Ford sees many sad elements in the westward expansion: the displacement of the Native Americans, the migration of discriminatory social patterns from the East and South to the West, the establishment of uncivilized towns, and the dissolution of moral character among the settlers. These issues are related to the setting in which the story takes place. Here and in his other westerns, Ford created his own vision of how the West was won. Most critics recognize that this vision is part real and part mythical, combining as it does the retelling of actual incidents with a strong overlay of Ford's ideas on how people behaved (or should have behaved).

One of Ford's persistent beliefs is that civilization occurs as a result of a genuine community built—in the wilderness—through heroism and shared values. In Ford's overall vision, American heroes are always fighting for their rights, whether the fight is against the British, the Native Americans, or the fascists. Precisely because the beauty of Monument Valley means so many different things to different people, it becomes a symbol of the many outcomes that can result from exploration, settlement, and the inevitable territorial disputes that follow. But there seems little doubt that Ford himself is speaking (through Dr. Boone) at the end of the film. As Ringo and Dallas ride off to freedom across the border, Dr. Boone utters the paradoxical observation, "Well, that's saved them the blessings of civilization."

Auditory Point of View as Narration in *Stagecoach*
Upon hearing the cavalry bugle and knowing that help is near, Lucy reacts with great emotion. This is a key turning point in the journey from Tonto to Lordsburg, and the arrival of the cavalry means—or at least the members of the stagecoach party hope it means—that they will end their journey safely.

Narration

As was typical of John Ford's style throughout his career, he relies on visual images and dialogue, not a narrator, to tell the *Stagecoach* story. His narration is omniscient (particularly in the exterior shots of the stagecoach hurtling across the territory) but also subjective in taking the direct and indirect points of view of both the audience and the characters. Although the movie uses neither narrator nor *interior monologue*, it features one especially interesting use of an auditory point of view when Lucy, a cavalry wife, is the first to recognize the bugle announcing the cavalry's impending arrival during the Apache attack. The situation is dire. She is praying, and Hatfield, who intends to shoot her so that she won't be captured by the Apaches, has pointed his revolver at her head. Just before he can pull the trigger, he is struck by an Apache bullet. Hearing the bugle at that moment, her face reacts with great emotion as she says: "Do you hear it? It's a bugle. They're blowing the charge." With a cut to the cavalry riding to save the stagecoach, the movie reaches its turning point. This powerful moment manipulates our expectations (we believe that Hatfield will perform the mercy killing), conventions of the western genre (we would expect the cavalry to announce itself directly, not through a fragile woman's perception), and diegesis (particularly the characterization and explicitly presented events). Lucy, unwittingly, becomes one of the heroes of the movie.

When he needs to show that the characters do not form a community—for example, at the noontime lunch stop at Dry Fork, where underlying tensions flare up because Ringo has seated Dallas at the same table as Lucy—Ford establishes and reinforces ideological and emotional differences by alternating between (1) shots from an omniscient point of view and (2) shots from the characters' subjective points of view. As a result, the space at the dinner table, even though it is physically larger, is as socially and morally restricted as the space inside the stagecoach. Ford's pattern of editing here establishes the camera's presence as narrator, the social stratification within the group, Lucy's inflexibility, Hatfield's protectiveness, and Gatewood's pretentiousness. But it also reveals Ringo's kindness, Dallas's vulnerability, and Ford's sympathy for them, which engage our sympathy.

→ Analyzing Narrative

Most of us can hardly avoid analyzing the narrative of a movie after we have seen it. We ask, "Why did the director choose *that* story?" "Why did he choose to tell it in *that* way?" "What does it mean?" At the simplest level, our analysis happens unconsciously while we're watching a movie, as we fill in gaps in events, infer character traits from the clues or cues we receive, and interpret the significance of objects. But when we're actively *looking at* a movie, we should analyze their narratives in more precise, conscious detail. The following checklist provides a few ideas about how you might do this.

Screening Checklist: Narrative

➤ Carefully reconstruct the *story* of the movie and note which events and elements of that story are explicitly presented in the movie's *plot*.

➤ Keep track of *nondiegetic elements* that seem essential to the movie's *plot* (voice-overs, for example). Do they seem natural and appropriate to the film, or do they appear to be "tacked on" to make up for a shortcoming in the overall presentation of the movie's narrative?

➤ Are the plot events presented in *chronological order*? What is the significance of the order of plot events in the movie?

➤ Keep track of the *hubs* and *satellites* in the movie's plot. Are any of the satellites unnecessary to the movie overall? If these satellites were removed from the movie, would it be a better movie? Why?

➤ Are there scenes that create a noticeable *summary relationship* between story duration and screen duration? Do these scenes complement or detract from the overall narrative?

Are you given all the information about the underlying story that you need in these scenes to understand what has happened in the elapsed story time?

➤ Do any scenes use *real time* or a *stretch relationship* between story duration and screen duration? If so, what is the significance of these scenes to the overall narrative?

➤ Is any major plot event presented onscreen more than once? If so, why do you think the filmmaker has chosen to use repetition of the event?

➤ Who is the movie's protagonist? Who are the major characters? Can you characterize each of them according to their depth (*round* characters versus *flat*) and motivation?

➤ How do the setting and the scope of the narrative complement the other elements?

➤ What is the narration of the movie? Does it use a narrator of any kind?

➤ What are the differences among omniscient, restricted, and unrestricted narration?

Questions for Review

1. Why do people tend to respond more readily to a movie's *narrative* than to any other element of its form?

2. How (and why) do we distinguish between the *story* and the *plot* of a movie?

3. What is meant by the *diegesis* of a story? What is the difference between *diegetic* and *nondiegetic* elements in the plot?

4. What are the differences among the *treatment*, *storyboard*, and *shooting script*?

5. What are *hubs* and *satellites*? What are they each supposed to do for the movie's plot?

6. Which of the following is the most common relationship of *screen duration* to *story duration*: *summary relationship*, *real time*, or *stretch relationship*? Define each one.

7. What is the difference between *suspense* and

surprise? Which one is more difficult for a filmmaker to create?

8. Can a *major character* be *flat*? Can a *minor character* be *round*? Explain your answer.

9. What is the difference between *narration* and *narrator*?

10. What are the differences between (a) *omniscient* and *restricted* narration and (b) *first-person* and *offscreen* narration?

DVD FEATURES: CHAPTER 2

The following tutorial on your DVD provides more information about film narrative:

■ Suspense and Surprise

Movies Described or Illustrated in This Chapter

Aguirre: The Wrath of God (1972). Werner Herzog, director.

Battleship Potemkin (1925). Sergei Eisenstein, director.

The Birds (1963). Alfred Hitchcock, director.

Blade Runner (1982). Ridley Scott, director.

Blue Velvet (1986). David Lynch, director.

Breaking the Waves (1999). Lars von Trier, director.

Casablanca (1942). Michael Curtiz, director.

Chinatown (1974). Roman Polanski, director.

Citizen Kane (1941). Orson Welles, director.

Clueless (1995). Amy Heckerling, director.

The Crying Game (1992). Neil Jordan, director.

Days of Heaven (1978). Terrence Malick, director.

The Divorcee (1930). Robert Z. Leonard, director (uncredited).

Dogville (2003). Lars von Trier, director.

Fight Club (1999). David Fincher, director.

Frances (1982). Graeme Clifford, director.

Gladiator (2000). Ridley Scott, director.

Great Expectations (1946). David Lean, director.

Great Expectations (1998). Alfonso Cuarón, director.

Irréversible (2002). Gaspar Noé, director.

The Last Emperor (1987). Bernardo Bertolucci, director.

The Last Laugh (1924). F. W. Murnau, director.

The Longest Day (1962). Ken Annakin and Andrew Marton, directors.

"The Lord of the Rings" trilogy (2001–03). Peter Jackson, director.

Lost in Translation (2003). Sofia Coppola, director.

The Magnificent Ambersons (1942). Orson Welles, director.

The Maltese Falcon (1941). John Huston, director.

The Manchurian Candidate (1962). John Frankenheimer, director.

Memento (2000). Christopher Nolan, director.

Napoléon (1927). Abel Gance, director.

Pulp Fiction (1994). Quentin Tarantino, director.

Raging Bull (1980). Martin Scorsese, director.

Raiders of the Lost Ark (1981). Steven Spielberg, director.

Red River (1948). Howard Hawks, director.

Rope (1948). Alfred Hitchcock, director.

Saving Private Ryan (1998). Steven Spielberg, director.

Scarface (1932). Howard Hawks, director.

The Silence of the Lambs (1991). Jonathan Demme, director.

Sin City (2005). Frank Miller and Robert Rodriguez, directors.

Some Like It Hot (1959). Billy Wilder, director.

Stagecoach (1939). John Ford, director.

The Sweet Hereafter (1997). Atom Egoyan, director.

The Thin Red Line (1998). Terrence Malick, director.

Titanic (1997). James Cameron, director.

2001: A Space Odyssey (1968). Stanley Kubrick, director.

Wonder Boys (2000). Curtis Hanson, director.

Mise-en-Scène

3

Master and Commander: The Far Side of the World (2003).
Peter Weir, director; William Sandell, production designer.

Learning Objectives

After reading this chapter, you should be able to

➤ Define *mise-en-scène* overall and in terms of its constituent parts.

➤ Describe the role of the production designer and the other personnel involved in designing a movie.

➤ Understand the importance of design elements to our sense of a movie's characters, narrative, and themes.

➤ Describe some of the major historical movements in film design.

➤ Explain how *composition* is different from, but complementary to, design.

➤ Describe how *framing* in movies is different from framing of static images such as paintings or photographs.

➤ Describe the relationship between *onscreen* and *offscreen* space, and explain why most shots in a film rely on both.

➤ Understand the difference between *open* and *closed* framing.

➤ Accurately distinguish between the two basic types of movement—that of figures within the frame and that of the frame itself—in any film you watch.

➤ Describe not only the details of any movie's mise-en-scène, but also the effects that the mise-en-scène has on the movie's characters, narrative, and themes.

What Is Mise-en-Scène?

The French phrase **mise-en-scène** (pronounced "meez-ahn-sen") means literally "staging or putting on an action or scene" and, thus, is sometimes called *staging*. In the critical analysis of movies, the term refers to the overall look and feel of a movie—the sum of everything the audience sees, hears,[1] and experiences while viewing it. A movie's mise-en-scène subtly influences our mood as we watch, much as the décor, lighting, smells, and sounds can influence our emotional response to a real-life place.

The two major visual components of mise-en-scène are design and composition. **Design** is the process by which the *look* of the settings, props, lighting, and actors is determined. Set design, décor, prop selection, lighting setup, costuming, makeup, and hairstyle design all play a role in shaping the overall design. **Composition** is the organization, distribution, balance, and general relationship of actors and objects within the space of each shot. The visual elements of mise-en-scène are all crucial to shaping our sympathy for, and understanding of, the characters shaped by them. As you consider how a movie's mise-en-scène influences your thoughts about it, ask yourself if what you see in a scene is simply appealing décor, a well-dressed actor, and a striking bit of lighting, or if these elements have a distinctive significance to your understanding of the narrative, characters, and action of the movie.

Although every movie has a mise-en-scène, in some movies the various elements of the mise-en-scène are so powerful that they enable the viewer to experience the aura of a place and time. A list of such films, chosen at random, might include historical spectacles such as Sergei Eisenstein and Dmitri Vasilyev's *Alexander Nevsky* (1938) or Andrei Tarkovsky's *Andrei Rublev* (1966); conventional dramas such as Stephen Frears's *My Beautiful Laundrette* (1985) or John M. Stahl's *Leave Her to Heaven* (1945); or the evocation of an unfamiliar place or culture, such as Satyajit Ray's *The Music Room* (1958), Bernardo Bertolucci's *The Last Emperor* (1987), or Lars von Trier's *Dogville* (2003). These movies challenge us to *read* their mise-en-scène and to relate it directly to the ideas and themes that the director is developing. Let's take a similar look at two such movies: Todd Haynes's *Far From Heaven* (2002) and Luchino Visconti's *The Leopard* (1963).

---

[1] As a scholarly matter, some critics and instructors, including me, consider sound to be an element of mise-en-scène. Other scholars consider mise-en-scène to be only the sum of *visual* elements in a film. Because of its complexity, we will discuss sound separately in Chapter 7. In this chapter, we will focus on the wholly visual aspects of mise-en-scène: on those filmmaking techniques and decisions that determine the placement, movement, and appearance of objects and people onscreen.

In *Far From Heaven* (production designer: Mark Friedberg), a melodrama about Cathy Whitaker's (Julianne Moore) personal and social problems, director Todd Haynes uses the style of such Hollywood women's melodramas as Michael Curtiz's *Mildred Pierce* (1945) and Douglas Sirk's *Imitation of Life* (1959)—a style in which mise-en-scène is absolutely essential to the director's defining (and our understanding) of character and action. But Haynes's story, set in the 1950s, couldn't have been told in those years: it's about Cathy, a "perfect" wife, mother, and community member; a husband who leaves her for a man; and the black man with whom she falls in love. Once Haynes establishes the ideas of perfection, regularity, and predictability (reinforced by periodic references to the changes of the seasons as reflected in the trees), he returns again and again to setting key moments of the action in the Whitakers' Connecticut house, located in a white suburb rife with racial prejudice. But the excellence of Cathy's house, clothes, appearance, entertaining, and civic activities is only surface perfection, because once it is shattered by her husband's confession that he loves a man, it quickly falls apart, leaving Cathy in limbo.

During the course of the movie, the leaves turn from red and gold in the beginning to spring blossoms in the final shots. These trees have a special significance to Haynes's view of Cathy's life. They indicate that nature changes, even though this town and its people will change little in the near future, and that, in any event, nothing will ever be the same for Cathy. Here, the director's viewpoint is in the many details he shows of Cathy's life. The mise-en-scène in *Far From Heaven* not only presents setting as a visual backdrop—as landscape or scenery—but also presents *ideas*.

Another dimension to mise-en-scène also contributes to our responses to a movie: how its surfaces, textures, sights, and sounds "feel" to us. There's nothing particularly surprising about this. Think about how real-life environments affect your emotions. For people who have lived in a rural or suburban environment their whole lives, for example, their first visit to a large city is a memorable experience that triggers an emotional response. That response flows directly from what we might

Far From Heaven Uses Mise-en-Scène to Reinforce Characters and Themes   The surface perfection of Cathy Whitaker (Julianne Moore, *far right*) is reflected in her annual New Year's Eve party: the house is tastefully decorated, the guests are well dressed, and Cathy is a lovely hostess. But the party is all hers, because her husband, Frank (Dennis Quaid, *sitting*) is already drunk.

call the city's mise-en-scène: the scale of the buildings, the proportion of steel and concrete to trees and grass, the appearance and demeanor of the people walking the streets, and the multitude of sounds. If you have ever experienced a city, your memory of it is at least partly filled with impressions of these sorts of details.

Similarly, nearly every movie immerses us in its mise-en-scène. When the mise-en-scène in a movie creates a feeling completely in tune with the movie's narrative and themes, we may not consciously notice it; it simply feels natural. But not all movies offer a mise-en-scène that successfully complements the movie's narrative and themes. Some movies overwhelm us with their mise-en-scène to the detriment of other elements. Baz Luhrmann's *Moulin Rouge!* (2001; cinematographer: Donald McAlpine; production designer: Catherine Martin), for example, aspired to reinvent the Hollywood musical for the twenty-first century, trying to match the inventiveness and spectacle of earlier high points of the genre, including Lloyd Bacon's *42nd Street* (1933), Bacon and Busby Berkeley's *Gold Diggers of 1937* (1936), Berkeley's *The Gang's All Here* (1943), and Francis Ford Coppola's visionary musical *One From the Heart* (1982; production designer: Dean Tavoularis). Luhrmann blended these influences and others into a pastiche of musical refer-

An Overpowering Mise-en-Scène in *Moulin Rouge!*
The Moulin Rouge nightclub in Paris is *all* mise-en-scène: fabulous sets and costumes, spectacular production numbers, and beautiful dancers. Baz Luhrmann's interpretation of the nightclub's famous cancan dance is different from any other version ever seen on the screen, giving a contemporary twist to the swirling dancers, colorful costumes, and uninhibited choreography of the original.

ences from many periods, movies, and styles. But the result has provoked some viewers to ask how much is too much before the mise-en-scène overwhelms the narrative with overripe colors, swirling movements (of characters and camera), manic editing, and nonnaturalistic acting. The movies can create the most imaginative spectacles, but when those spectacular effects do not help to tell the story, viewers are left with cinematic fireworks and little else.

In contrast, Italian director Luchino Visconti's *The Leopard* (1963; production designer: Mario Garbuglia) is an example of a film whose mise-en-scène perfectly complements its narrative and themes. The movie explores the gradual submergence and transformation of the aristocracy in Sicily after the unification of Italy in 1861. More than anyone else in his family, Prince Don Fabrizio Salina (Burt Lancaster) makes sincere efforts to adjust to the emerging middle class, but at the same time he continues to enjoy the rituals he has always loved—masses in the family chapel, lavish banquets, travel to his other houses, and fancy balls. The forty-five-minute ball sequence (out of 185 minutes total), in fact, is the movie's set piece. Its length makes it more or less extraneous to the overall sequence of events in the movie, but its gorgeous surface beautifully reveals the social change beneath.

Visconti immerses us in the atmosphere of the ball: the grand rooms in the candlelit palazzo; the formalities of arrival and welcome; the ladies in elegant gowns and gentlemen in white-tie or military attire; the champagne and the food; the music; the room with a dozen chamber pots; the excitement of the young and the boredom of some of their elders; the endless gossiping and flirting; and the dancing of quadrilles, mazurkas, and waltzes. Visconti's care with the minute details of the décor, costumes, and characters' relationship to this environment is true to the time, space, and rhythm of life in the period.

The prince wanders from room to room, greeting old friends, reflecting on change. His only moment of real engagement in this sweepingly romantic ball is the powerful moment when he dances a waltz with Angelica (Claudia Cardinale), the fiancée of Tancredi (Alain Delon), the prince's nephew. The daughter of a crude but wealthy bourgeois, Angelica is unquestionably the most beautiful woman in the room, and the prince's dance with her is a sign to everyone at the ball of just how far

Mise-en-Scène as Perfect Complement to Narrative in *The Leopard* Luchino Visconti, one of the world's great masters of mise-en-scène, was at the height of his creative powers in making the ballroom sequence in *The Leopard*. In this forty-five-minute sequence, Visconti creates a virtual microcosm of aristocratic Sicilian life at a time of great social transformation. This still image from a sequence full of movement—swirling dancers, active guests, and an almost constantly moving camera—shows the lavish, candlelit setting, the elegant décor, the guests in uniforms and gowns, and three of the principals—Tancredi (Alain Delon) in the far-left background, and Angelica (Claudia Cardinale) and Prince Don Fabrizio Salina (Burt Lancaster) dancing a waltz in the left middle ground. Notice how the composition is balanced between them and the two guests with the their backs toward us in the right foreground. During these moments, the old world is still very much alive.

1

2

Stanley Kubrick Tightly Controls Mise-en-Scène in
Eyes Wide Shut Two types of finely controlled mise-en-scène in Stanley Kubrick's *Eyes Wide Shut* (1999): [1] In this indirect-point-of-view shot, we see through the eyes of Dr. William Harford (Tom Cruise, not pictured) as he is brought before a ritualistic tribunal. Painterly framing concentrates our attention and thus accentuates the scene's harrowing, hallucinatory effects. Every particular in this image—the elaborate architecture, the beautiful masks and cloaks, the color scheme, the staging—makes clear that Harford is headed into the center of power within this cinematic underworld. [2] In contrast, a scene in which Harford

searches for a costume in New York City's Greenwich Village seems natural, chaotic, even haphazard—but this illusion has been constructed as carefully as every other one in the movie. Here, the darkly clad Harford is the focal point amid more visual information than we can absorb. We note the urgency of his quest, not the details of the surroundings. (In fact, Kubrick filmed the Greenwich Village scenes not in his native New York but on sets in his adopted home, London. That the street names and shop names do not correspond to real ones in New York alerts sharp-eyed viewers to the sets' artificiality.)

the society has been transformed. He blesses the marital union as he accedes to the larger societal change. You can see and hear this transformation occurring, just as you can almost feel the silken texture of the gowns and the wall coverings, and almost taste the wine and the food. Visconti's moving camera, and changing angles, brings us into the action and makes us a participant, yet his control of the compositional elements keeps us focused on the main character. Throughout *The Leopard*, Visconti helps us to understand not only how his mise-en-scène has been constructed, but also how it guides our reading of the scene's meaning. That room of colors, rituals, and music is a perfect lens through which to understand the change inside and outside.

The creation of a movie's mise-en-scène is nearly always the product of very detailed planning of each shot in the movie. Planning a shot involves making advance decisions about the placement of people, objects, and elements of décor on the set;

determining their movements (if any); setting up the lighting; figuring out the camera angles from which they will be photographed; determining the initial framing of the shot; choreographing the movement of the camera during the shot (if any); and creating the sounds that emanate from the shot. Mise-en-scène is the *result* of all that planning.

To be sure, impressive aspects of a movie's mise-en-scène can occur by chance, *without* planning, whether through an act of nature (a sudden rainstorm, for example), an actor's deviating from script, or some other accident. Although some directors display strict control of mise-en-scène and some don't, they generally collaborate with their teams to control every aspect of it. Consciously and deliberately put there by someone, *staged* for the camera, mise-en-scène happens because directors and their creative colleagues have envisioned it.

You should find the term *mise-en-scène* quite useful for explaining how all the formal elements of cinema contribute to your interpretation of a film's meanings. Indeed, the more familiar you become with film history, the more you will see that mise-en-scène can be used to distinguish the work of many great directors noted for their consummate manipulation of cinematic form from each other and from filmmakers whose mastery of mise-en-scène is less impressive. The work of some directors—Tim Burton, Sergei Eisenstein, John Ford, Howard Hawks, Alfred Hitchcock, Buster Keaton, Stanley Kubrick, Fritz Lang, Kenji Mizoguchi, F. W. Murnau, Max Ophüls, Yasujiro Ozu, Otto Preminger, Nicholas Ray, Satyajit Ray, Jean Renoir, Josef von Sternberg, Erich von Stroheim, and Orson Welles, to name a few—calls our attention to scope as well as to detail, to light as well as to shadow, to action as well as to nuance.

Although mise-en-scène can be highly personal and can help us distinguish one director's work from another's, it can also be created through a predetermined formula, as it was, for instance, by the studios during the classical Hollywood studio era, when, typically, each studio had its own look. In addition, there is the powerful influence that genre formulas can have on the mise-en-scène of individual films within that genre. Every director of a new film within a genre understands the pressure to make the mise-en-scène of that film correspond to the viewers' expectations of that genre. Nonetheless, each new film within a genre offers some new twist on the preceding formula, and those new twists may be the product of just a single collaborator's efforts.

Design

Sometimes the way the actors, setting, and décor in a movie *look* is the most powerful impression we take away from a first viewing. But design involves more than first impressions. Whatever its style and ultimate effect, design should help express a movie's vision; be appropriate for the narrative; create a convincing sense of times, spaces, and moods; suggest a character's state of mind; and relate to developing themes. The director counts on a team of professionals to design the look of the movie with these important criteria in mind. Chief among these professionals is the production designer.

The Production Designer

Generally one of the first collaborators that a director hires, the **production designer** works closely with the director, as well as with the director of photography, in visualizing the movie that will appear on the screen. The production designer is both an artist and an executive, responsible for the overall design concept, the *look* of the movie—as well as individual sets, locations, furnishings, props, and costumes—and for supervising the heads of the many departments that create that look. These departments include

> Art (the design personnel responsible for sketching out the movie's look, including sketch artists, painters, and computer graphics specialists)
> Costume design and construction
> Hairstyling
> Makeup
> Wardrobe (maintaining the costumes and having them ready for each day's shooting)
> Location (personnel responsible for finding appropriate locations, for contracting for their use, and for coordinating the logistics necessary for transporting the cast and crew back and forth between the studio and the locations)
> Properties (personnel responsible for finding the right piece of furniture or object for a movie, either from a studio's own resources or from specialized outside firms that supply properties)
> Carpentry
> Set construction and decoration
> Greenery (real or artificial greenery, including grass, trees, shrubs, and flowers)
> Transportation (supplying the vehicles used in the film)

During shooting, the production designer also works closely with the camera and lighting crews.

The title *production designer* is a relatively new one. In the classical Hollywood studio system of the 1930s, each studio had an art department, headed by an executive (called the **art director**) who, in addition to creating and maintaining the studio's distinctive visual style, took full screen credit and any awards the film received for art direction. The art department collaborated with the other departments that bore any responsibility for a film's visual look. The supervising art director, though nominally in charge of designing all the studio's films, in fact assigned an individual art director to each movie. Most art directors were trained in drafting or architecture and this brought to their work a fundamental understanding of how to draw and how to construct a building. In addition to having a thorough knowledge of architecture and design, art directors were familiar with decorative and costume styles of major historical periods and were acquainted with all aspects of film production. As a result, the most accomplished art directors worked closely with film directors in a mutually influential and productive atmosphere.[2]

By the 1960s, the title *production designer*, which we shall use, began to replace the title *art director*.[3] This shift in title wasn't merely a matter of ego or whim; it signaled an expansion of this important executive's responsibilities.

Design begins with the intensive previsualization done by the director and production designer—imagining, thinking, discussing, sketching, planning—that is at the core of all movies. If the collaboration succeeds, the production designer inspires the director to understand not only how the characters, places, objects, and so on will look, but also the relationships among these things. Responsible for everything on the screen except the actors' performances, the production designer helps create visual continuity, balance, and dramatic emphasis; indeed, the production designer "organizes the narrative through design."[4] Of course, the production designer's control over the final appearance of the movie is limited to a certain extent by the cinematographer's decisions about how to shoot the film.

Many art directors have become directors. Mitchell Leisen, for example, who began his career designing films for Cecil B. DeMille and Ernst Lubitsch, was the director of a long string of stylish studio films between 1934 and 1967. Edgar G. Ulmer, who began his career designing several of the classic German expressionist films—including F. W. Murnau's *The Last Laugh* (1924), as well as Murnau's Hollywood debut film, *Sunrise: A Song of Two Humans* (1927)—directed some fifty movies, most of which have cult status, including *The Black Cat* (1934), *Bluebeard* (1944), *Detour* (1945), and *The Strange Woman* (1946). From his early career as an art director, Alfred Hitchcock learned much about creating visual and special effects. Ridley Scott began his career as a set designer for England's BBC television and has directed a series of visually stylish films, including *Alien* (1979), *Blade Runner* (1982), *Thelma & Louise* (1991), and *Gladiator* (2000). David Fincher, who began his career doing special effects for Richard Marquand's *Return of the Jedi* (1983) and Steven Spielberg's *Indiana Jones and the Temple of Doom* (1984) and went on to do music videos for Madonna and other artists, has since directed *Alien[3]* (1992), *Se7en* (1995), *Fight Club* (1999), and *Panic Room* (2002).

[2] Despite their importance to the production process, most art directors worked in relative obscurity. Cedric Gibbons, supervising art director at MGM for thirty-two years, was the one art director for much of the twentieth century that the general public knew by name, not only because the quality of MGM's style was so high but also because he was nominated forty times for the Academy Award for Art Direction, an honor he won eleven times.

[3] Actually, the title *production designer* was first used to acknowledge William Cameron Menzies's contributions to *Gone With the Wind* (1939), but it came into common use only in the 1960s. Menzies had drawn every shot of *Gone With the Wind*, and those meticulous drawings held the production together through four directors, many writers, and constant interventions by the producer, David O. Selznick. Before that—and through the 1950s—the credit title *art director* was generally used; in fact, Menzies won the first two Academy Awards for Art Direction, for movies made in 1927 and 1928.

[4] Charles Affron and Mirella Jona Affron, *Sets in Motion: Art Direction and Film Narrative* (New Brunswick, N.J.: Rutgers University Press, 1995), 12.

Elements of Design

During the process of envisioning and designing a film, the director and production designer (in collaboration with the cinematographer) are concerned with several major elements. The most important of these are (1) *setting*, *décor*, and *properties*; (2) *lighting*; and (3) *costume*, *makeup*, and *hairstyle*.

Setting, Décor, and Properties The spatial and temporal *setting* of a film is the environment (realistic or imagined) in which the narrative takes place. In addition to its physical significance, the setting creates a mood that has social, psychological, emotional, economic, and cultural significance. Movies made in England often incorporate the design of the setting and décor to reflect that country's awareness of class distinctions—what we sometimes call the *upstairs/downstairs* theme. Such movies form a distinct tradition that includes

Design of Literary Adaptations Literary adaptations pose special problems for movie designers: How faithfully should the period and the narrative details be reproduced? How can images do justice to the author's prose textures? For the design team behind Jane Campion's *The Portrait of a Lady* (1996; production designer: Janet Patterson), the primary task was surely to find visual equivalents for the intricate, exquisitely wrought prose of Henry James's 1881 novel, considered by many critics to be his finest work. Patterson uses expressive lighting that is alternately diffuse and intense, warm and cool, borrowing the palettes and qualities of light common in paintings of the period. Here, the lighting echoes and complements the emotions felt by the Lady of this literary-cinematic portrait, Isabel Archer (Nicole Kidman, *foreground*), as she reacts coldly to the presence of Madame Merle (Barbara Hershey) at the convent school.

Alfred Hitchcock's *Rich and Strange* (1931), Mike Newell's *Dance With a Stranger* (1985), and Joseph Losey's *The Servant* (1963).

Robert Altman's *Gosford Park* (2001; production designer: Stephen Altman), set at an English country house in 1932, follows the familiar upstairs/downstairs treatment, this time of the lives of the upper and serving classes at a weekend house party. The design and execution of the many rooms (drawing rooms, bedrooms, servants' quarters, and kitchens) are accurate in establishing time and place, and the overall design underscores the social, psychological, and economic disparities that exist between the living style of, say, a titled lady and her maid. Altman's design is realized on a grand scale with consummate style in décor, costuming, hairstyle, and makeup. These elements provide not only visual pleasure, but also a solid base for seeing and understanding the differences between those who play upstairs and those who toil below.

Perhaps the most important decision that a filmmaker must make about setting is to determine when to shoot **on location** and when to shoot on a **set**. In the first two decades of moviemaking, the first preference was to shoot in exterior locations, for both authenticity and natural depth. But location shooting proved expensive, and the evolution of larger studios made possible interiors (or sets) that were large, three-dimensional spaces that permitted the staging of action on all three planes and that could also accommodate multiple rooms. Interior shooting involves the added consideration of **décor**—the color and textures of the interior decoration, furniture, draperies, curtains—and **properties** (or *props*)—objects such as paintings, vases, flowers, silver tea sets, guns, or fishing rods that help us understand the characters by showing us their preferences in such things.

A movie set is not reality, but a fragment of reality created as the setting for a particular shot, and it must be constructed both to look authentic and to photograph well. The first movie sets were no different from theater sets: flat backdrops erected, painted, and photographed in a studio, observed by the camera as if it were a spectator in the theater. Indoor lighting was provided by skylights and

[1]

[2]

[3]

[4]

Setting in *Gosford Park* The grand life at the grand English country house depicted in Robert Altman's *Gosford Park* is made possible by the legion of servants and the hard work they do. Both servants and guests are expected to behave according to certain codes, depending on where they are at any moment. [1] When "below stairs," the house servants (and those who accompany their employers for the weekend house party) are informal and friendly with one

artificial lights. (Outdoors, filmmakers often left natural settings unadorned and photographed them realistically.) The first spectacular sets to be specifically constructed for a film were made in Italy; and with Giovanni Pastrone's epic *Cabiria* (1914; no credits for art director or costume designer), "the constructed set emerged completely developed and demanding to be imitated."[5] Indeed, it was imitated in D. W. Griffith's *Intolerance* (1916), which featured the first colossal outdoor sets constructed in Hollywood. Other directors soon began to commission elaborate sets, constructed as architectural units out of wood, plaster, and other building materials or created from drawings that were manipulated by optical printers to look "real." (Today, computers and computer-generated imagery [CGI] have replaced optical printers.)

⊙ WEB Design in Historical Dramas

The old Hollywood studios kept backlots full of classic examples of various types of architecture, which were used again and again, often with new paint or landscaping to help them meet the requirements of a new narrative. Today the Universal Studios theme park in Hollywood preserves some of the sets from those lots. Sometimes, however, filmmakers construct and demolish a set as quickly as possible to keep the production on schedule. Only those aspects of a set that are necessary for the benefit of the camera are actually built, whether to scale (life-size) or in miniature, human-made or computer-modeled. For example, the exterior front of a house may look complete, with bushes and flowers, and curtains in the

[5] Affron and Affron, *Sets in Motion*, 12.

another. Here the visiting servants are being shown to their quarters by the head housekeeper, Mrs. Wilson (Helen Mirren, *right*). [2] While having dinner together, served by the butler, Jennings (Alan Bates), the servants are seated according to the social station of their employers—in other words, just like upstairs. [3] Upstairs, the guests include Lady Constance Trentham (Maggie Smith, *right*), who, in this image, is telling another guest that she is "simply worn out" from breaking in a new maid. [4] The formally dressed guests are shown here in the elegant dining room.

[1]

[2]

[3]

First Spectacular Movie Sets Created for *Cabiria*
Produced over six months at a cost equivalent to $2 million today, Giovanni Pastrone's *Cabiria* is regarded by many as the greatest achievement of the era of Italian blockbusters (roughly from 1909 through 1914). Its settings were the most complex and elaborate, yet they were created for a motion picture and, along with location shooting in Tunisia, Sicily, and the Alps, helped convince audiences that they were witnessing history in action (in this case, the Second Punic War between Rome and Carthage, which raged from 218 to 201 BCE). Italian pioneers of set design were later recruited by Hollywood producers and directors—including D. W. Griffith—to produce ever more convincing (and expensive) backdrops for epic historical dramas. Three images give an idea of Pastrone's attempt at historical accuracy: [1] the Temple of Moloch; [2] Hannibal (Emilio Vardannes) and his troops crossing the Alps; and [3] Princess Sophonisba (Italia Almirante-Manzini) with her pet leopard, drinking milk.

windows, and so on, but there may be no rooms behind that façade. Constructed on a **soundstage**—a windowless, soundproofed, professional shooting environment, which is usually several stories high and can cover an acre or more of floor space—will be only the minimum parts of the rooms needed to accommodate the actors and the movement of the camera: a corner, perhaps, or three sides.

On the screen, these parts will appear, in proper proportions to one another, as whole units. Lighting helps sustain this illusion. In *Citizen Kane* (1941; art directors: Van Nest Polglase and Perry Ferguson), Orson Welles, like many others before him, was determined to make his sets look more

authentic and thus photographed them from high angles (to show four walls) and low angles (to include both ceilings and four walls). In *The Shining* (1980; production designer: Roy Walker), Stanley Kubrick mounted a special camera (called a *Steadicam*; see Chapter 4) on a wheelchair that could follow Danny (Danny Lloyd) on his Big Wheel to provide the boy's close-to-the-floor view of the Overlook Hotel sets, which included ceilings, rooms with four walls, and a seemingly endless series of corridors.

Lighting During the planning of a movie, most production designers include an idea of the lighting in their sketches. When the movie is ready for shooting, these sketches help guide the cinematographer in coordinating the camera and the lighting. Light not only is fundamental to the recording of images on film but also has many important functions in shaping the way the final product looks, guiding our eyes through the moving image and helping to tell the movie's story. Light is an essential element in *drawing* the composition of a frame and realizing that arrangement on film. Through highlights, light calls attention to shapes and textures; through shadows, it may mask or conceal things. Often, much of what we remember about a film is its expressive style of lighting faces, figures, surfaces, settings, or landscapes. Both on a set and on location, light is controlled and manipulated to achieve expressive effects; except in rare instances, there is no such thing as wholly "natural" lighting in a movie.

The cinematographer Stanley Cortez said that in his experience, only two directors understood the uses and meaning of light: Orson Welles and Charles Laughton.[6] Both directors began their careers on the stage in the 1930s, when theatrical lighting had evolved to a high degree of expressiveness. One of the great stage and screen actors of the twentieth century, Laughton directed only one film, *The Night of the Hunter* (1955; art director: Hilyard Brown), an unforgettable masterpiece of suspense. For his cinematographer, he chose Cortez, a master of **chiaroscuro**—the use of deep gradations and subtle variations of lights and darks within an image.

Cortez once remarked that he "was always chosen to shoot weird things,"[7] and *The Night of the Hunter* is a weird film in both form and content. Its story focuses on Harry Powell (Robert Mitchum), an itinerant, phony preacher who murders widows for their money. His victims include the widow of a man who had stolen $10,000 to protect his family during the Depression, hidden the money inside his daughter's doll, and sworn both of his children to secrecy. After Harry marries and murders their

widowed mother, the children flee, ending up at a farm downriver kept by Rachel Cooper (Lillian Gish), a kind of fairy godmother devoted to taking in homeless children. When Harry tracks down the kids and begins to threaten the safety of Rachel and her "family," Rachel sits on her porch, holding a shotgun to guard the house while Harry, lurking outside, joins her in singing a religious hymn, "Lean on Jesus." Laughton uses backlighting that has a hard quality associated with the evil, tough Harry, but he also uses it on Rachel—not to equate her with his evil, but to intimate that she is a worthy adversary for him. Later in the same scene, she is suddenly lit differently—softer light, from a different direction, creates a halo effect through light behind her—because at this moment in the movie the director wants to emphasize not her resolve or her ability to stand up to Harry, but her purity of spirit.

⊚ DVD Lighting and Familiar Image

The story and emotional tones of Fernando Meirelles and Kátia Lund's *City of God* (2002; cinematographer: César Charlone), to cite another example, are closely linked with the movie's use of light. The co-directors and production designer Tulé Peak work with the contrasts between bright sunlight on the beach, the various kinds of lighting in the houses and apartments in the Brazilian slums, and, in a climactic moment in the movie, in a crowded disco. The lighting in the disco is true to the source: the flickering spangles that come from the revolving mirrored ball high above the dancers; spotlights that are moved restlessly; banks of bright lights to which the camera returns again and again rhythmically, increasing our awareness that the situation is getting out of control. During this scene, Benny (Phellipe Haagensen), a drug dealer who has decided to go straight, is murdered by his friend Li'l Zé (Leandro Firmino) after a heated quarrel. The pulsating strobe lighting ramps up the chaos of the scene, and although it is perfectly natural to the world of the disco, it underscores the violent struggle between Benny's desire to get out of the terrible world in which he has been a leader and lead a good life, and the evil Zé's equally strong desire to stop Benny from accomplishing his goal.

[6] See Charles Higham, "Stanley Cortez," in *Hollywood Cameramen: Sources of Light* (London: Thames & Hudson in association with the British Film Institute, 1970), 99.
[7] Stanley Cortez, qtd. in Higham, *Hollywood Cameramen*, 102.

Costume, Makeup, and Hairstyle During the years of the classical Hollywood studio system, an actor's box-office appeal depended on that individual's ability to project a screen image that audiences would love. Makeup and hair were the two most personal aspects of that image. The studios frequently took actors with star potential and "improved" their looks by having their hair dyed and restyled, their teeth fixed or replaced, or their noses reshaped or sagging chins tightened through cosmetic surgery. Such changes were based on each studio's belief that its overall look included a certain "ideal" kind of beauty, both feminine and masculine. To that end, each studio had the right to ask actors under contract to undergo plastic or dental surgery to improve their images on and off the screen. Today's audiences have learned to love actors for their individual looks and styles, not for their conformity to ideals determined by the studios, which, as a result, led to the typecasting of actors in certain kinds of roles with which they became identified. An actor's ability to break out of stereotyped casting, when possible, was often due to the work of members of the studio's design staff who gave the actor a new look.

Today's actors, unfettered by rigid studio contracts, tend to play a wider variety of roles than they would have in the 1930s and '40s. Although the actors' range and skill are important in making these different roles believable, perhaps even more important is the work of the art departments' professional staff to render the actor's appearance appropriate to the role.[8] For example, Jennifer Jason Leigh and Jack Nicholson, very versatile actors, have taken on many different parts, often changing their appearances (through costume,

Expressive Lighting in *City of God* Lighting plays a powerful role in establishing the setting (as well as character and mood) in Fernando Meirelles and Kátia Lund's *City of God*, a violent story of constantly changing moods that is told with equally rapid changes in style. [1] For a playful day on the beach, the lighting is bright sunlight, probably intensified by reflectors. [2] For a drug deal in a decaying slum building, the strong sunlight is filtered through a brick screen into the creepy hallway. [3] Strobe lights and reflections underscore the rapidly developing chaos at a disco party.

[8] For those who think that makeup is just a matter of smearing some foundation or powder on a face, or that hairstyle is a good haircut, it might come as a surprise that makeup and hairstyle in the movies require a far more complex process. Who would have thought of skin tones? Receding hair lines? Aging the face? A modern movie like *Forrest Gump* (1994) involved major makeup work, but the makeup does not call attention to itself. To learn more, check out the "Magic of Makeup" special feature in the DVD special collector's edition release of the film.

[1]

Costume, Makeup, and Hairstyle Jack Nicholson has created a memorable list of characters, ranging from edgy and creepy to charming and sophisticated. No matter what role he plays, he manages to personify the character, largely because of his acting talent, but also because of the artists who helped create his screen image. [1] In Danny DeVito's *Hoffa*, Nicholson plays Jimmy Hoffa, the legendary leader of the Teamsters' union, who is speaking here to the press before beginning a prison term. Although Nicholson was the same age as Hoffa at this time, he put on extra weight, copied Hoffa's hairstyle, and altered his voice to sound like Hoffa. [2] In Mike Nichols's *Wolf*, Nicholson is Will Randall, a book editor who turns into a werewolf. With yellow eyes, facial hair, and ferocious animal agility, Nicholson is truly terrifying. [3] In Nancy Meyers's *Something's Gotta Give*— as Harry Sanborn, an aging playboy who goes after only younger women until he meets Erica Barry (Diane Keaton)— Nicholson looks pretty much as he does today in "real" life.

[2]

[3]

makeup, and hairstyle) to suit the roles. Leigh has played a teenager in Amy Heckerling's *Fast Times at Ridgemont High* (1982), a prostitute in Uli Edel's *Last Exit to Brooklyn* (1989), a married phone-sex operator in Robert Altman's *Short Cuts* (1993), a high-powered journalist in Joel Coen's *The Hudsucker Proxy* (1994), the world-weary American humorist Dorothy Parker in Alan Rudolph's *Mrs. Parker and the Vicious Circle* (1994), a highly neurotic journalist in Taylor Hackford's *Dolores Claiborne* (1995), a physically unattractive nineteenth-century heiress in Agnieszka Holland's *Washington Square* (1997), and the downtrodden wife of a hit man in Sam Mendes's *Road to Perdition* (2002), as well as eight more movies since then.

Tackling similarly diverse roles, Nicholson has played a classical pianist turned oil field worker in Bob Rafelson's *Five Easy Pieces* (1970), a crusty sailor in Hal Ashby's *The Last Detail* (1973), a suave but doomed private detective in Roman Polanski's *Chinatown* (1974), a convict feigning mental illness in Milos Forman's *One Flew Over the Cuckoo's Nest* (1975), a demented writer in Stanley Kubrick's *The Shining* (1980), the 1920s American dramatist Eugene O'Neill in Warren Beatty's *Reds* (1981), the Joker in Tim Burton's *Batman* (1989), an irritable marine commander in Rob Reiner's *A Few Good Men* (1992), the aging labor leader Jimmy Hoffa in Danny DeVito's *Hoffa* (1992), a werewolf in Mike Nichols's *Wolf* (1994), a retired businessman in Alexander Payne's *About Schmidt* (2002), an aging swinger in Nancy Meyers's *Something's Gotta Give* (2003)—one different role after another, each requiring his attention to character development and the meticulous attention of designers and technicians to his appearance.

Costume The setting of a film generally governs the design of the **costumes** (the clothing worn by an actor in a movie, sometimes known as *wardrobe*), which can contribute to that setting and suggest specific character traits, such as social station, self-image, the image that the character is trying to project for the world, state of mind, overall situation, and so on. Thus, costumes are another element that help tell a movie's story. When the setting is a past era, costume designers may need to undertake extensive and lengthy research to ensure authenticity. Even with such research, however, the costumes in historical films often do not accurately depict such details as women's necklines, breast shapes, and waistlines. Hats tend to look more contemporary, and undergarments more lavish, than they would have historically. Designing costumes for a movie set in the contemporary world is equally rigorous, perhaps even more so. Because the characters will wear clothes similar to our own, the designer understands that we will read these costumes more closely and interpret them on the basis of our experiences. The same can be said of makeup and hair design.

Although verisimilitude is a factor in costume design, there are other factors—style, fit, condition, patterns, and color of the clothing—that can also define and differentiate characters. In Tim Burton's *Edward Scissorhands* (1990; costume designer: Colleen Atwood; makeup designer: Ve Neill), Edward's (Johnny Depp) outsider status and otherness is emphasized by his costume and makeup, as are the other characters' various conformity, sexual neediness, brutality, and other character traits.

Historical films tend to reflect both the years they hope to represent and the years in which they were created. Nonetheless, they shape our ideas of historical dress. For example, although Walter

The Importance of Costume Design in *Edward Scissorhands* Tim Burton's *Edward Scissorhands* is about Edward (Johnny Depp), a man who was "invented" (not born) with scissors for hands. He lives in a Gothic castle high above a cookie-cutter subdivision, and when he moves to this town, he finds out just how different he is. Although he's something of a sensation, the costumes reinforce his individuality in contrast to the bland conformity of the other characters. [1] Peg (Dianne Wiest), the Avon lady, dressed primly to match the pastel colors of the town's houses, calls on a customer who wears curlers in her hair and a sloppy outfit more to her taste. [2] Another housewife, Joyce (Kathy Baker), is dressed in a sultry outfit that suggests she wants more from the appliance repairman than a working dishwasher. [3] Edward meets the husbands of these and other housewives; tanned and healthy-looking, and all wearing short-sleeved golf shirts, they look almost identical. By contrast, Edward has a pasty, scarred face and wears a long-sleeve shirt and suspenders. In the end, however, we realize that the townspeople are every bit as individual in their costumes, makeup, and hairstyle as Edward Scissorhands is.

Plunkett's clothing designs for Victor Fleming's *Gone With the Wind* (1939; production designer: William Cameron Menzies) are often quite anachronistic, audiences usually see them as truly reflecting what people wore during the Civil War. Even though we have plenty of evidence to show what people wore in the mid 1800s, Vivien Leigh's appearance as Scarlett O'Hara only approximates how a woman of her social class might have dressed. Still, the costume design in *Gone With the Wind* often supports the narrative very well. Scarlett's green dress made from a curtain plays a major role in one scene and tells us a great deal about her character: the green reminds us of her Irish background, and the use of curtains reminds us of her newfound practicality and frugality. Ann Roth's costumes for Anthony Minghella's *Cold Mountain* (2003), another movie about the Civil War, were based not only on diligent research, but also on her belief that costumes help an actor to create character by restricting movement or facilitating it. For Joseph L. Mankiewicz's *Cleopatra* (1963), Irene Sharaff created spectacular costumes for Elizabeth Taylor that were basically contemporary gowns designed to accentuate the actress's beauty; experts agree that they bear very little resemblance to the elaborate styles of the late Greco-Roman period.

When a film involves the future, as in science fiction, the costumes must both reflect the social structure and values of an imaginary society and look the way we expect "the future" to look. Ironically, these costumes almost always reflect historical influences. The characters may live on other planets, but the actors' costumes recall, for example, the dress of ancient Greeks and Romans (as in Richard Marquand's *Return of the Jedi*, 1983; costume designers: Aggie Guerard Rodgers and Nilo Rodis-Jamero), Asian samurai and geisha (as in Daniel Haller's *Buck Rogers in the 25th Century*, 1979; costume designer: Jean-Pierre Dorléac), or medieval knights and maidens (as in Leonard Nimoy's *Star Trek III: The Search for Spock*, 1984; costume designer: Robert Fletcher).

The movies have always been associated with the greatest style and glamour. Beautiful clothes worn by beautiful people attract audiences, and

Design of Historical Dramas In W. S. Van Dyke's *Marie Antoinette* (1938; costume designer: Adrian), one of the most lavish costume epics ever made, the French queen (Norma Shearer) looks as glamorous as a movie star; Adrian, the designer, did everything within his power to embellish Shearer's screen image rather than make her resemble the queen, whose comparatively plain face is familiar from many paintings and other representations. Although much of the film is true to history, many scenes seem to exist only to reinforce MGM's peculiar notions of royal behavior. In one preposterous scene, Marie Antoinette, still a princess in the French court, greets King Louis XV (John Barrymore) and his mistress, Mme. du Barry (Gladys George), and attempts to assert her royal prerogatives by insulting them both. We see and remember not the personal and political tensions in the air, the issue of succession to the French throne, the power of the royal mistress, or the difficulties posed by the Austrian-born princess, but rather the décor, costumes, makeup, dancing, and music.

since the second decade of the twentieth century, filmmakers have invested considerable effort and expense in costume design. Giovanni Pastrone's Italian epic *Cabiria* (1914) was the first major film in which costumes were specifically designed to create the illusion of an earlier period (in this case, the Second Punic War, about 200 BCE), and it influenced

D. W. Griffith when he made *The Birth of a Nation* (1915; costume designer: Robert Goldstein) and *Intolerance* (1916; costume designer: Clare West, uncredited)—both notable for their authentic costumes. The first, concerned with the Civil War, featured Ku Klux Klan robes that helped provoke the public outrage against the film; the second told stories set in four different periods in history, each requiring its own costumes, some of which, as in the Babylon sequence, were researched carefully and realized extravagantly. Prior to those films, actors wore their own clothes, whether or not those garments were appropriate for the setting of a film. During the 1920s, costume design became a serious part of the glamour of such stars as Gloria Swanson (in Erich von Stroheim's *Queen Kelly*, 1929), Theda Bara (in J. Gordon Edwards's *Cleopatra*, 1917), and Clara Bow (in Clarence G. Badger's *It*, 1927).

In the 1930s, with the studio and star systems in full swing, Hollywood began to devote as much attention to costume as to setting. One measure of the impact of such fashionable design work was that the public bought huge quantities of copies of the clothing originally created for movie stars. Yet Hollywood has tended to regard costume design less seriously than some of the other design areas in film. From its establishment in 1928, the Academy of Motion Picture Arts and Sciences gave awards for art direction, but it did not establish awards for costume design until 1948.

Makeup   Traditionally, whether films took place in modern or historical settings, stars' makeup invariably had a contemporary look. This approach to makeup preserved the stars' images and also led to new beauty products being developed that actors could advertise, enabling female consumers to use the makeup worn by their favorite stars. In fact, the history of the commercial makeup industry roughly parallels the history of the movies. The single most important person in the manufacture of movie makeup was Max Factor. In 1908, he began supplying wigs and makeup to the small movie studios cropping up around Los Angeles. In the early 1920s, makeup was usually the responsibility of the actors, but Factor standardized makeup procedures—and thus created the position of makeup designer. His

The Expressive Power of Makeup   [1] For David Lynch's *The Elephant Man* (1980), makeup designers Beryl Lerman, Michael Morris, Wally Schneiderman, and Christopher Tucker convincingly rendered the title character, John Merrick (John Hurt), to help evoke our sympathy for this grotesquely deformed historical figure. [2] For Tim Burton's *Batman* (1989), makeup designers Paul Engelen and Nick Dudman transformed Jack Napier (Jack Nicholson), a cheap hood, into the Joker—a darkly comic deformation and a visual parallel to the character's combination of humor and evil.

products became the industry standard. Through research, the Max Factor Company continued to provide new forms of makeup to meet the challenges created by new camera lenses, lighting, and film stocks, especially color film, which required a very different approach to makeup than that required by black-and-white film. The most important names in the history of makeup design are those of George Westmore and his six sons; succeeding generations of the Westmore family have continued to dominate the field.

Although many directors favor makeup that is as natural as possible, we tend to notice makeup design when it helps create an unusual or fantastic character: Boris Karloff as the Monster in James Whale's *Frankenstein* (1931; makeup designer: Jack P. Pierce); the self-transformation through science of Fredric March from the mild Dr. Jekyll into the evil side of his own character, the lustful and hideous Mr. Hyde, in Rouben Mamoulian's *Dr. Jekyll and Mr. Hyde* (1931; makeup designer: Wally Westmore); James Cagney as the great silent-screen actor Lon Chaney in Joseph Pevney's *Man of a Thousand Faces* (1957; makeup designers: Bud Westmore and Jack Kevan); the ape-men in Stanley Kubrick's *2001: A Space Odyssey* (1968; makeup designer: Stuart Freeborn); or the varied creatures in the "Lord of the Rings" trilogy (makeup designer: Peter King).

Hairstyle During the studio years, hairstyles were based on modified modern looks rather than on the period authenticity favored in costumes. Exceptions to this rule—such as Bette Davis's appearing as Queen Elizabeth I with shaved eyebrows and hairline in Michael Curtiz's *The Private Lives of Elizabeth and Essex* (1939), and with a bald head in the same role in Henry Koster's *The Virgin Queen* (1955)—are rare, because few studios were willing to jeopardize their stars' images. The idea of achieving historical accuracy in hairstyle was completely undercut in the late 1930s, when the studios developed a "Hollywood Beauty Queen" wig serviceable for every historical period. This all-purpose wig was worn by, among many others, Norma Shearer in W. S. Van Dyke's *Marie Antoinette* (1938) (see illustration on p. 105) and Glynis Johns in Norman Panama and Melvin Frank's medieval comedy *The Court Jester* (1956). Generic as this wig was, hairstylists could obviously cut and style it to conform to the requirements of the individual production. Thus, one hairstyle served to depict two different characters at two different times in history.

In fact, until the 1960s, actors in almost every film, whether period or modern, were required to wear wigs designed for the film, for reasons both aesthetic and practical. In shooting out of sequence, in which case continuous scenes can be shot weeks apart, it is particularly difficult to re-create colors, cuts, and styles of hair. Once designed, a wig never

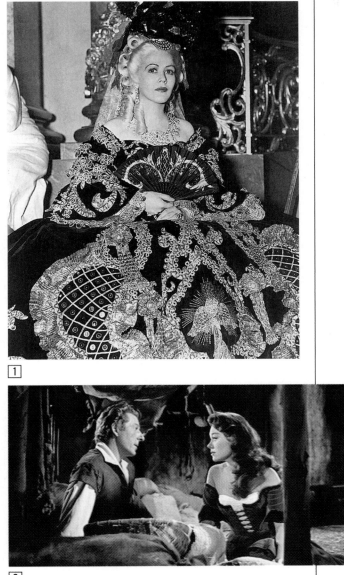

[1]

[2]

Hairstyles Because putting stars before the camera in hairstyles from, say, the Greek or Roman period, the Middle Ages, or even eighteenth-century France could threaten an actor's image with the public, American studios in the 1930s devised the "Hollywood Beauty Queen" (HBQ) wig, which could be cut and styled in a manner that was usually most flattering to the wearer. [1] The stylized wig worn by Mme. du Barry (Gladys George) in *Marie Antoinette* (1938) is, in fact, quite true to the spectacular wigs of the court of Louis XVI. [2] The HBQ wig worn by Maid Jean (Glynis Johns) in *The Court Jester*, however, has been styled more in keeping with the 1950s than the Middle Ages, and although Hubert Hawkins (Danny Kaye) is presumably wearing his own hair, he also looks very contemporary.

changes, ensuring, at least, that an actor's hair won't be the source of a continuity "blooper." Such aspects of continuity are the responsibility of the **script supervisor**, who once kept a meticulous log of each day's shooting. Today, script supervisors use a tiny **video assist camera**, which is mounted in the viewing system of the film camera and provides instant visual feedback, enabling them to view a scene (and thus compare its details with those of surrounding scenes) before the film is sent to the laboratory for processing. Although hairstylists receive screen credit, the Academy of Motion Picture Arts and Sciences has never recognized hair design as a craft within its awards system. However, hair design is so important in today's styles that many actors have their own hairdressers under personal contract.

International Styles of Design

Although there are as many styles of design as there are production designers, there are arguably only two *fundamental* styles of film design: the realistic and the fantastic. These two styles were established in France in the very first motion pictures. The Lumière brothers pioneered the nonfiction film, shooting short, realistic depictions of everyday activities. Georges Méliès created the fictional film, using illusions he had learned in the theater. As Méliès employed all kinds of stage tricks, mechanisms, and illusions, he invented a variety of cinematic effects. In so doing, he also invented the film set, and thus we can consider him the first art director in film history.

In Russia, after the 1917 revolution, the avant-garde constructivists and futurists reshaped the entire concept of cinema: what it is, how it is shot, how it is edited, and *how it looks*. The great Russian filmmakers of the 1920s and '30s—Dziga Vertov, Lev Kuleshov, Sergei Eisenstein, Vsevolod Pudovkin, and Aleksandr Dovzhenko—were influenced by two seemingly contradictory forces: (1) the nonfiction film with its "documentary" look and (2) a highly dynamic style of editing. Their films—masterpieces both of cinematic design and of political propaganda involving so-called Socialist Realism—combined highly realistic exterior shots with an editing

rhythm that, ever since, has affected the handling of cinematic time and space.

In 1922, Russian artists working in Paris introduced scenic conventions from the Russian realistic theater to French cinema and also experimented with a variety of visual effects influenced by contemporary art movements—cubism, dadaism, surrealism, and abstractionism. In the following decades, the look of the Russian film changed in many ways, including an increased use of art directors, studio and location shooting, and constructed sets and artificial lighting. Notable are Isaac Shpinel's designs for two great Eisenstein films—*Alexander Nevsky* (1938), whose medieval helmets, armor, and trappings for horses rival any historical re-creation ever seen on the screen, and *Ivan the Terrible: Parts I and II* (1944, 1958)—and, much later, Yevgeni Yenej and Georgi Kropachyov's designs for two Shakespearean films: Grigori Kozintsev's adaptations of *Hamlet* (1964) and *King Lear* (1969). This version of *Hamlet*, in particular, is noteworthy for being filmed at Kronborg Castle in Elsinore, Denmark; the director uses its mighty staircases for highly choreographed movement, and the sounds and sights of the surrounding sea for emotional effect.

However, most important early developments in art direction took place in Germany. Expressionism, which emerged in the first decades of the twentieth century, influenced almost every form of German art, including the cinema. Its goal was to give objective expression to subjective human feelings and emotions through the use of such objective design elements as structure, color, or texture; it also aimed at heightening reality by relying on such nonobjective elements as symbols, stereotyped characters, and stylization. In German cinema, in the years immediately following World War I, expressionism gave rise to a new approach to composition, set design, and directing. The object was to create a totally unified mise-en-scène that would increase the emotional impact of the production on the audience.

Expressionist films were characterized by extreme stylization in their sets, décor, acting, lighting, and camera angles. The grossly distorted, largely abstract sets were as expressive as the actors, if not more so. To ensure complete control

Expressionism The imagery in Robert Wiene's *The Cabinet of Dr. Caligari*, a sample of which is shown here, ushered in an era of expressionist cinematography, design, and mise-en-scène in German cinema that subsequently influenced filmmaking in the United States and elsewhere. That influence is clear in, for example, Charles D. Hall's designs for James Whale's *Frankenstein* (1931) and *Bride of Frankenstein* (1935), Jack Otterson's designs for Rowland V. Lee's *Son of Frankenstein* (1939), Van Nest Polglase and Perry Ferguson's designs for Orson Welles's *Citizen Kane* (1941), and the designs of countless film noirs.

and free manipulation of the décor, lighting, and camera work, expressionist films were generally shot in the studio even when the script called for exterior scenes—a practice that was to have an important effect on how movies were later shot in Hollywood. Lighting was deliberately artificial, emphasizing deep shadows and sharp contrasts; camera angles were chosen to emphasize the fantastic and the grotesque; and the actors externalized their emotions to the extreme.

The first great German expressionist film was Robert Wiene's *The Cabinet of Dr. Caligari* (1920), designed by three prominent artists (Hermann Warm, Walter Reimann, and Walter Röhrig), who used painted sets to reflect the anxiety, terror, and madness of the film's characters and thus reflected psychological states in exterior settings. *Dr. Caligari* gave space—interior and exterior—a voice. Its highly experimental and stylized setting, décor, costumes, and figure movement influenced the design of later German silent classics such as F. W. Murnau's *Nosferatu* (1922) and Fritz Lang's *Destiny* (1921), *Siegfried* (1924), *Kriemhild's Revenge* (1924), and *Metropolis* (1927). Furthermore, its exaggerated and distorted look strongly influenced horror films, thrillers, and the American film noir.

◉DVD Setting and Expressionism

At the same time that the expressionist film was evolving, the Germans developed a realist cinema (known as *Kammerspielfilm*), the masterpiece of which is F. W. Murnau's *The Last Laugh* (1924; production designer: Edgar G. Ulmer). This film radically changed the way shots were framed, actors were blocked, and sets were designed and built, thanks mainly to Murnau's innovative use of the moving camera and the subjective camera. His "unchained camera" freed filmmakers from the limitations of a camera fixed to a tripod; his subjective camera used the camera eye as the eyes of a character in the film, so that the audience saw only what the character saw. These new developments intensified the audience's involvement in events onscreen, extended the vocabulary by which filmmakers could tell and photograph stories, and thus influenced the conception and construction of sets.

British films of the 1930s and '40s were, in most instances, indistinguishable in look from Hollywood films, but the two major exceptions were the films directed by Alfred Hitchcock and those designed by Vincent Korda. Because of his background as a designer, Hitchcock created films that were always unusually stylish, including such early works as the first version of *The Man Who Knew Too Much* (1934), *Sabotage* (1936), and *The Lady Vanishes* (1938). Korda's distinctive, lavish style can be seen in Ludwig Berger, Michael Powell, and Tim Whelan's *The Thief of Bagdad* (1940), a colorful adaptation of an Arabian Nights tale, and in most of the films produced by London Films, which was

[1]

[4]

[2]

[3]

Camera Use in *The Last Laugh* F. W. Murnau's *The Last Laugh* is one of the most poignant, yet ultimately happy, movies ever made. Emil Jannings plays an aging, weary hotel doorman who is demoted to the job of men's washroom porter; in the process, he is stripped of his magnificent uniform coat and given a simple white jacket to wear. Because the character has no name, we can assume that he is "everyman." With great sensitivity to this man's predicament, Murnau pays careful attention to camera point of view as he photographs the character's descent from a job of great dignity to one of humiliation. The drama begins when the hotel manager notices that the doorman is so weary that he has to sit down and rest. [1] From the manager's point of view, the camera looks through the glass revolving doors and sees the resplendent doorman formally greeting a guest; however, the manager has previously decided that the doorman is too old and tired to continue in these responsibilities. [2] Later, in the manager's office, from the manager's point of view, we see an assistant remove the doorman's symbolic coat—a shameful moment in which the old man's pride and self-esteem are stripped away from him, like the skin flayed from an animal. [3] Still later, because the doorman does not want to be seen by anyone now, Murnau uses an objective camera to show us his descent to the basement to begin his new position; notice that, in contrast to image 1, the former doorman cowers in fear of being seen. [4] Once he is in the new job, because he is tired and weary here (just as he was when the manager decided to demote him), the former doorman dozes while holding a towel for a hotel guest, from whose point of view (through a mirror) this shot is photographed. Thus, with the exception of image 3, we see only what the characters see. The movie's title refers to the fact that, at the last moment, the doorman (through a plot twist you'll have to see to appreciate) becomes a rich man, returns to the hotel to dine, and has the last laugh.

headed by Korda's brother Alexander, including the historical epics *The Private Life of Henry VIII* (1933) and *Rembrandt* (1936). In addition, Vincent Korda helped design the sets for designer-director William Cameron Menzies's stylish science fiction film *Things to Come* (1936) and was one of several designers on Carol Reed's *The Third Man* (1949), set in a decadent Vienna after World War II and perhaps the most stylish of all black-and-white movies in the film noir style. Michael Powell and Emeric Pressburger, as creative partners, co-produced and co-directed a body of major films that reflect serious attention to design elements, including *The Life and Death of Colonel Blimp* (1943; production designer: Alfred Junge), *Black Narcissus* (1947; production designer: Alfred Junge), and *The Red Shoes* (1948; production designer: Hein Heckroth).

Italian neorealism, developed during World War II, influenced how cinema worldwide handled both narrative and design (or, in this case, absence of design). Its use of nonprofessional actors, handheld cameras, and location sets all diverged strongly from the practices of studio-bound productions, even those shot on location, and opened the door for new styles in Europe, India, and Hollywood. Its humanism and concerns with social conditions during and after the war broke away from conventional movie narrative and established a "new realism" in both story and style in the early films of Roberto Rossellini (*Rome, Open City*, 1945), Vittorio De Sica (*Shoeshine*, 1946; and *The Bicycle Thieves*, 1948), Michelangelo Antonioni (*L'Avventura*, 1960), and Federico Fellini (*I Vitelloni*, 1953).

Shooting in "real" locations—a seeming lack of design—actually reflects the work of an art director or a production designer who makes a well-orchestrated selection of streets and buildings, and produces a very definite look and feel—a mise-en-scène as recognizable as the most elaborately designed picture. This approach has been very influential on the design of countless films, both in Hollywood, where, after 1950, the increasing production of stories set in real locations owed much to the postwar Italian cinema. It was also notably influential in India, where Satyajit Ray, that country's most distinctive stylist, was deeply influenced by *The Bicycle Thieves* in making his classic Apu tril-

The Third Man   If, as already noted, movies such as Stanley Kubrick's *Eyes Wide Shut* (1999), Charles Laughton's *The Night of the Hunter* (1955), and Tim Burton's *Sleepy Hollow* (1999) all owe visual and even thematic debts to Robert Wiene's *The Cabinet of Dr. Caligari* (1920), then the missing link connecting them all might be Carol Reed's hugely influential thriller, *The Third Man* (1949; art directors: Vincent Korda, Joseph Bato, and John Hawkesworth). In this masterpiece of design and mise-en-scène, a pulp writer, Holly Martins (Joseph Cotten), finds himself in a shadowy, angular, mazelike Vienna. Because Martins's investigation into the mysterious death of a long-lost friend yields as much deceit as truth, the city becomes not just a backdrop but a kind of major character, the troubled Martins's alter ego. The film's climactic chase scene—set in the labyrinthine sewer system, with bright lights revealing the sweating tunnel walls and police officers splashing through the dark waters—is one of the most memorable nightmare visions in movie history. That Harry Lime, the subject of the police chase, is played by Orson Welles has led some viewers to regard *The Third Man* as an homage to both *Dr. Caligari* and Welles's *Citizen Kane* (1941). Indeed, because of its characteristically Wellesian "look," some other viewers mistakenly think Welles directed it.

ogy: *Pather Panchali* (1955), *The Unvanquished* (1957), and *The World of Apu* (1959).

Art direction and design is a very important element in the films of the three Japanese directors best known in the West: Akira Kurosawa, Kenji Mizoguchi, and Yasujiro Ozu. Yoshirô and Shinobu Muraki's design brings visual simplicity and dramatic power to Kurosawa's *Ran* (1985), for example. In Mizoguchi's *Sansho the Bailiff* (1954), Kisaku Ito and Shozaburo Nakajima's design is both poetic

Italian Neorealism Vittorio De Sica's *The Bicycle Thieves* is perhaps the best-loved movie from Italy's neorealist period, in part because its simple story speaks to many people by focusing on the details and chance events of ordinary lives. As Antonio Ricci (Lamberto Maggiorani) and his son Bruno (Enzo Staiola) pursue an old man who can identify the thief of Antonio's bicycle, for example, a rainstorm delays them and enables the old man to get away. The rainstorm was real, and the scene was filmed on location.

One Type of Japanese Mise-en-Scène A distinctive feature of many of Yasujiro Ozu's movies, including *Late Spring* (1949; art director: Tatsuo Hamada), from which this still is taken, is the low but level camera angle that seems to imply the presence of a houseguest sitting on a traditional Japanese floor mat. The resulting mise-en-scène is intimate, relaxed, and generally very still.

and realistic in its considerable beauty. Design credits seldom appear on Ozu's films, but we can discern a consistent visual style, austere and beautifully balanced in composition, in many of his films, including *An Autumn Afternoon* (1962) and *Late Spring* (1949). This style is based in part on Japanese culture itself—on the way contemporary Japanese people live, how they design their houses and furniture, and eat their meals—and is therefore not exportable.

⇥WEB Culture, Nation, Auteur: Four Japanese Filmmakers

In India, the films of Satyajit Ray, who was successful as a graphic designer before he turned to film directing, are noted for their adherence to the principles of Italian neorealism, particularly the emphasis on shooting in real locations. But Ray was also influenced by the movies of Jean Renoir and John Ford, to name but two Western directors, which is one reason his movies stand out from the traditional Indian cinema, which—like that of Japan

or China—mostly reflects the uniqueness of its culture and, therefore, is not particularly influential on the filmmaking of other countries. Ray is highly esteemed by audiences and his fellow film directors for his mastery of design details that reveal setting, a character's state of mind, and mood in such films as *The Music Room* (1958), *The Goddess* (1960), *Charulata* (1964), and *The Home and the World* (1984).

Chinese films display diverse visual styles. In the People's Republic of China, distinctive directors include Kaige Chen (*Yellow Earth*, 1984) and Yimou Zhang, whose films *Red Sorghum* (1987) and *Raise the Red Lantern* (1991) exploit color in impressive ways. In Hong Kong, a new cinema emerged in the 1960s, characterized by its focus on the local Cantonese culture and on technological sophistication, rather than style. Its distinctive achievements include Ann Hui's political *Ordinary Heroes* (1998), Hark Tsui's epic *Peking Opera Blues* (1986), and John Woo's superviolent *The Killer* (1989), a strong influence on director Quentin Tarantino and others.

In Taiwan, several important directors have

emerged, including Edward Yang, whose *The Day on the Beach* (1983) reflects Antonioni's austere style, and Hsiao-hsien Hou, whose *City of Sadness* (1989) adheres to a more traditional Chinese cinematic style. Most famous internationally is Ang Lee, whose early films include *The Wedding Banquet* (1993) and *Eat Drink Man Woman* (1994). Since crossing over into mainstream Western film production, Lee has made movies set in utterly disparate worlds: *Sense and Sensibility* (1995), based on the 1811 novel by English writer Jane Austen; *The Ice Storm* (1997), based on the 1994 novel by American writer Rick Moody; and *Crouching Tiger, Hidden Dragon* (2000), which tells a Chinese love story in the highly kinetic style reminiscent of Hong Kong martial-arts films. Each of these movies displays a mastery of the principles of production design.

Apart from such postmodern filmmaking efforts as the Danish *Dogme* movement (with its location shooting, using handheld cameras and natural light), most movie design today tends to strive for the seamless integration of studio and natural settings. And with the exception of today's highly popular and hugely successful science fiction and fantasy movies, the majority of today's stories involve recognizable people, wearing recognizable clothes, and moving through recognizable settings. The design work, however, is as challenging and involved as it was during the classical studio era, and the results, created with sophisticated technologies, are no less impressive.

Composition

Composition is part of the *process* of visualizing and planning the design of a movie. More precisely, composition is the organization, distribution, balance, and general relationship of stationary objects and **figures** (any significant things that move on the screen—people, animals, objects), as well as of light, shade, line, and color *within the frame*. Ensuring that such organization helps develop a movie's narrative and meanings requires much thought and discussion, so filmmakers use drawings and models—general sketches of the look of overall scenes, specific set designs, costume designs, storyboards for particular shot sequences, and so on—to aid them in visualizing each shot and achieving a unified whole. As filmmakers visualize and plan each shot, they must make decisions about two aspects of composition: **framing** (what we see on the screen) and **kinesis** (what moves on the screen).

This is true whether the movie strives for verisimilitude or fantasy. Certain visionary directors are known for making shots that resemble the canvas of an enormous painting and, in so doing, giving impressive amounts of attention to all aspects of composition. Such directors, to name only a few, include David Lynch (*The Elephant Man*, 1980; *Blue Velvet*, 1986; and *Mulholland Drive*, 2001), Terry Gilliam (*Brazil*, 1985; *Fear and Loathing in Las Vegas*, 1998; and *The Brothers Grimm*, 2005), Roy Andersson (*World of Glory*, 1991; and *Songs From the Second Floor*, 2000), and Francis Ford Coppola (*One From the Heart*, 1982; and *Apocalypse Now Redux*, 2001 [director's cut of *Apocalypse Now*, 1979]).

Composition is important because it helps to ensure the aesthetic unity and harmony of the movie, as well as to guide our looking—how we read the image and its component parts and, particularly, how we interpret the characters' physical, emotional, and psychological relationships to one another. Composition can produce a flat image, one in which figures and objects are arranged and photographed in the foreground of the screen, or an image that has the illusion of depth.

◆▶**WEB** Composition and Mise-en-Scène

Framing: What We See on the Screen

The frame is the border between what the filmmaker wants us to see and everything else—the dimensions of height and width that provide the shape of the movie's images. However, unlike the static frame around a painting, the frame around a motion picture image can move and thus change its point of view (this process of **reframing** results from what is called a **moving frame**). The movie frame is therefore not merely a container for

[1]

[2]

Composition and Mise-en-Scène Two shots from William Wyler's *The Best Years of Our Lives* (1946; art directors: Perry Ferguson and George Jenkins) illustrate the relationship between composition and mise-en-scène. In the movie, the lives of three veterans are intertwined, and triangular compositions reinforce that theme visually. [1] Early in the film, Fred Derry (Dana Andrews, *top*), Al Stephenson (Fredric March, *lower right*), and Homer Parrish (Harold Russell, *lower left*) return home after serving in World War II. Their tight physical grouping in the nose of a bomber reflects the tight emotional bond that they have only recently established. [2] Much later, a similar tri-point pattern establishes a different relationship among the men. Here, a shot in Butch's bar, with Derry using the phone in the background and a noticeable gap between Stephenson and Parrish, reflects the new and estranged relationship. Time has changed their lives, and the same old patterns have different meanings within the larger context.

a movie's visual elements, but is itself an important and dynamic visual element.

Framing also implies point of view (POV). At times, the framing seems to be presenting us with the point of view of a single character (*subjective POV*). At other times, the framing implies a view that seems to be coming from no one in particular (*omniscient POV*). However, sometimes the framing can be so varied that it creates a desirable ambiguity, one in which viewers are required to reach their own conclusions about the moral issues at hand. For example, Krzysztof Kieslowski's *The Decalogue* (1988; cinematographer: Slawomir Idziak; art director: Ewa Smal), composed of ten one-hour films, each of which is devoted to a contemporary interpretation of one of the biblical commandments, places particular attention on the point of view of the camera that, visually, narrates each of the stories. Kieslowski, a Catholic who experienced the Communist-controlled Poland of the 1960s and '70s, was not overtly religious, and thus he does not espouse any particular doctrinal interpretation of the commandments, leaving interpretation to the viewer.

Thou Shalt Not Kill, the fifth film, is perhaps the most demanding of the series, both because it deals with a murder so random and horrifying that it provokes our strongest moral outrage, and because Kieslowski's approach to the framing, which employs both traditional and innovative techniques, creates the sense of a coldly "objective" perspective on the crime even as it reveals subjective points of view. Kieslowski achieves this effect by shooting the actors and settings from a variety of angles, using a very close framing so that we become intimate with all of the characters, and shifting the camera's point of view so that, for example, as the murder is about to take place, we see shots of the murderer coiling a rope around his fist while drinking a cup of coffee and flirting with two young girls, hailing a taxi, staring at the driver's face in the rearview mirror, calmly looking out the window, and then murdering the driver. In other words, we see (1) the murderer's objective actions as observed by the camera, as if it were a documentary movie, including his garroting the driver, bludgeoning him, and dragging him to the riverside, where he smashes his face with a rock; (2) facial expressions that reveal some of the murderer's subjective thoughts; and (3) reaction shots of the driver as he picks up the passenger, discusses a change of route that leads him onto a deserted road where he is killed, and struggles to stay alive. At other times, the scene begins with the murderer in one corner of the frame, so that we see what he's seeing, and then the camera reframes so that he is central to the action. Because he has no apparent motive, we are appalled at the extraordinary brutality that we see. Even he seems shocked by what he has done. Obviously, the director's choices in such techniques as camera angle, framing, and camera movement contribute to our reactions, but they do not *lead* those reactions in one way or another. In fact, the continual use of reflections in windows and mirrors makes us wonder which images to trust.

Onscreen and Offscreen Space How filmmakers envision the look of a film, and how the camera interprets that vision, depends on the fundamental fact that cinematic seeing *is* framing. The frame of the camera's **viewfinder** (the little window you look through when taking a picture) indicates the boundaries of the camera's point of view. To demonstrate for yourself the difference between the camera's point of view and your everyday vision, put your hands together to form a rectangular frame, then look through it using one eye. If you move it to the left or the right, move it closer or farther away from your face, or tilt it up or down, you will see instantly how framing (and moving the frame) changes what you see.

Because the frame is dynamic, it often makes us aware of the **offscreen space** outside the frame as well as the **onscreen space** inside it. As the frame moves, it presents on the screen details that were previously offscreen, thus prompting us to be aware of the dynamic between offscreen and onscreen spaces. As the film theorist Noël Burch first suggested, the entire visual composition of a shot depends on the existence of both onscreen and offscreen spaces; both spaces are equally important to the composition and to the viewer's experience of it.[9] Burch divides offscreen space into six segments: the four infinite spaces that lie beyond the four borders of the frame; the spaces beyond the movie settings, which call our attention to entrances into and exits from the world of the frame; and the space behind the camera, which helps the viewer define the camera's point of view and identify a physical point beyond which characters may pass. Offscreen space has power, as Burch emphasizes: "The longer the screen remains empty, the greater the resulting tension between screen space and off-screen space and the greater the attention concentrated on off-screen space as against screen space."[10] In any movie—a verisimilar one, in particular—most shots depend on both onscreen and offscreen space, and our awareness of their interdependence reinforces the illusion of a larger spatial world than what is contained in any single frame.

In *Chinatown* (1974; production designer: Richard Sylbert), Roman Polanski uses offscreen space to accentuate the suspense of the second meeting between the prying detective J. J. Gittes (Jack Nicholson) and the menacing tycoon Noah Cross (John Huston) at the house of Evelyn Mulwray (Faye Dunaway), who is both Cross's daughter and Gittes's client. Cross is a ruthless man who will do anything to keep his loathsome personal life and corrupt public activities from further notice, and Gittes knows he's now in danger when Cross arrives at the house. From a camera viewpoint on an exterior terrace (foreground), we look through a door into an interior foyer (middle ground) and beyond to the front door of the house and its exterior front porch (background). As the scene begins, no one is in the frame, but a puff of cigarette smoke enters

[9] Noël Burch, *Theory of Film Practice*, trans. Helen R. Lane (1973; reprint, Princeton, N.J.: Princeton University Press, 1981), 25.
[10] Ibid.

[1]

[2]

[3]

Onscreen and Offscreen Space in *Chinatown* (Above)
[1] Because of the smoke from his cigarette (*screen left*), we know that J. J. Gittes (Jack Nicholson) is in the space depicted here, and not being able to see him accentuates the suspense in this climactic scene from Roman Polanski's *Chinatown*. [2] Noah Cross (John Huston) enters, looking for Gittes, and sees him offscreen left. [3] Gittes enters the frame and begins their conversation.

the left side of the frame and lets us know that Gittes is waiting there. This may be one of the rare instances when a puff of smoke can produce a powerful reaction from the viewers. Although it's been put there for a reason, its meaning is more metaphorical than literal: a transitional moment of vagueness before a powerful confrontation between two antagonists. Cross steps onto the front porch,

Onscreen and Offscreen Space in *Stagecoach*
(Opposite)   In John Ford's *Stagecoach* (1939; art director: Alexander Toluboff), a scene set in the noontime lunch stop at Dry Fork illustrates social division among the characters through the use of onscreen and offscreen spaces. [1] The scene opens by establishing the location, showing two of the room's four walls. Following this *establishing shot*, a series of cuts fills in parts of the room not seen here. [2] Revealing a third wall but keeping us oriented by showing the chairs and part of the table, this shot takes us to what had been offscreen space and remains marginal territory, where Ringo (John Wayne) and Dallas (Claire Trevor) interact before he seats her at the table. [3] Opposed to Ringo and Dallas, on the other side of the room, are Gatewood (Berton Churchill, *seated left*), Hatfield (John Carradine, *standing right*), and Lucy (Louise Platt, *seated right*)—three characters who consider themselves socially superior to the others. [4] From yet another perspective, we see the room's fourth wall and Lucy, who stares coldly and haughtily at [5] Dallas, who yields no ground. [6] When Ringo defies the anger rising across the table (a reinforcement of his position in image 2), [7] Hatfield escorts Lucy away from Dallas (a reinforcement of their position in image 3) to [8] the opposite end of the table, which we see from an entirely new perspective. Thus an area that had been largely offscreen, hardly registering, takes prominence, especially in contrast to the brightly lit, vacant, and exposed end of the table.

enters the house, crosses the foyer, appears on the terrace, looks offscreen at Gittes, and says, "Oh, there you are," as if he weren't prepared for the meeting. Gittes then enters the frame, and their conversation begins.

Open and Closed Framing   The first and most obvious function of the motion picture frame is to control our perception of the world by enclosing what we see within a rectangular border, generally wider than it is high. Because it shapes the image in a configuration that does not allow for peripheral vision, and thus does not conform to our visual perception, we understand framing as one of the many conventions through which cinema gives *form* to what we see on the screen. Film theorist Leo Braudy, one of many writers to study the relationship between cinematic arrangement and viewer perception, distinguishes between *open* and *closed* films (or forms) as two ways of designing and representing the visible world through

1

5

2

6

3

7

4

8

[1]

[4]

[2]

[5]

[3]

[6]

Open and Closed Framing   To understand the sometimes subtle distinctions between open and closed framings, compare two very different American crossroads: one featured in Alfred Hitchcock's *North by Northwest* (1959; production designer: Robert Boyle), the other in Robert Zemeckis's *Cast Away* (2000; production designer: Rick Carter). In *Cast Away*, Chuck Noland (Tom Hanks) [1] receives directions from Bettina Peterson (Lari White), [2] considers his options, and [3] wonders if Peterson's path is the one he should follow. His choices are as limitless as the expansive plain surrounding him. In *North by Northwest*, Roger Thornhill (Cary Grant) [4] finds himself in a similarly vast landscape that leaves him completely vulnerable to [5] the plane that [6] pursues him no matter where he runs. As vast and as similar as these physical places are, they represent very different psychological spaces: Noland ponders an open-ended choice (and thus Robert Zemeckis has established an open frame), while Thornhill faces diminishing options for escape (and thus Hitchcock has transformed an open landscape into a closed frame).

framing it, as well as two ways of perceiving and interpreting it.

Each of these cinematic worlds—open and closed—is created through a system of framing that should remain fairly consistent throughout the film so as not to confuse the viewer. Although both types of films are planned and designed, the **open frame** is designed to depict a world where characters move freely within an open, recognizable environment, and the **closed frame** is designed to imply that other forces (such as fate; social, educational, or economic background; or a repressive government) have robbed characters of their ability to move and act freely. The open frame is generally employed in realistic (*verisimilar*) films, the closed frame in antirealistic films. In the realistic, or verisimilar, film, the frame is a "window" on the world—a window that provides many views. Because the "reality" being depicted changes continuously, the movie's framing changes with it. In

TABLE 3.1 Open and Closed Frames		
	Open	**Closed**
Visual Characteristics	Normal depth, perspective, light, and scale. An overall look that is realistic, or verisimilar.	Exaggerated and stylized depth; out of perspective; distorted or exaggerated light and shadow; distorted scale. An overall look that is not realistic, or verisimilar.
Framing the Characters	Characters may move freely in and out of the frame. They are free to go to another place in the movie's world and return.	Characters are controlled by outside forces and do not have the freedom to come and go as they wish. They have no control over the logic that drives the movie's actions.
Relationship of Characters to Design Elements	The characters are more important than the sets, costumes, and other design elements. The design elements support the development of character and story.	Design elements call attention to themselves and may be more important than the characters. Design elements drive the story's development.
The World of the Story	The world of the story is based on reality. It changes and evolves, and the framing changes with it. The frame is a window on this world.	The world of the story is self-contained; it doesn't refer to anything outside of itself. It is rigid and hierarchical: everything has its place. The frame is similar to a painting.
Examples	*Wonderland* (1999; Michael Winterbottom, dir.), *Vera Drake* (2004; Mike Leigh, dir.), *La Promesse* (1996; Jean-Pierre and Luc Dardenne, dir.), *The River* (1951; Jean Renoir, dir.); *My Darling Clementine* (1946; John Ford, dir.); *Junebug* (2005; Phil Morrison, dir.)	*We Don't Live Here Anymore* (2004; John Curran, dir.), *Vertigo* (1958; Alfred Hitchcock, dir.), *Barry Lyndon* (1975; Stanley Kubrick, dir.), *The Big Heat* (1953; Fritz Lang, dir.), *The Wizard of Oz* (1939; Victor Fleming, dir.); *Mean Creek* (2004; Jacob Aaron Estes, dir.); *Elephant* (2003; Gus Van Sant, dir.)

Source: Adapted from Leo Braudy, *The World in a Frame: What We See in Films* (1976; reprint, Chicago: University of Chicago Press, 1984).

the antirealistic film, the frame is similar to the frame of a painting or photograph, enclosing or limiting the world by closing it down and providing only one view. Because only that one view exists, everything within the frame has its particular place. As with all such distinctions in film analysis, these differences between open and closed frames aren't absolute; they are a matter of degree and emphasis.

In Phil Morrison's *Junebug* (2005; production designer: David Doernberg), an open film, characters move freely from Chicago to Greensboro, North Carolina, and back to Chicago. They respond to their own feelings, do what they must, and pay the consequences. Life flows, with its crises and turning points, but does not bring any of the characters to a conclusion that they cannot walk away from or reverse. The characters are more important than the design—in the largest sense of that word—of this world. By contrast, Gus Van Sant's *Elephant* (2003; art director: Benjamin Hayden) is a closed movie in which the design of the film and the framing are more important than the characters. Meticulous in its observation of an ordinary high school that doubles for Columbine High School in Littleton, Colorado, *Elephant* features real teenagers improvising their own dialogue and going about their business, but we soon realize that they are caught in a labyrinth of the halls and classrooms that define their world. They are trapped. Some of the students like this reality, and those who don't try to destroy it. The activities of these students are deliberately repetitive; even the same stroll through the hallways is repeated several times, each from a different camera angle. This repetition calls our attention to the director's manipulation of the students' world and to their confinement.

The formulaic nature of these distinctions does not mean that you should automatically categorize movies that you see and analyze as open or closed, for there will be no profit in that. Instead, you can recognize the characteristics of each type of film (as described in Table 3.1), and you can be aware that certain directors consistently depict open worlds (Jean Renoir, John Ford, Robert Altman), while others are equally consistent in making closed ones (Alfred Hitchcock, Stanley Kubrick, Lars von Trier).

Kinesis: What Moves on the Screen

Because the movies move in so many ways, our perception of *kinesis* (movement) in a movie is influenced by several different factors at once—including the use of music in an otherwise static scene—but we perceive movement mainly when we *see* (1) the movement of objects and characters within the frame and (2) the apparent movement of the frame itself (the *moving frame*). Although their particular applications will differ depending on the specific work, both types of movement are part of any movie's composition and mise-en-scène.

Of course, all movies *move*, but some move more than others and differently. The kinetic quality of many movies is determined by their genre: action pictures, cartoons, and comedies tend to include more and faster movement than do love stories or biographical films. Many great films—Carl Theodor Dreyer's *The Passion of Joan of Arc* (1928), Robert Bresson's *Diary of a Country Priest* (1951), Yasujiro Ozu's *Tokyo Story* (1953), and Michelangelo Antonioni's *The Outcry* (1957), for example—use little movement and action. That *lack* of action represents not only a way of looking at the world (framing it) but also an approach to the movie's narrative and themes.

Which movie, then, is the more *cinematic*—one that moves all the time or one that moves hardly at all? Because kinetic power is only one of the inherent creative possibilities of movies, not an essential quality of every movie, we can answer this question only by examining the relationships among the movement, narrative, and overall mise-en-scène. In this way, we can determine what movement is appropriate and, furthermore, what movement *works* to control perceptions. To condemn *Tokyo Story*'s lack of movement when compared to the frenetic movement in, say, Yimou Zhang's *Hero* (2002; production designers: Tingxiao Huo and Zhenzhou Yi) is equivalent to condemning Shakespeare for not writing in the style of contemporary playwright Harold Pinter. In other words, the comparison is unfair to both sides.

Kinesis in Action Films Throughout the history of film—from the swashbuckling of Hollywood legend Douglas Fairbanks, to the cinematic portrayals of Shakespeare's Hamlet by Laurence Olivier, Mel Gibson, Kenneth Branagh, and many others, to the movie careers of martial artists such as Bruce Lee and Jackie Chan—the old-fashioned art of swordplay has always been one of the most exciting forms of movement onscreen. Ang Lee's *Crouching Tiger, Hidden Dragon* (2000), a contemporary update of Hong Kong sword-and-sorcery movies, combines martial arts with elaborate choreography. In playing the nobleman's-daughter-turned-warrior, Jen Yu, shown here in one of many fight sequences, actress Ziyi Zhang used her training in dance as well as her martial-arts skills.

WEB Action Scenes and Kinesthetic Art

Movement of Figures Within the Frame

The word *figure* applies to anything concrete within the frame: an object, an animal, a person. The most important figure is usually the actor, who is cast, dressed, made up, and directed for the film and thus is a vital element in the composition and resulting mise-en-scène. Figures can move in many ways: across the frame (in a horizontal, diagonal, vertical, or circular pattern), from foreground to background (and vice versa), or from on and off the screen. A character can float weightlessly in outer space, as Frank Poole (Gary Lockwood) does in Stanley Kubrick's *2001: A Space Odyssey* (1968); dance without danger to himself up a wall and across the ceiling, as Tom Bowen (Fred Astaire) does in Stanley Donen's *Royal Wedding* (1951); or break free from leg braces and run like the wind, defying a childhood spine problem and gravity itself, as the title character, played by Tom Hanks,

does in Robert Zemeckis's *Forrest Gump* (1994). These and other kinds of figure movement—which can be as prosaic or as poetic as the story requires—not only show *where* a character is moving, but *how* (on foot, in a vehicle, through the air in a fight), and sometimes (explicitly or implicitly) also *why*.

For each scene, the director and his team must plan the positions and movements of the actors and the cameras, and, in rehearsals, familiarize the cast and camera operators with their plan—a process known as **blocking**. In the early stages of blocking, the director often places pieces of tape on the floor to indicate the position of the camera and the actors; once crew and cast are familiar with their positions, the tape is removed. In designing a film, another essential element to be considered is how all the figures move within the space created to tell the story, as well as how they are placed in relation to each other. The physical placement of characters can suggest the nature

[1]

[2]

[3]

Movement of Figures Within the Frame Movies can make anything and anyone move in any way the story calls for. All three movements in the images here are in the realm of the unbelievable. [1] Astronaut Frank Poole (Gary Lockwood)—betrayed by an onboard computer that severs his lifeline—floats weightlessly to his death in *2001: A Space Odyssey*. [2] Expressing his love for a woman, Tom Bowen (Fred Astaire) in *Royal Wedding* dances his way up a wall and eventually across the ceiling. [3] Forrest Gump (Tom Hanks), in the movie of that name, acts from complete willpower to shed his leg braces and run free.

and complexity of whatever relationship may exist between them, and thus their placement and proximity are relevant to our understanding of how the composition of a shot helps to create meaning. (Analyzing placement and proximity is the study of *proxemics*, a topic we will discuss more fully in Chapter 4.)

Ordinarily, close physical proximity implies emotional or other kinds of closeness. Federico Fellini's *I Vitelloni* (1953; cinematographers: Carlo Carlini, Otello Martelli, and Luciano Trasatti; production designer: Mario Chiari) goes against this convention by employing a very rigorous compositional plan that involves placing the characters in symmetrical proximity. In one memorable shot, Fellini suggests group indolence by seating each character at a separate café table, with half of them facing in one direction and the other half facing in the other. In *Love and Death* (1975; cinematographer: Ghislain Cloquet; production designer: Willy Holt), a low comedy about life's big issues, director Woody Allen shows that physical proximity between two characters can also mean the absence of romantic closeness. On the night before he is to fight a duel, Boris (Woody Allen) asks Sonja (Diane Keaton) to marry him. They are very tightly framed in the shot, and he starts intoning a nonsensical monologue: "To die before the harvest, the crops, the grains, the fields of rippling wheat—all there is in life is wheat." The shot continues as she, looking offscreen left, confesses her innermost feelings about him; and, although he does not seem to hear what she is saying, his reaction is to mug all sorts of exaggerated facial reactions as he mumbles more nonsense about wheat. As he does with so many other aspects of film, Allen manipulates proxemics for brilliant comic effect.

DVD Composing the Frame

Looking at Mise-en-Scène

The better the fit between mise-en-scène and the rest of a movie's elements, the more likely we are to take that mise-en-scène for granted. A movie's mise-en-scène may be so well thought out and put together that it seems merely something *given* for the director and the cinematographer to film, rather than the deliberately produced result of labor by a team of artists and craftspeople. A fully realized mise-en-scène plays a crucial role in creating the illusion of naturalness that encourages our enjoyment of movies as spectators, but we must consciously *resist* that illusion if we hope to graduate from being spectators to being students of film, people who *look at movies* rather than just watch them. Looking at mise-en-scène critically does not mean taking the fun away from movies. You may still have as much fun as you like with (or is the better word *in*?) *The Matrix* (1999) while realizing that everything you see, hear, and feel in it was put there for a purpose.

Let's look closely at three movies in which mise-en-scène produces a rich viewing experience: Tim Burton's *Sleepy Hollow* (1999), Sam Mendes's *American Beauty* (1999), and Michael Almereyda's *Hamlet* (2000).

Tim Burton's *Sleepy Hollow*

Tim Burton is a visionary director who has created imaginative fantasies that reveal great visual ingenuity and a wicked sense of humor. His movies are always a treat to look at, and they offer abundant opportunities for analyzing their design and mise-en-scène, even when these aspects do not always serve the narrative well. Among his most successful movies are *Batman* (1989), *Edward Scissorhands* (1990), *Ed Wood* (1994), *Sleepy Hollow* (1999), *Planet of the Apes* (2001), *Charlie and the Chocolate Factory* (2005), and *Corpse Bride* (2005).

The highly stylized reimagining of Washington Irving's tale "The Legend of Sleepy Hollow" (1819–20) so totally transforms its source that, in effect, it leaves the text behind; it emphasizes instead the director's stunning vision and his production team's meticulous realization of that vision. The story concerns the efforts of Ichabod Crane (Johnny Depp), a forensic scientist, to solve three murders in the village of Sleepy Hollow, in which the victims were beheaded. The ending is so muddled that we don't really know if he succeeds, but at least he escapes with his head. The movie's unified design plan and mise-en-scène create the correct

Mise-en-Scène Creates *Sleepy Hollow*'s Unified Look
[1] *Sleepy Hollow*'s primary palette, tending toward slate-gray and bluish gray, and the overcast, foreboding look used in most of the outdoor shots enhance our sense of the mystery and danger lurking within the village. [2] Punctuating this overall grayness are magnificent homages to classic horror films, including a windmill straight out of James Whale's *Frankenstein* (1931).

times, place, and moods—according to Burton's vision—and go beyond the superficial to reveal characters, provide the appropriate settings for the extraordinary action of the film, and develop its themes. Burton's overall goal in production design seems to have been to make this film as weird and scary as possible. Verisimilitude has nothing to do with it. Although Washington Irving's story describes the valley of Sleepy Hollow as a place filled with rippling brooks, cheerful birdcalls, and unchanging tranquility, Burton's version of Sleepy Hollow is dark and foreboding from the start. The visual presentation of the village is clearly inspired by the design vocabularies of horror and gothic movies.

Such movies include James Whale's *Frankenstein* (1931), which ends with an angry mob trapping the Monster in a windmill that they set afire. Burton similarly places the spectacular climax of his film in an ominous windmill, where Ichabod Crane lures the Headless Horseman (Christopher Walken), whose mysterious powers save him from death in the fiery explosion. In addition, Burton draws on Mario Bava's visually sumptuous vampire movie *Black Sunday* (1960), Roman Polanski's *The Fearless Vampire Killers* (1967), and films from Britain's Hammer Studios (the foremost producer of gothic horror films in movie history), whose style was characterized by careful attention to detail—including, of course, lots of blood—in such films as Terence Fisher's *The Curse of Frankenstein* (1957) and *Horror of Dracula* (1958). Burton also pays homage to the horror genre by casting Christopher Lee, who plays the Creature in *The Curse of Frankenstein*, as the Burgomaster in *Sleepy Hollow*.

Sleepy Hollow features many of the prominent characteristics of the horror and gothic genres, including

> A spooky setting—the almost colorless village of Sleepy Hollow and the creepy woods that surround it
> A forensic scientist, Ichabod Crane (played by Johnny Depp, an actor whose fey style has added much to several of Burton's movies) forced to struggle with a demonic antagonist (or, perhaps the illusion of one), the Headless Horseman (Christopher Walken)
> A seemingly virginal heroine who dabbles in witchcraft—Katrina Anne Van Tassel (Christina Ricci)—and her wicked stepmother, Lady Mary Van Tassel (Miranda Richardson), the wife of the lord of the manor who moonlights as a witch
> Various other eccentric and deranged locals

In addition, there are glimpses of the spirit world, and other frightening, mysterious, and supernatural events.

Burton and his collaborators were also inspired

Different Characters in *Sleepy Hollow* Require Different Looks [1] Baltus Van Tassel (Michael Gambon, *standing left*) is among the many characters in *Sleepy Hollow* who might have stepped out of period paintings. Indeed, most of the village's residents seem stuck in an antiquated, vaguely European style of dress. [2] By contrast, the darkly and sleekly dressed Ichabod Crane (Johnny Depp) is a "modern" American man of science, here wearing the ambitious but wonderful instrument that he has designed to perform forensic inspections. [3] In a flashback, the "Hessian" (Christopher Walken), who in death will become the Headless Horseman, is all spikes and sharp angles, looking very much like the vampire in F. W. Murnau's classic, *Nosferatu* (1922).

by the visual style of drawings and paintings by the eighteenth-century British artists William Hogarth and Thomas Rowlandson. In such works as *A Rake's Progress* (1735), Hogarth created a series of anecdotal pictures (similar to movie storyboards) that had both a moral and a satirical message. Rowlandson created an instantly recognizable gallery of social types, many of whom seem to have served as models for the characters we meet at Van Tassel's mansion. When Crane steps into the house, a "harvest party" is taking place, and the guests are dancing, drinking, and quietly talking. The color palette changes from the exterior gloom to soft browns, grays, greens, and blacks. The interior colors are very subdued but warmed by a patterned tile floor, orange jack-o'-lanterns, candles, and firelight. (Here, as throughout the movie's interior scenes, candles seem to be the principal source of illumination.) Baltus Van Tassel (Michael Gambon) wears a suit of beautiful dark green velvet decorated with gold brocade, under which his cream-colored silk shirt is fastened with a bow; unlike many of the other men, he does not wear a wig. His beautiful, younger wife, Lady Mary Van Tassel, wears an elaborate gown of yellow silk velvet decorated with an overlaid pattern in cut brown velvet. Her hair is swept back from her high forehead. The Van Tassels' dress and manner leave no question as to who heads society in Sleepy Hollow.

In a scene that could have come straight from Hogarth, Crane is introduced to the other ranking members of the community. We are in Van Tassel's study, with its muted green wallpaper, leather chairs, books, portraits, Oriental carpet, blazing fire on the hearth, and candles mounted in wall sconces. Each man in the scene is striking in dress and manner. The Reverend Steenwyck (Jeffrey Jones) wears the most distinctive wig in the movie, and Magistrate Samuel Philipse (Richard Griffiths), seen pouring the contents of his flask into his teacup, has the stock red face of a drinking man that one sees so often in portraits of British aristocrats by George Romney, another of Hogarth's contemporaries.

Rick Heinrichs, the production designer, said of the design scheme for the village, "One of the things we were trying to do was inspire a sense of

Contrasting Colors Emphasize Narrative Contrasts in *Sleepy Hollow* Blood-red sealing wax [1] and blood spattered on a menacing jack-o'-lantern [2] are the sorts of bold design details that stand out against *Sleepy Hollow*'s generally muted palette, as seen in the "harvest party" scene [3], in which Katrina Anne Van Tassel (Christina Ricci), blindfolded, first encounters Ichabod Crane (Johnny Depp). Note, in contrast to the smiling children on the right, the jack-o'-lantern in the upper left corner, echoing the sour expression on the face of Crane's eventual romantic rival, Brom Van Brunt (Casper Van Dien).

scary portentousness in the village. I think it's different from Irving's Sleepy Hollow which is described as a dozing Dutch farming community. If our Sleepy Hollow is asleep, it's a fitful sort of sleep with nightmares."[11] *Sleepy Hollow* is clearly a closed film that depicts a singular, self-enclosed world in which almost everyone and everything are held in the grip of powerful personal, societal, and supernatural forces. Director Tim Burton is, of course, the strongest, most controlling force in this world.

To create this gloomy atmosphere, Burton and his collaborators use a muted, even drab color palette, punctuated here and there by carefully placed bright details. (The only consistent deviation is in the sequences depicting Crane's dreams of his mother.) As the movie begins with prologue and title credits, however, the dominant color is not muted, but the red of dripping wax being used to seal a last will and testament—a red so evocative that we momentarily mistake it for blood. After sealing his will, Peter Van Garrett (Martin Landau, in an uncredited performance), a pale figure wearing a pale yellow silk jacket, flees by carriage with the Headless Horseman in pursuit. The Horseman lops off the head of the coachman and then of Van Garrett, whose blood spatters all over an eerie orange pumpkin head mounted on a stake. Decapitation, a central theme of *Sleepy Hollow*, produces lots of blood, and blood continually spurts throughout the movie in the murders committed by the Horseman as well as in self-inflicted wounds and the gory examinations of dead bodies.

As Ichabod Crane travels by a closed, black carriage between New York City and Sleepy Hollow in the opening scene of the film, we are introduced to the principal color palette of late fall and early winter: gray river, gray wintry skies, trees almost barren of leaves, and rime on the ground. As day turns to twilight, Crane arrives at the village entrance, marked by two pillars topped by stone stags' heads, and walks down the road through the village and across the fields to the Van Tassel mansion. The entire scene appears to have been shot in black and

[1]

[2]

Expressive Details Define Characters in *Sleepy Hollow* In a movie as brilliantly stylized as Tim Burton's *Sleepy Hollow*, one in which the story hangs on the struggle between superstition and reason, many of the characters are defined in part by their costumes, makeup, or the props with which they are associated. For example, [1] Katrina Van Tassel's (Christina Ricci) book, *A Compendium of Spells, Charms and Devices of the Spirit World*, associates her clearly with the witchcraft that bedevils Sleepy Hollow, while [2] Ichabod Crane's (Johnny Depp) wonderful eyeglasses and bag of medical instruments, including some of his own devising, tell the town's inhabitants, as well as the movie's viewers, that he is a man of science.

white, rather than color, for Crane's extremely pale face provides the only color here, signifying, as we have already learned in theory but will now learn in fact, that the townspeople are drained of all life by their fear of the Horseman. Completely skeptical of what he considers the "myth" of the Horseman, Crane wears black and looks pallid, perturbed, and wary throughout the early part of the movie.

The village, the movie's most elaborate outdoor

[11] Rick Heinrichs, qtd. in Denise Abbott, "Nightmare by Designs," *Hollywood Reporter*, international weekly edition, February 29–March 6, 2000, S-6.

set, was constructed in England in a style that Heinrichs calls "Colonial Expressionism"; it includes a covered wooden bridge, church, general store, midwife's office, tavern, notary public, blacksmith, bank, mill house, warehouses, and several residences. Even the houses are scary, with their gray façades, doors, and shutters. Recalling English and Dutch architecture of the seventeenth and eighteenth centuries, many of these exteriors were also duplicated inside London studios, where heavy layers of artificial fog and smoke and controlled lighting helped create the illusion of a dark, misty valley under a leaden sky.

This meticulously created mise-en-scène encourages us not only to escape into the past but also to suspend our disbelief. On this ground, two worlds collide: one is represented by Crane, a "modern" criminal investigator using the latest technology (most of it of his own invention); the other is represented by the community of Sleepy Hollow, which itself ranges from the rich to the poor, all afraid of the Headless Horseman. Burton tells the story in part through fantastic objects and details, including Crane's notebook containing his drawings and notes, various forensic instruments, and peculiar eyeglasses; Katrina's book of witchcraft and evil-eye diagrams, over which an ominous spider creeps; the fairy tale witch's cave deep in the forest and her potions made of bats' heads and birds' wings; the mechanical horse used to propel the Horseman through the village and surrounding woods; the "Tree of Death," where the Horseman lives between murders; the windmill, where he almost meets his end; and the fountain of blood at the climactic moment, when the Horseman's head is restored to him and he returns to life. Impressionist, even expressionist, much of what we see in this creepy place, with its frightening inhabitants and their eccentric costumes and hairstyles, was created through special effects.

Although it is necessary to be precise in analyzing all of the design elements in a single scene or clip from a movie, we can only generalize in discussing them in a movie as stylistically rich as Sleepy Hollow. Throughout, however, Burton's mise-en-scène reflects a fairly consistent use of framing and camera movement. Reinforcing the closed nature of the movie, the frame is tightly restricted on the characters being photographed. Even many shots of the landscape are equally tight, providing little sense of the sky above, or even the earth below; and when they do, the sky is invariably overcast.

The lighting creates a very moody atmosphere. The exterior lighting—where mist, chimney smoke, and flashes of lightning are constant motifs—is slightly less dim than the interior lighting, which is provided seemingly by candles and firelight. The total impact of the design elements in Sleepy Hollow is that they produce distinct emotional responses in the viewer that perfectly complement our emotional responses to the narrative's twists and turns. We are repelled by the superstitious fears of the entire community and are made uncomfortable by the conspiracy among the townspeople to hide the secret of the Horseman, and the mise-en-scène reinforces our discomfort, even as it mesmerizes our eyes.

Sam Mendes's *American Beauty*

American Beauty (1999; production designer: Naomi Shohan), about two families in crisis, the Burnhams and the Fittses, is essentially a verisimilar movie, totally different from the fantastic world of *Sleepy Hollow*. But it is also subtly satirical, and its overall mise-en-scène is central to making us aware of its satirical slant. Director Sam Mendes and production designer Naomi Shohan use many aspects of their design scheme to define characters and comment on various aspects of contemporary American society, including consumerism and corporate culture, violence, puritanical sexual mores, mindless patriotism, self-empowerment jargon, peer pressure, drug use, unemployment, loneliness, and discrimination. These details are integral elements in an overall vision, patiently creating and revealing the characters while establishing the context for their lives and conflicts. *American Beauty* is a movie whose total mise-en-scène makes us laugh and feel terrified at the same time.

The Burnham family includes Lester (Kevin Spacey), an advertising salesman who quits his job in an attempt to free himself from the limits of middle-class life; his wife, Carolyn (Annette Bening), a real estate agent who is a compulsive perfec-

[1]

[2]

Details Within a Shot Help to Create Mood in
American Beauty Lester and Carolyn Burnham's
estrangement is established early in *American Beauty* by
simple shots such as these two images. [1] Lester (Kevin
Spacey), alone in bed and shot from above, is clearly wearied
by his life. [2] Carolyn (Annette Bening), meanwhile, decisively
snips a rose in bloom, and eerily inspects it. Clearly, these
visual elements are important *figuratively* as well as *literally*.

tionist; and Jane (Thora Birch), their teenage
daughter, who coolly regards her parents as "gross."

The movie opens with a moving aerial shot that
establishes the classic suburban scene of tree-lined
streets in an upper-middle-class neighborhood.
Another overhead shot, this one inside Lester and
Carolyn's bedroom, sets the scene of the Burnhams' loveless marriage. We see Lester just before
the alarm clock awakens him, alone in a big bed,
which is flanked by two identical end tables. Next,
we see him masturbating in the shower ("This will
be the high point of my day. It's all downhill from
here"), followed by a shot of a perfect rose growing
outside, and then another of Carolyn cutting the
rose from its stem. Roses are traditionally symbols
of love, but Carolyn's decisive use of the scissors
pointedly underscores her emasculating behavior
toward her husband.

The design creates a recognizable time and
place, but it is also highly symbolic in establishing
and developing the movie's themes. These two
families live in what the movies have often tried
to make us believe is a "typical" neighborhood. In
keeping with this type of film—one that explores
bright domestic surfaces and murky angst-filled
depths and, in so doing, strips away many aspects
of the American Dream—the exterior shots are
bathed in clear, abundant sunlight, making everything look new, bright, and welcoming. The interiors of both houses are frequently dimly lit: at the
Burnhams' house, it's likely by design, but at the
Fittses', it underscores the gloominess of their
family life. Unlike the lighting in *Sleepy Hollow*,
however, this lighting does not call attention to
itself or have much effect on the composition of
scenes.

The Burnhams live in a two-story white house,
surrounded by a white picket fence, with blue shutters and a bright red door. Bright red is used

[1]

[2]

***American Beauty* Uses Color for Symbolic Emphasis**
The color red appears often in *American Beauty*, [1] sometimes
subtly punctuating a shot, as in this image of the Burnhams'
home, and [2] sometimes dominating the frame, as in this
image from one of Lester's many fantasies about Angela.

An Attractive House in *American Beauty* Cannot Conceal the Marital Disharmony Inside The members of the Burnham family are surrounded by a picture-perfect décor that many Americans dream of. This aspect of the mise-en-scène makes the psychological distance between them all the more striking. They have attained the outward appearances of the American Dream, but at what cost? [1] The décor of the Burnhams' dining room reflects Carolyn's pretensions to formality: drapes, curtains, framed pictures, a tablecloth (with place mats to protect it), candles, and each person seated in a specific place at the table. Somewhat oddly, though, the floor is bare (a touch of coldness?). [2] When Lester has been drinking beer and then attempts to make love to Carolyn on the sofa, she worries that he will spill the beer. [3] In the ensuing argument, this element of décor provides a defining moment for them both. Carolyn shrieks, "It's a $4,000 sofa upholstered with Italian silk!" to which Lester responds, "This isn't life—it's just *stuff!*"

prominently throughout the movie: for that red door, Carolyn's red roses, Lester's fantasies of his daughter's friend Angela (Mena Suvari) in a bathtub filled with red rose petals, his red car, and, almost the last thing we see in the film, Lester's blood splattered on the white kitchen wall.

Inside, the house looks "perfect" in the choice and maintenance of its décor. For example, the kitchen, where Carolyn prepares "nutritious but savory meals," is immaculate. Everything has a place, and Carolyn has no doubt placed everything exactly where she wants it. Cooking pans hang over the island work space; a bowl of ripe fruit provides healthy snacks; small appliances are lined up neatly on the counters; dish towels are folded and hung; no dirty dishes linger in the sink; no messages are fastened with magnets to the refrigerator door. Whereas Carolyn thinks it's lovely to listen to Frank Sinatra during dinner, Jane calls it "elevator music," and Lester calls it "Lawrence Welk shit." In fact, Carolyn is so much in control of her environment that, as Lester tells us, "the handle of her gardening shears matches her gardening clogs—and that's no accident!"

The Fittses, who have recently moved in next door, include Colonel Frank Fitts (Chris Cooper), a marine obsessed with guns, discipline, and homophobia; his disturbed, unresponsive wife, Barbara (Allison Janney); and their teenage son, Ricky (Wes Bentley), who is part student, part drug dealer, part poet (he shoots moody videos featuring dead birds and plastic bags in the wind), and, even though his father abuses him terribly, the most stable and happy person in the film. The Fittses' is a more modest house, also immaculately kept, no doubt reflecting Frank's military background. They appear to be less materialistic and have not tried to keep up with the Burnhams—their chairs are covered in plastic, Barbara does not bring home a second income—and they have no pretensions to style. Inside Frank's den, a locked cabinet holds a gun collection and a dinner plate from Hitler's private service. Ricky pretends that he buys his state-of-the-art audio and video equipment with money earned from a job working for a caterer, not from the drugs he sells—a perfect indicator that all is not what it seems in these lives.

[1]

[2]

[3]

Stern, Dark Décor in _American Beauty_ Reflects a Family's Dysfunctional State   Like the Burnhams next door, the Fitts family is plagued by dysfunction. The dark and stern décor of their house reflects the family's state of mind, which is largely dictated by the father, Colonel Frank Fitts. [1] Barbara (Allison Janney), Frank (Chris Cooper), and Ricky (Wes Bentley) Fitts watch a military movie on TV (in all likelihood, Colonel Fitts's choice of entertainment). [2] Jane Burnham (Thora Birch) holds a plate from Colonel Fitts's basement collection of Nazi memorabilia, a chilling reminder of Fitts's brutal repression of his son, Ricky. [3] Barbara sits alone in the dining room, staring blankly ahead, nearly dead to the world.

Clothing also helps us understand these characters. Carolyn Burnham, who is always beautifully coiffed and made up, wears the sort of "power" outfits favored by some professional women, except when she strips down to her slip to clean a house she

[1]

[2]

Clothing Can Reveal a Character's Personality Clothing, makeup, and hairstyle in _American Beauty_ complement our sense of each character's personality. Ricky (Wes Bentley) [1], wearing a white shirt and tie, strikes stylish Angela (Mena Suvari) [2, _left_] as a "weirdo," but Jane (Thora Birch) [2, _right_], whose style is inspired by alternatives to name-brand fashion, sees something in Ricky (maybe the knit hat is a tip-off) that intrigues her.

hopes to sell that day, ironic behavior considering the badly dressed yokels to whom she shows it. By contrast, Barbara Fitts, who never seems to leave the house, sitting at the kitchen and dining room tables in a near-catatonic state, has dark circles under her eyes and wears drab clothing. Once he has quit his job, Lester wears jeans when he is relaxing and next to nothing when he is working out with weights in his garage. His goal is to "look good naked," as he tells the gay couple who live next door. These men, by the way, meet Carolyn Burnham's standards: "I _love_ your tie . . . that _color_," she tells one of them. Both men are successful professionals, yet they particularly upset Colonel Fitts when they present him with a welcome basket and tell him that they are "partners," which, at first, he understands to mean business partners.

Frank Fitts wears white T-shirts and pressed khakis, an outfit as close as he can get to a uniform

[1]

[3]

[2]

[4]

[5]

Different Settings in *American Beauty* Provoke Different Behaviors From Different Characters In *American Beauty*, male and female gazes play a central role in the developing drama. [1] Lester Burnham's (Kevin Spacey) overheated imagination turns Angela's (Mena Suvari) cheerleading performance into a seductive striptease performed only for his benefit. [2] Lester reacts with dumbfounded amazement at Angela's charms. [3] Meanwhile, Lester's daughter, Jane (Thora Birch), has attracted fellow student Ricky Fitts (Wes Bentley), who is shooting footage of her in his bedroom. [4] When Jane gets tired of telling Ricky how much she hates her father, she grabs the video camera and turns her gaze on him as he tells her about his past. [5] The bond between Jane and Ricky is sealed when he shares with her a poignant and poetic film of a simple, random occurrence: a plastic bag floating on a breeze.

without actually wearing one. The serious, confident Ricky—who probably makes more money from dealing drugs than anyone else in the movie—looks decidedly different from his fellow high school students, wearing a white shirt, tie, dark pants, dark sweater, and dark ski cap. Jane looks down-to-earth, like the rest of the students, wearing simple T-shirts, pants, and sweaters. She usually wears a strand of beads, has on a little lipstick, and pulls her hair back in a ponytail. Angela, who has delusions about her attractiveness and potential as a model, appears somewhat more sophisticated than Jane and the

other young women at school, wearing heavy makeup, sporting a shoulder bag, wearing her blond hair long, and smoking cigarettes. She thinks Ricky is a weirdo and asks Jane, "Why does he dress like a Bible salesman?"

American Beauty is an open film, one in which the characters have free will, even though it usually results in behavior that is out of control. The meticulous framing and consistently moving camera are two very important elements in establishing the mise-en-scène. To begin with, the film is shot in widescreen format, meaning that the frame is a rectangle, the perfect shape for revealing the design and furnishings of an entire room. Director Mendes and Conrad Hall—one of Hollywood's greatest cinematographers—invariably place two or more characters in the middle of this format, thereby emphasizing relationships, or use the zoom lens to highlight the characters in the frame. Characters frequently walk in and out of the frame, reminding us of the offscreen space. The framing most frequently adopts an omniscient POV, but this perspective is punctuated by subjective-POV framing that implicates us in voyeuristic moments, such as Lester's first vision of Angela during a cheerleading routine, or the many scenes in which Ricky uses his video camera.

Voyeurism is clearly a theme of *American Beauty*; in fact, it is the source of the bond that forms between Ricky and Jane: their friendship begins when Ricky photographs Jane from his window, first secretly, then openly, and finally with her complete cooperation. At one point, she even uses the camera herself. Ricky is on the left side of the screen, but his image is being fed by the video camera to a monitor on the right side. Thus, we not only have his movies within the larger movie, but both of these movies use screens within screens—wall mirrors in the houses, rearview mirrors in cars, and windows—to reflect what they are shooting.

The acting in *American Beauty* is as notably consistent as the design; all the characters are edgy and strung out, some of them more than others. The only sure thing in these lives, the only "American beauty," is death, and Ricky, who finds beauty in photographing dead birds, smiles knowingly after looking into the dead Lester's eyes. What he sees there, however, is left for us to decide. Perhaps that red door is a warning—that, to paraphrase Dante, we should abandon any hope when entering this particular vision of suburban hell.

Michael Almereyda's *Hamlet*

Hamlet was first filmed in 1900, under the direction of Clément Maurice and with the legendary actress Sarah Bernhardt as the prince. Since then, more than fifty film and video versions have been made of Shakespeare's most famous play. A century later, in the year 2000, Michael Almereyda created an adaptation for the MTV generation and made it speak *to* and *for* them, turning it inside out with

Mirrors and Self-Confrontation in *Hamlet* To depict Shakespeare's theme of self-confrontation, many shots in Michael Almereyda's movie version of *Hamlet* are reflected images of characters, such as this one of Hamlet (Ethan Hawke) studying his face in the mirror.

visual and verbal images that complement and clash with one another. The result is a unique vision both of *Hamlet* and of the United States, and the production designer, Gideon Ponte, makes startling design choices in bringing it to the screen. One key to this film's design scheme comes from Hamlet's (Ethan Hawke) advice to the players—"to hold as 'twere the mirror up to nature, to show virtue her own feature, scorn her own image, and the very age and body of the time his form and pressure."[12] To convey the theme of self-confrontation, interior scenes are reflected on rooms' windows—giving us two images of action at once—and faces are reflected in mirrors, on the glass door of a washing machine, and on security video screens.

Here the focus is on Manhattan, the principal setting, not suburbia. But like Sam Mendes in *American Beauty*, Almereyda directs our attention both to the surface and to what's beneath. The transformations are dazzling. Shakespeare's Danish royal house becomes the Denmark Corporation, with its headquarters in a Times Square skyscraper; the new king, Claudius (Kyle MacLachlan), becomes its president and CEO; his wife, Gertrude (Diane Venora), becomes his business collaborator; Hamlet, scholar-poet-playwright-actor on the page, becomes student-poet-filmmaker-videographer on the screen; the ghost of his dead father appears frequently, not on

[12] William Shakespeare, *The Tragedy of Hamlet*, act 3, scene 2.

[1]

[2]

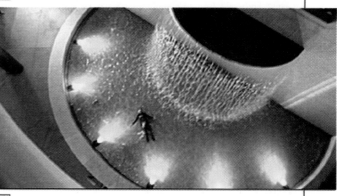

[3]

[4]

Hamlet's Characters and Settings Transformed for Modern Adaptation   Part of the creative excitement of Almereyda's version of _Hamlet_ is its transformations of Shakespeare's characters, positions, and settings from Denmark to Manhattan. [1] The new Claudius (Kyle MacLachlan), the CEO of the Denmark Corporation, is giving a press conference at his New York headquarters. [2] The ghost of the former Claudius (Sam Shepard) is seen haunting the terrace of a Manhattan apartment building. [3] Ophelia (Julia Stiles) commits suicide, not in a country river, but in the lobby pool of a skyscraper. [4] Hamlet (Ethan Hawke) kills Claudius not with Shakespeare's poisoned blade, but with a pistol.

foggy battlements like a figment of the imagination but right in front of Hamlet, on terraces, in rooms, on security camera images. While delivering part of the "Rogue and peasant slave" speech, Hamlet uses his portable DVD unit to watch James Dean (a moody, Hamlet-like actor) in Nicholas Ray's _Rebel Without a Cause_ (1955), as well as the late, legendary actor John Gielgud playing Hamlet. The play within the play, of course, has become a film within the film. Ophelia (Julia Stiles) remains a bewildered and dreamy young woman, but she's also a hip photographer living in a SoHo loft. In the end, Laertes (Liev Schreiber) and Hamlet are not killed by foils; instead, Laertes uses a gun (without which this could not be an "action" film) to kill Hamlet and then himself. And instead of killing Claudius with a poisoned rapier, the mortally wounded Hamlet takes Laertes's gun and shoots him. We are introduced to many of these aspects in the opening sequence.

In this world and in this _Hamlet_, technology abounds. Hamlet's apartment contains an array of electronic equipment, including portable video cameras, editing machines, and DVD players. Hamlet relies on computers as well, cunningly using the cut-and-paste function of his word processor to alter Claudius's secret order to kill him by substituting the names of Rosencrantz and Guildenstern for his own. Even the final fencing match is conducted with the aid of computerized sensors that register each "hit." Elsewhere, important messages

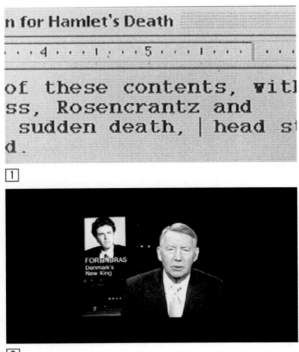

[1]

[1]

[2]

[2]

Modernized *Hamlet* Emphasizes Characters' Dependence on Technology   Technology, a key component of contemporary New York life, figures extensively in Almereyda's movie version of *Hamlet*. [1] Instead of altering a death warrant by hand, as he does in Shakespeare's play, Hamlet uses his word processor to substitute the names of Rosencrantz and Guildenstern for his own. [2] An epilogue added to the movie was transferred from the Player King's speech (in the *Mousetrap* scene) of the play, and transformed into a television newscast, spoken by real-life TV news anchor Robert MacNeil.

***Hamlet*'s Characters Obsessed With Visual as Well as Verbal Imagery**   Cameras of many kinds figure prominently in *Hamlet*. Hamlet himself [1] is obsessed with his video camera, and Ophelia [2] with her Polaroid camera.

emanate from fax machines; a video screen provides entertainment to limousine passengers; and another screen serves as a TelePrompTer for the anchorman (played by real-life TV news anchor Robert MacNeil) who delivers an "epilogue" that, in Shakespeare's text, is actually spoken by the Player King before the performance of *The Mousetrap*:

> Our wills and fates do so contrary run
> That our devices still are overthrown,
> Our thoughts are ours,
>   their ends none of our own.[18]

[18] Shakespeare, *Hamlet*, act 3, scene 2.

(As in life outside the movies, the anchorman has the last word on the day's events.)

The *camera* may be the single most important object in the film, for cameras are everywhere. Video security cameras reveal moments of great importance, including the Ghost's first appearance and Ophelia's body floating in a reflecting pool. Media representatives interview and photograph Claudius and Gertrude as if they were rock stars. Hamlet's cameras and other devices are his constant companions. In her mad scene, filmed at the Guggenheim Museum, Ophelia discards Polaroid pictures of pansies, fennel, columbine, rosemary, violets, and rue, the flowers mentioned in Shakespeare's text.

Costumes, makeup, and décor further develop milieu, story, and character. Hamlet wears black or pin-striped suits with T-shirts and a knitted hat from Peru. He has an incipient mustache and beard; wears tinted, wraparound sunglasses; and carries a shoulder bag. Ophelia wears stylish outfits and clumsy shoes. Gertrude is usually dressed in stylish black, including a black leather pantsuit that she wears to bid farewell to Hamlet and a large black feather hat at Ophelia's funeral. Claudius and his henchmen are also in black. Polonius (played here by Bill Murray as a tedious fool) is unkempt and unstylish. The Ghost (Sam Shepard) wears a tweed jacket. People smoke, drink Carlsberg beer from Denmark, and, as good Americans, chew gum.

Almereyda further refashions the play by cutting major speeches, restructuring the plot, and transforming Shakespeare's verbal images into visual ones. For example, here Hamlet delivers the "To be or not to be" soliloquy both directly and through interior monologue as he strolls through aisles of action videos at a Blockbuster store. Filled with indecision, he does not select a film, for what film could equal the revenge he contemplates? He also reveals his conflicted state of mind through the images he makes and keeps in his video diary. In this way, Almereyda's radical vision of *Hamlet* relies

Hamlet's "To be or not to be . . ." Photographed in a Video Store   Shakespeare's most famous soliloquy has been envisioned by theater and movie directors in countless different ways. In this version, Michael Almereyda thought it appropriate to his contemporary setting of the play to have Hamlet thinking about whether or not to act while he walks through the aisles of a video store.

on his design strategies. In fact, the visual images compete with the words, sometimes replacing them, a technique that provides a tacit criticism of contemporary media- and image-saturated American society. Thus Shakespeare's play proves both its timelessness and its timeliness.

→ Analyzing Mise-en-Scène

This chapter has introduced the major elements that together form any film's mise-en-scène. You should now understand that the term *mise-en-scène* denotes all of those elements taken together—the overall look and feel of the film—and that mise-en-scène plays a crucially important role in shaping the *mood* of the film. Using what you have learned in this chapter, you should be able to characterize the mise-en-scène of any movie (or any shot) in precise terms, referring to the framing, composition in depth, the lighting, the setting, the design and use of objects, and the placement and appearance of characters.

Screening Checklist: Mise-en-Scène

➤ As you watch the film or clip, be alert to the overall design plan and *mise-en-scène* and to your emotional response to them. Are you comforted or made anxious by them? Are your senses overwhelmed or calmed by what you see onscreen?

➤ Identify the elements of the mise-en-scène that seem to be contributing the most to your emotional response.

➤ Does the design in the movie or clip create the correct times, spaces, and moods? Does it go beyond surfaces and relate to developing themes?

➤ Be alert to the framing of individual shots, and make note of the composition within the frame. Where are *figures* placed? What is the relationship among the figures in the foreground, middle ground, and background?

➤ Is the framing of this film or clip *open*, or is it *closed*? How can you tell? What is the effect of this framing on your understanding of the narrative and characters?

➤ Does the use of light in the movie or clip call attention to itself? If so, describe the effect that it has on the composition in any shot you analyze.

➤ Does the film or clip employ lots of movement? Very little movement? Describe how the use of movement in the film or clip complements or detracts from the development of the narrative.

➤ Note the type of movement (movement of figures within the frame or movement of the frame itself) in important shots, and describe as accurately as possible the effect that that movement has on the relationships among the figures in the frame.

➤ Does the movie's design have a unified feel? Do the various elements of the design (the sets, props, costumes, makeup, hairstyles, etc.) work together, or do some elements work against others? What is the effect either way?

➤ Was achieving *verisimilitude* important to the design of this film or clip? If so, have the filmmakers succeeded in making the overall mise-en-scène feel *real*, or *verisimilar*? If verisimilitude doesn't seem to be important in this film or clip, what do you suspect the filmmakers were attempting to accomplish with their design?

➤ How does the design and mise-en-scène in this movie or clip relate to the narrative? Is it appropriate for the story being told? Does it quietly reinforce the narrative and development of characters? Does it partly *determine* the development of narrative and characters? Does it render the narrative secondary or even overwhelm it?

Questions for Review

1. What is the literal meaning of the phrase *mise-en-scène*? What do we mean by this phrase more generally when we discuss movies?
2. What are the two major visual components of mise-en-scène?
3. Does a movie's mise-en-scène happen by accident? If not, what or who determines it?
4. What are the principal responsibilities of the production designer?
5. Name and briefly discuss the major elements of cinematic design.
6. What is composition? What are the two major elements of composition?
7. What is the difference between the *static frame* and the *moving frame*?
8. Why do most shots in a film rely on both *onscreen* and *offscreen spaces*?
9. What are the essential differences between the *open frame* and the *closed frame*?
10. What are the two basic types of movement that we see onscreen?

DVD FEATURES: CHAPTER 3

The following tutorials on the DVD provide more information on mise-en-scène:

- Lighting and Familiar Image
- Setting and Expressionism
- Composing the Frame

Movies Described or Illustrated in This Chapter

American Beauty (1999). Sam Mendes, director.
The Best Years of Our Lives (1946). William Wyler, director.
Buck Rogers in the 25th Century (1979). Daniel Haller, director.
The Cabinet of Dr. Caligari (1920). Robert Wiene, director.
Cabiria (1914). Giovanni Pastrone, director.
Cast Away (2000). Robert Zemeckis, director.
Chinatown (1974). Roman Polanski, director.
Citizen Kane (1941). Orson Welles, director.
City of God (2002). Fernando Meirelles and Kátia Lund, directors.
The Decalogue (1988). Krzysztof Kieslowski, director.
Elephant (2003). Gus Van Sant, director.
Far From Heaven (2002). Todd Haynes, director.
Gone With the Wind (1939). Victor Fleming, director.
Gosford Park (2001). Robert Altman, director.
Hamlet (2000). Michael Almereyda, director.
Hero (2002). Yimou Zhang, director.
I Vitelloni (1953). Federico Fellini, director.
Intolerance (1916). D. W. Griffith, director.
Junebug (2005). Phil Morrison, director.
The Last Laugh (1924). F. W. Murnau, director.
Late Spring (1949). Yasujiro Ozu, director.
The Leopard (1963). Luchino Visconti, director.
Marie Antoinette (1938). W. S. Van Dyke, director.
Master and Commander: The Far Side of the World (2003). Peter Weir, director.
Metropolis (1927). Fritz Lang, director.
Moulin Rouge! (2001). Baz Luhrmann, director.
The Night of the Hunter (1955). Charles Laughton, director.
North by Northwest (1959). Alfred Hitchcock, director.
The Portrait of a Lady (1996). Jane Campion, director.
Return of the Jedi (1983). Richard Marquand, director.
Road to Perdition (2002). Sam Mendes, director.
The Shining (1980). Stanley Kubrick, director.
Sleepy Hollow (1999). Tim Burton, director.
Stagecoach (1939). John Ford, director.
Star Trek III: The Search for Spock (1984). Leonard Nimoy, director.
The Third Man (1949). Carol Reed, director.

Cinematography

The Last Emperor (1987). Bernardo Bertolucci, director; Vittorio Storaro, cinematographer.

What Is Cinematography?

Cinematography is the process of capturing moving images on film or some other medium. The word comes to us from three Greek roots—*kinesis*, meaning "movement"; *photo*, meaning "light"; and *graphia*, meaning "writing"—but the word was coined only after motion pictures themselves were invented. Cinematography is closely related to still photography, but its methods and technologies clearly distinguish it from its static predecessor. This chapter introduces the major features of this unique craft.

Although cinematography might seem to exist solely to please our eyes with beautiful images, it is in fact an intricate language that can (and in the most complex and meaningful films *does*) contribute to a movie's overall meaning as much as the story, mise-en-scène, and acting do. The cine-matographer (also known as the *director of photography*, or *DP*) uses the camera as a maker of meaning, just as the painter uses the brush or the writer uses the pen: the angles, heights, and movements of the camera function both as a set of techniques and as expressive material, the cinematic equivalent of brush strokes or of nouns, verbs, and adjectives. Thus, to make an informed analysis and evaluation of a movie, we need to consider whether the cinematographer, in collaboration with the other filmmakers on the project, has successfully harnessed the powers of this visual language to help tell the story and convey the meaning(s) of the movie. As director Satyajit Ray puts it, "There is no such thing as good photography *per se*. It is either right for a certain kind of film, and therefore good; or wrong—however lush, well-composed, meticulous—and therefore bad."[1]

The Director of Photography

Every aspect of a movie's preproduction—writing the script, casting the talent, imagining the look of the finished work, designing and creating the sets and costumes, and determining what will be placed in front of the camera and in what arrangement and manner—leads to the most vital step: representing the mise-en-scène on film or video. Although what we see on the screen reflects the vision and design of the filmmakers as a team, the director of photography is the primary person responsible for transforming the other aspects of moviemaking into moving images.

Freddie Young, who won Best Cinematography Oscars for three David Lean movies—*Lawrence of Arabia* (1962), *Doctor Zhivago* (1965), and *Ryan's Daughter* (1970)—defines the DP's job within the overall process of film production:

> [The cinematographer] stands at the natural confluence of the two main streams of activity in the production of a film—where the imagination meets the reality of the film process.

[1] Satyajit Ray, *Our Films, Their Films* (1976; reprint, New York: Hyperion, 1994), 68.

Imagination is represented by the director, who in turn is heir to the ideas of the scriptwriter, as he is to those of the original author of the story. Three minds, and three contributing sources of imagination have shaped the film before the cameraman can begin to visualize it as a physical entity.[2]

In the ideal version of this working relationship, the director's vision shapes the process of rendering the mise-en-scène on film, but the cinematographer makes very specific decisions about how the movie will be photographed.

When the collaboration between the director and the cinematographer has been a good one, the images that we see onscreen correspond closely to what the director expects the DP to capture on film. As cinematographer John Alton explains,

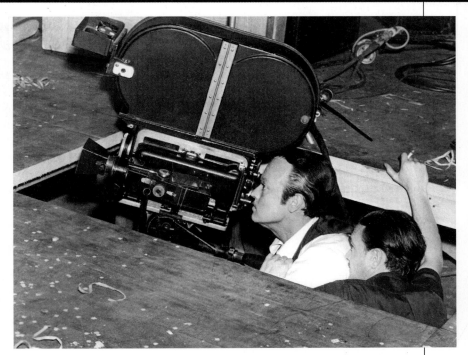

Setting Up a Shot   On the set of *Citizen Kane*, cinematographer Gregg Toland (*bottom left*) and director Orson Welles (*bottom right*) set up a shot. When Welles was preparing to shoot the movie—his first—Toland was one of the world's most famous cinematographers. Yet Toland approached Welles and offered to shoot it, saying, "I want to work with somebody who never made a movie. That's the only way to learn anything—from somebody who doesn't know anything."

> The screen offers the advantage of an ability (although we do not always utilize it) to photograph the story from the position from which the director thinks the audience would like to see it. The success of any particular film depends a great deal upon the ability of the director to anticipate the desires of the audience in this respect . . .
>
> . . . the director of photography visualizes the picture purely from a photographic point of view, as determined by lights and the moods of individual sequences and scenes. In other words, how to use angles, set-ups, lights, and camera as means to tell the story.[3]

As cinematographers translate visions into realities, however, they follow not inflexible rules but, rather, conventions, which are open to interpretation by the artists entrusted with them. "You will accomplish much more," advises Gregg Toland—

the cinematographer famous for such classics as John Ford's *The Grapes of Wrath* (1940) and William Wyler's *The Best Years of Our Lives* (1946), as well as Orson Welles's *Citizen Kane* (1941)—"by fitting your photography to the story instead of limiting the story to the narrow confines of conventional photographic practice. And as you do so you'll learn that the movie camera is a flexible instrument, with many of its possibilities still unexplored."[4]

The three key terms used in shooting a movie are *shot*, *take*, and *setup*. A **shot** is one uninterrupted run of the camera. It can be as short or as

[2] Freddie Young and Paul Petzold, *The Work of the Motion Picture Cameraman* (New York: Hastings House, 1972), 23.

[3] John Alton, *Painting With Light* (Berkeley: University of California Press, 1995), 33.

[4] Gregg Toland, "How I Broke the Rules in *Citizen Kane*," in *Focus on Citizen Kane*, ed. Ronald Gottesman (Englewood Cliffs, N.J.: Prentice-Hall, 1971), 77.

long as necessary, with the obvious condition that it not exceed the time limitations of the medium on which the moving images are being recorded. The term **takes** refers to the number of times a particular shot is taken. A **setup** is one camera position and everything associated with it. Whereas the shot is the basic building block of the film, the setup is the basic component of the film's production process, and the component on which the director and the cinematographer spend the most time collaborating.

The cinematographer's responsibilities for each shot and setup (as well as for each take) fall into four broad categories:

1. Cinematographic properties of the shot (film stock, lighting, lenses)
2. Framing of the shot (proximity to the camera, depth, camera angle and height, scale, camera movement)
3. Speed and length of the shot
4. Special effects

Although these categories necessarily overlap, we will look at each one separately. In the process, we will also examine the tools and equipment involved and what they enable the cinematographer to do.

In carrying out these responsibilities, the DP relies on the assistance of the **camera crew**, which is divided into one group of technicians concerned with the camera, and another concerned with electricity and lighting. The camera group consists of the **camera operator**, who does the actual shooting, and the **assistant camerapersons** (ACs). The **first AC** oversees everything having to do with the camera, lenses, supporting equipment, and the material on which the movie is being shot. The **second AC** prepares the **slate** that is used to identify each scene as it is shot; files camera reports; and, when film stock is being used, feeds that stock into magazines that are then loaded onto the camera. The group concerned with electricity and lighting consists of the **gaffer** (chief electrician), **best boy** (first assistant electrician), other electricians, and **grips** (all-around handypeople who work with both the camera crew and the electrical crew to get the camera and lighting ready for shooting).

Cinematographic Properties of the Shot

The director of photography controls the cinematographic properties of the shot, those basics of motion picture photography that make the movie image appear the way it does. These properties include the *film stock*, *lighting*, and *lenses*. By employing variations of each property, the cinematographer modifies not only the camera's basic neutrality, but also the look of the finished image that the audience sees.

Film Stock

The cinematographer is responsible for choosing a recording medium for the movie that has the best chance of producing images corresponding to the director's vision. Among the alternatives available are film stocks of various sizes and speeds, videotape, and direct-to-digital media. A skilled cinematographer must know the technical properties and cinematic possibilities of each option, and must be able to choose the medium that is best suited to the project as a whole.

Even though more movies are being shot on digital media with each passing year, the majority of feature films are still shot on traditional **film stock**. The two basic types of film stock—one to record images in black and white, the other to record them in color—are completely different and have their own technical properties and cinematic possibilities. Film stock is available in several standard **gauges** (widths measured in millimeters): 8mm, Super 8mm, 16mm, 35mm, 65mm, 70mm, as well as special-use formats, such as IMAX, which is ten times bigger than a 35mm frame. Before the advent of camcorders, 8mm and Super 8mm were popular gauges for amateurs (for home movies). Many television or student movies, as well as low-budget productions, are shot on 16mm. Most professional film productions use either 16mm or 35mm. Generally, the wider the gauge, the more expensive the film and, all other factors being equal, the better the quality of the image.

Another variable aspect of film stock is its **speed** (or *exposure index*)—the degree to which it is light-

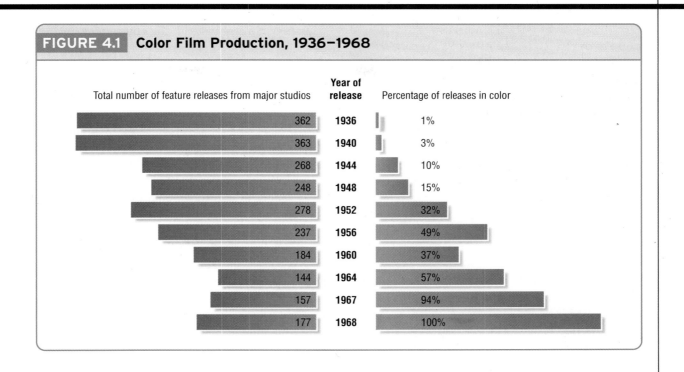

FIGURE 4.1 Color Film Production, 1936–1968

Total number of feature releases from major studios	Year of release	Percentage of releases in color
362	1936	1%
363	1940	3%
268	1944	10%
248	1948	15%
278	1952	32%
237	1956	49%
184	1960	37%
144	1964	57%
157	1967	94%
177	1968	100%

sensitive. Film stocks that are extremely sensitive to light, and thus are useful in low-light situations, are called *fast*; those that require a lot of light are called *slow*. There are uses for both slow and fast film stock, depending on the shooting environment and the desired visual outcome.

Which stock is right for a particular film depends on the story being told. With only a few outstanding exceptions, however, virtually all movies are now shot in color, for that is what the public is accustomed to and therefore expects. As Fig. 4.1 shows, when Hollywood began to use color film stock, only 1 percent of the feature releases from major studios in 1936 were in color; the growth of color production slowed during World War II because all film stock, especially color, was in short supply; but by 1968 virtually all feature releases were in color.

Although color can heighten the surface realism (if not the verisimilitude) and the spectacle of many stories, it is not suitable for all films. For example, films in the expressionist or film noir styles are deliberately conceived to be shot in black and white; it's almost impossible to imagine anyone having shot F. W. Murnau's *Nosferatu*

(1922), John Ford's *The Informer* (1935), or Fritz Lang's *The Big Heat* (1953) in color. During the 1970s and '80s, certain television executives tried to "improve" the "old" movies they were showing on television with the process of **colorization**: using digital technology, they "painted" colors on movies meant by the original filmmakers to be seen in black and white. The unimpressive results were limited by the state of computer graphics at the time, but even though computer technology has improved since then, the practice has abated. Many viewers, even those who grew up with color movies, could see that colorization was not an improvement for movies that had been shot in black and white. Film artists breathed a sigh of relief once it became clear that colorization was a failed experiment.

Although today the default choice for feature film production is color, the period from 1940 to 1970 was a time during which the choice between color and black and white needed to be carefully considered, and many films shot in color during that period might have been even stronger if they had been shot instead in black and white. John Ford's *The Searchers* (1956; cinematographer:

[1]

[2]

Black and White Versus Color *Stagecoach* [1], made in 1939, was the first film that John Ford shot in Arizona's Monument Valley. Bert Glennon's black-and-white cinematography in *Stagecoach* provided a portrayal of the Old West that was different from Winton C. Hoch's depiction using color cinematography in *The Searchers* (1956) [2], one of the last films that Ford shot in Monument Valley. Although the expressive photography was state-of-the-art in both films, the use of black and white and of color was not a matter of aesthetics but was dictated by industry standards.

Winton C. Hoch), a psychological western that is concerned less with the traditional western's struggle between good and evil than with the lead character's struggle against personal demons, might have been an even more powerful film had it been shot in black and white instead of color. Doing so might have produced a visual mood, as in film noir, that complemented the darkness at the heart of the

movie's narrative. Instead, the choice of color film stock for *The Searchers* seems to have been inspired by industry trends at the time—designed to improve flagging box-office receipts—rather than by strictly artistic criteria.

Ironically, audiences who had grown to love Ford's black-and-white movies set in Monument Valley reacted badly to his first color feature set there: *She Wore a Yellow Ribbon* (1949; cinematographer: Winton C. Hoch). The vibrant colors they were seeing in this movie and in *The Searchers*— the reds and browns of the earth, the constantly changing blues of the sky—accurately captured the appearance of Monument Valley in real life, but for viewers whose expectations were shaped by Ford's earlier movies, such as *Stagecoach* (1939), Monument Valley existed only in black and white. In color, *The Searchers* is magnificent; we can only guess at what it might have been in black and white.

Black and White   Black-and-white movies are not pictures that lack color, for black and white (and the range in between) *are* colors. Black-and-white film stock offers compositional possibilities and cinematographic effects that are impossible with color film stock, yet today—apart from some very prominent exceptions—it is used almost exclusively for nonprofessional productions. Because of its use in documentary films (before the 1960s) and in newspaper and magazine photographs (before the advent of color newspaper and magazine printing), we have, ironically, come to associate black-and-white photography and cinematography with a stronger sense of gritty realism than that provided by color film stock. But the distinct contrasts and hard edges of black-and-white cinematography can express an abstract world (that is, a world from which color has been abstracted or removed) perfectly suited for the kind of morality tales told in westerns, film noirs, and gangster films. In fact, although many excellent color films have been made in these same genres—such as Roman Polanski's neo-noir *Chinatown* (1974; cinematographer: John A. Alonzo) or Quentin Tarantino's gangster film *Pulp Fiction* (1994; cinematographer: Andrzej Sekula)—we gen-

Tonal Range This shot from Fred Zinnemann's *High Noon* (1952; cinematographer: Floyd Crosby) illustrates the tonal range possible in black-and-white cinematography: from absolute white (in the shirt), through a series of grays, to absolute black (in the bottom of the hat's brim). For the purposes of explanation, this illustration includes only six tones out of the complete range. Note that, although he is the movie's protagonist, Marshal Will Kane (Gary Cooper) wears a black hat—typically, in less sophisticated morality tales, the symbolic mark of the bad guy.

Black-and-White Tonality The opening scene of Alexander Mackendrick's *The Sweet Smell of Success* (1957) takes place near midnight in Times Square, which is alive with activity. The thousands of incandescent and neon lights create a brash black-and-white environment in which the space lacks both depth and shadows. The people packed on the streets are members of a crowd, not individuals. In other movies, such bold blacks and whites might suggest the contrast of good and evil, but the lighting here gives no clue as to which is which.

erally view their distinctive black-and-white predecessors as the templates for the genres.

Tonality—the system of tones—is the distinguishing quality of black-and-white film stock. This system includes the complete range of tones from black to white. Anything on the set—furniture, furnishings, costumes, and makeup—registers in these tones. Even when a film is shot in black and white, it is customary to design its settings and costumes in color. Black-and-white cinematography achieves its distinctive look through such manipulation of the colors being photographed, as well as through the lighting of them. During the height of the classical Hollywood studio system, set and costume designers worked in close collaboration with directors of photography to ensure that the colors used in their designs produced the optimal varieties of tones in black and white. Their goal was to ensure a balance of "warm" and "cold" tones to avoid a muddy blending of similar tones. Sometimes the colors chosen for optimal tonality on film were unattractive, even garish, on the set. Audiences were none the wiser, however, because they saw only the pleasing tonal contrasts in the final black-and-white movie.

Manipulation of tonal range makes black-and-white movies visually interesting, but that isn't all it does. For good or ill, tonality in black-and-white films often carries with it certain preconceived interpretations (e.g., black = evil, white = good). As simplistic, misleading, and potentially offensive as these interpretations may be, they reflect widespread cultural traditions that have been in effect for thousands of years. The earliest narrative films, which greatly appealed to immigrant audiences (most of whom could neither read nor speak English), often relied on such rough distinctions to establish the moral frameworks of their stories. Later, even though both audiences and cinematography became more sophisticated, these distinctions held together the narratives of countless films in diverse genres.

After tonality, the next thing we notice about black-and-white films is their use of, and emphasis on, *texture* and *spatial depth* within their images. The cinematographer can change the texture of an image by manipulating shadows and can control the depth of the image by manipulating lighting and lenses. The best-loved black-and-white movies employ such visual effects to underscore and enhance their stories. Looking at the work of cinematographer James Wong Howe on Alexander Mackendrick's *The Sweet Smell of Success* (1957), for example, we are immediately struck by how his deft manipulation of tone, texture, and spatial depth have captured the sleazy allure of New York City's once notorious Times Square, and how the look of this movie is absolutely essential to its story of urban menace, corruption, and decay.

Color

Although almost all movies today are shot in color, for nearly sixty years of cinema history color was an option that required much more labor, money, and artistic concession than black and white did. Color movies made prior to 1960 were typically elaborate productions, and the decisions to use color were made with the expectation from producers that the movies would justify the expense with impressive box-office returns. To gain a better understanding of the period prior to 1968, when color was not necessarily the default choice, let's take a moment to review briefly the history of color film technology.

Full-scale color film production arrived only in the 1930s, but it was possible to create color images from the movies' beginning. The earliest method was to *hand-paint* each frame—a process so tedious that at first only selected frames were colored. Because silent film had sixteen frames per second, hand-tinting even a ten-minute film meant painting each of 9,600 frames separately. Edwin S. Porter's *The Great Train Robbery* (1903), the best-known and most commercially successful American film of the pre–D. W. Griffith era, includes hand-painted frames, as do some of Georges Méliès's films, made in France around the same time.

Tinting, one of two other early methods for creating color images, involved dyeing the base of the film so that the light areas appeared in color; this technique provided shots or scenes in which a single color set the time of day, distinguished exterior from interior shots, created an emotional mood, or otherwise affected the viewer's perception. D. W. Griffith used this technique very effectively in such films as *Broken Blossoms* (1919; cinematographer: G. W. Bitzer), as did Robert Wiene in *The Cabinet of Dr. Caligari* (1920; cinematographer: Willy Hameister). *Toning*, the other process, offered greater aesthetic and emotional control over the image; it used chemicals that converted the image from black and white to color.

As imaginative as hand-painting, tinting, and toning are, they do not begin to accurately reproduce the range of colors that exists in nature. The Technicolor *additive* two-color process, developed in 1915, could reproduce a specific color by adding and mixing combinations of the three primary colors (red, yellow, and blue) in their required proportions. This process was used for color sequences in such films as Cecil B. DeMille's *The Ten Commandments* (1923; cinematographers: Bert Glennon, J. Peverell Marley, Archie Stout, and Fred Westerberg) and Erich von Stroheim's *The Merry Widow* (1925; cinematographer: Oliver T. Marsh), as well as in such complete features as Irvin Willat's *Wanderer of the Wasteland* (1924; cinematographer: Arthur Ball) and Albert Parker's *The Black Pirate* (1926; cinematographer: Henry Sharp).

By the early 1930s, the additive process had given way to the three-color *subtractive* process (introduced by Technicolor in 1932), which works by simultaneously shooting three separate black-and-white negatives through three light filters, each representing a primary color. These three *color separation* negatives are then superimposed and printed as a positive in natural color. The term *subtractive* is used because the final color results from the removal of certain color components from each of the three emulsion layers. The first films to be made with the subtractive process were Walt Disney's short "Silly Symphony" cartoons *Flowers and Trees* (1932) and *The Three Little Pigs* (1933)—both directed by Burt Gillett—and Pioneer Pictures' live-action film *La Cucaracha* (1934; director: Lloyd Corrigan). The first feature-length film made in the three-color subtrac-

Gone With the Wind and Color Filmmaking Victor Fleming's *Gone With the Wind* (1939) marked a turning point in Hollywood film production, ushering in an era of serious filmmaking in color. Its vibrant and nostalgic images of the antebellum South delighted audiences and earned it a special commendation at the 1939 Academy Awards for "outstanding achievement in the use of color for the enhancement of dramatic mood."

tive process was Rouben Mamoulian's *Becky Sharp* (1935; cinematographer: Ray Rennahan).

Making a Technicolor movie was complicated and cumbersome and cost almost 30 percent more than comparable black-and-white productions. The Technicolor camera, specially adapted to shoot three strips of film at one time, required a great deal of light. Its size and weight restricted its movements and potential use in exterior locations. Furthermore, the studios were obliged by contract to employ Technicolor's own makeup, which resisted melting under lights hotter than those used for shooting black-and-white films, and to process the film in Technicolor's labs, initially the only place that knew how to do this work.

For all these reasons, in addition to a decline in film attendance caused by the Great Depression, producers were at first reluctant to shoot in color. By 1937, however, color had entered mainstream Hollywood production; by 1939, it had proved itself much more than a gimmick in movies such as Victor Fleming's *Gone With the Wind* (cinematographer: Ernest Haller) and *The Wizard of Oz* (cine-

matographer: Harold Rosson), and John Ford's *Drums Along the Mohawk* (cinematographers: Bert Glennon and Ray Rennahan), all released that year.

In 1941, Technicolor introduced its Monopack, a multilayered film stock that could be used in a conventional camera. Because the bulky three-strip camera was no longer necessary, Technicolor filming could now be done outdoors. Eventually, Kodak's rival Eastman Color system—a one-strip film stock that required less light, could be used in any standard camera, and could be processed at lower cost—replaced Technicolor. This single-strip process, developed by Kodak and used also by Fuji and Agfa, remains the standard color film stock in use today. But just as Hollywood took several years to convert from silent film to sound, so, too, the movie industry did not immediately replace black-and-white film with color. During the 1950s, Hollywood used color film strategically, like the widescreen ratio, to lure people away from their television sets and back into theaters.

Now that color film dominates, a new naturalism has become the cinematographic norm, where what we see on the screen looks very much like what we would see in real life. By itself, however, color film stock doesn't necessarily produce a naturalistic image. Film artists and technicians can manipulate the colors in a film as completely as they can any other formal element. Ultimately, just like its black-and-white counterpart, color film can capture realistic, surrealistic, imaginary, or expressionistic images.

Much of Stanley Kubrick's *Barry Lyndon* (1975; cinematographer: John Alcott), for example, employs a color palette that reflects its temporal setting very well; it's the world of soft pastels and gentle shadows depicted in the paintings of such eighteenth- and nineteenth-century artists as Thomas Gainsborough, William Hogarth, and Adolph von Menzel. However, this palette wasn't achieved merely by pointing the camera in a certain direction and accurately recording the colors found there. Instead, the filmmakers specifically manipulated the images through careful planning and art direction, as well as technical know-how, to render the naturally occurring colors in more subtle and "painterly" shades.

Evocative Use of Color   Because we experience the world in color, color films may strike us as more realistic than black-and-white films. Many color films, however, use their palettes not just expressively, but also evocatively. For Stanley Kubrick's *Barry Lyndon* (1975), cinematographer John Alcott has helped convey both a historical period and a painterly world of soft pastels, gentle shading, and misty textures.

Exaggerated Color   Federico Fellini's *Juliet of the Spirits* (1965; cinematographer: Gianni Di Venanzo) tells the story of a mousy wife, Giulietta Boldrini (Giulietta Masina), who, as a result of her husband's affair with another woman, increasingly lives in a world of her dreams, memories, and bogus spiritual quests—a martyr to her undying love for him. In a flashback to her past, she remembers her convent school and a religious pageant in which, as a child, she played the role of a martyred saint. Her exaggerated memory recalls a stylish production that is hardly what we would expect from such a school. In this scene, in which she is burned to death on a flaming grate, the soldiers are dressed in costumes of pale beige, green, and lilac, but the "flames" that consume her are a surreal orange-red, emphasizing her pain and suffering.

In a different vein, the interplay of fantasy and reality is brilliantly and vibrantly conveyed in Federico Fellini's first color film, *Juliet of the Spirits* (1965; cinematographer: Gianni Di Venanzo), through the use of a rich, varied, and sometimes surreal palette. To underscore the movie's theme, Fellini and Di Venanzo often interrupt seemingly naturalistic scenes with bursts of intense and dreamlike color. The effect is disorienting but magical, much like dreams themselves.

Lighting

⊙DVD Seeing the Lighting

During preproduction, most designers include an idea of the lighting in their sketches, but in actual production, the cinematographer determines the lighting once the camera setups are chosen. Ideally, the lighting shapes the way the movie looks and helps tell the story. As a key component of composition, lighting creates our sense of cinematic space by illuminating people and things, creating highlights and shadows, and defining shapes and textures. Among its properties are its *source*, *quality*, *direction*, and *style*.

Source   The two sources of light are *natural* and *artificial*. Daylight is the most convenient and economical source, and in fact the movie industry made Hollywood the center of American movie production in part because of its almost constant sunshine. Even when movies are shot outdoors on clear, sunny days, however, filmmakers use reflectors and artificial lights because they cannot count on nature's cooperation. And even if nature does provide the right amount of natural light at the right time, that light may need to be controlled in various ways, as the accompanying photograph of *reflector boards* being used in the filming of John Ford's *My Darling Clementine* (1946) shows.

Artificial lights are called *instruments* to distinguish them from the light they produce. Among the many kinds of these instruments, the two most basic are **focusable spotlights** and **floodlights**, which produce, respectively, *hard* (mirrorlike) and *soft* (diffuse) light. A focusable spotlight can pro-

Reflector Boards Many scenes of John Ford's *My Darling Clementine* (1946) were shot in the sunny, desert terrain of Monument Valley in Arizona and Utah, but, as this photo shows, a large bank of reflector boards was used when the sunshine was insufficient or when the director wanted to control the lighting.

Softening Shadows Outdoor shots in direct sunlight pose a risk of casting harsh shadows on actors' faces. This shot from James Cameron's *Titanic* (1997) shows the effect of using a reflector board to soften shadows and to cast diffuse light on the bottom of the chin and the nose and under the brow, thus giving Leonardo DiCaprio's face a softer, warmer look onscreen.

Suggestive Use of Lighting In Billy Wilder's comedy *Some Like It Hot* (1959), the beam from a spotlight suggestively doubles as a virtual neckline for Marilyn Monroe during her famous performance of "I Wanna Be Loved by You." As he often did during his long career as a screenwriter and director, Wilder was playfully testing the boundaries of Hollywood moviemaking—seeing what he could get away with.

duce either a hard, direct spotlight beam or a more indirect beam. When it is equipped with black metal doors (known as *barn doors*), it can be used to cut and shape the light in a variety of ways. In either case, it produces distinct shadows. Floodlights produce diffuse, indirect light with very few to no shadows. The most effective floodlight for filmmaking is the *softlight*, which creates a very soft, diffuse, almost shadowless light.

Another piece of lighting equipment, the **reflector board**, is not really a lighting instrument, because it does not rely on bulbs to produce illumination. Essentially, it is a double-sided board that pivots in a *U*-shaped holder. One side is a hard, smooth surface that reflects hard light; the other is a soft, textured surface that provides a softer fill light. Reflector boards come in many sizes and are used frequently, both in interior and especially in exterior shooting; most often they are used to reflect sunlight into shadows during outdoor shooting.

Quality The *quality* of light on a character or situation is a very important element in helping a movie tell its story. Quality refers to whether the light is hard (shining directly on the subject, creating crisp details and a defined border and high contrast between illumination and shadow) or soft (diffused so that light hits the subject from many slightly varying directions, softening details, blurring the line between illumination and shadow, and thus decreasing contrast). We can generally (but not always) associate hard, high-contrast lighting featuring deep shadows (known as *low-key lighting*) with serious or tragic stories; and soft, even lighting (*high-key lighting*) with romantic or comic stories.

Lighting and Setting   A good way to understand the importance of how lighting influences our impressions of the setting is to compare the quality of two movies that were filmed in the same setting. Both Alexander Mackendrick's *The Sweet Smell of Success* (1957; cinematographer: James Wong Howe) and Woody Allen's *Manhattan* (1979; cinematographer: Gordon Willis) use the Queensborough Bridge (the 59th Street Bridge made famous in Simon and Garfunkel's song of the same name) for a key scene. Both scenes are shot at night in the environs of the bridge.

[1] This scene from *The Sweet Smell of Success* takes place outside a nightclub located on a street that runs alongside and below the bridge. In this image, Sidney Falco, the unscrupulous assistant to J. J. Hunsecker, the city's most powerful gossip columnist, has just planted drugs in the coat of Steve Dallas, an innocent jazz guitarist who wants to marry Hunsecker's sister, Susan. We see Falco (Tony Curtis, *left*) confirming the setup with NYPD Lieutenant Harry Kello (Emile Meyer, *right*) and one of his assistants (unidentified actor, *center*).

Hunsecker has ordered Falco, as well as the Kello, whom he controls, to make Dallas the victim of this scheme to keep the musician from marrying his sister. Shadows are deep, and the streetlights cast sharp pools of light on streets wet with rain. This atmosphere is made even more menacing by the noisy sounds of the bridge traffic overhead.

[2] In *Manhattan*, two of the typically self-deprecating New Yorkers that populate Allen's movies—Isaac Davis (Woody Allen) and Mary Wilkie (Diane Keaton)—meet for the second time at a cocktail party, desert their dates and leave together, and take a joyous walk through the streets, which ends on a bench in Sutton Square, a quiet, elegant neighborhood a few blocks closer to the river than the site of the scene in image 1, but close enough that this scene is also set alongside and below the bridge. The world of *Sweet Smell of Success* could be a million miles away. The bridge stretches above the two characters and across the frame, its supporting cables twinkling with lights, the early morning sky soft and misty behind. The only sound is the lovers' voices and George and Ira Gershwin's romantic ballad "Someone to Watch Over Me." Woody Allen is no starry-eyed fool, but the Manhattan in this movie is all romance, soft lights, and human relationships that (mostly) end happily.

Soft Versus Hard Lighting   Gregg Toland's use of lighting in *Citizen Kane* (1941) creates a clear contrast between Charles Foster Kane (Orson Welles) [1] and Susan

Alexander (Dorothy Comingore) [2] that signals important differences between them in age (Kane is 45; Alexander is 22) and experience.

The way the cinematographer lights and shoots an actor invariably suggests an impression of the character to the audience. A good example of how the quality of lighting can affect how we look at and interpret characters in a scene can be found in Orson Welles's *Citizen Kane* (1941; cinematographer: Gregg Toland). When Kane (Welles) first meets and woos Susan Alexander (Dorothy Comingore), the light thrown on their respective faces during close-up shots reveals an important distinction between them. Susan's face, lit with a soft light that blurs the border between illumination and shadow, appears youthful and naïve. In contrast, Kane's face is lit with a hard and crisp light, making him appear older and more worldly.

Direction   Light can be thrown onto a movie actor or setting (exterior or interior) from virtually any direction: front, side, back, below, or above. By direction, we also mean the angle of that throw, for the angle helps produce the contrasts and shadows that suggest the location of the scene, its mood, and the time of day. As with the other properties of lighting, the direction of the lighting must be planned ahead of time by the cinematographer in cooperation with the art director so that the lighting setup achieves effects that complement the director's overall vision.

The effects possible with any one lighting setup are extensive, but not limitless. If anything, the pioneering work of one cinematographer may make such an impression on moviegoers and filmmakers alike that it limits the freedom of subsequent filmmakers to use the same lighting setup in different ways. In other words, as with most other aspects of filmmaking, lighting is subject to *conventions*. Perhaps the best-known lighting convention in feature filmmaking is the **three-point system**. Employed extensively during the Hollywood studio era, the three-point system was used to cast a glamorous light on the studios' most valuable assets during these years—their stars—and it remains the standard by which movies are lighted today.

The three-point system employs three sources of light, each aimed from a different direction and position in relation to the subject: *key light, fill light,* and *backlight.* The backlight is the least essential of

Three-Point Lighting   In the history of over-the-top mise-en-scène, few directors surpass Josef von Sternberg. *The Scarlet Empress* (1934; cinematographer: Bert Glennon), a ravishing, high-camp historical drama, is also the director's visual tribute to the allure of Marlene Dietrich, who plays Russian Empress Catherine the Great. von Sternberg consistently photographs her with three-point lighting that accentuates her exquisite beauty. In this example, notice how the *key light*, positioned to the side and slightly below the actor, casts deep shadows around her eyes and on her right cheek; the fill light, which is positioned at the opposite side of the camera from the key light, softens the depth of the shadows created by the brighter key light; and the backlight (a von Sternberg trademark in lighting Dietrich), which is positioned behind and above the actor on two sides, not only creates highlights along the edges of her hair but also separates her from the background and thus increases the appearance of three-dimensionality in the image.

these three sources. The overall character of the image is determined mainly by the relationship between the key and fill lights. The **key light** (also known as the *main*, or *source*, *light*) is the primary source of illumination, and, thus, customarily set first. Positioned to one side of the camera, it creates hard shadows. The **fill light**, which is positioned at the opposite side of the camera from the key light, adjusts the depth of the shadows created by the brighter key light. Fill light may also come from a reflector.

The primary advantage of three-point lighting is that it permits the cinematographer to adjust the relationship and balance between illumination and shadow—the balance between the key

High-Key Lighting George Lucas's use in *THX 1138* (1971) of an austere setting and intense white lighting that creates a shadowless environment is as chilling as the futuristic society it records. This society has outlawed sexual relations and controls inhabitants with a regimen of mind-changing drugs. Those who rebel are thrown into a prison that is a vast, white void.

and fill lights—a balance known as the **lighting ratio**. When little or no fill light is used, the ratio between bright illumination and deep shadow is very high; the effect produced is known as **low-key lighting**. Low-key lighting produces the overall gloomy atmosphere that we see in horror films, mysteries, psychological dramas, crime stories, and film noirs, where its contrasts between light and dark often imply ethical judgments.

High-key lighting, which produces an image with very little contrast between the darks and the lights, is used extensively in dramas, musicals, comedies, and adventure films; its even, flat illumination does not call particular attention to the subject being photographed. When the intensity of the fill light equals that of the key light, the result will be the highest of high-key lighting: no shadows at all.

You may have noticed that these terms—*low-key lighting* and *high-key lighting*—are counterintuitive: we increase the contrasts to produce low-key lighting and decrease them to produce high-key lighting. The cinematographer lowers the fill light to achieve a higher ratio and contrast between shadow depth and illumination, and raises the fill light to lower the ratio and contrast.

The third source in three-point lighting is the **backlight**, usually positioned behind and above the subject and the camera, and used to create highlights along the edges of the subject as a means of separating it from the background and increasing its appearance of three-dimensionality (such highlights are also known as *edge lights* or *rim lights*). In exterior shooting, the sun is often used as a backlight. Although it is less important to the three-point system than key light and fill light, backlight can be used on its own to achieve very expressive effects. One effect is to create depth in a shot by separating a figure from the background, as in the projection room scene in Orson Welles's *Citizen Kane* (1941), in which Mr. Rawlston (Philip Van Zandt) and Jerry Thompson (William Alland) are outlined by the strong backlight from the projector.

Lighting from underneath a character (sometimes called *Halloween lighting*) creates eerie, ominous shadows on the actor's face by reversing the normal placement of illumination and shadow. This sort of lighting is especially appropriate in the horror genre, as in James Whale's *The Bride of Frankenstein* (1935; cinematographer: John J. Mescall), in which the lighting thrown on Dr. Preto-

Backlighting Backlighting can provide a dramatic sense of depth, especially when it is the sole light source, as in the projection room scene in Orson Welles's *Citizen Kane*. The intensity of light coming from the projection booth's windows provides clear visual cues to the depth of the onscreen space by creating a deep shadow in the foreground, a bright focus in the middle ground, and murky gray in the background. The shape of the beams of light—receding to a vanishing point behind the wall—not only contributes to our sense of depth but also accentuates the two main characters in the scene: Jerry Thompson (William Alland, *left*), the reporter who prepared the "News on the March" sequence, and his boss, Mr. Rawlston (Philip Van Zandt, *right*).

Lighting From Below   In this scene from *The Bride of Frankenstein* (1935), Dr. Pretorius (Ernest Thesiger), with lighting cast from below, watches his monstrous creation come to life.

Lighting From Above   In this scene from *The Godfather*, Don Corleone (Marlon Brando) has just been told by his consigliere, Tom Hagen (Robert Duvall), of the murder of Sonny (James Caan), his eldest son and heir to mob power. It's late at night, and Corleone has been awakened; stunned by the news, he starts to cry. Light thrown on him from above, emphasizing his scruffy appearance, makes him—for that fleeting moment—appear old, vulnerable, and sad.

rius (Ernest Thesiger) from below accentuates the diabolical nature of his scientific ambitions.

Lighting thrown on a character from above can be used for many different effects, but a common result is to make a character appear threatening, mysterious, or—in the example from Francis Ford

Coppola's *The Godfather* (1972; cinematographer: Gordon Willis) shown in the accompanying photo—vulnerable.

Style   The overall style of a film is determined by its **production values,** or the amount and quality of human and physical resources devoted to the image. Among the elements that determine production values is the style of a film's lighting. During the height of the classical Hollywood studio era, studios distinguished themselves from each other by adopting distinctive lighting styles and production values: for example, somber, low-key lighting in black-and-white pictures from Warner Bros.; sharp, glossy lighting in the films from 20th Century Fox; and bright, glamorous lighting for MGM's many color films, especially the musicals. The studios cultivated (and, in many cases, *enforced*) their distinct styles with an eye to establishing brand identities, and the filmmakers working for them were expected to work within the limits of the company style.

Cinematographers working within the constraints of a well-established genre often find that their decisions about lighting style are at least partly determined by the production values and lighting styles of previous films in that genre. Film noir lighting, for example, conventionally uses high-contrast white-and-black tones to symbolize the opposing forces of good and evil. The very name *film noir* (*noir* means "black" in French) implies that lighting style is an important aspect of the genre. Filmmakers working within a genre with well-established conventions of lighting must at the least be aware of those conventions.

Of course, the lighting conventions that define a genre can be altered by daring and imaginative filmmakers. For example, cinematographer John Alton deviates from the film noir lighting formula in Anthony Mann's *T-Men* (1947) in order to develop a sense of moral ambiguities rather than a hard-edged distinction between good (light) and evil (darkness). A hard-edged crime story about U.S. Treasury Department agents' successful busting of a counterfeit ring, *T-Men* incorporates many shots made in near-total darkness—a black so deep that sometimes you can barely see the action. Bright

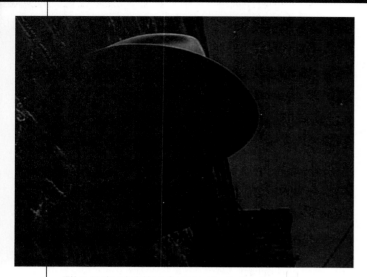

Film Noir Lighting for Mood In this image from Anthony Mann's *T-Men* (1947), U.S. Treasury agent Dennis O'Brien (Dennis O'Keefe) is trailing a dangerous forgery suspect in the early morning hours. He is shot from below, with a key light outlining the brim of his hat, and we cannot see his face. If this shot weren't preceded by others in which his face is visible, we wouldn't have a clue to this man's identity. By deviating from the expectations traditionally raised by film noir lighting—in which the good guys would be clearly visible to the viewer—Alton accentuates the peril of O'Brien's assignment (his partner has just been murdered) and, thus, influences our interpretation of the narrative.

lighting occasionally punctuates this gloom, but the overall tendency is to place everyone—cops and counterfeiters alike—in a dark and murky atmosphere. Alton lighted his sets for mood rather than for making them completely visible to the viewer, and with this approach, he rewrote the textbook on film noir lighting. In doing this, he also changed the expectations traditionally raised by film noir lighting in order to direct and complicate our interpretation of the film's narrative.

The various aspects of lighting—its source, quality, and direction—work together with other elements to determine the overall mood and meaning of a scene. Lars von Trier's *Dogville* (2003; cinematographer: Anthony Dod Mantle), a misanthropic vision of the United States in the Depression-era 1930s, is set in a town of the same name that is located high on a plateau and populated by selfish, bored losers and miscreants. Grace (Nicole Kidman)

arrives out of nowhere as a "gift" to the town's residents, whose primary reactions to her presence involve humiliating and torturing her, even as she does their chores to seek their acceptance. What is this place? Who is Grace? Why is she treated as an outsider? Lighting helps us answer these questions. The town's setting is a schematic design constructed on a vast, dark studio floor and often photographed from a very high angle that permits us to see its entire layout and total isolation from the surrounding countryside (which we never see). However, in contrast to the high-key lighting that floods the overall set with an even light, the scene we are considering (which takes place in one of the "houses" outlined on the floor) uses expressively lighted close-ups to record a turning point in the action.

Grace is frustrated by her lot in life and tries to provoke Jack McKay (Ben Gazzara) into taking a more open view of the world, which is ironic, since he is blind. We are in McKay's residence, where the window is heavily draped to emphasize his condition. The scene opens with Grace sitting in a chair as she taunts Jack, telling him that she's walked outside and noticed the windows: "It must be a wonderful view." The lighting that illuminates her is a classic example of three-point lighting (image 1 in the illustration on page 155): Grace, on the right side of the frame, in semiprofile, faces down; the light is falling on her from no identifiable source, highlighting her right cheek, part of the ridge of her nose, and her right shoulder; her heavily made-up eyes are in the shadows of her bangs. From this lighting, we clearly see that she is determined to get somewhere with her provocation; in addition to encouraging Jack to "see" more of the world, she may also be making sexual overtures toward him.

Next, Grace boldly takes the liberty of pulling open the drapes. Standing with her back toward us, and holding the drapes apart with her widespread arms, she faces bright, almost surreal sunlight and trees (significantly, there is little other greenery in the town), as the background music builds in a soft crescendo that suggests both spiritual and sexual release (image 2). The reflection of her brightly lighted face in the window accentuates the passage from darkness to light. She then turns, transfixed

[1]

[2]

[3]

[4]

Aspects of Lighting in *Dogville* [1] Grace provokes Jack. [2] Graces faces the sunlight. [3] Grace, in profile, is transfixed by the sunlight. [4] Grace turns toward Jack, astonished at how easy it was to bring light into darkness.

by the light: her profile, in the far right of the frame, faces directly left and toward the sunlight, which is evenly thrown onto her face; her lips are open in an ecstatic expression; the remaining two-thirds of the screen is dark (image 3). Finally she turns toward Jack, the bright sunlight behind her (an excellent example of backlighting), her face now in shadows, but her parted lips continue to underscore her sense of astonishment at how easy it was to bring light into darkness—a microcosm of her larger hope of achieving acceptance in Dogville (image 4). As the scene ends, Jack remains trapped in his blindness. It is Grace, not Jack, who is able to see the light.

Lenses

In its most basic form, a camera **lens** is a piece of curved, polished glass or other transparent material. As the "eye" of the camera, its primary function is to bring the light that emanates from the subjects in front of the camera (actors, objects, settings) into a focused image on the film, tape, or other sensor inside the camera. This was as true of the lens in the fifteenth-century camera obscura (in which the sensor was the wall on which the image was seen; see Fig. 1.1 on page 17) as it is of the lenses of today.

The basic properties shared by all lenses are *aperture*, *focal length*, and *depth of field*. The **aperture** of a lens is usually an adjustable **iris** (or diaphragm) that limits the amount of light passing through a lens. The greater the size of the aperture, the more light it admits through the lens. The **focal length** of the lens is the distance (measured in millimeters) from the optical center of the lens to the focal point on the film stock or other sensor if the image is sharp and clear (*in focus*). Focal length affects how we perceive perspective—the appearance of depth—in a shot, and it also influences our perception of the size, scale, and movement of the subject being shot. The four major types of lenses are designated by their respective focal lengths:

1. The **short-focal-length lens** (also known as the **wide-angle lens**, starting as low as

Short-Focal-Length Lens This shot from Stanley Kubrick's *Dr. Strangelove* (1964; cinematographer: Gilbert Taylor) comically reinforces our sense of the powerlessness of Group Captain Lionel Mandrake (Peter Sellers, *facing the camera*) as he meets with his superior officer, Brigadier General Jack D. Ripper (Sterling Hayden). The resulting wide-angle composition makes Mandrake look almost like a toy doll standing on the powerful general's desk.

Long-Focal-Length Lens This image from Stanley Kubrick's *Barry Lyndon* (1975) shows the flattening effect of a long-focal-length lens. The marching soldiers' forward progress seems more gradual as a result.

12.5mm) produces wide-angle views. It makes the subjects on the screen appear farther apart than they actually are, and because this lens elongates depth, characters or objects moving at a normal speed from background to foreground through this stretched depth might appear to be moving faster than they actually are.

2. The **long-focal-length lens** (also known as the **telephoto lens**, focal lengths ranging from 85mm to as high as 500mm) brings distant objects close, makes subjects look closer together than they do in real life, and flattens space and depth in the process. Thus, it alters the subject's movement, so that a subject moving from the background toward the camera might appear to be barely moving at all.

3. Although the short and long extremes are used occasionally to achieve certain visual effects, most shots in feature films are made with a **middle-focal-length lens**— from 35mm to 50mm—often called the *normal lens*. Lenses in this range create images that correspond to our day-to-day experience of depth and perspective.

Middle-Focal-Length Lens This shot from Billy Wilder's *Sunset Blvd.* (1950; cinematographer: John F. Seitz) includes the movie's three principal characters (*from left to right*): Max von Mayerling (Erich von Stroheim), with his back to us, in the near left foreground; Norma Desmond (Gloria Swanson) and Joe Gillis (William Holden) in the middle ground, facing us. A small orchestra is in the background. The middle-focal-length lens used to make this shot keeps the three principal subjects in normal focus, and the overall image corresponds to our day-to-day experience of depth and perspective.

1

2

Zoom Lens In John Singleton's *Boyz N the Hood* (1991; cinematographer: Charles Mills), a zoom lens pulls us closer to Tré Styles (Desi Arnez Hines II) even as he walks toward the camera. These combined movements of lens and actor increase the pace at which we're brought close enough to read his reaction to the arrest of his neighbors (*offscreen*).

4. The **zoom lens**—also called a *variable-focal-length lens*—permits the cinematographer to shrink or increase the focal length in a continuous motion, and thus simulates the effect of movement of the camera toward or away from the subject. However, it does not actually move through space, but simply magnifies the image.

Short-focal-length, long-focal-length, and middle-focal-length lenses all have a fixed focal length and are known as **prime lenses**, but zoom lenses are in their own category. Both prime and zoom lenses have their specific optical qualities, and because they are thought to produce sharper images, prime lenses are generally used more than zoom lenses. In the hands of an accomplished cinematographer, the zoom lens can produce striking effects, but when it is used indiscriminately, as it often is by less skilled filmmakers, it not only feels artificial to an audience but can unintentionally disorient viewers. As with all other aspects of cinematography, the lens used must be appropriate for the story being told.

Depth of field is a property of the lens that permits the cinematographer to decide what **planes**, or areas of the image, will be in focus. As a result, depth of field helps create emphasis, either on one or more selected planes or figures, or on the whole image. The term *depth of field* refers to the distances in front of a camera and its lens in which the subjects are in apparent sharp focus. The short-focal-length lens offers a nearly complete depth of field, rendering almost all objects in the frame in focus. The depth of field of the long-focal-length lens is generally a very narrow range, and it leaves the background and foreground of the in-focus objects dramatically out of focus. In the middle-focal-length lens, the depth of field keeps all subjects in a "normal" sense of focus.

In virtually all shooting, cinematographers keep the main subject of each shot in sharp focus to maintain clear spatial and perspectival relations within frames. One option available to cinematographers, however, is a **rack focus** (also known as *select focus*, *shift focus*, or *pull focus*)—a change of the point of focus from one subject to another. This technique guides our attention to a new clearly focused point of interest while blurring the previous subject in the frame.

Rack focus is used in Jonathan Demme's *Philadelphia* (1993; cinematographer: Tak Fujimoto) to show us within one shot both the face of a lawyer, Belinda Conine (Mary Steenburgen), as she makes her aggressively supercilious opening statement to the jury, and, behind her, the reaction of the plaintiff, Andrew Beckett (Tom Hanks), and his lawyer, Joe Miller (Denzel Washington), to her words. After she attempts to denigrate Beckett's competence by telling the jury the "fact" that

[1]

[2]

Rack Focus   Two successive shots in Jonathan Demme's *Philadelphia* (1993), the second of which begins with a rack focus, show us how changing the focus guides our attention to a new, clearly focused point of interest and, thus, influences our interpretation of the scene. [1] Belinda Conine (Mary Steenburgen) makes her opening allegations against the plaintiff, Andrew Beckett (Tom Hanks). [2] In the next shot, which begins with a rack focus, we see the reactions of Beckett and his lawyer, Joe Miller (Denzel Washington) to Conine's remarks.

TABLE 4.1	Types of Images Produced by Different Lenses
Type of Lens	**Characteristics of Images Produced by Aperture, Focal Length, and Depth of Field**
Prime Lenses Short-focal-length lens (wide-angle lens)	• Produces wide-angle views. • Makes subjects appear farther apart than they actually are. • Through its nearly complete depth of field, renders almost all objects in the frame in focus.
Long-focal-length lens (telephoto lens)	• Produces deep-angle views. • Brings distant objects close. • Flattens space and depth. • Makes subjects look closer together than they actually are. • Narrow depth of field leaves most of the background and foreground of the in-focus objects dramatically out of focus.
Middle-focal-length lens (normal lens)	• Produces images that correspond to our day-to-day experience of depth and perspective. • Keeps all subjects in a normal sense of focus.
Zoom lens Zoom lens (variable-focal-length lens)	• Produces images that simulate the effect of movement of the camera toward or away from the subject. • Rather than actually moving through space, merely magnifies the image. • Can make a shot seem artificial to an audience.

Beckett was "oftentimes mediocre" (image 1 in the illustration on page 158), there is a cut. The camera reframes, putting Conine out of focus on the right side of the image as she adds "sometimes flagrantly incompetent," and revealing Beckett's and Miller's reactions clearly in focus at their table (image 2). Conventionally, when a director keeps characters in focus, we typically assume that they are truthful; putting them out of focus raises questions in the viewer's mind. The result of this maneuver in *Philadelphia* is to make Conine appear as foolish as her line of argument will eventually turn out to be, record the reactions of her adversaries, and establish a pattern—repeated many times during the trial—of the director's empathy with Beckett's case.

🅓🅥🅓 Focal Length

The images you see on the screen are produced by a complex interaction of optical properties associated with the camera lens. Table 4.1 provides a ready reference on how the different lenses discussed here produce different images.

Framing of the Shot

Framing is the process by which the cinematographer determines what will appear within the borders of the image during a shot. Framing turns the comparatively infinite sight of the human eye into a finite movie image, an unlimited view into a limited view. This process requires decisions about each of the following elements: the *proximity to the camera* of main subjects, the *depth* of the composition, *camera angle and height*, the *scale* of various objects in relation to each other, and the type of *camera movement*, if any.

At least one decision about framing is out of the cinematographer's hands: although a painter can choose any size of canvas as the area in which to create a picture—large or small, square or rectangular, oval or round, flat or three-dimensional—cinematographers find that their choices for a "canvas" are limited to a small number of dimensional variations on a rectangle. This rectangle results from the historical development of photographic technology. Nothing *absolutely* dictates that our experience of moving images must occur within a rectangle; however because of the standardization of equipment and technology within the motion picture industry, we have come to know this rectangle as the shape of movies.

The relationship between the frame's two dimensions is known as its **aspect ratio** (Fig. 4.2), the ratio of the width of the image to its height. Each movie is made to be shown in one aspect ratio from beginning to end. The most common aspect ratios are

> 1.33:1 Academy (35mm flat)
> 1.66:1 European widescreen (35mm flat)
> 1.85:1 American widescreen (35mm flat)
> 2.2:1 Super Panavision and Todd-AO (70mm flat)
> 2.35:1 Panavision and CinemaScope (35mm anamorphic)
> 2.75:1 Ultra Panavision (70mm anamorphic)

Until the 1950s, when the widescreen image became popular, the standard aspect ratio for a flat film was the Academy ratio of 1.33:1, meaning that the frame is 33 percent wider than it is high—a ratio corresponding to the dimensions of a single frame of 35mm film stock. Today's more familiar widescreen variations provide wider horizontal and shorter vertical dimensions. Most commercial releases are shown in the 1.85:1 aspect ratio, which is almost twice as wide as it is high. Other widescreen variations include a 2.2:1 or 2.35:1 ratio when projected.

From the earliest days, movie directors have experimented with alternative shapes to the rectangle. To do so, they have often used a **mask**—an opaque sheet of metal, paper, or plastic with a cutout (known as an **iris** when circular) that is placed in front of the camera and admits light to a specific area of the frame—to create a frame within the frame. The obvious function of the mask is to draw our eyes to that particular place and thus to emphasize what we see there. In *The Night of the Hunter* (1955; cinematographer: Stanley Cortez), Charles Laughton uses an **iris-out**—a transitional effect in which the iris contracts from larger to smaller—in which we see Harry Powell (Robert Mitchum) walking toward a ground-level window behind which his

FIGURE 4.2 Basic Aspect Ratios

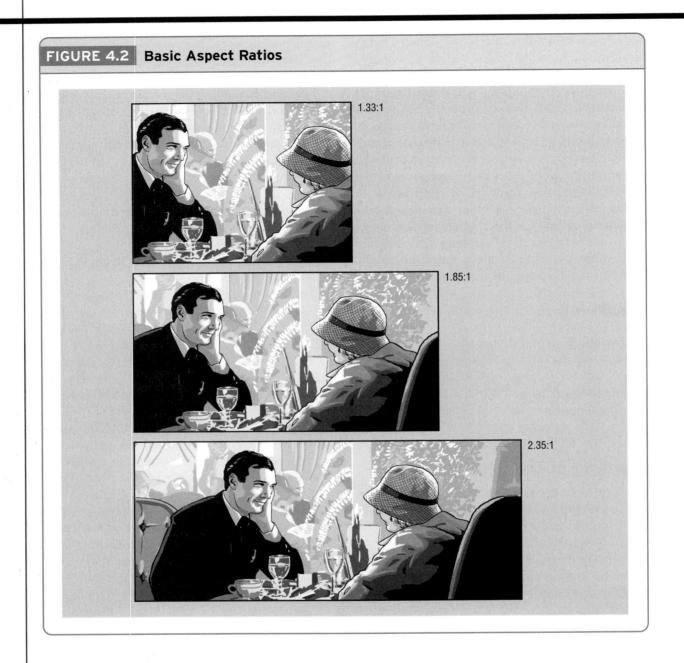

stepchildren are hiding from him. Masks can also be created by lighting, as when Laughton isolates a stripper within the frame by accentuating the spotlight in which she is performing.

Architectural details are frequently used to mask a frame, and a person placed between the camera and its subject can also mask the frame. In Mike Nichols's *The Graduate* (1967; cinematographer: Robert Surtees), during her initial seduction scene of Benjamin Braddock (Dustin Hoffman), Mrs. Robinson (Anne Bancroft) sits at the bar in her house and raises one leg onto the stool next to her, forming a triangle through which Benjamin is framed, or, perhaps, trapped. Despite these modest attempts to break up the rectangular movie frame into other shapes through frames within the frame, movies continue to come to us as four-sided images that are wider than they are tall.

Iris-Out In this shot from Charles Laughton's *The Night of the Hunter* (1955), Harry Powell (Robert Mitchum) makes his way nonchalantly toward the house in which his stepchildren are hiding from him. Although he acts as though he cannot see them, the iris-out that follows his progress toward the house (a technique that eventually frames the children's fearful faces peering out of the basement window) makes clear to us that he knows *exactly* where they are hiding.

Masking in *The Graduate* Mike Nichols's *The Graduate* (1967) features one of the most famous (and amusing) maskings of the frame in movie history. As the scene ends, Ben Braddock (Dustin Hoffman), framed in the provocative bend of Mrs. Robinson's (Anne Bancroft) knee, asks, "Mrs. Robinson, you're trying to seduce me . . . aren't you?"

Implied Proximity to the Camera

DVD **Shot Types and Implied Proximity**

The names of the most commonly used shots employed in a movie—*extreme long shot, long shot, medium long shot, medium shot, medium close-up, close-up,* and *extreme close-up*—refer to the implied distance between the camera lens and the subject being photographed. From our earlier discussion of mise-en-scène (see Chapter 3), we know that, in the vast majority of movies, everything we see on the screen—including subjects within a shot and their implied proximity to each other—has been placed there to develop the narrative's outcome and meaning. Our interpretations of these onscreen spatial relationships happen as unconsciously and automatically as they do in everyday life.

To get a sense of the importance of proximity, imagine yourself on a crowded dance floor at a club or party. Among all the other distracting things in your field of vision, you see an attractive person looking at you from the opposite end of the room. You may assign that person some significance

from that distance, but if that same person walks up to you, virtually filling your field of vision, then the person suddenly has much greater significance to you and may provoke a much more profound reaction from you. No matter what the outcome of this encounter, you have become visually involved with this person in a way that you wouldn't have if the person had remained at the other end of the room.

Similarly, the implied proximity of the camera to the subjects being shot influences our emotional involvement with those subjects. Think of how attentive you are during a close-up of your favorite movie actor, or how shocked you feel when, as in Gore Verbinski's horror movie *The Ring* (2002; cinematographer: Bojan Bazelli), an actor moves quickly and threateningly from a position of obscurity in the background to a position of vivid and terrifying dominance of the frame. We all have favorite scenes from horror films that have shocked us in this way, violating and then virtually erasing the distance between us and the screen. Of course, nearness is not the only degree of proximity that engages our emotions. Each of the possible arrangements of subjects in proximity to each other and to the camera has the potential to convey something meaningful about the subjects onscreen, and thankfully, most of those meanings come to us naturally.

The best way to remember and recognize the different types of shots is to think in terms of the scale of the human body within the frame, so we'll describe them in terms of that scale. In the **extreme long shot** (**XLS** or **ELS**), typically photographed at a great distance from the subject, that subject is often too small to be recognized, except through the context we see, which usually includes a wide view of a location, as well as general background information. When used to provide such informative context, the ELS is also an **establishing shot**.

These characteristics are evident in Charles Chaplin's *The Great Dictator* (1940; cinematographers: Karl Struss and Roland Totheroh), in which Chaplin, lampooning Adolf Hitler as Adenoid Hynkel, is dwarfed by his enormous office. The abstract swastika-like symbol also provides a specific background reference to fascism. Stanley Kubrick begins *The Shining* (1980; cinematographer: John Alcott) with a helicopter shot of majestic mountains and a wide river—a landscape in which the small car appears even smaller by contrast and whose occupants, the principal characters in the movie, are not yet visible.

In a **long shot** (**LS**), we see the character's full body (almost filling the frame but with some area above and below also visible) and some of the sur-

Long Shot Stanley Donen and Gene Kelly's *Singin' in the Rain* (1952), one of the most popular Hollywood musicals of all time, features several great dancers. Here, Kathy Selden (Debbie Reynolds) and Don Lockwood (Gene Kelly) are photographed in a long shot as they run through their rehearsal routine. We see the full bodies of both dancers (almost filling the frame but with some area above and below also visible), as well as some of the equipment on the studio's soundstage.

Extreme Long Shot An extreme long shot from Charles Chaplin's *The Great Dictator* (1940) leaves the dictator (Chaplin) overwhelmed by his surroundings. The effect makes this character, a lampoon of Adolf Hitler, ridiculous rather than menacing.

roundings. Also known as the **full-body shot**, the LS is used frequently in musicals and comedies, allowing us to see the dexterity of such dancers as Gene Kelly and Donald O'Connor in Stanley Donen and Gene Kelly's *Singin' in the Rain* (1952; cinematographer: Harold Rosson), or the physical-humor high jinks of Charles Chaplin in his *Modern Times* (1936; cinematographers: Ira H. Morgan and Roland Totheroh).[5]

The **medium long shot** (**MLS**, also known as the *two-shot,* the *plan américain,* or the *American shot*) is neither a long shot nor a medium shot, but one in between. It is used to photograph one or more characters, usually from the knees up, as well as some of the background. This very essential shot permits the director to have two characters in conversation and to shoot them from a variety of angles.

[5] As with the dancers, early film comedians such as Charlie Chaplin, Buster Keaton, and Harold Lloyd used the full-body shot to prove conclusively that they were responsible for their own comic stunts.

When the shot includes two characters, it is called a **two-shot**.

A **medium shot (MS)**, somewhere between the long shot and the close-up (which we discuss below), shows a character, usually from the waist up, or her full figure if she is seated. The MS is the most frequently used type of shot because it replicates our human experience of proximity without intimacy; it provides more detail of the body than the LS does. Unlike the close-up, the MS can include several characters, but it reveals more nuance in the characters' faces than can be captured in the MLS.

The **medium close-up (MCU)** shows a character from the middle of the chest to the top of the head. It provides a view of the face that catches minor changes in expression, and also provides some detail about the character's posture.

The **close-up (CU)** is produced when the camera is shooting from very near to the subject. Although it traditionally shows the full head (sometimes including the shoulders), it can also be used to show a hand, eye, or mouth. When focused on a character's face, the close-up provides an exclusive view of a character's emotions or states of mind. A variation on the close-up is the **extreme close-up (XCU or ECU)**, which is a very close shot of some detail. In John Ford's *The Grapes of Wrath* (1940), Ma Joad (Jane Darwell) goes through her possessions before the family

Medium Long Shot A representative medium long shot of "Sport" Matthew (Harvey Keitel, *left*) and Travis Bickle (Robert De Niro, *right*), taken from Martin Scorsese's *Taxi Driver* (1976; cinematographer: Michael Chapman). Because two figures are in the frame, this is also a two-shot.

Medium Shot In this medium shot from John Ford's *The Quiet Man* (1952; cinematographer: Winton C. Hoch), Sean Thornton (John Wayne) has just returned to the Irish town of Innisfree, where he was born, and sees for the first time Mary Kate Danaher (Maureen O'Hara). It's love at first sight, at least for him, but there will be plenty of brawls before we see them together in a peaceful MS.

Medium Close-Up The MCU provides more detail of facial expression than the MS, as you can see in this shot from Rouben Mamoulian's *Love Me Tonight* (1932; cinematographer: Victor Milner), in which Maurice Courtelin (Maurice Chevalier) admits to Princess Jeanette (Jeanette MacDonald) that he is not an aristocrat, but rather an ordinary tailor. After the princess gets over her temporary shock—reflected in this image—their affair continues happily.

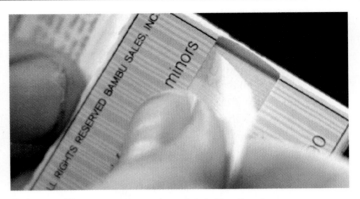

Extreme Close-up Darren Aronofsky's *Requiem for a Dream* (2000; cinematographer: Matthew Libatique) uses the extreme close-up extensively to show the repetitive motions and rituals of drug use.

Close-up The CU traditionally shows the full head (sometimes including the shoulders), as in this shot of John McFarland (John Robinson) in Gus Van Sant's *Elephant* (2003; cinematographer: Harris Savides).

1

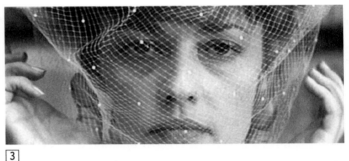

3

2

4

Types of Shots in *Jules and Jim* In François Truffaut's *Jules and Jim* (1962), this scene follows immediately after the title characters have returned from a trip to the Adriatic, where they have seen a beautiful statue, which reminds

them of the women they love. Truffaut uses all the major shot types to give us multiple perspectives on Catherine (Jeanne Moreau), with whom both Jules (Oskar Werner) and Jim (Henri Serre) will be obsessed for the rest of the movie.

heads to California. As she picks up a little ceramic dog, the camera frames an XCU on this object to emphasize that it reminds her of happier, more carefree times in her life. This detail might have been lost if Ford had used an MS or LS, but her recollections register clearly when isolated in a sustained XCU.

Filmmakers often mix shots of differing proximities in a single scene. In *Jules and Jim* (1962; cinematographer: Raoul Coutard), François Truffaut uses all the major shot types to give us multiple perspectives on Catherine (Jeanne Moreau), as both Jules (Oskar Werner) and Jim (Henri Serre) meet her for the first time. Truffaut celebrates the moment and pays tribute to the power of Moreau's legendary beauty by first introducing her in an LS on a staircase with two other women; gently reframing to an MCU; and concluding with a rapid montage of CUs of her face, some made with a zoom lens to exaggerate the power of the shot.

Depth

Because the image of the movie screen is two-dimensional and thus appears flat (in all but the few movies shot with 3-D cinematography), one of the most compelling challenges faced by cinematographers has been how to give that image an illusion of depth. From the earliest years of film history, filmmakers have experimented with achieving different illusions of depth. D. W. Griffith was a master at using huge three-dimensional sets in such movies as *Intolerance* (1916). A more sustained effort to make the most of *deep-space composition* began in the late 1920s. Many directors and cinematographers during this decade, especially those who were directing musicals with large casts and big production budgets, experimented with the technique of creating lines of movement from background to foreground to foster the illusion of depth.

For example, in *Applause* (1929; cinematographer: George S. Folsey), Rouben Mamoulian created spatial depth by organizing a line of burlesque dancers to move from the stage in the back of the image, across the catwalk that ran through the audience in the middle of the image, to the viewer, sitting, presumably, in the right-hand corner of the

Illusion of Depth   During the Great Depression, director-choreographer Busby Berkeley helped bring to the screen a series of musical-comedy extravaganzas whose titles all began with *Gold Diggers*. The first—Mervyn LeRoy's *Gold Diggers of 1933* (1933), choreographed by Berkeley—begins on a prosaic stage ("real," "open" space), enters a realm of complete fantasy (representing what happens to the space in the minds of the characters, as shown here), and then returns to the stage on which it opened. Note that the costumes copy the structure on which the women are standing, whose form repeats the contours of the neon violins that they're playing. Furthermore, in keeping with the public's fascination with precision ensembles such as this, these actors' gowns, hairstyles, and smiles are identical.

foreground of the screen. Director Mervyn LeRoy achieved a more elaborate effect with Busby Berkeley's choreography in *Gold Diggers of 1933* (1933).

Although these elaborately choreographed scenes reveal progress toward the goal of creating a cinematic image with greater depth, during the 1930s the traditional method of suggesting cinematic depth was to use an LS and place significant characters or objects in the foreground or middle-ground planes and then leave the remainder of the image in a soft-focus background. The filmmaker could also reverse this composition and place the significant figures in the background of the image with a landscape, say, occupying the foreground and middle ground. Thus, in both of these examples the cinematic space is arranged to draw the viewer's eyes toward or away from the background. With such

Depth   From the earliest years of film history, filmmakers have experimented with achieving different illusions of depth. [1] Rouben Mamoulian created a very effective illusion of spatial depth in *Applause* (1929) by organizing a line of burlesque dancers to move from the stage in the back of the image, across the runway that bisects the audience in the middle of the image, to the viewer, sitting, presumably, in the right-hand corner of the foreground of the screen. Even though it was not yet possible to maintain clear focus from

[2]

the foreground to background, the illusion of depth is there. [2] Three years later, in his dazzling comedy *Trouble in Paradise* (1932; cinematographer: Victor Milner), Ernst Lubitsch adhered to the traditional method of the time: suggesting depth by using an LS, placing the two main characters in the foreground plane, and leaving the remainder of the image in a soft-focus background. In both of these examples, the cinematic space is arranged to draw the viewer's eyes either away from or toward the background.

basic illusions, our eyes automatically give depth to the successive areas of the image as they seem to recede in space.

Also during the 1930s, however, various cinematographers experimented with creating a deeper illusion of space through cinematographic rather than choreographic means. Of these cinematographers, none was more important than Gregg Toland, who was responsible for bringing the previous developments together, improving them, and using them most impressively in John Ford's *The Long Voyage Home* (1940) and soon after in Orson Welles's *Citizen Kane* (1941). By the time he shot these two films, Toland had already rejected the soft-focus, one-plane depth of the established Hollywood style; experimented with achieving greater depth; created sharper black-and-white images; used the high-powered Technicolor arc lights for black-and-white cinematography; used Super XX film stock, which produced a clearer image and was four times faster than previously available black-

and-white stock; coated his lenses (to cut down glare from the lights); and used self-blimped cameras so that he could work in confined spaces.

In *Citizen Kane*, these methods came together in two related techniques: a deliberate use of **deep-space composition**, a total visual composition that can place significant information or subjects on all three planes of the frame and thereby creates an illusion of depth, coupled with **deep-focus cinematography**, which, using the short-focal-length lens, keeps all three planes in sharp focus. Deep-space composition permits the filmmaker to exploit the relative size of people and objects in the frame to convey meaning and conflict.

Toland's pioneering work on *Citizen Kane* had a profound influence on the look of subsequent movies, and helped to distance Hollywood even further from the editing-centered theories of the Russian formalist directors (e.g., Sergei Eisenstein) and to bring American moviemaking closer to the realism of such European directors as Jean Renoir.

Deep-Space Composition   An excellent example of the expressive potential of deep-space composition can be found in Alfred Hitchcock's *Notorious* (1946; cinematographer: Ted Tetzlaff). Alicia Huberman (Ingrid Bergman), an American counterspy working in Brazil to discover enemy secrets, marries Alexander Sebastian (Claude Rains), a German spy, at the request of her government. Sebastian and his mother, Madame Konstantin (Leopoldine Konstantin), eventually discover Alicia's duplicity, and in this scene they have already begun to kill her by poisoning her coffee. As Alicia complains of feeling ill, Madame Konstantin places a small cup on the table near her, putting it in the immediate foreground of the frame. The tiny cup, no more than a few inches tall, appears almost as large as Alicia's head in the middle ground, heightening the menace facing her and raising the level of suspense.

French film critic André Bazin emphasized that deep-focus cinematography "brings the spectator into a relation with the image closer to that which he enjoys with reality"; and "implies, consequently, both a more active mental attitude on the part of the spectator and a more positive contribution on his part to the action in progress."[6] In preserving the continuity of space and time, deep-focus cinematography seems more like human perception.

Toland also understood that a scene involving deep-space composition did not necessarily have to be shot with deep-focus cinematography, as he demonstrated in William Wyler's *The Little Foxes*

[6] André Bazin, "The Evolution of the Language of Cinema," in *What Is Cinema?* trans. Hugh Gray (Berkeley: University of California Press, 1967–71), 1:35–36.

(1941). Perhaps the best example is found in a scene in which Regina Giddens (Bette Davis) confronts her severely ill husband, Horace Giddens (Herbert Marshall), a man she detests for his overall opposition to her scheming brothers and their plan to expand her family's wealth by exploiting cheap labor. The sequence takes place in their parlor after Horace has returned home from a long hospital stay for treatment of his serious heart condition. When Regina asks him to put more funds into strengthening the family enterprise, he tells her that he has changed his will, leaving her nothing but bonds, which, he does not realize, members of the family have already stolen for the same purpose. Realizing that a man she despises has unknowingly trapped her in a difficult and illegal situation, Regina retaliates by telling him that she has always hated him. During her tirade, Horace has the first seizures of a heart attack. While attempting to take his medicine, he drops the bottle; and when he asks Regina to get the spare bottle upstairs, she makes the decision to let him die and sits perfectly still as he staggers toward the stairs and collapses. As Horace struggles toward the stairs behind Regina in the foreground, he grows progressively more out of focus, but he and his actions certainly are significant subject material. He goes out of focus for a specific reason—he is dying—and the shot is still very much deep-space composition, but not deep focus. Even though he is out of focus in the deep background of the frame, Horace remains significant to the outcome of the story.

The coupling of deep-space composition and deep-focus cinematography is useful only for scenes in which images of extreme depth within the frame are required, because the planning and choreography required to make these images are complex and time-consuming. Most filmmakers employ less complicated methods to maximize the potential of the image, put its elements into balance, and create an illusion of depth. Perhaps most important among these methods is the compositional principle known as the **rule of thirds**. This rule, like so many other "rules" in cinema, is a convention that can be adapted as needed. It takes the form of a grid pattern that, when superimposed on the image, divides it into horizontal thirds representing the foreground, middle

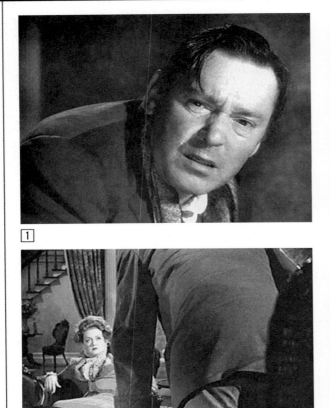

Use of Deep-Space Composition in *The Little Foxes*
At the climax of William Wyler's *The Little Foxes* (1941), Horace (Herbert Marshall) responds [1], begins having a heart attack, and rises [2] while Regina (Bette Davis) remains rigidly in place [3], offering Horace no help as he staggers to his death in the background, helpless and out of focus [4].

ground, and background planes and into vertical thirds that break up those planes into further elements. This grid assists the designer and cinematographer in visualizing the overall potential of the height, width, and depth of any cinematic space.

You can watch the rule of thirds in action in a motion picture by placing four strips of quarter-inch masking tape on your television screen (to conform to the interior lines in the grid) and then looking at any movie being shown in the standard Academy aspect ratio (1.33:1). The lines will almost invariably intersect those areas of interest within the frame to which the designer and cinematographer wish to draw your attention. Simple as it is, the rule of thirds takes our natural human ability to create balance and gives it an artistic form. Furthermore, it helps direct our eyes to obvious areas of interest within a cinematic composition, reminding us yet again that movies result from a set of deliberate choices.

The rule of thirds, like other filmmaking conventions, is not a hard-and-fast law. Compositions that consciously deviate from the rule of thirds can be effective, too, especially when they contrast with other compositions in the same film. In Stanley Kubrick's *Spartacus* (1960), for example, the opening title sequence rejects the rule of thirds in favor

[1]

[2]

The Rule of Thirds Stanley Kubrick's *Spartacus* (1960; cinematographer: Russell Metty) offers many shots in which classical compositions take full advantage of the rule of thirds. For example, [1] as the Roman legion marches out of Rome, Marcus Licinius Crassus (Laurence Olivier) proclaims to Antoninus (Tony Curtis, *offscreen*), "There boy, is Rome; the might, the majesty, the terror of Rome." The center of the frame is uncluttered, and the composition provides a strong foreground (the veranda of the villa), middle ground (soldiers crossing on the other side of the river), and background (the beautiful homes on the distant hillside). Meanwhile, Crassus is placed almost directly at the upper-left intersection point of the frame.

[2] By contrast, the opening title sequence of the film, designed by one of Hollywood's great visual designers, Saul

Bass, relies on very strong bias toward the center of the frame, rejecting the rule of thirds. Because at the beginning of *Spartacus*, Rome is at the height of its power and its central place in the world seems secure, this emphasis on the center of the frame makes thematic sense. But it also places the director's name in the center of the frame against a fully lighted, sculpted head—a clear acknowledgment of his power and central place in the world of the movie. With the exception of the credits for the production company and the movie's title, there is only one other individual—Alex North, the composer—whose name also appears in the exact middle of the screen, yet even there, the head behind his name is not fully lighted. Such are the important signals that can be sent by titles about an individual's significance in the production of a movie.

of a series of perfectly centered compositions that complement the narrative and that contrast with the classically composed shots throughout the rest of the film.

Another common deviation from the rule of thirds is any shot that places the action extremely close to the camera, thus offering little or no visual depth. This is perhaps the most effective method for the filmmaker to indicate that this action is the most important thing at the moment—for example, at a turning point or climax. Such a composition occurs in the final shot of Lewis Milestone's *The Strange Love of Martha Ivers* (1946; cinematographer: Victor Milner).

Sometimes a filmmaker both uses the rule of thirds and partially rejects it in a single shot. Such shots are generally composed in depth, presenting one part of the action in the foreground and another, equally important part in either the middle ground or background. The shot may begin looking like a classically composed shot that is following the rule of thirds but then, because of the

movement of several objects in the frame on all three planes, become less balanced and more complex. Such shots are complex for a reason: the filmmaker is probably attempting to call special attention to the relationship between the action in the foreground and that in the middle ground or background in order to establish a theme or to convey a number of narrative ideas simultaneously. In the long shot from Terrence Malick's *Days of Heaven* (1978; cinematographer: Néstor Almendros) pictured on page 170, composition of this sort establishes a very important hierarchical relationship between the characters in the foreground and the character (represented by his distant and visually aloof mansion) in the background.

In addition to helping filmmakers achieve distribution and balance in the general relationship of what we see on the screen, the rule of thirds helps cinematographers ensure that compositions flow appropriately from one shot to another. Without that visual consistency, the editor will be unable to establish continuity—though he or she may choose

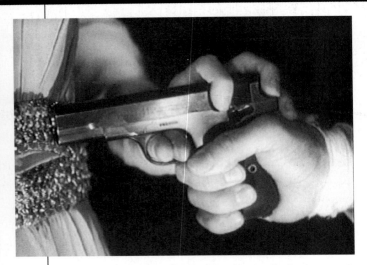

Composition With Limited Depth   In the final scene of Lewis Milestone's *The Strange Love of Martha Ivers* (1946), Walter O'Neil (Kirk Douglas) points a gun at Martha Ivers (Barbara Stanwyck), who places her thumb over his finger on the trigger and causes the gun to fire, killing her. The camera eye's proximity to the actors' bodies produces an image with no depth—just the beautifully balanced composition of their hands on the gun next to her waistline.

Composition in Depth in *Days of Heaven*   This shot from Terrence Malick's *Days of Heaven* (1978) establishes complex relationships, both spatially and thematically. The workers in the foreground are, as the direction of the woman's glance toward the house implies, curious about their employer, but they are physically (and culturally) removed from him. His house looms deep in the background; and although it is necessarily small within the frame, we can tell that it represents the position of power, mainly because it occupies the very edge of the high ground. Underscoring this relationship, the employer's agent walks (*left*) around the front of the car to explain that the workers are forbidden to go near the house.

to preserve graphic discontinuity as part of telling the story. For the viewer, such visual continuity suggests meanings through the placement and interrelationships of figures on the screen.

Camera Angle and Height

DVD Camera Angles

The camera's **shooting angle** is the level and height of the camera in relation to the subject being photographed. For the filmmaker, it is another framing element that offers many expressive possibilities. The normal height of the camera is *eye level*, which we take for granted because that's the way we see the world. Because our first impulse as viewers is to identify with the camera's point of view, and because we are likely to interpret any deviation from an eye-level shot as somehow different, filmmakers must take special care to use other basic camera angles—*high angle, low angle, Dutch angle,* and *aerial view*—in ways that are appropriate to and consistent with a movie's storytelling.

The phrases *to look up to* and *to look down on* reveal a physical viewpoint, as well as connoting admiration or condescension. In our everyday experience, a high angle is a position of power over what we're looking at, and we intuitively understand that the subject of a high-angle view is inferior, weak, or vulnerable in light of our actual and cultural experiences. A filmmaker shooting a shot from a high angle must be aware of this traditional interpretation of that view, whether or not the shot will be used to confirm or undermine that interpretation. Even a slight upward or downward angle of a camera may be enough to express an air of inferiority or superiority.

Eye Level   An **eye-level shot** is made from the observer's eye level and usually implies that the camera's attitude toward the subject being photographed is neutral. An eye-level shot used early in a movie—as part of establishing its characters, time, and place—occurs before we have learned the full context of the story, so we naturally tend to read its attitude toward the subject as neutral.

Thus, when Miss Wonderly (Mary Astor) introduces herself to Sam Spade (Humphrey Bogart) at the beginning of John Huston's *The Maltese Falcon* (1941; cinematographer: Arthur Edeson), the director uses an omniscient eye-level camera to establish a neutral client–detective relationship that seems to be what both characters want. This effect deliberately deceives us, as we learn only later in the film, when we discover that Miss Wonderly is not the innocent person she claims to be (as the eye-level angle suggested).

By contrast, an eye-level shot that occurs in *The Grifters* (1990; cinematographer: Oliver Stapleton), comes later in the movie, after the director, Stephen Frears, has established a narrative context for interpreting his characters and their situation. From the beginning of the film, we know that Lilly Dillon (Anjelica Huston) and her son, Roy (John Cusack), are grifters, or con artists. After an eight-year estrangement, they meet again, but each still regards suspiciously everything the other says or does. The eye-level shot reveals the hollow dialogue and tension of their reunion and is thus ironic, since they know, as we do, that their relationship is off balance (not "on the level").

Eye-Level Shot In John Huston's *The Maltese Falcon* (1941), this eye-level shot, used throughout the initial meeting of Miss Wonderly (Mary Astor) and Sam Spade (Humphrey Bogart), leads us to the false belief that the facts of their meeting are "on the level."

High Angle

A **high-angle shot** (also called a *high shot* or *down shot*) is made with the camera above the action and typically implies the observer's sense of superiority to the subject being photographed. In Rouben Mamoulian's *Love Me Tonight* (1932; cinematographer: Victor Milner), Maurice Courtelin (Maurice Chevalier) finally admits to Princess Jeanette (Jeanette MacDonald) that he is not an aristocrat, but rather an ordinary tailor. Although the princess loves him, she runs from the room in confusion, and the camera looks down on Maurice, who is now left to assess his reduced status with the symbolic measuring tape in his hands.

Sometimes, however, a high-angle shot can be used to play against its traditional implications. In Alfred Hitchcock's *North by Northwest* (1959; cinematographer: Robert Burks), one of the villains, Phillip Vandamm (James Mason), tells his collaborator, Leonard (Martin Landau), that he is taking his mistress, Eve Kendall (Eva Marie Saint), for a trip on his private plane. Vandamm knows that Kendall is part of an American spy ring that has discovered his selling of government secrets to the enemy, and he plans to kill her by pushing her out of the aircraft. As he speaks, the crane-mounted camera rises to a very high angle looking down at the two men, and Vandamm concludes, "This matter is best disposed of from a great height. Over water." The overall effect of this shot depends completely on this unconventional use of the high angle: it does not imply superiority, but rather emphasizes Vandamm's deadly plan. Its ironic, humorous effect depends as well on James Mason's wry delivery of these lines.

Low Angle

A **low-angle shot** (or *low shot*) is made with the camera below the action and typically places the observer in the position of feeling helpless in the presence of an obviously superior force, as when we look up at King Kong on the Empire State Building or up at the shark from the underwater camera's point of view in *Jaws*. In Spike Lee's *Do the Right Thing* (1989; cinematographer: Ernest R. Dickerson), Radio Raheem (Bill Nunn), who both entertains and intimidates the neighborhood by playing loud music on his boom

[1]

[2]

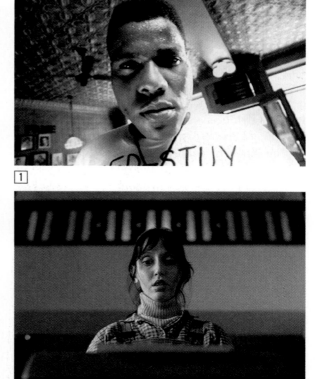

[1]

[2]

Low-Angle Shot   Two faces, both shot at low angle, convey two different meanings. [1] A low-angle shot of Radio Raheem (Bill Nunn) from Spike Lee's *Do the Right Thing* (1989) puts us in the position of Sal (Danny Aiello, *not pictured*), a pizzeria owner who is intimidated and angered by his boom box–carrying customer. [2] In Stanley Kubrick's *The Shining* (1980), a low-angle shot from an omniscient point of view reveals the depth of Wendy's (Shelley Duvall) panic and despair.

High-Angle Shot   [1] In this scene from Rouben Mamoulian's *Love Me Tonight* (1932), the high-angle shot has the traditional meaning of making the subject seem inferior. After Maurice Courtelin (Maurice Chevalier) admits that he is not an aristocrat, but rather an ordinary tailor, the camera looks down on him as he is left to assess his future with a symbolic measuring tape in his hands. [2] This shot from Alfred Hitchcock's *North by Northwest* (1959), although taken from a high angle, makes Phillip Vandamm (James Mason) and Leonard (Martin Landau), who are planning to murder Vandamm's mistress by pushing her out of his private airplane, appear even more menacing than they have up to this point.

box, appears menacing when photographed from a low, oblique angle during a confrontation with Sal, the owner of the neighborhood pizzeria.

However, filmmakers often play against the expectation that a subject shot from a low angle is menacing or powerful. In Stanley Kubrick's *The Shining*

(1980; cinematographer: John Alcott), when Wendy (Shelley Duvall) discovers a manuscript that suggests her husband, Jack, is insane, a low-angle shot emphasizes her anxiety, fear, and vulnerability. The shot also reminds us that the visual and narrative context of an angle affects our interpretation of it. The shot places Jack's typewriter in the foreground, thus making it appear very large, which implies its power over her and the threatening nature of what she is seeing (even before it is revealed to us). The low angle also denies us the ability to see what is

1

3

2

4

Camera Angles in *M* This scene from Fritz Lang's *M* (1931; cinematographer: Fritz Arno Wagner)—in which an innocent man becomes the object of a crowd's suspicions—uses eye-level, low-angle, and high-angle shots to provide a context for us to distinguish real threats from perceived ones. [1] A neutral (and accidental) meeting between a short man and a little girl occurs in a context of suspicion (the city of Berlin has suffered a number of child murders in a short span of time). [2] A high-angle shot from the perspective of a tall man who has brusquely asked, "Is that your kid?" reinforces the short man's modest stature and relative powerlessness. [3] The short man's perspective, an exaggerated low-angle shot, makes the question "Why were you bothering that kid?" even more ominous than the man's tone of voice makes it. [4] Here we return to an LS, as the short man protests his innocence and a crowd—soon to be a mob—gathers round.

going on behind her at a moment that we fear (and expect) the newly mad Jack to creep up behind her—thus elevating the suspense and making a character seen in extreme low angle appear more vulnerable than any high-angle shot could have.

In most scenes, obviously, different angles are used together to convey more complex meanings. Neil Jordan's *The Crying Game* (1992; cinematogra-pher: Ian Wilson), for example, uses alternating camera angles to convey and then resolve tensions between two characters. The scene begins with a confrontation between Fergus (Stephen Rea), an IRA gunman, and Jody (Forest Whitaker), a British-born black soldier whom Fergus and his terrorist cohorts have taken hostage. Power, race, and politics separate them, as confirmed by an alternating use of high- and low-angle shots from the perspectives of both characters during their dialogue. They start to relax when Jody shows Fergus a picture of his "wife," and by the time Jody talks about his experiences as a cricket player, they are speaking as men who have much in common—a transition that is signaled by a series of shots taken at eye level. These final shots help demonstrate that the men have more in common than their differences had at first suggested.

Dutch Angle   In a **Dutch-angle shot** (also called a *Dutch-tilt shot* or *oblique-angle shot*), the camera is tilted from its normal horizontal and vertical position so that it is no longer straight, giving the viewer the impression that the world in the frame is out of balance.[7] Two classic films that use a vertiginously tilted camera are John Ford's *The Informer* (1935; cinematographer: Joseph H. August) and Carol Reed's *The Third Man* (1949; cinematographer: Robert Krasker). For the sequence in *Bride of Frankenstein* (1935; cinematographer: John J. Mescall) in which Dr. Frankenstein (Colin Clive) and Dr. Pretorius (Ernest Thesiger) create a bride (Elsa Lanchester) for the Monster (Boris Karloff), director James Whale creates a highly stylized mise-en-scène—a tower laboratory filled with grotesque, futuristic machinery—that he shoots with a number of Dutch angles. The Dutch angles accentuate the unnatural nature of the doctors' unnatural actions, which are both funny and frightening.

Aerial View   An **aerial-view shot** (or *bird's-eye-view shot*), an extreme type of point-of-view shot, is taken from an aircraft or very high crane and implies the observer's omniscience. A classic example of the aerial view comes, naturally enough, from Alfred Hitchcock's *The Birds* (1963; cinematographer: Robert Burks). After showing us standard

[1]

[2]

Dutch-Angle Shot   In *Bride of Frankenstein* (1935), James Whale uses Dutch-angle shots to enhance the campy weirdness of the lab work in this film [1]. This scene culminates in one of the most famous Dutch-angle shots of all time—that of the Bride (Elsa Lanchester) first seeing the Monster [2].

high-angle shots of a massive explosion at a gas station, the director cuts to a high aerial shot (literally a bird's-eye view) in which the circling birds seem almost gentle in contrast to the tragedy they have just caused below. Hitchcock said he used this aerial shot to show, all at once, the gulls massing for another attack on the town, the topography of the region, and the gas station on fire. Furthermore, he

[7] The adjective *Dutch* (as in the phrases *Dutch uncle*, *Dutch treat*, and *Dutch auction*) indicates something out of the ordinary or, in this case, out of line. This meaning of *Dutch* seems to originate with the English antipathy for all things Dutch at the height of Anglo-Dutch competition during the seventeenth century. I am grateful to Russell Merritt for clarifying this for me.

did not want to "waste a lot of footage on showing the elaborate operation of the firemen extinguishing the fire. You can do a lot of things very quickly by getting away from something."[8]

Scale

Scale is the size and placement of a particular object or a part of a scene in relation to the rest—a relationship determined by the type of shot used and the position of the camera. Scale may change from shot to shot. From what you learned in the preceding sections, it should be clear that the type of shot affects the scale of the shot *and* thus the effect and meaning of a scene. In *Jurassic Park* (1993; cinematographer: Dean Cundey), as in most of his movies, Steven Spielberg exploits scale to create awe and delight. The director knows that we really want to see dinosaurs—the stars of the film, after all—and he slowly builds our apprehension by delaying this sight. When he introduces the first dinosaur, he maximizes—through the manipulation of scale and special-effects cinematography—the astonishment that characters and viewers alike feel.

At Jurassic Park, jeeps carrying the group arrive on a grassy plain, clearly establishing the human scale of the scene. But Drs. Grant (Sam Neill) and Sattler (Laura Dern), preoccupied with scientific talk, take a moment to realize that Hammond (Richard Attenborough) has just introduced them to a live dinosaur, as benign as it is huge, which looks down upon them. ELSs make the dinosaur seem even taller. When the dazed Grant asks, "How did you do this?" Hammond replies, "I'll show you." It's impossible to forget what Spielberg then shows us: not just the first dinosaur, but also a spectacular vista in which numerous such creatures move slowly across the screen. Creating a sense of *wonder* is one of Spielberg's stylistic trademarks, and his use of scale here does just that as it also helps create meaning. Because this is a science fiction film, we are prepared for surprises when we are introduced to a world that is partly recogniza-

[1]

[2]

Scale In Steven Spielberg's *Jurassic Park* (1993), [1] the reaction of Dr. Sattler (Laura Dern, *left*), and Dr. Grant (Sam Neill, *right*) to their first dinosaur sighting prepares us for an impressive image onscreen, and we are not disappointed. In placing the reaction before the action itself, Spielberg heightens the suspense of the scene. [2] The scale of the brontosaurus is exaggerated by the framing of this shot too, which implies that the beast is so gargantuan that it can't fit into the frame.

ble and partly fantastic. Once the dinosaurs make their actual appearance, we know that humans, however powerful in their financial and scientific pursuits, are not alone among the many species on Earth but also smaller than some and thus highly vulnerable.

Of course, the scale of small objects can be exaggerated for meaningful effect too, as in the example from Alfred Hitchcock's *Notorious* (1946) mentioned earlier (see page 167). When a tiny cup (or any other small object) looms larger than anything else in the frame, we can be sure that it is important to the film's meaning.

[8] Alfred Hitchcock, qtd. in François Truffaut, *Hitchcock*, rev. ed. (New York: Simon & Schuster, 1985), 292–94.

Camera Movement

⊙ DVD The Moving Camera

Any movement of the camera within a shot automatically changes the image we see because the elements of framing that we have discussed thus far—camera angle, level, height, types of shots, and scale—are all modified when the camera moves within that shot. The moving camera opens up cinematic space, and thus filmmakers use it to achieve many effects. It can search and increase the space, introduce us to more details than would be possible with a static image, choose which of these details we should look at or ignore, follow movement through a room or across a landscape, and establish complex relationships between figures in the frame—especially in shots that are longer than the average. It allows the viewer to accompany or follow the movements of a character, object, or vehicle, as well as to see the action from a character's point of view. The moving camera leads the viewer's eye, or focuses the viewer's attention and, by moving *into* the scene, helps create the illusion of depth in the flat screen image. Furthermore, it helps convey relationships: spatial, causal, and psychological.

Within the first decade of movie history, D. W. Griffith began to exploit the power of simple camera movement to create associations within the frame and, in some cases, to establish a cause-and-effect relationship. In *The Birth of a Nation* (1915; cinematographer: G. W. Bitzer), within one shot, he establishes a view of a Civil War battle, turns the camera toward a woman and small children on a wagon, and then turns back to the battle. From that instinctive, fluid camera movement, we understand the relationship between the horror of the battle and the misery that it has created for innocent civilians. Of course, Griffith could have cut between shots of the battle and the bystanders, but breaking up the space and time with editing would not achieve the same subtle effect as a single shot does.

In the 1920s, German filmmakers took this very simple type of camera movement to the next level, perfecting fluid camera movement within and between shots. In fact, F. W. Murnau, who is associated with some of the greatest early work with the moving camera in such films as *The Last Laugh* (1924; cinematographer: Karl Freund) and *Sunrise: A Song of Two Humans* (1927; cinematographers: Charles Rosher and Karl Struss), referred to it as the *unchained* camera, thereby suggesting that it has a life of its own, with no limits to the freedom with which it can move. Since then, the moving camera has become one of the dominant stylistic trademarks of a diverse group of directors, including Orson Welles, Max Ophüls, Jean Renoir, Martin Scorsese, Lars von Trier, Terrence Malick, and Pedro Almodóvar.

Almodóvar uses the moving camera throughout *Talk to Her* (2002; cinematographer: Javier Aguirresarobe), perhaps most effectively at the very beginning of the movie. After a brief prologue photographed at a dance performance, we see a close-up of Benigno Martín (Javier Cámara), going about his work while he talks about this performance to someone we do not see. Although we don't yet know for certain where he works, we get a clue from his collarless blue shirt, one often worn by hospital nurses or orderlies. As the camera moves down from his face, we see that he is manicuring someone's nails, probably a woman's, but we don't yet know her identity or if she is interested in the story he is telling her. Still within the first shot, the camera moves to the right and reframes to a close-up of a woman, lying in a bed, her eyes closed and a serene look on her face.

This gradual unfolding of the context of this scene grabs our interest and prompts us to ask, as each new detail is revealed by the moving camera, more questions about the relationship between these two people. After a series of shots immediately following this first one, we come to understand that the woman is Alicia (Leonor Watling), a young ballet student who has been in a coma in this hospital for four years, and that she is totally unaware of what is happening to and around her. Benigno, a respected member of the hospital staff, has fallen in love with her—a doomed endeavor it would seem, considering that he is homosexual and she is unlikely to recover. Throughout this complex story, Almodóvar uses the most subtle moving-camera shots to reveal the psychological relationship between Benigno and Alicia.

The smoothly moving camera helped change the way movies were made and thus the ways in which we see and interpret them. But before the camera was capable of smooth movement, directors and their camera operators had to find ways to create steady moving shots that would imitate the way the human eye/brain sees. When we look around a room or landscape, or see movement through space, our eyes dart from subject to subject, from plane to plane, and so we "see" more like a series of rapidly edited movie shots than a smooth flow of information. Yet our eyes and brain work together to smooth out the bumps. Camera motion, however, must itself be smooth in order for its audience to make sense of (or even tolerate) the shots that result from that motion.

There are exceptions, of course: during the 1960s, nonfiction filmmakers began what was soon to become a widespread use of the *handheld camera*, which both ushered in entirely new ways of filmmaking, such as *cinéma vérité* and *direct cinema*, and greatly influenced narrative film style. For the most part, however, cinematographers strive to ensure that the camera does not shake or jump while moving through a shot. To make steady moving shots, the camera is usually mounted on a *tripod*, where it can move on a horizontal or vertical axis, or on a *dolly*, *crane*, car, helicopter, or other moving vehicle that permits it to capture its images smoothly.

The basic types of shots involving camera movement are the *pan*, *tilt*, *tracking*, *dolly*, and *crane* shots, as well as those made with the *Steadicam*, *handheld camera*, or the *zoom lens*. Each involves a particular kind of movement, depends on a particular kind of equipment, and has its own expressive potential.

Pan Shot   A **pan shot** is the horizontal movement of a camera mounted on the gyroscopic head of a stationary tripod. This head ensures smooth panning and tilting and keeps the frame level. The pan shot offers us a larger, more panoramic view than a shot taken from a fixed camera; guides our attention to characters or actions that are important; makes us aware of relationships between

subjects that are too far apart to be shown together in the frame; allows us to follow people or objects; and attempts to replicate what we see when we turn our heads to survey a scene or follow a character. Pan shots are particularly effective in settings of great scope, such as the many circus scenes in Max Ophüls's *Lola Montès* (1955; cinematographer: Christian Matras) or the ballroom sequence in Orson Welles's *The Magnificent Ambersons* (1942; cinematographer: Stanley Cortez), where he used several pan shots that moved almost 360 degrees.

Tilt Shot   A **tilt shot** is the vertical movement of a camera mounted on the gyroscopic head of a stationary tripod. Like the pan shot, it is a simple movement with dynamic possibilities for creating meaning. Orson Welles makes excellent use of this shot in *Citizen Kane* (1941; cinematographer: Gregg Toland). When Susan Kane (Dorothy Comingore) finally summons the psychological and emotional strength to leave her tyrannical husband, he reacts by destroying her bedroom. At the peak of his violent rage, he seizes the glass globe with an interior snow scene; the camera tilts upward from the ball to Kane's (Welles) face; he whispers "Rosebud" and leaves the room. The tilt links the roundness and mystery of the glass ball with Kane's round, bald head; furthermore, it reminds us that the first place we saw the glass ball was on Susan's dressing table in her rooming-house bedroom, thus further linking the meaning of *Rosebud* with her.

Dolly Shot   A **dolly shot** (also known as a *tracking shot* or *traveling shot*) is one taken by a camera fixed to a wheeled support, generally known as a **dolly**. The dolly permits the cinematographer to make noiseless moving shots. When a dolly runs on tracks, the resulting shot is called a *tracking shot*. The dolly shot is one of the most effective (and consequently most common) uses of the moving camera. When the camera is used to **dolly-in** on (move toward) a subject, the subject grows in the frame, gaining significance not only through being bigger in the frame, but also through those moments in which we actually see it growing bigger.

The **dolly-out** movement (moving away from the subject) is often used for *slow disclosure*, which occurs when an edited succession of images leads from A to B to C as they gradually reveal the elements of a scene. Each image expands on the one before, thereby changing its significance with new information. A good example occurs in Stanley Kubrick's *Dr. Strangelove or: How I Learned to Stop Worrying and Love the Bomb* (1964) when—in a succession of images—the serious, patriotic bomber pilot is revealed to be concentrating not on his instruments, but instead on a copy of *Playboy* magazine.

A **tracking shot** is a type of dolly shot that moves smoothly with the action (alongside, above, beneath, behind, or ahead of it) when the camera is mounted on a wheeled vehicle that runs on a set of tracks. Some of the most beautiful effects in the movies are created by tracking shots, especially when the camera covers a great distance. Director King Vidor used an effective lateral tracking shot in his World War I film, *The Big Parade* (1925; cinematographers: John Arnold and Charles Van Enger) to follow the progress of American troops entering enemy-held woods. This shot, which has a documentary quality to it because it puts us in motion beside the soldiers as they march into com-

[1]

[2]

Tilt Shot In Orson Welles's *Citizen Kane* (1941), the camera presents the first half of this shot [1], then tilts upward to present the second half [2]. Of course, Welles could have shown us both halves, even Kane's entire body, within one static frame. The camera movement directs our eyes, however, and makes the symbolism unmistakable.

This gradual intensification effect is commonly used at moments of a character's realization and/or decision, or as a point-of-view shot of what the character is having a realization about. The scene in Hitchcock's *Notorious* (1946), illustrated on page 167, in which Alicia Huberman (Ingrid Bergman) realizes that she is being poisoned via the coffee, uses both kinds of dolly-in movements, as well as other camera moves that explicitly illustrate cause and effect (the camera moves from the coffee to Bergman at the moment she complains about not feeling well, for example).

A Dolly in Action Camera operators race alongside a speeding chariot on a *dolly* during the filming of Ridley Scott's *Gladiator* (2000; cinematographer: John Mathieson).

Tracking Shot In Jean Renoir's *The Grand Illusion* (1937), the contradictory aspects of Captain von Rauffenstein's (Erich von Stroheim) life are engagingly and economically captured by the long tracking shot that catalogs the objects in his living quarters. The pistol on top of a volume of Casanova's memoirs is an especially telling detail: von Rauffenstein is a lover and a fighter.

bat, has been repeated many times in subsequent war films.

Jean Renoir used the moving camera to create the feeling of real space, a rhythmic flow of action, and a rich mise-en-scène. In *The Grand Illusion* (1937; cinematographer: Christian Matras), Renoir's brilliant film about World War I, we receive an intimate introduction to Captain von Rauffenstein (Erich von Stroheim), the commandant of a German prison camp, through a long tracking shot (plus four other brief shots) that reveals details of his life.

Zoom The zoom is both a lens (as discussed earlier) and a type of camera movement. It has a variable focal length, which permits the camera operator during shooting to shift from the wide-angle lens (short focus) to the telephoto lens (long focus), or vice versa, without changing the focus or aperture settings. It is not a camera movement per se, but a lens. Because the optics inside the lens are able to move in relation to each other and thus shift the focal length, the zoom can provide the illusion of the camera moving toward or away from the

subject. One result of this shift is that the image is magnified (when shifting from short to long focal length) or demagnified by shifting in the opposite direction.

That magnification is the essential difference between **zoom-in** and dolly-in movements on a subject. When dollying, a camera actually moves through space; in the process, spatial relationships between the camera and the objects in its frame shift, causing relative changes in position between onscreen figures or objects. By contrast, because a zoom lens does not move through space, its depiction of spatial relationships between the camera and its subjects does not change. All a zoom shot does is magnify the image.

(◎DVD) Zoom and Moving Camera Effects

The result of zoom shots, as we've noted before, can be "movement" that appears artificial and self-conscious. Of course, there are dramatic, cinematic, and stylistic reasons for using this effect, but for the most part, the artificiality of the zoom (and the fact that viewers naturally associate the zoom effect with its overuse in amateur home videos) makes it a technique that is rarely used well in professional filmmaking. When the zoom shot *is* used expressively, however, it can be breathtaking. In *Goodfellas* (1990; cinematographer: Michael Ballhaus), during the scene in which Henry Hill (Ray Liotta) meets Jimmy Conway (Robert De Niro) in a diner, director Martin Scorsese achieves a memorable effect with the moving camera and the zoom lens. He tracks *in* (while moving the zoom lens *out*) and tracks *out* (while moving the zoom lens *in*) to reflect Henry's paranoid, paralyzed state of mind. As the camera and lens move *against* one another, the image traps Hill inside the hermetic world of the mob and us inside a world of spatial disorientation in an ordinary diner.

Crane Shot A **crane shot** is made from a camera mounted on an elevating arm that, in turn, is mounted on a vehicle capable of moving by its own power. A crane may also be mounted on a vehicle that can be pushed along tracks to smooth its movement. The arm can be raised or lowered to the degree that the particular crane permits. Shots made with a crane differ from those made with a camera mounted on a dolly or an ordinary track (each of which is, in theory, capable only of horizontal or vertical movement) because the crane has the full freedom of horizontal and vertical movement, as well as the capability of lifting the camera high off the ground. Thus a filmmaker can use a crane to shoot with extraordinary flexibility. As equipment for moving the camera has become more versatile, crane shots have become more commonplace.

Any list of memorable crane shots would include a shot in Victor Fleming's *Gone With the Wind* (1939; cinematographer: Ernest Haller) in which the camera soars up over ground near the Atlanta railroad station to reveal the hundreds of Civil War dead, or the smooth, graceful shot in Alfred Hitchcock's *Notorious* (1946; cinematographer: Ted Tetzlaff) in which the camera swoops down alongside a staircase and across a crowded ballroom. In Oliver Stone's *Alexander* (2004; cinematographer: Rodrigo Prieto), the Macedonian warrior Alexander the Great (Colin Farrell) looks up to see the eagle that is his personal symbol. The camera soars up to assume the eagle's point of view and then looks down over the field on which Alexander and his troops will shortly fight the Persians.

Perhaps the most famous crane shot in movie history occurs at the opening of Orson Welles's *Touch of Evil* (1958; cinematographer: Russell Metty). The scene takes place at night in Los Robles, a seedy town on the U.S.–Mexico border. After the Universal International logo dissolves from the screen, we see a close-up of a man's hand swinging toward the camera and setting a timer that will make the bomb he holds explode in about three minutes. The camera pans left to reveal two figures approaching the camera from the end of a long interior corridor; the bomber, Manelo Sanchez (Victor Millan), runs left into the frame, realizes that these people are his targets, and runs out of the frame to the right as the camera pans right to follow him. He places the bomb in the trunk of a luxurious convertible, the top of which is down, and disappears screen right just as the couple enters the frame at top left; the camera tracks backward and reframes to an LS.

As the couple gets into the car, the camera (mounted on a crane that is, in turn, mounted on a truck) swings to an extreme high angle. The car pulls forward alongside a building and turns left at the front of the building as the camera reaches the roof level at its back. We momentarily lose sight of the car, but the camera, which has oriented us to where the car is, merely pans left and brings it back into the frame as it moves left across an alley into a main street. The camera cranes down to an angle slightly higher than the car, which has turned left and now heads toward the camera on a vertical axis moving from background to foreground. When the car pauses at the direction of a policeman, who permits other traffic to cross in the foreground on a horizontal axis, the camera begins tracking backward to keep the car in the frame. The camera continues to track backward, reframes to an XLS, and pans slightly to the left. The car stops at an intersection.

A man and a woman ("Mike" Vargas, a Mexican narcotics agent played by Charlton Heston, and Susan Vargas, whom he has just married, played by Janet Leigh) enter the intersection at screen right and continue across the street as the camera lowers to an eye-level LS. The car turns left onto the street on which the Vargases are walking, and they scurry to get out of its way as the car moves out of the frame. They continue walking with the camera tracking slightly ahead of them; it keeps them in the frame as they pass the car, which is now delayed by a herd of goats that has stopped in another intersection. The camera continues to track backward, keeping the couple and the car in the frame; this becomes a deep-space composition with the car in the background, crossway traffic in the middle ground, and the Vargas couple in the foreground. The Vargases reach the kiosk marking the entrance to the border crossing and pass it on the right, still walking toward the camera, which now rises, reframing into a high-angle LS that reveals the car driving past the left side of the kiosk. The frame now unites the two couples (one in the car, the other walking) as they move forward at the same time to what we, knowing that the bomb is in the car, anticipate will be a climactic moment.

The camera stops and reframes to an MS with

1

5

2

6

3

7

4

8

The Crane Shot in *Touch of Evil* These stills from the opening crane shot in Orson Welles's *Touch of Evil* (1958) show the progress of the camera over a wide-ranging space through a continuous long shot that ends only at the point where the car blows up [1–7]. A reaction shot of Mike and Susan Vargas (Charlton Heston and Janet Leigh) follows [8], and as the Vargases run toward the site of the explosion, the mystery at the heart of the movie begins to unfold.

the Vargases standing on the right and the car stopped on the left. While the first border agent begins to question the newlyweds, soon recognizing Vargas, the second agent checks the car's rear license plate. The agents and Vargas discuss smashing drug rings, but Vargas explains that he and his wife are crossing to the American side so that his wife can have an ice cream soda. Meanwhile, the driver of the targeted car, Mr. Linnekar (actor not credited), asks if he can get through the crossing. The Vargases walk out of the frame, continuing the discussion about drugs, then apparently walk around the front of the car and reenter the frame at the left side; the camera pans slightly left and reframes the Vargases, border agents, and Linnekar and Zita (Joi Lansing), his companion.

After a few moments of conversation, the Vargases walk away toward the back and then left of the frame; the car moves slowly forward; and Zita complains to one of the guards—in a moment of delicious black humor—that she hears a "ticking noise." As the car leaves the frame, the camera pans left to another deep-focus composition with the Vargases in the background, two military policemen walking from the background toward the camera, and pedestrians passing across the middle ground. The camera tracks forward and reframes to an MS; the Vargases embrace as the bomb explodes. Startled, they look up and see the car in flames.

The final two shots in this extraordinary sequence are, first, a rapid *zoom-in* on the explosion, and second, a low-angle, *handheld* shot of Vargas running toward the scene. These shots, more self-conscious and less polished than the preceding, fluid crane shots, cinematically and dramatically shift the tone from one of controlled suspense to out-of-control chaos that changes the normal world and sets the scene for the story's development. This is also an excellent example of how movies exploit the establishment and breaking of narrative forms.

With extraordinary virtuosity, Welles has combined nearly all types of shots, angles, framings, and camera movements. He accomplishes the changes in camera height, level, angle, and framing by mounting the camera on a crane that can be raised and lowered smoothly from ground level to an extreme high angle, reframed easily, and moved effortlessly above and around the setting (parking lot, market arcade, street, intersections, border inspection area). Here the moving camera is both unchained and fearless, a thoroughly omniscient observer as well as a voyeur, particularly in its opening observations of the bomber. But what is the function of this cinematographic tour de force? Is it just one of Welles's razzle-dazzle attempts to grab the audience's attention, or does it create meaning?

The answer, of course, is that it has both purposes. Its virtuosity astonishes, but with a point. In addition to witnessing the inciting device for the plot, we learn that Los Robles is a labyrinth of activity, lights, shadows, and mysteries; and that the destinies of Linnekar, Zita, Vargas, and Susan are in some way tangled. The odd and extreme camera angles (at both the beginning and the end of the scene) reinforce the air of mystery and disorient us within the cinematic space. All the while, the bold black-and-white contrasts pull us into the deep shadows of vice, corruption, and brutal crime.

Handheld Camera The last two shots in the scene from *Touch of Evil* (1958) described in the previous section were made with a handheld camera, a small, portable, and lightweight instrument that is held by the camera operator during shooting. At one time, handheld cameras were limited to 8mm or 16mm film stock, but now they can handle a variety of film gauges. In contrast to the smooth moving-camera shots that we have been discussing, the inherent shakiness of the handheld camera can be exploited when a loss of control, whether in the situation or in the character's state of mind, is something the filmmaker wants to convey to the viewer. *Touch of Evil* does just that, with an elaborately choreographed and fluid moving-camera sequence suddenly interrupted by an explosion, which is photographed with the shaky handheld. We feel that the world has changed because the way we see the world has shifted so dramatically .

However, the uses of the handheld camera go beyond that. After nearly fifty years of viewing news coverage of unfolding events, nonfiction films in the direct cinema style, and reality television shows, audiences have been conditioned to associ-

Handheld Camera The handheld camera is used to great advantage in keeping the viewer disoriented during Paul Greengrass's high-action thriller, *The Bourne Supremacy* (2004), as in this shot of Jason Bourne (Matt Damon) trying to elude the pursuing police.

ate the look of handheld camera shots with documentary realism—that is, with the assumption that something is really happening, and the photographer (and thus the viewer) is *there*. Narrative feature films can take advantage of that intuitive association to heighten or alter our experience of a particular event, such as the attack on the military base in Stanley Kubrick's *Dr. Strangelove or: How I Learned to Stop Worrying and Love the Bomb* (1964: cinematographer: Gilbert Taylor), or cinematographer Haskell Wexler's influential documentary-style work in such movies as Milos Forman's *One Flew Over the Cuckoo's Nest* (1975) and John Sayles's *Matewan* (1987), or the cinematographer Oliver Wood's astonishing, disorienting handheld shots in Paul Greengrass's *The Bourne Supremacy* (2004).

Steadicam From the beginning of the movies, movie cameras (handheld as well as those mounted on tripods, dollies, or other moving devices) have allowed filmmakers to approach their subjects, as when they move in for close-ups. But the handheld camera frequently produces a jumpy image, characteristic of avant-garde filmmaking and usually not acceptable in the mainstream. Thus, mainstream filmmakers embraced the **Steadicam**, a camera actually *worn* by the cameraperson (so it is not "handheld"), which removes that jumpiness and is now much used for smooth, fast, and intimate camera movement. The Steadicam system, which is perfectly balanced, automatically compensates for any movements made by the camera oper-

ator, whether in running down stairs, climbing a hill, or maneuvering in tight places where dollies or tracks cannot fit.

The Steadicam is used so frequently that it has all but ceased to call attention to itself, but there are many great, exhilarating uses of this camera that are worth remembering, including the work of Garrett Brown, the Steadicam operator in Stanley Kubrick's *The Shining* (1980; cinematographer: John Alcott), perhaps the most memorable being the long sequence that follows Danny Torrance's (Danny Lloyd) determined tricycle ride through the halls of the Overlook Hotel.

Another memorable example is Larry McConkey's Steadicam shot of Henry and Karen (Ray Liotta and Lorraine Bracco) entering the Copacabana in Martin Scorsese's *Goodfellas* (1990; cinematographer: Michael Ballhaus). As in *The Shining*, the camera stays behind the subjects as they enter the club's rear entrance and move through the kitchen and various service areas, where everyone knows and greets Liotta's character, to the club's main room, where a table is set up for the couple near the stage. This Steadicam sequence is very different from the one used in *The Shining*. In the Kubrick film, the Steadicam (mounted on a wheelchair) takes us on a dizzying

Steadicam in Action A camera operator uses a Steadicam to film the action during one of the gladiatorial combat scenes in Ridley Scott's *Gladiator* (2000).

ride through the hotels' labyrinthine halls, echoing the actual labyrinth in the garden and emphasizing the intense mystery of the story. We are left breathless at the end of it. In the *Goodfellas* sequence, however, the Steadicam leads the viewer, like a guide, as we follow a brash, young gangster trying to impress his future wife as they enter the glamorous world of a New York nightclub.

WEB The Steadicam and Camera Movement

Framing and Point of View

As the preceding discussion has illustrated, the framing of a shot—including the type of shot and its depth, camera angle and height, scale, and camera movement—has several major functions. In the most basic sense, framing controls what we see (explicitly, what is on the screen; and implicitly, what we know has been left out) and how we see it (up close, far away, from above or below, and so on). Framing also calls attention to the technique of cinematography, allowing us to delight in the variety of possibilities that the director and cinematographer have at their disposal. It also implies *point of view* (*POV*), which can mean the POV of the screenwriter, director, or one or more characters, or the actual POV of the camera itself. Of course, all of these POVs can be used in any one movie.

The camera's POV, the eyes through which we view the action, depends on the physical position from which the camera shoots. In most movies, the camera is omniscient: virtually able to go anywhere and see anything, either at average human eye level or above it. Eye-level, high, and low shooting angles, however, raise questions of objectivity and subjectivity; sometimes, as we have seen, directors use them to play against our expectations, to control or mislead us. In looking at movies, we experience frequent shifts in the camera's POV. The dominant neutral POV gives us the facts and background that are the context in which the characters live. The **omniscient POV** shows what the omniscient camera sees, typically from a high angle; a **single character's POV**, in which the shot is made with the camera close to the line of sight of a character (or animal or surveillance camera), shows what that person would be seeing of the action; and

the **group POV** shows us what a group of characters would see at their level.

Consider a very fast and active scene in Alfred Hitchcock's *The Birds* (1963; cinematographer: Robert Burks), in which a classic use of camera angle and point of view establishes and retains the viewer's orientation as the townspeople of Bodega Bay become increasingly agitated because of random attacks by birds. During one such attack, frightened people watch from the window of a diner as a bird strikes a gas station attendant, causing a gasoline leak that results in a tragic explosion. Chief among these spectators are Melanie Daniels (Tippi Hedren) and Mitch Brenner (Rod Taylor).

The basic pattern of camera angles alternates between shots from a high angle in the restaurant, looking out and down, to those from eye level, looking from the exterior through the window of the restaurant. These alternating points of view give the sequence its power. How does Hitchcock's use of alternating points of view create meaning in the sequence? It shows us (not for the first time) that the birds really do maliciously attack unsuspecting people. It also demonstrates that, at least in this cinematic world, people close to an impending tragedy—people like Mitch, Melanie, and the man with the cigar—can do virtually nothing to stop it.

DVD Point of View

Types of Shots in *The Birds* (Opposite) In this action-packed scene from *The Birds* (1963), Alfred Hitchcock orients us by manipulating types of shots, camera angles, and points of view. It includes [1] an eye-level medium close-up of Melanie (Tippi Hedren) and two men, who [2] see a gas station attendant hit by a bird; [3] an eye-level medium shot of Melanie and another woman, who [4] through high-angle shots such as this close-up, watch gasoline run through a nearby parking lot; [5] a slightly low-angle close-up of a group warning [6] a man in the parking lot, seen in this high-angle long shot, not to light his cigar, though he doesn't hear the warning; [7] the resulting explosion and fire, seen in a long shot from high angle; and [8] Melanie watching [9] the fire spread to the gas station, which [10] the birds observe from on high.

1

2

3

4

5

6

7

8

9

10

Speed and Length of the Shot

Up to this point we have emphasized the spatial aspects of how a shot is composed, lighted, and photographed. But the image we see on the screen has both spatial *and* temporal dimensions. Its length can be as important as any other characteristic. Although a shot is one uninterrupted run of the camera, no convention governs what that length should be. Before the arrival of sound, the average shot lasted about five seconds; after sound arrived, that average doubled to approximately ten seconds. Nonetheless, a shot can (and should) be as long as necessary to do its part in telling the story.

By controlling the length of shots, not only do filmmakers enable each shot to do its work—establish a setting, character, or cause of a following event—but they also control the relationship of each shot to the others and thus to the rhythm of the film. The length of any shot is controlled by three factors: the screenplay (the amount of action and dialogue written for each shot), the cinematography (the duration of what is actually shot), and the editing (what remains of the length of the actual shot after the film has been cut and assembled).

Here we will concentrate on the second of these factors: the relationship between cinematography and time. What kind of time does the camera record? As you know from Chapter 1, when we see a movie we are aware of basically two kinds of time: *real time*, time as we ordinarily perceive it in life outside the movie theater; and *cinematic time*, time as it is conveyed to us through the movie. Through a simple adjustment of the camera's motor, cinema can manipulate time with the same freedom and flexibility that it has to manipulate space and light.

Slow motion decelerates action by photographing it at a rate greater than the normal 24 fps (frames per second), so that it takes place in cinematic time less rapidly than the real action that took place before the camera. One effect of slow motion is to emphasize the power of memory, as in Sidney Lumet's *The Pawnbroker* (1964; cinematographer: Boris Kaufman), in which Sol Nazerman (Rod Steiger), a pawnbroker living in the Bronx, remembers pleasant memories in Germany before the Nazis and the Holocaust. Martin Scorsese frequently uses slow motion to suggest a character's heightened awareness of someone or something. In *Taxi Driver* (1976), for example, Travis Bickle (Robert De Niro) sees in slow motion what he considers to be the repulsive sidewalks of New York; and in *Raging Bull* (1980), Jake LaMotta (De Niro) fondly remembers his wife Vickie (Cathy Moriarty) in slow motion. Both films were shot by cinematographer Michael Chapman. Finally, slow motion can be used to reverse our expectations, as in Andy and Larry Wachowski's *The Matrix* (1999; cinematographer: Bill Pope), where Neo (Keanu Reeves) dodges the bullets shot by Agent Smith (Hugo Weaving) while shooting back with a spray of slow-motion bullets as he does cartwheels on the walls—a scene made possible, of course, with advanced special-effects techniques.

By contrast, **fast motion** accelerates action by photographing it at less than the normal filming rate, then projecting it at normal speed so that it takes place cinematically more rapidly. Thus, fast motion often depicts the rapid passing of time, as F. W. Murnau uses it in *Nosferatu* (1922; cinematographers: Fritz Arno Wagner and Günther Krampf), an early screen version of the Dracula story. The coach that Count Orlok (Max Schreck) sends to fetch his agent, Hutter (Gustav von Wangenheim), travels in fast motion, and although this effect may seem silly today, its original intent was to place us in an unpredictable landscape. In *Rumble Fish* (1983; cinematographer: Stephen H. Burum), director Francis Ford Coppola employs fast-motion, high-contrast, black-and-white images of clouds moving across the sky to indicate both the passing of time and the unsettled lives of the teenagers with whom the story is concerned. In *Requiem for a Dream* (2000; cinematographer: Matthew Libatique), director Darren Aronofsky uses fast motion to simulate the experience of being high on marijuana—an effect also used by Gus Van Sant in *Drugstore Cowboy* (1989; cinematographer: Robert D. Yeoman).

Perhaps no modern director has used and abused slow and fast motion, as well as virtually every other manipulation of cinematic space and

The Long Take and the Close-up   Great cinematographers love great female beauty, as demonstrated by these four images from Jonathan Glazer's *Birth* (2004), in which cinematographer Harris Savides holds the camera steady on Nicole Kidman's face for two minutes. The slight changes in her expression and the position of her head, eyes, and lips as she listens to music that absorbs her attention reveal, however slightly, the depth of her thoughts.

time, more than Godfrey Reggio in his "Qatsi" trilogy: *Koyaanisqatsi* (1983: cinematographer: Ron Fricke); *Powaqqatsi* (1988: cinematographers: Graham Berry and Leonidas Zourdoumis); and *Nagoyqatsi* (2002: cinematographer: Russell Lee Fine). Although Reggio's sweeping vision of the cultural and environmental decay of the modern world is lavishly depicted in poetic, even apocalyptic images, he often relies too heavily on manipulation to make his point.

Whereas the average shot lasts ten seconds, the **long take** can run anywhere from one to ten minutes. (An ordinary roll of film runs for ten minutes, but specially fitted cameras can accommodate longer rolls of film that permit takes of anywhere from fourteen to twenty-two minutes.) One of the most elegant techniques of cinematography, the

long take has the double potential of preserving both real space and real time. Ordinarily, we refer to a sequence as a series of edited shots characterized by inherent unity of theme and purpose. The long take is sometimes referred to as a *sequence shot* because it enables filmmakers to present a unified pattern of events within a single period of time in one shot. However, with the exception of such extraordinary examples as the opening of Orson Welles's *Touch of Evil* (1958; discussed earlier), the long take is rarely used for a sequence filmed in one shot. Instead, even masters of the evocative long take—directors such as F. W. Murnau, Max Ophüls, Orson Welles, William Wyler, Kenji Mizoguchi, and Stanley Kubrick—combine two or more long takes by linking them, often unobtrusively, into an apparently seamless whole.

Coupled with the moving camera, the long take also eliminates the need for separate setups for long, medium, and close-up shots. It permits the internal development of a story involving two or more lines of action without use of the editing technique, called *crosscutting*, that is normally employed to tell such a story. Furthermore, if a solid sense of cause and effect is essential to developing a sequence, the long take permits both the cause and the effect to be recorded in one take.

Conventional motion picture technology limited the fluid long take that these directors were striving for, but digital technology has enabled a director to achieve it. Using a Steadicam fitted with a high-definition video camera, Russian director Aleksandr Sokurov made *Russian Ark* (2002; cinematographer: Tilman Büttner), a ninety-six-minute historical epic filmed in one continuous shot—to date, the longest unbroken shot in film history.

A very effective use of a long take combined with a close-up occurs in Jonathan Glazer's *Birth* (2004; cinematographer: Harris Savides), a thriller that skirts the boundaries between the believable and the absurd. Anna (Nicole Kidman), a young widow, is torn between memories of her husband, Sean, and her obsession with a ten-year-old boy, also named Sean (Cameron Bright), who claims to be the reincarnation of her dead husband. At a concert that she attends with her fiancé, Joseph (Danny Huston), Anna listens intently to a selection from an opera that is concerned partly with the incestuous relationship between two mythical characters. This theme obviously invades Anna's thoughts, as does her unnerving sexual attraction to young Sean. Cinematographer Harris Savides devotes a full two minutes to a long take of Kidman's face, capturing the subtle shifts in her expression in a way that seems inspired by cinematographer Rudolph Maté's adoration of the face of Maria Falconetti in Carl Theodor Dreyer's *The Passion of Joan of Arc* (1928; see page 227). On one hand, Savides's haunting, long take is a declaration of love for an actor's face (one of the prime purposes of the close-up), but the length of the shot gives Kidman the time to convey the depth of Anna's thoughts without the use of dialogue or overt action.

Special Effects

Cinema itself is a *special effect*, an illusion that fools the human eye and brain into perceiving motion. **Special effects** (abbreviated **SPFX** or **FX**) is a term reserved for technology that creates images that would be too dangerous, too expensive, or, in some cases, simply impossible to achieve with the traditional cinematographic materials that we have already discussed. As spectacular as SPFX technologies and their effects can be, however, the goal of special-effects cinematography is generally to create verisimilitude—an illusion of reality, or a believable alternative reality—within the imaginative world of even the most fanciful movie. Special-effects expert Mat Beck says, "The art of visual effects is the art of what you can get away with, which means you really have to study a lot about how we perceive the world in order to find out how we can trick our perceptions to make something look real when it isn't."[9]

In-Camera, Mechanical, and Laboratory Effects

The ability of movies to create illusion has always been one of their major attractions for audiences. Indeed, the first special effect appeared in Alfred Clark's *The Execution of Mary Stuart* in 1895, the year the movies were born. To depict the queen's execution, Clark photographed the actor in position, stopped filming and replaced the actor with a dummy, then started the camera and beheaded the dummy. (Incidentally, this film involved another kind of illusion: a man, Robert Thomae, played Queen Mary.)

From that point forward, special effects appeared regularly in the films of Georges Méliès, the great illusionist, who used multiple exposures and stop-motion animation. Edwin S. Porter's *The Great Train Robbery* (1903) featured matte and composite shots, and J. Searle Dawley's *Rescued From an Eagle's Nest* (1908; cinematographer:

---

[9] Mat Beck, qtd. in "Special Effects: Titanic and Beyond," *Nova*, produced for PBS by the Science Unit at WGBH Boston, November 3, 1998.

Porter) included a mechanical eagle, created by Richard Murphy, that was the forerunner of "animatronic" creatures in contemporary films. By the mid 1920s, extraordinary effects were featured in such films as Fritz Lang's *Metropolis* (1927), for which designer Otto Hunte created the city of the future in miniature on a tabletop; Cecil B. DeMille's first version of *The Ten Commandments* (1923), in which technicians could part the Red Sea because it was made of two miniature slabs of Jell-O;[10] and the first of four versions of *The Lost World* (1925), directed by Harry O. Hoyt. The special effects in *The Lost World* were the work of Willis H. O'Brien, who went on to create the special effects in Merian C. Cooper and Ernest B. Schoedsack's *King Kong* (1933), in which the giant ape terrorizing New York City from the top of the Empire State Building was, in fact, a puppet.

Until the advent of *computer-generated imagery* in the late 1960s, such illusions were accomplished in essentially three ways: through **in-camera effects** created in the production camera (the regular camera used for shooting the rest of the film) on the original negative, through **mechanical effects** that create objects or events mechanically on the set and in front of the camera, and through **laboratory effects** created on a fresh piece of film stock.

Although computer-generated graphics and animation have virtually eclipsed the way special effects are now made, as you study and analyze SPFX in movies from the past, it is helpful to know how the principal types were made. Traditionally, the first category—in-camera effects—has included such simple illusory effects as *fade, wipe, dissolve,* and *montage.* (Although these are shots in themselves, together with editing they create transitional effects or manipulate time; for definitions and examples, see "Conventions of Continuity Editing" in Chapter 6.) Other in-camera effects include *split screen, superimposition, models and miniatures,*

Early Special Effects   For Fritz Lang's *Metropolis* (1927), a pioneering science fiction film, the city of the future was a model created by designer Otto Hunte. Special-effects photography (coordinated by Eugen Schüfftan, who developed trick-shot techniques that are still in use today) turned this miniature into a massive place onscreen, filled with awe-inspiring objects and vistas.

glass shots, matte paintings, in-camera matte shots, and *process shots.*

The second category—mechanical effects—includes objects or events that are created by artists and craftspeople and placed on the set to be photographed. There are, of course, endless examples of such special effects, including the different Frankenstein masks used in the many movies that feature that character (e.g., Mel Brooks's *Young Frankenstein* (1974; cinematographer: Gerald Hirschfeld; makeup artist: Edwin Butterworth); the beast in Ishirô Honda's Japanese cult film, *Godzilla* (1954; cinematographer: Masao Tamai; special effects: Teisho Arikawa); or the menacing shark in Steven Spielberg's *Jaws* (1975; cinematographer: Bill Butler; special effects: Robert A. Mattey and Kevin Pike).

In the third category—laboratory effects—are more complicated procedures, such as *contact printing* and *bipack,* as well as *blow-ups, cropping, pan and scan, flip shots, split-screen shots,* and *day-for-night shooting.* These complex technical procedures are outside the scope of this book, but you can find complete information on them in the books by Raymond Fielding, Bruce Kawin, and Ira

[10] DeMille's 1956 version of this parting of the Red Sea (cinematographically engineered by Loyal Griggs), which cost $2 million—the most expensive special effect to that time—involved matte shots, miniatures, six hundred extras, and a thirty-two-foot-high dam channeling tens of thousands of gallons of water.

Konigsberg listed in the bibliography at the back of this book.

⬤ WEB Evolution of Special Effects

Computer-Generated Imagery

Since it was first used in the late 1960s, computer-generated imagery (**CGI**) has transformed the motion picture industry, particularly the making of animated, fantasy, and science fiction movies. During the subsequent forty years, CGI improved so rapidly that the major films that used it during that time now seem almost as old-fashioned as the process shot. (A **process shot** is made of action in front of a rear projection screen that has on it still or moving images for the background.) Yet certain achievements are memorable for innovations that are landmarks in the development of CGI. Stanley Kubrick's *2001: A Space Odyssey* (1968; special effects designer and director: Kubrick; supervisors: Wally Veevers, Douglas Trumbull, Con Pederson, and Tom Howard; cinematographer: Geoffrey Unsworth) was the first film to seamlessly link footage shot by the camera with that prepared by the computer, and, now some four decades later, its look continues to amaze audiences. Indeed, it set a standard of technical sophistication, visual elegance, integration with the story, and power to create meaning that remains unsurpassed.

Other CGI landmarks include Steven Lis-

Special Effects and Historical Footage Special effects make the seemingly impossible possible. In some movies, such as Stanley Kubrick's *2001: A Space Odyssey* (1968), the effects situate us in a believable otherworld. In others, such as Robert Zemeckis's *Forrest Gump* (1994), they insert characters into historical situations. Using CGI and other techniques, the filmmakers spliced footage of Gump (Tom Hanks) into real footage of Presidents Richard Nixon and Lyndon Johnson and former Beatle John Lennon. In this picture, Gump appears to sit next to Lennon on the set of Dick Cavett's 1970s talk show. In the original footage, Lennon's wife, Yoko Ono, sat in the middle chair.

berger's *Tron* (1982; cinematographer: Bruce Logan), which, through comparatively simple SPFX, transports a computer hacker inside a computer; the "Star Wars" trilogy, consisting of *Star Wars* (1977; director: George Lucas; cinematographer: Gilbert Taylor), *The Empire Strikes Back* (1980, director: Irvin Kershner; cinematographer: Peter Suschitzky), and *Return of the Jedi* (1983, director: Richard Marquand; cinematographer: Alan Hume); Barry Levinson's *Young Sherlock Holmes* (1985; cinematographers: Stephen Goldblatt and Stephen Smith), which, in the "Glass Man" sequence, created a new standard for image resolution by laser-scanning the image directly onto the film stock; and James Cameron's *The Abyss* (1989; cinematographer: Mikael Salomon), which introduced the first three-dimensional CGI. Cameron's other movies, including *Terminator 2: Judgment Day* (1991; cinematographer: Adam Greenberg) and *Titanic* (1997; cinematographer: Russell Carpenter) were equally innovative.

In 1993, Steven Spielberg's *Jurassic Park* (cinematographer: Dean Cundey) became an instant classic with its believable computer-generated dinosaurs, and Cundey's work on Brad Silberling's *Casper* (1995) introduced the first computer-

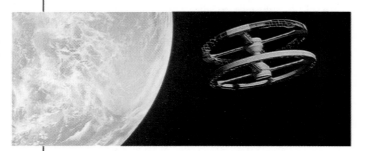

Modern Special Effects The special effects in Stanley Kubrick's *2001: A Space Odyssey* took up more than 60 percent of the movie's production budget and required nearly eighteen months to complete. When the movie was released in 1968, the results were immediately celebrated. A year before the first moon landing, this was human beings' closest look at outer space.

generated lead and talking figure. In 1988, Robert Zemeckis's *Who Framed Roger Rabbit* (1988; cinematographer: Dean Cundey) combined computer-generated imagery with actual settings and characters, so cartoonlike images entered the real world. Zemeckis reversed that pattern in *Forrest Gump* (1994; cinematographer: Don Burgess), by using CGI to insert footage of Gump (Tom Hanks) into real footage of Presidents Richard Nixon and Lyndon Johnson and former Beatle John Lennon.

In the last ten years, the major CGI achievements have been even more astonishing. Andy and Larry Wachowski's *The Matrix* (1999; cinematographer: Bill Pope) used still cameras to photograph actors in flight from all angles and then digitized them into moving images to replicate what might have been a shot from a moving camera if any moving camera were capable of such complex work. In this new world, movies are more likely to be set in wholly imaginary places such as those depicted in Peter Jackson's "Lord of the Rings" trilogy (2001–03; cinematographer: Andrew Lesnie). Thus, it is refreshing to see CGI used to re-create ancient Rome in Ridley Scott's *Gladiator* (2000; cinematographer: John Mathieson).

Much of the research and development that makes so many of these movies possible comes from George Lucas's special-effects company Industrial Light & Magic, where the visual-effects supervisor, Stefen Fangmeier, was behind the technology that made possible some of the movies mentioned here—including *Terminator 2: Judgment Day* and *Casper*—as well as the impressive historical re-creation of the world of the eighteenth-century British navy in Peter Weir's *Master and Commander: The Far Side of the World* (2003: cinematographer: Russell Boyd). With the increasing complexity of CGI, and the investment in human and technical resources required for its production, independent companies—whose artists and technicians usually work in consultation with the director, production designer, and director of photography—have become increasingly responsible for creating these effects. This artistry, now virtually a separate industry within the film industry, is expensive, but it has achieved astonishingly realistic effects at costs acceptable to producers. In addi-

tion to Industrial Light & Magic, other principal CGI firms are Pixar Animation Studios, Blue Sky Studios (Fox), Pacific Data Images (DreamWorks SKG), and Walt Disney Studios.

Yimou Zhang's *Hero* (2002; cinematographer: Christopher Doyle) has actors flying through the air, and sword fights like you've never seen before, all seamlessly integrated into a beautiful live-action movie. Brad Bird's *The Incredibles* (2004; cinematographers: Andrew Jimenez, Patrick Lin, and Janet Lucroy) combines various styles and CGI techniques in an imaginative, exciting, and witty format that proved entertaining to children and adults alike. Kerry Conran's *Sky Captain and the World of Tomorrow* (2004; cinematographer: Eric Adkins) is a CGI fantasy based on movie series of the past featuring heroes such as Buck Rogers and Flash Gordon. In shots similar to but more flexible than the process shots already described, the actors worked in front of a blue screen, and with the exception of that single set, the costumes, and

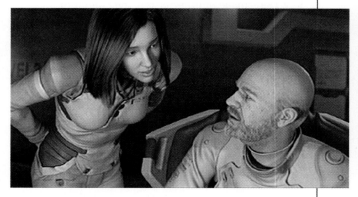

CGI and the "Uncanny Valley" Hironobu Sakaguchi and Moto Sakakibara's *Final Fantasy: The Spirits Within* (2001; cinematographer: Sakakibara) broke new ground in the world of special effects and CGI by being the first motion picture to feature a cast that—while convincingly human in features and motions—was entirely computer-generated. The result, as you can see here, is uncannily realistic—perhaps too much so. Some viewers and critics have reacted badly to movies such as *Final Fantasy* and Robert Zemeckis's *The Polar Express* (2004: cinematographers: Don Burgess and Robert Presley), describing a feeling of discomfort or revulsion while watching them. This negative response may be explained by the "uncanny valley," a theoretical notion originally conceived to explain why we tend to react negatively to robotic designs that mimic human appearance and mannerisms too faithfully.

any items that the live actors had to handle, everything you see on the screen was created in the computer and added after the fact. It is a provocative sign of what might happen to the design and production of movies in years to come.

Wherever special effects take movie production in the future, there is the ever-present danger that all the SPFX in action, adventure, and science fiction films will dazzle us but do little to increase our understanding of the world we live in or the drama of human life.

WEB The "Uncanny Valley"

➡ Analyzing Cinematography

This chapter has provided an overview of the major components of cinematography—the process by which a movie's mise-en-scène is recorded onto film or some other motion picture medium. More than just a process, however, cinematography is very much a *language* through which directors and their collaborators (most notably, directors of photography) can convey meaning, transmit narrative information, and influence the emotional responses of viewers. Now that you know something about the basic cinematographic tools available to filmmakers, you can pay greater attention to the particulars of this language while looking at movies.

Screening Checklist: Cinematography

➤ Determine whether or not the cinematographic aspects of the film—the qualities of the film stock, lighting, lenses, framing, angles, camera movement, and use of long takes—add up to an overall *look*. If so, try to describe its qualities.

➤ Take note of moments in the film in which the images are conveying information that is not reflected in characters' action and dialogue. These moments are often crucial to the development of a movie's themes, narrative, and meaning.

➤ Pay close attention to the length of shots in the film. Is there a recognizable pattern? Are long takes used? To what extent? For what purpose?

➤ Keep track of instances in which the film uses shots other than the medium shot (MS)—for instance, extreme close-ups (ECUs) or extreme long shots (ELSs). What role are these shots playing in the film?

➤ Also keep track of camera angles other than eye-level shots. If there are high- or low-angle shots, determine whether or not they are POV shots; that is, is the high or low angle meant to represent another character's point of view? If so, what does the angle convey about that character's state of mind? If not, what does it convey about the person or thing in the frame?

➤ As you evaluate crucial scenes, pay attention to the composition of shots within the scene. Are the compositions balanced in a way that conforms to the rule of thirds, or are the elements within the frame arranged in a less "painterly" composition? In either case, try to describe how the composition contributes to the scene overall.

➤ Pay attention to camera movement in the film. Sometimes camera movement is used solely to produce visual excitement or to demonstrate technological virtuosity on the part of the filmmaker. Other times it is playing an important functional role in the film's narrative. Be alert to these differences, and take note of meaningful uses of camera movement.

➤ Note when the cinematography calls attention to itself. Is this a mistake or misjudgment on the filmmakers' parts, or is it intentional? If intentional, what purpose is served by making the cinematography so noticeable?

Questions for Review

1. What are the differences among a *setup*, a *shot*, and a *take*?
2. A cinematographer depends on *two crews* of workers. What is each crew responsible for?
3. How the *lighting* for any movie looks is determined, in part, by its *source* and *direction*. Explain these terms and the effect each has on the overall lighting.
4. What are the *four major lenses* used on movie cameras? What is the principal characteristic of the image that each lens creates?
5. In terms of proximity to the camera, what are the *three most commonly used shots* in a movie? What is the principle by which they are distinguished?
6. What is the *rule of thirds*?
7. The movie camera can shoot from various angles. What are they? What does each *imply* in terms of meaning? Do these implications always hold true?
8. What are the basic types of *camera movement*?
9. What is a *long take*? What can it achieve that a *short take* cannot? What is the difference between a *long take* and a *long shot*?
10. Special effects create images that might not be possible with traditional cinematography. What are the basic ways to create special effects?

DVD FEATURES: CHAPTER 4

The following tutorials on the DVD provide more information about cinematography:

- Seeing the Lighting
- Focal Length
- Shot Types and Implied Proximity
- Camera Angles
- The Moving Camera
- Zoom and Moving Camera Effects
- Point of View

Movies Described or Illustrated in This Chapter

The Abyss (1989). James Cameron, director.
Barry Lyndon (1975). Stanley Kubrick, director.
The Birds (1963). Alfred Hitchcock, director.
Birth (2004). Jonathan Glazer, director.
The Birth of a Nation (1915). D. W. Griffith, director.
The Bourne Supremacy (2004). Paul Greengrass, director.
Bride of Frankenstein (1935). James Whale, director.
Citizen Kane (1941). Orson Welles, director.
The Crying Game (1992). Neil Jordan, director.
Days of Heaven (1978). Terrence Malick, director.
Do the Right Thing (1989). Spike Lee, director.
Dogville (2003). Lars von Trier, director.
Dr. Strangelove or: How I Learned to Stop Worrying and Love the Bomb (1964). Stanley Kubrick, director.
Drugstore Cowboy (1989). Gus Van Sant, director.
Elephant (2003). Gus Van Sant, director.
Forrest Gump (1994). Robert Zemeckis, director.
The Godfather (1972). Francis Ford Coppola, director.
Gone With the Wind (1939). Victor Fleming, director.
Goodfellas (1990). Martin Scorsese, director.
The Graduate (1967). Mike Nichols, director.
The Grand Illusion (1937). Jean Renoir, director.
The Grifters (1990). Stephen Frears, director.
High Noon (1952). Fred Zinnemann, director.
Jules and Jim (1962). François Truffaut, director.
Juliet of the Spirits (1965). Federico Fellini, director.
Jurassic Park (1993). Steven Spielberg, director.
The Little Foxes (1941). William Wyler, director.
Lola Montés (1955). Max Ophüls, director.
"The Lord of the Rings" trilogy (2001–2003). Peter Jackson, director.
Love Me Tonight (1932). Rouben Mamoulian, director.
M (1931). Fritz Lang, director.
The Maltese Falcon (1941). John Huston, director.
Manhattan (1979). Woody Allen, director.
The Matrix (1999). Andy and Larry Wachowski, directors.
Modern Times (1936). Charles Chaplin, director.
The Night of the Hunter (1955). Charles Laughton, director.
North by Northwest (1959). Alfred Hitchcock, director.

Nosferatu (1922). F. W. Murnau, director.

Notorious (1946). Alfred Hitchcock, director.

The Passion of Joan of Arc (1928). Carl Theodor Dreyer, director.

Philadelphia (1993). Jonathan Demme, director.

Powaqqatsi (1988). Godfrey Reggio, director.

The Quiet Man (1952). John Ford, director.

Raging Bull (1980). Martin Scorsese, director.

Requiem for a Dream (2000). Darren Aronofsky, director.

Return of the Jedi (1983). Richard Marquand, director.

Rumble Fish (1983). Francis Ford Coppola, director.

The Searchers (1956). John Ford, director.

The Shining (1980). Stanley Kubrick, director.

Sky Captain and the World of Tomorrow (2004). Kerry Conran, director.

Spartacus (1960). Stanley Kubrick, director.

The Strange Love of Martha Ivers (1946). Lewis Milestone, director.

The Sweet Smell of Success (1957). Alexander Mackendrick, director.

T-Men (1947). Anthony Mann, director.

Talk to Her (2002). Pedro Almodóvar, director.

The Third Man (1949). Carol Reed, director.

Touch of Evil (1958). Orson Welles, director.

2001: A Space Odyssey (1968). Stanley Kubrick, director.

Million Dollar Baby (2004). Clint Eastwood, director. Pictured: Hilary Swank and Morgan Freeman.

Learning Objectives

After reading this chapter, you should be able to

➤ Explain how the *coming of sound* into the movie industry affected acting.

➤ Describe how movie acting today differs from that of the classical studio era.

➤ Explain why the *relationship between the actor and the camera* is so important.

➤ Describe the criteria used to *cast* actors.

➤ Explain the differences between *naturalistic* and *nonnaturalistic* movie acting.

➤ Define *improvisational acting.*

➤ Explain the potential effects on acting of *framing, composition, lighting, shot types,* and *shot lengths.*

What Is Acting?

When Richard M. Nixon was president of the United States, the public generally regarded him as a cold, calculating politician. So when Anthony Hopkins played him in Oliver Stone's *Nixon* (1995), many were astonished at the depth of humanity they saw onscreen. Hopkins persuaded audiences that Nixon had unexpected dimensions, turning him into a far more sympathetic *character*.

Screen acting of this kind is an art, in which an actor uses imagination, intelligence, psychology, memory, vocal technique, facial expressions, body language, and an overall knowledge of the filmmaking process to realize, under the director's guidance, the character created by the screenwriter. The performance and effect of that art can seem mysterious and magical when we're enjoying a movie, and acting turns out to be even more complex than we might at first assume.

Our initial interest in a movie is almost always sparked by the actors featured in it. As the critic Pauline Kael said, "I think so much of what we respond to in fictional movies is acting. That's one of the elements that's often left out when people talk theoretically about the movies. They forget it's

the human material we go to see."[1] The power of some actors—Julia Roberts or Tom Cruise, for example—to draw an audience is frequently more important to a movie's financial success than any other factor. For this reason, some observers regard screen actors as mere commodities, cogs in a machine of promotion and hype designed only to generate revenue. Although even the most accomplished screen actors can be used as fodder for promotional campaigns, such a view overlooks the many complex and important ways that skillful acting can influence the narrative, style, and meanings of a film. Writer-director-producer-actor Orson Welles, who questioned nearly every other aspect of filmmaking dogma, firmly believed in the importance of acting: "I don't understand how movies exist independently of the actor—I truly don't."[2]

Despite its central importance, acting is also the aspect of filmmaking over which directors have the least precise control. Directors may describe literally what they want from their principal collaborators—for example, screenwriters or costume designers—but they can only *suggest* to actors what they want. Screen actors, or at least *experienced* screen actors, know that the essential relationship is between them and the camera—not between them and the director, or even the audience. Actors interpret the director's guidance in the area between them and the lens—an intimate and narrowly defined space that necessarily concentrates much of the actors' energy on their faces. Through composition, close-ups, camera angles and movements, and other cinematic techniques, movie actors always come *closer* to the audience, and appear *larger*, than actors on the stage do.

The camera makes possible an attention to detail that was impossible before the invention of cinema, mainly because stage acting forced actors to project their voices and their gestures to the back of the theater. Screen acting, as an experience, can be as tight and intimate as examining a

[1] Leonard Quart, "I Still Love Going to Movies: An Interview with Pauline Kael," *Cineaste* 25, no. 2 (2002): 10.
[2] Orson Welles and Peter Bogdanovich, *This Is Orson Welles*, ed. Jonathan Rosenbaum (New York: HarperCollins, 1992), 262.

The Camera and the Actor English film actor Michael Caine has compared the movie camera to an impossibly attentive lover who "hangs on your every word, your every look; she can't take her eyes off you. She is listening to and recording everything you do, however minutely you do it."[4] That appears to be exactly what the camera is doing in this expressive close-up of Caine as Thomas Fowler in Phillip Noyce's *The Quiet American* (2002). The business and art of Hollywood moviemaking intersect when "bankable" stars such as Michael Caine (and, in this example, his costar Brendan Fraser, *left, back to camera*) take on challenging, unglamorous roles that transcend their physical attractiveness.

painting at arm's length. As American screen actor Joan Crawford put it, "A movie actor paints with the tiniest brush."[3]

Movie Actors

The challenges facing movie actors in interpreting and pretending to be their characters, and the responsibilities involved in performing those characters on the screen, are very different from the challenges and responsibilities facing stage actors. Stage actors convey their interpretations of the characters they play directly to the audience through voice, gesture, and movement. By contrast, movie actors, using gesture and movement—and *voice* since the coming of sound—convey their characters directly to the camera. In turn, that camera is the single element that most radically differentiates the movie actor's performance. Stage actors play to a large audience and must project the voice so that it can be

heard throughout the theater, and avoid the soft speech, subtle facial expressions, or small gestures that are fundamental tools of the movie actor.

Stage actors, who must memorize their lines, have the advantage of speaking them in the order in which they were written, which, in turn, makes it much easier to maintain psychological, emotional, and physical continuity in a performance as the play proceeds. By contrast, movie actors, who are subject to the shooting schedule—which, for budgetary and logistical reasons, determines that most shots are made out of the sequence in which they appear in the screenplay—learn only those lines that they need for the moment. Therefore, movie actors bear the additional burden, particularly on their memory, of creating continuity between related shots, even though the shots may have been made days, weeks, or even months apart.

Toward the goal of maintaining continuity (as we will discuss in Chapter 6), editing is a major factor in putting shots together and, thus, helping to create the performance. During the presentation of a play, the stage actor performs each scene only once; during the shooting of a movie, the actor may be asked to do many *takes* before the director is satisfied with the performance. Before a shot is made, the movie actor must be prepared to wait, sometimes for long periods, while camera, lighting, or sound equipment is moved or readjusted; the stage actor faces no such delays or interruptions.

Although the theater and the movies are both collaborative arts, once the curtain goes up, stage actors need not think much about the backstage crew, for the crew will perform scenery or lighting changes according to a fixed schedule. Movie actors, however, while playing directly to the camera, are always aware of dozens of people standing around just outside the camera's range, doing their jobs but also watching and listening to everything the actors do. Some of people are there because they have to be (e.g., the director, script supervisor, cinematographer, sound recordist, makeup artist, hairstylist); others are there waiting to make the necessary changes in scenery, properties, or lighting required for the next shot. Over the years, some temperamental actors have succeeded in having removed from the set all but the most essential

[3] Joan Crawford, qtd. in Lillian and Helen Ross, *The Player: A Profile of an Art* (New York: Simon and Schuster, 1962), 66.
[4] Michael Caine, *Acting in Film: An Actor's Take on Moviemaking* (New York: Applause, 1990), 4.

personnel, but that is an exception to conventional practice. Traditionally, however, movie sets have been closed to visitors, particularly the media.

Although there are many types of actors—probably as many types as there are actors themselves—we can, for the purposes of this discussion, identify four key types:

1. Actors who take their personas from role to role (*personality* actors)
2. Actors who deliberately play against our expectations of their personas
3. Actors who seem to be different in every role (*chameleon* actors)
4. Actors, often nonprofessionals or people who have achieved success in another field (sports or music, for example), who are cast to bring verisimilitude to a part

In our everyday lives, each of us creates a *persona*, the image of character and personality that we want to show the outside world. For movie actors, those personas are their appearance and mannerisms of moving and delivering dialogue—unique creations that are consistent at least on some level from role to role, and from performance to performance. Actors' personas are usually (but not always) rooted in their natural behavior, personality, and physicality. Current actors defined by their personas include Tom Cruise, Cameron Diaz, and Will Smith. Paul Giamatti is not, by Hollywood standards, a leading man, yet in Alexander Payne's *Sideways* (2004), this actor—whose persona might be described as an overweight, balding, neurotic but likable loser—channels these attributes and attitudes in a way that makes us care about his character, Miles Raymond, a recently divorced man who just might have another chance at romance. Even more-versatile actors—not just those who are popular action or comedy stars—rely on persona, including Susan Sarandon, Sean Penn, Morgan Freeman, Jack Nicholson, William H. Macy, Chris Cooper, Ewan McGregor, and Benicio Del Toro.

⊙ DVD Persona and Performance

For many movie actors, the persona is the key to their career, as well as an important part of film marketing and why we choose particular movies over others. One reason audiences go to movies is to see a certain kind of story. That's a big part of what the concept of *genre* is all about. You go to a romantic comedy, an action movie, a horror film, or a comic-book adaptation because you *know* what to expect and you *want* what you expect. Having made your choice on the basis of story, you should get familiar and appealing narrative structures, cinematic conventions, character types, dramatic situations, and payoffs.

The same thing goes for persona-identified actors like Tom Cruise. He's not only good-looking, but he projects an interesting balance of arrogance and vulnerability that appeals to many viewers. When you go to a Tom Cruise movie (the kind where the star's name is the most important factor in your choice), you have an expectation of the kind of performance he's going to give you, based on his persona, and you expect to see that performance, that persona, within the context of a certain kind of story. Part of the fun comes from seeing that persona in different kinds of movies, enjoying your favorite persona interacting with a particular role or genre. So part of the reason you might go to see Cruise in Stanley Kubrick's *Eyes Wide Shut* (1999) is to see what he makes of Dr. William Harford, a Manhattan physician facing serious sexual and moral issues; or, in Michael Mann's *Collateral* (2004), how he portrays Vincent, a hit man; or how he pushes the vulnerable side of his persona and unfortunately becomes the stereotype of a concerned dad in Steven Spielberg's *War of the Worlds* (2005).

Sometimes an actor with a familiar, popular persona takes on a role that goes against what we expect—for example, Jack Nicholson as Warren Schmidt in Alexander Payne's *About Schmidt* (2002); or Charlize Theron as Aileen Wuornos in Patty Jenkins's *Monster* (2005). A major factor affecting our enjoyment of actors in such roles is not just the role, but the strange sensation of seeing an actor whose persona we have come to know well play a totally different sort of role—in Nicholson's case, the normally crafty, strong, menacing man as a powerless, mundane, befuddled, and cuckolded insurance salesman. In Theron's case, we are astonished to see an actor known heretofore for her beauty—delightful in such lightweight comic roles as Laura Kensington in Woody Allen's *Curse of the Jade Scorpion* (2001) or Candy Kirkendall in Jordan Brady's *Waking Up in Reno* (2002)—undergo a complete physical transformation (facial and physical appearance, voice, gestures, and movement) in order to play the challenging role of Aileen, an ugly, menacing serial murderer.

On the other side of the acting scale is the chameleon actor—named for the lizard that can make quick, frequent changes in its appearance in response to the environment. Chameleon actors adapt their look, mannerisms, and delivery to suit the role. They surprise us as persona actors when they are cast, as Nicholson or Theron, in a role we do not expect—one that extends their range. Take, for example, actor Robert Duvall, who often looks so different in roles that he's unrecognizable at first: Tom Hagen, the wing-tipped consigliere in Francis Ford Coppola's *The Godfather* (1972); Lieutenant Colonel Bill Kilgore, the napalm-loving warmonger in Coppola's *Apocalypse Now* (1979); or alcoholic country singer Mac Sledge in Bruce Beresford's *Tender Mercies* (1983).

Johnny Depp is a chameleon actor who has reached star status without any fixed persona. Although he's earned the reputation as the ideal *nonnaturalistic* actor for such Tim Burton movies as *Edward Scissorhands* (1990), *Sleepy Hollow* (1999), and *Charlie and the Chocolate Factory* (2005), he's also played very different roles with different directors: Raoul Duke/Hunter S. Thompson in Terry Gilliam's *Fear and Loathing in Las Vegas* (1998); the cocaine king George Jung in Ted Demme's *Blow* (2001); Sir James Matthew Barrie, the author of *Peter Pan*, in Marc Forster's *Finding Neverland* (2004); and Lord Rochester, the seventeenth-century English poet, in Laurence Dunmore's *The Libertine* (2004).

Finally, there is the nonprofessional actor—someone who has achieved success in another field who is cast to bring verisimilitude to a part. Examples include football great Brett Favre playing himself in Bobby and Peter Farrelly's *There's Something About Mary* (1998); rap star Eminem playing Jimmy "B-Rabbit" Smith, Jr., a rapper whose rise to super-star status parallels his own, in Curtis Hanson's *8 Mile* (2002); fashion designer Isaac Mizrahi playing an art director in Woody Allen's *Hollywood Ending* (2002); and rapper 50 Cent playing Marcus, a character loosely based on his own life, in Jim Sheridan's *Get Rich or Die Tryin'* (2005). With these actors essentially playing themselves, there is very little distinction between the person and the part.

Whereas previous generations of stage actors knew that their duty was to convey emotion through recognized conventions of speech and gesture (mannerisms), screen actors have enjoyed a certain freedom to adopt individual styles that communicate emotional meaning through subtle—and highly personal—gestures, expressions, and varieties of intonation. American screen actor Barbara Stanwyck credited director Frank Capra with teaching her that "if you can think it, you can make the audience know it . . . On the stage, it's mannerisms. On the screen, your range is shown in your eyes."[5] In addition, many different types of inspiration fuel screen acting; many factors guide actors toward their performances in front of the camera.

Consider American movie actor Sissy Spacek, who has been nominated six times for the Academy Award for Best Actress, and who won for her performance as country singer Loretta Lynn in Michael Apted's *Coal Miner's Daughter* (1980). We might say that Spacek's appearance—diminutive figure; pale red hair; large, open, very blue eyes; sharp, turned-up nose; abundant freckles; and Texas twang—has destined her to play a certain type of role: a sweet, seemingly simple and frail, but ultimately strong, perhaps strange and even otherworldly woman. Spacek brings out the depths within her characters, however, making each unique, believable, and easy to connect with or at least care about.

Depending on what the role calls for, Spacek can make herself look plain (avoiding makeup and hairstyling) or beautiful. Between the ages of twenty-four and twenty-seven, she played three characters in their teens, all childlike and somewhat naïve. In

---

[5] Barbara Stanwyck, qtd. in *Actors on Acting for the Screen: Roles and Collaborations*, ed. Doug Tomlinson (New York: Garland, 1994), 524.

Terrence Malick's *Badlands* (1973), she plays Holly, whose unemotional narration, taken from her flat yet poetic diary entries, contrasts markedly with her physical passion for Kit (Martin Sheen), a murderer who takes her on a horrifying odyssey. In Brian De Palma's *Carrie* (1976), a horror movie based on a novel by Stephen King, she plays the title character, a lonely, misunderstood teenager raised by a fundamentalist mother, tormented by her conceited schoolmates, and possessing the telekinetic ability to perform vengeful acts. In Robert Altman's *3 Women* (1977), she plays Pinky Rose, perhaps the most enigmatic of these three characters: vulnerable, unsophisticated, sensitive to what others think of her, and clumsy, but also shrewd in getting what she wants and psychologically haunted by what seems to be a dream of the past.

Spacek recalls how three very different directors helped bring out these three very different types of screen performance:

> From Terry Malick I learned how to approach a character. . . . With Terry you feel an incredible intimacy. We spent a lot of time just talking about our lives, remembering things that help you to tie the character [to] your own life. . . . Bob [Altman] works by bringing elements together, not expecting anything—he brings things together to capture the unexpected. Brian [De Palma] approaches films more like a science project. With Brian I learned to work with the camera . . . [E]verything was storyboarded. . . . You can act your guts out and the camera can miss it. But one little look, if you know how it's going to be framed, can have a thousand times more impact.[6]

Each directorial style requires something different from actors. Malick, encouraging actors to identify with characters, promotes a style loosely referred to as *method acting*. Altman, favoring spontaneity and unpredictability in actors' performances, encourages *improvisation*. De Palma, choosing neither of these two roads, pushes his actors to see their performances from a cinematographic point of view, to explicitly imagine how

[6] Sissy Spacek, qtd. in *Actors on Acting for the Screen*, ed. Tomlinson, 518.

[1]

[2]

The Versatility of Sissy Spacek A contemporary actress of style and substance, Sissy Spacek has exhibited great flexibility not only in the roles she chooses, but also in the techniques she employs to convey her characters' often complex emotional lives. [1] In Terrence Malick's *Badlands* (1973), she embodies the innocent sexuality and dreaminess of romance novels. [2] In Robert Altman's *3 Women* (1977), as Pinky Rose, she is an enigmatic combination of childlike innocence and manipulative cunning.

their gestures and expressions will *look* onscreen. In doing so, he essentially encourages actors to think more than to feel, to perform their roles almost as if they are highly skilled technicians whose main task is to control one aspect of the mise-en-scène (performance), much as set designers control the look and feel of sets, sound mixers control sound, directors of photography control cinematography, and so on.

No matter what type a movie actor is—how definite or changeable the persona is, how varied the roles are, how successful the career—we tend to blur the distinction between the actor onscreen and the person offscreen. The heroes of today's world are performers—athletes, musicians, actors—and a vast media industry exists to keep them in the public eye and to encourage us to believe that they are every bit as fascinating in real life as they are on the screen. Inevitably some movie actors become rich and famous without having much art or craft in what they do. Essentially they walk through their movies, seldom playing any character other than themselves. Fortunately, for every one of these actors there are many more talented actors who take their work seriously; try, whenever possible, to extend the range of roles that they play; and learn to adapt to the constantly shifting trends of moviemaking and public taste.

One definition of great acting is that it should look effortless—an achievement that takes talent, training, discipline, experience, and hard work. It also takes the skills necessary for dealing with the pressures that range from getting older (and, thus, becoming more apt to be replaced by a younger, better-looking actor) to fulfilling a producer's expectation that you will succeed in carrying a multimillion dollar production and making it a profitable success.

As we continue this discussion of acting, remember that it is not actors' personal lives that count, but rather their ability to interpret and portray certain characters. In today's world, where the media report actors' every offscreen activity, especially indiscretions, maintaining the focus required for good acting poses a challenge. Although the media have always done this, the behavior of some of today's actors is not only more reckless, but also seldom covered up by a studio public relations department as it was in Hollywood's golden age.

The Evolution of Screen Acting

Early Screen-Acting Styles

The people on the screen in the very first movies were not actors, but ordinary people playing themselves. The early films caught natural, everyday actions—feeding a baby, leaving work, yawning, walking up and down stairs, swinging a baseball bat, sneezing—in a simple, realistic manner, and "acting" was simply a matter of trying to ignore the presence of the camera as it recorded the action. In the early 1900s, filmmakers started to tell stories with their films and thus needed professional actors. Most stage actors at the time scorned film acting, however, and refused to take work in the fledgling industry.

The first screen actors were thus usually rejects from the stage or fresh-faced amateurs eager to break into the emerging film industry. Lack of experience (or talent) wasn't the only hurdle facing them. Because no standard language of cinematic expression, nor any accepted tradition of film direction, existed at the time, these first actors had little option but to adopt the acting style favored in the nineteenth-century theater and try to adapt it to their screen roles. The resulting quaint, unintentionally comical style consists of exaggerated gestures, overly emphatic facial expressions, and a bombastic mouthing of words (which could not yet be recorded on film) that characterized the stage melodramas popular at the turn of the twentieth century.

In 1908, the Société Film d'Art ("Art Film Society"), a French film company, was founded with the purpose of creating a serious artistic cinema that would attract equally serious people who ordinarily preferred the theater. Commercially, this was a risky step, not only because cinema was in its infancy, but also because, since the sixteenth century, the French had seen theater as a temple of expression. Its glory was (and remains) the Comédie-Française, the French national theater; and to begin its work at the highest possible level, the Société Film d'Art joined creative forces with this revered organization, which agreed to lend its actors to the society's films. In addition, the society commissioned leading theater playwrights, directors, and designers, as well as prominent composers, to create its film productions. The most famous of these productions were André Calmettes and Charles Le Bargy's *The Assassination of the Duke de Guise* (1908), and Henri Desfontaines and Louis Mercanton's *Queen Elizabeth* (1912).

Early Film Acting Sarah Bernhardt (1844–1923), known as *La voix d'or* ("the golden voice") and *La divine Sarah*, was a star of the French stage and the first great theatrical actress to appear in a movie, Clément Maurice's *Hamlet* (1900). Despite her very mixed feelings about the new medium, Bernhardt made a series of critically and commercially successful movies with the Société Film d'Art, including André Calmettes's *Camille* (1912) and Henri Desfontaines and Louis Mercanton's *Queen Elizabeth* (1912), pictured here. In this silent, filmed play, Bernhardt employs the emphatic gestures that served her so well on the stage; she even bows at the end. To see just how film-acting styles have developed, compare two other portrayals of Elizabeth I: Bette Davis's in Michael Curtiz's *The Private Lives of Elizabeth and Essex* (1939) and Cate Blanchett's in Shekhar Kapur's *Elizabeth* (1998).

As interesting as it is to see Sarah Bernhardt, one of the early twentieth century's greatest actors, as Elizabeth I, it is even more interesting to observe how closely this "canned theater" resembled an actual stage production. The space we see is that of the theater, limited to having actors enter and exit from stage left or right, not that of the cinema, where characters are not confined to the physical boundaries imposed by theater architecture. For all her reputed skill, Bernhardt's acting could only echo what she did on the stage. Thus we see the exaggerated facial expressions, strained gestures, and clenched fists of late-nineteenth-century melodrama. Although such artificiality was conventional and thus accepted by the audience, it was all wrong for the comparative intimacy between the spectator and the screen that existed even in the earliest movie theaters.

Despite its heavy-handed technique, Desfontaines and Mercanton's *Queen Elizabeth* succeeded in attracting an audience interested in serious drama on the screen, made the cinema socially and intellectually respectable, and therefore encouraged further respect for the industry and its development. What remained to be done was not to teach Sarah Bernhardt how to act for the camera, but to develop cinematic techniques uniquely suitable for the emerging narrative cinema, as well as a style of acting that could help actors realize their potential in this new medium.

D. W. Griffith and Lillian Gish

American film pioneer D. W. Griffith needed actors who could be trained to work in front of the camera, and by 1913 he had recruited a group that included some of the most important actors of the time: Mary Pickford, Lillian and Dorothy Gish, Mae Marsh, Blanche Sweet, Lionel Barrymore, Harry Carey, Henry B. Walthall, and Donald Crisp. Some had stage experience, some did not. All of them earned much more from acting in the movies than they would have on the stage, and all enjoyed long, fruitful careers (many lasting well into the era of sound films).

Because the cinema was silent during this period, Griffith worked out more-naturalistic movements and gestures for his actors rather than training their voices. The longer stories of such feature-length films as *The Birth of a Nation* (1915), *Intolerance* (1916), *Hearts of the World* (1918), and *Broken Blossoms* (1919) gave the actors more screen time and thus more screen space in which to develop their characters. Close-ups required them to be more aware of the effects that their facial expressions would have on the audience, and actors' faces increasingly became more important than their bodies (although, in the silent comedies of the 1920s, the full presence of the human body was virtually essential to conveying humor).

Under Griffith's guidance, Lillian Gish invented the art of screen acting. Griffith encouraged her to study the movements of ordinary people on the street or in restaurants, to develop her physical skills with regular exercise, and to tell stories through her face and body. He urged her to watch the reactions of movie audiences, saying, "If they're held by what you're doing, you've succeeded as an actress."[7] Gish's performance in *Broken Blossoms* was the first great film performance by an actor. Set in the Limehouse (or Chinatown) section of London, the movie presents a very stylized fable about the love of an older Chinese merchant, Cheng Huan (Richard Barthelmess), for an English adolescent, Lucy Burrows (Gish). Lucy's racist father, the boxer Battling Burrows (Donald Crisp), beats her for the slightest transgression. Enraged by her friendship with the merchant, Burrows drags her home; and when Lucy hides in a tiny closet, he breaks down the door and beats her so savagely that she dies soon after.

The interaction of narrative, acting, extremely confined cinematic space, and exploitation of the audience's fears gives this scene its beauty, power, *and* repulsiveness. Seen from various angles within the closet, which fills the screen, Lucy clearly cannot escape. Hysterical with fear, she finally curls up as her father breaks through the door. At the end, she dies in her bed, forcing the smile that has characterized her throughout the film. Terror and pity produce the cathartic realization within the viewer that Lucy's death, under these wretched circumstances, is truly a release.

In creating this scene, Gish invoked a span of emotions that no movie audience had seen before and few have seen since. Her performance illustrates the qualities of great screen acting: appropriateness, expressive coherence, inherent thoughtfulness/emotionality, wholeness, and unity. Amazingly, the performance resulted from Gish's own instincts—her sense of what was right for the climactic moment of the story and the mise-en-scène in which it took place—rather than from Griffith's direction:

Lillian Gish in *Broken Blossoms* Lillian Gish was twenty-three when she played the young girl Lucy Burrows in D. W. Griffith's *Broken Blossoms* (1919). It was, incredibly, her sixty-fourth movie, and she gave one of her long career's most emotionally wrenching performances.

The scene of the terrified child alone in the closet could probably not be filmed today. To watch Lucy's hysteria was excruciating enough in a silent picture; a sound track would have made it unbearable. When we filmed it I played the scene with complete lack of restraint, turning around and around like a tortured animal. When I finished, there was a hush in the studio. Mr. Griffith finally whispered: "My God, why didn't you warn me that you were going to do that?"[8]

Gish gives a similar, powerful performance—her character shoots the man who raped her—in Victor Sjöström's *The Wind* (1928); and her work in confined spaces influenced such later climactic scenes as Marion Crane's (Janet Leigh) murder in the shower in Alfred Hitchcock's *Psycho* (1960) and Jack Torrance's (Jack Nicholson) attempt to get out of a bathroom in which he is trapped in Stanley Kubrick's *The Shining* (1980).

[7] Lillian Gish, with Ann Pinchot, *The Movies, Mr. Griffith, and Me* (Englewood Cliffs, N.J.: Prentice-Hall, 1969), 97–101; quotation, 101. See also Jeanine Basinger, *Silent Stars* (New York: Knopf, 1999).

[8] Gish, *The Movies, Mr. Griffith, and Me*, 200. For another version of how this scene was prepared and shot, see Charles Affron, *Lillian Gish: Her Legend, Her Life* (New York: Scribner, 2001), 125–31.

The Influence of Sound

It was not long after Griffith and Gish established a viable and successful style of screen acting that movie actors were faced with the greatest challenge yet: the conversion from silent to sound production. Instead of instantly revolutionizing film style, the coming of sound in 1927 began a period of several years in which the industry gradually converted to this new form of production (see Chapter 7). Filmmakers made dialogue more comprehensible by developing better microphones; finding the best placements for the camera, microphones, and other sound equipment; and encouraging changes in actors' vocal performances. Initially they encased the camera, whose overall size has changed relatively little since the 1920s, in either a bulky soundproof booth or the later development known as a **blimp**—a soundproofed enclosure somewhat larger than a camera, in which the camera may be mounted so that its sounds do not reach the microphone.

Such measures prevented the sounds of the camera's mechanism from being recorded, but also restricted the freedom with which the camera—and the actors—could move. Actors accustomed to moving around the set without worrying about speaking now had to curtail their movements inside the circumscribed sphere where recording took place. Furthermore, technicians required time to adjust to the recording equipment, which restricted their movements as well. Eventually, technicians were able to free the camera for all kinds of movement and to find ways of recording sound that allowed the equipment and actors alike more mobility.

As monumental as the conversion to sound was—in economic, technological, stylistic, and human terms—Hollywood found humor in it, making it the subject of one of the most enjoyable of all movie musicals: Stanley Donen and Gene Kelly's *Singin' in the Rain* (1952), which vividly and satirically portrays the technical difficulties of using the voice of one actor to replace the voice of another who hasn't been trained to speak, trying to move a camera weighted down with soundproof housing, and forcing actors to speak into microphones concealed in flowerpots. As film scholar Donald Crafton writes, "Many of the clichés of the early sound cinema (including those in *Singin' in the Rain*) apply to films made during this period: long static takes, badly written dialogue, voices not quite in control, poor-quality recording, and a speaking style with slow cadence and emphasis on 'enunciated' tones, which the microphone was supposed to favor."[9]

How did the "talkies" influence actors and acting? Although sound enabled screen actors to use all their powers of human expression, it also created a need not only for screenplays with dialogue, but also for dialogue coaches to help the actors "find" their voices and other coaches to help them master foreign accents. The more actors and the more speaking that a film included, the more complex the narrative could become. Directors had to make changes too. Before sound, a director could call out instructions to the actors during filming; once the microphone could pick up every word uttered on the set, directors were forced to rehearse more extensively with their actors, thus adopting a technique from the stage to deal with screen technology. Though many actors and directors could not make the transition from silent to sound films, others emerged from silent films ready to see the addition of sound less as an obstacle than as the means to a more complete screen verisimilitude.

→WEB Voice Acting

An innovative production from this period is Rouben Mamoulian's *Applause* (1929; sound-recording technician: Ernest Zatorsky). After several years of directing theater productions in London and New York, Mamoulian made his screen-directing debut with *Applause*, which is photographed in a style that mixes naturalism with expressionism. From the opening scene, a montage of activity that plunges us right into the lively world of burlesque, the film reveals Mamoulian's mastery of camera movement. But when the camera does not move, as in the many two-shots

9 Donald Crafton, *The Talkies: American Cinema's Transition to Sound, 1926–1931* (New York: Scribner, 1997), 14.

Early Sound-Film Acting On the set of Alexander Korda's *Lilies of the Field* (1930), actors Corinne Griffith and Ralph Forbes are filmed by cinematographer Lee Garmes and observed by producer Walter Morosco. By this time, filmmakers had overcome many of the technological problems that plagued early sound productions. Wheels delivered camera mobility, and cloth "blimps" and other coverings kept camera noise from interfering with the recording of dialogue, here being captured by an overhead microphone (unseen). By the mid 1930s, film sound was on its way to becoming a routine part of movie production.

full of dialogue, we can almost *feel* the limited-range microphone boom hovering over the actors, one step beyond the use of flowerpots. In contrast to the vibrant shots with the moving camera, these static shots are lifeless and made even more confusing by the loud, expressionist sounds that overwhelm ordinary as well as intimate conversations.

Obviously such limitations have an impact on how we perceive the acting, which is *Applause*'s weak point throughout. In all likelihood because Mamoulian knew that symphonies of city sounds and noises would be the main impression of many scenes, the actors have little to say or do. However, the movie remains interesting because of a new technique in sound recording that Mamoulian introduced and that soon became common practice. Earlier, all sound in a particular shot had been recorded and manipulated on a single sound track. Mamoulian persuaded the sound technicians to record overlapping dialogue in a single shot using two separate microphones and then to mix them together on the sound track. When April Darling (Joan Peers), her head on a pillow, whispers a prayer while her mother, Kitty (Helen Morgan), sits next to her and sings a lullaby, the actors almost seem to be singing a duet—naturally, intimately, and convincingly.[10]

Acting in the Classical Studio Era

From the early years of moviemaking, writes film scholar Robert Allen, "the movie star has been one of the defining characteristics of the American cinema."[11] Most simply, a **movie star** is two people: the actor and the character(s) he or she has played. In addition, the star embodies an image created by the studio to coincide with the kinds of roles associated with the actor. That the star also reflects the social and cultural history of the period in which that image was created helps explain the often rapid rise and fall of stars' careers. But this description reveals at its heart a set of paradoxes, as Allen points out:

> The star is powerless, yet powerful; different from "ordinary" people, yet at one time was "just like us." Stars make huge salaries, yet the work for which they are handsomely paid does not appear to be work on the screen. Talent would seem to be a requisite for stardom, yet there has been no absolute

[10] In his next films, Mamoulian made other innovations in sound, including the sound flashback in *City Streets* (1931) and the lavish use of contrapuntal sound in the opening of *Love Me Tonight* (1932).

[11] For a study of stars in Hollywood from which this section liberally draws, see Robert C. Allen and Douglas Gomery, *Film History: Theory and Practice* (New York: Knopf, 1985), 172–89, quotation, 174 (reprinted as Robert C. Allen, "The Role of the Star in Film History [Joan Crawford]," in *Film Theory and Criticism: Introductory Readings*, 5th ed., ed. Leo Braudy and Marshall Cohen [New York: Oxford University Press, 1999], 547–61).

correlation between acting ability and stardom. The star's private life has little if anything to do with his or her "job" of acting in movies, yet a large portion of a star's image is constructed on the basis of "private" matters: romance, marriage, tastes in fashion, and home life.[12]

The golden age of Hollywood, roughly from the 1930s until the 1950s, was the age of the movie star, and acting in American movies generally meant *star acting*. During this period, the major studios gave basic lessons in acting, speaking, and movement; but because screen appearance was of paramount importance, they were more concerned with enhancing actors' screen images than with improving their acting.

During this period, when the studio system and the star system went hand in hand, the studios had almost complete control of their actors. Every six months, the studio reviewed an actor's standard seven-year **option contract**: if the actor had made progress in being assigned roles and demonstrating box-office appeal, the studio picked up the option to employ that actor for the next six months and gave him or her a raise; if not, the studio dropped the option and the actor was out of work. The decision was the studio's, not the actor's. Furthermore, the contract did not allow the actor to move to another studio, stop work, or renegotiate for a higher salary. In addition to those unbreakable terms, the contract had restrictive clauses that gave the studio total control over the star's image and services; it required an actor "to act, sing, pose, speak or perform in such roles as the producer may designate"; it gave the studio the right to change the name of the actor at its own discretion and to control the performer's image and likeness in advertising and publicity; and it required the actor to comply with rules covering interviews and public appearances.[13]

These contracts turned the actors into the studios' chattel. To the public, perhaps the most fascinating thing about making actors into stars was the process of changing their names. Issur Danielovitch became Kirk Douglas, Julia Jean Mildred Frances Turner became Lana Turner, and Archibald Leach became Cary Grant. Name and image came first, with acting ability often considered secondary to an actor's screen presence or aura, physical or facial beauty, athletic ability or performance skills, or character "type." Although many stars were also convincing actors, capable of playing a variety of parts (e.g., Bette Davis, Henry Fonda, Barbara Stanwyck, Jimmy Stewart), surprisingly little serious attention was paid to screen acting. As Charles Affron observes:

> An almost total absence of analytical approaches to screen acting reflects the belief that screen acting is nothing more than the beautiful projection of a filmic self, an arrangement of features and body, the disposition of superficial elements. Garbo is Garbo is Garbo is Garbo. We mortals are left clutching our wonder, and victims of that very wonder, overwhelmed by our enthusiasm and blinded by the light of the star's emanation.[14]

Today, film acting has become the subject of new interest among theorists and critics in semiology, psychology, and cultural studies who wish to study acting as an index of cultural history and an aspect of ideology.[15] This approach stresses that stars are a commodity created by the studio system through promotion, publicity, movies, criticism, and commentary. As Richard Dyer notes, "Stars are involved in making themselves into commodities; they are both labour and the thing that labour produces. They do not produce themselves alone."[16]

[12] Allen and Gomery, *Film History*, 174.

[13] Tino Balio, *Grand Design: Hollywood as a Modern Business Enterprise*, 1930–1939 (New York: Scribner, 1993), 145.

[14] Charles Affron, *Star Acting: Gish, Garbo, Davis* (New York: Dutton, 1977), 3. See also Roland Barthes, "The Face of Garbo," in *Film Theory and Criticism*, ed. Braudy and Cohen, 536–38; and Alexander Walker, *Stardom: The Hollywood Phenomenon* (New York: Stein and Day, 1970).

[15] See Richard Dyer, *Stars*, new ed. (London: British Film Institute, 1998); and *Heavenly Bodies: Film Stars and Society* (New York: St. Martin's Press, 1986). See also Richard DeCordova, "The Emergence of the Star System in America," *Wide Angle* 6, no. 4 (1985): 4–13; Carole Zucker, ed., *Making Visible the Invisible: An Anthology of Original Essays on Film Acting* (Metuchen, N.J.: Scarecrow Press, 1990); and Christine Gledhill, *Stardom: Industry of Desire* (New York: Routledge, 1991).

[16] Dyer, *Heavenly Bodies*, 5.

[1]

[2]

The Movie Star   Jimmy Stewart once said that his first impression of Joan Crawford was of glamour, and Bette Davis characterized Crawford as the personification of the "Movie Star." A classic figure of the studio-driven "star system," Crawford was a chorus-line dancer before moving to Hollywood and landing her first movie roles. During a career of more than fifty years, she changed course several times, adapting to times and circumstances. [1] In Harry Beaumont's *Our Dancing Daughters* (1928), her breakthrough film with MGM, Crawford (*foreground*) played Diana Medford, a free-spirited flapper who, along with her friends Beatrice (Dorothy Sebastian, *background*) and Ann (played by Anita Page, *not pictured*), embraces the liberated lifestyle of the American Jazz Age. [2] Almost twenty years later, Crawford played the title character in Michael Curtiz's *Mildred Pierce* (1945), a drama/murder mystery about a successful restaurateur trying to raise her spoiled and willful daughter.

Such analyses tend to emphasize the ways in which culture makes meaning rather than the art and expressive value of acting, the ways in which actors make meaning.

Materialistic as it was, the star system dominated the movie industry until the studio system collapsed, at which time it was replaced by a similar industrial enterprise powered essentially by the same motivation of making profits for its investors. However, because every studio had its own system, creating different goals and images for different stars, there was no typical star. For example, when Lucille Fay Le Sueur (also known early in her career in the theater as Billie Cassin) went to Hollywood in 1925, MGM decided that her name must be changed and that her image would be that of an ideal American "girl." Through a national campaign conducted by a fan magazine, the public was invited to submit names; the first choice, "Joan Arden," was already being used by another actress, so Lucille Le Sueur became Joan Crawford, a name to which she objected for several years.

Crawford's career soon took off, reaching a high level of achievement in the mid 1930s, when she became identified with the "woman's film." Subsequently, in a long series of films, she played women who, whether by family background or social circumstances, triumphed over adversity and, usually, paid a price for independence. No matter what happened to them, her characters remained stylish and distinctive in their looks—chic, self-generated survivors. Like many other stars, Crawford became indelibly associated with the roles she played. Yet she received little serious acclaim for her acting until the mid 1940s, when she left MGM for Warner Bros. For Michael Curtiz's *Mildred Pierce* (1945), her first film there, Crawford won the Academy Award for Best Actress—her only Oscar, though she received two more nominations. After her success at Warner Bros., Crawford worked for various major studios and independents, shedding her image as the stalwart, contemporary American woman. Sometimes her performances were excellent as in Curtis Bernhardt's *Possessed* (1947), David Miller's *Sudden Fear* (1952), and, costarring with Bette Davis, Robert Aldrich's *What Ever Happened to Baby Jane?* (1962).

Davis was a star of another sort, leading a principled and spirited fight against the studio and star systems' invasion into virtually every aspect of actors' personal and professional lives. In fact, Davis's career (from 1931 to 1989) comes as close to any as demonstrating these systems at their best and worst. In the mid 1930s, when she walked out of Warner Bros. demanding better roles, the studio successfully sued her for breach of contract. Though she returned to work rewarded by increased respect, a new contract, and better roles, her career sagged after World War II, for she had reached her early forties, an age at which female actors are seldom offered good parts. Ironically, playing just such a character—an older stage actress in danger of losing roles because of her age—she triumphed in Joseph L. Mankiewicz's *All About Eve* (1950), generally regarded as her greatest performance. During her long career, Davis was nominated eleven times for the Oscar for Best Actress, winning for Alfred E. Green's *Dangerous* (1935) and William Wyler's *Jezebel* (1938). Nominations for an Oscar involve a peer-review process in which only actors vote for acting nominations. Davis's record of nominations is exceeded only by Meryl Streep (thirteen nominations), Katharine Hepburn (twelve) and Jack Nicholson (twelve).

Method Acting

During the studio years, movie acting and the star system were virtually synonymous. Although acting styles were varied, the emphasis was on the star's persona and its effect at the box office—on the product, not the process of acting. And as production processes were regularized, so, too, was acting. That's not to say that screen acting in the 1930s and 40s was formulaic or unimaginative; quite the contrary. On Broadway, however, stage actors were becoming acquainted with a Russian technique that became known as *method acting*. Method acting did not make a major impact on Hollywood until the 1950s, but it marks a significant point in the evolution of screen acting from the studio system's reliance on "star acting" in the 1930s and 1940s to a new style in which actors draw on their own personal experiences and feelings in an attempt to become the character.

What Americans call *method acting* was based on the theory and practice of Konstantin Stanislavsky, who cofounded the Moscow Art Theater in 1898 and spent his entire career there. Developing what became known as the **Stanislavsky system** of acting, he trained students to strive for realism, both social and psychological, and to bring their own past experiences and emotions to their roles. This intense psychological preparation required the actors' conscious efforts to tap their unconscious selves. On one hand, they had to portray living characters onstage; on the other, they could not allow their portrayals to detract from the acting ensemble and the play as a whole and as written text.

Stanislavsky's ideas influenced the Soviet silent-film directors of the 1920s—Sergei Eisenstein, Aleksandr Dovzhenko, Lev Kuleshov, and Vsevolod I. Pudovkin—all of whom had learned much from D. W. Griffith's work. But they often disagreed about acting, especially about how it was influenced by actors' appearances and by editing, which could work so expressively both for and against actors' interpretations.

Among this group, Pudovkin, whose *Film Acting* (1935) was one of the first serious books on the subject, has the most relevance to mainstream movie acting today. Although he advocates an explicitly Stanislavskian technique based on his observations of the Moscow Art Theater, he writes from the standpoint of film directors and actors working together. Because film consists of individual shots, he reasons, both directors and actors work at the mercy of the shot and must strive to make acting (out of sequence) seem natural, smooth, and flowing while maintaining expressive coherence across the shots. He recommends close collaboration between actors and directors, with long periods devoted to preparation and rehearsal. He also advises film actors to ignore voice training because the microphone makes it unnecessary, notes that the close-up can communicate more to the audience than overt gestures can, and finds that the handling of "expressive objects" (e.g., Charlie Chaplin's cane) can convey emotions and ideas even more effectively than close-ups can.

Outside the Soviet Union, Stanislavsky's books *My Life in Art* (1924) and *An Actor Prepares* (1936) had a lasting impact. In the mid 1930s, Stella Adler studied privately with him in Moscow—perhaps the first American actor to do so. Soon after, she returned to New York and taught principles of method acting to members of the experimental Group Theatre, including Elia Kazan. In 1947, Kazan and Lee Strasberg, now directors, founded the Actors Studio in New York City; two years later, Adler founded the Stella Adler Studio of Acting, where Marlon Brando was her most famous and successful student.

These teachers loosely adapted Stanislavky's ideas—not only his principle that actors should draw on their own emotional experiences to create characters, but also his emphasis on the importance of creating an ensemble and expressing the subtext, the nuances that lay beneath the lines of the script. The naturalistic style that they popularized (and called **method acting**, more popularly known as *the method*) encourages actors to speak, move, and gesture not in a traditional stage manner but just as they would in their own lives. Thus it is an ideal technique for representing convincing human behavior on the stage and on the screen. The method has led to a new level of realism and subtlety, influencing such actors as Marlon Brando, Montgomery Clift, James Dean, Robert De Niro, Faye Dunaway, Robert Duvall, Morgan Freeman, Gene Hackman, Dustin Hoffman, Dennis Hopper, Holly Hunter, Harvey Keitel, Walter Matthau, Paul

Elia Kazan and Method Acting Elia Kazan is notable, among many other things, for directing two of the iconic method-acting achievements: [1] Marlon Brando's as Terry Malloy in *On the Waterfront* (1954)—here we see Kazan (*center*) and Brando (*right*) on location during the filming—and [2] James Dean's as Cal Trask, a troubled teenager, in *East of Eden* (1955).

Newman, Jack Nicholson, Al Pacino, Sidney Poitier, Jon Voight, and Shelley Winters.[17]

To understand method acting, you have to see it. Fortunately, there are some wonderful examples, including James Dean's three movie roles—Cal Trask in Elia Kazan's *East of Eden* (1955), Jim Stark in Nicholas Ray's *Rebel Without a Cause* (1955), and

[17] See Carole Zucker, "An Interview with Lindsay Crouse," *Post Script: Essays in Film and the Humanities* 12, no. 2 (winter 1993): 5–28. See also Foster Hirsch, *A Method to Their Madness: The History of the Actors Studio* (New York: Norton, 1984), and Steven Vineberg, *Method Actors: Three Generations of an American Acting Style* (New York: Schirmer Books, 1991).

Jett Rink in George Stevens's *Giant* (1956); and Marlon Brando's equally legendary performances as Stanley Kowalski in Elia Kazan's *A Streetcar Named Desire* (1951)—reprising the stage role that made him famous—and as Terry Malloy in Kazan's *On the Waterfront* (1954). Other notable performances, out of many, include those given by Paul Newman as Eddie Felson in Robert Rossen's *The Hustler* (1961), Shelley Winters as Charlotte Haze Humbert in Stanley Kubrick's *Lolita* (1962), and Faye Dunaway as Evelyn Cross Mulwray in Roman Polanski's *Chinatown* (1974). Each of these performances exhibits the major characteristics of method acting: intense concentration and internalization on the actor's part (sometimes mistaken for discomfort); low-key, almost laid-back delivery of lines (sometimes described as *mumbling*); and an edginess (sometimes highly neurotic) that suggests dissatisfaction, unhappiness, and alienation.

Screen Acting Today

From the earliest years, the development of movie acting has relied on synthesizing various approaches, including those already discussed. Contemporary actors employ a range of physically or psychologically based approaches, with some action stars, like Arnold Schwarzenegger or Jamie Foxx, relying entirely on physical effect, and others, like Bruce Willis, relying both on physical prowess and a very defined persona that has evolved from his early wise-guy days to a more world-weary persona. Directors also take different approaches toward actors. Robert Altman, for example, who is particularly good at capturing the mood of an ensemble of actors within a narrative, encourages improvisation and the exploration of individual styles. Joel Coen, in contrast, tends to regard acting as a critical component of the highly stylized mise-en-scène within the often cartoonlike movies that he creates with his brother, Ethan.

In Altman's *The Player* (1992), Tim Robbins plays Griffin Mill, a Hollywood producer, at once emotively and satirically. He uses his big, open face and charming manner to draw us into Mill's professional and existential crises, then turns edgy enough to distance us as Mill becomes a murderer

and ruthless careerist. In Altman's *Kansas City* (1996), Jennifer Jason Leigh delivers an emotional hurricane of a performance as the cheap, brassy, tough Blondie O'Hara, a Jean Harlow wannabe. Her scowl, furrowed brow, rotten teeth under big red lips, and screeching-cat voice leave no room for the kind of gently ironic distance that Robbins creates in *The Player*.

In Coen's *The Hudsucker Proxy* (1994), however, both Robbins and Leigh tailor their performances to fit the madcap mood and mannered décor of an art deco screwball comedy. Indeed, part of the movie's appeal lies in watching an ensemble of actors working in this style. Channeling Cary Grant and Rosalind Russell in Howard Hawks's *His Girl Friday* (1940) and Spencer Tracy and Katharine Hepburn in Walter Lang's *Desk Set* (1957), Robbins plays Norville Barnes, a goofy mailroom clerk who becomes company president, and Leigh plays Amy Archer, a hard-boiled, wisecracking newspaper reporter. Robbins and Leigh's zany comic interaction fits perfectly in Coen's jigsaw puzzle, which lovingly pays tribute to an era when movie style often transcended substance.

Today, actors struggle to get parts and to create convincing performances and, like their earlier counterparts, seldom have the chance to prove themselves across a range of roles. Once **typecast**—that is, cast in particular kinds of roles because of their looks or "type" rather than for their acting talent or experience—they continue to be awarded such parts as long they bring in good box-office receipts. No star system exists to sustain careers and images, but now, as in earlier periods of movie history, some individuals use films to promote themselves; and music or sports stars, or other celebrities, sometimes appear in a movie or two, leaving no mark on the history of film acting.

The transition from studio production to independent production has markedly affected the livelihood of actors and the art of acting. The shape of the average career has fundamentally changed; because fewer major movies appear each year, actors supplement film work with appearances on television shows, in advertisements, and in theater. (Salaries and contractual benefits, such as residual payments for television reruns, provide excellent

Contemporary Star Power   With the success of one or two major movies, contemporary actors can become stars almost overnight. Benicio Del Toro has been appearing in movies since 1988, with varying degrees of success and recognition, but he began attracting serious attention in independent films such as Bryan Singer's *The Usual Suspects* (1995) and Julian Schnabel's *Basquiat* (1996). Del Toro remained relatively unknown to American audiences until his breakthrough performance, here, as the Mexican police officer Javier Rodriguez in Steven Soderbergh's *Traffic* (2000), for which he won the Academy Award for Best Supporting Actor.

financial security.) In addition, because today the average movie is a comedy targeted at—indeed, mass-marketed to—the under-thirty audience (and a comedy relying on physical humor, often of a scatological nature, rather than verbal wit), fewer quality roles are available to actors.

Some extremely versatile actors—Russell Crowe, Benicio Del Toro, Johnny Depp, Leonardo DiCaprio, Samuel L. Jackson, Nicole Kidman, Julianne Moore, Kevin Spacey, and Hilary Swank, to name a few—have, with two or three successful films, become stars quickly. The greater their drawing power at the box office, the greater the urgency to promote them to top rank and cast them in more films. As independent agents, however, they can contract for one film at a time and thus hold out for good roles, rather than having to make a specific number of films for a given studio. In addition, these newcomers can negotiate a new salary for each film, and they routinely make more money from a *single* picture than some of the greatest stars of classical Hollywood made in their *entire* careers. Furthermore, they usually work under their own names. But because audience reaction, and not a studio's

publicity office, maintains their status, such actors often face highly unpredictable futures.

WEB The Star System and "Star Vehicles"

Finally, for every advance in the world of special effects, the narrative and the acting that propels it lose some of their importance. Movies such as Stanley Kubrick's *2001: A Space Odyssey* (1968) and Steven Spielberg's *E.T. the Extra-Terrestrial* (1982) made us familiar, even comfortable, with nonhuman creatures that had human voices and characteristics; John Lasseter, Ash Brannon, and Lee Unkrich's *Toy Story 2* (1999), with its shiny, computer-generated graphics, took this process another step forward.

With technology now revolutionizing filmmaking, will actors be replaced by digitally created *synthespians* (a name coined by the digital-effects expert Jeff Kleiser, who with Diana Walczak created the first synthespian for the 1988 short *Sextone for President*)? Yes and no. Today's computer-generated "actors" in Hironobu Sakaguchi and Moto Sakakibara's *Final Fantasy: The Spirits Within* (2001), Andrew Niccol's *S1m0ne* (2002), and Robert Zemeckis's *Polar Express* (2004) seem to be another stage in this evolution. George Lucas, as successful and influential as anyone in the industry, seems, as a director, to be more interested in perfecting digital technology than in directing actors and developing a character's emotions. For example, he "directed" the CGI character Jar Jar Binks (voice of Ahmed Best) to interact with live actors in three of his "Star Wars" movies: *The Phantom Menace* (1999), *Attack of the Clones* (2002), and *Revenge of the Sith* (2005). However, this strategy turned out to be particularly unpopular with his "Star Wars" fans, many of whom demanded that the character be eliminated from future movies. Nonetheless, the CGI character of Gollum (voice of Andy Serkis) in Peter Jackson's "Lord of the Rings" trilogy (2001–03) is a fully realized character created in a very different way from a typical Lucas cardboard cutout.

Computer-generated characters might even meet with the fate of some of the other innovations that Hollywood has periodically employed to keep the world on edge, such as the widescreen ratio (see "Framing of the Shot" in Chapter 4); the short-lived

"Synthespians" What will be the future of acting if more and more performances in narrative films are the product of computer-generated imagery? In Robert Zemeckis's *The Polar Express* (2004), through the computer technology known as *performance capture*, Tom Hanks plays multiple roles, including the Hobo, seen here talking with Hero Boy (whom he also "plays") on top of the train.

In a world where video games are aggressively challenging the movies, the use of CGI characters raises many questions in the minds of movie fans. If CGI frees the director's imagination, does it capture the viewer's? If one actor can play multiple roles in a movie, no matter how well, what's to become of the more individual characterization that inevitably results from having different actors in different roles? Is the result verisimilar or creepy? Will CGI characters work as effectively in movies made for adult audiences as it seems to in those made primarily for children? Will they move viewers emotionally and intellectually in the manner of great human performances?

Sensurround, which relied on a sound track to trigger waves of high-decibel sound in the movie theater, making viewers feel "tremors" during Mark Robson's *Earthquake* (1974); or the even shorter-lived Odorama process, involving scratch-and-sniff cards, for John Waters's *Polyester* (1981). Indeed, the use of computer technology to replace actors is one side effect of our current fascination with virtual reality. Although the evolving film technology may enable filmmakers to realize their most fantastic visions, we should remember, as film theorist André Bazin has so persuasively argued, that such developments may extend and enrich the illusions that the movies create at the expense of the film artists themselves, including directors, designers, cinematographers, editors, *and* actors.[18]

[18] André Bazin, "The Myth of Total Cinema," in *What Is Cinema?*, trans. Hugh Gray (Berkeley: University of California Press, 1967–71), 1:17–22.

Casting Actors

Casting is the process of choosing and hiring actors for a movie, and there are various ways to do it. Although casting usually takes place during preproduction after the script has been written, it may also occur during development, if scripts are written for specific actors. In the studio system, each studio ran its casting department and thus tended to restrict casting to its own actors. Today, professional casting directors work under contract to independent producers and also have their own professional association, the Casting Society of America (CSA). Casting can be done either by professionals hired for a particular film or by a casting agency. In either case, the people in charge generally work closely with the producer, director, and screenwriter when first determining casting needs. To aid in the initial selection of candidates, they maintain files of actors' résumés and photographs.

Similarly, there is no one way for actors to find out about parts that they may want to play. Producers, directors, screenwriters, or casting directors may alert agents or contact actors directly. Audition calls may be published in trade papers such as *Variety*, *The Hollywood Reporter*, and *Back Stage*; or word may spread through networks of movie professionals.

Regardless of actors' experience, they may be asked to read for parts, either alone or with other actors, or to take **screen tests** (trial filmings). If they are chosen for the parts, negotiations will, in most cases, be handled by their agents; but if they belong to one of the actors' unions—the Screen Actors Guild (SAG) or the American Federation of Television and Radio Artists (AFTRA)—the conditions of their participation will be governed by union contract.

Factors Involved in Casting

The art of casting actors takes many factors into account. In theory, the most important considerations are the type of role and how an actor's strengths and weaknesses relate to it. In reality, casting—like every other aspect of movie production—depends, in one way or another, on the budget and expected revenues. Here, gender, race, ethnicity, and age also come into play. The American film industry has tended to produce films with strong, white, male leads, usually younger than fifty. Thus, in a major 2005 poll of favorite movie stars, this heterogeneous group of ten actors topped the list (in descending order): Tom Hanks, Mel Gibson, Julia Roberts, Johnny Depp, Harrison Ford, Denzel Washington, John Wayne (even though he died in

The Faces of Contemporary Casting The diversity of contemporary film actors is apparent whenever we go to the Cineplex to see the latest releases. Among the most popular actors working today are [1] Denzel Washington, seen here in his role as Ben Marco in Jonathan Demme's *The Manchurian Candidate* (2004); [2] Jennifer Lopez, shown here as Charlie in Robert Luketic's *Monster-in-Law* (2005); [3] Antonio Banderas, here playing the role of Carlos Rueda in Christopher Hampton's *Imagining Argentina* (2003); and [4] Lucy Liu, in this image portraying O-Ren Ishii in Quentin Tarantino's *Kill Bill: Vol. 1* (2003).

1979), Clint Eastwood, Sean Connery, and George Clooney. Each of these actors has a well-defined persona, but we cannot confidently predict what roles they will undertake or how they will play them. For example, the George Clooney of Joel Coen's *O Brother, Where Art Thou?* (2000) or Steven Soderbergh's *Ocean's Eleven* (2001) is not the George Clooney of, say, *Good Night, and Good Luck* (2005), a movie he also directed, or of Stephen Gaghan's *Syriana* (2005). Casting Clooney in his familiar image of a loose, easy swinger has given way to casting him in more socially and politically conscious roles.

It is also true, however, that today gender, race, ethnicity, and age have become important issues in the movies, as in other areas of American popular culture. Both the characters depicted on the screen and the actors playing them have grown more diverse, particularly in terms of race and ethnicity; and this diversification has, in turn, changed the people who make movies, the audiences for movies, and the financing that makes them possible. Twenty years ago, to see a movie about African Americans meant waiting for the next Spike Lee release, and anyone wanting to see a mainstream movie about Hispanic, Latino, or Asian Americans was generally out of luck. By contrast, now every week—depending, of course, on the distribution of movies in a particular part of the country—audiences can choose from a range of movies that reflect contemporary North America's social diversity in the stories they tell and the filmmakers and actors who made them. Here, the industry has learned that significant profits can be gained by targeting film releases to different demographics.

For decades, movie producers intentionally contradicted social reality by casting actors who are *not* of a certain race or ethnicity to portray that race or ethnicity: Richard Barthelmess as Cheng Huan in D. W. Griffith's *Broken Blossoms* (1919; see "D. W. Griffith and Lillian Gish," earlier in this chapter), Luise Rainer as O-Lan in Sidney Franklin's *The Good Earth* (1937), Marlon Brando as Sakini in Daniel Mann's *The Teahouse of the August Moon* (1956), and Mickey Rooney as Mr. Yunioshi in Blake Edwards's *Breakfast at Tiffany's* (1961), to name just a few. The practice is nearly but not completely extinct today. In Julian Schnabel's *Before

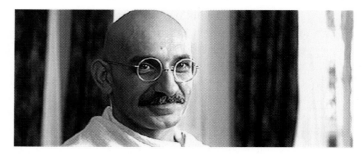

Casting *Gandhi* In Richard Attenborough's *Gandhi* (1982), the English actor Ben Kingsley plays the Indian political and spiritual leader Mahatma Mohandas K. Gandhi (1869–1948) from his youth until his assassination. Born Krishna Bhanji, the son of an Indian doctor and an English fashion model, Kingsley looks so much like Gandhi and inhabits the role so completely that, for many viewers, the two men are inextricably linked.

Night Falls (2000), for example, Sean Penn plays a dark-skinned Cuban, Cuco Sánchez. The somewhat darker-skinned Johnny Depp plays both Bon Bon, a transvestite, and Lieutenant Victor, a Cuban military officer. An even more striking example was the casting of Anthony Hopkins as a light-skinned African American in Robert Benton's *The Human Stain* (2003)—a decision that struck many critics as a critical casting error.

The long-standing explanation for this custom among movie executives was that they could not find the appropriate actors. Instead, they gave such all-purpose actors as Anthony Quinn, an Irish Mexican, roles of different races and ethnicities. Using costume, makeup, and accents to change himself, Quinn played a Spaniard, an Italian, a Greek, a Frenchman, an Arab, and a Native American, while Alec Guinness, a great British actor famous for his facility in international accents, played an Indian, an Arab, and a Scotsman. Laurence Olivier played an equally diverse set of roles on the stage and screen, including Shakespeare's Moor, Othello. This does not mean that Quinn, Guinness, and Olivier took these roles because they could not get other work; or that they did not look or sound appropriate in these roles, which they most often did; or even that actors should be limited to roles matching their own genders, races, ethnicities, or ages (since acting is, after all, about the *creation* of a character). But it is clear that producers simply felt more comfortable casting roles in this manner, that minority actors were disqualified as a result, and that, absent public opposition, the custom continued unabated.

Such barriers were not always in place, or at least not so firmly. Beginning in the 1920s, in reaction to the stereotyping of African Americans in D. W. Griffith's *The Birth of a Nation* (1915), some African Americans strove to make their own films. Producer, director, and exhibitor Oscar Micheaux was the most prominent among the leaders of this effort. Although he made about forty feature films, only ten survive. And although Hollywood also tried appealing to the African American audience with all-black musicals, its efforts were few and disappointing. From the beginning, however, Hollywood drew many actors from various racial backgrounds.

In the 1930s, the great comic actor Stepin Fetchit was the first African American to receive featured billing in the movies. Butterfly McQueen, Louise Beavers, and Hattie McDaniel (who won an Oscar for Best Supporting Actress for her performance in *Gone With the Wind*, 1939) all had durable careers playing maids and mammies. Paul Robeson, a great actor and singer on the Broadway stage, was featured in several movies, most notably Dudley Murphy's *The Emperor Jones* (1933), James Whale's *Show Boat* (1936), and Julien Duvivier's *Tales of Manhattan* (1942). In the 1950s, Sidney Poitier and Dorothy Dandridge became the first African American movie *stars*. Poitier has enjoyed an extraordinarily successful career, but Dandridge was not so fortunate. She began by playing stereotypical African American roles in twenty-one movies and was later nominated for the Oscar for Best Actress for her leading role in Otto Preminger's sumptuous musical production *Carmen Jones* (1954), but ended her career after starring (opposite Poitier) in Preminger's *Porgy and Bess* (1959).

Among the African Americans who have since become stars are Pearl Bailey, Halle Berry, Diahann Carroll, Bill Cosby, Laurence Fishburne, Jamie Foxx, Morgan Freeman, Pam Grier, Samuel L. Jackson, James Earl Jones, Eddie Murphy, Denzel Washington, and Forest Whitaker. Among the many Hispanic, Latino, and Asian stars are Anto-

"This Door Tonight Has Been Opened" In Martha Coolidge's *Introducing Dorothy Dandridge* (1999), Halle Berry plays Dandridge, who is shown here starring as the title character in Otto Preminger's *Carmen Jones* (1954). For her role in that film, which featured an all-black cast, Dandridge was the first black woman to receive an Academy Award nomination for Best Actress; Grace Kelly received the Oscar that year (for her performance in George Seaton's *The Country Girl*). Nearly fifty years later, Halle Berry became the first African American woman to win the Academy Award for Best Actress, for her performance in Marc Forster's *Monster's Ball* (2001). Berry began her acceptance speech, "This moment is for Dorothy Dandridge, Lena Horne, Diahann Carroll . . . and it's for every nameless, faceless woman of color that now has a chance because this door tonight has been opened."

nio Banderas, Joan Chen, Dolores del Rio, José Ferrer, Li Gong, Raul Julia, Nancy Kwan, Fernando Lamas, Lucy Liu, Jennifer Lopez, Keye Luke, Toshirô Mifune, Alfred Molina, Ricardo Montalban, María Montez, Rita Moreno, Haing S. Ngor, Edward James Olmos, Cesar Romero, Lupe Velez, Anna May Wong, and Chow Yun-Fat.

WEB Contemporary Treatments of Race in Popular Cinema

Traditionally, because audiences have shown little interest in films about women older than forty-five, the industry has produced few of them. Some women older than this cutoff—Joan Crawford, Bette Davis, Angela Lansbury, Shirley MacLaine, Debbie Reynolds, Elizabeth Taylor, Shelley Winters—have taken roles as stereotyped eccentrics, where the camp value of their performances translates into the triumphant statement "I'm still here!" Furthermore, audiences love it when a great star from a former era makes a rare comeback, as Gloria Swanson did in Billy Wilder's *Sunset Blvd.* (1950). But even though many excellent movies have featured older male actors—Henry Fonda, Jack Lemmon, Walter Matthau, Jason Robards, Jimmy Stewart, Spencer Tracy—the apparent bias against older female actors remains a box-office fact and thus a reality of casting in Hollywood. By contrast, the British seem to lack such prejudices, for their actors—including Judi Dench, Alec Guinness, Laurence Olivier, Peter O'Toole, Joan Plowright, Vanessa Redgrave, Ralph Richardson, Margaret Rutherford, and Maggie Smith—generally work as long as they can. Their popularity in the United States may say something about American audiences' cultural stereotypes—namely, that they'll accept and even expect aging, as long as it happens to other people.

Complicating the issue of age is the ability of young actors, in part through the magic of makeup, to play characters older than themselves: think of Jane Fonda as writer Lillian Hellman in Fred Zinnemann's *Julia* (1977), Leonardo DiCaprio as Howard Hughes in Martin Scorsese's *The Aviator* (2004), or Frank Langella as the CBS network boss in George Clooney's *Good Night, and Good Luck* (2005). Or they can play characters who mature onscreen from youth to old age, as did Orson Welles in his own *Citizen Kane* (1941), Dustin Hoffman as Jack Crabb in Arthur Penn's *Little Big Man* (1970), Ben Kingsley in Richard Attenborough's *Gandhi* (1982), and Robert Downey Jr. in Attenborough's *Chaplin* (1992). In the standard variation on this approach, two or more actors play the same character during different stages of the character's life, as Kate Winslet and Gloria Stuart did in James Cameron's *Titanic* (1997).

Aspects of Performance

Types of Roles

Actors may play major roles, minor roles, character roles, cameo roles, and walk-ons. In addition,

roles may be written specifically for bit players, extras, stuntpersons, and even animal performers. Actors who play **major roles** (also called *main, featured,* or *lead roles*) become principal agents in helping to move the plot forward. Whether stars or newcomers, they appear in many scenes and—ordinarily, but not always—receive screen credit preceding the title.

In the Hollywood studio system, major roles were traditionally played by stars such as John Wayne, whose studios counted on them to draw audiences regardless of the parts they played. Their steadfastness was often more important than their versatility as actors, although Wayne surprises us more often than we may admit. One of the strengths of the studio system was its grooming of professionals in all its creative departments, including actors at all levels, from leads such as Henry Fonda and Katharine Hepburn to character actors such as Thelma Ritter and Andy Devine—best remembered as, respectively, the wisecracking commentator on "Jeff's" (James Stewart) actions in Alfred Hitchcock's *Rear Window* (1954), and the Ringo Kid's (John Wayne) loyal friend in John Ford's *Stagecoach* (1939). Indeed, one of the joys of looking at movies from this period comes from those character actors whose faces, if not names, we always recognize: Mary Boland, Walter Brennan, Harry Carey Jr., Ray Collins, Laura Hope Crews, Gladys George, Marjorie Main, Butterfly McQueen, Una O'Connor, Franklin Pangborn, Erskine Sanford, and Ernest Thesiger, to name a distinctive few out of hundreds.

Stars may be so valuable to productions that they have **stand-ins**, actors who look reasonably like them in height, weight, coloring, and so on and who substitute for them during the tedious process of preparing setups or taking light readings. Because actors in major roles are ordinarily not hired for their physical or athletic prowess, **stuntpersons** double for them in scenes requiring special skills or involving hazardous actions, such as crashing cars, jumping from high places, swimming, and riding (or falling off) horses. Through special effects, however, filmmakers may now augment actors' physical exertions so that they appear to do their own stunts, as in Andy and Larry

Character Actors Although Franklin Pangborn was never a household name, his face was instantly recognizable in the more than 200 movies he made over a career that spanned four decades. With his intimidating voice and fastidious manners, he was best known for playing suspicious hotel clerks, imperious department store floorwalkers, and sourpuss restaurant managers. Here he's the threatening bank examiner J. Pinkerton Snoopington in the W. C. Fields classic *The Bank Dick* (1940; director: Edward F. Cline).

highly recognizable actors or personalities. As a favor to his friend Orson Welles, with whom he'd worked several times before, Joseph Cotten played such a role in Welles's *Touch of Evil* (1958), where he had a few words of dialogue and literally walked on and off the set.

Animal actors, too, play major, minor, cameo, and walk-on roles. For many years, Hollywood made pictures built on the appeal of such animals as the dogs Lassie, Rin Tin Tin, Asta, and Benji; the cat Rhubarb; the parakeets Bill and Coo; the chimp Cheta; the mule Francis; the lion Elsa; the porpoise Flipper; and the killer whale Willy. Most of these animals were specially trained to work in front of the camera, and many were sufficiently valuable that they, like other stars, had stand-ins for setups and stunt doubles for hazardous work. Working with animal performers often proves more complicated than working with human

Wachowski's *The Matrix* (1999) and McG's *Charlie's Angels* (2000). In effect, the computer becomes the stunt double. Nonetheless, ten stunt boxers were cast for Clint Eastwood's *Million Dollar Baby* (2004), indicating, at least, that some activities cannot be faked on the screen, particularly activities that could cause damage to an actor's looks or other serious injuries.

Actors who play **minor roles** (or *supporting roles*) rank second in the hierarchy. They also help move the plot forward (and thus may be as important as actors in major roles), but they generally do not appear in as many scenes as the featured players. They may hold **character roles**, which represent distinctive character types (sometimes stereotypes): society leaders, judges, doctors, diplomats, and so on. **Bit players** hold small speaking parts, and **extras** usually appear in nonspeaking or crowd roles and receive no screen credit. **Cameos** are small but significant roles often taken by famous actors, as in Robert Altman's Hollywood satire *The Player* (1992), which features appearances by sixty-five well-known actors and personalities. **Walk-ons** are even smaller roles, reserved for

The Importance of Minor Roles In John Huston's *The Maltese Falcon* (1941), Humphrey Bogart stars as the hard-boiled private eye Sam Spade. Gladys George has a small part as Iva Archer, Spade's former lover and the widow of his business partner, Miles Archer (Jerome Cowan). In this scene, George delivers a strongly emotional performance, against which Bogart displays a relative lack of feeling that fills us in on relations between the characters. Stars' performances often depend on the solid and even exceptional work of their fellow actors. The unusually fine supporting cast in this movie includes Hollywood greats Mary Astor, Peter Lorre, and Sydney Greenstreet, who received an Oscar nomination for Best Supporting Actor.

actors. For example, six Jack Russell terriers, including three puppies, played the title character in Jay Russell's *My Dog Skip* (2000), a tribute to that indomitable breed.

Preparing for Roles

In creating characters, screen actors begin by synthesizing basic sources, including the script and the director's advice, their own experiences and observations, and the influences of other actors. Different roles have different demands, and all actors have their own approaches, whether they get inside their characters, get inside themselves, or do further research. Bette Davis, whose roles were often assigned her by studios, said, "It depends entirely on what the assignment happens to be . . . [But] I have never played a part which I did not feel was a person very different from myself."[19] Jack Lemmon, a method actor who generally chose his own roles, explained, "It's like laying bricks. You start at the bottom and work up; actually I guess you start in the middle and work to the outside."[20]

Building a character "brick by brick" is an approach also used by Harvey Keitel and John Malkovich, who might have varied this approach slightly when he played himself in Spike Jonze's *Being John Malkovich* (1999). Liv Ullmann and Jack Nicholson believe that the actor draws on the subconscious mind. Ullmann says, "Emotionally, I don't prepare. I think about what I would like to show, but I don't prepare, because I feel that most of the emotions I have to show I know about. By drawing on real experience, I can show them."[21] In describing his work with director Roman Polanski on *Chinatown* (1974), Nicholson says that the director "pushes us farther than we are conscious

Olivier's *Henry V* Sir Laurence Olivier in the first screen adaptation of *Henry V* (1944); this very popular film during a troubled time (World War II) was uniformly praised for the quality of its acting. The many previous screen adaptations of Shakespeare's plays had been mainly faithful records of stage productions, but Olivier's film, his first as a director, benefited from his understanding of cinema's potential as a narrative art, his extensive acting experience, his deep knowledge of Shakespeare's language, and his sharp instincts about the national moods in Great Britain and the United States. *Henry V* received an Oscar nomination for Best Picture, and Olivier received a Best Actor nomination, as well as an Oscar for his outstanding achievement as actor, producer, and director for bringing *Henry V* to the screen.

of being able to go; he forces us down into the subconscious—in order to see if there's something better there."[22] Jodie Foster works from instinct, doing what she feels is right for the character.[23] To create The Tramp, Charlie Chaplin started with the character's costume: "I had no idea of the character. But the moment I was dressed, the clothes and the make-up made me feel the person he was."[24] Alec Guinness said that he was never happy with his preparation until he knew how the character walked; Laurence Olivier believed that he would not be any good as a char-

[19] "Bette Davis: The Actress Plays Her Part," in *Playing to the Camera: Film Actors Discuss Their Craft*, ed. Bert Cardullo, Harry Geduld, Ronald Gottesman, and Leigh Woods (New Haven, Conn.: Yale University Press, 1998), 177–85: quotation, 179.

[20] "Jack Lemmon: Conversation with the Actor," in *Playing to the Camera*, ed. Cardullo et al., 267–75: quotation, 267.

[21] "Liv Ullmann: Conversation With the Actress," in *Playing to the Camera*, ed. Cardullo et al., 157–65: quotation, 160.

[22] See the entry on Nicholson in *Actors on Acting for the Screen*, ed. Tomlinson, 404–7: quotation, 405.

[23] See the entry on Foster in *Actors on Acting for the Screen*, ed. Tomlinson, 196–97.

[24] Charles Chaplin, *My Autobiography* (New York: Simon & Schuster, 1964), 260.

acter unless he "loved" him,[25] and Morgan Freeman says that some of his preparation depends on the clothes he is to wear.[26]

Olivier, one of the greatest stage and screen actors of the twentieth century, defined acting in various ways, including as "convincing lying."[27] Although Olivier stands out for the extraordinary range of the roles he undertook, on both stage and screen, and for his meticulous preparation in creating them, this remark suggests that he had little patience with theories of acting. Indeed, when asked how he created his film performance as the king in *Henry V* (1944; director: Olivier), he replied simply, "I don't know—I'm England, that's all."[28] Olivier had made this film to bolster British morale during the last days of World War II, and thus he wanted Henry V to embody traditional British values.

The great silent-era director F. W. Murnau emphasized intellect and counseled actors to restrain their feelings, to *think* rather than *act*. He believed actors to be capable of conveying the intensity of their thoughts so that audiences would understand. Director Rouben Mamoulian gave Greta Garbo much the same advice when she played the leading role in his *Queen Christina* (1933). The film ends with the powerful and passionate Swedish queen sailing to Spain with the body of her lover, a Spanish nobleman killed in a duel. In preparing for the final close-up, in which the queen stares out to sea, Garbo asked Mamoulian, "What should I be thinking of? What should I be doing?" His reply: "Have you heard of *tabula rasa*? I want your face to be a blank sheet of paper. I want the writing to be done by every member of the audience. I'd like it if you could avoid even blinking your eyes, so that you're nothing but a beautiful mask."[29] Is she remembering the past? Imagining the future? With the camera serving as an apparently neutral mediator between actress and audience, Garbo's blank face asks us to transform it into what we *hope* or *want* to see.

Naturalistic and Nonnaturalistic Styles

We have all seen at least one movie in which a character, perhaps a whole cast of characters, is like no one we have ever met, nor like anyone we *could* ever meet. Either because the world they inhabit functions according to rules that don't apply in our world or because their behaviors are extreme, such characters aren't realistic in any colloquial sense of the word. But if the actors perform skillfully, we are likely to accept the characters as believable within the context of the story. We might be tempted to call such portrayals *realistic*, but we'd do better to use the term *naturalistic*.

Actors who strive for appropriate, expressive, coherent, and unified characterizations can render their performances naturalistically and/or nonnaturalistically. Screen acting appears naturalistic when actors re-create recognizable or plausible human behavior for the camera. The actors not only look like the characters should (in their costume, makeup, and hairstyle) but also think, speak, and move the way people would offscreen. By contrast, nonnaturalistic performances seem excessive, exaggerated, even overacted; they may employ strange or outlandish costumes, makeup, or hairstyles; they might aim for effects beyond the normal range of human experience; and they often intend to distance or estrange audiences from characters. Frequently they are found in horror, fantasy, and action films.

What Konstantin Stanislavsky was to naturalistic acting, German playwright Bertolt Brecht was to nonnaturalistic performance. Brecht allied his theatrical ideas with Marxist political principles to create a nonnaturalistic theater. Whereas Stanislavsky strove for realism, Brecht believed that audience members should not think they're watching

[25] See the entry on Guinness in *Actors on Acting for the Screen*, ed. Tomlinson, 232–33; and Laurence Olivier, *Confessions of an Actor: An Autobiography* (1982; reprint, New York: Penguin, 1984), 136–37.

[26] From an interview with James Lipton, "James Lipton Takes on Three," on disk 2 ("Special Features") in the widescreen DVD release of *Million Dollar Baby*.

[27] Olivier, *Confessions of an Actor*, 20.

[28] Olivier, qtd. in Donald Spoto, *Laurence Olivier: A Biography* (New York: HarperCollins, 1992), 111–12.

[29] Mamoulian, qtd. in Tom Milne, *Rouben Mamoulian* (Bloomington: Indiana University Press, 1969), 74.

something actually happening before them. Instead, he wanted every aspect of a theatrical production to limit the audience's identification with characters and events, thereby creating a psychological distance (called the **alienation effect** or **distancing effect**) between them and the stage. The intent of this approach is to remind the audience of the artificiality of the theatrical performance.

Overall, this theory has not had much influence on mainstream filmmaking; after all, unlike theater, cinema can change—as often as it wants—the relationship between spectators and the screen, alternately alienating them from or plunging them into the action. However, we do see this approach when actors step out of character, face the camera, and directly address the audience (a maneuver, more common in theater than cinema, that is called *breaking the fourth wall*—the imaginary, invisible wall that separates the audience from the stage). Although it is a device that can destroy a movie if used inappropriately, breaking the fourth wall works effectively when audience members are experiencing things as the character does *and* the character has the self-confidence to exploit that empathy.

Tom Edison (Paul Bettany) frequently addresses his idealistic views directly to the viewer in Lars von Trier's *Dogville* (2003), which in overall style owes much to Bertolt Brecht's influence. In Max Ophüls's *Lola Montès* (1955), the Circus Master (Peter Ustinov) addresses the circus audience, of which, we understand, we are members. For comic effect, Tom Jones (Albert Finney) breaks the fourth wall in Tony Richardson's *Tom Jones* (1963), as does Alfie (Michael Caine) in Lewis Gilbert's *Alfie* (1966) and (played by Jude Law) in Charles Shyer's 2004 remake. Various characters speak directly to the viewer in Spike Lee's *Do the Right Thing* (1989). There is a much more solid tradition of direct address in the European theatrical cinema of such directors as Jean-Luc Godard, Chantal Akerman, and Eric Rohmer, among others.

In Wayne Wang's *Smoke* (1995), Harvey Keitel gives a naturalistic performance as Auggie Wren, a middle-aged, white Brooklynite who runs a cigar store, lives alone, and maintains an idiosyncratic photographic record of his neighborhood. In Boaz

Naturalistic Versus Nonnaturalistic Performances
Naturalistic and nonnaturalistic performances sometimes overlap, but these categories help us relate actors' contributions to a filmmaker's overall vision. [1] In *Fresh* (1994), Sean Nelson's naturalistic performance becomes part of director Boaz Yakin's clear-eyed depiction of contemporary American urban life. Yakin's film is about truth, "the way it is." [2] Johnny Depp's nonnaturalistic performance as the title character in *Edward Scissorhands* (1990) enables director Tim Burton to draw us into the exaggerated, downright weird world of this story. Burton's film is about fantasy, the way things might be in that world. Nelson's and Depp's performances differ widely, but they suit their respective movies. Imagine how out of place either character would be in the other's world!

⟶WEB **Naturalistic and Nonnaturalistic Performances**

Yakin's *Fresh* (1994), Sean Nelson naturalistically plays the title character—a young, black Brooklynite working as a courier for a dope dealer between going to school and looking out for his older sister. In Tim Burton's *Edward Scissorhands*

(1990), Johnny Depp gives a nonnaturalistic performance as the title character, a kind of Frankenstein's monster—scary, but benevolent—created by a mad inventor who died before his work was finished. Edward lives in a deteriorating Gothic castle on a mountaintop that overlooks a nightmarishly pastel suburb, to which he eventually moves. The décor and costumes identify him immediately as a metaphor for the ultimate outsider. But the challenge to Depp as an actor is not only to acknowledge just how different he appears to others ("hands," scars, makeup, hairstyle), which he does in a very self-conscious and often comic manner (e.g., using his hands to shred cabbage for cole slaw), but also to humanize this character so that he can be accepted as a member of the community.

Improvisational Acting

Improvisation can mean extemporizing—that is, delivering lines based only loosely on the written script or without the preparation that comes with studying a script before rehearsing it. It can also mean *playing through* a moment, making up lines to keep scenes going when actors forget their written lines, stumble on lines, or have some other mishap. Of these two senses, the former is most important in movie acting, particularly in the poststudio world; the latter is an example of professional grace under pressure.

Improvisation can be seen as an extension of Stanislavsky's emphasis that the actor striving for a naturalistic performance should avoid any mannerisms that call attention to technique. Occupying a place somewhere between his call for actors to bring their own experiences to roles and Brecht's call for actors to distance themselves from roles, improvisation often involves collaboration between actors and directors in creating stories, characters, and dialogue, which may then be incorporated into scripts. According to film scholar Virginia Wright Wexman, what improvisers

> seem to be striving for is the sense of discovery that comes from the unexpected and unpredictable in human behavior. If we think of art as a means of giving form to life, improvisation can be looked at as one

way of adding to our sense of the liveliness of art, a means of avoiding the sterility that results from rote recitations of abstract conventional forms.[30]

For years, improvisation has played a major part in actors' training, but it was anathema in the studio system—where practically everything was preprogrammed—and it remains comparatively rare in narrative moviemaking. Actors quite commonly confer with directors about altering or omitting written lines, but this form of improvisation is so limited in scope that we can better understand it as the sort of fertile suggestion making that is intrinsic to collaboration. Although certain directors encourage actors not only to discover the characters within themselves, but also to imagine what those characters might say (and how they might act) in any given situation, James Naremore, an authority on film acting, explains that even great actors, when they improvise, "tend to lapse into monologue, playing from relatively static, frontal positions with a second actor nearby who nods or makes short interjections."[31]

Among the director–actor collaborations that have made improvisation work effectively are Bernardo Bertolucci and Marlon Brando (*Last Tango in Paris*, 1972); Robert Altman and a large company of actors (*Nashville*, 1975; *Short Cuts*, 1993; *Gosford Park*, 2001); Mike Leigh and various actors (*Life Is Sweet*, 1990; *Naked*, 1993; *Topsy-Turvy*, 1999; *All or Nothing*, 2002); and John Cassavetes and Gena Rowlands (*Faces*, 1968; *A Woman Under the Influence*, 1974; *Gloria*, 1980).

The Cassavetes–Rowlands collaboration is particularly important and impressive, not only for what it accomplished but also for the respect it received as an experimental approach within the largely conventional film industry. "John's theory," Rowlands explains,

> is that if there's something wrong, it's wrong in the writing. If you take actors who can act in other

[30] Virginia Wright Wexman, "The Rhetoric of Cinematic Improvisation," *Cinema Journal* 20, no. 1 (fall 1980): 29. See also Maurice Yacowar, "An Aesthetic Defense of the Star System in Films," *Quarterly Review of Film Studies* 4, no. 1 (winter 1979): 48–50.

[31] James Naremore, *Acting in the Cinema* (Berkeley: University of California Press, 1988), 45.

Improvisation "You talkin' to me? . . . You talkin' to me?" Screenwriter Paul Schrader wrote no dialogue for the scene in Martin Scorsese's *Taxi Driver* in which Travis Bickle (Robert De Niro) rehearses his dreams of vigilantism before a mirror. Prior to filming, De Niro improvised the lines that now accompany this well-known moment in film history, a disturbing, darkly comic portrait of an unhinged mind talking to itself.

things and they get to a scene they've honestly tried to do, and if they still can't get it, then there's something wrong with the writing. Then you stop, you improvise, you talk about it. Then he'll go and rewrite it—it's not just straight improvisation. I'm asked a lot about this, and it's true, when I look at the films and I *see* that they look improvised in a lot of different places where I know they weren't.[32]

Improvised acting requires directors to play even more active roles than if they were working with prepared scripts, because they must not only elicit actors' ideas for characters and dialogue but also orchestrate those contributions within overall cinematic visions. Ultimately, directors help form all contributions, including those of actors. Nearly all directors who employ improvisation have the actors work it out in rehearsal, then lock it down for filming, perhaps radically changing their plans for how such scenes will be shot. This is how, for example, Martin Scorsese and Robert De Niro worked out the originally silent "You talkin' to me?" scene in *Taxi Driver* (1976). Unless directors and actors have talked publicly about their work, we

[32] Gena Rowlands, in *Actors on Acting for the Screen*, ed. Tomlinson, 482.

seldom know when and to what extent improvisation has been used in a film. Because we know that Cassavetes prepared his actors with precise scripts that they refined with extensive improvisational exercises, by studying the original script we can prepare to look for the improvisation, to judge its usefulness, and to determine whether improvised performances seem convincing or, ironically, less convincing than scripted ones.

Directors and Actors

Directors and actors have collaborated closely since the days when D. W. Griffith established screen acting with Lillian Gish. Inevitably, such relationships depend on the individuals: what each brings to their work, what each can do alone, and what each needs from a collaborator. Such different approaches taken by different directors in working with actors are as necessary, common, and useful as the different approaches taken by different actors as they prepare for roles.

Some veterans of the studio system, such as William Wyler and George Cukor, are known as "actors' directors," meaning that the directors inspire such confidence that they can actively shape actors' performances. Although Wyler may have enjoyed the trust of Bette Davis, Fredric March, Myrna Loy, Barbra Streisand, and other notable actors, the atmosphere on the set was considerably tenser when Laurence Olivier arrived in Hollywood for his first screen role, Heathcliff in Wyler's *Wuthering Heights* (1939). Olivier had already earned a considerable reputation on the London stage and was frankly contemptuous of screen acting, which he thought serious actors did only for the money. Wyler, on the other hand, was one of Hollywood's great stylists, a perfectionist who drove actors crazy with his keen sense of acting and love of multiple takes. Everyone on the set perceived the tension between them. Wyler encouraged Olivier to be patient in responding to the challenges involved in acting for the camera, and eventually Olivier overcame his attitude of condescension to give one of his greatest film performances.

In developing his relationships with actors, director John Ford encouraged them to create their characters to serve the narrative. He preferred to work with the same actors over and over, and his working method never changed. John Wayne, who acted in many of Ford's films and has been described as the director's alter ego, said Ford gave direction "with his entire personality—his facial expressions, bending his eye. He didn't verbalize. He wasn't articulate, he couldn't really finish a sentence. . . . He'd give you a clue, just an opening. If you didn't produce what he wanted, he would pick you apart."[33] Newcomers faced a challenge in getting it right the first time.

However rigid Ford's approach may at first seem, we find it in similarly fruitful collaborations between Rouben Mamoulian and Greta Garbo, Josef von Sternberg and Marlene Dietrich, John Huston and Humphrey Bogart, François Truffaut and Jean-Pierre Léaud, Akira Kurosawa and Toshirô Mifune, Satyajit Ray and Soumitra Chatterjee, Martin Scorsese and Robert De Niro, Spike Lee and Denzel Washington, and Tim Burton and Johnny Depp. These directors know what they want, explain it clearly, select actors with whom they work well, and then collaborate with them to create movies that are characterized in part by the seamless line between directing and acting.

By contrast, the line that *can* exist between directing and acting is evident in the work of director Alfred Hitchcock, who tends to place mise-en-scène above narrative, and both mise-en-scène and narrative above acting. Hitchcock's movies were so carefully planned and rehearsed in advance that actors were expected to follow his direction closely, so that even those with limited talent (e.g., Tippi Hedren in *The Birds*, 1963; and Kim Novak in *Vertigo*, 1958) gave performances that satisfied the director's needs.

On the other hand, Stanley Kubrick, who was as rigidly in control of his films as Hitchcock, was more flexible. When directing *Barry Lyndon* (1975), a film in which fate drove the plot, Kubrick gave his principal actors—Ryan O'Neal and Marisa Berenson—almost nothing to say and then moved them about his sumptuous mise-en-scène like pawns on a chessboard. When working with a more open story, however, he encouraged actors to improvise in rehearsal

or on the set. The results included such memorable moments as Peter Sellers's final monologue as Dr. Strangelove (and the film's last line, "*Mein Führer*, I can walk!") and Jack Nicholson's manic "Heeeere's Johnny!" before the climax of *The Shining* (1980). Malcolm McDowell in *A Clockwork Orange* (1971), and Tom Cruise and Nicole Kidman in *Eyes Wide Shut* (1999), are also said to have worked out their performances in improvisations with the director. Perhaps the most extreme example is director Werner Herzog, who, in directing *Heart of Glass* (1976), hypnotized the entire cast each day on the set to create what he called "an atmosphere of hallucination, prophecy, visionary and collective madness."

How Filmmaking Affects Acting

Actors must understand how a film is made, because every aspect of the filmmaking process can affect performances and the actors' contributions to the creation of meaning. At the same time, audiences should understand what a movie actor goes through to deliver a performance that, to their eyes, seems effortless and spontaneous. Here are some of the challenges an actor faces.

Although there are certain exceptions, most production budgets and schedules do not have the funds or the time to give movie actors much in the way of rehearsal. Thus, actors almost always perform a character's progression entirely out of sequence, and this out-of-continuity shooting can also force those who are being filmed in isolation to perform their parts as though they were *inter*acting with other people. When these shots are edited together, the illusion of togetherness is there, but the actors must make it convincing. Actors must time their movements and precisely hit predetermined marks on the floor so that a moving camera and a focus puller know where they will be at every moment; they must often direct their gaze and position their body and/or face in unnatural-feeling poses to allow for lighting, camera position, and composition. These postures usually appear natural onscreen but don't feel natural to the actors performing them on the set.

[33] John Wayne, qtd. in Joseph McBride, *Searching for John Ford: A Life* (New York: St. Martin's Press, 2001), 299.

Movie actors must repeat the same action/line/emotion more than once—not just for multiple takes from a single setup, but also for multiple setups—which means that they may perform the close-up of a particular scene an hour after they performed the same moment for a different camera position. Everything about their performance is fragmented, and thus they must struggle to stay in character. Finally, actors are sometimes required to work with acting and dialogue coaches, physical trainers, and stunt personnel. For all the reasons listed here, delivering a convincing screen performance is very challenging.

In the following chapters we will examine editing and sound and the ways they relate to acting and meaning. Here we'll look briefly at how acting is affected by framing, composition, lighting, and the types and lengths of shots.

Framing, Composition, Lighting, and the Long Take

Framing and composition can bring actors together in a shot or keep them apart. Such inclusion and exclusion create relationships between characters, and these, in turn, create meaning. The physical relation of the actors to each other and to the overall frame (height, width, and depth) can significantly affect how we see and interpret a shot.

The inciting moment of the plot of Orson Welles's *Citizen Kane* (1941) and one of the principal keys to understanding the movie—for many viewers, its most unforgettable moment—occurs when Charles Foster Kane's (Welles) mother, Mary Kane (Agnes Moorehead), signs the contract that determines her son's future. It consists of only six shots, two of which are long takes. Relying on design, lighting, cinematography, and acting, Welles creates a scene of almost perfect ambiguity.

In designing the scene, Welles puts the four principal characters involved in the incident in the same frame for the two long takes but, significantly, divides the space within this frame into exterior and interior spaces: a young Charles (Buddy Swan) is outside playing with the *Rosebud* sled in the snow, oblivious to how his life is being changed forever; while Mary, her husband, Jim (Harry Shannon),

and Walter Parks Thatcher (George Coulouris) are in the house for shots 1-3 (images [1] to [5], *opposite*) and outside for shot 4 (image [6]). In shot 3, this division of the overall space into two separate physical and emotional components is dramatically emphasized after Mary signs the contract and Jim walks to the background of the frame and shuts the window, symbolically shutting Charles out of his life and also cutting us off from the sound of his voice. Mary immediately walks to the same window and opens it, asserting her control over the boy by sharply calling "Charles!" before going out to explain the situation to him.

The two long takes carry the weight of the scene and, thus, require the adult actors to work closely together in shot 3 (image [4], *opposite*) and with the boy in shot 4 (image [6]). They begin inside the house as a tightly framed ensemble confronting one another across a small table—their bodies composed and their faces lighted to draw attention to the gravity of the decision they are making—and continue outdoors, where these tensions break into the open as young Charles learns of his fate.

The lighting also helps create the meaning. Lamps remain unlit inside the house, where the atmosphere is as emotionally cold as the snowy landscape is physically cold. Outside, the light is flat and bright; inside, this same bright light, reflected from the snow, produces deep shadows. This effect appears most clearly after the opening of shot 3, when Mary Kane turns from the window and walks from the background to the foreground. As she does, lighting divides her face, the dark and light halves emphasizing how torn she feels as a mother in sending Charles away.

To prepare for the long take, Welles drilled his actors to the point of perfection in rehearsals, giving them amazing things to do (such as requiring Moorehead to pace up and down the narrow room), and then letting this preparation pay off in moments of great theatrical vitality. Look closely, for example,

Acting and Composition in *Citizen Kane*   (*opposite*)
The contract-signing scene in *Citizen Kane*: [1] from shot 1, [2] from shot 2, [3, 4] from shot 3, [5, 6] from shot 4, [7] from shot 5, [8] from shot 6.

1

2

3

4

5

6

7

8

at the performance of Agnes Moorehead, with whom Welles had worked in radio productions.[34] Moorehead knew exactly how to use the tempo, pitch, and rhythm of her voice to give unexpected depth to the familiar melodramatic type she plays here. In the carefully designed and controlled setting—the long room, dividing window, and snowy exterior—Mrs. Kane, whose makeup, hairstyle, and costume are those of a seemingly simple pioneer woman, reveals herself to be something quite different. She is both unforgettably humane as she opens the window and calls her son sharply to the destiny she has decreed, and—given that her only business experience has been in running a boardinghouse—surprisingly shrewd in obviously having retained Thatcher to prepare the contract that seals this moment. In fact, this is one of the few scenes in the movie in which a female character totally dominates the action—not surprising, for it is a scene of maternal rejection.

As Mary Kane throws open the window, she cries out, "Charles!" in a strained, even shrill voice that reveals her anxiety about what she is doing; yet a moment later, sounding both tender and guilty, she tells Thatcher that she has had Charles's trunk packed for a week. Should we read the cold mask of her face as the implacable look of a woman resigned to her decision or as a cover for maternal feelings? Does it reflect the doubt, indecision, and dread any person would feel in such a situation? Is it the face of sacrifice? Is it all of these possibilities and more? And how should we read Charles, who, in the span of a moment, goes from playful to wary to angry to antagonistic?

Although the downtrodden Jim Kane protests his wife's actions, when Thatcher coolly informs him that he and his wife will receive $50,000 per year, he feebly gives in, saying, "Well, let's hope it's all for the best"—a remark that invariably, as it should, provokes laughter from viewers. And Thatcher, wearing a top hat and dressed in the formal clothes of a big-city banker, sends contradictory signals. He's precise in overseeing Mrs. Kane's signature, dismissive of Mr. Kane, fawning as he

[34] Welles reportedly called Agnes Moorehead "the best actor I've ever known"; qtd. in Simon Callow, *Orson Welles: The Road to Xanadu* (New York: Viking, 1995), 512.

meets Charles, and angry when Charles knocks him to the ground. In encouraging this kind of richly nuanced acting, and its resulting ambiguity, Welles shifts the challenge of interpretation to us.

As this scene shows, the *long take*, used in conjunction with *deep-focus cinematography*, provides directors and actors with the opportunity to create scenes of greater-than-usual length, as well as broader and deeper field of composition. In addition, the long take encourages *ensemble acting* that calls attention to acting, not editing between shots. Although we tend to think of actors and their performances as acts of individual creativity, we should not neglect the fact that one actor's performance often very much depends on another's. Indeed, it may rely on an ensemble, or group, of actors.

Ensemble acting—which emphasizes the interaction of actors, not the individual actor—evolved as a further step in creating a verisimilar mise-en-scène, for both the stage and the screen. Typically experienced in the theater, ensemble acting is used less in the movies because it requires the provision of rehearsal time that is usually denied to screen actors. However, when a movie director chooses to use long takes and has the time to rehearse the actors, the result is a group of actors working together continuously in a single shot. Depending on the story and plot situation, this technique can intensify the emotional impact of a specific plot situation by having all the involved characters on the screen at the same time.

As with so many other innovations, Orson Welles pioneered ensemble acting in *Citizen Kane* (1941) and *The Magnificent Ambersons* (1942), and its influence was quickly seen in the work of other directors, notably William Wyler in *The Little Foxes* (1941) and *The Best Years of Our Lives* (1946). Other excellent examples of ensemble acting can be found in Akira Kurosawa's *The Lower Depths* (1957), Fred Schepisi's *Last Orders* (2001), Clint Eastwood's *Mystic River* (2003), Peter Weir's *Master and Commander: The Far Side of the World* (2003), Peter Jackson's "Lord of the Rings" trilogy (2001–03), and Stephen Daldry's *The Hours* (2002). Two examples of impressive acting by an ensemble of child actors are Lasse Hallström's *My Life as a Dog* (1985) and Jacob Aaron Estes's *Mean Creek* (2004).

Acting and the Close-up Carl Theodor Dreyer's *The Passion of Joan of Arc* (1928) vividly and unforgettably illustrates the power of the close-up. Most of this silent movie's running time is taken up with contrasting close-ups of Joan (played by Maria Falconetti, a French stage actress who never again appeared on film) and of her many interrogators during the course of her trial. As Joan is questioned, mocked, tortured, and finally burned at the stake, we witness an entire, deeply moving story in her face. Thus, we respond to a single character's expressions as they are shaped by the drama and the camera.

The Camera and the Close-up

The camera creates a greater naturalism and intimacy between actors and audience than would ever be possible on the stage, and thus it serves as screen actors' most important collaborator. Nowhere is the camera's role—that is, its effect on the actor's role—more evident than in a close-up. The *true* close-up isolates an actor, concentrating on the face; it can be active (commenting on something just said or done, reminding us who is the focus of a scene) or passive (revealing an actor's beauty). Thus, actors' most basic skill is understanding how to reveal themselves to the camera during the close-up.

All great movie actors understand, instinctively or from experience, what to do and not do with their faces when the camera moves in. They must temporarily forget their bodies' expressive possibilities, must stand as close to the camera as they would to a person in real life, must smoothly balance their voices because of the closeness of the microphone, and must focus on the communicative power of even the slightest facial gesture.

Close-ups can shift interpretation to the viewer, as in the two-minute-long close-up of Anna (Nicole Kidman) in Jonathan Glazer's *Birth* (2004; see page 187), or they can leave little room for independent interpretation, as in Marlene Dietrich's opening scene as Amy Jolly in Josef von Sternberg's *Morocco* (1930; cinematographer: Lee Garmes). On the deck of a ship bound for Morocco, the mysterious and beautiful Amy drops her handbag. A sophisticated,

Artistic Collaboration and The Close-up In *Morocco* (1930), Marlene Dietrich's beautiful face is made to appear even more haunting and enigmatic by director Josef von Sternberg's mise-en-scène and Lee Garmes's black-and-white cinematography. Dietrich, too, instinctively understood the kind of lighting and camera placement that was right for her role and the narrative, as well as for the glamorous image she cultivated in all her movies. In this MCU, she stands on deck of a ship at night and appears distant, almost otherworldly, as she is bathed in soft, misty "Rembrandt lighting." One half of her face is bright, part of the other half is in shadow. Her face is further framed and softened by her hat and veil, and by shooting her against a background that is out-of focus. In all likelihood, Garmes also placed thin gauze fabric over the lens to further soften the image. This is the first appearance of Dietrich's character in the movie, so we know little about her, but can already discern that she is not only alluring, but mysterious. But one thing we know for sure: the Dietrich face, as it appeared on the screen, was the conscious creation of the actress, director, and cinematographer.

older Frenchman—Monsieur La Bessiere (Adolphe Menjou)—kneels at her feet to retrieve her things and then offers to assist her in any way he can when she arrives at her destination. In a relatively quick close-up, Amy looks off into space and tells him she will not need any help. Design elements further distance us from the actress and the character: Dietrich wears a hat with a veil, and thus the shot is "veiled by the 'Rembrandt' light, by the fog, by the lens, and by the diaphanous fabric."[35] Although we do not yet know who Amy is, what she does, or why she's going to Morocco, we certainly understand La Bessiere's interest.

Close-ups can also reveal both the process of thinking and the thoughts at its end. In a close-up during the climactic moment of John Ford's *The Searchers* (1956), Ethan Edwards (John Wayne) transforms from a hateful to a loving man as he halts his premeditated attempt to murder his niece, Debbie (Natalie Wood), and instead lifts her to the safety of his arms. The shot doesn't give us time to analyze *why* he has changed his mind—only to see the results of that change.

In a bar scene in Elia Kazan's *On the Waterfront* (1954), Terry Malloy (Marlon Brando), playing the tough guy, tells Edie Doyle (Eva Marie Saint) his philosophy: "Do it to him before he does it to you." Up to this point, he has remained aloof after witnessing the mob's murder of Edie's brother, an attitude he continues to display until Edie, who is trying to do something about the corruption on the waterfront, asks for his help. Stopped in his tracks, Terry sits down, and a series of close-ups reveals the shakiness of his unfeeling posture. In a soft, caring, but slightly nervous voice (in this bar setting, surrounded by other tough guys, he's a little self-conscious of being tender with a woman), he tells her, "I'd like ta help"—thus revealing to her, the camera, and the audience a more sensitive man under the macho mannerisms.

Acting and Editing

Because a screen actor's performance is fragmented, the editor has considerable power in shaping it. We've already emphasized that the actor is responsible for maintaining the emotional continuity of a performance, but even the most consistent actor delivers slightly different performances on each take. Editors can patch up mistakes by selecting, arranging, or juxtaposing shots to cover the error. They control the duration of an actor's appearance on the screen and how that time is used. When aspects of an actor's performance that was originally deemed acceptable appear in the editing stage to interrupt the flow of the narrative, the development of the character, or the tone of the movie, the editor, in consultation with the director, can dispense with it completely by leaving that footage on the cutting-room floor. In short, the editor can mold a performance with more control than most directors and even the actors themselves can.

🄳🅅🅳 **Editing and Performance in *Snapshot***

Looking at Acting

Given all the elements and aspects in our discussion of an actor's performance, how do we focus our attention on analyzing acting? Before we look at some recognized criteria, let's discuss how we can bring our own experiences to the task. An actor's performance on the screen is not only what we see and hear, but also includes many intangibles and subtleties. That alone makes the analysis of acting much more challenging. Breaking down and cataloging other elements of cinematic language—whether narrative, mise-en-scène, production design, or cinematography—and using that information to analyze their usefulness and effectiveness is much easier than analyzing acting. Yet acting (perhaps second only to narrative) is the component most people use to assess movies. We feel an effective, natural, moving performance in a more direct way than other cinematic aspects of most films, and we feel both qualified and compelled to judge films by their performances.

What accounts for this sense of entitlement? Why are we so fixated on actors, and so frequently judge the quality of the movie by the (often intangible) quality of their performances? There are several reasons. First, we identify with characters.

---

[35] Naremore, *Acting in the Cinema*, 141.

Although cinematic language has a considerable effect on the way we look at a movie, we also *identify* with characters and, of course, with the actors who inhabit those characters. Second, we identify with characters who pursue a goal. We get involved with this pursuit—one that is driven by and embodied by the actors who inhabit the characters—because a movie narrative is constructed to exploit what most involves us. We don't even have to like the characters, as long as we believe them. Third, we identify with characters because of our own behavior as people. Although cinematic language draws from our instinctive responses to everyday visual and audio information, we don't consciously notice and process it as much as we do human behavior. We are people watchers by nature, necessity, and desire. We are constantly analyzing behavior. When you say hello to a friend or ask a professor a question or order a cup of coffee from a waiter, you are noticing and processing and reacting to human behavior. Is the friend happy? Does the professor think you're stupid? Is the waiter paying attention?

Finally, our identification with characters and the actors who play them has something to do with the fact that we, too, behave in a way that is consistent with our general character or state of mind, and beyond that, we are also engaged in role-playing. You present yourself differently, depending on where you are, what's going on, and who you're with. You behave differently with a police officer than you do with your mother or your professor, differently with a new friend than with an old one.

These are some of the reasons *why* we react as we do to actors and acting. But *how* do we analyze performance? What are the criteria of a good performance? In their everyday moviegoing, people tend to appreciate acting very subjectively. They like an actor's performance when he or she looks, speaks, and moves in ways that confirm their expectations for the character (or type of character). Conversely, they dislike a performance that baffles those expectations.

This approach, though understandable, can also be limiting. How many of us have sufficient life experiences to fully comprehend the range of characters that appear on the screen? What background do we bring to an analysis of the perform-

ance of Humphrey Bogart as a cold-blooded private eye in John Huston's *The Maltese Falcon* (1941); Carlo Battisti as a retired, impoverished bureaucrat in Vittorio De Sica's *Umberto D* (1952); Giulietta Masina as a childlike circus performer in Federico Fellini's *La Strada* (1954); Toshirô Mifune

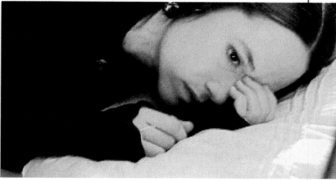

[1]

[2]

Assessing Acting Performances   [1] Toshirô Mifune in the death scene of Lord Washizu in Akira Kurosawa's *Throne of Blood* (1957) and [2] Holly Hunter in Jane Campion's *The Piano* (1993), a performance for which she won the Academy Award for Best Actress. To analyze an actor's performance, we need to consider its context—the particular movie in which it appears. Kurosawa's film draws on a specific genre—the *jidai-geki*, or historical drama—that is traditionally full of action; Campion's film draws on history but focuses more on psychology than on action. Thus, Mifune uses ritualized, nonnaturalistic facial expressions and body language; and Hunter, who speaks only in voice-over, appears more naturalistic, inner-directed, *muted* (subdued).

as a Japanese warlord (based on Shakespeare's *Macbeth*) in Akira Kurosawa's *Throne of Blood* (1957); Marlon Brando as a Mafia don in Francis Ford Coppola's *The Godfather* (1972); Holly Hunter as a mute Victorian relocated from Scotland to New Zealand in Jane Campion's *The Piano* (1993); Sissy Spacek as the mother of a murdered son in Todd Field's *In the Bedroom* (2001); Brad Pitt as the leader of a male aggression movement in David Fancher's *Fight Club* (1999); or Philip Seymour Hoffman as author Truman Capote in Bennett Miller's *Capote* (2005)?

Movie acting may be, as legendary actor Laurence Olivier once said, the "art of persuasion."[36] Yet it is also a formal cinematic element, one as complex as design or cinematography. To get a sense of how movie acting works, on its own and ultimately in relation to the other formal elements, we need to establish a set of criteria more substantial than our subjective feelings and reactions.

Because every actor, character, and performance in a movie is different, it is impossible to devise standards that would apply equally well to all of them. Furthermore, different actors, working with different directors, often take very different approaches to the same material, as you can judge for yourself by comparing the many remakes in movie history. Within the world of a particular story, your goal should be to determine the quality of the actor's achievement in creating the character and how that performance helps tell the story. Thus you should discuss an actor's specific performance in a specific film—discussing, say, Peter Sellers's acting in Hal Ashby's *Being There* (1979) as it serves to create the character of Chance and tell the story of that film without being influenced by expectations possibly raised by your having seen Sellers in other movies.

In analyzing any actor's performance, you might consider

> *Appropriateness.* Does the actor look and act naturally like the character he or she portrays, as expressed in physical appearance, facial expression, speech, movement, and ges-

ture? If the performance is nonnaturalistic, does the actor look, walk, and talk the way that character might or should?

Paradoxically, we expect an actor to behave as if he or she were *not* acting but were simply living the illusion of a character we can accept within the context of the movie's narrative. Such appropriateness in acting is also called *transparency*, meaning that the character is so clearly recognizable —in speech, movement, and gesture—for what he or she is supposed to be that the actor becomes, in a sense, invisible. Most actors agree that the more successfully they create characters, the more we will see those characters and not them.

> *Inherent thoughtfulness or emotionality.* Does the actor convey the character's thought process or feelings behind the character's actions or reactions? In addition to a credible appearance, does the character have a credible inner life?

An actor can find the *motivations* behind a character's actions and reactions at any time before or during a movie's production. They may come to light in the script (as well as in any source on which it is based, such as a novel or play), in discussions with the director or with other cast members, and in spontaneous elements of inspiration and improvisation that the actor discovers while the camera is rolling. No matter which of these aspects or combinations of them delineate the character's motivation, we expect to *see* the actor reflect them within the character's consciousness, or as part of the illusion-making process by which the character appears. Another way of saying this is that characters must appear to be *vulnerable* to forces in the narrative, capable of thinking about them, and, if necessary, changing their mind or feelings about them.

> *Expressive coherence.* Has the actor used these first two qualities (appropriateness and inherent thoughtfulness/emotionality) to create a characterization that holds together?

[36] Olivier, *Confessions of an Actor*, 51.

Whatever behavior an actor uses to convey character, it must be intrinsic, not extraneous to the character, "maintaining not only a coherence of manner, but also a fit between setting, costume, and behavior."[37] When an actor achieves such a fit, he or she is *playing in character*. Maintaining expressive coherence enables the actor to create a very complex characterization and performance, to express thoughts and reveal emotions of a recognizable individual without veering off into mere quirks or distracting details.

> *Wholeness and unity.* In spite of the challenges inherent in most film productions, has the actor maintained the illusion of a seamless character, even if that character is purposely riddled with contradictions?

Whereas expressive coherence relies on the logic inherent in an actor's performance, wholeness and unity are achieved through the actor's ability to achieve aesthetic consistency while working with the director, crew, and other cast members; enduring multiple takes; and projecting toward the camera rather than to an audience. However, wholeness and unity need not mean uniformity. The point is this: as audience members we want to feel we're in good hands; when we're confused or asked to make sense of seemingly incoherent elements, we want to know that the apparent incoherence happened intentionally, for an aesthetic reason, as part of the filmmakers' overall vision. For example, if a given character suddenly breaks down or reveals himself to be pretending to be somebody he isn't, the actor must sufficiently prepare for this change in the preceding scenes, however he chooses, so that we can accept it.

To begin applying these criteria, let's examine the work of two very distinctive, successful actors: Barbara Stanwyck as Stella Dallas in King Vidor's *Stella Dallas* (1937) and Hilary Swank as Maggie Fitzgerald in Clint Eastwood's *Million Dollar Baby*

[37] Naremore, *Acting in the Cinema*, 69.

(2004). In these roles, both actors play strong, assertive women and bring a significant amount of physicality to their portrayals. However, in looking at these two movies, and analyzing them, we must remember that they are separated by a wide chronological and cultural gap, and take into consideration how those elements influence the narrative and acting.

Each actor started in the movies in a different way. Stanwyck, who was born Ruby Stevens in Brooklyn in 1907, started on the Broadway stage and went to Hollywood at the age of twenty-one. The studios changed her name (*Stanwyck* has the vaguely British aura that Hollywood admired—all the more amusing considering that Ms. Stevens never really lost her New York accent). Overall, she made more than 100 movies and was nominated four times for the Oscar for Best Actress, for her work in *Stella Dallas*, Howard Hawks's *Ball of Fire* (1941), Billy Wilder's *Double Indemnity* (1944), and Anatole Litvak's *Sorry, Wrong Number* (1948). She never won.

Hilary Swank was born in Lincoln, Nebraska, in 1974 and was active in amateur theater there. At sixteen, she went to Hollywood, and although she kept her own name, ironically *Hilary Swank* sounds like a name that was invented by a studio. Today, in her early thirties, she has already made some nineteen movies and won Best Actress Oscars for her portrayals in Kimberly Peirce's *Boys Don't Cry* (1999) and *Million Dollar Baby*. Coincidentally, Stanwyck specialized in what used to be called *tough-girl* parts, and Swank's role in *Million Dollar Baby* is the kind of role Stanwyck might have played if the studios in the 1930s and '40s had been making movies in which women played prizefighters. The closest that Stanwyck came to such a role was playing a prizefighter's love in Rouben Mamoulian's *Golden Boy* (1939).

Barbara Stanwyck in King Vidor's *Stella Dallas*

Stella Dallas, based on Olive Higgins Prouty's 1923 novel of the same title, tells the story of a brassy, scheming, but charming young woman from a working-class family who is openly derided by members of the middle and upper middle classes but who has married Stephen Dallas (John Boles), a socially prominent man.[38] Although they have a daughter, Laurel (Anne Shirley), the Dallases separate when they realize that their social and educational backgrounds are too different for them to be happy together.

Stella is a formidable character for any actress to attempt, but Stanwyck beautifully meets the challenge of balancing the character's nonnaturalistic and naturalistic qualities. On one hand, Stella is loud and overdressed in clothes of her own making; on the other, she is a tender mother who sacrifices everything for her daughter's happiness. After Stephen has returned to his former fiancée, Helen Morrison (Barbara O'Neil), Stella visits Helen, offering to divorce Stephen if he and Helen will marry and raise Laurel as their own. Stella wears a gaudy fur coat, ridiculous hat, and fussy blouse. Her blunt way of speaking, mannish walk, and nervous fidgeting with her hands set her apart completely from the elegant, cultured, simply dressed, and well-groomed Helen.

When Laurel becomes engaged to marry Richard Grosvenor (Tim Holt), Stella is pleased that her daughter will achieve the upper-middle-class married life that has eluded her, but she realizes that she will be an embarrassment to Laurel. She pretends to leave the country but instead stands outside the New York townhouse in which the marriage takes place, watching the ceremony through a big window. All the movie's major themes culminate here, in the Depression-era contrasts between those born to wealth and those born to work; in the contrast between the warm, secure interior and the cold, rainy exterior, where envious strangers grab a quick glimpse at what's going on inside before being hurried along; and in the contrast between Laurel in her white wedding dress and her mother, who is dressed plainly.

[38] *Stella Dallas* has been of interest to many feminist critics; see E. Ann Kaplan, "The Case of the Missing Mother: Maternal Issues in Vidor's *Stella Dallas*," and Linda Williams, "'Something Else Besides a Mother: *Stella Dallas* and the Maternal Melodrama"—both in *Feminism and Film*, ed. E. Ann Kaplan (New York: Oxford University Press, 2000), 466–79, 480–504.

Barbara Stanwyck in *Stella Dallas* In King Vidor's *Stella Dallas* (1937), the title character (Barbara Stanwyck) pleads with a police officer to allow her one more minute to watch through the window of the townhouse in which her daughter, Laurel (Anne Shirley), has just been married. Stanwyck received an Oscar nomination for Best Actress; Shirley, for Best Supporting Actress. To compare their performances to other actors' handling of the same roles, see Henry King's *Stella Dallas* (1925), starring Belle Bennett and Lois Morgan; and John Erman's *Stella* (1990), starring Bette Midler and Trini Alvarado.

Indeed, although she is wearing her usual heavy makeup, Stella's appearance has changed. Having always set herself apart from the ordinary, she now wears clothes that help her blend into the crowd— a cloth coat with fur trim and a simple felt hat—and she is not wearing jewelry. Stanwyck called this her favorite scene in the movie: "I had to indicate to audiences, through the emotions shown by my face, that for Stella joy ultimately triumphed over the heartache she had felt."[39] We do not know whether Stanwyck arrived at this interpretation intuitively or at Vidor's suggestion.

Let's look more closely at what Stanwyck expresses facially and through gestures with a handkerchief, which film scholar James Naremore, borrowing Russian director Vsevolod Pudovkin's term, calls an "expressive object."[40] As the wedding

[39] Stanwyck, qtd. in Ella Smith, *Starring Miss Barbara Stanwyck* (New York: Crown, 1974), 99.
[40] See Naremore's excellent discussion of this scene in *Acting in the Cinema*, 86–87; quotation, 85.

progresses, Vidor cuts between long and middle shots of the interior from Stanwyck's point of view and middle shots and close-ups of Stanwyck's face—a classic method for emphasizing the contrasts inherent in the scene.

As the ceremony begins, Stella's face is open and curious, but what is she thinking? Within the narrative context, it must be how happy she is to be there. As Richard places the ring on Laurel's hand, however, Stella runs through a range of emotions. She smiles tenderly, she shudders slightly, tears well up in her eyes, and finally she swallows hard to suppress her emotion. When a police officer asks the crowd to disperse, Stella asks for another minute, the only time she speaks in the scene, which otherwise is underscored by the kind of highly charged music intended to make the audience cry. After the officer gives Stella extra time to see the bride and groom kiss, Stanwyck brings the handkerchief into play. Looking like she's about to lose control of her emotions, she slowly lifts the handkerchief as though to wipe away tears. Instead, she puts a corner of it in her mouth and, like a child, begins to chew and suck on it. She looks down in a moment of perfect maternal happiness, then looks up, her eyes shining and brimming with tears.

Vidor then cuts to a long shot of Stanwyck walking confidently toward the camera, looking fulfilled and swinging the handkerchief back and forth freely. As she crumples the handkerchief into her hand, squares her shoulders, and straightens her posture, the film ends. This is the sort of tearjerking ending that made Hollywood's "women's films" so popular, and Stanwyck's performance is consistent not only with the character she plays but also with the melodramatic narrative. She gives us Stella's range of character between tough and sensitive, but, with her final self-confident stride, she also emphasizes the fulfillment in a mother's dream of seeing her daughter happily married.

Ultimately, Stanwyck's performance transcends the story's melodrama. In her natural physical appearance, movements, and gestures (especially with the handkerchief); expressive coherence (aided by our belief that Stella is doing the right thing); and emotional consistency (alternating feelings of happiness and sorrow, determination and

doubt), Stanwyck remains true to the good-hearted character that she has been building from the first scene.

Hilary Swank in Clint Eastwood's *Million Dollar Baby*

Paul Haggis's screenplay for *Million Dollar Baby* is based on *Rope Burns*, a book of short stories by boxing manager F. X. Toole. Although the plot unravels at a slow, methodical pace, it is straightforward and follows the classic five-part structure (see Chapter 2). During the exposition, we are introduced to the setting of the Hit Pit Gym in Los Angeles and the three main characters: Frankie Dunn (Clint Eastwood), an aging boxing coach who owns the gym; Eddie "Scrap Iron" Dupris (Morgan Freeman), Dunn's friend and employee; and Maggie Fitzgerald (Hilary Swank), self-identified as Missouri "trash," a young woman who works as a waitress but is determined by her dual qualities of will and naïveté to become a successful boxer. Undeterred by Dunn's repeated insistence that "I don't train girls," she perseveres in an all-male environment.

The action picks up when Dupris persuades Dunn to train Maggie. The ensuing struggle is underlined by Maggie's saying that she's tough, and Dunn's response: "Girlie, tough ain't enough." But once he's hooked, he's in it for the duration—tough means training—and she, indeed, becomes one "tough girl." After an unbroken string of successes, the climax occurs during a championship bout when Maggie is viciously attacked and paralyzed by a ruthless German boxer. The falling action—Dunn's determination to see Maggie rehabilitated, and Maggie's resilience during the ordeal, which includes a visit from her hateful family—precede the denouement, in which, after several suicide attempts ("I've seen it all," she admits), Dunn commits euthanasia.

Although Dupris narrates the movie in voiceover, the story also reflects two other points of view: Frankie takes the long view based on his lifetime experiences, and Maggie takes the short view based on her expectations of rewards. Maggie is a character that audiences can easily identify with because her goals, though abstract, are specific.

Hilary Swank in *Million Dollar Baby* Although she is well over the age for beginning a boxing career, Maggie Fitzgerald (Hilary Swank) in Clint Eastwood's *Million Dollar Baby* (2004) makes up for lost time as she wins yet another fight on her rapid ascent to the hair-raising championship title bout that puts an end to her aspirations.

Starting with Buster Keaton's *Battling Butler* (1926), boxing movies have been a perennial favorite in the sports genre. Classics include Robert Rossen's *Body and Soul* (1947); John G. Avildsen's *Rocky* (1976, and four sequels, one directed by Avildsen and three by Sylvester Stallone, who plays Rocky); John Huston's *Fat City* (1972); and Martin Scorsese's *Raging Bull* (1980). *Million Dollar Baby*, which incorporates some of the standard clichés of the genre, is the first feature film about a female boxer. It includes a backstory about Dunn's estrangement from his daughter (and obvious transference of his affection to Maggie).

For the most part, *Million Dollar Baby* avoids the sentimental. Its ending caused a momentary outcry from those opposed to the violence of the sport, as well as from disability rights activists and far-right conservatives (who opposed the idea of euthanasia), sportswriters (who found technical faults), and even devotees of the Gaelic language who were upset that Eastwood misspelled *mo chuisle*, a term of Gaelic endearment meaning "pulse of my heart." It is, indeed, a movie that encompasses several major topics, and avoids others, such as the lack of any punishment for the woman who destroyed Maggie. In this sad, depressing, and thought-provoking movie, Eastwood never manipulates the viewer in developing its concerns with serious life-and-death issues.

Hilary Swank has the reputation of preparing for a role with great dedication, reportedly to the point of "living" the part. She is athletic by nature, bringing considerable physical agility and stamina to the role of Maggie Fitzgerald, and it is hard to imagine any other actor being cast for the part. Furthermore, she says that she brought her similar life experiences—someone who went from Nebraska to Hollywood at sixteen with little but a dream—to her characterization of Maggie as a sweet, genuine, somewhat naïve but determined woman of thirty-one. Hers is not a subtle performance, because Maggie is not a particularly subtle character, but Swank effectively balances Maggie's combination of quiet dignity and Irish grit. Physically, she has a taut, agile body, hair pulled back into a heavy braid, wide eyes and distinctive eyebrows, and a large, downturned mouth with very large teeth. To her naturally broad, flat midwestern accent, she added a softness that is consistent with Maggie's unpretentious character. Her body language is convincing as she moves about the gym, works with the punching bag, and, eventually, triumphs in the ring.

In this movie, as well as in Kimberly Peirce's *Boys Don't Cry* (1999), Swank seems to enjoy looking as plain, unglamorous, and—yes—boyish as possible. Since the credits list ten stunt women, it is clear that Swank was well covered in the ring, but it is also clear that she learned the rudiments of boxing, and that preparation, coupled with very skillful cinematography, creates a credible illusion of her as a boxer. Although Swank probably wore only the minimum amount of makeup necessary for lighting and cinematography, a great deal of attention is paid to Maggie's makeup as her face is bashed during fights and, especially, in the harrowing scenes in the hospital, where she suffers constantly.

One key to Maggie's character (and Swank's performance) is her response to the training regimen—how Swank shows us that she's learning to be "tough." The characteristics include heart, determination, willingness to risk everything for a dream, belief in yourself, forgetting what you know in order to learn the correct way, and always protecting yourself. Time moves slowly in *Million Dollar Baby*, and it takes more than a year before Swank gets into the ring, so she persistently *shows* us (primarily through her very pleasant nature and expressive body language) how she learns and eventually masters these qualities.

In portraying such a character as Maggie, Hilary Swank was faced with formidable challenges, but she maintains expressive coherence—understanding what it means to follow her dream, no matter what the consequences—and brings unity and wholeness to her characterization. Maggie shows the same qualities when she trains, wins, and then is beaten and paralyzed. Although the movie has other flaws, the unity and credibility of Swank's performance are not among them. She not only looks and acts like such a character in physical appearance, facial expression, speech, movement, and gesture, but also understands and *can make us understand* all kinds of feelings, from extreme vulnerability to invincible strength.

Stella Dallas and *Million Dollar Baby*: two different movies—both concerned with strong, natural women confronted by social barriers—and two different actors, both playing with strong emotion. Which is the better performance? Look at them, apply the criteria you've learned here, and decide for yourself.

➡️ Analyzing Acting

Because our responses to actors' performances onscreen are perhaps our most automatic and intuitive responses to any formal aspect of film, it is easy to forget that acting is as much a formal component of movies—something *made*—as mise-en-scène, cinematography, and editing are. And yet, acting is clearly something that must be planned and shaped in some manner; the very fact that films are shot out of continuity demands that actors approach their performances with a rigor and consciousness that mirrors the director's work on the film as a whole. This chapter has presented several different things to think about as you watch film acting from this point forward. Using the criteria described in the previous section, remaining sensitive to the context of the performances, and keeping the following checklist in mind as you watch, you should be able to incorporate an intelligent analysis of acting into your discussion and writing about the movies you screen for class.

Screening Checklist: Acting

➤ Why was this actor, and not another, cast for the role?

➤ Does the actor's performance create a coherent, unified character? If so, how?

➤ Does the actor look the part? Is it necessary that the actor look the part?

➤ Does the actor's performance convey the actions, thoughts, and internal complexities that we associate with natural or recognizable characters? Or does it exhibit the excessive approach we associate with nonnaturalistic characters?

➤ What elements are most distinctive in how the actor conveys the character's actions, thoughts, and internal complexities: body language, gestures, facial expressions, language?

➤ What special talents of imagination or intelligence has the actor brought to the role?

➤ How important is the filmmaking process in creating the character? Is the actor's performance overshadowed by the filmmaking process?

➤ Does the actor work well with fellow actors in this film? Do any of the other actors detract from the lead actor's performance?

➤ How, if at all, is the actor's conception of the character based on logic? How does the performance demonstrate *expressive coherence*?

➤ Does the actor's performance have the expressive power to make us forget that he or she is acting? If it does, how do you think the actor achieved this effect?

Questions for Review

1. How is *movie acting* today different from movie acting in the period from the 1930s through the 1960s?
2. Why is the *relationship between the actor and the camera* so important in making and looking at movies?
3. How did the *coming of sound* influence movie acting and actors?
4. What's the difference between movie *stars* and movie *actors*? Why do some critics emphasize that movie stars are a commodity created by the movie industry?
5. What factors influence the *casting* of actors in a movie?
6. How are *naturalistic* and *nonnaturalistic* movie acting different?
7. What is *improvisational acting*?
8. How do *framing, composition, lighting*, and the *long take* affect the acting in a movie?
9. Given the range of techniques available to movie actors, why do we say that their most basic skill is understanding how to reveal themselves to the camera during the close-up?
10. What do you regard as the most important criteria in analyzing acting?

DVD FEATURES: CHAPTER 5

The following tutorials on the DVD provide more information about cinematography:

- Persona and Performance
- Editing and Performance in *Snapshot*

Movies Described or Illustrated in This Chapter

About Schmidt (2002). Alexander Payne, director.

Apocalypse Now (1979). Francis Ford Coppola, director.

Applause (1929). Rouben Mamoulian, director.

Badlands (1973). Terrence Malick, director.

Birth (2004). Jonathan Glazer, director.

Blow (2001). Jonathan Demme, director.

Broken Blossoms (1919). D. W. Griffith, director.

Carrie (1976). Brian De Palma, director.

Charlie and the Chocolate Factory (2005). Tim Burton, director.

Chinatown (1974). Roman Polanski, director.

Citizen Kane (1941). Orson Welles director.

Coal Miner's Daughter (1980). Michael Apted, director.

Collateral (2004). Michael Mann, director.

East of Eden (1955). Elia Kazan, director.

Edward Scissorhands (1990). Tim Burton, director.

Eyes Wide Shut (1999). Stanley Kubrick, director.

Fear and Loathing in Las Vegas (1998). Terry Gilliam, director.

Finding Neverland (2004). Marc Foster, director.

Giant (1956). George Stevens, director.

The Godfather (1972). Francis Ford Coppola, director.

Henry V (1944). Laurence Olivier, director.

The Hudsucker Proxy (1994). Joel Coen, director.

Kansas City (1996). Robert Altman, director.

Lolita (1962). Stanley Kubrick, director.

Million Dollar Baby (2004). Clint Eastwood, director.

Morocco (1930). Josef von Sternberg, director.

The Player (1992). Robert Altman, director.

Queen Christina (1933). Rouben Mamoulian, director.

Queen Elizabeth (1912). Henri Desfontaines and Louis Mercanton, directors.

Rebel Without a Cause (1955). Nicholas Ray, director.

The Searchers (1956). John Ford, director.

Sideways (2004). Alexander Payne, director.

Sleepy Hollow (1999). Tim Burton, director.

Smoke (1995). Wayne Wang, director.

Stella Dallas (1937). King Vidor, director.

A Streetcar Named Desire (1951). Elia Kazan, director.

Tender Mercies (1983). Bruce Beresford, director.

3 Women (1977). Robert Altman, director.

Editing | 6

Memento (2000). Christopher Nolan, director; Dody Dorn, editor.

What Is Editing?

Editing, the basic creative force of cinema, is the process by which the editor combines and coordinates individual shots into a cinematic whole. Orson Welles said, "For my vision of the cinema, editing is not simply one aspect. It is *the* aspect."[1] Both a stylistic and a technical system, editing consists of two parts. The first begins when the editor takes the footage that was shot by the cinematographer and director and then selects, arranges (as shots to be used by themselves or combined into scenes or sequences), and assembles these components into the movie's final visual

form. The second part includes the mixing of all the sound tracks into the master sound track and then matching that sound track with the visual images (see Chapter 7).

Film editor and scholar Ken Dancyger distinguishes between the *technique*, the *craft*, and the *art* of editing. The *technique* (or method) is the actual joining together of two shots—often called **cutting** or **splicing** because, prior to the era of digital editing software, the editor had to first cut (or splice) each shot from its respective roll of film before gluing or taping all the shots together. The *craft* (skill) is the ability to join shots and produce a meaning that does not exist in either one of them individually. The *art* of editing, Dancyger declares, "occurs when the combination of two or more shots takes meaning to the next level—excitement, insight, shock, or the epiphany of discovery."[2]

The basic building block of film editing is the **shot** (as defined in Chapter 4), and its most fundamental tool is the **cut**. Each shot has two explicit values: the first value is determined by what is *within* the shot itself; the second value is determined by how the shot is situated *in relation to other shots*. The first value is largely the responsibility of the director, cinematographer, production designer, and other collaborators who determine what is captured on film. The second value is the product of editing.

The early Soviet film theorist and filmmaker Lev Kuleshov reputedly demonstrated the fundamental power of editing by producing a short film (now lost, unfortunately) in which an identical shot of an expressionless actor appeared after each of these shots: a dead woman, a child, and a dish of soup. The audience viewing this film reportedly assumed that the actor was reacting to each stimulus by changing his expression appropriately—showing sorrow (for the dead woman), tenderness (for the young child), and hunger (for the food)—when in fact his expression remained the same.

This tendency of viewers to interpret shots in relation to surrounding shots is the most fundamental assumption behind all film editing. Editing takes advantage of this psychological tendency in

---

[1] Orson Welles, qtd. in A. O. Scott, "Inside the Editing Room, Where Movies Are Built," *New York Times* (September 8, 2005), E5.

[2] Ken Dancyger, *The Technique of Film and Video Editing: Theory and Practice*, 2nd ed. (Boston: Focal Press, 1997), xiv–xv.

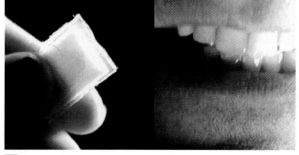

1

2

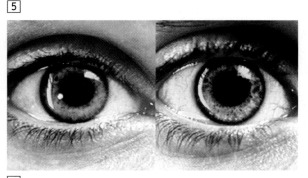

3

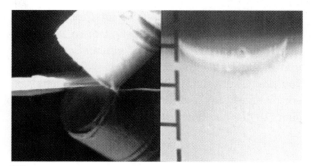

4

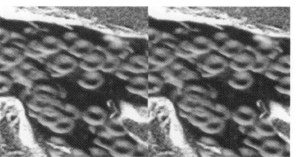

5

6

The Power of Editing These images, taken from a roughly half-minute sequence from Darren Aronofsky's *Requiem for a Dream* (2000; editor: Jay Rabinowitz), illustrate the potential power of film editing. As pictures are juxtaposed—in this case literally placed side by side using an editing technique called *split screen*—the meaning of one affects the meaning of the other. That is, together the shots influence our creation of their meaning—and their combined meaning then affects how we see the following two halves, whose meaning undergoes a transformation similar to that of the first two, and so on. This interpretive process goes on through the sequence, into the following shot, the following sequence, and ultimately the entire movie. Our creation of meaning proceeds from increment to increment, though at a much faster rate of calculation than this caption can convey.

All of these images, in this context, relate to drug use.

Focusing on minute details of the rituals of drug use, the sequence seeks to approximate the characters' frantic experience and to represent the perceptual changes that accompany their intake of narcotics. Through the language of editing, Aronofsky has given us a fresh look at a phenomenon that is often portrayed in clichéd and unimaginative ways.

As an experiment, try to imagine different juxtapositions of these same images, taken not in sequence but in isolation. Outside the context of drugs, what might George Washington's image on a dollar bill next to a widened, bloodshot eye mean? What might gritting teeth next to that reddish flow mean? For that matter, to what use might someone, maybe the creator of television commercials or public-service messages, put each image alone?

order to accomplish various effects: to help tell a story, to provoke an idea or feeling, or to call attention to itself as an element of cinematic form. No matter how straightforward a movie may seem, you can be sure that (with very rare exceptions) the editor had to make difficult decisions about which shots to use and how to use them.

The Film Editor

The person primarily responsible for such decisions is the *film editor*. The bulk of the film editor's work occurs after the director and collaborators have shot all of the movie's footage. In many major film productions, however, the editor's responsibilities as a collaborator begin much earlier in the process. During preproduction and production—even from the moment the movie is conceived—a trusted editor may make suggestions to the director and cinematographer for composition, blocking, lighting, and shooting that will help the editing itself. Editors literally work behind the scenes, but their contributions can make the difference between artistic success and artistic failure, between an ordinary movie and a masterpiece.

A good film editor must be focused, detail-oriented, well organized, disciplined, able to work alone for long stretches of time, and willing to take as much time as necessary to fulfill the director's vision. Throughout their work, film editors must collaborate with the director and be resilient enough to withstand the producer's interference. In short, a good editor practices a rigorous craft. Even in a well-planned production, one for which the director has a clear vision of what to shoot and how it will look, the editor will face countless difficult decisions about what to use and what to cut.

⟩WEB Evolution of Editing Technology

That has always been the case, but today's movies run longer and contain more individual shots than movies did fifty years ago, so the editor's job has become more involved. For example, a typical Hollywood movie made in the 1940s and '50s runs approximately one to one-and-a-half hours long and is composed of about a thousand shots; today's movies typically run between two and three hours, but because they consist of approximately two to three thousand shots, they have a faster tempo than earlier films had. That factor alone increases the editor's work of selecting and arranging the footage. It is not uncommon for the ratio between unused and used footage in a Hollywood production to be as high as twenty to one, meaning that for every minute you see on the screen, twenty minutes of footage has been discarded. The postproduction problems that really challenge editors, however—the ones we sometimes read about in the press—tend to inflate this ratio of unused to used footage to extremes.

Perhaps the best-known extreme example is Francis Ford Coppola's *Apocalypse Now* (1979). Working for two years, Walter Murch and his editorial team eventually shaped 235 hours of footage into a (mostly) coherent movie that runs two hours and thirty-three minutes (resulting in a ratio of unused to used footage of just under a hundred to one). Sifting through the mountain of footage to find the best shots, making thousands of little decisions along the way, Murch and his team gave narrative shape to what many people at the time—including, occasionally, Coppola himself—considered a disaster of directorial self-indulgence. Twenty-two years later, Coppola asked Murch and his team to restore forty-nine minutes that they had originally cut; that version, known as the *director's cut*, was released in 2001 as *Apocalypse Now Redux*.

Clearly, the creative power of the editor comes close to that of the director. But in most mainstream film productions, that creative power is put in service of the director's vision. "One gives as much as possible," says film editor Helen van Dongen, "as much as is beneficial to the final form of the film, without overshadowing or obstructing the director's intentions . . . The editor working with a great director can do no better than discover and disclose the director's design."[3]

---

[3] Helen van Dongen, qtd. in Richard Barsam, "Discover and Disclose: Helen van Dongen and *Louisiana Story*," in *Filming Robert Flaherty's "Louisiana Story": The Helen van Dongen Diary*, by Helen Durant, ed. Eva Orbanz (New York: Museum of Modern Art, 1998), 86.

The Editor's Responsibilities

The editor is responsible for constructing the overall form of the movie and helping the production team realize its collective artistic vision by selecting, manipulating, and assembling its constituent visual and aural parts. Specifically, the editor is responsible for managing the following aspects of the final film:

> Spatial relationships between shots
> Temporal relationships between shots
> The overall rhythm of the film

Let's examine these responsibilities more closely.

Spatial Relationships Between Shots One of the most powerful effects of film editing is the creation of a sense of space in the mind of the viewer. When we are watching any single shot from a film, our sense of the overall space of the scene is necessarily limited by the height, width, and depth of the film frame during that shot. But as other shots are placed in close proximity to that original shot, our sense of the overall space in which the characters are moving shifts and expands. The juxtaposition of shots within a scene can cause us to have a fairly complex sense of that overall space (something like a mental map) even if no single shot discloses more than a fraction of that space to us at a time.

For example, as the opening titles roll in Kimberly Peirce's *Boys Don't Cry* (1999; editor: Lee Percy), through a short sequence of tightly framed shots we see cars dangerously passing one another on a rural highway, the exterior of a trailer park, an interior of a trailer where Teena Brandon (Hilary Swank) is getting a haircut to make her look like a teenage boy, the exterior of a skating rink, and, finally, the refashioned young woman inside introducing herself to her female blind date as "Brandon." The shots themselves and the manner in which they are edited introduce the space clearly, tightly, and unambiguously. These shots also introduce characters, mood, and conflict. The foreboding mood is established by the steady rhythm of the editing and the equally steady drumbeat on the sound track. There seems to be no turning back for Teena, and,

as a result, we sense that a conflict may arise over this young woman's identification of her gender.

The power of editing to establish spatial relationships between shots is so strong, in fact, that there is almost no need for filmmakers to ensure that there is a real space whose dimensions correspond to the one implied by editing. Countless films—especially historical dramas and science fiction films—rely heavily on the power of editing to fool us into perceiving their worlds as vast and complete even as we are shown only tiny fractions of the implied space. Because our brains effortlessly make spatial generalizations from limited visual information, George Lucas was not required, for example, to build an entire to-scale model of the *Millennium Falcon* to convince us that the characters in *Star Wars* are flying (and moving around within) a vast spaceship. Instead, a series of cleverly composed shots filmed on carefully designed (and relatively small) sets could, when edited together, create the illusion of a massive, fully functioning spacecraft.

In addition to painting a mental picture of the space of a scene, editing manipulates our sense of spatial *relationships* among characters, objects, and their surroundings. For example, the placement of one shot of a person's reaction (perhaps a look of concerned shock) after a shot of an action by another person (falling down a flight of stairs) immediately creates in our minds the thought that the two people are occupying the same space, that the person in the first shot is visible to the person in the second shot, and that the emotional response of the person in the second shot is a reaction to what has happened to the person in the first shot. The central discovery of Lev Kuleshov, the Soviet film theorist mentioned at the beginning of this chapter, was that these two shots need not have *any actual relationship at all* to one another for this effect to take place in a viewer's mind. The effect of perceiving such spatial relationships even when we are given minimal visual information or when we are presented with shots filmed at entirely different times and places is sometimes called the *Kuleshov effect*.

⊙ DVD *The Kuleshov Experiment* Experiment

[1]

[2]

[3]

[4]

[5]

[6]

The Kuleshov Effect In Joel Coen's *Raising Arizona* (1987; editor: Michael R. Miller), a simple example of the Kuleshov effect is used for comic effect to depict a moment when H. I. "Hi" McDonnough (Nicolas Cage), a kidnapper, has a guilt-induced fantasy in which Leonard Smalls (Randall "Tex" Cobb), an avenging bounty hunter, is on his trail. After speeding across the desert, throwing grenades at rabbits to show his power, Smalls rides up a road [1–2] and over a hill

[3], where, with a cut to the next shot [4], he enters [5] an entirely different place [6]. The action is edited in such a way as to fool us into perceiving the jump and the landing as a single, continuous action taking place in a single, continuous space, even though the first shot (images 1–3) is completely different in time, terrain, and vegetation from the second (images 4–6).

Temporal Relationships Between Shots

We have already learned that the *plot* of a narrative film is very often shaped and ordered in a way that differs significantly from the film's underlying *story*. In fact, the pleasure that many contemporary movies give us has its source in the bold decisions made by some filmmakers to manipulate the presentation of the plot in creative and confusing ways. Films such as Christopher Nolan's *Memento* (2000; editor: Dody Dorn), Spike Jonze's *Adaptation* (2002; editor: Eric Zumbrunnen), or Michel Gondry's *Eternal Sunshine of the Spotless Mind* (2004; editor: Valdis Oskarsdottir), are interesting in part because their plots are presented in a fragmented, out-of-order fashion that we as viewers must reshuffle in order to make sense of the underlying story. But even in more traditional narrative films in which the plot is presented in a more or less chronological manner, editing is used to manipulate the presentation of plot time onscreen.

For example, **flashback** (the interruption of chronological plot time with a shot or series of shots that show an event that has happened earlier in the story) is a very common editing technique. Used in virtually all movie genres, it is a traditional storytelling device that typically explains how a situation or character developed into what we see at the present time. For example, after a scene in George Clooney's *Confessions of a Dangerous Mind* (2003; editor: Stephen Mirrione) in which a TV personality, Chuck Barris (Sam Rockwell), stands naked and stares at a television screen, there is a flashback to the events that contributed to his astonishing life.

The flashback can be as stimulating as it is in Orson Welles's *Citizen Kane* (1941; editor: Robert Wise), where our sense of Charles Foster Kane is created by the memories of those who knew him; or as straightforward as Walter Neff's (Fred MacMurray) onscreen narration of Billy Wilder's classic film noir, *Double Indemnity* (1944; editor: Doane Harrison); in fact, the flashback is frequently used in film noir. It can also serve as the backbone for the structure of a complicated narrative, as in Alain Resnais's *Hiroshima mon amour* (1959; editors: Jasmine Chasney, Henri Colpi, and Anne Sarraute) or Quentin Tarantino's *Pulp Fiction* (1994; editor: Sally Menke).

Much less common than the flashback is the **flashforward**, the interruption of present action by a shot or series of shots that shows images from the plot's future. Often, flashforwards reflect a character's desire for someone or something, a premonition of something that might happen, or even a psychic projection. Flashforward is a problematic element in any film that strives for realism because it implies that the characters in the film are somehow seeing the future. Once employed, flashforward sends the signal that the movie we are watching is at least partly fantastical, and that we should be ready to suspend our disbelief. For example, in Steven Soderbergh's brilliant thriller *The Limey* (1999; editor: Sarah Flack), Wilson (Terence Stamp) imagines that he is shooting Terry Valentine (Peter Fonda). The scene, at a crowded party, is repeated three times; in each repetition, Wilson approaches from a slightly different direction, carries a different pistol, and hits Valentine in a different part of his body. The last attempt is lethal, but the sequence, we learn later, is wish fulfillment—a fantasy, not a fact.

The most common manipulation of time through editing is **ellipsis**, an omission between one thing and another. In a quotation, for example, an ellipsis mark (. . .) signifies the omission of one or more words. In filmmaking, an ellipsis generally signifies the omission of time—the time that separates one shot from another. Ellipsis in movies is first and foremost a *practical* tool; it economizes the presentation of plot, skipping over portions of the underlying story that do not need to be presented onscreen to be understood or inferred. But its use requires the filmmaker to have carefully established the time, place, location, characters, and action so that viewers are able not only to follow what they see, but also to make the intuitive inferences that fill in the material that was left out. This is what happens in Gus Van Sant's *Drugstore Cowboy* (1989; editors: Mary Bauer and Curtiss Clayton) when a policeman asks Bob (Matt Dillon), a heroin addict, "Are you going to tell us where you hid the drugs, or are we going to have to tear the place apart bit by bit?" When the next shot shows Bob's house torn apart, the cut implies an ellipsis of time, and it presents us with everything we need

[1]

[2]

[3]

Ellipsis Causing Disorientation Steven Soderbergh's *Erin Brockovich* (2000) demonstrates how an ellipsis can be used to cause the viewer's momentary disorientation. A sharp cut leads from [1] Erin Brockovich's car being hit broadside to [2] Ed Masry (Albert Finney) being told by his secretary (Conchata Ferrell) that Brockovich is waiting to see him. Next [3] Masry is seen greeting Brockovich (Julia Roberts), who is wearing a neck brace. Images 2 and 3 take place sequentially; although we don't know how much time has elapsed between images 1 and 2, it was at least enough to permit Brockovich to get the brace and make an appointment to see a lawyer.

to know about the period of story time that has elapsed.

The effect of an ellipsis on viewers is determined by how much story time is implied between shots, as well as by the manner in which the editing makes the transition from the first shot to the second. In some cases, such as the example from *Drugstore Cowboy* just mentioned, an ellipsis can seem a very natural progression and may signal a straightforward cause-and-effect relationship. In others, an ellipsis may span a much longer period of implied story time, or the transition may be so unexpected and sudden that the effect on viewers is shock or disorientation.

For example, in Steven Soderbergh's *Erin Brockovich* (2000; editor: Anne V. Coates), the title character (played by Julia Roberts), while driving away from an unsuccessful job interview, is hit broadside. We don't see what happens as the immediate result of this incident, for there is a sharp elliptical cut to a scene in which lawyer Ed Masry (Albert Finney) arrives at his office and is told by his secretary that a woman named Erin Brockovich is waiting to see him: "car accident; not her fault, she says." When he enters his office, he sees Erin wearing a neck brace. However, we don't know how much time has elapsed between the accident and this meeting.

An ellipsis may also span a longer period of implied story time. David Lean's *Lawrence of Arabia* (1962; editor: Anne V. Coates) contains a very effective cut that suggests an unspecified amount of elapsed time. T. E. Lawrence (Peter O'Toole) receives his charge from Mr. Dryden (Claude Rains), a British officer in Cairo; as he does so, he lights a cigarette, blows out the match, and says, "It's going to be fun," as the scene suddenly cuts to a shot of Lawrence enjoying coffee and food on the Arabian desert. We learn that he's made the trip from Cairo by boat, but we don't know how long it took.

Playing with time, and particularly with ellipses of all kinds, has become one of Steven Soderbergh's stylistic trademarks. In *The Limey* (1999; editor: Sarah Flack), the time and space of the entire movie are edited to be disorienting. The engine that drives the narrative is a continual use of the ellipsis for shock and/or disorientation.

England and California are constantly juxtaposed, as are the present, past, and future; and memory, imagination, flashbacks, and flashforwards. Some shots identify characters in full frames; others do not. We are never quite sure where or when the action is taking place. However, the cumulative progress of disorientation eventually leads us to put the pieces together, to see repeating patterns, and to become oriented.

Whether sudden and unexpected or seemingly natural, ellipses are also frequently used to provide an instant, sometimes comic, resolution to a situation. In *Out of Sight* (1998; editor: Anne V. Coates), for example, director Soderbergh tells the story of an improbable romance between two highly attractive people: Jack Foley (George Clooney), a notorious bank robber, and Karen Sisco (Jennifer Lopez), a federal marshal. Sisco has witnessed Foley and a buddy bust out of prison, and they take her hostage, but she escapes. The next day, she learns that Foley is in Miami, and, with gun in hand, she enters his hotel room and discovers him relaxing in the bathtub. As she bends over him with her gun pointed at his head, he pulls her into the water on top of him, she lays down the gun, and they kiss.

There is a quick cut, and an obvious ellipsis, for the next shot is of Sisco's father standing over her in a hospital bed with a dark bruise on her forehead. From earlier in the movie, we know that she got to the hospital as a result of a car crash that occurred during her escape from Foley and his buddy. However disorienting this ellipsis may be, it is also funny because, in such romantic comedies, it is conventional for opposites to fall for one another, perhaps even to become partners in crime, à la Bonnie and Clyde, whose portrayals on the screen (in Arthur Penn's *Bonnie and Clyde*, 1967) Sisco and Foley have previously discussed with admiration.

Another method for controlling the presentation of time in a film is **montage**. *Montage*—from the French verb *monter*, "to assemble or put together"—is the French word for "editing." In the former Soviet Union in the 1920s, *montage* referred to the various forms of editing that expressed ideas developed by Eisenstein, Kuleshov, Vertov, Pudovkin, and others. In Hollywood, beginning in the 1930s, *montage* designates a sequence of shots, often with superimposi-

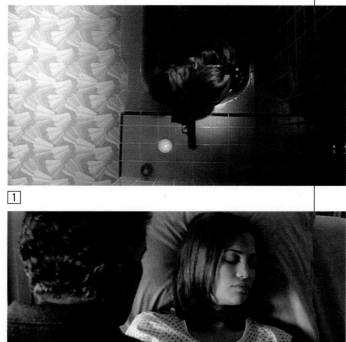

[1]

[2]

Ellipsis for Comic Effect An ellipsis shortens the time between two actions, but it can also have comic implications. In Steven Soderbergh's *Out of Sight* (1998), [1] Karen Sisco (Jennifer Lopez), a federal marshal, starts out to nab an escaped convict, Jack Foley (George Clooney), but instead is pulled into a bathtub and kisses him. [2] A quick cut, an obvious ellipsis, shows her later in a hospital bed with a nasty bruise on her forehead. Considering that she thinks little about being in a bathtub with a convicted felon, we might reach various fanciful conclusions—until we remember that she was put in that hospital earlier in the movie for another reason.

tions and optical effects, that shows a condensed series of events. For example, a montage of flipping calendar pages was a typical (if trite) way to show the passage of time. In Wes Anderson's *Rushmore* (1998; editor: David Moritz), after the headmaster identifies Max Fischer (Jason Schwartzman) as "one of the worst students we've got," a twenty-one-shot montage unexpectedly shows Max as the key person in virtually every club at the school.

The hilarious *Team America: World Police* (2004; editor: Tom Vogt), an irreverent comedy from

[1]

[2]

[3]

[4]

[5]

Montage Although these still shots do not convey the pace of the lively lyrics in the "Montage!" sequence of Trey Parker's *Team America: World Police* (2004), imagine a driving disco beat accompanying these images of Spottswoode overseeing the process by which Gary Johnston is being made into a complete soldier: close-up of Johnston [1]; Johnston practicing on firing range [2], running on a treadmill [3], lifting weights [4], and engaging in karate with Spottswoode [5].

director Trey Parker (creator of *South Park*), has more targets than it can possibly reach in ninety-seven minutes, but it hits dead right on the montage technique. At the end of the movie, Spottswoode (voice of Daran Norris), the sinister mastermind of Team America, believes that his protégé, Gary Johnston (voice of Parker), is the man to thwart the plan of Kim Jong Il (voice of Parker) to use weapons of mass destruction to end the world. The problem is that Spottswoode has to make a complete soldier of Johnston in "*very little time.*" Johnston naïvely asks: "How are we gonna do that?" and Spottswoode replies, "I think I know *just* what we need." Thus begins a musical sequence called "Montage!"—set to a lively disco beat—in

which a time-condensing montage sequence (using many split screens) is accompanied by lyrics breathlessly announcing the technique and style of the conventional montage sequence:

> . . . show us the passage of time—we're gonna need a montage!
> . . . show a lot of things that are happening at once to remind everyone of what's going on
> . . . with every shot, show a little improvement; to show it all would take too long—that's called a montage!;
> . . . even *Rocky* had a montage

and

. . . always fade-out in a montage; if you fade-out, it seems more time has passed in a montage.

This sequence provides an excellent example of a montage as it simultaneously satirizes action movies. The "Montage!" song itself was borrowed from *South Park*.

In order for these various editorial manipulations of time to be understandable to viewers, editors must employ accepted conventions of editing to signal the transitions from shot to shot. Luckily, our minds are able to understand these conventions and to infer correctly the progression of plot and story from them, even when the plot is presented in nonchronological order and is riddled with ellipses. It's not entirely clear why our brains are able to do this, but for the sake of film history, it's a good thing. As Walter Murch puts it,

> When you stop to think about it, it is amazing that film editing works at all. One moment we're on top of Mauna Kea and—*cut!*—the next we're at the bottom of the Mariana Trench. The instantaneous transition of the cut is nothing like what we experience as normal life, which seems to be one continuous shot from the moment we wake until we close our eyes at night. It wouldn't have been surprising if film editing had been tried and then abandoned after it was found to induce a kind of seasickness. But it doesn't: we happily endure, in fact even enjoy, these sudden transitions for which nothing in our evolutionary history seems to have prepared us.[4]

Rhythm Among other things, editing determines the **duration** of a shot. Thus it controls the length of time you can look at each shot and absorb the information within it. An editor can control the rhythm (or, to use musical terminology, the beat) of a film—the pace at which it moves forward—by varying the duration of the shots in relation to one another, and thus control the speed (tempo) and accents (stress or lack of it on certain shots). Sometimes the editing rhythm allows us time to think about what we see; other times it moves too quickly to permit thought.

The musical analogy is useful, but only to a point, because a movie serves a narrative, while rhythm seldom does. However, there are some landmarks in the development of movie editing—among them the "Odessa Steps" sequence in Sergei Eisenstein's *Battleship Potemkin* (1925; editors: Grigori Akesandrov and Eisenstein), the diving sequence in Leni Riefenstahl's *Olympiad* (1938; editor: Riefenstahl), Jean-Luc Godard's *Breathless* (1960; editors: Cécile Decugis and Lila Herman), Andy and Larry Wachowski's *The Matrix* (1999; editor: Zach Staenberg), and Tom Tykwer's *Run Lola Run* (1998; editor: Mathilde Bonnefoy)—in which the editing (its patterns, rhythms, etc.) seem almost to take precedence over the narrative. A movie narrative has its own internal requirements that signal the editor how long to make each shot and with what rhythm to combine those shots. Many professional editors say that they *intuitively* reach decisions on these matters.

What happens, however, when the rhythm is imposed autocratically *before* a film is made? To find out, you might look at Jørgen Leth and Lars von Trier's *The Five Obstructions* (2004; editors: Morten Højbjerg and Camilla Skousen). In the movie, von Trier, one of the founders of the Danish *Dogme* movement, views Leth's twelve-minute film *The Perfect Human* (1967) and, in an interesting reversal of roles—Leth was one of von Trier's idols—"orders" the older director to remake the film five times, each version tightly controlled by limitations ("obstructions") that he specifies. The first version is to be composed of single shots of no more than twelve frames, each shot appearing for approximately one-half of a second on the screen. The result, a charming look at Cuba, closely resembles a television advertisement or an MTV spot.

Of course, the images "tell" a kind of story simply by the rhythm that links them, but this rigid imposition of a fixed rhythm makes traditional editing, and thus traditional storytelling, impossible. Why? Because editing requires the editor to make decisions about shot length, rhythm, emphasis, and the like; and von Trier's formula (as successfully applied by Leth) ties the editor's hands and puts all

[4] Michael Ondaatje, *The Conversations: Walter Murch and the Art of Editing* (New York: Knopf, 2004), 49.

of the decision making in the mind of the viewer. Looking at *The Five Obstructions*, we can understand the value of experimentation, particularly for those who prefer intellectual schematics to be applied to art.

Experimentation in editing does not have to be formulaic, as demonstrated by Mathilde Bonnefoy, the editor of Tom Tykwer's *Run Lola Run* (1998). Bonnefoy handles the editor's traditional tasks—fixing the duration and frequency of shots, and thus controlling the film's emphasis on a person, setting, or object—with such a sense of joy that the movie is more about the editing than about the narrative. In the opening sequence, Lola (Franka Potente) receives a phone call from her boyfriend, Manni (Moritz Bleibtreu), who implores her to help him return $100,000 to the criminal gang for which he works. If he does not do so in twenty minutes, the gang will kill him. Lola hangs up, imagines what her task will involve, and then sets off, running through the rooms of her apartment, down the stairs, and out into the city streets.

Although the principal action is composed of shots of Lola running, there are breaks in that rhythm for scenes of other action that introduce several of the characters relevant to Lola's quest. Tykwer uses a constantly moving camera, live and animated footage, time-lapse cinematography, slow motion and fast motion, different camera positions and angles, hard cuts, dissolves, jump cuts, and ellipses. Accents within the shots create their own patterns: different camera angles and heights, changes in the direction from which we see Lola's run on the screen (e.g., left to right, right to left, toward us, away from us, or diagonal across the frame). Underscoring the resulting visual rhythm is an equally exciting sound track: basically, the familiar disco beat scored for a synthesizer, piano, and percussion, with accents of glass breaking and camera shutters clicking, and Lola's voice repeating, "I wish I was a . . . ," and other voices chanting "Hey, hey, hey."

Together, editing and sound create the steady pace of Lola's run, make us empathize with her dilemma, and establish suspense (will Lola get the money? will she save Manni?) that continues until the last moment of the film. Editor Mathilde Bonnefoy's handling of the complex rhythms in this scene not only dazzles us with its pacing, but also maintains the focus on what Lola is doing and why. The editing of this movie—its rhythm, in particular—has been particularly influential on such films as Paul Greengrass's *The Bourne Supremacy* (2004; editors: Richard Pearson and Christopher Rouse).

The tempo of a movie can also be strictly measured in *slow* rather than fast terms, as it is in another Tykwer work, *Heaven* (2002; editor: Mathilde Bonnefoy), a moral fable-cum-thriller based on a script by the great Polish director-writer Krzysztof Kieslowski. Here the action—a bomb going off in the wrong place, a woman admitting responsibility for placing it, a police officer falling in love with the woman because of her sense of moral duty, the destruction of critical evidence by a corrupt police captain, a jailbreak and flight from the police—all takes place at a very deliberate pace established by a piano and violin score that is heard in virtually every shot in the movie. The music and editing are not only measured in tempo but also devoid of accents, causing the viewer to wonder when something is going to happen that will break that tempo, signal a turning point, or provide a climax. Then, in the final moment, in a burst of gunfire, the two fugitives seize a helicopter and rise slowly toward heaven until they are out of sight—a moment of elation that contrasts with the previously unwavering tempo established by the rhythms of both the editing and the piano–violin music.

Varying the duration and rhythm of shots guides our eyes just as varying the rhythm in jazz guides the almost involuntary tapping of our fingers or feet as we listen to it. When the rhythms of the visual and aural images match up, this is obvious, but when the visual images move with a rhythm that has little or nothing to do with the sound, we intuitively recognize and react to that rhythm. In the scene where the gulls attack a gas station attendant in *The Birds* (1963; see page 185 in Chapter 4), director Alfred Hitchcock and his editor, George Tomasini, masterfully use the rhythm of editing to build up excitement. If you attempt to tap the rhythm with your finger at each of the thirty-nine

1

4

2

5

3

6

Rhythm in Editing In Tom Tykwer's *Run Lola Run* (1998), the title character (played by Franka Potente) [1] receives word of her boyfriend, Manni's (Moritz Bleibtreu) [2], dire situation—a matter of money and time [3], which is running out. Close-ups show Lola facing facts [4] and imagining the possibilities [5]. Finally, she has no choice but to run for help [6]. From here on, the pace and rhythm of the editing will match the pace and rhythm of dramatic developments and Lola's sometimes split-second decision making.

cuts in the scene, you'll find that you're able to keep a discernible rhythm at first, but as the scene reaches its climax, you'll find that you can barely keep pace with the cuts.

The choices that an editor makes regarding the rhythm of scenes can in turn create larger patterns of shot duration. These patterns can be built and broken for dramatic emphasis and impact, as in Sergio Leone's *Once Upon a Time in the West* (1968; director's cut DVD version released 2003; editor: Nino Baragli). During the opening title and credits, the editor has created a sequence of almost fifteen minutes that is extraordinary for the patterns both of what we see (an isolated railroad station on the prairie where three desperate-looking characters are waiting for a train to arrive) and of what we hear (an equally extraordinary montage of sounds, the slow, steady rhythm of which establishes an ominous mood).

These visual and aural images establish a slow, deliberate pattern of duration, sound, and movement. The shots of waiting for the train's arrival last a very long time, made to seem even longer by the views of the vast prairie on the widescreen format, but they feature little or no action or movement by the characters. Because we have very little information to take in, ordinarily we would expect the director to use shots of a shorter duration, and to cut from one to the next at the peak of what is known as the **content curve**, the point at which we have absorbed all we need to know. However, by *not* cutting where we expect it, Leone traps us in each shot, making us wait along with the bored desperadoes.

The montage of natural sounds in Leone's opening sequence in this film has a different rhythm from that of the visual images; its purpose is to underscore the tedium of the wait. The duration of each sound is shorter than the duration of the shots, and what we hear are repetitions of the same sounds: wind, squeaking windmill, footsteps, telegraph machine, water dripping, fly buzzing, knuckles cracking, and silence. Suddenly this pattern, pace, and mood are broken by a shot—taken from a camera positioned underneath the tracks—of a train speeding toward the station. The pattern of editing speeds up, with cuts between close-ups of three men loading their guns; the train approaching at dramatic angle, its sounds now taking precedence over the others; and finally the train coming to a stop at a right angle to the screen, in front of the camera, wheels grinding to a halt and whistle blowing. In a moment, the train departs, leaving behind Harmonica (Charles Bronson).

The short, abrupt change in editing associated with the train's arrival takes on added significance because of Harmonica, who is to become one of the heroes of the film. In completing this scene, Leone returns to the overall pattern established in this sequence, with slow, quiet, static shots of the four-way face-off between Harmonica and the desperadoes building up to a rapid-fire shooting sequence (in terms of both the action being filmed and the

camera shots that are capturing it) in which every gunman, even Harmonica, catches a bullet.

Major Approaches to Editing: Continuity and Discontinuity

Because the editing of most contemporary narrative movies is made to be as inconspicuous as possible, the process and the results of editing may not be apparent to people unfamiliar with filmmaking. In the editing of such movies, the point is to tell the story as clearly, efficiently, and coherently as possible. Thus, we often refer to it as *seamless* or *invisible* editing because it flows so smoothly that we are not distracted by the cuts. This style of editing, called **continuity editing**, is certainly the most prevalent in mainstream filmmaking, and it's the sort of editing that we'll spend most of this chapter discussing. But it's not the only possible approach to film editing. When filmmakers deliberately choose to manipulate shots so that the transitions between them are *not* smooth, continuous, or coherent—in other words, when the editing calls attention to itself rather than invisibly propelling the film forward—**discontinuity editing** is being employed.

Like the tension between realism (verisimilitude) and antirealism more generally, continuity and discontinuity are not absolute values but are instead tendencies along a continuum. An average

Relationship Between Continuity and Discontinuity Editing Eight frames from Sergei Eisenstein's groundbreaking *Battleship Potemkin* (1925) illustrate the relationship between continuity editing and discontinuity editing. [1–4] A starving sailor (Mikhail Gomorov), enraged by the words "Give us this day our daily bread" printed on a plate, brings the plate up behind his head and then flings it down. The continuity of these shots and the action within them leads us to believe that the plate has broken, but the next thing we see [5–8] is that same sailor, through the same framing, smashing the same plate. Again, the shots and action here are continuous, but their juxtaposition with the previous sequence creates visual, temporal, and logical discontinuity. Only in the following shot, which shows the plate in pieces, is continuity restored. Why might Eisenstein have interrupted our expectations in this way?

1

5

2

6

3

7

4

8

Hollywood movie may exhibit continuity in some parts and discontinuity in others, even if the overall tendency of the movie is toward classical continuity. Similarly, an avant-garde film that is mostly discontinuous can include scenes that employ continuity editing. We don't need to look any further than Michel Gondry's *Eternal Sunshine of the Spotless Mind* (2004) or Fernando Meirelles and Kátia Lund's *City of God* (2002)—to cite just two cases—to find examples that use both of these major approaches to editing, as well as many of the specific tools of editing described in this chapter.

The Evolution of Editing: The Lumières to Eisenstein

Conventions of Continuity Editing

Continuity editing, now the dominant style of editing throughout the world, seeks to achieve logic, smoothness, sequential flow, and the temporal and spatial orientation of viewers to what they see on the screen. As with so many conventions of film production, the conventions of continuity editing remain open to variation, but in general, continuity editing ensures that

> What happens on the screen makes as much narrative sense as possible.
> Screen direction is consistent from shot to shot.
> Graphic, spatial, and temporal relations are maintained from shot to shot.

The fundamental building blocks of continuity editing are to establish the scene through a *master shot* and maintain *screen direction* through the *180-degree system*.

Master Shot A **master shot**, sometimes called an *establishing shot*, is more a shot type than an editing technique. However, the master shot is very important to continuity editing for two reasons: (1) it provides film editors with the sorts of tools they need to do the job effectively, and (2) it orients the viewer in preparation for the shots that follow. In making a master shot, the cinematographer essentially shoots the entire shot in a continuous take,

generally in a long shot (or extreme long shot) that covers all of the action. The master shot serves as the foundation for, and ordinarily begins, a sequence of shots by showing the location of ensuing action, suggesting the mood, and giving the viewer additional information, such as time, weather, and overall environment.

The master shot can also be photographed from many other different setups and angles, as appropriate, such as full shots, medium shots of each character (single shots or two-shots, depending on which their spatial relationship allows), and close-ups. Then the editors have the freedom to cut the scene however the action, performances, and script dictate, because they have all of the scene's action available in each shot and take. Typically, an editor starts a scene or sequence of shots with the master shot in order to establish location, situation, spatial relationships, and so on, then cuts gradually in on various subjects as the drama and action dictate, regularly cutting back to the master to reacquaint viewers with location, what's happening, who's doing it, and how the characters are positioned in relation to one another. The master shot is also called a *cover shot* because the editor can repeat it later in the film to remind the audience of the location, thus providing "coverage" to the director by avoiding the need to **reshoot** (or make *additional photography*).

Although some of today's mainstream directors are far more experimental with continuity (we discuss several in this chapter) and do not always adhere to such conventions as establishing shots, note that other directors have traditionally used establishing shots to open films in which place is paramount, including westerns. For example, John Ford opens *The Searchers* (1956; editor: Jack Murray) with a shot of spectacular Monument Valley framed in the doorway of a darkened house. The point of view is that of Martha Edwards (Dorothy Jordan), who has an instinct that someone is outside, coming to her house. She steps out on her porch and—in an extreme long shot—soon sees a horseman riding in her direction. An exterior shot shows us the isolation of her house in the vast landscape, and we will soon learn why she has had this intuition and why this horseman is so important in her life.

[1]

[4]

[2]

[5]

[3]

[6]

Establishing Shot These six shots from the opening of John Ford's *The Searchers* (1956) very economically establish both the place and some of the themes of this complex movie: the vastness of the desert valley in which Aaron and Martha Edwards's home is situated; the intimacy of family life in this isolated spot; and the return home of Ethan Edwards, who became a mercenary soldier in the Civil War after his brother married Martha, who, nonetheless, still yearns for Ethan, as he does for her. [1] Martha (Dorothy Jordan), framed in the doorway, looks out at Monument Valley in the background; [2] she stands on the porch; [3] she shields her eyes to try to focus on someone approaching; [4] Ethan Edwards (John Wayne) rides toward the house; [5] Martha is joined by her husband, Aaron (Walter Coy), and their children; finally, [6] the two brothers meet for the first time in years.

FIGURE 6.1 The 180-Degree System

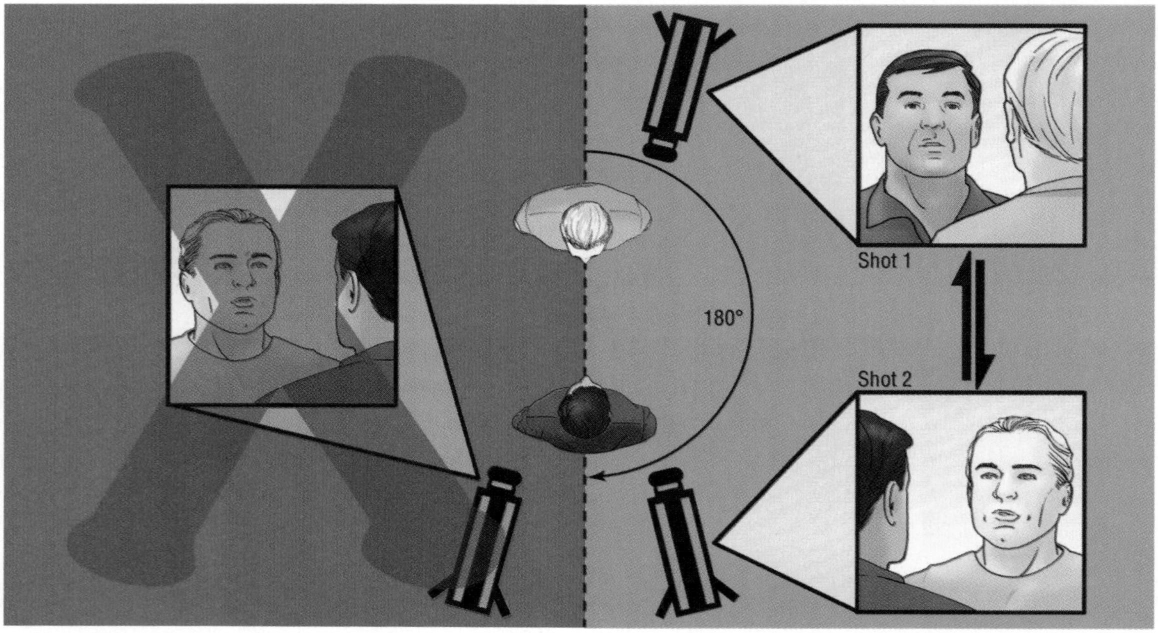

Shots 1 and 2 are taken from positions within the same 180-degree space (green background). When viewers see the resulting shots onscreen, they can make sense of the actors' relative positions to one another. If a camera is placed in the opposite 180-degree space (red background), the resulting shot reverses the actors' spatial orientation and thus cannot be used in conjunction with either Shot 1 or Shot 2 without confusing the viewer.

Martha is joined by her husband, Aaron (Walter Coy), and their children, by which time they sense also that the lone rider is Ethan Edwards (John Wayne), her husband's brother. In a few shots of great economy, Ford establishes that Ethan has been away for a long period of time, but that, somehow, his home is here. These shots establish two motifs—the vastness of the desert valley and the intimacy of the pioneer home—that Ford will develop throughout the movie.

Screen Direction In the early years of cinema, the evolution of films containing many shots from a variety of angles (especially those containing the types of action shots that occur in a chase scene) demanded that filmmakers find a way to maintain consistent **screen direction**, the direction of a figure's or object's movement on the screen. The fundamental result of their search—established as early as 1903, and used with occasional inconsisten-cies (often for deliberate comic purposes) until about 1912, when filmmakers first began to adhere to it—is the **180-degree system** (also called the *180-degree rule*, the **axis of action**, the *imaginary line*, and the *line of action*).

The axis of action, an imaginary horizontal line between the main characters being photographed, determines where the camera should be placed to preserve screen direction and thus one aspect of continuity (Fig. 6.1). Once this axis of action is determined, the camera must remain on the same side of the line. The resulting shots orient the viewer within the scene, ensure consistent screen direction across and between cuts, and establish a clear sense of the space in which the action occurs (because something, an object or person, remains consistent in the frame, to identify the relations between sequential spaces). The axis of action shifts, though, as the characters move within the frame and as the camera moves.

To summarize, in reaching the goals of continuity, the 180-degree system depends on three factors working together *in any single shot*: (1) the action in a scene must move along a *hypothetical* line that keeps the action on a single side of the camera; (2) the camera must shoot consistently on one side of that line; and (3) everyone on the production set—particularly the director, cinematographer, editor, and actors—must understand and adhere to this system.

⊚ DVD The 180-Degree Rule

This means that in a scene of dialogue, say, in which character A is on the left and character B is on the right, the viewer is oriented to that spatial relationship between them because the camera stays on one side of the imaginary line; however, if the camera crosses the imaginary line between the characters and moves to a position 180 degrees opposite its original position, the position of the characters in the image is reversed: character A is now on the right, character B is on the left.

This is easy to understand if you pretend for a moment to be a cinematographer and do the following practical exercise. First, ask two of your friends or classmates to represent characters A and B, standing (or sitting) as just described. Second, using your hands to make a rectangular frame, position them in front of your eyes as if they were the camera's viewfinder, and stand in front of your "actors" so that they both fit in that "frame." You can choose to make it a long shot, medium shot, or close-up, and use any angle you wish, as long as you see characters A and B on the left and right, respectively. Next, with the characters remaining in exactly the same position, move around 180 degrees from your first hypothetical camera position. Look through your handmade viewfinder, and of course you'll find that the characters' positions have been reversed in the image—again regardless of what framing, camera position, or camera angle you use. If you were making an actual movie and crossed the imaginary line without providing any explanation—direct or indirect—for changing the characters' positions on the screen, your viewers would immediately become disoriented and wonder why the characters' positions were flipped on the screen.

In another example—this time a car chase—if, in shot A, the car travels across the screen from the right to the left side of the frame, in shot B it must enter from the right side of the frame to maintain continuity of screen direction. Otherwise the viewer will be disoriented and perhaps wonder if the driver made a U-turn without the viewer seeing it. Once the screen direction is established, the director can make shots from any angle or height desired; when those shots are edited together, the viewer will continue to understand the direction in which the car is moving.

Screen direction can also suggest meaning in an abstract or symbolic way. For example, the earlier discussion of *Run Lola Run* described how Lola runs *against* a deadline. If you study the patterns of her running, you'll see that she actually does run *against* time by continuously going in a counterclockwise pattern. Thus the screen movement and rhythm of editing reinforce the major theme: her need to beat the clock if she's going to save her boyfriend's life.

The 180-degree system remains a *convention* (not a rule) that can be broken if the director desires. Sometimes, for example, the director might wish to use a **reverse-angle shot** (one in which the angle of shooting is opposite to that in a preceding shot) or to dolly or zoom out to include more people or actions. In any case, if the director asks the cinematographer to cross the line, both the shooting and the editing must be done carefully so as not to confuse the audience.

In Michael Mann's *The Insider* (1999; editors: William Goldenberg, David Rosenbloom, and Paul Rubell), the director, cinematographer, and editors created one scene in which they maintain the 180-degree system and then purposely break it. The movie tells the story of Dr. Jeffrey Wigand (Russell Crowe), the man who blew the whistle on the tobacco industry's use of nicotine for addictive purposes, and Lowell Bergman (Al Pacino), the *60 Minutes* producer who broke the story that, after prolonged legal action, resulted in the industry's $246 billion settlement. The relationship of these two volatile men reaches one of several turning points as they are having dinner in a Japanese restaurant. The scene begins with a

[2]

[1]

Violating the 180-Degree Rule Intentionally In *The Insider* (1999), director Michael Mann conforms to the 180-degree system and then purposely breaks it to visually heighten the tension in a discussion about ethics between Dr. Jeffrey Wigand (Russell Crowe) and Lowell Bergman (Al Pacino). [1] Most of the scene is shot from this perspective, with Wigand on the left and Bergman on the right, and with a blank wall in the background. [2] This shot—onscreen for less than four seconds—breaks the 180-degree line, which is confirmed by the reversal of their seating positions and the latticework screen behind them. Although the amount of time that the second shot is onscreen is very short, making it almost subliminal to the viewer, it nonetheless strengthens our understanding of the tension that divides the two men.

series of medium two-shots taken from an angle that places the imaginary line as a diagonal crossing from lower left to upper right. Wigand and Bergman are seated in the traditional Japanese position on the floor, across from one another, in the middle of a low rectangular table, Wigand on the left and Bergman on the right. The background wall is blank. Throughout the scene, both actors are shot in profile so that screen direction, eyelines, and the imaginary line are very clearly defined.

As this tense conversation heats up (typical of the overall relationship between the two men), the camera shifts position, shooting from floor level. In the first shot of this new camera setup, Wigand challenges Bergman's belief in the power of television journalism to raise the public consciousness on major issues, but Bergman reaffirms his belief. In the second shot, a moment of high tension, the camera has moved to a position 180 degrees opposite where it was; we know this because, obviously, the characters have shifted position (Bergman on the right, Wigand on the left), and the wall behind them is a latticework screen. In the third shot, the original camera setup is restored, as Wigand insultingly challenges Bergman's motives. Bergman, angry but tactful, challenges Wigand's skepticism about journalism and his apparent inability to go public with the vital information he possesses.

At this point the camera setup returns to where it was when the scene began: medium two-shots taken from an angle that places the imaginary line as a diagonal crossing from lower left to upper right. After a few moments the scene ends without resolution of the conflict. This is a straightforward, powerful example of how the 180-degree system maintains screen continuity; then is purposely broken at a moment of high tension, giving added emphasis to the tension and conflict; and finally returns to the system and continuity to complete the scene.

Editing Techniques That Maintain Continuity

In addition to the fundamental building blocks—the master shot and maintaining screen direction with the 180-degree system—various editing techniques are used to ensure that graphic, spatial, and temporal relations are maintained from shot to shot.

Shot/Reverse Shot A **shot/reverse shot**, one of the most common and familiar of all editing patterns, is a technique in which the camera (and editor) switches between shots of different characters, usually in a conversation or other interaction. When used in continuity editing, the shots are typically framed over each character's shoulder to preserve screen direction. Thus, in the first shot the camera is behind character A, who is looking right, and records what character B says to A; in the second shot, the camera is behind character B, who is looking left, and records that character's response.

Again, Michael Mann's *The Insider* (1999) provides a good example. In one of their first discussions, Dr. Wigand and Mr. Bergman are sitting in the closed confines of Wigand's car. As their conversation begins, Wigand is on the right of the frame, in the driver's seat, and Bergman is in the front passenger's seat, the imaginary line being the backs of the seats. But, as you first might expect, the scene is *not* shot through the windshield. Instead, the camera shoots Wigand through the window adjacent to Bergman, and vice versa. Although the two characters are essentially facing the windshield, they continually turn to face the other and maintain eyeline contact. The conversation is tense, and perfectly suited to this closed, conspiratorial space.

The shot/reverse shot is one of the most fundamental of all filmmaking conventions, and because it is so frequently used, directors over the years have developed many variations on its basic technique. Besides playing an essential role in maintaining continuity, the shot/reverse shot helps ease some of the logistical challenges of making a movie. For example, this editing technique fools our eyes by bringing together two characters on the screen that could have been photographed in completely different locations or at completely different times. Thus we are reminded that a movie is not shot in the order we see it on the screen and that the editor has the power to make it appear that it was.

Match Cuts   Match cuts—those in which shot A and shot B are matched in action, subject, graphic content, or two characters' eye contact—help create a sense of continuity between the two shots. There are several kinds of match cuts. *Technically*, they are identical; the differences between them are in *what* is depicted.

Match-on-Action Cut   A **match-on-action** cut shows us the continuation of a character's or object's motion through space without actually showing us the entire action. It is a fairly routine

editorial technique for economizing a movie's presentation of movement. Of course, the match-on-action cut has both *expressive* and practical uses.

Michel Gondry's *Eternal Sunshine of the Spotless Mind* (2004), a black comedy based on the absurd idea that you can erase people's brains, employs match-on-action cuts for different effects. The editor frequently cuts between the present and the past to depict Joel Barish (Jim Carrey) doing similar actions at different ages; thus, a shot of young Joel is followed by a cut to the mature Joel running inside and getting under the kitchen table. In another scene, a shot of mature Joel wearing a red cape and walking out of the frame is followed by a cut to young Joel, also wearing a red

Match-on-Action Cut   Among its many startling effects, Michel Gondry's *Eternal Sunshine of the Spotless Mind* (2004) employs match-on-action cuts for different effects. In trying to remember his past, Joel Barish (Jim Carrey) remembers himself as a child seeking shelter from a rainstorm [1], a shot that is immediately followed by Joel taking shelter at the present time under a table in the kitchen [2], the surface of which resembles the roof of the shelter in image 1. These two moments, in fact divided by some twenty-five years of Joel's life, blur the idea that there is a distinction between past and present.

cape, completing the action of walking out of the frame. These cuts preserve a sense of seamless action within an extended passage of time (see the earlier discussion of ellipses).

In another example from this movie—a tense moment between a technician, Stan (Mark Ruffalo), and his employer, Dr. Howard Mierzwiak (Tom Wilkinson)—a shot of Stan wiping his forehead is followed by a cut to the doctor *simultaneously* wiping *his* forehead. Ironically, match cuts are a motif in a film about seemingly ill-matched people. At the beginning, for example, where Joel meets Clementine Kruczynski (Kate Winslet), the *lack* of seamless match cuts underscores the difficulty they're having in getting to know one another.

Graphic Match Cut In a **graphic match cut**, the similarity between shots A and B is in the shape and form of what we see. In this type of cut, the shape, color, or texture of objects matches across the edit, providing continuity. The prologue of Stanley Kubrick's *2001: A Space Odyssey* (1968; editor: Ray Lovejoy) contains a memorable exam-

ple of a graphic match cut in which the action continues seamlessly from one shot to the next: a cut that erases millions of years, from a bone weapon of the Stone Age to an orbiting craft of the Space Age. The weapon and the spacecraft match not only in their tubular shapes but also in their rotations.

Alfred Hitchcock gives us another classic example of the graphic match cut in *Vertigo* (1958; editor: George Tomasini) when John "Scottie" Ferguson (James Stewart) places a necklace around the neck of Judy Barton (Kim Novak). This action occurs in a sequence: a medium shot of Barton and Ferguson in front of a mirror as Ferguson fastens the necklace, followed by a dolly-in right to a close-up of him looking at her reflection; cut to a dolly-in to a close-up of the necklace on Barton's neck, followed by the match cut to a dolly-out from a close-up of a similar necklace in a portrait.

Graphic matches often exploit basic shapes—squares, circles, triangles—and provide a strong visual sense of design and order. For example, at the end of the shower murder sequence in *Psycho* (1960;

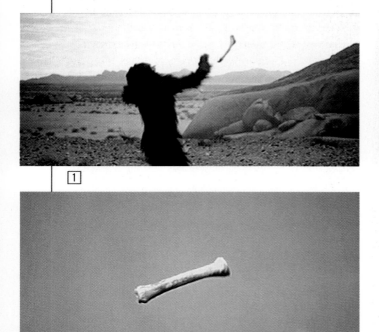

[1]

[2]

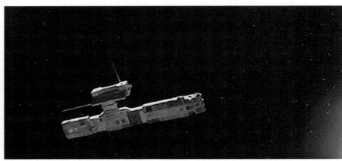

[3]

Graphic Match Cut In Stanley Kubrick's *2001: A Space Odyssey* (1968), a graphic match (and simultaneously match-on-action) cut enables humanity to rocket from prehistory into outer space. An ape-man [1] rejoices in his newfound weaponry, a bone, by tossing it into the air [2], at which point it becomes technology of a far more sophisticated kind [3]. This astonishing leap of sight, space, and time introduces several of the movie's principal themes: the relativity of time, the interaction of inventiveness and aggressiveness, and the desire of the human race to conquer the unknown.

1

2

Eyeline Match Cut in *Now, Voyager* As we know from looking at "old" movies, everyone smoked in them. For one thing, tobacco companies paid the studios to feature stars with cigarettes, cigars, or pipes; for another, public censorship of smoking was decades away. Today it's seldom that we see stars smoking onscreen, but in early years Bette Davis was Hollywood's most memorable smoker. In Irving Rapper's *Now, Voyager* (1942), the affair between Charlotte

Vale (Davis) and Jerry Durrance (Paul Henreid), is repeatedly punctuated by his signature custom of lighting two cigarettes and giving one to her. In the eyeline match cut pictured here, as Charlotte asks for Jerry's help, he says "Shall we just have a cigarette on it?" This signals the viewer that he will do all she asks, even if it means that their relationship is going up in a puff of smoke.

editor: George Tomasini), Hitchcock matches two circular shapes: the eye of Marion Crane (Janet Leigh), tears streaming down, with the round shower drain, blood and water washing down—a metaphorical visualization of Marion's life ebbing away.

Eyeline Match Cut The **eyeline match cut** joins shot A, a point-of-view shot of a person looking off-screen in one direction, and shot B, the person or object that is the object of that gaze. In Irving Rapper's *Now, Voyager* (1942; editor: Warren Low), Jerry Durrance (Paul Henreid) lights two cigarettes, one for him, the other for Charlotte Vale (Bette Davis). As he hands one to her and looks into her eyes, an eyeline match cut joins a shot of her eyes looking into his, the culmination of an intensely romantic moment that, ironically, ends their relationship.

Parallel Editing **Parallel editing** is the cutting together of two or more lines of action that occur simultaneously at different locations or that occur

at different times. Although the terms *parallel editing*, *crosscutting*, and *intercutting* are often used interchangeably, you should understand the differences among them. *Parallel editing* is generally understood to mean two or more actions happening at the same time in different places, as in the "Baptism and Murder" scene in Francis Ford Coppola's *The Godfather* (1972; see page 14).

Crosscutting refers to editing that cuts between two or more actions occurring at the same time, and usually in the same place. Joel Coen's *Raising Arizona* (1987; editor: Michael R. Miller) uses crosscutting to link several simultaneous actions: Hi (Nicolas Cage) fleeing the police after robbing a convenience store; the police chasing him; his enraged wife, Ed (Holly Hunter), rescuing him from the police; the hapless clerk at the convenience store reacting to Hi's robbery; and a pack of runaway dogs also pursuing Hi. The complex choreography of this scene, accentuated by the brilliant crosscutting, creates a hilarious comic episode. But when crosscutting is used excessively—as it is in the final scenes of Tim Robbins's *Cradle Will Rock*

[1]

[4]

[2]

[5]

[3]

[6]

Eyeline Match Cut in *Vertigo* In Alfred Hitchcock's *Vertigo*, John "Scottie" Ferguson (James Stewart) [1] has followed Madeleine Elster (Kim Novak) [2] into the California Palace of the Legion of Honor, an art museum, where she stares, obsessed, at a painting of the long-dead Carlotta Valdes. Match cuts (eyeline match cuts that are also graphic match cuts, as described on pages 257–59) establish continuity between Madeleine's bouquet [3] and Carlotta's [4]; and between Carlotta's bun [5] and Madeleine's [6]. Through these subjective-point-of-view shots, we experience Ferguson's "detective" work.

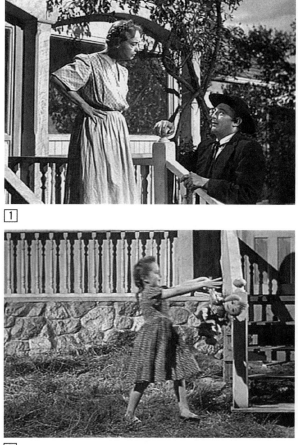

Eyeline Match Cut in *The Night of the Hunter* In Charles Laughton's *The Night of the Hunter* (1955; editor: Robert Golden), Harry Powell (Robert Mitchum) confronts Rachel (Lillian Gish) [1], who is providing refuge for the children he seeks. As one of the children (Pearl, played by Sally Jane Bruce) enters the scene [2], she drops a doll containing something very valuable to Harry and runs to him. Harry, clearly more interested in the doll than in Pearl, betrays his true interest by looking directly at the doll [3], which we understand by the eyeline match shot of the doll that follows [4].

(1999; editor: Geraldine Peroni), where the chaotic jumping back and forth among three simultaneous actions (the production of Orson Welles's *The Cradle Will Rock*, the destruction of a Diego Rivera mural in Rockefeller Center, and a mock funeral parade in the streets) signifies nothing more than vigorous editing—it can be disorienting to the viewer.

Intercutting refers to editing of two or more actions taking place at the same time but with the difference that it creates the effect of a single scene rather than of two distinct actions. Nicholas Roeg's thriller *Don't Look Now* (1973; editor: Graeme Clifford) contains an explicit sexual scene between John and Laura Baxter (Donald Sutherland and Julie Christie). The two, long devastated by the death of a daughter, are having sex for the first time since the tragedy. Yet, because the highly erotic shots are intercut with shots of the couple's postcoital routine of getting dressed for dinner afterward, there is also something matter-of-fact, even comic, about this scene. The editing combines the pre- and postcoital moments into one unforgettable sequence that leaves its meaning up to the viewer. Steven Soderbergh pays tribute to this classic scene with a similar one between Jack Foley (George Clooney) and Karen Sisco (Jennifer Lopez) in *Out of Sight* (1998; editor: Anne V. Coates).

Parallel editing and crosscutting permit us to experience at least two sides of related actions, and both have long been very familiar conventions in chase or rescue sequences (as we saw earlier in D. W. Griffith's *Way Down East* [1920]; see page 9). Intercutting brings together two directly related actions, often slowing them down or speeding them up, and sometimes omitting some action that might have occurred between the two actions, thus also creating a sort of ellipsis.

Point-of-View Editing   As we saw in the discussion of the point-of-view shot in Alfred Hitchcock's *The Birds* (1963; see page 185), **point-of-view editing** is used to cut from shot A (a point-of-view shot, with the character looking toward something off-screen) directly to shot B (using a match-on-action shot or an eyeline match shot of what the character is actually looking at). Point-of-view editing is editing of *subjective* shots that show a scene exactly the way the character sees it; be careful not to confuse point-of-view editing with, say, the eyeline match cut, which joins two comparatively *objective* shots, made perhaps by an omniscient camera.

In *Rear Window* (1954; editor: George Tomasini), Hitchcock uses a similar editing technique, this time alternating between shot A (taken from the character's point of view) and shot B (taken from an omniscient camera). In an early scene, Hitchcock alternates subjective and omniscient points of view in an ABABAB pattern. As we watch the temporarily sidelined photographer L. B. "Jeff" Jeffries (James Stewart) sitting near the window of his apartment and watching the activities of his neighbors, one of whom he believes has committed a murder, we begin to realize that this movie is partly about what constitutes the boundaries of our perceptions and how ordinary seeing can easily become snooping, even voyeurism.

To emphasize this concept, one of the movie's principal design motifs is the frame within a frame—established when we see the opening titles

Point-of-View Editing   Alternating subjective and omniscient POVs in Alfred Hitchcock's *Rear Window* (1954): [1, 3, 5, 7] From his wheelchair, L. B. "Jeff" Jeffries (James Stewart) observes his neighbors: [2] a dancer (Georgine Darcy), known as Miss Torso; [4] a sculptor (Jesslyn Fax), known as Miss Hearing Aid because she adjusts hers to silence the noise of Miss Torso's dancing; [6] a songwriter (Ross Bagdasarian); and [8] Lars Thorwald (Raymond Burr) and his wife, Anna (Irene Winston).

framed within a three-panel window frame, in which blinds are raised automatically to reveal the setting outside. Similarly, Jeffries, immobilized in his chair by a broken leg, has his vision limited by the height and position of his chair, as well as by the window frame. This frame within a frame (or inner frame) is used throughout the movie, determining—along with the point-of-view editing—what we see, and further defining the idea of perception that is at the movie's core.

Hitchcock's use of these two basic camera points of view—the omniscient POV and the single character's POV—is often heightened by Jeffries's use of his binoculars or his camera's telephoto lens. These POVs complement, even mirror, one another and are reinforced by the point-of-view editing, which continually keeps us aware of one of the movie's developing meanings: not to trust completely what anyone or any camera sees.

Other Transitions Between Shots

The Jump Cut   The **jump cut** presents an instantaneous advance in the action—a sudden, perhaps illogical, often disorienting *ellipsis* between two shots caused by the absence of a portion of the film that would have provided continuity. Because such a jump in time can occur either on purpose or because the filmmakers have failed to follow continuity principles, this type of cut has sometimes been regarded more as an error than as an expressive technique of shooting and editing.

In one of the first major films of the French New Wave—*Breathless* (1960; editors: Cécile Decugis and Lila Herman)—Jean-Luc Godard employs the jump cut deliberately and effectively to create the movie's syncopated rhythm. In one scene, for exam-

1

2

3

4

5

6

7

8

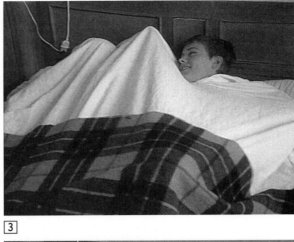

1

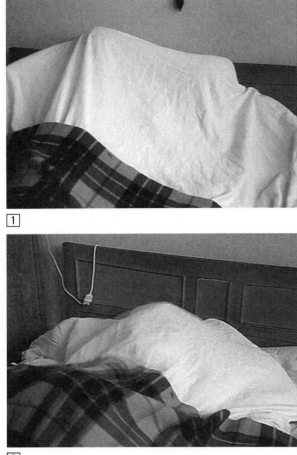

2

3

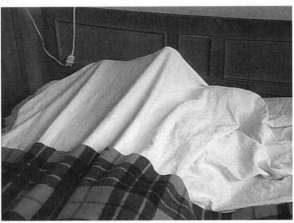

4

Jump Cut   In the hands of director Jean-Luc Godard, the jump cut creates a disregard for continuity but at the same time establishes a tempo that provides structure to the action. In this scene from *Breathless* (1960), Michel Poiccard (Jean-Paul Belmondo) and Patricia Franchini (Jean Seberg) are in bed together, talking under the covers. The fragments of their inconsequential conversation are linked by jump cuts between four images. [1] She says, "I see my reflection in your eyes." [2] From a slightly wider camera angle we see them rolling around under the covers. Michel says, "I'm laughing because this is truly a Franco-American encounter." [3] Patricia, head outside the covers, says, "We'll hide like elephants when they're happy." [4] Both are again under the covers, as Michel says, "A woman's hips . . . this really gets me."

ple, Michel Poiccard (Jean-Paul Belmondo) and Patricia Franchini (Jean Seberg) are in bed together under the covers. As she says, "I see my reflection in your eyes," there is a jump cut to a slightly wider angle as they roll around under the covers. This cut establishes a pattern: Another remark; another jump cut to Patricia's head alone outside the sheets. Another remark; another jump cut to the couple under the covers again.

New Wave stylistic elements—such as the jump cut and the *freeze-frame* (which we'll discuss later)—had an important influence on the New American Cinema of the 1970s, including Arthur Penn's *Bonnie and Clyde* (1967; editor: Dede Allen) and Sam Peckinpah's *The Wild Bunch* (1969; editor: Lou Lombardo), by introducing new cinematic techniques to supplant the conventions that had dominated filmmaking since the 1930s. In *Buffalo '66* (1998; editor: Curtiss Clayton), Vincent Gallo uses a sequence of jump cuts to emphasize the extreme physical discomfort that Billy Brown (Gallo) feels as he tries vainly to find an open men's room in a bus station. As the jump cuts separate each unsuccessful effort, we get a sense of the station's enormous size and we come to understand that its facilities are closed at night for cleaning, but still, because of the jumpiness of the images, we empathize with Billy's predicament.

Fade The **fade-in** and **fade-out** are transitional devices that allow the opening or closing of a scene slowly. In a fade-*in*, a shot appears out of a black screen and grows gradually brighter; in a fade-*out*, a shot grows rapidly darker until the screen turns black for a moment. Traditionally, such fades have suggested a break in time, place, or action.

Fades can be used *within* a scene, as in John Boorman's *The General* (1998; editor: Ron Davis). Martin Cahill, aka "The General" (Brendan Gleeson), is one of Dublin's most notorious criminals, as famous for his audacious capers as he is for his ability to outwit the police. In one scene, he enters the house of a wealthy couple when almost everyone is asleep and steals several valuable items. The scene opens with a fade-in and closes with a fade-out; in between are eleven brief segments, each separated by a fade-out or fade-in. Cahill's stealth and self-confidence are underscored by the almost buoyant rhythm of these fades, and his evident arrogance and satisfaction are echoed on the sound track: Van Morrison's "So Quiet in Here," which contains the lyric "This must be what paradise is like, it's so peaceful in here, so quiet." The fades convey both the passage of time and the character's thoughts.

Fades can also be used *between* scenes, as in Ingmar Bergman's *Cries and Whispers* (1972; editor: Siv Lundgren). In this dreamlike movie, Agnes

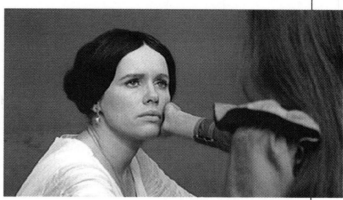

[1]

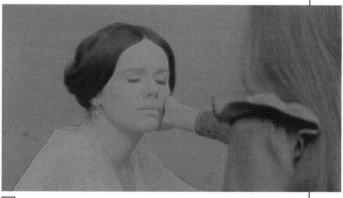

[2]

[3]

Fade-in and Fade-out In *Cries and Whispers* (1972), Ingmar Bergman builds the emotional intensity of his story by cutting back and forth between scenes of the past and the present, and ending most of those scenes with a fade-out to a blood-red screen. Bergman has said that he thinks of red as the color of the human soul, but it also functions here as a symbolic system that has much to do with the film's focus on women. Just before this brief scene, Agnes (Rosanna Mariano, playing her as a child) has been hiding behind a curtain watching her mother (Liv Ullmann, who also plays Agnes's sister); when her mother sees Agnes, she summons the girl to her side. Agnes fears that she will be reprimanded, but instead Bergman gives us a moment of great simplicity and tenderness that unfolds in three shots: [1] Agnes touches her mother; [2] her mother is moved by the caress; [3] the image fades to the blood-red screen. Can we find words to explain the purpose of this fade-out to red?

(Harriet Andersson) is dying, attended by her two sisters, Karin (Ingrid Thulin) and Maria (Liv Ullmann), and a servant, Anna (Kari Sylwan). Color is central to understanding the fades and the film, for the predominant reds hold a key to its meanings, suggesting the cycles of life, love, and death with which the story is concerned. Whole rooms are painted red, and the plot, which moves back and forth across the lives of these women, is punctuated with frequent fades to a completely blood-red screen (sometimes the next scene begins with a fade-in from such a red screen).

Dissolve   Also called a *lap dissolve*, the **dissolve** is a transitional device in which shot B, superimposed, gradually appears over shot A and begins to replace it midway through the process. Like the fades described in the preceding section, the dissolve is essentially a transitional cut, primarily one that shows the passing of time or implies a connection or relationship between what we see in shot A and shot B. But it is different from a fade in that the process occurs simultaneously on the screen, whereas a black screen separates the two parts of the fade. Fast dissolves can imply a rapid change of time or a dramatic contrast between the two parts of the dissolve. Slow dissolves can mean a gradual change of time or a less dramatic contrast.

In John Ford's *My Darling Clementine* (1946; editor: Dorothy Spencer), a dissolve establishes a thematic connection between its parts. In the first scene, on the prairie outside of Tombstone, Wyatt Earp (Henry Fonda) and his brothers discuss the troublemakers who have killed their younger brother. After a fast dissolve to the wide-open town of Tombstone, we instinctively understand that the troublemakers might be there. This dissolve makes an important connection for our understanding of Earp, who quells a ruckus in a saloon and, as a result, is made the town's sheriff.

Wipe   Like the dissolve and the fade, the **wipe** is a transitional device—often indicating a change of time, place, or location—in which shot B wipes across shot A vertically, horizontally, or diagonally to replace it. A line between the two shots suggests something like a windshield wiper. A soft-edge wipe is indicated by a blurry line; a hard-edge wipe, by a sharp line. A jagged line suggests a more violent transition.

Although the device reminds us of early eras in filmmaking, directors continue to use it. In fact, some directors use it to call to mind these earlier eras. In *Star Wars* (1977; editors: Richard Chew, Paul Hirsch, and Marcia Lucas), for example, George Lucas refers to old-time science fiction serials that inspired him by using a right-to-left horizontal wipe as a transition between the scene in which Luke Skywalker (Mark Hamill) meets Ben Obi-Wan Kenobi (Alec Guinness) and a scene on Darth Vader's (David Prowse) battle station.

Iris Shot   In the **iris shot**, everything is blacked out except for what is seen through a keyhole, telescope, crack in the wall, or binoculars, depending on the actual shape of the iris or the point of view with which the viewer is expected to identify. Sometimes, of course, the point of view is that of the director, who wants to call our attention to this heightened way of seeing. Tom Tykwer's *Heaven* (2002; editor: Mathilde Bonnefoy) contains a superb iris shot: Two fugitives, Philippa (Cate Blanchett) and Filippo (Giovanni Ribisi), board a train, riding with their backs to the train's direction. When it enters a tunnel, the screen turns black, but after a moment or two, a tiny light appears at the end of the otherwise black tunnel. This iris shot grows as quickly as the train is moving toward it, then opens out in a burst of color as the train continues its journey through the golden Tuscan countryside.

The **iris-in** and **iris-out**—named after the iris diaphragm, which controls the amount of light passing through a camera lens—are wipe effects (made in a special-effects laboratory, not in the camera) in which the wipe line is usually a circle. Thus, the iris-in, which brings a shot gradually into view, begins with a small circle that expands to a partial or full image; the iris-out, which gradually closes an image, works in the reverse direction. When used to open out or close down to a partial image, an iris shot can approximate a close-up that is isolated within an otherwise dark frame.

Employed to great advantage by D. W. Griffith

[1]

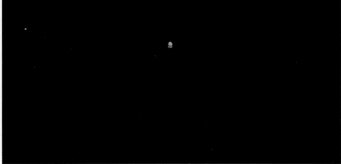

[2]

[3]

Iris-in Shot   In *Heaven* (2002), director Tom Tykwer plays with the idea of the iris shot by having the viewer see what the characters cannot. They are riding with their backs to the train's direction [1]; the camera is theoretically mounted on the front of the train, so they cannot see the light at the end of the dark tunnel [2] or the burst of scenic color as the train leaves the tunnel [3].

Iris-out Shot   In this shot from Robert Weine's *The Cabinet of Dr. Caligari* (1920), Jane (Lil Dagover) begins a search for her father, whom she does not yet know is suspected by the police of murder. Hers is a lonely endeavor, emphasized by isolating her in this shot which irises-out into a continuation of the action that shows her still isolated on one of the painted sets characteristic of the expressionist movie. In this use of the sepia-tinted iris-out shot, Weine was influenced by the work of D. W. Griffith, who pioneered the use of these stylistic conventions a few years earlier.

and other early filmmakers, this effect is used less widely today because of the fluidity with which editors can cut between close-ups and other shots, but it remains a very expressive design figure. Some directors—such as Steven Spielberg, Francis Ford Coppola, and Martin Scorsese—use it to pay homage to their predecessors. In *The Night of the Hunter* (1955; editor: Robert Golden), Charles Laughton uses the iris-out both for its own sake and perhaps as homage to Griffith and Lillian Gish, who plays a main character in the movie and was a frequent star of Griffith's films.

Freeze-Frame   The **freeze-frame** (also called *stop-frame* or *hold-frame*) is a still image within a movie, created by repetitive printing in the laboratory of the same frame so that it can be seen without movement for whatever length of time the filmmaker desires. It stops time and functions somewhat like an exclamation point in a sentence, halting our perception of movement to call attention

[1]

[2]

[3]

Freeze-Frame Freeze-frames are often used to underscore a significant emotional change in a character—to "freeze" time, as it were, for the character's reflection on what's happening. In the final moments of François Truffaut's *The 400 Blows* (1959), Antoine Doinel (Jean-Pierre Léaud), having escaped from reform school, arrives at a beach. Doinel runs along the shore, the camera following, until he abruptly turns and heads straight toward the camera. The freeze-frame [1] that ends the movie clearly doesn't tell us where Doinel goes next, but it conveys just how unsure he feels, here and now, about the possibilities that surround him. In Alfonso Cuarón's *Y tu mamá también*, Julio Zapata (Gael García Bernal) feels "great pain" at learning of his best friend's betrayal in having sex with an older woman whom Julio adores, and he sinks below the surface of the leaf-filled swimming pool [2] to think about it. [3] During this freeze-frame from Martin Scorsese's *Goodfellas* (1990), we actually hear young Henry Hill (Christopher Serrone) tell us what he thinks of his father's beating him for being a truant from school and working for the mob: "I didn't care. The way I saw it, everybody takes a beating sometimes." At roughly the same age as the other two boys described here, Henry has the greater self-realization at this moment of epiphany in his life.

change that comes with autumn; the screen freezes as we hear a rooster crowing, underscoring Julio's realization of change.

Cuarón uses the freeze-frame here, in all likelihood, to pay homage to one of the most famous uses of the freeze-frame: the conclusion of François Truffaut's *The 400 Blows* (1959; editor: Marie-Josèphe Yoyotte). The poignant freeze-frame close-up of young Antoine Doinel (Jean-Pierre Léaud) that concludes that movie not only stops his movement on a beach, but also points toward the uncertainty of his future. In both examples, the freeze-frame ironically underscores a significant emotional change in the characters depicted.

Martin Scorsese uses the freeze-frame in *Goodfellas* (1990; editors: Thelma Schoonmaker and James Y. Kwei) to show a character who actually acknowledges an emotional change as it is happening. The scene begins with young Henry Hill (Christopher Serrone) doing odd jobs for the mob, his offscreen narration telling us that this makes him feel like a grown-up. At home, when Henry lies about his school attendance, his father (Beau Starr) savagely beats him with a belt. During an unusually long freeze-frame (fifteen seconds) that suspends the beating, Henry continues

to an image. In Alfonso Cuarón's *Y tu mamá también* (2001; editors: Cuarón and Alex Rodríguez), it is used to emphasize an important moment of passage in a young man's life. Julio Zapata (Gael García Bernal) has just felt what he calls "great pain" at learning of his best friend's getting the advantage over him with a woman they both desire. He retreats to a swimming pool. In an overhead shot, we see him sink underwater through a surface covering of brown leaves, a traditional symbol of the his narration, and then the violence resumes. The effect is ironic: while the film "stops" the violence (as Henry's mother cannot) so that we linger on its wrath, the boy continues his narration in a matter-of-fact voice suggesting his awareness that domestic violence and mob violence are now part of his life.

Split Screen The **split screen**, which has been in mainstream use since Phillips Smalley and Lois Weber's *Suspense* (1913), produces an effect that is similar to parallel editing in its ability to tell two or more stories at the same cinematic time, whether or not they are actually happening at the same time or even in the same place. Among its most familiar uses is to portray both participants in a telephone conversation simultaneously on the screen. Unlike parallel editing, however, which cuts back and forth between shots for contrast, the split screen can tell multiple stories within the same frame.

In *Napoléon* (1927; editor: Gance), Abel Gance introduced Polyvision, a multiscreen technique, as in the epic pillow fight between the young Napoleon (Vladimir Roudenko) and other boys in their school dormitory. The fight begins on a single screen; continues on a screen split into four equal parts, then on one split into nine equal parts; reaches its climax on a single screen with multiple, superimposed full-size images; and ends, as it began, on a single screen. Other movies in which the split screen has been used significantly and effectively include Paul Morrissey and Andy Warhol's *Chelsea Girls* (1966; editing uncredited), Norman Jewison's *The Thomas Crown Affair* (1968; editors: Hal Ashby, Byron Brandt, and Ralph E. Winters), Michael Wadleigh's *Woodstock* (1970; editors: Thelma Schoonmaker, et al.), Richard L. Bare's *Wicked, Wicked* (1973; editor: John F. Schreyer), George Lucas's *American Graffiti* (1973; editors: Verna Fields and Marcia Lucas), Brian De Palma's *The Bonfire of the Vanities* (1990; editors: Beth Jochem Besterveld, Bill Pankow, and David Ray), Guy Ritchie's *Snatch* (2000; editor: Jon

Harris), Mike Figgis's *Timecode* (2000; editing uncredited), and Quentin Tarantino's *Kill Bill: Vol. 1* and *Vol. 2* (2003–04; editor: Sally Menke).

Perhaps the most ambitious use of the split screen in the history of cinema is found in Duncan Roy's *AKA* (2002; editors: Lawrence Catford, John Cross, and Jackie Ophir). This film tells the story of a British, gay, working-class young man—Dean Page/Lord Gryffoyn (Matthew Leitch)—who wants a life different from the one into which he was born. After he insinuates himself into upper-class society posing as a lord, he ends up in jail for credit card fraud. The entire film was shot by multiple cameras; the resulting footage was edited not as single shots, but compiled into triptychs, with three panels appearing simultaneously on the screen, each shot (panel) taken from a different angle and revealing a different aspect of the action.

The entire movie is told through these continuous triptychs. Each one shapes the story in a way we've never seen before, and, consequently, these triptychs create a movie that challenges almost everything we know about looking at movies, especially their handling of time. In one scene, for example, the left-hand panel is a long shot of Dean talking with his mother, Georgie (Lindsey Coulson), at the kitchen table; the center panel is a close-up of the mother at a slightly different angle; the right-hand panel, a medium shot of Dean's stepfather, Brian (Geoff Bell), running upstairs to his stepson's bedroom, where he begins to abuse him sexually. The first two images take place simultaneously, but the third occurs at a later (or earlier) time. Sometimes these triptychs imply a cause-and-effect relationship among the three panels; other times they simply provide three different perspectives on, say, a glamorous party. Compelling as this is, it is ultimately an experimental technique that has limited usefulness in mainstream cinema. (Note: The full triptych version of *AKA* was screened only in theaters; the DVD release is a full-screen version that contains only one triptych segment.)

→ Analyzing Editing

When we watch a movie, we *see* the mise-en-scène, design, and acting; we *hear* the dialogue, music, and sound effects; but we *feel* the editing, which has the power to affect us directly or indirectly. Good editing—editing that produces the filmmakers' desired effects—results from the editor's intuition in choosing the right length of each shot, the right rhythm of each scene, the right moment for cutting to create the right spatial, temporal, visual, and rhythmic relationships between shots A and B. In answer to the question "What is a good cut?" Walter Murch says,

> At the top of the list is Emotion . . . the hardest thing to define and deal with. *How do you want the audience to feel*? If they are feeling what you want them to feel all the way through the film, you've done about as much as you can ever do. What they finally remember is not the editing, not the camerawork, not the per-formances, not even the story—it's how they felt.[5]

As a viewer, you can best understand the overall effects of an editor's deci-sions by studying a film as a creative whole. But you can most effectively *ana-lyze* an editor's contributions to a film by examining individual scenes, paying attention to the ways in which individual shots have been edited together. Indeed, the principles of editing are generally most evident within the parts that make up the whole.

[5] Walter Murch, *In the Blink of an Eye: A Perspective on Film Editing* (Los Angeles: Silman-James Press, 1995), 18.

Screening Checklist: Editing

➤ Does the editing overall seem to create *conti-nuity* or *discontinuity*? If the editing is mostly creating continuity, are there nonetheless moments when the editing creates discontinu-ity? What is the significance of those moments?

➤ As each shot cuts to the next shot in the movie or clip, tap your finger on a tabletop or other surface, to get a feeling for the *rhythm* of the editing. How would you describe that rhythm? Does it stay constant, or does it speed up or slow down? How does the rhythm affect your emotional response to the movie?

➤ Keep track of the types of *transitions* from shot to shot. Does the editor use one transi-tional effect more than others? Are the tran-sitions seamless and nearly unnoticeable, or do they call attention to themselves?

➤ Look for the different types of *match cuts* in the film. What sort of visual or narrative infor-mation is each match cut conveying?

➤ Are there any moments in the movie in which the traditional conventions of Hollywood *con-tinuity editing*—including use of the master shot, the 180-degree system, shot/reverse shot, match cuts, and parallel editing—are violated in some way? Describe how these moments appear onscreen. What do you think is the significance of these moments in the film?

➤ Does the editing seem to indicate what the filmmakers want the audience to *feel*? What is that intended feeling? Do you feel it? Is it an appropriate feeling for the narrative and themes of the movie?

Questions for Review

1. What is *editing*? Why is it regarded as a *language*?

2. What is the *basic building block* of film editing? What is film editing's *fundamental tool*?

3. What are the film editor's principal responsibilities?

4. What is *continuity editing*? What does it contribute to a movie?

5. What is the purpose of the *180-degree system*? How does it work?

6. What is *discontinuity editing*? Given the dominance of continuity editing in mainstream filmmaking, what role does discontinuity editing usually play?

7. Name and describe the various types of *match cuts*.

8. How does the match cut differ from and compare to *parallel editing*?

9. What is a *jump cut*? What is the typical effect of a jump cut on a viewer?

10. Given the magnitude of the editor's overall responsibility during the postproduction stage of filmmaking, why is it considered desirable, if not essential, that the editor also collaborate during the preproduction phase?

DVD FEATURES: CHAPTER 6

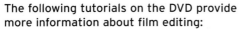

The following tutorials on the DVD provide more information about film editing:

- *The Kuleshov Experiment* Experiment
- The Evolution of Editing
- The 180-Degree Rule
- Editing Techniques in *Snapshot*

Movies Described or Illustrated in This Chapter

Adaptation (2002). Spike Jonze, director.

AKA (2002). Duncan Roy, director.

Apocalypse Now (1979). Francis Ford Coppola, director.

Battleship Potemkin (1925). Sergei Eisenstein, director.

Boys Don't Cry (1999). Kimberly Peirce, director.

Breathless (1960). Jean-Luc Godard, director.

Buffalo '66 (1998). Vincent Gallo, director.

Cradle Will Rock (1999). Tim Robbins, director.

Cries and Whispers (1972). Ingmar Bergman, director.

Don't Look Now (1973). Nicholas Roeg, director.

Drugstore Cowboy (1989). Gus Van Sant, director.

Erin Brockovich (2000). Steven Soderbergh, director.

Eternal Sunshine of the Spotless Mind (2004). Michel Gondry, director.

The Five Obstructions (2004). Jørgen Leth and Lars von Trier, directors.

The 400 Blows (1959). François Truffaut, director.

The General (1998). John Boorman, director.

Goodfellas (1990). Martin Scorsese, director.

Heaven (2002). Tom Tykwer, director.

The Insider (1999). Michael Mann, director.

The Limey (1999). Steven Soderbergh, director.

Memento (2000). Christopher Nolan, director.

My Darling Clementine (1946). John Ford, director.

Napoléon (1927). Abel Gance, director.

The Night of the Hunter (1955). Charles Laughton, director.

Now, Voyager (1942). Irving Rapper, director.

Once Upon a Time in the West (1968; director's cut DVD version released 2003). Sergio Leone, director.

Out of Sight (1998). Steven Soderbergh, director.

Psycho (1960). Alfred Hitchcock, director.

Raising Arizona (1987). Joel Coen, director.

Rear Window (1954). Alfred Hitchcock, director.

Requiem for a Dream (2000). Darren Aronofsky, director.

Run Lola Run (1998). Tom Tykwer, director.

Rushmore (1998). Wes Anderson, director.

Star Wars (1977). George Lucas, director.

Team America: World Police (2004). Trey Parker, director.

2001: A Space Odyssey (1968). Stanley Kubrick, director.

Vertigo (1958). Alfred Hitchcock, director.

Y tu mamá también (2001). Alfonso Cuarón, director.

Sound 7

Ray (2004), Taylor Hackford, director; Steve Cantamessa, sound designer.

Learning Objectives

After reading this chapter, you should be able to

➤ Explain the assumptions influencing contemporary *sound design*.

➤ Differentiate among *sound recording*, *sound editing*, and *sound mixing*.

➤ Describe the difference between *diegetic* and *nondiegetic* sound.

➤ Understand the perceptual characteristics of sound: *pitch*, *loudness*, and *quality*.

➤ Name and define the principal *sources* of film sound.

➤ Distinguish between the four major *types* of film sound.

➤ Explain the *functions* of film sound.

➤ Describe how sound can call attention to both the *spatial* and *temporal* dimensions of a scene.

➤ Explain how sound helps to create meaning in a movie.

What Is Sound?

The movies engage two senses: vision and hearing. Although some viewers and even filmmakers assume that the cinematographic image is paramount, what we *hear* from the screen can be at least as significant as what we see on it, and sometimes what we hear is more significant. Director Steven Spielberg says, "The eye sees better when the sound is great." Sound—talking, laughing, singing, music, and the aural effects of objects and settings—can be as expressive as any of the other narrative and stylistic elements of cinematic form. What we hear in a movie is often technologically more complicated to produce than what we see. In fact, because of the constant advances in digital technology, sound may be the most intensively creative part of contemporary moviemaking. Spielberg, for one, has also said that, since the 1970s, breakthroughs in sound have been the movie industry's most important technical and creative innovations. He means not the sort of gimmicky sound that takes your attention away from the story being told—"using the technology to show off"—but rather sound used as an integral storytelling element.[1]

Stanley Kubrick's *The Shining* (1980; sound: Dino Di Campo, Jack T. Knight, and Wyn Ryder) opens with a series of helicopter point-of-view shots that, without the accompanying sound, might be mistaken for a TV commercial. In these shots we see a magnificent landscape, a river, and then a yellow Volkswagen driving upward into the mountains on a winding highway. Whereas we might expect to hear a purring car engine, car wheels rolling over asphalt, or the passengers' conversation, instead we hear music: an electronic synthesis by composers Wendy Carlos and Rachel Elkind of the *Dies Irae*, one of the most famous melodies of the Gregorian chant that became the fundamental music of the Roman Catholic Church. The *Dies Irae* (literally, "the day of wrath") is based on Zephaniah 1:14–16, a reflection on the Last Judgment, and is one section of the Requiem Mass, or mass for the dead. Experiencing the shots together with the sound track, we wonder about the location, the driver, and the destination. What we hear gives life to what we see and offers some clues to its meaning. The symbolic import and emotional impact of this music transforms the footage into a movie pulsating with ominous energy and dramatic potential.

After the opening credits of Terrence Malick's *Days of Heaven* (1978; sound: James Cox, et al.), we see Bill (Richard Gere) working in a Chicago steel mill, where the sounds of the manufacturing process are so loud that we cannot hear what Bill or the foreman say when they begin to fight with one another. This ambient sound may be true to the actual noises in such a factory, but by sustaining its loudness at this level, the director lets us know that the sound is more important than the dialogue, more important even than what we see. He thereby creates a scene that illustrates as clearly and concisely as possible that the sounds of Bill's impersonal, alienating, and unhealthy working conditions correspond to his anger, which makes him strike and kill his boss. Indeed, this scene establishes the frustration and violence that will characterize Bill.

[1] Rick Lyman, "A Director's Journey Into a Darkness of the Heart," *New York Times*, June 24, 2001, sec. 2, p. 24.

Sound as Meaning   In the opening scene of Terrence Malick's *Days of Heaven* (1978), Bill (Richard Gere, *left*), a steel mill worker, confronts the foreman (Stuart Margolin, *right*), whom he impetuously kills soon after. Throughout this scene, the loud, maddening industrial noise matches the intensity of the furnace, whose heat we can practically feel; the characters' surroundings thus enlighten us about and even represent their internal states. In later scenes, sound plays equally expressive roles: a haunting silence accompanies shots of windswept fields, the dialogue seems as natural as the acting looks (perhaps, in both cases, thanks to improvisation), and Ennio Morricone's understated score combines his own music with expressionist pieces by the French Romantic composer Camille Saint-Saëns (performed by the Vienna Philharmonic Orchestra), contemporary American folk guitarist Leo Kottke, and contemporary American Cajun/country singer Doug Kershaw.

The sound in the scenes just described (or in any movie scene) operates on both physical and psychological levels. For most narrative films, sound provides cues that help us form expectations about meaning; in some cases, sound actually shapes our analyses and interpretations. Sound calls attention not only to itself but also to silence, to the various roles that each plays in our world and in the world of a film. The option of using silence is one crucial difference between silent and sound films; a sound film can emphasize silence, but a silent film has no option. As light and dark create the image, so sound and silence create the sound track. Each property—light, dark, sound, silence—appeals to our senses differently.

Like every other component of film form, film sound is the product of very specific decisions by the filmmakers. The group responsible for the sound in movies—the **sound crew**—generates and controls

the sound physically, manipulating its properties to produce the effects that the director desires. Let's look more closely at the various aspects of sound production controlled by the sound crew.

Sound Production

Sound production consists of four phases: *design, recording, editing,* and *mixing.* Although we might suppose that the majority of sounds in a movie are the result of recording during filming (such sounds are called *production sounds*), the reality is that most film sounds are constructed during the post-production phase (and thus are called *postproduction sounds*). But before any sounds are recorded or constructed, the overall plan for a movie's sound must be planned. That planning process is called *sound design.*

Design

Sound design, or creating the sound for a film, has in the past been the responsibility of a sound crew composed of the artists and technicians who record, edit, and mix its component parts into the **sound track**. In conventional filmmaking with film stock, the sound track is a narrow band to one side of the image on which the sound is recorded. In digital filmmaking, depending on the recording method being used, the sound track basically consists of a digital code being placed somewhere on the digital recording medium. (Sound recorded with the Dolby system further requires a theater equipped with a Dolby playback system.)

As motion picture sound has become increasingly innovative and complex, as a result of comprehensive sound design, the role of the sound designer has become more well known. Given its name by film editor Walter Murch, *sound design* combines the crafts of editing and mixing and, like them, involves matters both theoretical and practical.[2] Although many filmmakers continue to understand

[2] Randy Thom, "Designing a Movie for Sound," 1998, <www.filmsound.org/articles/designing_for_soundelder.htm> (accessed February 4, 2006).

and manipulate sound in conventional ways, sound design has produced major advances in how movies are conceived, made, viewed, and interpreted. Prior to the 1970s, the vast majority of producers and directors thought about sound only after the picture was shot. They did not design films with sound in mind and, frequently, did not fully recognize that decisions about art direction, composition, lighting, cinematography, and acting would ultimately influence how sound tracks would be created and mixed. They considered sound satisfactory if it could distract from or cover up mistakes in shooting and create the illusion that the audience was hearing what it was seeing. They considered sound *great* if it was loud, either in earsplitting sound effects or in a heavily orchestrated musical score.

By contrast, the contemporary concept of sound design rests on the following basic assumptions:

> Sound should be integral to all three phases of film production (preproduction, production, and postproduction), not an afterthought to be added in postproduction only.
> A film's sound is potentially as expressive as its images.
> Image and sound can create different worlds.
> Image and sound are co-expressible.

Thus, sound is not subordinate to image.

A sound designer treats the sound track of a film the way a painter treats a canvas. That is, for each shot, after all the necessary sounds are identified in terms of the story and plot, the designer starts by laying in all the background tones (different tones equal different colors) to create the support necessary for adding the specific sounds that help the scene to function. According to Tomlinson Holman (the creator of Lucasfilm's THX technology), "sound design is the art of getting the right sound in the right place at the right time."[3] Today, many directors—Joel Coen and David Lynch, among others—are notable for their comprehensive knowledge and expressive use of sound.

Prior to the wide acceptance of sound design,

the responsibilities for sound were divided among recording, rerecording, editing, mixing, and sound effects crews; these crews sometimes overlapped but often did not. In attempting to integrate all aspects of sound in a movie, from planning to postproduction, the *sound designer* supervises all these responsibilities—a development that was initially resented by many traditional sound specialists, who felt their autonomy was being compromised. It is now conventional for sound designers (or supervising sound editors) to oversee the creation and control of the sounds (and silences) we hear in movies. They are, in a sense, advocates for sound.

During preproduction, sound designers encourage directors and other collaborators to understand that what characters hear is potentially as significant as what they see—especially in point-of-view shots, which focus characters' (and audiences') attention on specific sights or sounds. Sound designers encourage screenwriters to consider all kinds of sound; working with directors, they indicate in shooting scripts what voices, sounds, or music may be appropriate at particular points. They also urge their collaborators to plan the settings, lighting, cinematography plan, and acting (particularly the movement of actors within the settings) with an awareness of how their decisions might affect sound. During production, sound designers supervise the implementation of the sound design. During postproduction, after the production sound track has been cut along with the images, they aid the editing team. But although their results may far exceed the audience's expectations of clarity and fidelity, sound designers keep their eyes and ears on the story being told. They want audiences not only to regard sound tracks as seriously as they do visual images but also to interpret sounds as integral to understanding those images.

Recording

The process of recording sound for the movies is very similar to the process of hearing. Just as the human ear converts sounds into nerve impulses that the brain identifies, so the microphone converts sound waves into electrical signals that are

[3] Tomlinson Holman, *Sound for Film and Television* (Boston: Focal Press, 1997), 172.

then recorded and stored. The history of recording movie sound has evolved from optical and magnetic systems to the digital systems preferred today in professional productions. The **digital format** offers greater flexibility in recording, editing, and mixing and thus is fast becoming the standard. Of the various types of *film sound* (which will be described later in the chapter), dialogue is the only type typically recorded during production. Everything else is added in the *editing* and *mixing* stages of postproduction.

The recording of production sound is the responsibility of the *production sound mixer* and a team of assistants, which includes, on the set, a sound recordist, a sound mixer, a microphone **boom** operator, and gaffers (in charge of the power supply, electrical connections, and cables). This team must place and/or move the microphones so that the sound corresponds to the space between actors and camera and the dialogue will be as free from background noise as possible. **Double-system recording** is the standard technique of recording film sound on a medium separate from the picture. At one time, sound was recorded directly on the film, but now the various media used to record sound include digital audiotape, compact discs, or computer hard drives. This system, which synchronizes sound and image, allows both for maximum quality control and for the manifold manipulation of sound during postproduction editing, mixing, and synchronization. Once the sound has been recorded and stored, the process of editing it begins.

WEB Vocal Performances in Film: Recording Technology and Techniques

Editing

The *editor* is responsible for the overall process of editing and for the sound crew, which consists of a supervising sound editor, sound editors (who usually concentrate on their specialties: dialogue, music, or sound effects), sound mixers, rerecording mixers, sound effects personnel, and Foley artists. The editor also works closely with the musical composer or those responsible for the selection of music from other sources. In the editing room, the

ADR in Action   For the American version of Hayao Miyazaki's animated movie *Spirited Away* (2001), it was necessary to rerecord the characters' voices using English-speaking actors and the ADR (automatic dialogue replacement) system. Here, Jason Marsden (the voice of Haku), standing in front of a microphone and holding his script, lip-synchs his lines to coordinate with the action on the monitor in the background.

editor is in charge, but producers, the director, screenwriters, actors, and the sound designer may also take part in the process. In particular, the producer and director may make major decisions about editing.

The process of editing, of both pictures and sounds, usually lasts longer than the shooting itself. Sound editing takes up a great deal of that time, because a significant portion of the dialogue and all of the sound effects and music are created and/or added during postproduction. Included in this process is adding *Foley sounds* (discussed later in the chapter) for verisimilitude and emphasis, creating and layering ambience with traffic, crowd voices, and other background sounds.

Filmmakers first screen the **dailies** (or *rushes*), which are synchronized picture/sound work prints of a day's shooting; select the usable individual shots from among the multiple takes; sort out the **outtakes** (any footage that will not be used); log the usable footage in order to follow it easily through the rest of the process; and decide which dialogue needs recording or rerecording and which sound effects are necessary. **Rerecording** of sound first recorded on the set (sometimes called *looping* or *dubbing*) can be done manually (with the actors watching the footage, synchronizing their lips with it, and rereading the lines) or, more likely today, by computer through **automatic dialogue replacement** (**ADR**)—a faster, less expensive, and more technically sophisticated process.

If ambient or other noises have marred the quality of the dialogue recorded during photography, the actors are asked to come back, view the scene in question, and perform the dialogue again as closely as possible. When an acceptable rerecording take has been made, an ADR editor inserts it into the movie. Finally, the sound-editing team synchronizes the sound and visual tracks. There can be a certain amount of overlap between the sound editing and mixing stages, facilitated by the fact that the entire editing and mixing process is now done digitally.

Mixing

Mixing is the process of combining different sound tracks onto one composite sound track synchronous with the picture. Each type of sound occupies an individual *sound track*. This term is used in several different ways. Here it refers to a single element (one track for vocals, one for sound effects, one for music, etc.) that can be combined in a multitrack sound design. However, the term is also familiarly used to describe a compilation of music included in a movie and typically released for consumers on a CD.

The number of sound tracks used in a movie depends on the kind and amount of sound needed to tell each part of the story; thus, filmmakers have an unlimited resource at their disposal. No matter how many tracks are used, usually they must be combined and compressed during the final mixing. Working with their crew, sound mixers adjust the loudness and various aspects of sound quality; filter out unwanted sounds; and create, according to the needs of the screenplay, the right balance of dialogue, music, and sound effects. The result may be an "audio mise-en-scène" that allows the filmmaker and the viewer to distinguish between background and significant elements that are arranged in relation to one another.

This process resembles the typical recording process for popular music, in which drums, bass, guitars, vocals, and so on, are recorded separately and then mixed and adjusted to achieve the desired acoustic quality and loudness. The ideal result of sound mixing is clear and clean; that is, whatever the desired effect is, the audience will hear it clearly and cleanly. Even if what the filmmakers want is distorted or cluttered sound, the audience will hear that distortion or clutter perfectly.

With this background on the four basic stages of sound production—the basics of what goes on during sound design, recording, editing, and mixing—we're ready now to look more closely at the actual characteristics that make up the sounds we hear in real life, as well as in the movies.

Describing Film Sound

When talking or writing about a movie's sound, you should be able to describe a sound in terms of its perceptual characteristics (determined by its *pitch*, *loudness*, *quality*, and *fidelity*), its source (where it comes from), and its type (vocal or musical, for example). To that end, let's take a closer look at the perceptual characteristics of sound.

Pitch, Loudness, Quality

The perceptual and physical characteristics of sound are linked as illustrated in Table 7.1. What the table shows in summary form, the discussion that follows explains in detail.

The **pitch** (or *level*) of a sound can be high (like the screech of tires on pavement), low (like the rumble of a boulder barreling downhill), or somewhere between these extremes. Pitch is defined by the **frequency** (or *speed*) with which it is produced (the number of sound waves produced per second). Most sounds fall somewhere in the middle of the scale, but the extremes of high and low, as well as the *distinctions* between high pitch and low pitch, are often exploited by filmmakers to influence our experience and interpretation of a movie.

TABLE 7.1 Connections Between the Perceptual and Physical Characteristics of Sound

Perceptual Characteristics (what we perceive in sound) →	Physical Characteristics ← (what constitutes the sound)
Pitch → (or level) Described as *high* or *low*.	← Frequency (or speed—that is, the number of sound waves produced per second)
Loudness → (or volume or intensity) Described as *loud* or *soft*.	← Amplitude (or degree of motion within the sound wave)
Quality → (or timbre, texture, or color) Described as *simple* or *complex*.	← Harmonic content (or texture resulting from a single sound wave or mix of sound waves)

In Victor Fleming's *The Wizard of Oz* (1939; sound: Douglas Shearer), the voice of the "wizard" has two pitches—the high pitch of the harmless man behind the curtain and the deep, booming pitch of the magnificent "wizard"—each helping us to judge the trustworthiness of the character's statements. Similarly, in the "all work and no play" scene in Stanley Kubrick's *The Shining* (1980), the pitch of the accompanying music changes from low to high to underscore Wendy's (Shelley Duvall) state of mind as she discovers Jack's (Jack Nicholson) writing (the low pitch corresponds to her anxiety and apprehension; the high pitch signals that her anxiety has turned into sheer panic).

Sound propagates through the air in a wave that is acted upon by factors in the physical environment. Think of this as analogous to the wave that ripples outward when you throw a rock into a pond—a wave that is acted upon by the depth and width of the pond. The **loudness** (or *volume* or *intensity*) of a sound depends on its **amplitude**, the degree of motion of the air (or other medium) within the sound wave. The greater the amplitude of the sound wave, the harder it strikes the eardrum, and thus the louder the sound. Again, although movies typically maintain a consistent level of moderate loudness throughout, filmmakers sometimes use the extremes (near silence or

shocking loudness) to signal something important, or to complement the overall mood and tone of a scene. In *The Shining*, during the scene in which Wendy and Jack argue and she strikes him with a baseball bat, Kubrick slowly increases the loudness of all the sounds to call attention to the growing tension.

The **quality** (also known as *timbre*, *texture*, or *color*) of a sound includes those characteristics that enable us to distinguish sounds that have the same pitch and loudness. In music, the same note played at the same volume on three different instruments (say, a piano, violin, and oboe) will produce tones that are identical in frequency and amplitude, but very different in quality. The sound produced by each of these instruments has its own **harmonic content**, which can be measured as wavelengths. In talking about movie sounds, however, we do not need scientific apparatus to measure the harmonic content, because most often we see what we hear.

In the opening sequence of Francis Ford Coppola's *Apocalypse Now* (1979; sound designer: Walter Murch), the sound comes from many sources—including helicopters, the fan in a hotel room, explosions, jungle noises, a smashed mirror, the Doors' recording of "The End," voice-over narration, and dialogue—each of which contributes its own qualities to an overall rich texture. Although

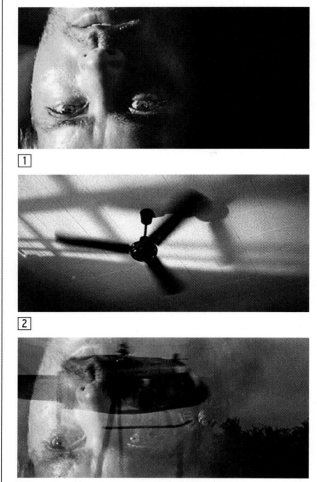

1

2

3

Exploiting the Perceptual and Physical Characteristics of Sound Francis Ford Coppola's *Apocalypse Now* (1979) opens with horrific images of war and continues with a scene of a very agitated Captain Benjamin L. Willard (Martin Sheen) in his Saigon hotel room. The first words in his voice-over narration—"Saigon. Shit!"—introduce the movie's counterintuitive logic. Between missions, Willard is distraught, not because he has not returned home to the United States, but because he is "still only in Saigon." The jungle is where he really wants to be. Intercut with shots of Willard, here seen upside down, are shots of his ceiling fan, the jungle, helicopters, napalm fires, and so on—all of which are represented in a ferocious and hugely ambitious sound track that combines sonic details, noise, dialogue, voice-over, and music. Together, pictures and sound prepare us for many of the movie's key themes, including the hellishness and surreality of the Vietnam War, the devastating power of military technology to destroy human beings and natural resources, and the complex roles within 1960s American society of countercultural forces such as rock music, drugs, and psychedelia.

many of these sounds are distorted or slowed down to characterize both the dreamlike, otherworldly quality of the setting and Captain Benjamin L. Willard's (Martin Sheen) state of mind, they have been recorded and played back with such accuracy that we can easily distinguish among them.

Fidelity

Fidelity is a sound's faithfulness or unfaithfulness to its source. Ang Lee's *The Ice Storm* (1997; sound effects designer: Eugene Gearty) faithfully exploits the sounds of a violent ice storm to underscore the tragic lives of two dysfunctional Connecticut families, the Hoods and the Carvers. At the climax of the movie, in the midst of the storm, Lee meticulously observes the phenomena and records the sounds of icy rain as it falls on the ground or strikes the windows of houses and cars; icy branches that crackle in the wind and crash to the ground; and the crunch of a commuter train's wheels on the icy rails. As the marriage of Ben and Elena Hood (Kevin Kline and Joan Allen), which is already on the rocks, completely falls apart, the ice storm has a powerful, even mystical effect on the lives of these characters, and its harsh breaking sounds not only serve as a metaphor for their frail lives, but also provide an audibly faithful reminder of the power of nature.

Nonfaithful Sound In *Mean Streets* (1973; sound: Glen Glenn), Martin Scorsese uses nonfaithful sound when Charlie (Harvey Keitel), after making love to Teresa (Amy Robinson, *back to camera*), playfully points his fingers at her as if they were a gun and pulls the "trigger." We hear a gunshot, but there is no danger, for this is just a lovers' quarrel.

An excellent early example of a sound effect that is not faithful to its source occurs in Rouben Mamoulian's *Love Me Tonight* (1932; sound: M. M. Paggi). During the farcical scene in which "Baron" Maurice (Maurice Chevalier) tells Princess Jeanette (Jeanette MacDonald), whom he is wooing, that he is not royalty but just an ordinary tailor, pandemonium breaks out in the royal residence. As family and guests flutter about the palace, singing of this deception, one of the princess's old aunts accidentally knocks a vase off a table. As it hits the floor and shatters, we hear the offscreen sound of a bomb exploding, as if to suggest that the social order is under attack.

Sources of Film Sound

By *source*, we mean the location from which a sound originates. Obviously, as mentioned already, most of the sounds heard in a movie literally originate from postproduction processes. But when we talk about source, we're speaking of the *implied* origin of that sound, whether it's a production sound or a postproduction sound. For example, the sound of footsteps that accompany a shot of a character walking along a sidewalk may have been constructed by Foley artists in a sound studio after filming was completed, but the *source* of that sound is implied to be onscreen—created by the character while walking.

The descriptive terms that are used to describe the source of a movie sound are *diegetic* or *nondiegetic*, *onscreen* or *offscreen*, and *internal* or *external*. Table 7.2 summarizes how these terms relate to each other, and the discussion that follows provides the details.

Diegetic Versus Nondiegetic

As you know from the "Story and Plot" section in Chapter 2, the word *diegesis* refers to the total world of a film's story, consisting perceptually of figures, motion, color, and sound. **Diegetic sound** originates from a source within a film's world; **nondiegetic sound** comes from a source outside that world. Most diegetic sound gives us an aware-

TABLE 7.2	Sources of Movie Sound	
	Diegetic Sound	Nondiegetic Sound
Spatial and Temporal Awareness		
Produces spatial awareness	X	
Produces temporal awareness	X	X
Source of Sound		
Internal	X	
External	X	
Onscreen	X	X
Offscreen	X	X
Simultaneous	X	
Nonsimultaneous	X	X

ness of *both* the spatial and the temporal dimensions of the shot from which the sound emanates; most nondiegetic sound has no relevant spatial or temporal dimensions. For example, the electronic music that plays during the opening sequence of Stanley Kubrick's *The Shining* (1980) is completely nondiegetic: we're not supposed to assume that the music is coming from the sky, or playing on the car radio, or coming from *any* location in the scene onscreen.

Diegetic sound can be either internal or external, onscreen or offscreen, and recorded during production or constructed during postproduction. The most familiar kind of movie sound is diegetic, onscreen sound that occurs simultaneously with the image. All of the sounds that accompany everyday actions and speech depicted onscreen—footsteps on pavement, a knock on a door, the ring of a telephone, the report from a fired gun, ordinary dialogue—are diegetic.

Nondiegetic sound is offscreen and recorded during postproduction, and it is assumed to be inaudible to the characters onscreen. The most familiar forms of nondiegetic sound are musical scores and narration that is spoken by a voice that

Diegetic Sound in Action In John Schlesinger's *Midnight Cowboy* (1969), right after stepping in front of an oncoming car (which screeches to a halt and honks its horn), "Ratso" Rizzo (Dustin Hoffman, *right*) interrupts his conversation with Joe Buck (Jon Voight, *left*) to shout one of the most famous movie lines of all time: "I'm walkin' here!" Even surrounded by everyday Manhattan pedestrian and traffic noise, Rizzo's nasal voice and heavy "Noo Yawk" accent help characterize him as the extremely eccentric and comic foil to Buck, a new and unseasoned arrival in the big city.

does not originate from the same place and time as the characters on the screen. When Redmond Barry (Ryan O'Neal) attracts the attention of the countess of Lyndon (Marisa Berenson) in Stanley Kubrick's *Barry Lyndon* (1975; sound: Robin Gregory and Rodney Holland), during a visually magnificent scene accompanied by the equally memorable music from the second movement of Franz Schubert's Trio in E-flat Major (D. 919, opus 100) for violin, cello, and piano, the instrumentalists are nowhere to be seen; furthermore, we do not expect to see them. We accept, as a familiar convention, that this kind of music reflects the historical period being depicted but does not emanate from the world of the story.

Nondiegetic music is used comically in Alfred Hitchcock's *North by Northwest* (1959; sound: Franklin Milton; music: Bernard Herrmann), when we see Roger Thornhill (Cary Grant) and Eve Kendall (Eva Marie Saint) climbing across the presidential faces sculpted on Mount Rushmore and hear Bernard Herrmann's fandango score, music that is not only nondiegetic but also completely absurd, given the danger facing these two characters.

The standard conventions of diegetic and non-diegetic sound may be modified for other effects. In Bobby and Peter Farrelly's *There's Something About Mary* (1998; supervising sound editor: Michael J. Benavente), for example, the "chorus" troubadour, Jonathan (Jonathan Richman), exists outside the story, which makes him and his songs nondiegetic, even though we can see him. The Farrellys play with this concept by having Jonathan get shot accidentally in the climactic scene and thus become part of the story.

1

2

Incongruous Nondiegetic Sound Emphasizes an Incongruous Scene Inappropriate and out-of-place things are responsible for much of the comedy in Alfred Hitchcock's extremely lighthearted thriller *North by Northwest* (1959). Mount Rushmore provides one of the movie's most incongruous and therefore comic settings, as the expensively dressed and perfectly coiffed Eve Kendall (Eva Marie Saint) and Roger Thornhill (Cary Grant) attempt to escape their pursuer and defy death by climbing all over the national monument. Bernard Herrmann, who wrote scores for seven Hitchcock films and is considered the quintessential Hitchcock composer, uses lively Spanish dance music here. (The same music provides the "Overture" under Saul Bass's title sequence.) Perfectly irrational in this setting, the music seems to come from some other world entirely, signaling that the situation's improbability is part of the fun.

Onscreen Versus Offscreen

Onscreen sound emanates from a source that we can see. **Offscreen sound**, which can be either diegetic or nondiegetic, derives from a source that we do not see. When offscreen sound is diegetic, it consists of sound effects, music, or vocals that emanate from the world of the story. When nondiegetic, it takes the form of a musical score or narration by someone who is not a character in the story. Note that onscreen and offscreen sound are also referred to, respectively, as *simultaneous* and *nonsimultaneous* sound. **Simultaneous sound** is diegetic and onscreen; **nonsimultaneous sound** occurs familiarly when a character has a mental flashback to an earlier voice that recalls a conversation or a sound that identifies a place. We recognize the sound, too, because its identity has previously been established in the movie.

Somewhere between onscreen and offscreen sound is **asynchronous sound**. We are aware of it when we sense a discrepancy between the things heard and the things seen on the screen. It is either a sound that is closely related to the action but not precisely synchronized with it, or a sound that either anticipates or follows the action to which it belongs. Because we cannot see its source, asynchronous sound seems mysterious and raises our curiosity and expectations. Thus it offers creative opportunities for building tension and surprise in a scene.

Asynchronous sound was used expressively in some of the first sound movies by such innovators as King Vidor, Rouben Mamoulian, and René Clair. For example, in his classic *Le Million* (1931), director René Clair uses asynchronous sound for humorous effect when we see characters scrambling to find a valuable lottery ticket and hear the sounds of a football game. Another classic example (with a variation) occurs in Alfred Hitchcock's *The 39 Steps* (1935; sound: A. Birch). A landlady enters a room, discovers a dead body, turns to face the camera, and opens her mouth as if to scream. At least, that's what we expect to hear. Instead, as she opens her mouth, we hear the high-pitched sound of a train whistle, and then Hitchcock cuts to a shot of a train speeding out of a tunnel. The sound seems to come from the landlady's mouth, but this is in fact an asynchronous *sound bridge*, linking two simultaneous actions occurring in different places.

Most movies provide a blend of offscreen and onscreen sounds that seems very natural and verisimilar, leading us to almost overlook the distinction between them. Some uses of sound, however, call attention to themselves; for example, when a scene favors offscreen sounds or excludes onscreen sounds altogether, we usually take notice. The total absence of diegetic, onscreen sound where we expect it most can be disturbing, as it is in the concluding, silent shots of a nuclear explosion in Sidney Lumet's *Fail-Safe* (1964; sound: Jack Fitzstephens); or comic, as it is at the conclusion of Stanley Kubrick's *Dr. Strangelove or: How I Learned to Stop Worrying and Love the Bomb* (1964; sound: John Cox), when the otherwise silent nuclear explosion is accompanied by nondiegetic music (Vera Lynn singing "We'll Meet Again").

In Robert Bresson's *A Man Escaped* (1956; sound: Pierre-André Bertrand), a member of the French Resistance named Lieutenant Fontaine (François Leterrier) is being held in a Nazi prison during World War II. Once he has entered the prison, he never sees outside the walls, although he remains very much aware, through offscreen sound, of the world outside. In fact, sounds of daily life—church bells, trains, trolleys—represent freedom to Fontaine.

Internal Versus External

An **internal sound** occurs whenever we hear what we assume are the thoughts of a character within a scene. The character might be expressing random thoughts or a sustained monologue. In the theater, when Shakespeare wants us to hear a character's thoughts, he uses a soliloquy to convey them, but this device lacks verisimilitude. Laurence Olivier's many challenges in adapting *Hamlet* for the screen included making the title character's soliloquies acceptable to a movie audience that might not be familiar with theatrical conventions. Olivier wanted to show Hamlet as both a thinker whose psychology motivated his actions and a man who could not make up his mind. Thus in his *Hamlet*

Internal Sound in *Hamlet*

To be, or not to be; that is the question:
Whether 'tis nobler in the mind to suffer
The slings and arrows of outrageous fortune,
Or to take arms against a sea of troubles,
And, by opposing, end them.[4]

Few lines cut deeper into a character's psyche or look more unflinchingly into the nature of human existence, and yet it's not hard to imagine how ineffective these well-known lines might be if simply recited at a camera. In his *Hamlet* (1948), actor-director Laurence Olivier fuses character and psyche, human nature and behavior, by both speaking his lines and rendering them, in voice-over, as the Danish prince's thoughts, while simultaneously combining, in the background, music and the natural sounds of the sea. Olivier's version of *Hamlet* was the first to apply the full resources of the cinema to Shakespeare's text, and his innovativeness is especially apparent in the sound.

[4] William Shakespeare, *The Tragedy of Hamlet*, act 3, scene 1.

(1948; sound: John W. Mitchell, Harry Miller, and L. E. Overton), Olivier (as Hamlet) delivered the greatest of all Shakespearean soliloquies—"To be, or not to be"—in a combination of both spoken lines and **interior monologue**. This innovation influenced the use of internal sound in countless other movies, including subsequent cinematic adaptations of Shakespeare's plays.

External sound comes from a place within the world of the story, and we assume that it is heard by the characters in that world. The source of an external sound can be either onscreen or offscreen. In John Ford's *My Darling Clementine* (1946; sound: Eugene Grossman and Roger Heman Sr.), Indian Charlie (Charles Stevens, uncredited) is drunk and shooting up the town of Tombstone. The townspeople are afraid of Charlie, and the sheriff (actor uncredited) resigns rather than confront him, so Wyatt Earp (Henry Fonda)—who is both on- and offscreen during the scene—is appointed sheriff and takes it upon himself to stop the chaos that Charlie has created.

The scene effectively combines both on- and offscreen sounds. The characters (and the viewer) hear the offscreen sounds of Charlie shooting his gun inside the saloon, followed by the offscreen sounds of women screaming; then the women appear onscreen as they run from the saloon with Charlie right behind them, still shooting his gun. When Earp onscreen starts to enter the building through an upstairs window, we hear the offscreen screams of the prostitutes who are in the room as he says, "Sorry, ladies." Offscreen, Earp confronts Charlie and conks him on the head, for we hear the thud of Charlie falling to the saloon floor. This is followed by an onscreen shot of Earp dragging Charlie out of the saloon to the waiting crowd. This use of sound not only demonstrates Earp's courage and skill, but also treats his serious encounter with Charlie with a comic touch.

Types of Film Sound

The types of sound that filmmakers can include in their sound tracks fall into four general categories: (1) vocal sounds (dialogue and narration), (2) environmental sounds (ambient sound, sound effects, and Foley sounds), (3) music, and (4) silence. As viewers, we are largely familiar with vocal, environmental, and musical sounds. Vocal sounds tend to dominate most films because they carry much of the narrative weight, environmental sounds usually provide information about a film's setting and action, and music often directs our emotional reactions. However, any of these types of sound may dominate or be subordinate to the visual image, depending on the relationship that the filmmaker desires between sound and visual image.

Vocal Sounds

Dialogue, recorded during production or rerecorded during postproduction, is the speech of characters who are either visible onscreen or speaking offscreen—say, from an unseen part of the room or from an adjacent room. Dialogue is a function of plot because it develops out of situations, conflict, and character development. Further, it depends on actors' voices, facial expressions, and gestures and is thus also a product of acting. Expressing the feelings and motivations of characters, dialogue is one of the principal means of telling a story. In most movies, dialogue represents what we consider ordinary speech, but dialogue can also be highly artificial.

During the 1930s, screwball comedies invented a fast, witty, and often risqué style of dialogue that was frankly theatrical in calling attention to itself. Among the most exemplary of these films are Ernst Lubitsch's *Trouble in Paradise* (1932; screenwriters: Grover Jones and Samson Raphaelson), Howard Hawks's *Bringing Up Baby* (1938; screenwriters: Dudley Nichols and Hagar Wilde), and Preston Sturges's *The Lady Eve* (1941; screenwriters: Sturges and Monckton Hoffe), each of which must be seen in its lunatic entirety to be fully appreciated but nonetheless provides countless rich individual exchanges. Today the screwball comedy genre has been transformed in such movies as Nora Ephron's *You've Got Mail* (1998) and Joel Coen's *Intolerable Cruelty* (2003). David Mamet, who writes and directs his own movies (e.g., *The Spanish Prisoner*, 1997; and *Heist*, 2001) is noted for dialogue that calls attention to itself with its sharp, terse, and often profane characteristics.

Movie speech can take forms other than dialogue. For example, French director Alain Resnais specializes in spoken language that reveals a character's stream of consciousness, mixing reality, memory, dream, and imagination. In Resnais's *Providence* (1977; screenplay: David Mercer; sound: René Magnol and Jacques Maumont), Clive Langham (John Gielgud), an elderly novelist, drinks heavily as he drifts in and out of sleep. Through the intertwining strands of his interior monologue, we learn of his projected novel—about four characters who inhabit a doomed city—and of his relationships with members of his family, on whom his fictional characters are evidently based. Langham's monologue and dialogues link the fantasy to the reality of what we see and hear; in this way, sound objectifies what is ordinarily neither seen nor heard in a movie.

Narration, the commentary spoken by either offscreen or onscreen voices, is frequently used in narrative films, where it may emanate from an omniscient voice (thus, not one of the characters) or from a character in the movie. In the opening scene of Stanley Kubrick's *The Killing* (1956; sound: Rex Lipton and Earl Snyder), when Marvin Unger (Jay C. Flippen) enters the betting room of a racetrack, an omniscient narrator describes him for us. The narrator knows details of Unger's personal life and cues us to the suspense of the film's narrative.

In Terrence Malick's *Badlands* (1973; sound: Maury Harris), Holly (Sissy Spacek) narrates the story, helping us understand her loneliness, her obsession with Kit (Martin Sheen), her participation in a series of brutal murders, and her inability to stop. This technique enhances our appreciation of her character, because rather than simply reinforcing what we are seeing, Holly's understanding and interpretation of events differ significantly from ours. She thinks of her life with Kit as a romance novel rather than a pathetic crime spree.

In *The Magnificent Ambersons* (1942; sound: Bailey Fesler and James G. Stewart), Orson Welles uses both offscreen and onscreen narrators. Welles himself is the offscreen, omniscient narrator who sets a mood of romantic nostalgia for the American

Onscreen Narration Billy Wilder's *Double Indemnity* (1944; sound: Stanley Cooley and Walter Oberst) uses onscreen narration in a unique way. Walter Neff (Fred MacMurray), a corrupt insurance investigator, is pictured here recording his confession of murder on an office Dictaphone. His story leads to flashbacks that fill us in on events leading to that confession.

past, while an onscreen "chorus" of townspeople—a device that derives from Greek drama—gossip about what is happening, directly offering their own interpretations. Thus the townspeople are both characters and narrators.

Environmental Sounds

Ambient sound, which emanates from the ambience (or background) of the setting or environment being filmed, is either recorded during production or added during postproduction. Although it may incorporate other types of film sound—dialogue, narration, sound effects, Foley sounds, and music—ambient sound should not include any unintentionally recorded noise made during production, such as the sounds of cameras, static from sound-recording equipment, car horns, sirens, footsteps, or voices from outside the production. Filmmakers regard these sounds as an inevitable nuisance and generally remove them electronically during postproduction. Ambient sound helps set the mood and atmosphere of scenes, and it may also contribute to the meaning of a scene.

Consider the ambient sound of the wind in John Ford's *The Grapes of Wrath* (1940; sound: Roger Heman Sr. and George Leverett). Tom Joad (Henry Fonda), who has just been released from prison, returns to his family's Oklahoma house to find it empty, dark, and deserted. The low sound of the wind underscores Tom's loneliness and isolation and reminds us that the wind of dust bowl storms reduced the fertile plains to unproductive wastes and drove the Joads and other farmers off their land. In Satyajit Ray's Apu trilogy—*Pather Panchali* (1955), *The Unvanquished* (1957), and *The World of Apu* (1959)—recurrent sounds of trains establish actual places, times, and moods; but they poetically express characters' anticipations and memories as well. These wind and train sounds, respectively, are true to the physical ambience of Ford's and Ray's stories, but filmmakers also use symbolic sounds as a kind of shorthand to create illusions of reality. In countless westerns, for example, tinkling pianos introduce us to frontier towns; in urban films, honking automobile horns suggest the busyness (and business) of cities.

Sound effects include all sounds artificially created for the sound track that have a definite function in telling the story. All sound effects, except those made on electronic equipment to deliberately create electronic sounds, come from "wild" recordings of *real things*, and it is the responsibility of the sound designer and the sound crew to pick and combine these sounds to create the hyper-reality of the film's sound track. (*Wild recording* is any recording of sound not made during synchronous shooting of the picture.) In Ray's *Pather Panchali* (sound: Bhupen Ghosh), two children, Apu (Subir Bannerjee) and Durga (Uma Das Gupta), find their family's eighty-year-old aunt, Indir Thakrun (Chunibala Devi), squatting near a sacred pond and think she is sleeping. As Durga shakes her, the old woman falls over, her head hitting the ground with a hollow sound—a diegetic, onscreen sound effect—that evokes death.

A special category of sound effects—**Foley sounds**—was invented in the 1930s by Jack Foley, a sound technician at Universal Studios. There are two significant differences between Foleys and the sound effects just described. The first is that tradi-

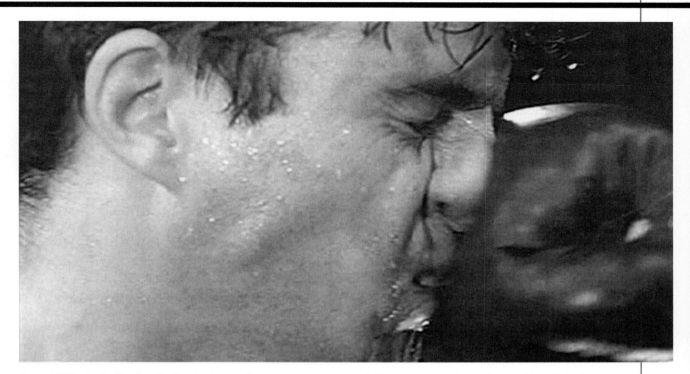

Sound Effects in *Raging Bull* The boxing film against which all others are measured, Martin Scorsese's *Raging Bull* (1980)—based on former middleweight champion Jake La Motta's memoir of the same title—fully employs every aspect of filmmaking technology as it re-creates the experience of being in the ring. Close-ups don't get much more vivid than this one, in which La Motta's (Robert De Niro) glove slams into and breaks fighter Tony Janiro's (Kevin Mahon) nose, blood spurts, and sweat flies. The image moves from powerful to unbearable, however, when accompanied by the Foley sounds of impact, collapse, and explosion.

tional sound effects are created and recorded "wild" and then edited into the film, whereas Foleys are created and recorded in sync with the picture. To do this, the technicians known as Foley artists have a studio equipped with recording equipment and a screen on which to view the movie as they create sounds in sync with it. The second difference is that traditional sound effects can be taken directly from a library of prerecorded effects (e.g., church bells, traffic noises, jungle sounds) or created specifically for the movie. By contrast, Foley sounds are unique. As an example of the latter, the sound technicians working on Peter Jackson's *The Fellowship of the Ring* (2001; sound designer: David Farmer) needed the sounds of arrows shooting through the air, so they set up stationary microphones in a quiet graveyard and shot arrows past the mikes to record those sounds.

Foley artists use a variety of props and other equipment to simulate everyday sounds—such as footsteps in the mud, jingling car keys, the rustling of clothing, or cutlery hitting a plate—that must exactly match the movement on the screen. Such sounds not only fill in the soundscape of the movie and enhance verisimilitude, but also convey important narrative and character information. Although these sounds match the action we see on the screen, they can also exaggerate reality—both loud and soft sounds—and thus may call attention to their own artificiality. Generally, however, we do not consciously notice them, so when they are truly effective, we cannot distinguish Foley sounds from real sounds.

In Martin Scorsese's *Raging Bull* (1980; sound: Frank Warner), brutal tape-recorded sounds from boxing matches are mixed with sounds created in the Foley studio, with many different tracks, including a fist hitting a side of beef, a knife cutting into the beef, water (to simulate the sound of blood spurting), animal noises, and the whooshes of jet airplanes and arrows—all working together to provide the dramatic illusion of what, in a real boxing match, would be the comparatively simpler sound of one boxer's gloves hitting another boxer's flesh.

Today's movies are particularly rich in their uses of sound. The artistry involved in using all the various sources and types of sound has permanently established the role of the sound designer and exponentially increased the number of sound-related job titles, and therefore new employment, in the field of movie sound—all of which is reflected in the large number of sound artists and technicians receiving screen credit. Furthermore, it has made necessary the invention and development of new equipment for sound recording, editing, and mixing, and has also brought change to many theaters, which have had to install expensive new equipment to process the superb sound made possible by the digital revolution.

WEB Foley Sounds and Other Sound Effects

Music and Ideas In the funeral procession that opens Orson Welles's *The Tragedy of Othello* (1952), the composers use heavy piano chords, insistent drums, and a chorus to underscore the director's interpretation that fate was the cause of the deaths of Othello (Welles) and Desdemona (Suzanne Cloutier).

Music

Although music is used in many distinct ways in the movies, in this discussion we are concerned principally with the kind of music that Royal S. Brown, an expert on the subject, describes as "dramatically motivated . . . music composed more often than not by practitioners specializing in the art to interact specifically with the diverse facets of the filmic medium, particularly the narrative."[5] Such music can be classical or popular in style, written specifically for the film or taken from music previously composed for another purpose, written by composers known for other kinds of music (e.g., Leonard Bernstein, Aaron Copland, Philip Glass, and Igor Stravinsky) or by those who specialize in movie scores (e.g., Elmer Bernstein, Carter Burwell, Georges Delerue, Bernard Herrmann, Ennio Morricone, David Raksin, Tôru Takemitsu, and

John Williams, among many others), or music played by characters in the film or by offscreen musicians, diegetic or nondiegetic.

Some of Hollywood's most prolific contemporary composers were formerly rock musicians: Oingo Boingo's Danny Elfman has scored many Tim Burton movies, including *Corpse Bride* (2005); Devo's Mark Mothersbaugh, another prolific composer, scored Catherine Hardwicke's *Lords of Dogtown* (2005) and Wes Anderson's *The Life Aquatic With Steve Zissou* (2004). Songwriter and singer Randy Newman, equally prolific, scored Gary Ross's *Seabiscuit* (2003) and Jay Roach's *Meet the Fockers* (2004).

Like other types of sound, music can be intrinsic, helping to tell the story, whether it pertains to plot, action, character, or mood; indeed, music plays an indispensable role in many movies. Perhaps the most familiar form of movie music is the large symphonic score used to set a mood or manipulate our emotions.[6] Few old-Hollywood films were without a big score by masters of the genre

[5] Royal S. Brown, *Overtones and Undertones: Reading Film Music* (Berkeley: University of California Press, 1994), 13.

[6] See Larry Timm, *The Soul of Cinema: An Appreciation of Film Music* (New York: Simon & Schuster, 1998), chap. 1.

[1]

[4]

[2]

[5]

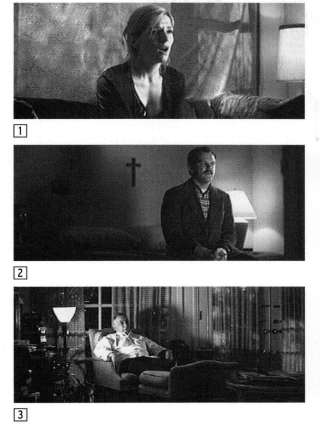

[3]

[6]

Songs Inspire a Movie   Miraculous things happen, and people and events connect in unexpected ways, throughout Paul Thomas Anderson's *Magnolia* (1999; sound designer: Richard King). Part of what inspired Anderson in writing his screenplay was hearing then-unreleased recordings by American pop-rocker Aimee Mann. In some cases, connections between the songs and the narrative are explicit, as when the lyrics to "Deathly"—"Now that I've met you / Would you object to / Never seeing / Each other again"—become a line of dialogue: "Now that I've met you, would you object to never seeing me again?" At the film's emotional climax, [1] Claudia Wilson Gator (Melora Walters), [2] Jim Kurring (John C. Reilly), [3] Jimmy Gator (Philip Baker Hall), [4] Quiz Kid Donnie Smith (William H. Macy), [5] "Big Earl" Partridge (Jason Robards, *left*) and his nurse, Phil Parma (Philip Seymour Hoffman, *right*), and [6] Stanley Spector (Jeremy Blackman)—all in different places and different situations—sing along with Mann's "Wise Up."

such as Max Steiner (who scored Victor Fleming's *Gone With the Wind*, 1939). Although recent movies have relied mainly on less ambitious scores, they are still used when large stories call for them, including Ridley Scott's *Gladiator* (2005; composers: Hans Zimmer and Lisa Gerrard); Peter Jackson's "Lord of the Rings" trilogy (2001–03; composer: Howard Shore); the Harry Potter movies (2001–07; various directors; composer: John Williams); and the three "Star Wars" prequels, for which Williams, who has been involved with the "Star Wars" series from the beginning, wrote the scores. Kar Hai Wong's stylish, futuristic *2046* (2004) has a lush symphonic score by Peer Raben and Shigeru Umebayashi that incorporates much Western classical and pop music.

Movie music can be equally effective when it creates or supports ideas in a film, as in Orson Welles's *The Tragedy of Othello: The Moor of Venice* (1952; music: Alberto Barberis and Angelo Francesco Lavagnino; 1999 sound restoration supervisor: John Fogelson; 1999 music restoration supervisor: Michael Pendowski). Welles takes a deterministic view of Othello's fate, but he depicts the two central characters, Othello (Welles) and Desdemona (Suzanne Cloutier), as being larger than life, even as they are each destined for an early death.

Accompanying their funeral processions is a musical score that leaves no question that these tragic circumstances are the result of fate. In fact, in their cumulative power the sights and sounds express the inexorable rhythm of all great tragedies. The complex musical score covers several periods and styles, but to most ears it resembles medieval liturgical music. Deep, hard, dirgelike piano chords combine with the chanting of monks and others in the processions, spelling out (even drawing us into) the title character's inevitable deterioration and self-destruction.

For John Curran's *We Don't Live Here Anymore* (2004), a dark melodrama about marital infidelities, composer Michael Convertino has written a score that builds with the suspense and establishes the mood of anxiety that hangs over everyone involved. By contrast, Don Davis's score for Andy and Larry Wachowski's *The Matrix* (1999) uses the sounds of brass and percussion instruments and songs by the Propellerheads and Rage Against the Machine to match the world of the story's synthetic technological environment. Davis also scored the music for the two sequels (*The Matrix Reloaded* and *The Matrix Revolutions*, both 2003).

Irony often results from the juxtaposition of music and image, because the associations we bring when we hear a piece of music greatly affect our interpretation of a scene. Take, for example, composer Ennio Morricone's juxtaposition of "Ave Maria" with shots of Brazilian natives and missionary priests being slaughtered by Portuguese slave traders in Roland Joffé's *The Mission* (1986), or Quentin Tarantino's use of Stealers Wheel's carefree, groovy "Stuck in the Middle With You" to choreograph the violent cop-torture scene in *Reservoir Dogs* (1992).

Neil Jordan makes a more sustained use of such juxtaposition in *The Crying Game* (1992), a political and psychological thriller that is also a frank, revealing movie about loneliness, desire, and love.

Its music helps underscore the surprises in its story. Fergus (Stephen Rea) is interested in Dil (Jaye Davidson), who appears to be an attractive black woman until Dil reveals that he is a transvestite. The personal and political plot twists are too complicated to discuss in this context, but Fergus falls in love with Dil and, because of his love, takes a prison rap for him. At the end of the movie, Dil is visiting Fergus in prison, and as the camera pulls back to the final fade-out and closing credits, we hear Tammy Wynette and Billy Sherrill's country-and-western classic, "Stand by Your Man," sung by Lyle Lovett. (This irony would be missed if the viewer did not stay for the credits, which today increasingly include music or other information vital to understanding the overall movie.) It's funny and touching at the same time, but especially ironic in light of the music under the opening credits: Percy Sledge singing the African American classic, "When a Man Loves a Woman" (by Cameron Lewis and Arthur Wright), the perfectly ironic introduction—although we do not know it then—to this story of desperate love.

Among directors, Tom Tykwer is notable for his use of music to enhance the pace, or tempo, of *Run Lola Run* (1998; music: Reinhold Heil, Johnny Klimek, Franka Potente, and Tykwer), in which the relentless rhythm of the techno music matches the sped-up, almost surreal pace of the action. Significantly, this music does not change with developments in the action, so it takes on a life of its own.

Ironic Music for an Ironic Story When Fergus (Stephen Rea) first meets Dil (Jaye Davidson) in "her" haircutting shop, he doesn't yet know that Dil is a transvestite. Eventually, they fall in love. Looking back after the movie ends, we realize the irony of the song 'When a Man Loves a Woman' that we heard under the opening credits.

[1]

[2]

Great Music, Bad Boy   One of the principal concerns of Stanley Kubrick's *A Clockwork Orange* (1971; sound editor: Brian Blamey), the loss of moral choice through psychological conditioning, is developed by a focus on [1] Alex (Malcolm McDowell), a worthless, violent character, here staring at [2] a poster of the German classical/Romantic composer Ludwig van Beethoven. Alex's only good trait is his love for Beethoven's Ninth Symphony—especially the setting in its finale of Friedrich von Schiller's "Ode to Joy," music that

represents all that is most noble in the human spirit. Here, however, this music is used ironically to underscore Alex's desire to preserve his freedom to do what he wants (which consists mostly of violent acts) even though society tries to socialize him away from these acts (using a fascistic treatment that attempts to turn him into a "clockwork orange"). In the somewhat muddled world of this controversial film, we're supposed to be glad that Alex is still sufficiently human to embrace Beethoven *and* resist brainwashing.

Indeed, any action movie with many exciting chase sequences, such as Paul Greengrass's *The Bourne Supremacy* (2004; composer: John Powell), could become routine if the music did not change significantly to suit the participants, location, and outcome of each chase. In *The Bourne Supremacy*'s most spectacular chase in Moscow traffic, Jason Bourne (Matt Damon), whose own musical theme is played by a bassoon, successfully eludes the Russian police but not before many vehicles are destroyed. The sound in this scene is a very expressive mix of ambient sounds, Foley sounds, sound effects, and John Powell's score. Indeed, it's impossible to disentangle these elements. The loud sounds of sirens, screeching tires, shattered glass, gunshots, and revving car engines accentuate the violent action, while the music, which is somewhat softer in volume, is a full orchestral score mixed with Russian folk themes and electronic sounds, including techno music. The chase ends with a final smash-up and silence.

Many directors use music to provide overall structural unity or coherence to a story, as in Otto Preminger's psychological thriller *Laura* (1944;

composer: David Raksin), about which Royal S. Brown writes:

> Almost every piece of music, diegetic and nondiegetic, heard in the film either is David Raksin's mysteriously chromatic fox-trot tune or else grows out of it, particularly in the nondiegetic backing. The detective (Dana Andrews) investigating Laura's "murder" turns on a phonograph: it plays "Laura." The journalist throws a party for Laura once she has "returned from the dead": the background music is "Laura." But the way in which the melody travels back and forth between the diegetic and the nondiegetic, making that distinction all but meaningless, likewise reinforces the overall obsessiveness.[7]

A movie such as Stephen Daldry's *The Hours* (2002), which tells a story spanning some eighty years in three different settings with three different women, presents a unique challenge to a musical

---

[7] Brown, *Overtones and Undertones*, 86.

composer to find some way to unify all these elements. The movie's narrative concerns the different ways these three women are affected by Virginia Woolf's 1925 novel *Mrs. Dalloway*, including the novelist herself (played by Nicole Kidman) in the 1920s; an American housewife, Laura Brown (Julianne Moore), in the 1940s; and a New York professional woman, Clarissa Vaughan (Meryl Streep), in the present. Therefore, one might expect a tripartite musical score with one distinct sound for each historical period and location and perhaps even a distinct theme for each principal character. However, composer Philip Glass chooses a very different course.

A New Age classical composer with minimalist tendencies, Glass links the three stories with certain recurring musical motifs, played by a chamber orchestra of a pianist and five string players. To create further unity among the lives of the three women, Glass emphasizes the bond that Woolf's novel has created among them by avoiding music from the periods in which they lived. The tensions in the score pull between the emotional and cerebral, underscoring the tensions that the characters experience in this psychological melodrama.

Musical themes are frequently associated with individual characters, and they may also help present a character's thoughts, as in Lasse Hallström's *My Life as a Dog* (1985), in which Björn Isfält's score reflects the poignant and melancholic state of mind of a boy yearning for his dead mother; or Joseph L. Mankiewicz's *The Ghost and Mrs. Muir* (1947), in which Bernard Herrmann's score reflects a widow's loneliness in an isolated house perched on a cliff overlooking the sea. James Horner's score for James Cameron's *Titanic* (1997) makes ample use of Rose's theme (Rose is played by Kate Winslet and Gloria Stuart). Roger Hickman, an expert on movie music, notes that this theme has qualities from Irish folk music, but that since "Rose is neither Irish nor a member of the folk class . . . [the] association of this theme with the character is vague. Nonetheless, the theme is hauntingly beautiful."[8] Indeed, beautiful and memorable is about all we

can expect from most musical themes associated with characters.

Finally, film music may emanate from sources within the story—a television, a radio or stereo set, a person singing or playing a guitar, an orchestra playing at a dance. For example, Joel Coen's *The Man Who Wasn't There* (2001) includes several scenes in which Rachel Abundas (Scarlett Johansson) plays a Beethoven piano sonata from which one theme also figures as a principal motif in Carter Burwell's score. Ridley Scott's *Black Hawk Down* (2001) depicts a complex and failed attempt by a group of U.S. Army Rangers to depose a Somalian warlord, a conflict between Americans and African Muslims. For this film, composer Hans Zimmer decided against writing the sort of score we hear in other classic war movies, such as Coppola's *Apocalypse Now* (1979; composers: Carmine and Francis Ford Coppola) or Oliver Stone's *Platoon* (1986; composer: Georges Delerue).

Instead of using familiar classical themes for theatrical effect, Zimmer relies heavily on diegetic music that emanates from soldiers' radios, street musicians, or mosques. Thus the score juxtaposes Western and African music: including Irish tunes, songs sung by Elvis Presley and popular groups such as Alice in Chains, Stone Temple Pilots, and Faith No More on one hand, and traditional Muslim prayer music and chants, mournful piano and strings, African pop music, and tribal drums on the other. At times, such as the beginning of the attack on the marketplace, Zimmer fuses elements of both. His "score" goes beyond music to include many sound effects that function as rhythmic elements (e.g., the constant hum of military and civilian vehicles, the beating of the helicopter rotor blades, the voices of the American soldiers and African crowds). In this expanded sense of a musical score, Zimmer and Jon Title, the sound designer, worked together to create an original, seamless entity in which there are few distinctions between music and other sounds. Of course, at times in *Black Hawk Down* music is just music and sound effects are just sound effects, but the major achievement here is the fusion of sounds.

With this score, Zimmer does not make conflict appear to be the work of godlike warriors (such as

[8] Roger Hickman, *Reel Music: Exploring 100 Years of Film Music* (New York: W. W. Norton, 2006), 431.

[1]

[2]

Diegetic Music   In Spike Lee's *Do the Right Thing* (1989), [1] Radio Raheem (Bill Nunn) and [2] Stevie (Luis Ramos) face off to determine whose music (and whose boom box) is superior. After a volley of insults and adjustments of volume, Stevie stands down, conceding Radio Raheem's audio supremacy. The diegetic rap and salsa music in this scene help convey one of the movie's themes: the clash of different cultures in contemporary America. During the movie, among the rap, reggae, soul, and pop records spun (in those pre-compact disc days) are Public Enemy's "Fight the Power," Take 6's "Don't Shoot Me," Steel Pulse's "Can't Stand It," Rubén Blades's "Tu y Yo," and Al Jarreau's "Never Explain Love."

the helicopter gunship in *Apocalypse Now*), but rather conveys the hell of war, reinforces the bond among the soldiers, and helps us understand the agony they suffer on each other's behalf. Near the end, we hear his "Leave No Man Behind," a beautiful tapestry of piano and strings that includes familiar patriotic musical motifs, and his soft, mar-

tial arrangement of the heartbreaking Irish ballad "Minstrel Boy," sung by Joe Strummer and the Mescaleros. This score, derived from many sources—both diegetic and nondiegetic—is not background music, but central to portraying the movie's almost unbearable tension.

Although a movie's characters and its viewers hear diegetic music, which can be as simple as sound drifting in through an open window, only viewers hear nondiegetic music, which usually consists of an original score composed for the movie, selections chosen from music libraries, or both. Nondiegetic music is recorded at the very end of the editing process so that it can be matched accurately to the images. In recording an original score, the conductor and musicians work on a specially equipped recording stage, which enables them to screen the film and tailor every aspect of the music's tempo and quality to each scene that has music (similar to the way that Foley sounds are created). Further adjustments of the sounds of individual musicians, groups of musicians, or an entire orchestra are frequently made after these recording sessions and before the final release prints are made. Similar efforts are made to fit selections taken from music libraries with the images that they accompany.

WEB Film Music

Silence

As viewers, we are familiar with all the types of film sound that have been described in this chapter, but we may be unfamiliar with the idea that *silence* can be a sound. Paradoxically, silence has that function when the filmmaker deliberately suppresses the vocal, environmental, or musical sounds we expect in a movie. When so used, silence frustrates our normal perceptions. It can make a scene seem profound or even prophetic. Furthermore, with careful interplay between sound and silence, a filmmaker can produce a new rhythm for the film—one that calls attention to the characters' perceptions.

Akira Kurosawa's *Dreams* (1990; no sound credit) consists of eight extremely formal episodes, each based on one of the director's dreams. The

The Sound of Silence In "The Blizzard," one of eight episodes in Akira Kurosawa's *Dreams* (1990), the specter of Death is a beautiful woman who tries to seduce an exhausted mountain climber to give in to her charms. She lulls him with poetic phrases and covers him with beautiful fabrics. During this sequence, the climber drifts in and out of consciousness; the sound track reflects his very limited consciousness, and we, too, hear only the ethereal woman and the low sounds of the wind.

third episode, "The Blizzard," tells of four mountain climbers trapped in a fierce storm. We hear what they hear when they are conscious, but when they are exhausted and near death, they (and we) hear almost nothing.

As the episode begins, we hear the climbers' boots crunching the snow, their labored breathing, and the raging wind. They are exhausted, but the leader warns them that they will die if they go to sleep. Nonetheless, they all lie down in the snow. The previous loud sounds diminish until all we hear is the low sound of the wind. Then, out of this, we hear the sweet, clear, high sounds of a woman singing offscreen. The leader awakens to see a beautiful woman onscreen—the specter of Death— who says, "The snow is warm . . . The ice is hot." As she covers the leader with shimmering fabrics, he drifts in and out of sleep, trying to fight her seductive powers—all in silence.

Ultimately, Death fails to convince the leader to give up. When it's clear that he has regained his consciousness and strength, he is able to hear the loud storm again. Death disappears, accompanied by wind and thunder. Perhaps her beauty has given the leader the courage to resist death and thus save the group. The other men awaken; they, of course, have

not seen or heard any of this. We then hear muted trumpets, horns, and Alpine music—all nondiegetic sounds signifying the climbers' victory over the weather and death. Ironically, when they awaken in the bright sunshine, the climbers recognize that they have slept in the snow only a few yards away from the safety of their base camp. What is the meaning of this dream? Perhaps that life equals consciousness and, in this instance, awareness of sound.

Types of Sound in Steven Spielberg's *War of the Worlds*

Let's take a close look at how important sound is to one movie in particular: Steven Spielberg's *War of the Worlds* (2005; sound designer: Richard King; musical score: John Williams). To do this, we'll catalog the *types of sounds* we hear in the movie. Because the sound design of this movie is so complex, it would be impossible to identify every one that we hear, but the following discussion will provide a sense of the numerous types of sound incorporated into the overall sound design.

The movie begins with shots of protoplasm as seen through a microscope, accompanied by the deep, soothing voice of the narrator (Morgan Freeman) speaking the opening lines of H. G. Wells's 1898 novel, *The War of the Worlds*, on which the screenplay was loosely based:

No one would have believed in the last years of the nineteenth century that this world was being watched keenly and closely by intelligences greater than man's and yet as mortal as his own; that as men busied themselves about their various concerns they were scrutinised and studied, perhaps almost as narrowly as a man with a microscope might scrutinise the transient creatures that swarm and multiply in a drop of water.

The ominous nature of this text, along with the grave voice of the narrator, lets us know that we're in for a thrilling story. Furthermore, these few lines establish the basis of the sound design. Those "intelligences greater than man's" inhabit the colossal tripods, which make thunderous noises. By contrast, humankind is a puny thing, prone to mak-

Sounds Introduce Conflict   At the beginning of Steven Spielberg's *War of the Worlds* (2005), we hear loud, high-pitched sounds (accompanying eerie atmospheric effects) and realize that something terrible is going to happen. Here, Ray Ferrier (Tom Cruise) and his daughter, Rachel (Dakota Fanning), brave the roaring winds to watch the darkening skies.

The Tripods' Warning   For the first time, Ray Ferrier sees and hears the foghornlike warning "voice" of the tripods. He and his neighbors, who do not yet understand what's happening, seem stunned by the tripods—as much by their massive size as by their ill-portending sounds.

ing incredulous assumptions about what is happening and then whimpering or crying about it. Big/little, loud/soft: that's the pattern underscoring this conflict.

As the action begins with Ray Ferrier (Tom Cruise) working at a New Jersey container port, we hear the ambient sounds of this industrial operation: traffic in and around the area; the television in Ray's apartment (bringing an ominous news report of violent lightning strikes in Ukraine); and dialogue between Ray, his ex-wife Mary Ann (Miranda Otto), and their children (Rachel, played by Dakota Fanning; and Robbie, played by Justin Chatwin), who are spending the weekend with their father. From this point on, however—when the movie rapidly enters the surreal world of the story—the majority of the sounds we hear are the work of sound engineers and technicians: the violent lightning storm that incites the action, sudden winds that make the laundry flap wildly on the line, shattering glass as a baseball breaks a window, the earthquake that splits the streets and enables the giant tripods to emerge, electrical flashes that emanate from the tripods, and the sounds of explosions, falling debris, shattered glass, and people being vaporized as the tripods wreak havoc. There are also implied sounds, such as what Robbie is listening to on his iPod, which we cannot hear.

Flight From Terror   Ferrier (at the wheel of a van that he has stolen) and his two children (who are hiding from danger on the floor of the car) flee their New Jersey town as it is destroyed by the tripods. Notable here are the sound effects of crumbling steel bridges, vaporizing concrete highways, and debris falling everywhere.

As the crisis in this New Jersey town worsens, we are overwhelmed by the sounds of fires, explosions, bridges and highways collapsing, and the screeching tires of the car as Ray drives frantically out of town. When Ray and his children reach the temporary safety of his ex-wife's new house, there are more light and lightning storms, heavy winds, and the sounds of a jet aircraft crashing on the front lawn. Many of these sounds were produced in the Foley lab.

During a lull before the tripods appear again, we hear more ambient sounds: Rachel's shrill screams, a radio report on the status of the emergency broadcast system, a passing convoy of army tanks and trucks, and car horns in the heavy traffic as the Ferriers approach a ferry on the Hudson River. At the ferry landing we hear the deafening roar of a freight train as it passes in the night, the jangling of the warning bells at the train's crossing, a female ferry employee shouting instructions through a megaphone, and the ferry's deep-sounding horns. The crowd there is furious at Ray for having a car in which to escape and begins to attack it; we hear loud crowd noises, individual voices, gunshots, and the sounds of the car's windows being smashed. In the midst of this pandemonium, Rachel looks up to the sky and hears geese honking as they fly by—a classic omen of the horror to come. There is very little music in this part of the film (the rising action of the plot), but we hear from a radio somewhere the sound of Tony Bennett singing "If I Ruled the World." Since viewers know that a new demonic force now rules the world, it's a particularly ironic use of music.

The Ferriers manage to get on the ferry boat, but their escape is thwarted when the boat is caught in a whirlpool and capsizes, throwing cars and passengers overboard. The sounds of this action are faithful and vivid. We also see and hear people thrashing underwater as they seek safety. By now, the tripods are on the scene, their huge tentacles (with their own peculiar noises) grabbing people out of the Hudson and gobbling them up into their nasty "mouths." Of course, the three members of the Ferrier family escape all of this.

On the riverbank, we see an Armageddon-like scene—what might be the final conflict between the tripods and humanity—and hear the sounds of the massive tripods crashing through the land-scape, army tanks firing missiles at them, and heli-copters and fighter jets above also firing missiles and dropping bombs. The scene is complete chaos, with ambient noises of the crowds rushing back and forth. In the midst of all this, Robbie Ferrier pleads with his father for independence and escapes into the fray.

As the crowds disperse, and a semblance of quiet and order return, Ray and Rachel are wel-comed into the basement of a nearby farmhouse by

Panic   The tripods cause a whirlpool that capsizes a ferry overcrowded with people trying to escape. Sounds here include the hornlike "voices" of the tripods, the screams of the crowd (those still on deck and those who have fallen or dived into the river), the buckling steel of the ferryboat, underwater sounds, and John Williams's musical score.

Armageddon   As the tripods attack the fleeing crowds and devastate the landscape, military jets and missiles fail in their attempts to subdue them. We hear the sounds of the tripods and the chaos they create, aircraft, music, and various electronic sounds that add to the doomsday atmosphere.

a Harlan Ogilvy (Tim Robbins). Soon the sounds of his sharpening a large blade provide another omen that the battle is not yet over and that this man, too, may become an evil force with which Ray will need to reckon. Actually we expect that Ogilvy is a murderer and that Ray and Rachel are in harm's way, but in fact he just wants to annihilate the tripods.

The basement is full of sounds that further establish the imminent evil: scurrying rats; the soft, whirring sound of a tripod's tentacle as it

Farmhouse Refuge   Rachel and her father take shelter in the house of Harlan Ogilvy (Tim Robbins, *far right*). Their initial meeting is a moment of comparative quiet that is rare for this movie; all we hear is Harlan's soft voice and the offscreen sounds of distant battles being fought outside.

Rachel Captured   As her father screams, "No! No!" a tentacle of one of the tripods swoops down and captures Rachel. Other sounds include Rachel's screams and the ominous, insistent musical score that suggests the inevitability of this incident.

searches the labyrinth of rooms; rippling water that is pooling there; and the sounds of the stealthy grasshopper-like creatures that have also emerged from inside the tripods. Meanwhile, as Rachel continues to scream, her father attempts to calm her by singing; she sings also. But Harlan has now decided to take on the tripods himself—an act that Ray knows will prove to be fatal for him and his daughter—so Ray kills Harlan (offscreen), apparently beating him to death with a shovel, as indicated by the accompanying heavy drumlike sound.

When Ray and his daughter emerge from the basement, they are confronted with a desolate landscape and an entire arsenal of eerie sounds associated with the tripods and other creatures. For an instant all is quiet (a rare moment in this very noisy movie), and then the tripods strike again with all the familiar sounds we have come to expect. Ray attempts to hide in a car, which is smashed by the tripods; Rachel and Ray scream as they are grabbed separately by the tentacles that are swirling everywhere like giant snakes.

It is already clear, though, that the Ferriers can withstand anything, and fulfilling that expectation, they once again escape, to Boston, where the tripods self-destruct in violent explosions and fire-works. We hear the last sputtering bursts of flame, the gushing red fluid, and the last gasps of the crea-

Home, Devastated Home   At the conclusion of Spielberg's *War of the Worlds*, Ray, his daughter, Rachel, and his son, Robbie are reunited with the children's mother. The soft, muted horns suggest a happy ending, but as Ray and his family tearfully celebrate their reunion, the camera reveals the full extent of the havoc the alien invaders have wrought. Whatever future the Ferriers may have is uncertain.

tures on board. At the conclusion, as leaves blow across a Boston street (reminding us of the winds in New Jersey at the beginning of this adventure), Rachel and Robbie reunite with their mother, who has been visiting her own mother for the weekend. We hear somber piano music and sad horns as the camera surveys the dead landscape.

As for the musical score, even though written by John Williams, the most famous composer of film music alive today, the fright that is at the heart of the story is realized more effectively with sound effects than with music. Contrary to our expectations (if we are, in fact, familiar with Williams's other work), Williams neither creates a musical theme for each of the major characters—although there is a recurring, low-key motif for the tripods—nor leaves us with one of his memorable "wall of sound" experiences. We are frightened when we see the unfamiliar tripods, and Williams underscores that fear with atonal music, but he also understands that what we see in this movie demands a level of sound effects that necessarily assigns music a secondary role.

It's interesting to compare Steven Spielberg's movie adaptation of *The War of the Worlds* with Orson Welles's classic radio adaptation. Spielberg spent some $135 million to make the movie and employed hundreds of artists and technicians in the fields of sound and special effects. Welles's budget (estimated at $2,000) paid for his eleven-person radio cast, small crew, and studio orchestra. We cannot easily compare a blockbuster movie released in 2005 with a radio show broadcast in 1938, not only because of the differences in the two media, but also because the radio audience then was less media-savvy than movie audiences of today are. But for anyone who has turned off the lights and listened to Welles's production—the most famous of all radio broadcasts—it's clear how he was able to convince millions of people in the audience that aliens had actually landed and that humankind was in mortal danger. At some level, Spielberg instinctively understood this, because, like Welles, ultimately he created fright through *sound*.

Functions of Film Sound

Primarily, sound helps the filmmaker tell a movie's story by reproducing and intensifying the world that has been partially created by the film's visual elements. A good sound track can make the audience aware of the spatial and temporal dimensions of the screen, raise expectations, create rhythm, and develop characters. Either directly or indirectly, these functions provide the viewer with cues to interpretation and meaning. Sounds that work directly include dialogue, narration, and sound effects (often Foley sounds) that call attention (the characters' or ours) to on- or offscreen events.

In John Ford's *My Darling Clementine* (1946; sound: Eugene Grossman and Roger Heman Sr.), "Doc" Holliday (Victor Mature) noisily tosses his keys on the hotel desk to underscore his desire to leave town if Clementine (Cathy Downs) won't keep her promise to leave before him. In Charles Laughton's *The Night of the Hunter* (1955; sound: Stanford Houghton), Harry Powell (Robert Mitchum), covets the large sum of money that he knows is hidden somewhere around the farm. His stepchildren, John (Billy Chapin) and Pearl (Sally Jane Bruce), have kept the money hidden inside Pearl's doll, but Pearl is too young to understand what's going on and has cut two of the bills into figures that she calls *Pearl* and *John*. When Harry comes out of the house to tell the children that it's bedtime, they quickly restuff the crackling bills into the doll. Although *we* hear this sound, Harry doesn't; but a moment later, in a small but easily missed visual moment in the wide frame, we see and hear the two *Pearl* and *John* bills blowing across the path toward Harry. This ominous coincidence adds tension to the scene because we fear that Harry will surely hear it too, look down, and discover the children's secret. Happily, at least for the moment, he doesn't. The sound effects in both of these films were created by Foley artists.

Sounds that function indirectly help create mood and thus may help the audience interpret scenes subconsciously. Tomlinson Holman, a sound expert, points out that viewers differentiate visual elements in a movie far more easily and analytically than they do sound elements. The reason is that they tend to hear sound as a whole, not as individual elements. Filmmakers can take advantage of viewers' inability to separate sounds into constituent parts and use sound to manipulate emotions, often via the musical score. In *Bride of Frankenstein* (1935; composer: Franz Waxman), director James Whale uses low-pitched music to accentuate the terror of the scene in which a lynch mob pursues the Monster (Boris Karloff) through the woods. In Steven Spielberg's *Jaws* (1975), composer John Williams uses four low notes as the motif for the shark—the sound of fear being generated in an otherwise placid environment.

Whether direct or indirect, sound functions according to conventions, means of conveying information that are easy to perceive and understand.

Audience Awareness

Sound can define sections of the screen, guide our attention to or between them, and influence our interpretation. *Once Upon a Time in the West* (1968; sound engineers: Fausto Ancillai, Claudio Maielli, and Elio Pacella), Sergio Leone's masterfully ironic reworking of the western genre, begins with a scene at the Cattle Corner railroad stop somewhere in the Arizona desert. This scene is notable for an overall mise-en-scène that emphasizes the isolation of the location and the menacing behavior of three desperadoes waiting for a man called Harmonica (Charles Bronson) to arrive on the Flagstone train. Within that setting, the director and his sound engineers have created a memorable audio mise-en-scène for the opening scene, running approximately 14 minutes. This sequence utilizes various diegetic sounds that we perceive as emanating from very specific points on and off the screen.

It's worth studying this scene both for its montage of sounds and for the convincing way in which it pinpoints their sources. This sound tapestry is composed almost entirely of sound effects: a creaking door inside the crude station, the scratch of chalk as the station agent writes on a blackboard, a squeaking windmill, the clackety clack of a telegraph machine, water slowly dripping from the ceiling, a man cracking his knuckles, various animals and insects (a softly whimpering dog, loudly buzzing fly, and chirping bird in a cage), the distant sound of a train approaching and the closer sounds of its chugging steam engine, the music from Harmonica's harmonica, and the sounds of the shootout in which Harmonica swiftly kills the three waiting desperadoes.

We see and hear clearly the source of each of these sounds. Because we are in the desert, there is no background sound per se (with the exception

[1]

[2]

Sound That Defines Cinematic Space The tapestry of sounds that underscores the opening of Sergio Leone's *Once Upon a Time in the West* (1968) is based on recurring sounds (squeaking windmill) [1], sounds heard only once (whimpering dog), sounds that advance the narrative (an approaching train), sounds that emphasize the tension of the situation in which three desperadoes wait for a train (buzzing fly, dripping water), and sounds that remind us of the outside world (the clackety clack of the telegraph—until it is disabled by one of the desperadoes) [2].

of the sound of the train approaching); at two brief moments we hear voices and, at the end, only a hint of Ennio Morricone's musical score. This sound design not only helps us distinguish the individual sounds, but also helps us understand how they are arranged in relation to one another. Furthermore, it creates a brooding suspense and raises fundamental questions about the narrative and characters: Who are these desperadoes? Who are they waiting for? Why do they seem to betray Harmonica the moment he arrives? Why does he kill them?

In addition to directing our attention to both the spatial and temporal dimensions of a scene, as in *Once Upon a Time in the West*, sound creates *emphasis* by how it is selected, arranged, and (if necessary)

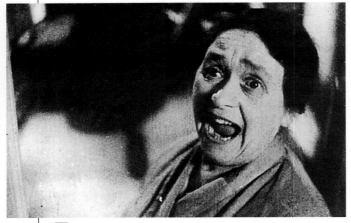

[1]

Sound That Thwarts Audience Expectations
A classic example of sound thwarting audience expectations occurs in Alfred Hitchcock's *The 39 Steps* (1935; sound: A. Birch). A landlady (actor not credited) enters a room, discovers a dead body, turns to face the camera, and opens her mouth as if to scream [1]. At least, that's what we expect to hear. Instead, as she opens her mouth we hear a sound

[2]

that *resembles* a scream but is slightly different—a sound that, because it is out of context, we may not instantly recognize. Immediately, though, Hitchcock cuts to a shot of a train speeding out of a tunnel [2], and the mystery is solved: instead of a scream, we have heard the train whistle blaring a fraction of a second before we see the train.

enhanced. In Robert Altman's *The Player* (1992; sound: Michael Redbourn), sound helps us eavesdrop on the gossip at one table in a restaurant and then, even more deliberately, takes us past that table to another in the distance where the protagonist is heading and where the gossip will be confirmed. Because the scene takes place on the terrace of an exclusive restaurant in Beverly Hills—the guests all seem to be in the motion picture business—the sound makes us feel as if we're among them, able to see the rich and famous come and go, and, more relevant here, able to hear what they're saying, even if they think they aren't being overheard.

Audience Expectations

Sounds create expectations. For example, in a scene between a man and a woman where you hear quiet music, the sounds of their movements, and a subtle sound of moving clothes, you might expect intimacy between the characters. However, in a similar scene where the characters are not moving and you cannot hear their clothes—and instead you hear the harsh sound of traffic outside or a fan in

the room—you might expect something other than intimacy. Sound also requires precise timing and coordination with the image. For example, when a simple scene of meeting in a doorway is accompanied by a musical chord, we know that the incident is significant, whether or not we know how it will evolve. But in a scene where a small boy is taken away by a bad guy at a carnival, and we hear only the carnival music and loud crowd sounds, and then see the look of terror on the parents' faces when they realize their child is gone, dramatic music is probably not needed.

When a particular sound signals an action and that sound is used repeatedly, it plays on our expectations. In Ridley Scott's *Alien* (1979; sound: Jim Shields), sound (along with visual effects) plays an impressive role in helping to create and sustain the suspenseful narrative. This science fiction/horror movie tells the story of the crew of a commercial spacecraft that takes on board an alien form of "organic life" that ultimately kills all but one of them, Lieutenant Ellen Ripley (Sigourney Weaver).

One device used to sustain this suspense is the juxtaposition of the familiar "meow" sounds made by Ripley's pet cat, Jonesy, against the unfamiliar sounds made by the alien beast. After the alien disappears into the labyrinthine ship, three crew members—Ripley, Parker (Yaphet Kotto), and Brett (Harry Dean Stanton)—attempt to locate it with a motion detector. This device leads them to a locked panel, which, when opened, reveals the cat, which hisses and runs away from them. Because losing the cat is Brett's fault, he is charged with finding it by himself. We hear his footsteps as he proceeds warily through the craft, calling "Here, kitty, kitty . . . Jonesy, Jonesy," and we are relieved when Brett finds the cat and calls it to him. Before the cat reaches Brett, however, it sees the alien behind him, stops, and hisses. Alerted, Brett turns around, but he is swiftly killed by the beast. This sound motif is repeated near the end of the film, when Ripley prepares to escape on the craft's emergency shuttle but is distracted by the cat's meow.

Expression of Point of View

By juxtaposing visual and aural images, a director can express a point of view. In countless movies, for example, the sounds of big-city traffic—horns honking, people yelling at one another, taxis screeching to a halt to pick up passengers—express the idea that these places are frenetic and unlivable. Similarly, when a movie is set in other distinct environments—seashore, desert, mountain valley—the natural sounds associated with these places (the placid, turbulent, and stormy rhythms of the sea; or the howling winds of the desert sands; or the cry of a lone wolf in an otherwise peaceful valley) reflect the director's point of view of landscape and, often as well, the thoughts or emotional mood of the characters.

Alfred Hitchcock is a master of expressing his point of view through sound. In *The Birds* (1963), for example, one of the few of his movies that does not have background music, Hitchcock uses a design of electronic bird sounds (by Remi Gassmann and Oskar Sala) to express his point of view about the human chaos that breaks out in an unsuspecting town that has been attacked by birds. Bernard Herrmann, who composed the scores for many Hitchcock movies, including *Psycho* (1960), was the uncredited sound designer on this one. It is a highly stylized sound track, consisting of a juxtaposition of natural sounds and computer-generated bird noises. Elisabeth Weis, an authority on film sound, writes:

> . . . [In] *The Birds*, screeches are even more important than visual techniques for terrorizing the audience during attacks. Indeed, bird sounds sometimes replace visuals altogether. . . . Hitchcock carefully manipulates the sound track so that the birds can convey terror even when they are silent or just making an occasional caw or flutter. . . . Instead of orchestrated instruments there are orchestrated sound effects. If in *Psycho* music sounds like birds, in *The Birds* bird sounds function like music. Hitchcock even eliminates music under the opening titles in favor of bird sounds.[9]

Directors of visionary movies—those that show the past, present, or future world in a very distinctive, stylized manner—rely extensively on sounds of all kinds, including music, to create those worlds. In *2001: A Space Odyssey* (1968), where the world created comes almost totally from his imagination, Stanley Kubrick uses sounds (and the absence of them) to help us experience what it might be like to travel through outer space. The barks and howling of the apes in the prologue reflect Kubrick's point of view that aggression and violence have always been a part of the world, indeed that such behavior removes the distinction between such concepts as *primitive* and *civilized*. The sounds of switches, latches, and doorways on the space shuttles have a peculiar hollow sound all their own. The electronic sounds emanating from the monolith reflect its imposing dignity, but also mirror the awe and fear of the astronauts who approach it.

Although Werner Herzog usually shoots his visionary movies with direct sound (meaning that it is recorded onsite), he frequently augments that sound with haunting musical scores by the German group Popol Vuh. These sounds, as well as Herzog's

[9] Elisabeth Weis, *The Silent Scream: Alfred Hitchcock's Sound Track* (Rutherford, NJ: Fairleigh Dickinson University Press, 1982), 138–39.

very deliberate use of silence, are part of what elevates such films as *Aguirre: The Wrath of God* (1972), *Nosferatu the Vampyre* (1979), and *The Enigma of Kasper Hauser* (1974) beyond being mere poetic movies to being philosophical statements about human life. *Aguirre* recounts the failed attempt of Don Lope de Aguirre (Klaus Kinski), a sixteenth-century Spanish explorer, to conquer Peru and find the fabled city of El Dorado. From the opening to the closing moments of this extraordinary movie, it is clear that Aguirre is mad. Indeed, Kinski's performance as Aguirre leaves no doubt that he is possessed by ruthless ambition and greed.

Herzog's style is frequently called *hallucinatory* (as well as *visionary*) because it produces a feeling in the viewer of being somewhere between fantasy and reality, which is exactly where Aguirre is. In the opening scene, in which Aguirre and his forces slowly descend a steep mountainside toward a river, most of the action is shot in real time, helping us to understand just how arduous and dangerous the expedition will be. The primary sounds are people's low voices, footsteps on the path, and Popol Vuh's minimalist score, which mixes electronic and acoustic sources with choral monotones. This music makes clear Herzog's view of the futility of Aguirre's quest. Thus, at the end, when Aguirre is alone on a drifting raft spinning slowly out of control on the river (photographed impressively from a helicopter, which of course we do not hear), we are not surprised to hear this musical score again—except that now Aguirre, too, seems to understand the futility of his quest. This re-use of music reinforces the prophetic nature of the director's point of view.

Rhythm

Sound can add rhythm to a scene, whether accompanying or juxtaposed against movement on the screen. In *Citizen Kane* (1941; sound: Bailey Fesler and James G. Stewart), in the comic scene in which Kane moves into the *Inquirer* office, Orson Welles uses the rhythms within overlapping dialogue to create a musical composition—one voice playing off another in its pitch, loudness, and quality (see "Sound in Orson Welles's *Citizen Kane*" later in this chapter). In Atom Egoyan's *The Sweet Hereafter* (1997; sound: Steve Munro), two conversations overlap, joined in time but separated in onscreen space: Wendell and Risa Walker (Maury Chaykin and Alberta Watson) talk with each other while Mitchell Stephens (Ian Holm) speaks with his daughter, Zoe (Caerthan Banks), on a cell phone.

A **montage** of sounds is a mix that ideally includes multiple sources of diverse quality, levels, and placement and, usually, moves as rapidly as a montage of images. Such a montage can also be *orchestrated* to create rhythm, as in the famous opening scene of Rouben Mamoulian's *Love Me Tonight* (1932; sound: M. M. Paggi)—one of the first films to use sound creatively—in which the different qualities of sounds made by ordinary activities establish the "symphony" that accompanies the start of the day in an ordinary Parisian neighborhood.

Jean-Pierre Jeunet and Marc Caro pay homage to Mamoulian's sound montage in *Delicatessen* (1991; sound: Vincent Arnardi and Laurent Zeilig). One comic scene in the film functions like a piece of music, with a classic verse-chorus-verse-chorus-verse-chorus pattern. When a butcher, Monsieur Clapet (Jean-Claude Dreyfus) makes love to his mistress, Mademoiselle Plusse (Karin Viard), the mattress and frame of the bed squeak noisily and in an increasing rhythm that matches their increasing ardor. As the tempo increases, we expect the scene to end climactically. Playing on our expectations, though, Jeunet and Caro cut back and forth between the lovers and other inhabitants of the building, who hear the squeaking bed and subconsciously change the rhythm of their daily chores to keep time with the sounds' escalating pace. The sequence derives its humor from the way it satisfies our formal expectations for closure (the sexual partners reach orgasm) but frustrates the tenants, who just become exhausted in their labors.

On a far grander scale—commensurate with the scope of the story—Francis Ford Coppola's *Apocalypse Now* (1979; sound designer: Walter Murch) includes a mix of more than 140 sound tracks during the exciting, horrifying helicopter assault on the beach of a Vietcong stronghold; prominent in

1

4

2

5

3

6

Sound and Characterization The opening montage in Francis Ford Coppola's *Apocalypse Now* (1979) sets a high visual and sonic standard, but Coppola and his collaborators meet and perhaps exceed that standard during the "Helicopter Attack" scene, in which the lunatic Lieutenant Colonel Kilgore (Robert Duvall, *standing in image 6*) leads a largely aerial raid on a Vietnamese village. Accompanying horribly magnificent images of destruction and death are the sounds of wind, footsteps, gunfire, explosions, airplanes, helicopters, crowd noise, shouting, dialogue, and Wagner's "Ride of the Valkyries." The grand operatic music gives unity, even a kind of dignity, to the fast-moving, violent, and disparate images, but what it accomplishes more than anything else is to underscore Kilgore's megalomania.

the mix is "The Ride of the Valkyries" from Richard Wagner's opera *Die Walküre* (1856). In a later film about Vietnam, Oliver Stone's *Platoon* (1986; sound designer: Gordon Daniel), the personal hatreds that divide a platoon are underscored by a montage that includes the roar of the helicopters, voices of frightened men, screams of the dying, and repeated excerpts from Samuel Barber's grief-stricken "Adagio for Strings" (1936).

Characterization

All types of sound—dialogue, sound effects, music—can function as part of characterization. In Mel Brooks's *Young Frankenstein* (1974; sound: Don Hall), when Frau Blücher's (Cloris Leachman) name is mentioned, horses rear on their hind legs and whinny. It becomes clear in context that she is so ugly and intimidating that even horses can't stand to hear her name; so for the rest of the movie, every time her name is mentioned, we hear the same sounds.

In *Jaws* (1975; sound: John R. Carter), Steven Spielberg uses a sound effect to introduce Quint (Robert Shaw), the old shark hunter. When Quint enters a community meeting called in response to the first killing of a swimmer by the shark, he draws his fingernails across a chalkboard to show his power and bravery: he is affected neither by a sound that makes most people cringe nor, by extension, by the townspeople or sharks. We might also observe that this sound is as abrasive as Quint is.

Musical themes often identify characters, occurring and recurring on the sound track as the characters make their entrances and exits on the screen. But music can also underscore characters' insights. In Sam Mendes's *American Beauty* (1999; composer: Thomas Newman), for example, Lester Burnham (Kevin Spacey) is having a midlife crisis. Although a wide variety of diegetic popular music helps identify the musical tastes of the Burnham family, it is an original theme that helps identify and sustain Lester's longing for a different life, literally a "bed of roses"—roses being the symbol of Lester's lust for his daughter's friend Angela (Mena Suvari). Lying on his bed, having this fantasy—shots of rose petals floating on him are intercut with shots of Angela naked among the rose petals on the ceiling above him—we hear a peaceful theme played by a Javanese gamelan orchestra. The repetitiveness and quality of this music emphasize Lester's mood of wanting to escape to another world.

Continuity

Sound can link one shot to the next, indicating that the scene has not changed in either time or space. **Overlapping sound** carries the sound from a first shot over to the next before the sound of the second shot begins. Charles Laughton's *The Night of the Hunter* (1955; sound: Stanford Houghton) contains an effective sound bridge: Harry Powell (Robert Mitchum), a con man posing as an itinerant preacher, has murdered his wife, Willa (Shelley

Winters), placed her in an automobile, and driven it into the river. An old man, Birdie Steptoe (James Gleason), out fishing on the river, looks down and discovers the crime.

Through shot A, an underwater shot of great poetic quality in which we see Willa in the car, her floating hair mingling with the reeds, we hear Harry singing one of his hymns; that music bridges the cut to shot B, where Harry, continuing to sing, is standing in front of their house looking for his stepchildren. Hearing Harry's hymn singing over Willa's submerged body affects the meaning of this scene in two ways: it both adds to the shot's eerie feeling of heavenly peace (with her gently undulating hair, diffused light, etc.) associated with what should be a grisly image, and connects Harry directly to the murder. In addition, the fact that he sounds calm, satisfied, even righteous, reinforces the interpretation that he sees his killings as acts of God. When the picture catches up with the sound to reveal Harry calmly stalking the murdered woman's children, the dramatic tension is increased as a result of the association between Harry and Willa's body that the sound bridge has reinforced.

Joel Coen's *The Man Who Wasn't There* (2001), a dark, twisted neo-noir film, contains a smoothly edited sequence of fifteen shots, thirteen of which are linked by overlapping, nondiegetic bits of a Beethoven piano sonata, and two of which show Ed Crane (Billy Bob Thornton) listening to Rachael Abundas (Scarlet Johansson) playing the sonata (diegetic music). In the midst of a life filled with conflict and tragedy, Ed has found "peace" listening to Rachael play this particular sonata, and this sequence is made all the more peaceful by its lyrical theme. But Carter Burwell, the movie's composer, must have chosen this sonata—No. 8 in C minor, op. 13—for its subtitle, the "Pathetique," a pointedly ironic reminder that Crane sees himself as a loser, as does everyone else.

Emphasis

A sound can create emphasis in any scene—that is, can function as a punctuation mark—when it accentuates and strengthens the visual image. Although some movies treat emphasis as if it were

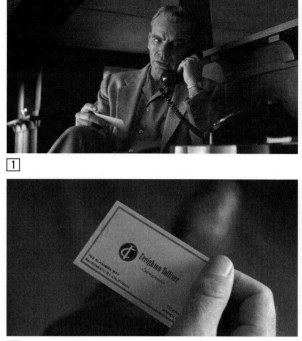

1

2

3

4

5

Overlapping Music   A fifteen-shot sequence in Joel Coen's *The Man Who Wasn't There* (2001) documents a futile attempt by Ed Crane (Billy Bob Thornton) to find a man who has swindled him out of $10,000. The sequence is one of many in the movie that show the decent but ineffectual Crane coming to grips with his life as an ordinary barber, while his wife and everyone else around him set higher goals. The sequence is underscored with the nondiegetic and diegetic sounds of Beethoven's "Pathetique" piano sonata. Here are five shots from the middle of the sequence: Crane [1] tries to locate Creighton Tolliver, the swindler (played by Jon Polito), by phone; [2] checks the man's business card; and [3] listens to Rachael "Birdy" Abundas (Scarlet Johansson), a teenage neighbor, playing a Beethoven piano sonata. [4] Rachael's father, Walter (Richard Jenkins), also listens. [5] Crane is back at his job in the barber shop. When he says, "How could I have been so stupid," we understand the appropriateness of the filmmakers' choice of this Beethoven sonata to underscore his self-insight.

a sledgehammer, others handle it more subtly. In Peter Weir's *The Truman Show* (1998; sound: Lee Smith), Truman Burbank (Jim Carrey) unknowingly has lived his entire life in an ideal world that is, in fact, a fantastic television set contained within a huge dome. When, after thirty years, he realizes the truth of his existence, he overcomes his fear of water and attempts to sail away. To deter him, the television producer orders an artificial storm, which temporarily disables Truman, but the sun comes out, he wakes up, and continues his journey, thinking he is free. Suddenly the boom of one of his sails pierces the inside of the great dome with a sound that is unfamiliar to him, indeed one of the most memorable sounds ever heard in a movie. His first reactions are shock, anguish, and disbelief. How could there be an "end" to the horizon?

Distinct as this sound is, it has nothing of the sledgehammer effect. Rather, it underscores

Truman's quiet, slow epiphany of who and where he is. His next reaction is the awareness that something is very wrong with his world. Cautiously touching the dome's metal wall, he says, "Aah," indicating a further insight into his situation. He walks along the edge of the "horizon," mounts a surreal staircase, pauses for a moment to talk with the show's producer, and finally walks through an exit door to the first free day of his life. The unique sound of the boom piercing the metal dome—underscored by the chord progressions of Burkhard Dallwitz's score—is nothing like the ordinary sound of a boat bumping against a dock. And although it is a *real* sound, it is not a natural one. This is a symbolic sound that both emphasizes Truman's captivity and heralds his liberation from a world of illusion.

In Adrian Lyne's version of *Lolita* (1997; sound: Michael O'Farrell), the sexual ambiguity of a confrontation between Humbert Humbert (Jeremy Irons) and his nemesis, Clare Quilty (Frank Langella), is punctuated by the insistent sound of an electric bug zapper. In action movies, such as *Sin City* (2005; directors: Frank Miller and Robert Rodriguez; sound designer: Paula Fairfield), the sounds of violent action are greatly emphasized so that fists hit with a bone-crunching "thunk" and cars crash with a deafening noise. The same exaggerated emphasis applies to many animated movies, in which the violence is loud but usually harmless.

Sound in Orson Welles's *Citizen Kane*

During the 1930s, the first decade of sound in film, many directors used sound as an integral part of their movies. Their innovations were all the more significant because most of them had little or no prior background in sound. Between 1933 and 1938, Orson Welles established himself as one of the most creative innovators in American radio broadcasting. Before Welles, radio broadcasting had been a wasteland lacking in creativity, but Welles approached the medium the way he approached the theater and, later, the movies: *experimenting and making things different.*

As always, Welles was a one-man show: writer, director, producer, actor. As writer, he specialized in making modern adaptations of classic literary works; as producer, he cast famous stage and movie actors, generally saving the most important part for himself; and as director, he orchestrated voices, sound effects, narration, and music in a complex mix that had never been tried before, at least on the scale that he created. There was no commercial television broadcasting at the time, and Welles understood the power of pure sounds, without images, to entertain, educate, and engage listeners. He also understood the power of radio to shock people, as his notorious 1938 production of H. G. Wells's *The War of the Worlds* proved. Indeed, it was the awesome imagination behind that one radio broadcast that not only made Orson Welles world famous overnight, but also was instrumental in his recruitment by Hollywood.

Welles's complex sound design for *Citizen Kane* (1941; sound: Bailey Fesler and James G. Stewart) is a kind of *deep-focus sound*, in that it functions much like deep-focus cinematography. Indeed, we can, with confidence, call Welles the first sound designer in American film history, because of the comprehensive way in which he used sound to establish, develop, and call our attention to the meanings of what we see. In this discussion we will look more closely at the impressive uses of sound in the party scene that celebrates Kane's acquisition of the *Chronicle* staff for the *Inquirer*. In addition to the combined staff of reporters, musicians, waiters, and dancers, the principal characters are Charles Foster Kane (Welles), Mr. Bernstein (Everett Sloane), and Jed Leland (Joseph Cotten). The setting for the party is the *Inquirer*'s offices, which have been decorated for the occasion. The room is both deep and wide, designed to accommodate the deep-focus cinematography. Welles made his complicated sound design possible by covering the ceilings with muslin, which concealed the many microphones necessary to record the multiple sounds as the scene was shot.

We hear these multiple sounds simultaneously, distinctly, and at the proper sound levels in relation to the camera's placement, so that the farther we are from the sound, the softer and less distinct the sound becomes. When Bernstein and Leland are

[1]

[2]

Sound Mise-en-Scène   The mise-en-scène of this party scene from Orson Welles's *Citizen Kane* (1941) clearly reflects what's going on—both visually and aurally. Leland (Joseph Cotten) and Bernstein (Everett Sloane) are talking, and even though there are competing sounds around them, their voices are distinct because they have been placed close to a microphone in a medium shot. Note that Kane (Welles), both visually and aurally, dominates this scene through his presence in the middle background of each shot.

additions were made during the rerecording process. Reversing the ordinary convention of composing the music after the rough cut of a film has been assembled, Bernard Herrmann wrote the music first, and Robert Wise edited the footage to fit the music's rhythm.

Sources and Types

The sound in this scene is diegetic, external, onscreen; was recorded during both production and postproduction; and is diverse in quality, level, and placement. The types include overlapping voices, ordinary dialogue, and singing; music from an onscreen band; sound effects; and ambient noise. Welles's handling of sound dominates this scene: he makes us constantly aware of the sources, the types, and the mix and (unsurprisingly) doesn't use much silence. However, two signs mounted on walls read "SILENCE" and thus, as relics of an earlier period, remind us how quiet these same offices were before Kane took over from the previous editor. Through this visual pun, Welles employs a touch of silence during the loudest sequence in *Citizen Kane*.

Functions

This sound montage

> Guides our attention to all parts of the room, making us aware of characters' relative positions (e.g., the contrast between Kane and the others).
> Helps define the spatial and temporal dimensions of the setting and the characters' placement within the mise-en-scène (e.g., sound is loud when the source is closer to the camera).
> Conveys the mood and the characters' states of mind (e.g., the sound is frantic and loud and gains momentum until it almost runs out of control, underscoring the idea that these men, Kane and reporters alike, are being blinded and intoxicated by their own success).
> Helps represent time (e.g., the sound here is synchronous with the action).
> Fulfills our expectations (e.g., of how a party of this kind might sound and of the fact that

talking, for example, they appear in medium shots, and their dialogue is naturally the loudest on the sound track; however, they literally have to shout to be heard because of the pitch, loudness, and quality of the competing sounds: the music, the dancing, the crowd noise.

We can say that the sound has its own mise-en-scène here. Although these diegetic, onscreen sounds were recorded directly on the set, some

Sound Creates Mood   At this party, where spirits are high, almost everyone joins in the act, including Kane, the performers, and Kane's staff of reporters, here pretending as if they were members of the band.

Complex Mix of Sound   In addition to the distinctive voices of the three main characters and the voices of the guests and performers, there is a brass marching band—all of this constituting a sound design and mix that was very advanced for its time.

Who Is This Man?   "Who is this man," a line in Kane's campaign song, "There Is a Man," might function as a subtitle for the movie itself, and allows Kane—singing, dancing, and mugging his way through the act—to show a lighter side of his many-faceted personality.

Kane is continuing on his rapid rise to journalistic and political power).

> Creates rhythm beyond that provided by the music (within the changing dramatic arc that starts with a celebration involving all the men and ends with one man's colossal display of ego).

> Reveals, through the dialogue, aspects of each main character (e.g., establishes a con-

flict between Kane and Leland over personal and journalistic ethics, one in which Bernstein predictably takes Kane's side).

> Underscores one principal theme of the entire movie (e.g., the song "There Is a Man" not only puts "good old Charlie Kane" in the spotlight—he sings and dances throughout it—but also serves as the campaign theme song when he runs for governor and becomes a dirge after his defeat; at the same time, while the lyric attempts to answer the question "Who is this man?" it has no more success than the rest of the movie).

> Arouses our expectations about what's going to happen as the film evolves (e.g., the marching band signals both that the *Inquirer* won over the *Chronicle* and that the *Inquirer* "declares" war on Spain—a war the United States will win).

> Enhances continuity with sound bridges (the smooth transitions from shot to shot and scene to scene within the sequence).

> Provides emphasis (e.g., the sound of the flashlamp when the staff's picture is taken punctuates Kane's bragging about having gotten his candy; after Kane says, "And now, gentlemen, *your complete attention*, if you

Sound Effects Welles rarely missed an opportunity to use sound effects expressively, as here, where the bright light of the old-fashioned flash unit not only illuminates the scene, but also punctuates his bragging about his acquisition of the *Chronicle* staff: "I felt like a kid in a candy store!"

please," he puts his fingers in his mouth and whistles; the trumpets' blare).

> Enhances the overall dramatic effect of the sequence.

This overwhelming sound mix almost tells the story by itself.

Characterization

All the functions named in the previous section are important to this particular sequence and the overall film. In this section we will look more closely only at how the sound helps illuminate the characters of Charles Foster Kane (Orson Welles), Mr. Bernstein (Everett Sloane), and Jed Leland (Joseph Cotten). Even though their dialogue is primarily a function of the narrative, its vocal delivery brings it to life. Long after you have seen the movie, you remember the characters, what they said, and the voices of those who portrayed them. As one legacy of his radio experience, Welles planned it that way.

Each of the actors playing these characters has a distinctive speaking voice that is a major part of their characterization. Indeed, their voices are part of the key to our understanding of their characters. The depth and resonance of Welles's voice, coupled

with its many colors (or qualities) and capabilities for both nuance and emphasis, enhance his ambiguous portrayal of the character. In several distinct areas, the sound of his voice deepens our understanding of this contradictory figure. It helps Kane flaunt his wealth and his power as the *Inquirer*'s publisher: when he brags to the new reporters about feeling like a "kid in a candy store" and having gotten his candy, his remarks are punctuated by the sound of the photographer's flashlamp. However, this sound may also be interpreted as Welles's way of mocking Kane's bragging.

Kane dominates the table of guests with the announcement that he is going to Europe for his health—"forgive my rudeness in taking leave of you"—but there is in fact nothing physically wrong with him, as we learn when he calls attention to his mania for collection (and wealth) by sarcastically saying, "They've been making statues for two thousand years and I've only been buying for five." This conversation between Kane and Bernstein is directed and acted as if it were a comedy routine on a radio show or in a vaudeville theater between the "top banana" (Kane) and the "straight man" (Bernstein). The implied nature of this exchange is something that 1940s audiences would have instinctively understood.

The sound in this scene helps Kane build on his power, not only as the boss *and* host of the party—"And now, gentlemen, *your complete attention*, if you please"—but also as the flamboyant and influential publisher: "Well, gentlemen, are we going to declare war on Spain, or are we not?" He's in charge because he's the boss, and the boss's voice also dominates his employees. As he asks this question, the band enters, playing "Hot Time in the Old Town Tonight" and is followed by women dancers carrying toy rifles. When Leland answers, "The *Inquirer* already has," Kane humiliates him by calling him "a long-faced, overdressed anarchist." Even though he says this humorously, he uses the tone of his voice, as well as his words, to humiliate his subordinate.

The song about "good old Charlie Kane"—here the excuse for more of Welles's vocal theatrics—later becomes his political campaign theme, so the sound in this scene connects us with later scenes in which we hear this musical theme again. By participating

[1]

[2]

[3]

in the singing and dancing, Kane continues to call "complete attention" (his words) to himself. Through both *visual and aural imagery*, Kane remains in the center of the frame for most of the scene, either directly onscreen himself or indirectly reflected in the windows. His voice dominates all the other sounds in this scene because it always seems to be the loudest.

Leland and Bernstein are different from one another in family background, education, level of sophistication, and relationship to Kane, and their conversation about journalistic ethics establishes another major difference: these characters' voices are also quite different from Kane's voice. Leland has the soft patrician voice of a Virginia gentleman, while Bernstein's voice reflects his New York immigrant-class upbringing. Leland gently questions Kane's motives in hiring the *Chronicle*'s staff and wonders why they can change their loyalties so easily, but the pragmatic Bernstein bluntly answers, "Sure, they're just like anybody else . . . They got work to do, they do it. Only they happen to be the best in the business." Their reading of these lines embodies one of the movie's major themes: journalistic ethics. Even their singing sets them apart. Bernstein sings as if he's having a good time, but Leland seems to sing only to show his good manners. Their differences, including the differences in their voices, ultimately determine their future relationship with Kane.

Sound Aids Characterization in Citizen Kane
[1] Standing at opposite ends of the banquet table, Bernstein (*background*) and Kane (*foreground*) banter back and forth as if they were a comedy duo. [2] Welles dominates the scene with sound. Putting his fingers between his lips, Kane gets the attention of his guests and loudly calls for their "complete attention." [3] Bernstein (*left*) and Leland (*right*) join in the singing of "There is a Man," but Leland, now disillusioned with Kane, sings only to be polite.

Themes

Sound serves many functions in this scene, including the development of several major themes and concerns:

1. *Kane's youthful longings fulfilled.* A major strand of the narrative conveys Kane's lifelong bullying of others, mania for buying

things, and egomania as a reaction to being abandoned by his parents at an early age. Here he begins the scene by addressing the new reporters and likening his acquisition of the *Chronicle* staff to a kid who has just gotten all the candy he wants. This statement is punctuated by the sound of a flashbulb.

2. *Kane's ruthless ambition.* The mix of burlesque dancing, loud music, and serious conversation about ethics only underscores Kane's determination to do whatever is necessary to attain his goals.

3. *Kane's disregard for ethics and principles and his relation with his two closest associates.* Kane's domination of the scene is made personal by his humiliation of Leland (throwing his coat at him, as if he were a lackey) and teasing of Bernstein ("You don't expect me to keep any of those promises, do you?"), a further reference to the "Declaration of Principles" that Kane flamboyantly writes and prints on the first page of the *Inquirer*. The dialogue in this scene (and those scenes that precede and follow it) further clarifies the relationships among Kane, Bernstein, and Leland.

The care and attention that Welles and his colleagues enthusiastically gave to the sound design of this scene was virtually unprecedented in 1941 and was seldom equaled until the 1970s. In giving this rowdy party the appearance of a real event, not something staged for the cameras, the sound— along with the visual design, mise-en-scène, acting, and direction, of course—plays a major role in depicting a crucial turning point in the narrative.

→ Analyzing Sound

By this point in our study of the movies, we know that sound (like everything else in a movie) is manufactured creatively for the purposes of telling a story. As you attempt to make more informed critical judgments about the sound in any movie, remember that what you *hear* in a film results from choices made by directors and their collaborators during and after production, just as what you *see* does. This chapter has provided a foundation for understanding the basic characteristics of film sound, and a vocabulary for talking and writing about it analytically. As you screen movies in and out of class, you'll now be able to thoughtfully appreciate and describe how the sound in any movie either complements or detracts from the visual elements portrayed onscreen.

Screening Checklist: Sound

➤ As you analyze a shot or scene, carefully note the specific *sources* of sound in that shot or scene.

➤ Also keep notes on the *types* of sound that are used in the shot or scene.

➤ Note carefully those moments when the sound creates *emphasis* by accentuating and strengthening the visual image.

➤ Does the sound in the shot, scene, or movie as a whole help develop *characterization*? If so, how does it do so?

➤ In the movie overall, how is music used? In a complementary way? Ironically? Does the use of music in this movie seem appropriate to the story?

➤ Do image and sound complement one another in this movie, or does one dominate the other?

➤ Does this film use *silence* expressively?

➤ In this movie, do you hear evidence of a comprehensive approach to sound—one, specifically, in which the film's sound is as expressive as its images? If so, explain why you think so.

Questions for Review

1. What is *sound design*? What are the responsibilities of the *sound designer*?
2. Distinguish among *recording, rerecording, mixing*, and *editing*.
3. What is the difference between *diegetic* and *nondiegetic* sources of sound?
4. What are the differences between sounds that are *internal* and *external*? *Onscreen* and *offscreen*?
5. Is a movie limited to a certain number of *sound tracks*?
6. How do *ambient sounds* differ from *sound effects*? How are *Foley sounds* different from *sound effects*?
7. Can the music in a movie be both diegetic and nondiegetic? Explain.
8. How does sound call our attention to both the *spatial* and *temporal* dimensions of a scene?
9. Cite an example of sound that is faithful to its *source*, and an example that is not.
10. What is a *sound bridge*? What are its functions?

DVD FEATURES: CHAPTER 7

The following tutorial on the DVD provides more information about sound:

- Sound in *Snapshot*

Movies Described or Illustrated in This Chapter

Aguirre: The Wrath of God (1972). Werner Herzog, director.

Alien (1979). Ridley Scott, director.

American Beauty (1999). Sam Mendes, director.

Apocalypse Now (1979). Francis Ford Coppola, director.

Badlands (1973). Terrence Malick, director.

Barry Lyndon (1975). Stanley Kubrick, director.

The Birds (1963). Alfred Hitchcock, director.

Black Hawk Down (2001). Ridley Scott, director.

The Bourne Supremacy (2004). Paul Greengrass, director.

Bride of Frankenstein (1935). James Whale, director.

Citizen Kane (1941). Orson Welles, director.

A Clockwork Orange (1971). Stanley Kubrick, director.

The Crying Game (1992), Neil Jordan, director.

Days of Heaven (1978). Terrence Malick, director.

Delicatessen (1991). Jean-Pierre Jeunet and Marc Caro, directors.

Double Indemnity (1944). Billy Wilder, director.

Dr. Strangelove or: How I Learned to Stop Worrying and Love the Bomb (1964). Stanley Kubrick, director.

Dreams (1990). Akira Kurosawa, director.

Fail-Safe (1964). Sidney Lumet, director.

The Fellowship of the Ring (2001). Peter Jackson, director.

The Ghost and Mrs. Muir (1947). Joseph L. Mankiewicz, director.

The Grapes of Wrath (1940). John Ford, director.

Hamlet (1948). Laurence Olivier, director.

The Hours (2002). Stephen Daldry, director.

The Ice Storm (1997). Ang Lee, director.

Jaws (1975). Steven Spielberg, director.

The Killing (1956). Stanley Kubrick, director.

Laura (1944). Otto Preminger, director.

Lolita (1997). Adrian Lyne, director.

Love Me Tonight (1932). Rouben Mamoulian, director.

The Magnificent Ambersons (1942). Orson Welles, director.

Magnolia (1999). Paul Thomas Anderson, director.

A Man Escaped (1956). Robert Bresson, director.

The Man Who Wasn't There (2001). Joel Coen, director.

The Matrix (1999). Andy and Larry Wachowski, directors.

Mean Streets (1973). Martin Scorsese, director.

The Mission (1986). Roland Joffé, director.

My Darling Clementine (1946). John Ford, director.

My Life as a Dog (1985). Lasse Hallström, director.

The Night of the Hunter (1955). Charles Laughton, director.

North by Northwest (1959). Alfred Hitchcock, director.

Once Upon a Time in the West (1968). Sergio Leone, director.

Pather Panchali (1955). Satyajit Ray, director.

The Player (1992). Robert Altman, director.

Providence (1977). Alain Resnais, director.
Raging Bull (1980). Martin Scorsese, director.
Reservoir Dogs (1992). Quentin Tarantino, director.
Run Lola Run (1998). Tom Tykwer, director.
The Shining (1980). Stanley Kubrick, director.
The Sweet Hereafter (1997). Atom Egoyan, director.
There's Something About Mary (1998). Bobby and Peter Farrelly, directors.
The 39 Steps (1935). Alfred Hitchcock, director.
Titanic (1997). James Cameron, director.

The Tragedy of Othello: The Moor of Venice (1952). Orson Welles, director.
The Truman Show (1998). Peter Weir, director.
War of the Worlds (2005). Steven Spielberg, director.
We Don't Live Here Anymore (2004). John Curran, director.
The Wizard of Oz (1939). Victor Fleming, director.
Young Frankenstein (1974). Mel Brooks, director.

Thinking About Movies, Theory, and Meaning

8

Wonder Boys (2000). Curtis Hanson, director.

Learning Objectives

After reading this chapter, you should be able to

➤ Explain what *film theory* is, as well as identify at least five of its many areas of investigation.

➤ Make a clear distinction between *film theory* and *film criticism*.

➤ Understand the differences between *realist* and *formalist* theory.

➤ Understand the distinctions among *explicit* meaning, *implicit* meaning, and *ideological* meaning.

➤ Explain the distinctions among three interpretive frameworks: *mimesis*, *catharsis*, and *binary oppositions*.

➤ Explain the major concerns of each of the major categories of film theories: *auteurism*, *psychological theories*, and *ideological theories*.

➤ Apply at least two of these theoretical approaches (e.g., auteurism and feminism) to a brief reading of a movie.

➤ Understand how to apply the concept of *genre* to a critical analysis.

➤ Describe the traditional approaches to the study of film history.

Movies and Meanings

Sometimes we are happy to be entertained by a movie without delving deeper into its meaning. More often than not, though, we leave a movie theater thinking about what the movie seems to be saying directly, implying, or hinting at. We wonder what, ultimately, the movie *means*. And we often find that other viewers have different ideas about the movie's meanings. Movies can mean a great number of things, and there is plenty of room for argument about those meanings. In addition, there is no one way to look at a movie or interpret it. Nonetheless, even before we see a movie, we are influenced by the comments of friends ("you've got to see it!"), critical reviews in the media ("best movie of the year!"), and our own free expectations

("my favorite actor is in it, so it's got to be good"). These influences are all vital, valid factors in the process of developing a first reaction to a movie. But when you want to explore more thoroughly why a movie has stimulated your intellectual or emotional responses, what is the next step?

Because this book has consistently encouraged you to go beyond expressing perfunctory reactions ("I loved—or hated—it") and to find convincing reasons within the movie to support your opinions, the next step is to introduce you to the many different theoretical and critical methods that are available to help you enrich both your participation in class discussions and your writing assignments.[1] Here you will see that interpreting movies can be an experience that is as diverse and rewarding as looking at them is.

Film Theory and Film Criticism

Although *film theory* and *film criticism* are distinct activities, the terms are often (but not accurately) used interchangeably. It is important to know the differences between them. When some of us hear the word *theory*, we think of the scientific model—one that requires hypothesis, experiment, analysis, and proof. In cinema studies (as well as other disciplines in the humanities and the arts), however, we rely on theories that need not—in fact, cannot—be proved. What, then, is film theory, and how does it work? **Film theory** is based on general principles concerning how we might analyze the movies. Its purpose is to give us a model for contemplating and understanding a movie's various meanings. As such, film theory is a way of looking at movies from a particular intellectual or ideological perspective. As we shall see in this section, there are many kinds of film theory, some as old as film itself, others reflecting more contemporary thought. Professional and student writers often

---

[1] For more help with writing papers about film, refer to the supplementary guide, *Writing About Movies*, that came packaged with this book (and can be found on the *Looking at Movies* website).

use several theories, all applicable, in studying a particular film, filmmaker, or group of films.

By contrast, **film criticism** is generally focused on evaluating a film's artistic merit and appeal to the public. Film criticism takes two basic forms: reviews that are written for a general audience and appear in the popular media, and essays that are published in academic journals for a scholarly audience. Each form of criticism focuses on analyzing and evaluating one or more movies in language that appeals to its particular audience. Reviews in the daily newspaper generally reflect the personality of the writer and the tastes of the paper's audience; those in scholarly journals are more likely to reflect an awareness of film theory, if not a straightforward application of it.

In the past twenty-five years, the moviegoing public has become increasingly more knowledgeable about the movies, chiefly as a result of the availability of college-level film studies courses, as well as improvements in the quality of movie reviewing. At the same time, the academic study of film has changed significantly, chiefly as a result of broad, interdisciplinary investigations into the nature of film itself, as well as the intersection of film studies with such traditional academic disciplines as psychology, economics, and history, and its revitalization by such newer disciplines as cultural studies. As a result, film theory and criticism now tend, in varying degrees, to influence one another.

Film theory is concerned with many areas of investigation, including

> The film text itself—its structural properties and its meanings.
> The film text's connection to culture and history.
> The relationship between film and reality, expressed in two fundamental points of view. The first (what we call *realist theory*) holds, among other beliefs, that cinematic language and technology are capable of bringing the movies closer to our experience of the phenomenal world—in short, of achieving an almost perfect representation of reality. The opposing viewpoint (*formalist theory*) holds that cinema is more than a mere reproduction of reality, and that the film artist gives *form* to reality.
> The production of movies as the result of a system of art form, economic phenomenon, cultural product, and technology.
> Our psychological relationship to the world projected on the screen.
> The distinctions and relationships among various types of film.

The history of film theory traditionally is divided into three phases. These overlap to some extent, but they nonetheless provide a framework that helps us understand the evolution of film theory. The first phase—a formalist movement that spanned 1916 to the mid 1930s—includes the work of Hugo Münsterberg, Rudolf Arnheim, and Sergei Eisenstein. The second phase—a realist reaction to formalism that began with the coming of sound in 1927 and helped further shape thinking about film until the 1960s—includes the work of Béla Balázs but was primarily influenced by Siegfried Kracauer and André Bazin.

The third phase, which began in the 1960s and continues today, reflects a wide range of new interpretive approaches. These approaches reflect, in turn, a wide range of academic disciplines that have influenced film theorists—including linguistics, social anthropology, cognitive psychology, psychoanalytic analysis, and cultural history in the humanities and social sciences, as well as such interdisciplinary approaches as feminism, Marxism, and queer studies, among others. More theorists than ever are writing today, and a list of even the principal theorists in these fields would be very long. A short list of the seminal writers in these new fields would include Jean-Louis Baudry, David Bordwell, Judith Butler, Noël Carroll, Stanley Cavell, Michel Foucault, Miriam Hansen, Claude Lévi-Strauss, Christian Metz, Laura Mulvey, Eve Kosofsky Sedgwick, and Peter Wollen.

Although formalist theory—reading the film text for itself—is a central concern of this book, we will devote this chapter to an overview of the diversity of theoretical, critical, and cultural perspectives that have influenced both advanced academic discourse on film and the teaching of introductory film courses. These perspectives are different from and yet relate to the kinds of analysis to which the previous seven chapters are an introduction. There is, of course, no single way to read and interpret a film, and of the many theories discussed today, some are more useful than others. Each approach has its advantages and disadvantages. Before we turn to the various theoretical approaches, however, let's clarify what we mean when we talk about a film's *meaning*.

Explicit, Implicit, and Ideological Meanings

In looking at movies, we traditionally find three kinds of meaning: explicit, implicit, and ideological.

Explicit meaning is a little more sophisticated than plot summary, but not overly interpretive; it is the sum of the things that a movie presents on its surface. George Lucas's *Star Wars* (1977), for example, is explicitly about many things: the training of a Jedi knight; the conflict between the Galactic Empire and the Rebel Alliance; the interactions among robots, humanoids, and non-humanoid life-forms; the belief that good will eventually triumph over evil. Although explicit meaning is on the surface of a film for all to observe, it is unlikely that every viewer or writer will remember and acknowledge every part of that meaning. Because movies are rich in plot and detail, good analyses or readings of movies must begin by taking into account the breadth and diversity of what has been explicitly presented. A viewer who recalls how Luke Skywalker's (Mark Hamill) childhood experience shooting the vile womp rats prepares him for the amazing shot that destroys the Death Star at the end of *Star Wars* will be organizing and associating just two of the thousands of pieces of information in the film. Our ability to discern a movie's explicit meanings is directly dependent on our ability to notice such associations and relationships.

Implicit meaning, which lies below the surface of explicit meaning, is closest to our everyday sense of the word *meaning*. It is an association, connec-

Explicit Meaning in *Star Wars*   One of the explicit meanings of the *Star Wars* movies is that Luke Skywalker (Mark Hamill) is a hero capable of using the Force for good. As *Star Wars* (1977; retitled *Star Wars: Episode IV—A New Hope*) comes to a conclusion, Luke's task in the Rebel Alliance is to destroy the Empire's Death Star ship. He says, "It's not impossible. I used to bull's-eye womp rats in my T-16 back home; they're not much bigger than two meters!" Tapping into the strength of the Force, he launches the missiles with bull's-eye accuracy and destroys the ship, achieving a major victory for the Rebellion against the Empire.

tion, or inference that a viewer makes on the basis of the given (explicit) story and form of a film. To recognize Ben Obi-Wan Kenobi (Alec Guinness) as a father figure to Luke Skywalker is to make a simple inference, a type of implicit meaning. To compare Han Solo (Harrison Ford) to a western outlaw hero, or to compare the silly bickering of R2-D2 (Kenny Baker) and C-3PO (Anthony Daniels) to comic buddy teams such as Laurel and Hardy or Abbott and Costello, is to make an implicit association, to *read between the lines*.

A very common type of implicit meaning occurs at the thematic level of narrative. **Themes** are shared, public ideas—metaphors, adages, myths, and familiar conflicts and personality types; thematic structures may or may not be made explicit over the course of the narrative, but perceptive viewers will recognize them. For instance, the theme of the Camelot legend (that is, the legend of King Arthur and his Knights of the Round Table) runs throughout *Star Wars*, but the film's closest explicit reference to this world of ideas is merely the term Jedi *knight*.

When a movie communicates beliefs—whether belonging to the filmmakers, to one or more characters in the movie, or to the time and place in

Implicit Meaning in *Star Wars* The presence and teachings of the Jedi Knight Ben Obi-Wan Kenobi (Alec Guinness, *right*) are a major factor in Luke's (Mark Hamill, *middle*) becoming a Jedi Knight and a hero. Obi-Wan was a close friend of Luke's father, Anakin Skywalker; now that Anakin is dead, it's implicit that Obi-Wan's role is that of a surrogate father. At a crucial moment in Luke's education, Obi-Wan gives Luke his father's light saber, the weapon of a Jedi Knight, and initiates him into the mysteries of the Force.

Ideological Meaning in *Star Wars* Although the world of the *Star Wars* movies is fictional, its highly complex structure is understandable through references and allusions to the world we live in. We can see two aspects of this connection in this image, in which the "good guy," Han Solo (Harrison Ford, *back to camera*), confronts the "bad guy," Jabba the Hutt (voice uncredited), an obese, loathsome, sluglike creature. Solo's costume—open-necked white shirt, leather vest, jeans, leather boots, and gun belt—suggests a cowboy in an American western, while everything about Jabba, from his reptilian skin to creepy voice, suggests a ruthless boss in the world of organized crime. Solo's charm, plus his he-man demeanor, prevents this confrontation from becoming violent.

which the movie was made—it expresses **ideological meaning**. Such meaning is the product of social, political, economic, religious, philosophical, psychological, and sexual forces that shape the filmmakers' perspectives; it may be either intentional or unconscious. It may be symptomatic of the time and place in which the film is made and of the people who make the movie and those who watch it.

The word *ideology* is not a simple synonym for *idea*. Instead, *ideology* implies a number of interrelated ideas—a worldview—about human life and culture. In a movie, ideology is the body of ideas that reflects the social needs and aspirations of an individual, a group, class, or culture. Ideological meaning is therefore generally complex and intertwined with a movie's explicit and implicit meanings. A movie's own ideology may be highly personal, may be at odds with others' views, and may lead viewers to interpretations that don't agree with all of the movie's explicit and implicit meanings.

For instance, an ideological reading of *Star Wars* might note that the film's galactic politics echo a particular American historical perspective, with the Empire evoking both the British Empire (through actors' English accents) and Nazi Ger-

many (through Darth Vader's helmet and other costume features) and its heroic depiction of the Rebel Alliance (Han Solo as cowboy hero and Luke Skywalker as all-American boy next door) working within a familiar celebration of American revolutionary democracy as leading a free and diverse galactic (international) coalition—a traditional American historical (and *ideological*) view of the nation's role in the Revolutionary and First and Second World Wars. There's no doubt that George Lucas and his collaborators intended viewers to see *Star Wars* as a classic struggle between good and evil, but once the ideological undercurrent described here is revealed, some viewers (viewers not as favorably disposed toward the United States or its ideological perspective) may feel ambivalent about the movie's implicit meaning.[2]

---

[2] This celebration of American ideology was even more forcefully developed in Roland Emmerich's *Independence Day* (1996), another blockbuster science fiction film, which ultimately drew criticism for its jingoistic plot, in which America saved the world from alien invasion.

Ideology and the Action Picture In Andrew Davis's *Collateral Damage* (2002), fireman Gordy Brewer (Arnold Schwarzenegger) loses his wife and young son in a terrorist attack and, determined to exact revenge, travels to Colombia to hunt down and kill the terrorist responsible. Originally scheduled for theatrical release on October 5, 2001, the movie was held for four months because of its uncomfortable resonances with the actual terrorist attacks of September 11, 2001. By all accounts a below-average action picture, the movie nonetheless provides an interesting opportunity for thinking about ideological meaning: produced before 9/11 but shown after, *Collateral Damage* on its opening day was already (to quote Roger Ebert) "a relic from an earlier ... time, a movie about terrorism made before terrorists became the subject of our national discourse."[3] Watching it in light of all that has happened after 9/11, we can easily discern and discuss the ideological underpinnings of the movie (and of pre-9/11 America). Like so many Hollywood action pictures, *Collateral Damage* ends with the lone American hero bringing the powerless and innocent to safety (in this case, a young Colombian boy named Mauro [played by Tyler Posey], whose adoptive mother just happened to be one of the terrorists).

Critical Approaches

Traditional criticism attempts to place a value on a work of art, a genre, or an artist; to establish hierarchies of good and bad, high and low; and to distinguish between timeless classics and forgettable pulp. Cultivating an appreciation and understanding of art, as practiced for thousands of years, is also the work of criticism. *Formalism* is a traditional type of criticism; when applied to film, it

[3] Roger Ebert, "*Collateral Damage*" (February 8, 2002) <http://rogerebert.suntimes.com/apps/pbcs.dll/article?AID=/20020208/REVIEWS/202080302/1023>.

entails seeing cinematic form as the most important source of a movie's meanings, concentrating on the filmmakers' handling of the elements of cinematic form, and attempting to explain how the filmmakers' techniques create (or imply) the movie's layered meanings. As a method, formalism can be applied by those espousing a wide range of theories, old and new. It does not require making value judgments on artworks. Formal analysis is the primary sort of analytic thinking, speaking, and writing that most beginning students of film are expected to practice.

Critical theories—Freudianism, feminism, Marxism, and others—represent loosely aligned ideas that attempt to explain how people and societies function. We might contrast formalism, which looks inward at a film, with the *contextualism* (which looks outward) of these theories. At their most basic and practical, theories offer specific worldviews that make expansive claims to explain the place of works of art within a larger context, and they offer critical lenses into the implicit and ideological meanings within those works of art. Theories also represent attitudes toward the activity of interpretation. But they are not rules, and the various isms overlap a great deal in ideas and methodology. Most analysis of movies, especially most professional writing about movies, takes a formalist's approach to some aspects of a film and a contextualist's approach to others, balancing them as appropriate. The more you learn about film theory, history, production, and criticism, the better able you will be to choose critical and theoretical perspectives that suit your interpretive goals.

Because you are using this textbook, which focuses on the formal language of cinema, your teacher likely encourages formal analysis to some degree; but the specific approach you adopt in your own analysis of movies will grow out of the unique context of your particular film course and your own interests. Some film teachers are generalists who see value in, and draw from, a variety of theories; some see themselves as specialists, advocating one theory over, and often against, others.

Your teacher may have several goals in teaching you about film: to help you develop an appreciation for great filmmaking, to prepare you for a career in

Catharsis and Violence in *The Passion of the Christ* Perhaps no movie in recent memory better exemplifies the complex issues in discussions about film violence than Mel Gibson's *The Passion of the Christ* (2004). Is the movie's two-hour-long portrayal of the torture and crucifixion of Jesus Christ (played by James Caviezel, *center*) merely an exploitation of "the popular appetite for terror and gore" on a par with Quentin Tarantino's *Kill Bill* series, as A. O. Scott of the *New York Times* would have it? Or is it (to quote Roger Ebert) a "visceral idea of what the Passion consisted of … ," a moving "visualization of the central event in the Christian religion"? Given the ultimate theological import of Jesus' death for Christians, is Gibson's explicitly brutal presentation of that death *cathartic* and ennobling, or does it (again quoting A. O. Scott) "succeed more in assaulting the spirit than in uplifting it"?[4]

media, to improve your ability to "read" the implicit meanings and formal structures of the movies you watch, or to reveal how films reinforce certain ideologies. Recognizing your teacher's academic interests and background will obviously help you navigate your course work, but even if you find yourself at odds with your teacher's beliefs, you should take this difference in opinion as an opportunity to develop your own arguments before a strong critic. You may find that your critical thinking about film becomes much more perceptive and interesting as you engage in genuine disagreement.

The following pages will introduce some of the most common critical movements in film studies (auteurism, Freudianism, cognitive psychology, Marxism, feminism, and cultural studies) and a few concepts that we'll call *interpretive frameworks* (mimesis, catharsis, and binary oppositions)—ideas so fundamental and resonant that they underlie most theoretical camps and disciplines. Learning about these forms of thought will help

you better appreciate many of the debates surrounding film and media and will offer productive strategies of analysis that can help with any film.

Interpretive Frameworks

Mimesis and Catharsis   In the Western tradition, the debate over the effect of art on people and society begins with Greek philosophers and dramatists, who were sharply split. On one side were those—most prominently Plato—who viewed the arts as dangerous in their potential influence. In part, Plato opposed the idea of *mimesis*, the Greek

---

[4] The two Scott quotes are from A. O. Scott, "Good and Evil Locked in Violent Showdown," *New York Times*, February 25, 2004 <http://query.nytimes.com/gst/fullpage.html?res=9A07 EFD6143CF936A15751C0A9629C8B63>. The Ebert quote is from Roger Ebert, "The Passion of the Christ" (February 24, 2004) <http://rogerebert.suntimes.com/apps/pbcs.dll/article? AID=/20040224/REVIEWS/402240301/1023>.

word for the imitative representation of the world in art and literature. Plato argued that art was at least two steps removed from reality: artists copied the ephemeral things around them, which were themselves imperfect copies of the eternal and unchanging ideas of those things. He was particularly concerned that poets, by representing bad behavior and bad people, would weaken society. Plato's fear that people will imitate the baser behaviors and emotions that they see depicted in art continues to this day. It drives ratings and censorship policies around the world, criticism and campaigns by groups across the political spectrum, and studies and debates about television viewing (in particular, the influence of television violence on children). Since its birth, Hollywood has remained a key target in these debates. Incidents of copycat violence, in which individuals commit acts very similar to fictional events that they have seen, are highly publicized and widely known, though uncommon.

On the other side of the Greek debate were the defenders of art, who found its influence beneficial. In the *Poetics*, Aristotle argued that humans acquire knowledge through imitation. More famously, he used the Greek medical term *katharsis* (meaning "purgation" or "purification")—in English, *catharsis* —to describe a therapeutic by-product of watching tragedy, which, through fear and pity, purged viewers of such emotions. This metaphor was taken up by later philosophers, art critics, psychologists, theorists, and social advocates to explain and justify the paradoxical presence of negative content (violence, criminality, and hatred) in art.

Today, a cathartic defense of art is commonly offered in nearly all arguments concerning its moral and social status. In film studies, particular genres (horror, thrillers, slapstick comedy, pornography) and especially violent films—for example, Mel Gibson's *Braveheart* (1995), Oliver Stone's *Natural Born Killers* (1994), David Fincher's *Se7en* (1995)—are sometimes seen as case studies demonstrating a cathartic or, alternatively, detrimental effect on society. Although most film analyses may not directly explore the issue, many assume either a general positive or negative influence of the medium on the viewer; therefore, you should begin to think about your own stance in this age-old dilemma.

Binary Oppositions in *It's a Wonderful Life* Frank Capra's lump-in-the-throat melodrama *It's a Wonderful Life* (1946) features James Stewart in a remarkable performance as George Bailey, a young man who lives in a movie-perfect small town, where he manages the savings bank founded by his father. At a critical turning point in the plot, the bank misplaces a significant sum, and George has no recourse but to appeal to Henry F. Potter (Lionel Barrymore), a villainous, miserly banker, to lend him sufficient funds until the money can be found. Bailey is totally honest, but Potter, who has always hated Bailey and his father, merely taunts the young man and threatens to call the police. In this image, Potter (*seated left*) shows why George (*right*) and other townsfolk consider him the "richest and meanest man" in the county (note the bust of Napoleon Bonaparte behind him). As a result of this confrontation between opposing forces—old man/young man, rich man/temporarily desperate man, selfishness/humanitarian values—George, who can't get a reasonable grasp on how changes in the post-World War II world have altered the social contract, is so upset that he considers suicide, no doubt prompted by Potter's comment, "You're worth more dead than alive."

Binary Oppositions (Dualism) According to structuralist anthropologist Claude Lévi-Strauss (born 1908), all human cultures share an underlying reliance on *dualism*, the tendency to see the world in terms of opposing *binary oppositions*— raw/cooked, nature/culture, man/woman, and darkness/light, for example. These binary oppositions are so much a part of the worldview of all cultures that they can be seen in their language, myths, and art. Binary thinking is a universal human condition, yet expressed differently in each culture and individual. In addition, each binary opposition reveals an underlying tension, a potential conflict that myth or art tries to reconcile. Of course, the form of such resolutions reflects the prevailing culture and its ideological paradigms.

Other theorists have applied this approach to the works of popular culture. For example, James Cameron's *Terminator* films exploit an opposition between machine and humanity, frequently challenging our more simplistic binary distinctions so that, by the end of the second film, *Terminator 2: Judgment Day* (1991), we have come to recognize the T-800 Terminator (Arnold Schwarzenegger) as akin to "human" while we continue to categorize the T-1000 Terminator (Robert Patrick) as a machine. This opposition becomes even more interesting (and productive for film analysis) when we note that both films explore it through the traits of their human characters (notice the emotionless intensity and physical prowess of Sarah Connor, played by Linda Hamilton, in the second film) as well as through their form—the costumes, lighting, sound effects, and so forth.

If we assume that Hollywood narratives are our culture's primary system of myths, we begin to understand something of the incredible success and generational resonance of films such as Victor Fleming's *The Wizard of Oz* (1939) and Frank Capra's *It's a Wonderful Life* (1946), because each film addresses recurring cultural tensions. Both movies treat similar oppositions between rural (small-town) and urban lifestyles, and both do so in the context of coming-of-age tales that exploit the more narrow tension arising when youthful idealism and wanderlust are set against traditional respect for family and home ("There's no place like home").[5] *The Wizard of Oz* and *It's a Wonderful Life* treat and ameliorate the fears and frustrations that develop out of evolving conceptions of American ideology. Because storytellers and scriptwriters design stories around dramatic conflict, it is almost impossible to find a film that is not structured

---

[5] A major demographic transformation of twentieth-century America was the tremendous shift of population from rural areas and small towns to urban areas and big cities, accompanied by a decline in extended families and a rise in nuclear and single-parent families.

around a number of traditional and specific cultural binary oppositions.

Major Film Theories

Auteurism The auteur theory postulates that the film director is the *auteur* ("author") of a film. **Auteurism** has roots in 1920s France; its popularity peaked there in the 1950s with the influential film journal *Cahiers du cinéma*, founded and edited by André Bazin. Contributors to this journal and early proponents of the theory (both as critics and directors) included the New Wave filmmakers François Truffaut, Jean-Luc Godard, Eric Rohmer, and Claude Chabrol. Bazin is most closely associated with the auteur theory. Very influential, widely interpreted, and often misunderstood, the auteurist approach is not a theory per se but rather an attitude. As such, it is personal, idiosyncratic, and flexible. Its application frequently takes two forms: a judgment of the whole body of a film director's work (not individual films) based on style, and a classification of great directors based on a hierarchy of directorial styles.

A director must have made a significant body of films to be considered an auteur. Auteurists believe, to varying degrees, that a film director's style can (and should, according to Alexandre Astruc, one of Bazin's followers) be as distinctive as a novelist's. If the director is the visionary, the one person who makes a film what it is, then cinematic style is the DNA by which that author can be identified.

In the early 1960s, the concept of director-as-author was introduced and popularized in the United States by Andrew Sarris, who was for twenty-nine years the influential film critic for the New York–based weekly newspaper *The Village Voice*. His pioneering work, *The American Cinema: Directors and Directions, 1929–1968* (1968)—one of the most provocative books ever published about American movies—employs the auteur theory to create a comprehensive ranking of American directors in terms of their personal visions of the world. Sarris's "pantheon" of fourteen directors has probably inspired more arguments among film enthusiasts than any other single list, and his overall theory so enraged Pauline Kael, a longtime critic for *The New Yorker* and one of this country's most influential voices on the movies in the twentieth century, that it ignited a long critical war between them and their followers.

Although its weaknesses—for example, its rigidity, its stress on artistic vision over technical competence, its tendency to view all movies by a single director as equally valuable—limit its application, the auteurist approach to film criticism can be very useful in identifying and appreciating those directors whose body of work displays ideological and stylistic consistency. Because the directors who shaped and influenced film history are often great innovators or stylists, we may refer to them as *auteurs*.

Psychological Theories

Freudianism Sigmund Freud, the Austrian founder of psychoanalysis, believed that each person has an unconscious that, although utterly beyond conscious reach, can manifest itself through accidents, slips of the tongue, dreams, and art. The unconscious holds one's darkest fears and desires, including one's desire for and aggression against one's own parents—thoughts that are so taboo that they resist conscious expression yet are so compelling that they are expressed indirectly, as through art. For Freud, *Hamlet* reflected Shakespeare's own oedipal desires and aggressions, projected, without the author's awareness, onto the characters of the play. Freudian theory holds that, just as a therapist can uncover the causes of a patient's hysteria, so a critic can uncover the implicit psychological meaning within a work of art.

At the societal level, Freudianism holds that a good deal of individual and collective desire and aggression is vented through art, narratives, and entertainment. From the Freudian perspective, this venting of the unconscious is generally therapeutic, cathartic, and good for individuals and society. As noted earlier, in almost every debate about the influence of art and film on individuals and society, a defense pointing to the utility of such catharsis is often used to counter the accusation that people will imitate the attitudes and behaviors presented in art and films.

Freudian Theory and *Hamlet* Laurence Olivier's pioneering film production of *Hamlet* (1948) begins with Olivier's own prologue: "This is the tragedy of a man who cannot make up his mind." Olivier's very personal adaptation of the play was influenced not only by Sigmund Freud's interpretation of Sophocles' *Oedipus Rex*, but also by Ernest Jones's elaboration of that interpretation in his study, *Hamlet and Oedipus*. Their ideas can help us understand Olivier's approach (both as director and actor). In an early scene, Olivier emphasized the idea that Hamlet's guilt, self-hatred, and suicidal tendencies are linked with his feeling that his mother's second marriage has tainted his own flesh. In this image, just after Hamlet has sat resentfully through King Claudius's praise of him—"Our chiefest courtier, cousin, and our son"—he begins (in interior monologue) this soliloquy: "O that this too too solid flesh would melt, / Thaw and resolve itself into a dew, / Or that the Everlasting had not fixed / His canon 'gainst self-slaughter" (act 1, scene 2).

Freudian theory is not only a major influence on film theory but has been explicitly incorporated into the stories of numerous films, from the psychological dramas of Ingmar Bergman's *Fanny and Alexander* (1982), Alfred Hitchcock's *Spellbound* (1945), and Jacques Tourneur's *Cat People* (1942; remade by Paul Schrader in 1982) to science fiction films such as Fred M. Wilcox's *Forbidden Planet* (1956) and Ken Russell's *Altered States* (1980). Though traditional Freudian theory has lost influence in film studies (as elsewhere), much of the film analysis and interpretation that we read and create is still informed by its most fundamental ideas, which can be stated as follows:

> Art may reveal emotional dynamics not deliberately fashioned by the artist (a significant counterpoint to the more traditional formalist and literary assumption that art reflects the artist's conscious choices).

> Expressions of sexual desire in art are intertwined with incompletely suppressed aggression, fear, and guilt.

> A critic can link an artwork and an artist's biographical background within an interpretation that reveals unconscious manifestations of desire, aggression, fear, and guilt.

Cognitive Psychology and *The Sixth Sense*   M. Night Shyamalan's *The Sixth Sense* (1999) draws us into the private world of a brilliant but troubled boy, Cole Sear (Haley Joel Osment), by showing us what the boy—but not the adults in the story—can see. In this image (from near the end of the movie), Cole has just revealed his big secret to his mother: "I see dead people. They want me to do things for them." Among other puzzling questions, viewers must ask themselves if Cole is actually seeing the ghosts of dead people just because the viewers see them too. Whatever the answer, seeing ghosts seems to make Cole more communicative with his mother, just as it makes his psychologist, Dr. Malcolm Crowe (Bruce Willis), more communicative with his wife. Viewers must interpret the details (and the absences of them) to determine for themselves the meaning of the movie's ending: is it happy, sad, believable, ambiguous, scary, or mawkish, supernatural kitsch?

Cognitive Psychology   Although Freudianism has had strong adherents over the years, others have reacted against it, preferring psychological explanations that deal with more practical perceptual, emotional, and conscious responses of viewers. Cognitive psychology—drawing on work in perceptual psychology, aesthetic studies, and artificial intelligence, among many other fields—seeks to explain how we recognize objects, fit disparate elements into orderly patterns, experience joy and sadness through art, simultaneously understand multiple meanings, and so forth. In recent decades, film scholars such as Richard Allen, Joseph Anderson, Gregory Currie, Carl Plantinga, Murray Smith, and especially David Bordwell and Noël Carroll have written articles and books that apply the ideas and findings of traditional cognitive psychology to questions of film reception. In practice, this cognitive approach shifts the critical emphasis from artist, artwork, or context to the viewer—a viewer seen as an active participant in the creation of a film's effects and meaning.

A foundational idea of cognitive psychology is that people use *schemas* to make sense of an always perceptually incomplete world. Schemas are mental concepts that filter our experience. When movie villains enter a dark bedroom and strike out at sleeping figures, we are as surprised as the villains when the covers are pulled back to reveal the old pillows-as-decoy ruse. This trick works again and again because both villains and spectators maintain a schema for the human body shape and the act of sleeping that a few pillows and darkness can evoke.

In film studies, cognitive approaches join nicely with formalist analysis, enabling us to explore how cues in a film activate schemas in viewers to help generate effects and meanings. Cognitive psychology helps explain how the storyteller's plot (what we see and hear) works with the viewer's understanding to create the story (something much larger than the plot; for more on the distinction between plot and story, see Chapter 2). By focusing on the viewer's minute-by-minute comprehension and experience of a film—of what is literally given to us perceptually—the cognitive approach helps counterbalance the traditional emphasis on the artist as the sole, active contributor to the effects and meanings of a film. Thrillers, horror movies, and mysteries like M. Night Shyamalan's *The Sixth Sense* (1999)—films that leave as much offscreen as they place onscreen—offer countless examples of forcing the viewer to play an active role in making sense of limited information.

Ideological Theories Many forms of contemporary film analysis focus on ideological concerns. Though ideological criticism is complex, diverse, and wide-ranging, some underlying general tendencies are worth recognizing. First, ideological criticism attends to the formal and informal beliefs, feelings, and habits of individuals, groups, and nations. When looking at art from an ideological critical stance, we assume that art reflects the ideologies from which it comes. In practice, this simple assumption—that films reflect ideology—can lead to sophisticated analyses and intense debate, largely because societies and art are so complex, diverse, and frequently contradictory, with theorists divided on the particularities of ideology's relation to art and on the methodology best suited to exploring this relation.

Overt examples of ideological expression can be seen in World War II–era propaganda films such as Leni Riefenstahl's *Triumph of the Will* (1935) and Frank Capra's "Why We Fight" series (1943–45), but contemporary ideological analysis holds that all films are a product of their ideological context, including those in genres such as romance, comedy, and horror. Unlike propaganda films or those treating overtly political subjects, genre films—even romantic comedies—may indirectly endorse ideological beliefs or obscure more radical solutions to social problems. No matter how drastic the problems exposed in a Hollywood film are, the familiar happy endings betray a tradition of finding resolutions and solutions from within *the system*. Like the Freudian approach and so much contemporary critical analysis, the ideological approach assumes a substructure of meaning that critics decode and reveal in their writing.

Marxism Marxism is a body of doctrine developed by Karl Marx and, to a lesser extent, Friedrich Engels in the mid nineteenth century. It originally consisted of three interrelated ideas: a philosophical (quasi-religious) view of humanity, a theory of history, and an economic and political program. Marxism has perhaps had its most significant influence in its philosophy. It has inspired people to rebel against tyranny and to seek the fulfillment of their hopes within a communal (sometimes communist) society. Its ideology fired up revolutions in many countries in the twentieth century, most notably in Russia and China.

Marxism can be called a *quasi religion* in that it requires of its followers fervent commitment and devotion to an ideal. Its view of history is that human and social progress occurs when the conflict between the bourgeoisie (middle class) and the proletariat (lower class) leads to the emergence of a classless society without a government. Ultimately, Marx predicted a revolution in advanced capitalist states, as the proletariat would dissolve all class distinctions and inaugurate a new era of harmony, peace, and prosperity for all humanity: communism.

During the twentieth century, the various socialist movements around the world adapted Marx and Engels's original ideas to meet their needs. In the West, neither of the two basic forms of Marxism—that of the traditional communist parties and the more diffuse "New Left" form, which has come to be known as *Western Marxism*—has resulted in the revolutionary change advocated by Marx. Even though orthodox Marxism has taken hold in developing nations, it has not proven particularly relevant in modern Western society, in which capitalism appears to have triumphed decisively. In the intellectual and academic world, however, Marxism remains very influential.

Many attempts have been made to incorporate Marxian doctrines into theoretical principles and analytic methods that could be used to relate cinema to the theory and practice of revolution. Following the 1917 Russian revolution, the party state paid special attention to the development of visual and sound materials that disseminated its ideas to the mainly illiterate populace. The result in the 1920s and early 1930s was a period of imaginative, ideological filmmaking by such innovators as Aleksandr Dovzhenko, Sergei Eisenstein, Lev Kuleshov, V. I. Pudovkin, Esfir Shub, and Dziga Vertov.

Perhaps the most resilient legacy of Marxism is its diagnostic and critical method—its ability to analyze power structures and class inequities. Starting in the 1930s, led by such European thinkers as Walter Benjamin and György Lukács, writers have produced a large body of Marxist aesthetic theory, which (despite the collapse of the

Soviet Union in the early 1990s) remains relevant today because of its concern with power and class.

The history of the American film industry, particularly the studio system, offers abundant opportunities for studying the interaction of the power relations in the production process. Some of the most influential Marxist criticism has focused on the portrayal of politics and the mass media in American films, past and present. However, the emphasis of Marxism on communal rather than individual life means that Marxist critics today are more likely to write about the class struggle as depicted in films from developing countries in the Middle East, Africa, and Latin America than they are to discuss films from the industrialized United States or European countries, where these subjects are treated less frequently. American fiction and nonfiction films concerned with social, economic, and political issues are nonetheless the subject of lively debates in such periodicals as *Jump Cut* and *Cinéaste*. Other critical perspectives, such as those concentrating on gender, race, feminism, and psychoanalysis, also benefit from incorporating the economically aware, class-conscious Marxist approach.

Feminism Feminist film theory brings to the study and criticism of the movies the same overall concerns that mark the feminist movement as a whole: a desire for equality with men, in society as well as in the arts that represent it; the roles that women have traditionally been expected to fulfill in society; the patriarchal structure of society; stereotyped representations of women; and gender discrimination against women. Feminist critics have focused particularly on calling attention to the media's representation of women as passive, dependent on men, or objects of desire. Influential since the 1960s, feminism has incorporated a variety of other critical perspectives, including psychoanalytic, semiotic, gender, and Marxist theories. The journals *Wide Angle, Cinema Journal, Women and Film*, and *Camera Obscura* frequently publish feminist film theory, and they are good places to chart how it has changed. Two of the many contentious issues in feminist film theory are worth addressing briefly here.

First, many feminist critiques focus on whether women and men can challenge or escape patriarchy, a social system in which men dominate. Laura Mulvey's landmark essay "Visual Pleasure and Narrative Cinema" (1975) takes the position that patriarchy is a systemic condition that neither film artists nor viewers can change, for the conventions of classic narrative cinema portray women in films as objects to be looked at, first by male protagonists in films and then by spectators forced to identify with the protagonists. Other writers advocate raising the consciousness of all women, protest negative portrayals of women on the screen, and insist that women be given an equal opportunity to take positions both in the film industry and in independent filmmaking.

In one of the first influential feminist film studies, *From Reverence to Rape: The Treatment of Women in the Movies* (1974), Molly Haskell surveys the unrealistic depictions of women throughout the history of the movies. She concludes that they are, essentially, stereotypes of what men want to believe about women, and she argues that these stereotypes of women as virgins, victims, and sex goddesses should be replaced with depictions that are more diverse, faithful to women's actual lives, and positive. We might call Mulvey's approach *deterministic* feminist theory and Haskell's approach *liberal-progressive* feminist theory. During the 1960s and early 1970s, feminist film theory leaned toward the former stance; today it tends to lean more toward the latter.

Second, some feminist critics seek to determine whether particular characters, stories, filmmakers, or film practices are pro- or antifeminist—attempts that naturally lead to disagreements. Although no single set of criteria exists for making such judgments, feminist film critics are more likely to find demeaning characterizations of women in films made before the 1960s than after that decade.

Cultural Studies An important legacy of Marxist criticism has been its influence on cultural studies, which began in the mid 1920s at the Frankfurt Institute of Social Research in Germany. There scholars attempted to incorporate politics, culture, psychology, and sociology into one discipline. During the next four decades, the work of such intellectuals as Theodor Adorno, Walter Benjamin, Erich Fromm, Max Horkheimer, Siegfried Kracauer, and Herbert Marcuse had a major impact on social and cultural thinking in the United States, to which many of them fled in the 1930s.

Thanks to such influential works as Benjamin's essay "The Work of Art in the Age of Mechanical Reproduction" (1936) and Kracauer's book *From Caligari to Hitler: A Psychological History of the German Film* (1947), cultural studies has opened a new perspective on the movies, one in which the movies are regarded more as a popular art or a cultural artifact than as a traditional art form. As a result, movies are increasingly being studied outside of film studies departments. Cultural studies has even made inroads on such critical perspectives as formalism as it has become the broadest theoretical and critical approach to movie criticism. It is concerned with the movies' function within popular culture, as well as with the influence of popular culture on the movies. Labels such as *high* and *low* have no place here; all products of culture play a role within culture, and all are relevant to how members of a society respond to those products.

For example, *reception theory* (a field within cultural studies) does not study the movie, its director, or its themes, but rather emphasizes how the audience received the movie. This is a complex undertaking because viewers bring different personal and cultural experiences to bear on their responses to a screening, but also because of other considerations. To what extent did the period in which the movie was made affect audience reception? How did such factors as age, politics, race, ethnicity, class, sexual identity, gender, income, and neighborhood affect their reception of the movie? Did they buy tickets at a theater, or rent or buy the movie for home viewing? Did they respond, in a measurable degree, to merchandise tie-ins connected with the movie's release? (To a certain degree, you will see an overlap between reception theory and social approach to film history studies in "Film History Study" later in this chapter.) In the light of reception theory, the hierarchies of the auteurist critics appear to be relics of an outmoded elitist undertaking. Thus "B" movies of the 1940s suddenly become cultural touchstones that enable us to understand wartime America. Cultural studies goes deep beneath the surface of a movie to explore implicit and hidden meanings.

Applied Readings

Let's now look at a number of films that are well suited to specific critical and theoretical approaches. Although all approaches are broadly applicable to almost any film, and although critics often combine various approaches to enrich their analyses, some movies yield more interesting answers to particular kinds of questions, as the explorations that follow will demonstrate.

Mimesis and Catharsis: *Die Hard*

Like most successful action films, John McTiernan's *Die Hard* (1988) presents violence in a form that can both horrify and entertain. Thus the movie provides fuel for the age-old debate about mimesis and catharsis. In the film, John McClane (Bruce Willis), a New York City cop, has flown to Los Angeles to attend the Christmas party of the Nakatomi Corporation with his estranged wife, Holly (Bonnie Bedelia), a company executive. The party takes place in the firm's beautiful, modern high-rise. Early in the festivities, international criminals arrive and seal off the nearly deserted building to crack a safe containing hundreds of millions of dollars' worth of negotiable bonds. McClane escapes the hostage roundup and battles the villains in an elaborate game of cat and mouse that smartly exploits the various spaces of the tower.

As in many action films, much of the hero's violence is justified as self-defense, protection of the weak, and thus legal force. In one scene, however, McClane uses plastic explosives to dispatch some villains and in the process blows up an entire floor—an act presented in the film as excessively zealous, if not vengeful. This scene and others in the film visually celebrate the destruction of the lush décor of the Nakatomi high-rise by machine gun, explosives, and fire.

To explore *Die Hard*'s treatment of violence, you could do basic research into the film's reception—

reading reviews, criticism, marketing materials, interviews of viewers and fans—to learn how the film's violence was marketed and received, and then carefully analyze the formal and narrative depictions of violence for evidence of tone, attitude, perhaps even contradictions. Do scenes such as the destruction of the Nakatomi high-rise provide catharsis for audiences, venting societal aggression? Do they suggest a more deep-seated human aggressiveness toward objects of great economic and social value? Do the film's release during the height of Japanese international economic ascendancy and the Germanic background of a number of the villains hint at collective U.S. envy and aggression toward the country's World War II enemies? Ultimately, has the movie struck the right balance between its condemnation and its celebration of violence? What role does the individual spectator play in judging the depictions of that violence?

Binary Oppositions: *Die Hard*

To begin working with binary oppositions, you should compose a simple list shortly after watching a film. These early notes might also include observations that could eventually become important points in or even the thesis of a paper. A typical Hollywood action film like *Die Hard* suggests dozens of binary oppositions, such as

> Man versus woman (in fact, a tough, working-class man versus a white-collar woman; notice that the kidnapping takes Holly out of her corporate world and places her into her husband's element: a physical battle for survival)
> Black versus white
> New York (East Coast, nervous, tough) versus Los Angeles (West Coast, laid-back, soft; notice that the film was released at a time of West Coast economic ascendancy)
> Local cops versus feds (FBI)
> America versus Japan
> America versus Europe
> Outlaw hero versus official hero

Notice how entries such as man/woman and East Coast/West Coast add detail to some very basic

Binary Oppositions in *Die Hard*   Although the action movie *Die Hard* (1988; director: John McTiernan) is as improbable as they come, it has genuine human moments, including the reunion between John McClane (Bruce Willis) and his estranged wife, Holly (Bonnie Bedelia), and the partnership that McClane, an NYPD cop, forges, through walkie-talkie communication, with LAPD Sergeant Al Powell (Reginald Veljohnson). After an unending series of bloody but thrilling scenes in an office tower held by terrorists— with John proving to be their most formidable adversary— John and Holly emerge on the ground floor thinking that they are finally safe. But, of course, one last challenge remains: a terrorist staggers out and points his machinegun at John; Al kills the terrorist with his pistol, and John, overcome with emotion and gratitude, tearfully embraces his newfound friend (in this image, John is on the right, and Al has his back to the camera). There is a considerable power in the image of the he-man New York cop embracing the calm, collected Los Angeles patrolman.

oppositions. All of the oppositions listed here are quite common and, at their most general, could apply to hundreds if not thousands of films. The last opposition, outlaw hero versus official hero, is pervasive in American narratives.[6] Hollywood buddy

[6] The outlaw hero/official hero binary opposition was best developed by Robert B. Ray, in *A Certain Tendency of the Hollywood Cinema, 1930–1980* (Princeton, NJ: Princeton University Press, 1985). Ray argues compellingly that American narratives—especially westerns, action films, and cop and crime stories—often develop a contrast between outlaw and official heroes and their respective modes of behavior. Beginning with the historical and legendary contrast between George Washington and Daniel Boone and continuing with cinematic heroes, Ray notes the difference between heroes that play by the rules in order to do good (official heroes) and those that bend and sometimes break the rules in the service of the good (outlaw heroes). Ray traces the need for an outlaw hero to a sort of Achilles' heel of Western democracies, whose broad protections and rights that are afforded to all citizens, including criminals, allow a certain latitude for nefarious types.

films such as the *Lethal Weapon* series (1987–98; director: Richard Donner) and *Rush Hour* series (1998–2001; director: Brett Ratner) series often team up an outlaw and official partner, whose significant differences in behavior and strategy help differentiate and spice up the characterizations and plots. In *Die Hard*, John McClane (Bruce Willis) follows the outlaw hero model: while combating the terrorists, McClane is technically out of his jurisdiction. By film's end, McClane looks and behaves more like a guerrilla fighter than like a uniformed police officer. In your own analysis, you could continue by finding elements of the plot, dialogue, costume, and setting suggesting that McClane is being depicted as an outlaw hero. Indeed, you could chart many of the film's characters in relation to their status as outlaw or official hero.

Die Hard is rich with oppositions that speak to tensions and issues in American culture, including the conflict and the possibility of constructive social interaction between African Americans and whites. Essentially alone as he battles a small army of criminals, McClane is befriended primarily by two black men: Argyle (De'voreaux White), the limo driver who brings him to the Nakatomi Tower, and Sergeant Al Powell (Reginald Veljohnson), the first police officer on the scene. Communicating with one another over walkie-talkies, sharing the experiences of their profession, McClane and Powell become so close during their ordeal that they embrace when they finally meet at the end of the movie.

In the context of contemporary America and especially Los Angeles, a hotbed of racial tensions and abuses of police power, *Die Hard*'s depiction of black and white unity and collective problem solving (against vaguely European villains) offers a therapeutic and hopeful resolution to tremendously difficult and historically fraught social problems. At the same time, the film traffics in stereotypes—for example, Argyle's costume and behavior suggest his less-than-serious attitude toward work and life. An analysis of this aspect of the movie could take these general notions and explore *Die Hard*'s treatment of race and of interracial interactions, perhaps in light of Los Angeles history and Hollywood's responses to current events.[7]

Freudianism: *Wall Street*

Oliver Stone's *Wall Street* (1987) provides an almost textbook example of a Freudian oedipal narrative. Bud Fox (Charlie Sheen) is a tremendously ambitious young stockbroker who begins working with Gordon Gekko (Michael Douglas), a corporate raider who buys companies and breaks them up, selling their assets and firing employees to make a profit. In the background is Carl Fox (Martin Sheen), Bud's father, a hardworking aircraft mechanic and union member who occupies the moral high ground of business: a concern for employees, the creation of good products and services. At first, Bud rejects his father's ethos and embraces Gekko's ruthless, win-at-all-costs philosophy; later, Bud battles with Gekko; finally,

Freud, the Oedipal Conflict, and *Wall Street* This image from Oliver Stone's *Wall Street* (1987) depicts a classic Freudian conflict between a caring and supportive father and his prodigal son. Carl Fox (Martin Sheen, *left*), a working-class airline mechanic, meets with his son Bud (Charlie Sheen, *right*) and berates him for his ambition as a stockbroker, with the unspoken implication that he has betrayed the family's values. Bud earns more than his father, but he can't make ends meet and asks his father for a temporary loan so that he can get through the month, and Carl complies. For audience members who know that Martin and Charlie Sheen are also father and son offscreen, the scene has even deeper resonance.

[7] During the 1980s a number of public incidents involving the police took place in Los Angeles. The Watts Riots of 1965 may provide the major historical context here.

Bud embraces Carl's philosophy and pulls a fast one on Gekko, thereby saving the airline his father works for. The fact that Martin Sheen is Charlie Sheen's biological father adds to the film's resonance.

Oliver Stone begins the film with a dedication to his own recently deceased father, "Louis Stone, stockbroker," with whom (as he has discussed in interviews) he came into conflict after his voluntary service in Vietnam left him opposed to the war. Though *Wall Street* overtly claims that Stone's father inspires its view of the best of American business practices, we might see the film as one artist's attempt to split the Father into good and bad elements, making it possible to renounce one half and embrace the other. To do a Freudian reading of *Wall Street*, you could investigate Stone's comments on his father and carefully explore the film's treatment of fathers and father figures, perhaps comparing it to that in other Stone films, such as *Born on the Fourth of July* (1989) and *Natural Born Killers* (1994)—always remaining mindful of Freud's central idea that oedipal aggression expresses itself indirectly, accidentally, unconsciously.

Cognitive Psychology: *Vertigo*

In Alfred Hitchcock's *Vertigo* (1958), Gavin Elster (Tom Helmore) asks an old friend, retired detective Scottie Ferguson (James Stewart), to watch his wife, Madeleine (Kim Novak), whom he fears is losing her grip on reality and coming to believe she is the reincarnation of Carlotta Valdes, who died in 1857. Infatuated with Madeleine, Scottie attempts to put to rest her troubling dreams by taking her to Carlotta's grave; there, Madeleine flees from Scottie, who, battling his fear of heights, chases her to the top of a bell tower; he arrives just in time to see her fall to her death in the courtyard below.

Recovering from the nervous breakdown that follows, Scottie revisits places associated with Madeleine and recognizes her in other women. One day, he sees Judy Barton (Kim Novak), who in profile looks exactly like Madeleine, though her dress and hair are different. Scottie approaches her and pleadingly asks to get to know her. When Scottie leaves, the audience learns Judy's story: Gavin Elster set Scottie up to believe that the murder of the real Madeleine Elster was a suicide by having his mistress, Judy, portray a psychologically disturbed Madeleine. Not knowing the truth, Scottie makes Judy over into his memory of Madeleine, and she reluctantly obliges.

Vertigo is interesting cognitively for a number of reasons: the point-of-view depiction of vertigo effects, the visually dramatic dream sequences, and the viewer's less spectacular but more significant sharing of Scottie's visions of Madeleine and then his memory of her through Judy. One of *Vertigo*'s strongest visual themes is the use of the profile for Kim Novak's various incarnations as Madeleine. The repeated silhouettes help link Scottie's obsession with Madeleine to the Western aesthetic conventions for representing feminine beauty. That is, Hitchcock transforms Madeleine (Novak) into a work of art: statuesque, reserved, posing, in profile—"those beautiful phony trances," Scottie angrily shouts when he discovers the artifice. Of course, these transformations are motivated dramatically, in that Gavin Elster and Judy know how to go about manufacturing a beautiful, mysterious woman because they are familiar with the conventions for representing feminine beauty, whether in high art, fashion, or Hollywood itself.

Vertigo exploits our most basic cognitive skills, particularly the ability to remember and recognize a familiar face (profile). Whereas Freudianism emphasizes the unconscious, cognitive science holds that many types of cognition can operate as unthinking habit. Facial recognition, like voice and language recognition, is typically a habituated process that functions as we're busy doing other things. *Vertigo* exploits this ability by habituating viewers (through Scottie's detective work and his obsession) to a Madeleine ideal, which is then destroyed—only to be reborn in front of our eyes in the guise of Judy. When Scottie sees Judy on the street for the first time, we have been set up to share Scottie's cognitive dissonance (she looks like but doesn't look like Madeleine).

A cognitive analysis might explore *Vertigo*'s many other hauntingly familiar treatments of feminine ideals, profiles, and hairstyles. More generally,

Hitchcock: The Auteur Who Signs His Movies
Although several other directors have appeared in their films, none has more consistently "signed" his movies with cameo appearances than Alfred Hitchcock. These appearances are less vanity than a reaffirmation of the director's awareness of the almost total control he maintained over his productions. However, they also reveal his playful approach to filmmaking. He said, "I always give a little thought to my appearances and come on as early as possible—don't want to hold them in suspense for the wrong

reason!"[8] Indeed, these appearances took on a life of their own, and you can actually feel a sense of relief in the theater as audiences catch a momentary glimpse of his imposing figure and realize that they can now concentrate on the mystery. Here we see his appearances in [1] *Rear Window* (1954), winding the clock in the songwriter's apartment (26 minutes after the movie begins); and [2] *Vertigo* (1958), walking past a shipyard and carrying a small trumpet case (11 minutes after the movie begins).

the idea of cognitive dissonance can apply to any number of Hitchcock films, which are famous for complicating "normal" human vision and classical Hollywood perspective.

Auteurism: *Rear Window*

The title of Alfred Hitchcock's *Rear Window* (1954) refers to Jeff Jeffries's (James Stewart) apartment window, which looks out onto a courtyard and a host of New York apartments. Stuck inside and practically immobile in his hip-to-toe cast, Jeff amuses himself by watching his neighbors. In addition, he is visited daily by his nurse, Stella (Thelma Ritter), and his girlfriend, Lisa Fremont (Grace Kelly). One day, the bedridden wife of his neighbor Lars Thorwald (Raymond Burr) disappears. Jeff suspects foul play. When Thorwald learns that Lisa and Jeff suspect him, he comes to Jeff's apartment, struggles with him, and pushes him out Jeff's rear window just as the police arrive in time to cushion his fall and save his life.

Rear Window encapsulates much of what has come to be identified with the Hitchcock film. The

director's obsession with "cool blondes" is embodied in Grace Kelly, whose Lisa Fremont is as elegant and beautiful as she is strong and funny. His penchant for leading men who could represent the average guy caught in outlandish situations is perfectly satisfied in James Stewart. Most importantly, Hitchcock's interest in voyeurism is profoundly evident in both the film's form (Jeff looks; the audience shares Jeff's point of view; the audience sees Jeff's reaction) and its themes (looking is exciting, dangerous, guilt-laden, and a compulsive group activity).

In terms of production, *Rear Window* is a good example of Hitchcock's well-documented desire for control and manipulation. The *Rear Window* set built at Paramount Studios was one of the largest and most elaborate ever created, and the film never leaves it—a restricted location similar to Hitchcock's experiments in *Lifeboat* (1944) and *Rope* (1948). In *Rear Window*, actors in the apartments across the way wore earpieces that Hitchcock

[8] Hitchcock, qtd. at MysteryNet.com: <www.mysterynet.com/hitchcock/cameos.shtml>.

could use to communicate directions, and the lighting for the entire set could be controlled from an electronic console.

An auteur analysis of a film and director is only as good as the writer's knowledge of the director's body of work. Because the main value of this approach is in drawing comparisons and tracing the evolution of the director's work across a number of films, a thorough familiarity is needed. Moreover, an auteur study should avoid the simplistic assumption that any director, even Hitchcock, is solely responsible for his films. Hollywood films, at least, are undertakings too large for any one person to control in the way that novelists and painters can govern every element of their art. A more nuanced application of auteurism might begin with the notion that Alfred Hitchcock was not only a dominating presence on all his films but also a smart collaborator who hired the best artists and actors in Hollywood and allowed them to contribute to his overall vision.

Film scholar Steven DeRosa's *Writing With Hitchcock: The Collaboration of Alfred Hitchcock and John Michael Hayes* (New York: Faber and Faber, 2001) is one of the more recent works to detail how films like *Rear Window* were collaborative affairs that strove for a Hitchcockian style and model that had, by the 1950s, outgrown the direct influence and control of the director himself. The auteur approach need not be undermined by a false dichotomy that sets total directorial control against collaboration; Hitchcock's films are excellent examples of how the director, together with his cast, crew, and writers, created unified and intelligent works.

Marxism: *Metropolis*

Fritz Lang's silent masterpiece *Metropolis* (1927) has influenced an extraordinary range of productions, from science fiction dystopias such as Ridley Scott's *Blade Runner* (1982) to music videos such as Madonna's "Express Yourself" (1989). Recognized as the high point of German expressionism, *Metropolis* borrows heavily from Marxist critiques of unrestrained modernism. Set in a futuristic high-rise city with a vast underground population, the film presents a social structure much like that described by Marx: the wealthy leisure and administrative classes of the upper world (the bourgeoisie) run Metropolis, while the laborers (the proletariat) of the lower world must tend the huge array of machinery that powers the upper world.

The film's sympathies are obviously with the suffering laborers and against the pampered and ruthless upper classes. Known for its striking compositions, elaborate sets, and expressionistic camerawork and lighting, *Metropolis* presents many images that boldly register the plight of the workers and the domination of the elite: legions of workers

Marxist Critique as a Central Element in *Metropolis*
Fritz Lang's *Metropolis* (1927) is a science fiction story set in a totalitarian corporate city-state called Metropolis (resembling an exaggerated Manhattan). The owners live aboveground, and the slave workers toil beneath, as we see in this image of the bizarre "M-Machine," which subjects them to mind-numbing, repetitive tasks. Lang was far ahead of his time in predicting such contemporary inventions as robotic factory workers, as well as in anticipating the debilitating effect modern technology would have on labor. The fact that machines could be both beautiful and horrifying at the same time excited many artists of his time, but the movie's suggestion that the heart is the mediator between the head and the hands, as well as between employers and employees, seems uniquely his. Lang's politics were continually changing, and he fled Hitler's regime (even though Hitler said *Metropolis* was his favorite film). There is little question, though, that the film's depiction of the oppression of workers, the need for rebellion against employers, and a mediated resolution of their conflicts lends itself particularly to Marxist analysis.

marching slowly and mechanically through underground tunnels at the start of their shift; workers stretched across the face of clocklike machine controls, constantly moving the controls as if shackled to them; elite, arrogant, smartly dressed functionaries and government engineers in a cloud-high command center.

A Marxist reading of *Metropolis* might attend to the basic historical context of the film—Weimar, Germany, in 1927, a time when some viewed communism as a solution to Germany and Europe's economic misery. The social upheavals of the 1920s led instead to the coming to power of the Nazis—deadly enemies of communism—in 1933. Lang obviously sympathized with the Marxist distrust of modern capital and industry, and he turned down the Nazis' offer to run the German film industry under the Third Reich; ironically, though, on the set of *Metropolis* the director's perfectionism and onerous working of his actors and extras seemed profoundly exploitive.

Marxism's central tenet—exploitation of workers by those who control capital—remains an undercurrent in all the various science fiction dystopias that *Metropolis* influenced, any of which might be examined in an analysis of the film. One might also compare the film, from a Marxist perspective, with classic Soviet films, such as Sergei Eisenstein's *Strike* (1925) and *Battleship Potemkin* (1925), or with more recent American films, such as Barbara Kopple's documentary *Harlan County, U.S.A.* (1976) and John Sayles's feature film *Matewan* (1987), which present worlds in which workers are obviously exploited.

Feminism: *Thelma & Louise*

In Ridley Scott's *Thelma & Louise* (1991), Thelma (Geena Davis) is married to a slob of a husband, and her friend Louise (Susan Sarandon) works as a waitress at the local diner, waiting for her musician boyfriend to get serious about their relationship. The two women decide to spend a long weekend together to get away from it all. They stop at a roadhouse for some drinks and dancing, and as they're leaving, Thelma is nearly raped in the parking lot. Louise pulls a gun on the offending man,

Female and Male Takes on the Road Picture and Buddy Genres It is both appropriate and useful to do a feminist reading of *Thelma & Louise* in comparison to a mainstream, male-centered film of the road picture or buddy genres, such as George Roy Hill's *Butch Cassidy and the Sundance Kid* (1969). The two films have a surprising number of similarities, as well as some important differences. Both comedies feature charismatic, likable actors portraying characters who escape one life for another: the women leave unhappy marriages for a more satisfying life; the men (with a female accomplice) move their criminal activities to Bolivia to escape being apprehended by U.S. authorities. In the process, the women kill a man in self-defense, and the men rob one too many banks. They are all wanted for these crimes. Whereas *Thelma & Louise* is a fresh take on the road and buddy genres, *Butch Cassidy* is a parody of those genres, as well as of the western. [1] Thelma (Geena Davis, *left*) and Louise (Susan Sarandon, *right*) speed across the desert in their Thunderbird, enjoying their newfound freedom. [2] Butch Cassidy (Paul Newman, *left*), Etta Place (Katharine Ross), and Sundance (Robert Redford, *right*) plan a bank robbery. Both stories are stylishly told with much action in wide-open spaces, but although they are comedies, they don't necessarily end happily. Both sets of characters enjoy their liberated, independent lives, but pay a heavy price for them. The women choose suicide rather than capture by the police; Louise drives their car off a cliff bordering Monument Valley (the iconic location of many classic westerns), and a freeze-frame, which catches the car in midair, ends the movie. Their fate is nonetheless clear. The men, also surrounded by police, emerge from their hiding place, and a final freeze-frame leaves their fate to the viewer.

who defiantly curses at her; Louise pulls the trigger, killing him. Thus begins a flight from the law and a strange road movie, in which Thelma and Louise bond as outlaws against a male-dominated western landscape. Refusing to surrender, the women take to robbing banks and, after a long chase ends with them surrounded by police, drive their T-bird over a majestic southwestern cliff.

At the time of its release, *Thelma & Louise* inspired a good deal of debate simply because it was one of the first big-budget Hollywood films to assert a feminist perspective. The details of the film's feminism remain debatable, however. First, at its most simplistic, the film traffics in stereotypes of male chauvinism: a lewd trucker, a sanctimonious highway patrolman, a husband more interested in beer and football than in his intelligent and beautiful wife, a young hunk who steals hearts as well as purses. In the Hollywood tradition, each stereotypical man in this film gets his comeuppance at the hands of the heroines; this pattern seemed appropriate to most mainstream viewers, although the results can be seen as being far from progressive or sophisticated.

Second, Thelma and Louise take on traditionally male roles as they replace the outlaw-buddy heroes of countless westerns and road movies. Both visually and thematically, the image of Thelma and Louise packing pistols and using them with gusto was a striking inversion of the cultural tradition.

Third, in the film's most sophisticated move, Callie Khouri's script presents two women who develop before our eyes into proud, fearless, and genuinely satisfied individuals. Thus the road picture and the western, each characterized by a separate search for identity, overlap with feminist concerns about the formation of new, truer identities for women.

Fourth, in the tradition of Hollywood liberal critiques of society, *Thelma & Louise* condemns the criminal justice system and its unwillingness to believe in and protect women victimized by sexual assault.

Finally, the movie deflects the traditional Hollywood male gaze, wherein a male character, the camera, and the viewer share a desire-filled view of a female character; this happens most particularly when Thelma ogles the handsome J.D. (Brad Pitt).

To do a feminist reading of *Thelma & Louise*, you might begin with any of these notions, finding similarities to and differences from mainstream, male-centered films of the road picture or buddy genres, such as George Roy Hill's *Butch Cassidy and the Sundance Kid* (1969) or Dennis Hopper's *Easy Rider* (1969). Or you might compare this movie with a smaller, independent feminist film such as Allison Anders's *Gas, Food Lodging* (1992), Julie Dash's *Daughters of the Dust* (1991), or Edward Zwick's *Leaving Normal* (1992), a female-buddy road film reminiscent of *Thelma & Louise*.

Cultural Studies: *Repo Man*

Alex Cox's *Repo Man* (1984) is the strange tale, set in Los Angeles, of Otto (Emilio Estevez), a disaffected urban punk who leaves behind his ex-hippie, born-again parents and a string of menial jobs for an apprenticeship with a group of repo men—automobile bounty hunters who repossess (in effect, steal) cars from owners who have failed to keep up their loan payments. Along the way, Otto survives a number of liquor store robberies carried out by old punk acquaintances; is attacked, beaten, and shot at during his various car repossession runs; meets and seduces a young woman working with a secretive UFO cult; is captured by federal agents and tortured; and flies off into the night inside a radioactive Chevy Malibu containing the bodies of four aliens.

Repo Man's low budget, black comedy, and cult status make it the kind of film that traditional criticism frequently dismisses as unworthy of study or analysis. But cultural studies, with its claim that any film—even a low-budget cult film—may speak eloquently about social conditions and attitudes, validates the study of such films and allows for serious appraisals of ostensibly unserious subject matter and genres. Because blatant humor helps the director to tell the truth, we find that *Repo Man* says a great deal about 1980s culture.

Besides its admittedly exaggerated portrayal of urban punk attitudes and behaviors, *Repo Man* parodies our spiritual yearnings, whether expressed through UFO mythology, Scientology, televangelism, or mainstream religion. Also parodied are mass marketing and advertising: characters sing jingles even as every consumer product in the film appears in white-and-blue "generic" packaging,

Cultural Criticism Alex Cox's *Repo Man* (1984) is a hilarious parody of many late-1970s conventions, including the short-lived idea that marketing generic food rather than name brands might alter our consumer culture. Thus, when characters want food or a drink, they invariably buy a box labeled "food" or a can labeled "drink." Cox takes this parody one step further when the lead character Otto Maddox (Emilio Estevez) returns to the home he shares with his stoned ex-hippie parents; asks, "Anything to eat?"; takes a can labeled "food" out of the refrigerator; and begins to eat out of it. His mother, not taking her eyes off the televangelist, fulfills her maternal obligations by saying, "Put it on a plate, son, you'll enjoy it more." This cult movie is filled with similar deadpan commentary on American social conditions and attitudes.

including large cans labeled "food." The film is full of what anthropologists and sociologists call *subcultures*: the distinctive milieus of punks, repo men, ufologists, scientists working on top secret projects, CIA agents. By exploring these subcultures and their interactions, *Repo Man* captures people's attitudes and manners of expression and dress better than most serious, big-budget films do.

Most importantly, the film traces certain American strains of paranoia, conspiracy theory, working-class cynicism, and millennialism. Ten years before *The X-Files* began its run on television, *Repo Man* was exploring this terrain of urban legend and mythology. Though the movie's plot is ridiculous, the attitudes, language, dress, and paraphernalia of popular culture offered up suggest actual subcultures and thinking. To do a cultural studies reading of *Repo Man*, you might examine the film's treatment of the punk movement, urban legends, and conspiracy theories, or you might compare this film with others that depict subcultures of disaffected youth, such as Stanley Kubrick's *A Clockwork*

Orange (1971), Francis Ford Coppola's *Rumble Fish* (1983), Richard Linklater's *Slacker* (1991), Kevin Smith's *Clerks* (1994), Larry Clark's *Kids* (1995), or Terry Zwigoff's *Ghost World* (2001).

Cult films, by definition, have small but devoted audiences that admire and value certain aspects of them. The films may then perpetuate attitudes and stances among the subcultures that embrace them. In an analysis of *Repo Man*, you might explore the narrow demographics of cult films, contrasting these audiences with our monolithic conception of a mainstream audience.

Other Forms of Film Analysis

In addition to the critical and theoretical approaches to studying movies that we have discussed already, there are other, very interesting, forms of film analysis—forms that introductory students aren't expected to undertake right away. However, if you pursue your study of film, either as a major or by taking elective courses, you will be able to learn more about at least two of them: the study of individual movies within a certain genre, and the study of many films over time. Following is an introduction to each of these fields.

Genre Study

Filmmakers and marketers depend greatly on the major Hollywood genres to ensure that a particular film has a decent chance of finding an appropriate audience (review "Genre" in Chapter 1). Genres offer familiar story formulas, conventions, themes, and conflicts, as well as immediately recognizable visual icons, all of which together provide a blueprint for creating and marketing a type of film that has proven successful in the past. Whether or not a particular analysis focuses on genre, nearly any kind of film analysis will benefit from an awareness of it. Understanding some basic ways in which genre functions will help you develop interesting critiques of genre films.

Music offers the notion of *variations on a theme*, the idea that multiple composers can take a melody and compose endless variations on it in which it remains recognizable. Some compositions will be more interesting and expert than others. In poetry, strict adherence to a prescribed form, such as the sonnet or haiku, also provides the challenge that inspires creativity and variation. The most fundamental film genre analysis thus consists of asking how a film, scene, or image varies or conforms to the genre's standard. For the genre filmmaker, the challenge is to offer enough original variation on the theme or genre to satisfy viewers who want both the familiar and the unfamiliar, who expect both *convention* and *invention*. A focus on genre involves asking where—in what plot developments, scenes, stylistic systems—the film attempts to invent and where it is following convention or even, as is frequently the case, paying homage to a classic forerunner of its genre.

One simple but very effective way of analyzing genre convention and a particular film's place within a genre is to break down a movie into three discrete temporal aspects: *story formula, scene convention,* and *iconic shot*.[9] This three-part breakdown helps isolate the basic conventions of every genre. Story formula is the overall plot structure found in a genre. In science fiction, one of the many types is that of *the alien visitor*, the structure of which follows a set pattern: status quo, arrival, discovery by an enlightened local, discovery by fearful members of the local populace, conflict with the local authorities, and resolution by death or departure. We recognize the formula in films as diverse as John Carpenter's *Starman* (1984), Iain Softley's *K-PAX* (2001), and Steven Spielberg's *E.T. the Extra-Terrestrial* (1982). We notice, too, familiar scene types in science fiction films of alien visitors: the point at which the visitor displays otherworldly powers to an appreciative audience, the moment in which fearful locals mistake alien overtures of peace for aggression, and so on. Finally, individual shots within a genre film offer iconic images (an *icon* being an immediately recognizable visual symbol, such as the Stetson cowboy hat or Colt six-shooter of the western). Some icons of the alien visitor story formula include lingering, homesick views of the night sky; the shiny metals and kaleidoscopic lights of the alien's mode of travel; and arrays of local police and military squared off against the invader.

Lately, as the major film genres have evolved, the filmmakers working within them have begun to display greater self-consciousness of genre history and conventions. This development is visible in such simple touches as a brief reference or homage to a previous film and in such complex endeavors as Wes Craven's *Scream* (1996), which self-consciously echoes and recasts Alfred Hitchcock's *Psycho* (1960), John Carpenter's *Halloween* (1978), and the horror genre itself. Parodies may be better than any other type of film at exposing narrative and stylistic conventions. The *Scary Movie* franchise (with the original release in 2000 followed by sequels in 2001, 2003, and 2006) parodies the melodrama, horror, and mystery genres. When one of these movies exaggerates the conventions of these genres, it explicitly draws attention to them—in effect, breaking the illusions of reality, representation, and invisible editing that a "straight" treatment of the conventions does not. While remakes, parodies, and sequels have long played with self-consciousness, the past decades have brought this approach into the main works of a number of genres.

Closely related is another recent development that could be termed *hybridization*—a tendency to combine genres (sometimes genres not often associated) within a single film with a free hand. Ridley Scott's *Blade Runner* (1982) is a classic example of an adventure movie that combines the thriller and science fiction genres. More recent films, such as Andy and Larry Wachowski's *The Matrix* (1999) and Andrew Adamson and Vicky Jenson's *Shrek* (2001), revel in this combinatory approach. Like *Blade Runner, The Matrix* combines adventure with the thriller and science fiction genres; and *Shrek*, an animated family movie, combines adventure, comedy, fantasy, and romance.

When studying any genre film, be sensitive to its ratio of inventiveness to conventionality; its expression of genre convention through formula, scene, and icon; its historical and cultural inflections; and

[9] This breakdown of genre into formula, scene, and icon is borrowed from Thomas Sobchack and Vivian C. Sobchack, "Genre Films," in *An Introduction to Film*, 2nd ed. (Boston: Little, Brown, 1987), 227–34.

the degree to which it self-consciously asserts its status *as* genre.

Remakes, sequels, and parodies, like genre films, provide good topics for papers. They offer illustrative comparisons and thus what we might call a built-in thesis, if you can find the most interesting and dramatic difference between them and the original films. As when musicians or singers cover other people's compositions, remakes frequently inspire artists to recast originals in provocative ways. Some notable makes and remakes include *Cape Fear* (directors: J. Lee Thompson, 1962; Martin Scorsese, 1991), *Great Expectations* (David Lean, 1946; Alfonso Cuarón, 1998), *The Man Who Knew Too Much* (Alfred Hitchcock, 1934 and 1956), *Scarface* (Howard Hawks, 1932; Brian De Palma, 1983), *Psycho* (Alfred Hitchcock, 1960; Gus Van Sant, 1998), *Alfie* (Lewis Gilbert, 1966; Charles Shyer, 2004), *Ocean's Eleven* (Lewis Milestone, 1960; Steven Soderbergh, 2001), *The Ring* (Hideo Nakata, 1998; Gore Verbinski, 2002), and *Pride and Prejudice* (Robert Z. Leonard, 1940; Joe Wright, 2005).

Comparing a sequel (even a poor one) to an original can help expose the formulas, themes, motifs, and stylistic approaches integral to the original film. Remember, poor and even bad films can teach us a good deal, both about film form and about other films' historical and cultural contexts. Even more than remakes, sequels seem obliged to repeat, but in new ways, many of the first films' best bits. Often movie sequels are criticized as being less creative because they build on a known success for profit, and therefore as artistically inferior. For example, many people believe that Francis Ford Coppola did not equal his masterpiece *The Godfather* (1972) in its sequels. Some directors, however, actually improve on weaknesses in the original; for example, James Whale's *The Bride of Frankenstein* (1935) is far more witty and stylish than his *Frankenstein* (1931).

Film History Study

What is the study of film history? In its broadest sense, film history, a branch of the academic discipline of cinema studies, examines the development of the movies from the invention of motion pictures in 1895 to the present. Scholars Robert C. Allen and Douglas Gomery define film history as follows:

> The term itself suggests a two-part definition. Film history involves the study of the phenomenon we commonly refer to as "film" (or cinema, the movies, motion pictures—these terms will be used interchangeably). Further it involves studying film from a particular perspective and with particular goals in mind—perspective and goals that are historical.[10]

The movies and history interconnect in several ways. Some Hollywood history movies tend to smooth history's facts and blur its moral ambiguities in order to create a pleasant account for audiences, particularly in movies about historical characters who are larger than life. Think of Marlene Dietrich as Catherine the Great (Josef von Sternberg's *The Scarlet Empress*, 1934), Ben Kingsley as Gandhi (Richard Attenborough's *Gandhi*, 1982), or Denzel Washington as Malcolm X (Spike Lee's *Malcolm X*, 1992). *The Scarlet Empress* is both eccentrically stylish and downright silly, and although Dietrich's portrayal of Catherine II of Russia captures the empress's luxurious life, the movie neglects Catherine's significant political and administrative contributions to her country. Kingsley, by contrast, looks, walks, and talks like Gandhi in a movie that takes the conventional biographical approach. As Malcolm X, the elusive but mythical African American leader, Washington not only looks the part, but conveys his elusive qualities. Spike Lee handles this complex historical subject with care and attention to detail.

By contrast, other movies about history or myth take a more biased approach and, thus, become notorious, actually making history of their own in the process (e.g., D. W. Griffith's *The Birth of a Nation*, 1915; or Martin Scorsese's *The Last Temptation of Christ*, 1988). Some, like Victor Fleming's *Gone With the Wind* (1939) trivialize history and transform it into myth. Nonfiction films, such as combat films made during battle, actually record

---

[10] Robert C. Allen and Douglas Gomery, *Film History: Theory and Practice* (New York: Knopf, 1985), p. 4. Material in this section owes much to this definitive study, especially parts 1 and 2 and their exemplary case studies.

history as it is being made (e.g., John Huston's *The Battle of San Pietro*, 1945).[11]

Although all movies, including history movies, are made to entertain, they may also succeed in inspiring and educating their audiences to the human conflict that is at the heart of all history. Indeed, the three hours you spend looking at Steven Spielberg's *Saving Private Ryan* (1998) might tell you more (and more quickly) about the human sacrifices involved in World War II than a dozen books could. But the movies do not provide a substitute for the more substantial analysis that professional historians have undertaken with all available materials. Ideally we should accept the emotional truth of *Saving Private Ryan* and understand that the D-Day invasion, which is its centerpiece, is only a part of the overall background of the war. Spielberg does not claim that his story is "truthful," and we should not assume that its verisimilitude is anything more than brilliant entertainment. However, it encourages anyone interested in the subject to explore further.

That further exploration is the subject of this section, as well as the focus of the academic discipline of film history. As we'll learn next, there are different types of historical writing about the cinema (the analysis and evaluation of source materials), which is also called *film historiography*.

Types of Historical Writing About the Movies   Within the relatively short history of the movies, the development of historical writing about them has been many-sided.[12] The first two film histories, by Robert Grau and Terry Ramsaye, published in 1914 and 1926 respectively,[13] helped establish the parameters of inquiry in the field. Today, there are various different approaches to

writing and studying film history, each of which has its advantages and disadvantages. By and large, however, the practice of film history—a confrontation between historians and their materials—has the fundamental goal of communicating the facts and the film historian's judgment of them.

The traditional approaches to film history are aesthetic, technological, economic, and social. We'll briefly consider each of these approaches:

> *The aesthetic approach.* Sometimes called the *masterpiece approach* or *great man approach*, the aesthetic approach seeks to evaluate individual movies, national cinemas, and/or directors on criteria that assess their artistic significance and influence. Historians who take the aesthetic perspective do not necessarily ignore the economic, technological, and cultural aspects of film history—indeed, it would be impossible to discuss many great movies without considering these factors— but generally they regard these factors as subordinate to the primary goal of charting the development of classic films. Genre study falls in this category. The films of John Ford—which, if rearranged in the order of the events in American history with which they are concerned (not in the order of their release)—have long provided a focus for discussing his traditional values (home, family, community, country) and his mythical and often sentimental view of our nation's early history. If you were interested in studying history versus myth in Ford's films, you might consider such issues as the director's style and overall body of accomplishment; works on subjects of Ford's films made by other filmmakers in the same period or genre; information about the politics, economics, social attitudes, and culture of the period in which the director lived and worked; ideas and influences that shaped the director's style; conventions of filmmaking at the time the film was made; a study of the director's life as it might help you understand the work; and the director's reasons for making the film in particular ways if, and only if,

[11] For an authoritative discussion by noted historians of many historical movies, see Mark C. Carnes, ed., *Past Imperfect: History According to the Movies* (New York: Holt, 1995).

[12] A useful source on the diversity of historical writing on the cinema is Steven Mintz, "A Guide to American Film History," <http://history.acusd.edu/gen/bibliographies/bibfilms.html>.

[13] Robert Grau, *The Theatre of Science; A Volume of Progress and Achievement in the Motion Picutre Industry* (New York: Broadway Publishing, 1914); Terry Ramsaye, *A Million and One Nights: A History of the Motion Picture*, 2 vols. (New York: Simon and Schuster, 1926).

he or she discussed such intentions. In delving further into the context in which the director lived and worked, you could read interpretive essays, reviews, and books; attend a lecture by a critic explaining the work; or take a course devoted to the director.

> *The technological perspective.* All art forms have a technological history that records the advancements in materials and techniques that have affected the nature of the medium. Of all the arts, though, cinema relies most heavily on the technology (optics, chemistry, digital processing, etc.) that has evolved in both large and small ways since 1895. The film historian who takes a technological perspective recognizes, and is thus concerned primarily with, how the major developments (including the coming of sound, the moving camera, deep-focus cinematography, color film stock, and digital cinematography, processing, and projection) have changed the ways in which movies are made. The film historian often finds that the aesthetic and technological approaches intersect. Students who are interested in this area of inquiry and who limit themselves to a distinct subject (e.g., the rise and fall of Smell-o-Vision) will have a manageable research project.

> *The economic approach.* It almost goes without saying that the motion picture industry, which spends vast amounts of money to make movies, has a huge impact on the economy. Film historians interested in the economics of the industry recognize that every movie released has an economic history of its own, as well as a place in the overall economic history of the period or country in which it was produced. They understand, for example, why certain movies are released at particular times of the year to attract a targeted audience, and why certain movie brands have a year-round appeal. Those who look at film history from a Marxist perspective criticize the profit-seeking nature of the industry, as well as its "cultural imperialism"

around the world. Today, a major focus of economic historians is the change in American film production that occurred as the so-called independent production system replaced the classical studio system and now seems to have resulted in a fluid kind of hybrid production system that combines elements of both. Students might encounter insurmountable obstacles in undertaking an economic analysis for an introductory course.

> *Social history.* As we have known from the beginning of film history, the movies are a social phenomenon. Social history and culture have a profound effect on the movies, which in turn often influence society and culture. Because the movies reflect, make, and influence history, they can be primary sources in studies of society. Thus, writing about movies as social history continues to be a major preoccupation of journalists, scholars, and students alike. Historian Ian Jarvie suggests that, in undertaking these studies, we ask the following basic questions: Who made the movies, and why? Who saw the films, how, and why? What was seen, how, and why? How were the movies evaluated, by whom, and why?[14] Hollywood itself—whose studio system is the most complex community in the world for making movies—is often the nexus of social histories of film, but at any point in movie history, Hollywood does not function in a vacuum, and scholars thus take into account such social factors as religion, politics, cultural trends and taboos, and the like. Thus, social historians ask to what extent, if any, a particular movie was produced to sway public opinion or effect social change (e.g., John Sayles's *Matewan*, 1987; Steven Soderbergh's *Erin Brockovich*, 2000; or Ang Lee's *Brokeback Mountain*, 2005).[15]

[14] This paraphrase of Jarvie comes from Allen and Gomery, *Film History*, p. 154.
[15] See "A Conversation Between Eric Foner and John Sayles" in Mark C. Carnes, ed., *Past Imperfect: History According to the Movies* (New York: Holt, 1995), 11–27.

Although some areas in the study of film history may require experience and analytic skills beyond those possessed by most introductory students, it is important to realize that one who becomes familiar with film history can use that familiarity to inform even the most basic analysis.

→ Analyzing Movies

Whatever your critical perspective is, the most important sources for interpreting and analyzing meaning are on the screen. In practice, you should begin any serious film analysis by viewing each film carefully (and as many times as necessary), concentrating on what you think are the most important cues to meaning. Having read the previous chapters of this book, you already know what to look for in terms of the formal qualities of film. The following checklist provides a few additional questions to ask yourself whenever you screen a film—questions that may help you tackle possible implicit and ideological meanings lying below the surface.

Screening Checklist: Movies, Theory, and Meaning

➤ Can you summarize in a paragraph or less what the movie is "about" *explicitly* and *implicitly*?

➤ Does the movie present a clear *ideological* perspective? Is it aware of its own ideological assumptions? Or does it seem to present itself as free from ideology?

➤ What sorts of *binary oppositions* does the movie present?

➤ Are the conflicts in the movie's narrative driven primarily by its characters' individual psychologies or by forces outside of them?

➤ Does the movie resort to stereotypes in its portrayal of certain characters? If so, are there patterns in such portrayals?

➤ Does the movie seem concerned, either explicitly or implicitly, with issues of class?

➤ Are there any curious gaps or puzzles in the movie that make you consciously aware of your role as a partial maker of the movie's meaning?

➤ Are female characters in the movie active and complex? Does it seem that these characters are fashioned after living, breathing women and girls, or are they made to play a limited role?

➤ Does the movie seem firmly rooted in an era? Does it comment on or vividly illustrate aspects of popular culture of the time of the movie's setting or of the actual time of its production?

➤ How would you characterize this movie's relationship to its *genre*? What is the proportion of convention to innovation? Is it a hybrid, parody, or other self-aware form of the genre?

➤ Is this movie about a historical event? What seems to be its approach to historical accuracy?

➤ Is this film (from whatever you know of it) considered a very important part of cinema history? If so, can you briefly summarize why? Does this importance seem to be a product of its intrinsic qualities, or more a result of its context?

Questions for Review

1. What are the differences between *film theory* and *film criticism*?
2. What is the principal difference between *realist* and *formalist* film theory?
3. What is the difference between *explicit* and *implicit* meaning?
4. What is *mimesis*, and how does it differ from *catharsis*?
5. What is *catharsis*? Why is it thought by many to be a beneficial part of looking at movies?
6. What is *ideology*? What is ideological meaning? Why are Marxism, feminism, and cultural studies considered ideological theories?
7. What are the fundamental principles of *auteur theory*?
8. What is *genre* study? Why are movie genres subject to remakes, parodies, sequels, and hybridization?
9. What is involved in the study of *film history*?
10. What is the difference between the *aesthetic* and *social* approaches to studying film history?

Movies Described or Illustrated in This Chapter

Alfie (1996). Lewis Gilbert, director.

Alfie (2004). Charles Shyer, director.

Altered States (1980). Ken Russell, director.

The Battle of San Pietro (1945). John Huston, director.

Battleship Potemkin (1925). Sergei Eisenstein, director.

The Birth of a Nation (1915). D. W. Griffith, director.

Blade Runner (1982). Ridley Scott, director.

Braveheart (1995). Mel Gibson, director.

The Bride of Frankenstein (1935). James Whale, director.

Brokeback Mountain (2005). Ang Lee, director.

Butch Cassidy and the Sundance Kid (1969). George Roy Hill, director.

Cape Fear (1962). J. Lee Thompson, director.

Cape Fear (1991). Martin Scorsese, director.

Cat People (1942). Jacques Tourneur, director.

Cat People (1982). Paul Schrader, director.

Clerks (1994). Kevin Smith, director.

Collateral Damage (2002). Andrew Davis, director.

Daughters of the Dust (1991). Julie Dash, director.

Die Hard (1988). John McTiernan, director.

E.T. the Extra-Terrestrial (1982). Steven Spielberg, director.

Easy Rider (1969). Dennis Hopper, director.

Erin Brockovich (2000). Steven Soderbergh, director.

Fanny and Alexander (1982). Ingmar Bergman, director.

Forbidden Planet (1956). Fred M. Wilcox, director.

Frankenstein (1931). James Whale, director.

Gandhi (1982). Richard Attenborough, director.

Gas, Food Lodging (1992). Alison Anders, director.

Ghost World (2001). Terry Zwigoff, director.

The Godfather (1972). Francis Ford Coppola, director.

Gone With the Wind (1939). Victor Fleming, director.

Great Expectations (1946). David Lean, director.

Great Expectations (1998). Alfonso Cuarón, director.

Halloween (1978). John Carpenter, director.

Hamlet (1948). Laurence Olivier, director.

Harlan County, U.S.A. (1976). Barbara Kopple, director.

Independence Day (1996). Roland Emmerich, director.

It's a Wonderful Life (1946). Frank Capra, director.

K-PAX (2001). Iain Softley, director.

The Last Temptation of Christ (1988). Martin Scorsese, director.

Leaving Normal (1992). Edward Zwick, director.

Malcolm X (1992). Spike Lee, director.

The Man Who Knew Too Much (1934, 1956). Alfred Hitchcock, director.

Matewan (1987). John Sayles, director.

The Matrix (1999). Andy and Larry Wachowski, directors.

Metropolis (1927). Fritz Lang, director.

Natural Born Killers (1994). Oliver Stone, director.

Ocean's Eleven (1960). Lewis Milestone, director.

Ocean's Eleven (2001). Steven Soderbergh, director.

The Passion of the Christ (2004). Mel Gibson, director.

Psycho (1960). Alfred Hitchcock, director.

Psycho (1998). Gus Van Sant, director.

Rear Window (1954). Alfred Hitchcock, director.

Repo Man (1984). Alex Cox, director.

Ring (1998). Hideo Nakata, director.

The Ring (2002). Gore Verbinski, director.

Rumble Fish (1983). Francis Ford Coppola, director.

Saving Private Ryan (1998). Steven Spielberg, director.

Scarface (1932). Howard Hawks, director.

Scarface (1983). Brian De Palma, director.

The Scarlet Empress (1934). Josef von Sternberg, director.

Scary Movie (2000) and *Scary Movie 2* (2001). Keenan Ivory Wayans, director.

Scary Movie 3 (2003) and *Scary Movie 4* (2006). David Zucker, director.

Scream (1996). Wes Craven, director.

Se7en (1995). David Fincher, director.

Shrek (2001). Andrew Adamson and Vicky Jenson, directors.

The Sixth Sense (1999). M. Night Shyamalan, director.

Slacker (1991). Richard Linklater, director.

Spellbound (1945). Alfred Hitchcock, director.

Star Wars (1977). George Lucas, director.

Starman (1984). John Carpenter, director.

Strike (1925). Sergei Eisenstein, director.

Terminator 2: Judgment Day (1991). James Cameron, director.

Thelma & Louise (1991). Ridley Scott, director.

Triumph of the Will (1935). Leni Riefenstahl, director.

Vertigo (1958). Alfred Hitchcock, director.

Wall Street (1987). Oliver Stone, director.

"Why We Fight" series (1943–45). Frank Capra, director.

The Wizard of Oz (1939). Victor Fleming, director.

Appendix: Hollywood Production Systems

The art of the movies—the primary concern of this book—is inseparable from its business. In his novel *The Last Tycoon*, F. Scott Fitzgerald attempted to explain how Hollywood works:

> You can take Hollywood for granted like I did, or you can dismiss it with the contempt we reserve for what we don't understand. It can be understood too, but only dimly and in flashes. Not half a dozen men have ever been able to keep the whole equation of pictures in their heads.[1]

In fact, however, that equation is quite simple: moviemaking is, above all, a moneymaking enterprise.[2]

In the movie industry, costs and profits are measured in hundreds of millions of dollars. Today the *average* Hollywood film costs about $64 million to produce and an additional $35 million to market. Thus, with the average movie costing about $100 million, the individuals and financial institutions that invest in the production of films, and the producers and studios in whom they invest, care first about money (ensuring the safety and potential return of their investments) and second—often a distant second—about art. They focus on movies as commodities and, for that reason, often consider release dates, distribution, and marketing as more important than the products themselves. In view of this reality, it is all the more impressive, then, that the movie industry produces a small number of films each year that can be appreciated, analyzed, and interpreted as genuine works of art rather than simply as commercial products to be consumed.

Because movie production involves a much more complicated and costly process than do most other artistic endeavors, very few decisions are made lightly. Unlike some arts—painting, for example—in which the materials and the process are relatively inexpensive, every decision in filmmaking has significant financial ramifications. Painters may paint over pictures many times without incurring significant costs, and thus their decisions can be dictated almost entirely by artistic inspiration. Movies, in contrast, involve a constant tug-of-war between artistic vision and profitability.

A great movie generally requires two key ingredients: a good script and a director's inspiration, vision, intelligence, and supervision (but not necessarily control) of all aspects of the film's production.

---

[1] F. Scott Fitzgerald, *The Last Tycoon* (New York: Scribner's, 1941), 3.
[2] David Thomson takes a nonfiction approach to defining the equation in *The Whole Equation: A History of Hollywood* (New York: Knopf, 2005).

Because the director plays the paramount role in the production process and in most cases has final authority over the result, we ordinarily cite a film in this way: Amy Heckerling's *Clueless* (1995). But although movie history began with staunchly individual filmmakers, movies have been carried forward through the years by teamwork. From the moment the raw film stock is purchased through its exposure, processing, editing, and projection, filmmakers depend on a variety of technology, technicians, and craftspeople. And no matter how clear filmmakers' ideas may be at the start, their work will change considerably, thanks to technology and teamwork, between its early stages and the final version released to the public.

Although many movie directors—working under such pressures as producers' schedules and budgets—have been known for taking their power all too seriously (being difficult on the set, throwing tantrums, screaming at and even physically assaulting members of the cast and crew, and raging at the front office), moviemaking is an essentially collaborative activity.[3] Even then, as film scholar Jon Lewis observes, "what ends up on the screen is not only a miracle of persistence and inspiration but also the result of certain practical concessions to the limitations of the studio system."[4]

Film production is complicated by the cost-effective, standard practice of shooting movies out of chronological order. This means that the production crew shoots the film not in the order that preserves narrative continuity but in an order that allows the most efficient use of human and financial resources. During production, a **script supervisor** stays as close to the director as possible, for this person is an invaluable source of factual information about the shooting. The script supervisor records all details of continuity from shot to shot, ascertaining that costumes, positioning and orientation of objects, and placement and movement of actors are consistent in each successive shot and, indeed, in all parts of the film. Overall, the pattern of production includes securing and developing a story with audience appeal; breaking the story into units that can be shot most profitably; shooting; establishing through editing the order in which events will appear onscreen; and then adding the sound, music, and special effects that help finish the movie. Today, however, because the use of a **video assist camera** permits a director to review each take immediately after shooting, it is much easier to match details from shot to shot.

The process once took place in the vast, factory-like studios that dominated Hollywood and other major film production centers around the world. Today it happens in the self-contained worlds of individual production units, which often operate in leased studio facilities. The differences between these two modes of production are, in a sense, reflected in movies' production credits. In older films, all the (brief) production credits generally appear at the beginning, with, sometimes, the names of the leading actors repeated in (and constituting) the closing credits. Today opening credits vary widely, but closing credits are lengthy and often include several hundred people, accounting for virtually every person who worked on a film or had something to do with it (e.g., caterers, animal handlers, accountants). Collective-bargaining agreements between producers and various labor unions—representing every person who works on a union production—impose clear definitions of all crewmembers' responsibilities, as well as the size and placement of their screen credits. These credits properly and legally acknowledge people's contributions to films.[5]

---

[3] Insights into the long hours and hard work that go into movie production are provided in movies about making movies, which show us that, in a world of large egos, collaboration can be a myth, and that many things go wrong on most movie sets. See "Further Viewing" at the end of this appendix for a list of such films. See also Rudy Behlmer and Tony Thomas, *Hollywood's Hollywood: The Movies About the Movies* (Secaucus, N.J.: Citadel, 1975).

[4] Jon Lewis, *Whom God Wishes to Destroy: Francis Ford Coppola and the New Hollywood* (Durham, N.C.: Duke University Press, 1955), 4.

[5] Because nonunion crews make many independent films, these conventions of the division of labor and screen credit do not necessarily apply to independent films. Often on such films, crew members may be relatively inexperienced, not yet qualified for union membership, or unwilling to play several roles in return for the experience and screen credit. Government agencies and volunteer individuals or organizations may also be credited for their contributions.

In order to understand certain aesthetic judgments made by film producers, directors, and their collaborators, you should be familiar with the fundamentals of how a movie is made—in particular, with the three phases of the moviemaking process: preproduction, production, and postproduction.

How a Movie Is Made

The making of a movie, whether by a studio or by an independent producer (as we'll discuss later), proceeds through three basic phases: *preproduction*, *production*, and *postproduction.*

Preproduction

Stage one, **preproduction**, consists of planning and preparation. It takes as long as necessary to get the job done—on average, a year or two. First, filmmakers develop an idea or obtain a script they wish to produce. They may secure from a publisher the rights to a successful novel or buy a writer's "pitch" for a story. The opening segment of Robert Altman's *The Player* (1992) provides a comic view of the start of a studio executive's typical day. The executive, Griffin Mill (Tim Robbins), has the responsibility of listening to initial pitches from writers and recommending to his boss the ones he likes. Moving blithely through a world of business politics, intrigue, and power games, he hears from people with and without appointments, losers, hangers-on, hacks, and even experienced authors. Everyone he meets wants to be a screenwriter, and everyone wants to cast Julia Roberts. The pitches are, for the most part, desperate attempts to make a new movie out of two previously successful ones, as when one scriptwriter—who cannot even agree with her partner on what they're talking about—summarizes a proposal as "*Out of Africa* meets *Pretty Woman.*" The final pitch before the credits end, about a "political thriller," serves as a transition to the thriller at the heart of Altman's film. One of Hollywood's most inventive and successful independent directors, Altman clearly knows the territory well enough to satirize it.

Once the rights to producing a story have been contracted and purchased, the producers can spend months arranging the financing for a production. The ease with which they accomplish this, and the funds that they secure, will largely depend on the film they offer to their backers and its projected financial returns. As we'll see, a director may spend another month or more discussing the script with the screenwriter and the key people responsible for design, photography, music, and sound. Another two or three months may be spent rewriting the script. During this process of previsualization, before the cameras start to roll, the director and the chief collaborators decide how they want the film to look, sound, and move. At least two to three weeks more can be devoted to organizational issues and details such as scheduling studio space and scouting locations, obtaining permissions to use those locations, and arranging for the design and construction of sets, costumes, and properties. Just before shooting begins, another two weeks will probably be devoted to rehearsals with the cast and crew.

Up to this point, almost a year has elapsed—assuming that all has gone smoothly. Though the entire process of making a movie may seem straightforward, this description does not take into account the inevitable delays, the continuing difficulties in pulling together the financial package, and the countless details that must be attended to. For example, a film made at the peak of the Hollywood studio system would have been carefully planned, budgeted, and supervised by the producer in the front office, whether it was shot in a studio or on location. Daily reports to and from the set ensured that everyone knew, to the minute and to the dollar, the progress and the cost.

Orson Welles extensively composed and planned the shots of his first film, *Citizen Kane* (1941), which was photographed entirely in the RKO studio and miraculously (considering Welles's later reputation as a spendthrift independent director) was completed in less than a year, almost within the allotted budget. By contrast, Francis Ford Coppola, already a highly experienced director by the time he made *Apocalypse Now* (1979), began without a clear plan of what he wanted to achieve, worked as an independent producer with financing from United

Artists, and shot the film in a foreign country under very difficult conditions, ultimately exposing 115 hours of film for every hour actually used. During the four years it took to complete the film, he spent more than twice his original budget.

In making a film, meticulous preparation is everything, and key people take the time to think out alternatives and choose the one that seems best for the film. Thorough planning does not stifle further creativity or improvisation during production but rather encourages it, because planning makes the alternatives clear. Director Sidney Lumet emphasizes the logistics:

> Someone once asked me what making a movie was like. I said it was like making a mosaic. Each setup is like a tiny tile [a *setup*, the basic component of a film's production, consists of one camera position and everything associated with it]. You color it, shape it, polish it as best you can. You'll do six or seven hundred of these, maybe a thousand. (There can easily be that many setups in a movie.) Then you literally paste them together and hope it's what you set out to do. But if you expect the final mosaic to look like anything, you'd better know what you're going for as you work on each tiny tile.[6]

Production

Production, the actual shooting, can last six weeks to several months or more. Although the producer and director continue to work very closely together, the director ordinarily takes charge during the shooting. The director's principal activities during this period are conducting blocking and lighting rehearsals on the set with *stand-ins*, followed by rehearsals with the cast; supervising the compilation of the records that indicate what is being shot each day and informing cast and crew members of their assignments; placing and, for each subsequent shot, re-placing cameras, lights, microphones, and other equipment; shooting each shot as many times as necessary until the director is satisfied and calls "print"; reviewing the results of each day's shooting

(called *rushes* or *dailies*) with key creative personnel and cast; and reshooting as necessary.

Every director works differently. Ordinarily, however, the director further breaks down the shooting script into manageable sections, then sets a goal of shooting a specified number of pages a day (typically, three pages is a full day's work). This process depends on the number of setups involved. Most directors try to shoot between fifteen and twenty setups a day when they're in the studio, where everything can be controlled; for exterior shooting, the number of setups varies. In any event, everyone involved in the production works a full day—usually from about 8:00 am to about 6:00 pm (depending on their jobs and contracts), five days a week, with overtime when necessary. When complicated makeup and costuming are required, the actors may be asked to report for work early enough to finish that preparation before the crew is due to report. After each day's shooting, or as soon thereafter as the processing laboratory can deliver them, the director and others review the rushes. (Movies shot digitally, or with a video assist camera, can be reviewed immediately, allowing retakes to be made with the same setup or a different one.)

Recently, watching a movie shoot in a Manhattan store, which was closed for the night to give the crew maximum access, I saw again why it can take a great deal of time to complete even the simplest shot. By actual count, forty crew members were there to support the director and four actors, who were ready to work. After the first setup was blocked, rehearsed, and lighted, the director made three takes. This process took three hours. However, the rest of the day's schedule was abandoned because the lighting that had been brought in for the shoot failed. Why? The gaffer, the chief electrician, had neglected to ensure that the store's electrical capacity could support it. By the time generators were located and trucked to the site, two hours had been lost. Of course, any one of a dozen problems—human and technical—could have kept the director and crew from meeting their schedule.

During production, the number of people required to film a particular shot depends on the needs of that shot or, more precisely, on the overall scene in which the shot occurs. Many factors deter-

---

[6] Sidney Lumet, *Making Movies* (New York: Vintage, 1996), 58.

mine the size of the crew for any shot or scene, including the use of studio or exterior locations, day or night shooting, shooting on an uncrowded exterior location or a crowded city street, camera and lighting setups, and the extent of movement by the camera and the actors. For example, a scene that involves two people in a simple interior setting, with a basic camera and lighting setup, may require a minimal crew, while a scene involving many people in an exterior setting, with several camera positions and carefully choreographed movement, normally requires a large crew. The creation of artificial weather (rain, wind, or snow) and the use of animals or crowds—all expensive factors—require additional personnel. Shooting on exterior locations is usually more expensive than shooting in a studio because it involves transportation and food, sometimes requires hotel accommodations, and depends to a considerable extent on the weather.

To better understand what's involved in shooting, we'll look briefly at the production of Robert Zemeckis's *Cast Away* (2000). The movie features Tom Hanks as Chuck Noland, a FedEx systems engineer based in Memphis, Tennessee. While he is en route from Moscow to the Far East, his plane crashes in the ocean, and Chuck, the only survivor, washes ashore on a desert island. After sustaining himself physically, emotionally, and spiritually for four years, Chuck builds a raft and attempts to return to civilization. Overwhelmed by the elements, and near death, he is picked up by a freighter and returned to Memphis, where he faces yet another emotional challenge.

In making *Cast Away*, the production crew faced daunting physical and logistical problems. Their largest challenge was to make the most efficient use of human, financial, and physical resources. The film, which cost $85 million to produce, was shot on sound stages in Hollywood, as well as on actual locations in Texas, Tennessee, Russia, and the Fijian island of Monuriki in the South Pacific; the task of planning the overall production schedule was relatively routine, however. Although the largest part of the film's three-part structure is set on Monuriki and features only one actor (Hanks), the cast actually includes nearly sixty other actors. The credits list another 123 members of the pro-duction crew, most involved in the creation of the visual and special effects.

When shooting on Monuriki, the crew had to endure real winds, storms, and floods; and when nature would not cooperate with their shooting schedule, they had to create their own bad weather. Furthermore, their work depended on the tides and available sunlight (Chuck would not have had artificial light on the island). The airplane crash was simulated in Hollywood, where considerable shooting was done underwater, and the scenes of Chuck's attempted escape by raft were shot on the ocean, as well as in the perilous surf off another Fijian island. After one month's shooting on Monuriki, capturing footage that established Chuck's overall challenge, the crew took a yearlong hiatus while Hanks lost the fifty pounds he had gained to portray Chuck in the early part of the film. This change helped create the illusion that Chuck had spent four years on the island. Meeting these challenges as successfully as the filmmakers did (while maintaining visual consistency within the footage) was central to maintaining the film's verisimilitude.

Postproduction

When the shooting on a film has been completed, **postproduction** begins. Postproduction consists of three phases: editing, preparing the final print, and bringing the film to the public (marketing and distribution). In brief, editing consists of assembling the visual images and sound recordings, adding the musical score and sound effects, adding the special effects, assembling the sound tracks, and doing any necessary dubbing. Preparing the final print consists of timing the color print, a process of inspecting each shot of a film and assigning color corrections and printer light values to maintain consistency of brightness and color from shot to shot; completing the first combined picture and sound print, in release form, of a finished film; possibly previewing the film; then possibly making changes in response to the comments of preview audiences. Bringing the film to the public consists of determining the marketing and advertising strategies and budgets, setting the release date and number of theaters, finalizing distribution rights and ancillary rights, and finally exhibiting the film.

In your study of movies, keep in mind that the art of the movies has been influenced not only by changes in technology and cinematic conventions, but also by changes in the production process. Thus, the Hollywood studio system process that created F. W. Murnau's *Sunrise: A Song of Two Humans* (1927) was very different from the independent production process that created Ang Lee's *Brokeback Mountain* (2005). The history of Hollywood production systems can be easily understood as comprising three basic periods: the studio system, the independent system, and a system today that manages to combine them. Let's look more closely at each of them.

The Studio System

Organization Before 1931

The studio system roots go back to the first decade of the twentieth century and the pioneering attempts of men such as Thomas Edison, Carl Laemmle, and D. W. Griffith to make, distribute, and exhibit movies. In 1905, Laemmle began to distribute and exhibit films, but by 1909 his efforts were threatened by the Motion Picture Patents Company (MPPC—not to be confused with the Motion Picture Production Code), a protective trade association (or trust) controlled by Edison, which sought both to control the motion picture industry completely and to eliminate competition by charging licensing fees on production and projection equipment. However, widespread resistance to the MPPC encouraged competition and laid the groundwork for both the studio and independent systems of production. The U.S. government broke the MPPC monopoly in 1915.

Between 1907 and 1913, a large number of movie production companies in New York and New Jersey migrated to various spots in warmer climates, including Florida, Texas, and New Mexico, but eventually the main companies settled in southern California, in and around Hollywood. They did so to take advantage of the year-round good weather, the beautiful and varied scenery, the abundant light for outdoor shooting, and the geographic distance from the greedy MPPC;[7] soon they had a critical mass of both capital and talent on which to build an industry. By 1915, more than 60 percent of the American film industry, employing approximately fifteen thousand workers, was located in Hollywood.

Before 1931, typical Hollywood studios were dominated by central producers such as Louis B. Mayer at Metro-Goldwyn-Mayer, Adolph Zukor at Paramount, and Harry and Jack Warner at Warner Bros. These men—known as *moguls*, a reference to the powerful Muslim Mongol (or Mogul) conquerors of India—controlled the overall and day-to-day operations of their studios. Executives in New York, generally called the "New York office," controlled the studios financially; various personnel at the studios handled the myriad details of producing films. *Central producers*, such as Irving Thalberg at MGM, supervised a team of associate supervisors (not yet called *producers*), each of whom had an area of specialization (sophisticated comedies, westerns, etc.). The associate supervisors handled the day-to-day operations of film production, but the central producer retained total control.

By the late 1920s, the film industry had come to see that the central-producer system encouraged quantity over quality and that less-than-stellar movies did not draw audiences into theaters. As a result, the industry sought a new system, one that would value both profits and aesthetic value.

Organization After 1931

In 1931, the film industry adopted the *producer-unit system*, an organizational structure that typically included a general manager, executive manager, production manager, studio manager, and individual production supervisors.[8] Each studio had its own configuration, determined by the New York

[7] This peculiar mixture of art, geography, and economics is the subject of Allen J. Scott's *On Hollywood: The Place, the Industry* (Princeton, N.J.: Princeton University Press, 2004).
[8] The material in this section was drawn from David Bordwell, Janet Staiger, and Kristin Thompson, *The Classical Hollywood Cinema: Film Style and Mode of Production to 1960* (New York:

FIGURE A.1 Producer-Unit System at MGM

General Manager
Irving Thalberg

Thalberg supervised the overall production of some fifty films each year: his responsibilities included selecting the property, developing the script (either by himself or in collaboration with writers), selecting the actors and key production people, editing the film, and supervising marketing. Thus, without ever leaving his office to visit the set, he could be intimately involved in every phase of every production at the studio. He generally received screen credit as "producer."

Executive Manager

Responsible for the studio's financial and legal affairs, as well as daily operations.

Production Manager

Responsible for all pre- and postproduction work; key liaison between the general manager, studio manager, and individual production supervisors.

Studio Manager

Responsible for the support departments (research, writing, design, casting, cinematography, marketing research, etc.) representing almost three hundred different professions and trades.

Individual Unit Production Supervisors

Ten men (e.g., Hunt Stromberg and Bernard Hyman), each responsible for the planning and production of the six to eight individual films per year to which they were assigned by the general manager and production manager, often called *associate* or *assistant producers*, and sometimes given screen credit as such. Each producer was sufficiently flexible to be able to handle various types of movies.

office. The producer-unit system as it functioned at MGM in the 1930s illustrates the structure. (Figure A.1 indicates the basic form and responsibilities of the producer-unit system. Note that the titles of these team members are generic; the actual titles varied with each studio.)

Columbia University Press, 1985), parts 2 and 5; Thomas Schatz, *The Genius of the System: Hollywood Filmmaking in the Studio Era* (1988; reprint, New York: Holt, 1996), parts 2 and 3; and Joel Finler, *The Hollywood Story* (New York: Crown, 1988), part 2.

The general manager, Irving Thalberg, who had been supervising MGM's production since 1924, continued this work in the new unit. At the time, MGM's annual output was some fifty films. Reporting directly to Thalberg was a staff of ten individual-unit production supervisors, each of whom was responsible for roughly six to eight films per year; the actual number varied widely because of the scope and shooting schedules of different productions. Each producer, who usually received screen credit with that title, was able to handle various types of movies. Such flexibility also enabled the general manager to assign these producers according to need, not specialization. This producer-unit management system (and its variations) helped create an industry that favored standardization, within which workers were always striving for the ideal relationship between "cost" and "quality."

The system produced movies that had a predictable technical quality, often at the cost of stylistic sameness, or what we call the studio "look"; and it resulted in an overall output that, inevitably—since hundreds of films were produced each year—valued profitability above all else. Yet although it could be stifling, standardization allowed for creative innovation, usually under carefully controlled circumstances. To help ensure such creativity, unit producers received varied assignments.

Let's look at a typical year for two of Thalberg's individual-unit production supervisors: Hunt Stromberg and Bernard Hyman.[9] (During this period, MGM had no female producers.[10])

In 1936, a busy year for MGM, the studio released six movies for which Stromberg received screen credit as producer, including W. S. Van Dyke's *After the Thin Man* (comic murder mystery), William A. Wellman's *Small Town Girl* (romantic comedy), Robert Z. Leonard's *The Great Ziegfeld*

(musical biopic), Clarence Brown's *Wife vs. Secretary* (romantic comedy), and W. S. Van Dyke's *Rose-Marie* (musical). In other words, Stromberg produced two musicals, two romantic comedies, and the second of four Thin Man movies.

Bernard Hyman, a Thalberg favorite among the MGM unit producers, produced four films that year, some of which were released in 1936 and some in 1937: W. S. Van Dyke's *San Francisco* (1936; a musical melodrama about the 1906 earthquake, starring Clark Gable and Jeanette MacDonald), George Cukor's *Camille* (1936; a romantic melodrama, starring Greta Garbo and Robert Taylor), Clarence Brown's *Conquest* (1937; a romantic historical epic about Napoleon and Countess Marie Walewska, his Polish mistress, starring Greta Garbo and Charles Boyer), and Jack Conway's *Saratoga* (1937; a romantic comedy starring Clark Gable and Jean Harlow). The first three were lavish productions; *Saratoga* was a bread-and-butter movie featuring two of MGM's most popular stars.

Although Hyman regularly produced fewer films each year than Stromberg, both were members of Thalberg's inner group. Reliable if not particularly imaginative (exactly what Thalberg liked in his subordinates), these producers made movies that enhanced MGM's reputation for making quality movies, kept its major stars in the public eye, and satisfied the studio's stockholders. That's what the studio system was all about. Finally, these producers were forerunners of what today we call a *line producer*, the person responsible for supervising the daily operations of a film production.

The Hollywood studio system established the collaborative mode of production that dominated American filmmaking during its golden age, concurrently influencing the mode of film production worldwide. The studio system also established an industrial model of production through which American filmmaking became one of the most prolific and lucrative enterprises in the world. Furthermore, although its rigidity ultimately led to its demise after some forty years, the system contained within itself the seeds—in the form of the independent producers that would replace it—to sustain American film production until the present day.

[9] In late 1932, because of his own ill health and Mayer's growing dislike of his power, Thalberg took a break, returning in 1933 not as general manager but as a unit producer. The production staff, answerable directly to Mayer, also included David O. Selznick (Mayer's son-in-law) and Walter Wanger, both of whom had left their jobs as central producer at, respectively, RKO and Columbia. And both soon left MGM: Wanger in 1934 to become an independent producer, Selznick in 1935 to found Selznick International Pictures, where he produced a series of major films that were successful artistically and commercially, including Victor Fleming's *Gone With the Wind* (1939).

[10] Good accounts of women in Hollywood include Rachel Abramovitz, *Is That a Gun in Your Pocket? Women's Experience of Power in Hollywood* (New York: Random House, 2000); Ally Acker, *Reel Women: Pioneers of the Cinema, 1896 to the Present* (New York: Continuum, 1991); Jeanine Basinger, *A Woman's View: How Hollywood Spoke to Women, 1930–1960* (Hanover, Mass.: Wesleyan University Press, 1995); and Cari Beauchamp, *Without Lying Down: Frances Marion and the Powerful Women of Early Hollywood* (New York: Scribner, 1997).

Organization During the Golden Age

By the mid-1930s, Hollywood was divided into four kinds of film production companies: majors, minors, "B" studios, and independent producers (Table A.1).[11] The five major studios—Paramount, MGM, Warner Bros., 20th Century Fox, and RKO—were all vertically integrated companies, meaning that they followed a top-down hierarchy of control, with the ultimate managerial authority vested in their corporate officers and boards of directors. These managers were, in turn, responsible to those who financed them: wealthy individuals (e.g., Cornelius Vanderbilt Whitney or Joseph P. Kennedy), financial institutions (e.g., Chase Manhattan Bank in New York or Bank of America in California), corporations related to or dependent on the film industry (e.g., RCA, manufacturers of sound equipment used in movie production), and stockholders (including studio executives and ordinary people who purchased shares on the stock market). Controlling film production through their studios and, equally important, film *distribution* (the marketing and promotion of a film) and *exhibition* (the actual showing of a motion picture in a commercial theater) through their ownership of film exchanges and theater chains, they produced "A" pictures, meaning those featured at the top of the double bill (ordinarily, for the price of a single admission, moviegoers enjoyed almost four hours of entertainment: two feature films, plus a cartoon, short subject, and newsreel).

The three minor studios—Universal, Columbia, and United Artists—were less similar. Universal and Columbia owned their own production facilities, but no theaters, and thus depended on the majors to show their films. By contrast, United Artists (UA)—founded in 1919 by Mary Pickford, Charlie Chaplin, Douglas Fairbanks, and D. W. Griffith—was considered a "studio" even though it was essentially a distribution company established by these artists to give them greater control over how their movies were distributed and marketed. During the 1930s, however, UA was distributing the work of many other outstanding producers, directors, and actors. Although UA declined during the 1940s, it was revived in the 1950s and today is part of MGM.

The five B studios (sometimes called the *poverty row* studios because of their relatively small budgets) were Republic Pictures, Monogram Productions, Grand National Films, Producers Releasing Corporation, and Eagle-Lion Films. Their "B" movies filled in the bottom half of double bills.

The most important independent producers in the 1930s, when independent production was still a relatively unfamiliar idea, were Hollywood titans Samuel Goldwyn, David O. Selznick, and Walt Disney. Each producer owned his own studio but released pictures through his own distribution company, one of the majors, or United Artists. Disney produced his classic animated films, such as *Pinocchio* (1940), at the Walt Disney Studios and released them through

[11] See David A. Cook, *A History of Narrative Film*, 4th ed. (New York: Norton, 2004), 239–255.

TABLE A.1	Structure of the Studio System Until 1950		
Major Studios	**Minor Studios**	**Most Significant "B" (Poverty Row) Studios**	**Most Significant Independent Producers**
1. Paramount 2. Metro-Goldwyn-Mayer 3. Warner Bros. 4. 20th Century Fox 5. RKO	1. Universal Studios 2. Columbia Pictures 3. United Artists	1. Republic Pictures 2. Monogram Productions 3. Grand National Films 4. Producers Releasing Corporation 5. Eagle-Lion Films	1. Samuel Goldwyn Productions 2. David O. Selznick Productions 3. Walt Disney Studios

his own distribution company, Buena Vista Productions. Goldwyn produced such major pictures as William Wyler's *The Best Years of Our Lives* (1946), which he released through RKO. In 1936, Selznick left MGM to establish Selznick International Pictures. In 1940, three of his films—Victor Fleming's *Gone With the Wind* (1939), Alfred Hitchcock's *Rebecca* (1940), and Gregory Ratoff's *Intermezzo* (1939)—together earned some $10 million in net profits—more than all the films of any of the majors, each of which produced roughly fifty-two films that year. Although he released his films through the major studios, including MGM, Selznick's prestige pictures and remarkable profits established the independent producer as a dominant force in Hollywood for the next sixty years and beyond.

The **producer** guides the entire process of making the movie from its initial planning to its release and is chiefly responsible for the organizational and financial aspects of the production, from arranging the financing to deciding how the money is spent. The studio system was dominated by producers who, in turn, depended on directors who were under studio contract to direct a specific number of films in each contract period.

The work of the **director** is to determine and realize on the screen an artistic vision of the screenplay; cast the actors and direct their performances; work closely with the production design in creating the look of the film, including the choice of locations; oversee the work of the cinematographer and other key production personnel; and, in most cases, supervise all postproduction activity, including sometimes the editing. Though some studio system directors—Alfred Hitchcock, John Ford, and Vincente Minnelli, for example—could be involved completely from preproduction through postproduction, most were expected to receive a script one day and begin filming shortly thereafter. They were seasoned professionals capable of working quickly and were conversant enough with various genres to be able to handle almost any assignment.

The career of Edmund Goulding, who directed thirty-eight movies, exemplifies very clearly the work of a contract director. After starting in silent films in 1925 and directing several films at Paramount Pictures, Goulding made an auspicious start as a director at MGM with *Grand Hotel* (1932), an all-star blockbuster. He followed that with *Blondie of the Follies* (1932), a comedy featuring Marion Davies; the melodrama *Riptide* (1934), starring Norma Shearer; and *The Flame Within* (1935), also a melodrama. From MGM Goulding moved to Warner Bros., where, as a contract director, he made *That Certain Woman* (1937), *Dark Victory* (1939), and *The Old Maid* (1939), all starring Bette Davis; *The Dawn Patrol* (1938), a World War I action film; *'Til We Meet Again* (1940), a wartime romance; and *The Constant Nymph* (1943), a romantic drama.

After World War II, Goulding moved to 20th Century Fox, where the declining quality of the movies he was assigned truly reflects the challenges facing a contract director. Starting with *The Razor's Edge* (1946; a quasi-philosophical movie nominated for an Oscar as Best Picture of 1946) and *Nightmare Alley* (1947), a melodramatic film noir, he went on to direct *We're Not Married!* (1952), an episodic comedy featuring Marilyn Monroe; *Teenage Rebel* (1956), a drama; and, for his last film, *Mardi Gras* (1958), a teenage musical starring Pat Boone. Goulding made the most of the challenges inherent in such variety. He was also popular with actors and noted for his screenwriting, which accounts for some of the gaps between pictures (most contract directors were expected to make three or four movies per year). Goulding was also noteworthy as an openly gay man who successfully pursued his career at a time when most Hollywood gays and lesbians remained in the closet.[12]

The actual, physical studios, called "dream factories" by anthropologist Hortense Powdermaker, were complex operations.[13] If you were fortunate enough to get past a studio's high walls and through its guarded gates, you would find yourself in a vast, industrial complex. MGM, for example, the largest studio, covered 117 acres, over which ten miles of paved streets linked 137 buildings. There were twenty-nine sound stages—huge air-conditioned and soundproofed production facilities, the largest of

[12] See William J. Mann, *Behind the Screen: How Gays and Lesbians Shaped Hollywood, 1910–1969* (New York: Penguin, 2001).
[13] See Hortense Powdermaker, *Hollywood, the Dream Factory: An Anthropologist Looks at the Movie-Makers* (Boston: Little, Brown, 1950).

which had a floor area of nearly one acre. The studio was a self-contained community with its own police and fire services, hospital, film library, school for child actors, railway siding, industrial section capable of manufacturing anything that might be needed for making a movie, and vast backlot containing sets representing every possible period and architecture. In the average year, MGM produced fifty full-length feature pictures and one hundred shorts. Depending on the level of production, the workforce consisted of four to five thousand people. The other major studios had smaller but similar operations.

Labor and Unions   Before the industry was centralized in Hollywood, movie production was marked by conflicts between management and labor. Strikes led to the formation of guilds and unions, which led to the division of labor; that development, as much as anything, led a hodgepodge of relatively small studios to prosper and grow into one of the world's largest industries. In 1926, the major studios and unions stabilized their relations through the landmark Studio Basic Agreement, which provided the foundation for future collective bargaining in the industry.[14]

Workers in the industry formed labor unions for the standard reasons: they sought worker representation, equity in pay and working conditions, safety standards, and job security. For example, the Screen Actors Guild, established in 1933, is the nation's premier labor union representing actors. In the 1940s, it fought the attempt of the studio system to break long-term engagement contracts; today, it faces new challenges in protecting artists' rights amid the movie industry's conversion to digital production. In addition, because of the uniquely collaborative nature of their jobs, industry workers needed a system that guaranteed public recognition of their efforts. Contracts between the labor unions and the studios covered the workers' inclusion in screen credits. Executive managers often had similar contracts.

[14] An excellent account of the power of labor unions in Hollywood, including the pervasive presence of organized crime, is Connie Bruck's, *When Hollywood Had a King: The Reign of Lew Wasserman, Who Leveraged Talent into Power and Influence* (New York: Random House, 2003).

In any manufacturing enterprise, *division of labor* refers to breaking down each step in that process so that each worker or group of workers can be assigned to and responsible for a specialized task. Although this system was designed to increase efficiency in producing steel, cars, and the like, it was applied very successfully in the film industry. Indeed, Hollywood has often been compared to Detroit. Both of these major industrial centers are engaged in the mass production of commodities. Detroit's output is more standardized, though manufacturer and model differentiate the automobiles that roll off the assembly line.

Like automobile manufacturers, each studio during the studio era specialized in certain kinds of films in its own distinctive style (e.g., MGM excelled in musicals; Warner Bros., in films of social realism); but unlike the Detroit product, each film was a unique creative accomplishment, even if it fit predictably within a particular genre such as film noir. For the most part, each studio had its own creative personnel under contract, though studios frequently borrowed talent from each other on a picture-by-picture basis. Once a studio's executive management—board of directors, chairman, president, and production moguls—determined what kinds of films would most appeal to its known share of the audience, the studio's general manager (here titles varied among studios) developed projects and selected scripts and creative personnel consistent with that choice.

In Hollywood, the activities in the three phases of making a movie—*preproduction*, *production*, and *postproduction*—are carried out by two major forces: management and labor. Management selects the property, develops the script, chooses the actors, and assigns the key production people, but the actual work of making the film is the responsibility of labor (the artists, craftspeople, and technicians belonging to labor unions). Members of management receive the highest salaries; the salaries of labor depend on the kind and level of skills necessary for each job. Such a division of labor across the broad, collaborative nature of creating a film shapes the unavoidable interaction between the work rules set by union contracts and the standards set by professional organizations.

Professional Organizations and Standardization Beyond the labor unions, other organizations are devoted to workers in the motion picture industry, including the American Society of Cinematographers (founded in 1916), the Society of Motion Picture and Television Engineers (1918), and the American Cinema Editors (1950), which set and maintain standards in their respective professions. These organizations engage in the activities of a traditional professional organization: conducting research related to equipment and production procedures, standardizing that equipment and those procedures, meeting, publishing, consulting with manufacturers in the development of new technologies, promulgating professional codes of conduct, and recognizing outstanding achievement with awards. Although they do not represent their membership in collective bargaining as do labor unions, they voice opinions on matters relevant to the workplace.

In 1927, the industry established the Academy of Motion Picture Arts and Sciences, which seeks, among its stated objectives, to improve the artistic quality of films, provide a common forum for the various branches and crafts of the industry, and encourage cooperation in technical research. Since ancient times, *academy* has been defined as a society of learned persons organized to advance science, art, literature, music, or some other cultural or intellectual area of endeavor. Although profits, not artistic merit, are the basic measure of success in the movie industry, using the word *academy* to describe the activities of this new organization suited early moviemakers' strong need for social acceptance and respectability.

A masterful stroke of public relations, the Academy is privately funded from within the industry and is perhaps best known to the public for its annual presentation of the Academy Awards, or Oscars. Membership in the Academy is by invitation only. Now numbering around five thousand, members fall into thirteen categories: actors, administrators, art directors, cinematographers, directors, executives, film editors, composers, producers, public relations people, short-subject filmmakers, sound technicians, and writers. Members in each category make the Oscar nominations and vote to determine the winners. All voting members are also eligible to vote for the Best Picture nominees.

The Decline of the Studio System

Fostered by aggressive competition and free trade, the studio system grew to maturity in the 1930s, reached a pinnacle of artistic achievement and industrial productivity in the 1940s, and then went into decline at the beginning of the 1950s. We can see this trajectory clearly by looking at the actual number of films produced and released by American studios during that downward swing. As Table A.2 indicates, the average number of films annually produced and released in the United States from 1936 to 1940 was 495; from 1941 to 1945, the war years, that number fell to 426; in the immediate postwar period,

TABLE A.2	Feature Films Produced and Released in the United States, 1936–1951

Year	Number of Feature Films Released
1936	522
1937	538
1938	455
1939	483
1940	477
1941	492
1942	488
1943	397
1944	401
1945	350
1946	378
1947	369
1948	366
1949	356
1950	383
1951	391

Source: Finler, *The Hollywood Story*, 280.
Note: These figures do not include foreign films released in the United States.

1946–1950, it fell even further, to 370. In 1951, the total number of U.S. films was 391, the highest it would be until 1990, when 440 films were released. In looking at these data, remember that the total film releases in any one year usually reflect two kinds of productions: those begun in that year and those begun earlier. In any case, one thing is clear: total Hollywood production between 1936 and 1951 fell by 25 percent.

By the mid 1930s, in fact, the system had reached a turning point, as a result of three intertwined factors. First, the studios were victims of their own success. The two most creative production heads—Darryl F. Zanuck, who dominated production at 20th Century Fox from 1933 until 1956, and Irving Thalberg, who supervised production at MGM from 1923 until his death in 1936—had built such highly efficient operations that their studios could function exceptionally well, both stylistically and financially, without the sort of micromanaging that characterized David O. Selznick's style at Selznick International Pictures. In a very real sense, these central producers and others had made themselves almost superfluous.

Second, several actions taken by the federal government signaled that the studios' old ways of doing business would have to change. President Franklin D. Roosevelt's plan for the economic revitalization of key industries—the 1933 National Industrial Recovery Act—had a major impact on Hollywood. On one hand, it sustained certain practices that enabled the studios to control the marketing and distribution of films to their own advantage; on the other, it fostered the growth of the labor unions, perennially unpopular with the studio heads, by mandating more thoroughgoing division of labor and job specialization than Hollywood had yet experienced. In 1938, however, the federal government began trying to break the vertical structure of the major studios—to separate their interlocking ownership of production, distribution, and exhibition—an effort that finally succeeded in 1948.

Third, the studios began to reorganize their management into the producer-unit system. Each studio had its own variation on this general model, each with strengths and weaknesses. Although the resulting competition among the units increased the overall quality of Hollywood movies, the rise of the unit producer served as a transition between the dying studio system and the emergence of the independent producer.

Three additional factors further undercut the studio system. The first was a shift in the relations between top management and creative personnel that loosened the studios' hold on the system. From the mid 1930s on, actors, directors, and producers sought better individual contracts with the studios—contracts that would give them and their agents higher salaries and more control over scripts, casting, production schedules, and working conditions. For example, in the early 1950s actor James Stewart had an agreement whereby he would waive his usual salary for appearing in two films (then $200,000 per picture) in exchange for 50 percent of the net profits. Equally significant, these profits would extend through the economic life of the film, whether it was shown on a theater screen, broadcast on television, or distributed via other formats.

The second factor was World War II, which severely restricted the studios' regular, for-profit operations (they were also making movies that supported government initiatives, such as films instructing people how to cope with food rationing or encouraging them to buy war bonds). As noted already, the production of feature films fell precipitously during the war. Because many studio employees (management and labor alike) were in the armed services and film stock was being rationed to ensure the supply needed by armed-services photographers, there were fewer people and materials to make films. Thus, even though audiences went to the movies in record numbers, fewer films were available for them to see.

The third blow to the studio system was the rise of television, to which Hollywood reacted slowly. When the federal government made the studios divest themselves of their theater holdings, it also blocked their plans to replicate this dual ownership of production and distribution facilities by purchasing television stations. At first, the major studios were not interested in television production, leaving it to the minors and to such pioneering independents as Desilu Productions (Desi Arnaz and Lucille Ball, producers). By 1955, though, the majors were reorganizing and retooling what remained of their studios to begin producing films for television. Some efforts were more successful than others, but even more profitable was the sale both of their real estate—on which the studios were built—for development and of the valuable films in their vaults for television broadcasting. Universal Studios had the best of both worlds, continuing to use part of its vast property at the head of the San Fernando Valley for film and television production and devoting the rest to a lucrative theme park devoted to showing how movies are made.

The Independent System

Through the 1930s and '40s, the independent system of production—sometimes called the *package-unit system*—coexisted with the studio system, as it continues to do with a much different set of studios. The package-unit system, controlled by a producer unaffiliated with a studio (independents such as Samuel Goldwyn, David O. Selznick, Walt Disney, and others), is a personalized concept of film production that differs significantly from the industrial model of the studio system. Based outside the studios but heavily dependent on them for human and technical resources, the package-unit system governs the creation, distribution, and exhibition of a movie (known as the *package*). The independent producer does what a movie producer has always done: chooses the right stories, directors, and actors to produce quality films.

Depending on many factors, the producer may also choose to be involved in creative responsibilities, ranging from developing the property, revising the screenplay, assembling the key members of the production team, supervising the actual production (including the editing), and marketing and distributing the finished product. Consider the career of Sam Spiegel, one of the most successful independent producers; his movies included John Huston's *The African Queen* (1951), Elia Kazan's *On the Waterfront* (1954), David Lean's *The Bridge on the River Kwai* (1957) and *Lawrence of Arabia* (1962), Joseph L. Mankiewicz's *Suddenly, Last Summer* (1959), and Elia Kazan's *The Last Tycoon* (1976), inspired by the life of his fellow producer Irving

Thalberg. Spiegel would have agreed with the successful Hollywood producer who said, "Since I control the money, I control the process."[15] Although that attitude may seem arrogant, it makes excellent business sense to a producer responsible for films like Spiegel's—which were characterized by high costs, high artistic caliber, and high profits.

The producer's team may include an **executive producer**, **line producer**, and **associate** or **assistant producers**. These variations on the overall title of producer reflect the changes that have occurred since the studio system collapsed and, in different ways, reinvented itself. By the nature of film production, titles must be flexible enough to indicate greater or fewer responsibilities than those listed here. Unlike the members of the craft unions—cinematographers or editors, for example—whose obligations are clearly defined by collective-bargaining agreements, producers tend to create responsibilities for themselves that match their individual strengths and experiences.

At the same time, the comparative freedom of independent filmmaking brings new benefits. Creative innovation is both encouraged and rewarded; actors, writers, and directors determine for themselves not only the amounts of compensation but also the ways in which they receive it; and though the overall number of movies produced each year has decreased, the quality of independently produced films has increased considerably from year to year. Whereas the producer helps transform an idea into a finished motion picture, the director visualizes the script and guides all members of the production team, as well as the actors, in bringing that vision to the screen.

The director sets and maintains the defining visual quality of the film, including the settings, costumes, action, and lighting—those elements that produce the total visual impact of the movie's image, its look and feel. When a film earns a profit or wins the Oscar for Best Picture, the producer takes a large share of the credit and accepts the award (true under the studio system also); but the

[15] Robert Simonds, qtd. in Bernard Weinraub, "What Makes Boys Laugh: A Philosophy Major Finds the Golden Touch," *New York Times*, July 23, 1998, sec. E, p. 5.

director usually bears artistic responsibility for the success or failure of a movie. When a film loses money, the director often is saddled with the major share of the blame.

Because creativity at this high level resists rigid categorization, we cannot always neatly separate the responsibilities of the producer and the director. Sometimes one person bears both titles; other times the director or the screenwriter may have initiated the project and later joined forces with the producer to bring it to the screen. But whatever the arrangement, both the producer and the director are involved completely in all three stages of production.

A quick snapshot of a few differences between the studio and independent systems will give you an idea of how moviemaking has changed. At first, each studio's facilities and personnel were permanent and capable of producing any kind of picture; and the studio owned its own theaters, guaranteeing a market for its product. Now, by contrast, an independent producer makes one film at a time, relying on rented facilities and equipment and a creative staff assembled for that one film; and—even figuring for those cost-saving elements—the expenses can be staggering.

Moviemaking entails various kinds of "costs." In both the "old" and the "new" American film industry, the total cost of a film is what it takes to complete the postproduction work and produce the *release negative*, as well as one or two positive prints for advance screening purposes. But this "total cost" does not include the cost of marketing or of additional prints for distribution, so it is useful only for the special purposes of industry accounting practices. You will generally see this figure referred to as the *negative cost* of a movie, where *negative* refers to the costs of producing the release negative.

For example, Orson Welles made *Citizen Kane* (1941) at RKO in four and a half months and completed postproduction in another three months; the cost of the release negative was $840,000 (approximately $11 million in 2006 dollars). Today the production stage of a feature film takes at least one year, with the release negative costing an *average* of $64 million. The average marketing costs per movie of $30 million bring that to a total cost of approximately $100 million. (Unlike expenses calculated today, the costs of the release negative of *Citizen Kane* included marketing and distribution, elements that were then simpler and less costly.)

James Cameron's *Titanic* (1997) cost $200 million, making it the most expensive movie produced to that time, and Steven Spielberg's *Saving Private Ryan* (1998) cost $65 million, a relatively low figure for such an epic film. The use of the most advanced special effects raised the costs of *Titanic*, but for *Saving Private Ryan* the costs remained low because both Spielberg and the star of the film, Tom Hanks, received only minimal fees up front rather than their usual large salaries. According to a clause in their contracts, each man was guaranteed 17.5 percent of the studio's first-dollar gross profit, meaning that thirty-five cents of every dollar earned on the film went to Spielberg and Hanks.

A similar arrangement applied to Spielberg's *Minority Report* (2002), which reportedly cost more than $100 million to make. With this movie, Spielberg and his star, Tom Cruise, also stand to make up to 17.5 percent of every dollar earned; thus, it is estimated that each man could earn $70 million once the revenues from all ticket receipts, DVD and video sales, promotional products, and sales of movie rights are computed. As in any other industry, costs and revenues are controlled by supply and demand. As costs increase for making the kind of blockbuster films that return sizable revenues, producers make fewer films, forcing people who work in the industry to become financially creative in negotiating the contracts that preserve their jobs.

Financing in the Industry

The pattern for financing the production of motion pictures, much like the establishment of labor practices, developed in the industry's early years. Within the two decades after the invention of the movies, there were two major shifts: first from individual owners of small production companies (e.g., Edison and Griffith) to medium-sized firms, and then to the large corporations that not only sold stock but also relied heavily on the infusion of major capital from the investment community. Because prudent investors have traditionally considered producing films to be a risky business, the motion picture industry recognized that it would need efficient management, timely production practices, and profitable results to attract the capital necessary to sustain it. As Hollywood grew, its production practices became more and more standardized. Today, producers aggressively seek the support of a newer breed of investors, including hedge funds.

From the beginning, however, the vertical organizational structure of the studios was challenged by independent producers. Although the studios dominated the distribution and exhibition of films (at least until 1948, when the federal government broke that monopoly), the independents did have access to many movie theaters and could compete successfully for the outside financing they required. The early success of independent producers—such as David O. Selznick in gaining the financing for such major undertakings as *Gone With the Wind* (1939)—demonstrates not only their individual strengths but also the viability and possible profitability of their alternative approach to the studio system.

No rule governs the arranging of financing—money may come from the studio, the producer, the investment community, or (most probably) a combination of these—just as no one timetable exists for securing it. By studying the production credits of films, you can see just how many organizations may back a project. For example, Figure A.2 lists, in the order of their appearance on the screen, the opening credits of Bill Condon's *Gods and Monsters* (1998). Universal Studios released the film, which involved the financial as well as creative input of six entities: Lions Gate Films, Showtime, Flashpoint, BBC Films, Regent Entertainment, and Gregg Fienberg. Separate title screens identify two line producers, three co-executive producers, two executive producers, and two more executive producers; finally, a "Produced By" screen credit lists three more names. Each person receiving credit as a producer was affiliated with one of the six entities listed at the beginning of the film and may also have had some creative responsibility beyond their financial and organizational concerns.

Some producers will have enough start-up financing to ensure that the preproduction phase can proceed with key people on the payroll; others will not be able to secure the necessary funds until they present investors with a detailed account of anticipated audiences and projected profits. Whether a movie is produced independently (in which case it is usually established as an independent corporation) or by one of the studios (in which case it is a distinct project among many), financial and logistical control is essential to making progress and ultimately completing the actual work of production, as well as to holding down costs. Initial budgets are subject to constant modification, so budgeting, accounting, and auditing are as important as they would be in any costly industrial undertaking.

In the old studio system, the general manager, in consultation with the director and key members of the production team, determined the budget for a film, which consisted of two basic categories: *direct costs* and *indirect costs*. Direct costs included everything from art direction and cinematography to insurance. Indirect costs, usually 20 percent of the direct costs, covered the studio's overall contribution to "overhead" (such items as making release prints from the negative, marketing, advertising, and distribution). Table A.3 shows the summary budget for Michael Curtiz's *Casablanca* (1942), including a line-item accounting for each major expense. Direct costs were 73 percent of the total budget.

Today, in the independent system, budgeting is done somewhat differently. Usually the producer or a member of the producer's team prepares the budget with the assistant director. The total cost of producing the completed movie generally breaks down into a ratio of 30 percent to 70 percent between *above-the-line costs* (the costs of the preproduction stage, producer, director, cast, screenwriter, and literary property from which the script was developed) and *below-the-line costs* (the costs of the production and postproduction stages and the crew).[16] Categorizing costs according to where they

---

[16] An excellent source of information on current budgeting practices is Deke Simon and Michael Wiese, *Film and Video Budgets*, 3rd ed. (Studio City, Calif.: Michael Wiese Productions, 2001).

FIGURE A.2 Producers' Credits on *Gods and Monsters*

UNIVERSAL
[Title superimposed over company logo]

LIONS GATE FILMS
SHOWTIME and FLASHPOINT
in association with
BBC FILMS
Present

A
REGENT ENTERTAINMENT
PRODUCTION

in association with
GREGG FIENBERG

A
BILL CONDON
FILM

Next, separate titles list the principal members of the cast, film title, and major members of the production crew

LINE PRODUCERS
JOHN SCHOUWEILER
&
LISA LEVY

CO-EXECUTIVE PRODUCERS
VALERIE MASSALAS
SAM IRVIN
SPENCER PROFFER

EXECUTIVE PRODUCERS
CLIVE BARKER
AND
STEPHEN P. JARCHOW

EXECUTIVE PRODUCERS
DAVID FORREST
BEAU ROGERS

PRODUCED BY
PAUL COLICHMAN
GREGG FIENBERG
MARC R. HARRIS

TABLE A.3 Summary Budget for *Casablanca*

	Subtotals	Totals	Grand Totals
DIRECT COSTS			**$638,222**
Story		$67,281	
Story	$20,000		
Continuity and treatment (writers, secretaries, and script changes)	$47,281		
Direction		$83,237	
Director: Michael Curtiz	$73,400		
Assistant Director: Lee Katz	$9,837		
Producer: Hal Wallis		$52,000	
Cinematography		$11,273	
Camera operators and assistants	$10,873		
Camera rental and expenses	$400		
Cast	$217,603		
Cast salaries: talent under contract to studio, including Humphrey Bogart, Sydney Greenstreet, Paul Henreid, and others	$69,867		
Cast salaries: outside talent, including Ingrid Bergman, Claude Rains, Dooley Wilson, Peter Lorre, and others	$91,717		
Talent (extras, bits, etc.)	$56,019		
Musicians (musical score, arrangers, etc.)		$28,000	
Sound expenses		$2,200	
Sound operating salaries		$8,000	
Art department		$8,846	
Wardrobe expenses		$22,320	
Makeup, hairdressers, etc.		$9,100	
Electricians		$20,755	
Editors' salaries		$4,630	
Special effects		$7,475	
Negative film stock		$8,000	
Developing and printing		$10,500	
Property labor		$10,150	
Construction of sets		$18,000	
Stand-by labor		$15,350	
Striking (dismantling sets and storing props)		$7,000	
Property rental and expenses		$6,300	
Electrical rental and expenses		$750	
Location expenses		$1,252	
Catering		$1,200	
Auto rental expenses and travel		$5,000	

	Subtotals	Totals	Grand Totals
Insurance		$2,800	
Miscellaneous expenses		$3,350	
Trailer (preview)		$2,000	
Stills		$850	
Publicity		$3,000	
INDIRECT COSTS			$239,778
General studio overhead (35%)	$223,822		
Depreciation (2.5%)	$15,956		
GRAND TOTAL COST (release negative)			$878,000

Source: Adapted from Joel Finler, *The Hollywood Story*, 39.

are incurred in the three stages of production is a change from the studio system method. Costs also vary depending on whether union or nonunion labor is being used. In some cases, producers have little flexibility in this regard, but usually their hiring of personnel is open to negotiation within industry standards. Finally, we must always remember that no matter what approach is taken to making movies, movie industry accounting practices traditionally have been as creative as, if not more creative than, the movies themselves.

Marketing and Distribution

After screening a movie's answer print (the first combined print of the film, incorporating picture, sound, and special effects) for executives of the production company, as well as for family, friends, and advisers, the producer may show it to audiences at previews. Members of preview audiences are invited because they represent the demographics of the audience for which the film is intended (e.g., female teenagers). After the screening, viewers are asked to complete detailed questionnaires to gauge their reactions. At the same time, the producer may also have chosen a smaller focus group from this audience and will meet with them personally after

the screening to get their reactions firsthand. After analyzing both the questionnaires and the responses of the focus group, the person in charge of the final cut—either the producer or the director—may make changes in the film. Although this procedure is presumably more "scientific" than that employed in previous years by the studios, it reflects the same belief in designing a film by the numbers. Since *most* major movies are intended as entertainment for the largest, broadest audience possible, the strategy makes business sense. Films intended to appeal to smaller, more homogeneous audiences must attract them through publicity generated by media coverage, festival screenings and awards, and audience word of mouth.

The mode of production determines how the activities in this final phase of postproduction are accomplished. Under the studio system, in the days of vertical integration, each studio or its parent company controlled production, distribution, and exhibition. Independent producers, however, have never followed any single path in distributing films. A small producer without a distribution network has various options, which include renting the film to a studio (such as Paramount) or to a producing organization (such as United Artists or Miramax) that will distribute it. These larger firms can also arrange for the film to be advertised and exhibited.

Deciding how and where to advertise, distribute, and show a film is, like the filmmaking process itself, the work of professionals. During the final weeks of postproduction, the people responsible for promotion and marketing make a number of weighty decisions. They determine the release date (essential for planning and carrying out the advertising and other publicity necessary to build an audience) and the number of screens on which the film will make its debut (necessary so that a corresponding number of release prints can be made and shipped to movie theaters). At the same time, they finalize domestic and foreign distribution rights and ancillary rights, contract with firms who make videotapes and DVDs, schedule screenings on airlines and cruise ships, and, for certain kinds of films, arrange marketing tie-ins with fast-food chains, toy manufacturers, and so on.

Some or all of this activity is responsive to the voluntary movie-rating system administered by the Motion Picture Association of America (MPAA),

the trade association of the industry (Table A.4). Because the rating helps determine the marketing of a film, and thus the potential size of its audience, it is very important. The release of Stanley Kubrick's last film, *Eyes Wide Shut* (1999), provides an excellent example of how a studio might try to influence the rating decision. Featuring top box-office stars Tom Cruise and Nicole Kidman, *Eyes Wide Shut* is a complex movie about sexual realities and fantasies—not for everyone, and certainly not for younger viewers. Because Kubrick died just after preparing a cut of the film, we do not know whether the released version represents his complete vision for it. However, we do know that Warner Bros. digitally obscured an orgy scene to avoid an NC-17 rating (no children under seventeen admitted), and some have suggested that the studio also tried to remove other material that might have proved offensive and thus harmful to the box office. *Eyes Wide Shut* was eventually rated R (for strong sexual content, nudity, language, and some drug-

TABLE A.4 MPAA Movie-Rating System

Rating Category	Explanation
G: General Audience	All ages admitted. Specifically: No material is thought to be unsuitable for children. Contains a minimum of violence, as well as no strong language, nudity, sex scenes, or drug use content.
PG: Parental Guidance Suggested	Some material may not be suitable for children. Specifically: May contain some profanity, violence, or brief nudity, but no drug use content.
PG-13: Parents Strongly Cautioned	Some material may be inappropriate for children under 13. Specifically: May contain nudity, but not sexually oriented nudity. May contain harsher profanity but not if used in a sexual context. May contain violence, but only if not too rough or persistent.
R: Restricted	Children under 17 must be accompanied by parent or adult guardian. Specifically: May include strong language, violence, nudity, and drug abuse.
NC-17: No Children Under 17 Admitted	No one 17 or under admitted. Specifically: May contain "excessive violence, sex, aberrational behavior, drug abuse or … other elements which … most parents would consider too strong and therefore off-limits for viewing by their children."

Source: Motion Picture Association of America, 1990, <www.mpaa.org/FlmRat_Ratings.asp> (accessed April 2005).

related material); after opening strong, it proved a financial disappointment.

Once initial marketing and distribution decisions have been made, all that remains is to show the film to the public, analyze the reviews in the media and the box-office receipts of the first weekend, and make whatever changes are necessary in the distribution, advertising, and exhibition strategies to ensure that the movie will reach its targeted audience.

Production in Hollywood Today

The production system in Hollywood today is an amalgam of (1) a studio system that differs radically from that of the golden age described earlier and (2) independent production companies, many of which are "small picture" or "prestige" (nongenre) divisions of the larger studios. The term *studio system* no longer means what it once did: a group of vertically integrated, meticulously organized factories, with large numbers of contract employees in the creative arts and crafts. Today there is no "system," and the studios exist to make and release movies, one at a time. In addition, now that almost every studio has its own prestige "indie" division, very few producers are truly independent.

Table A.5 summarizes this new arrangement. In 2005, there were seven studios and some thirty independent production companies; altogether they produced 398 films and grossed $8.5 billion. With the exception of Sony and DreamWorks, the major studios have been in business since the 1920s.[17] However, the major studios accounted for 80 percent of that gross income, a percentage that would be even greater if the grosses of their smaller, independent production units were included. Not reflected in Table A.5, but nonetheless very significant, is the fact that, in 2006, females were the top business or creative executives at five of these seven studios, burying forever the idea that Hollywood is a man's world.

Dominating the market worldwide, the major studios continue to define the nature of movie production in the United States. When one of these smaller studios has a larger corporate owner, the parent firm is usually the distributor. In addition, countless independent producers must distribute their movies through the "big six" studios if they want the largest possible audience and the maximum profits on their investments.[18]

To get a better sense of how this arrangement works today, consider Table A.6, which shows how the five Oscar nominees for Best Picture of 2005 were produced and released. All five were independent productions involving multiple co-production deals. As for distribution, only Steven Spielberg's *Munich* was distributed by a major studio; Bennett Miller's *Capote* and George Clooney's *Good Night, and Good Luck* were distributed by the "prestige" divisions of major studios; and Ang Lee's *Brokeback Mountain* and Paul Haggis's *Crash* were distributed by large independent producers.

Today the American film industry is healthy, but changing, as the following brief discussion shows.[19] Although movie theater attendance dropped about 10 percent between 2004 and 2005, rentals and sales of videotapes and DVDs during that period increased. (On average, U.S. residents have attended at least five movies per year between 2000 and 2004.) The industry employed close to 200,000 people in production and related services alone, with another 141,000 people employed in the theaters and rental stores.

As for the ratings, there has been a distinct shift in the past few years toward a more lenient approach, provoking children's advocates and critics

[17] Columbia Pictures, a minor studio founded in 1924, is now owned by Sony Pictures. See Benjamin M. Compaine and Douglas Gomery, *Who Owns the Media?: Competition and Concentration in the Mass Media Industry*, 3rd ed. (Mahwah, N.J.: Erlbaum, 2000), especially Chapter 6. The biggest surprise on the list is that MGM, a victim of continual corporate reorganization, has dropped from its place as Hollywood's largest studio to the bottom of the list of large independent producers. Also noteworthy is the departure of Harvey and Bob Weinstein from Miramax, which remains under the ownership of Disney, to found a new production outfit, The Weinstein Company.

[18] Compaine and Gomery, *Who Owns the Media?*, 373.

[19] This discussion is based on 2004 statistics supplied by the Motion Picture Association of America (MPAA); Table A.5 is based on 2005 data.

TABLE A.5	2005 Production Figures and Gross Receipts of Hollywood Studios and Independent Producers and Distributors		
		Number of Films Released	2005 Gross Receipts[a]
MAJOR STUDIOS			
Major Studios and Owners			
20th Century Fox (News Corporation)		19	$1.32 b
Warner Bros. Pictures (Time Warner Inc.)		20	$1.28 b
Sony Pictures (Sony Corporation)		27	$1.05 b
Universal Studios (Vivendi Universal)		27	$1.01 b
Walt Disney Pictures (Walt Disney Pictures)		16	$918.6 m
Paramount (Viacom Corporation)		13	$736.6 m
DreamWorks SKG (Steven Spielberg, Jeffrey Katzenberg, David Geffen)		9	$485.6 m
SUBTOTALS (Major Studios)		**131**	**$6,800,800,000**
INDEPENDENT PRODUCTION COMPANIES			
Large Independents and Studio Owners (where applicable)			
New Line Cinema (Time Warner Inc.)		10	$398.9 m
Miramax (Walt Disney Pictures)		20	$308.1 m
Lions Gate Films		21	$267.5 m
Focus Features (Universal Studios)		10	$207.3 m
Warner Independent Pictures (Warner Bros. Pictures)		6	$113.4 m
Fox Searchlight Pictures (20th Century Fox)		7	$110 m
The Weinstein Company		5	$67 m
Sony Pictures Classics (Sony Pictures)		24	$61 m
MGM		6	$56 m
Subtotals		**109**	**$1,589,200,000**
Medium-Sized Independents and Studio Owners (where applicable)			
Paramount Classics (Paramount)		6	$30 m
IDP		9	$17.6 m
ThinkFilm		19	$11 m
Magnolia Pictures		7	$9.3 m
IFC Films		13	$6.8 m
Newmarket Films		5	$6.5 m
Picture House		5	$2.6 m
Wellspring Media		11	$2.1 m
Fine Line Features (subsidiary of New Line)		4	$2 m
Shadow		4	$2.2 m
Subtotals		**83**	**$90,100,000**

	Number of Films Released	2005 Gross Receipts[a]
Small Independents		
Tartan Films USA	7	$1.7 m
Strand Releasing	12	$1.3 m
Palm Pictures	7	$1.1 m
Zeitgeist Films	5	$1.07 m
Empire Pictures	3	$0.78 m
Kino International	8	$0.65 m
New Yorker Films	8	$0.49 m
The Cinema Guild	3	$0.32 m
TLA Releasing	7	$0.25 m
Koch Lorber Films	5	$0.18 m
First Run Features	10	$0.18 m
Subtotals	**75**	**$8,020,000**
SUBTOTALS (Independent Production Companies)	**267**	**$1,687,320,000**
GRAND TOTALS	**398**	**$8,488,120,000**
Percentage of total grosses:		
Major studios	80%	
Independent producers	20%	

Source: Material adapted and expanded from "Bulls & Bears," *Film Comment*, 42, no. 2 (March/April 2006).
[a] b = billion; m = million.

TABLE A.6 **Production and Distribution Data for the 2005 Oscar Nominees for Best Picture**

Title	Producers[a]	Number of Co-production Companies	Distributor
Brokeback Mountain	Diana Ossana and James Schamus	6	Focus Features
Capote	Caroline Baron, William Vince, and Michael Ohoven	5	Sony Pictures Classics
Crash	Paul Haggis and Cathy Schulman	6	Lions Gate Films
Good Night, and Good Luck	Grant Heslov	8	Warner Independent Pictures
Munich	Kathleen Kennedy, Steven Spielberg, and Barry Mendel	8	Universal Pictures

[a] Names recognized by the Academy of Motion Picture Arts and Sciences for legal and award purposes; thus, this table does not include the names of the executive, associate, and line producers.

of the rating system to condemn the increase of violent and sexually explicit content in movies rated PG or PG-13. The MPAA ratings of the top five grossing movies of 2004 were as follows:

> Roland Emmerich's *The Day After Tomorrow*: PG-13 for intense situations of peril
> Paul Greengrass's *The Bourne Supremacy*: PG-13 for violence, intense action, and brief language
> Jon Turteltaub's *National Treasure*: PG for action violence and scary images
> Robert Zemeckis's *The Polar Express*: G
> Jay Roach's *Meet the Fockers*: PG-13 for crude and sexual humor, language, and a brief drug reference

Of the five films that attracted the largest audiences of the year, only one, the innocuous *Polar Express*, was deemed suitable for the entire family. The PG and PG-13 ratings of the remaining four movies place large responsibilities on parents who are concerned with the moviegoing of their children.

The Impact of Digital Production and Exhibition

Motion picture film stock is an *analog* medium, although it was not described as such until the introduction of digital cameras. In the traditional film camera, images are created by light that passes through the lens onto the photosensitive chemical surface of the celluloid negative stock inside. Thus, as light is converted into a film image, we can say that it creates a measurable physical *analog* of the actual scene. Although the initial image created in this process may be as good as light, lens, and chemistry permits, it is also subject to degradation over time. Such film is, in fact, unstable, and unless great care is taken with archival preservation of motion picture film, it eventually disintegrates. This is why so many movies have been lost forever.

By contrast, the *digital* camera does not convert light into images on another medium (film stock), but rather captures and stores images in a series of binary numbers that, unlike the analog image, have no physical relationship to the original. Thus, the result is not an *image* but a digital file that is stored on a computer hard drive (or similar storage device) and, simply put, can be used to reconstruct the original image or create different ones.

During the past ten years, digital-imaging technology began to transform certain aspects of mainstream filmmaking, primarily the computer-generated graphics so essential to making animated and action movies as popular and successful as they are. There is a great deal of talk about the "digital revolution" and how its impact will change the cinema as we know it. Several directors—including James Cameron, David Fincher, George Lucas, David Lynch, Robert Rodriguez, and Lars von Trier—have claimed that celluloid film is dead and that future filmmaking will be an all-digital medium. Yet other directors—including Tim Burton, Martin Scorsese, Ridley Scott, Oliver Stone, and Quentin Tarantino—have said that they will continue to shoot on film.

In any event, as yet there has been no revolution. The shift to digital filmmaking is moving very slowly, and the facts show that its impact differs with each stage of the production process. Table A.7 summarizes the current state of digital cinema. This table indicates that, with the exception of digital editing, to which the industry will have completely converted in 2006, the impact of digital technology has so far been minimal. Filming, distribution, and exhibition all have a long way to go before completing the transition to digital. Although 5 percent of distribution is handled digitally, less than 1 percent of all Hollywood production and exhibition is digital (the first feature film shot without using any film at all was George Lucas's *Star Wars: Episode II—The Attack of the Clones*, 2002).

The obstacles to initial adoption and eventual conversion include debates over the relative quality of the film and digital image, technical standards, and piracy issues. Costs are also a factor, although less in filming and editing than in distribution and exhibition, where the expenses of converting theaters to digital projection are estimated at between $50,000 and $150,000 per screen. Once these many

TABLE A.7	The State of Digital Cinema in 2006				
	Percentage of Films Using Digital Activity in Category	Aesthetic Advantages of Digital Filmmaking	Cost Advantages of Digital Filmmaking	Obstacles to Adoption of Digital Filmmaking	Predicted Timeline for Conversion to an All-Digital Medium
Filming	Less than 1%	An issue of great debate. More vivid colors, lack of grain and scratching on image; easier integration with special effects; instant replay; image and audio on same medium; faster and more flexible editing.	Faster shooting at lower cost; no costs for developing. Studios can rent digital and analog cameras for about the same price.	Debate over aesthetic quality of the image; varying quality of response to light, especially direct sunlight; archival longevity unknown.	2025
Editing	99%	Filmmakers can experiment endlessly with different editing approaches.	Digital film editing suites are reasonably priced.	None	2006
Distribution	5%	Cheap reprints with consistent quality; movies are e-mailed or downloaded by theaters from satellites.	In contrast to the high costs of making and shipping film prints, DVDs are lightweight, and easy to duplicate without additional costs. Digital movies can also be downloaded directly to a theater.	Lack of uniform technical standards; concern over downloading by pirates.	First stage 2005.
Exhibition	Less than 1%	Spotless picture; ability to screen a variety of content and move it quickly among theaters.	At present, almost none. Upgrading theaters for digital projection costs $50,000-150,000 per screen.	High cost of conversion and who pays for it; low monetary incentive for theater owners.	2010–2012

Source: Information adapted from Xeni Jardin, "The Cuban Revolution," *Wired*, no. 13.04 (April 2005), p. 121.

issues are settled—probably on the issue of cost rather than quality—the conversion of the film industry to an all-digital medium will begin on a large scale. Although it is generally predicted that this transition will not be completed until 2025—and it is risky to make predictions about the movie business—the situation may change much earlier than anticipated with the introduction of newer, better, and cheaper technologies.

The eventual conversion to an all-digital medium raises a closely related issue: the impact of the DVD on the movie industry. Return for a moment to Table A.5, where you'll see that the total gross receipts for 2005 were close to $8.5 billion. Of that total, 65 percent came from sales of DVD or VHS versions of movies sold in retail stores; 21 percent came from selling theater tickets; and the remaining 14 percent came from other sources. The fact is that encouraging consumers to purchase packaged movies in retail stores has become more important than getting them into the theaters, at least in the nonmetropolitan areas of the country.

More and more people own DVD playback machines, and the DVD will have virtually replaced VHS within the next year or two. Consumers can buy DVDs in every town in the country, large or small, permitting them to see movies that may not have been released in their local theaters. The fact that the big chain stores (e.g., Wal-Mart, Costco, Target) control the DVD market indicates just how pervasively the total sales of DVDs depend on suburban and rural customers. Wherever they live, however, consumers can also install home theater systems, making commercial theaters even more redundant. In 2006, six of the studios began competing with retailers by selling and downloading movies over the Internet. Thus, it is no surprise that theater owners seem reluctant to convert their projection systems to digital technology.

Theater owners have every reason to be nervous. Some theater owners see the DVD as a threat to their business and are attempting to lure people away from their home "theaters" and back into the world of the big screen by installing more comfortable seating (often reserved), improved projection and sound systems, and even comparatively private viewing areas where patrons can purchase upscale food and alcoholic beverages. Other owners regard the DVD as a boon to their business, because the revenues from retail sales of tapes and disks funnel more money back into the studios and, in turn, provide more money for movie production.

On the other hand, in 2006, it became clear that DVD sales were slowly beginning to shrink in response to several factors: a conflict over emerging high-definition formats (e.g., Blu-Ray and HD-DVD), consumer dissatisfaction with overly-priced, elaborately packaged DVD units ("special" or "anniversary" editions), the success of on-line DVD rental sources (e.g., Netflix and Blockbuster), and direct downloading (for specific viewing periods) of DVDs from distributors to consumers. Nonetheless, even in an industry where the technology seems to change monthly, experts believe some form of DVD technology will continue to produce the lion's share of Hollywood's profits through the next decade.

Maverick Producers and Directors

Hollywood has always had its maverick producers and directors, people who refuse to conform to the accepted way of making movies. Today's most successful maverick, independent producers are Scott Rudin, Jerry Bruckheimer, and Brian Grazer. Among directors, there is a do-it-yourself trend exemplified by John Sayles and Robert Rodriguez, both of whom work entirely outside the Hollywood system. Sayles not only writes, directs, and edits his films, but also finances them with income earned as a scriptwriter and script doctor. His films, which reflect a strong moral and political sensibility, include *Lone Star* (1996) and *Sunshine State* (2002). Rodriguez, who has his own studio in Texas, produces, directs, and sometimes writes the script as well as the musical score, and does the special effects. His films (e.g., *Sin City*, 2005, which he co-directed with Frank Miller; and *Spy Kids*, 2001) attract large audiences, garner solid critical reviews, and are very profitable, but their semi-improvised look reflects the fact that they are made on comparatively low budgets and fast schedules. Mel Gibson is another maverick director who does it himself while overtly bucking the system. *The*

Passion of the Christ (2004), which he produced, wrote, and directed, ranks twenty-eighth on the list of all-time, worldwide box-office successes.

Other mavericks include Robert Altman, Steve Buscemi, Francis Ford Coppola, Spike Lee, George Lucas, and Martin Scorsese, each of whom has long held considerable control over the making of his films. Steven Soderbergh, who works inside the Hollywood system and is responsible for such box-office hits as *Traffic* (2000) and *Ocean's Eleven* (2001), also experiments with movies made and distributed outside the system, such as *Bubble* (2005). In either mode, he produces and directs, and often shoots and edits his movies as well. Many filmmakers, working in other countries where the Hollywood conventions are less restrictive or nonexistent, flourish as mavericks. Among them are Jean-Pierre and Luc Dardenne, French brothers who produced, wrote, and directed the critically acclaimed, documentary-style *L'Enfant* (2005); and Michael Haneke, the German who wrote and directed the mystery thriller *Caché* (2005). Fortunately for movie lovers everywhere, the list of maverick filmmakers goes on and on.

Further Viewing

You can learn more about moviemaking, especially about the long hours and hard work that go into production, from the following movies, which are about making movies or are set within the film industry:

The Bad and the Beautiful (1952). Vincente Minnelli, director.

The Big Knife (1955). Robert Aldrich, director.

Contempt (1963). Jean-Luc Godard, director.

Day for Night (1973). François Truffaut, director.

The Day of the Locust (1975). John Schlesinger, director.

Ed Wood (1994). Tim Burton, director.

8½ (1963). Federico Fellini, director.

The Extra Girl (1923). F. Richard Jones, director.

Frances (1982). Graeme Clifford, director.

Full Frontal (2002). Steven Soderbergh, director.

The Goddess (1958). John Cromwell, director.

Gods and Monsters (1998). Bill Condon, director.

In a Lonely Place (1950). Nicholas Ray, director.

Inside Daisy Clover (1965). Robert Mulligan, director.

Jeanne Eagels (1957). George Sidney, director.

The Last Tycoon (1976). Elia Kazan, director.

The Legend of Lylah Clare (1968). Robert Aldrich, director.

Living in Oblivion (1995). Tom DiCillo, director.

Mommie Dearest (1981). Frank Perry, director.

The Player (1992). Robert Altman, director.

Show People (1928). King Vidor, director.

Singin' in the Rain (1952). Stanley Donen and Gene Kelly, directors.

Stand-In (1937). Tay Garnett, director.

The Star (1952). Stuart Heisler, director.

A Star Is Born (1937). William A. Wellman, director.

A Star Is Born (1954). George Cukor, director.

State and Main (2000). David Mamet, director.

Sunset Blvd. (1950). Billy Wilder, director.

Two Weeks in Another Town (1962). Vincente Minnelli, director.

What Ever Happened to Baby Jane? (1962). Robert Aldrich, director.

What Price Hollywood? (1932). George Cukor, director.

Further Viewing

Now that you've learned the basics of film "language" and have gotten a taste of film history and film production, you're probably eager to see more movies. In addition to the lists of movies at the end of each chapter, the following "best" lists should provide you with a lifetime of viewing options.

Academy Award Winners for Best Picture

The following is a list of all "Best Picture"[1] Academy Award winners, from the first year of the award to 2005. Although the Academy of Motion Picture Arts and Sciences is organized by crafts—for example, cinematographers vote for the cinematography awards, film editors vote for the editing awards, and so on—all Academy members vote for the Best Picture award.

[1] The phrase *Best Picture* was not always the designation that the Academy reserved for this award. In 1928 and 1929, the designation was *Outstanding Picture*; from 1930 to 1940, *Outstanding Production*; from 1941 to 1943, *Outstanding Motion Picture*; from 1944 to 1961, *Best Motion Picture*; and since 1962, *Best Picture*.

Year of Award	Title	Director(s)
1927/28	*Wings*	William A. Wellman
1928/29	*The Broadway Melody*	Harry Beaumont
1929/30	*All Quiet on the Western Front*	Lewis Milestone
1930/31	*Cimarron*	Wesley Ruggles
1931/32	*Grand Hotel*	Edmund Goulding
1932/33	*Cavalcade*	Frank Lloyd

Year of Award	Title	Director(s)
1934	*It Happened One Night*	Frank Capra
1935	*Mutiny on the Bounty*	Frank Lloyd
1936	*The Great Ziegfeld*	Robert Z. Leonard
1937	*The Life of Emile Zola*	William Dieterle
1938	*You Can't Take It With You*	Frank Capra
1939	*Gone With the Wind*	Victor Fleming
1940	*Rebecca*	Alfred Hitchcock
1941	*How Green Was My Valley*	John Ford
1942	*Mrs. Miniver*	William Wyler
1943	*Casablanca*	Michael Curtiz
1944	*Going My Way*	Leo McCarey
1945	*The Lost Weekend*	Billy Wilder
1946	*The Best Years of Our Lives*	William Wyler
1947	*Gentleman's Agreement*	Elia Kazan
1948	*Hamlet*	Laurence Olivier
1949	*All the King's Men*	Robert Rossen
1950	*All About Eve*	Joseph L. Mankiewicz
1951	*An American in Paris*	Vincente Minnelli
1952	*The Greatest Show on Earth*	Cecil B. DeMille
1953	*From Here to Eternity*	Fred Zinnemann
1954	*On the Waterfront*	Elia Kazan
1955	*Marty*	Delbert Mann
1956	*Around the World in 80 Days*	Michael Anderson
1957	*The Bridge on the River Kwai*	David Lean
1958	*Gigi*	Vincente Minnelli
1959	*Ben-Hur*	William Wyler
1960	*The Apartment*	Billy Wilder
1961	*West Side Story*	Robert Wise and Jerome Robbins
1962	*Lawrence of Arabia*	David Lean
1963	*Tom Jones*	Tony Richardson
1964	*My Fair Lady*	George Cukor
1965	*The Sound of Music*	Robert Wise
1966	*A Man for All Seasons*	Fred Zinnemann
1967	*In the Heat of the Night*	Norman Jewison
1968	*Oliver!*	Carol Reed
1969	*Midnight Cowboy*	John Schlesinger
1970	*Patton*	Franklin J. Schaffner
1971	*The French Connection*	William Friedkin
1972	*The Godfather*	Francis Ford Coppola

Year of Award	Title	Director(s)
1973	*The Sting*	George Roy Hill
1974	*The Godfather: Part II*	Francis Ford Coppola
1975	*One Flew Over the Cuckoo's Nest*	Milos Forman
1976	*Rocky*	John G. Avildsen
1977	*Annie Hall*	Woody Allen
1978	*The Deer Hunter*	Michael Cimino
1979	*Kramer vs. Kramer*	Robert Benton
1980	*Ordinary People*	Robert Redford
1981	*Chariots of Fire*	Hugh Hudson
1982	*Gandhi*	Richard Attenborough
1983	*Terms of Endearment*	James L. Brooks
1984	*Amadeus*	Milos Forman
1985	*Out of Africa*	Sydney Pollack
1986	*Platoon*	Oliver Stone
1987	*The Last Emperor*	Bernardo Bertolucci
1988	*Rain Man*	Barry Levinson
1989	*Driving Miss Daisy*	Bruce Beresford
1990	*Dances With Wolves*	Kevin Costner
1991	*The Silence of the Lambs*	Jonathan Demme
1992	*Unforgiven*	Clint Eastwood
1993	*Schindler's List*	Steven Spielberg
1994	*Forrest Gump*	Robert Zemeckis
1995	*Braveheart*	Mel Gibson
1996	*The English Patient*	Anthony Minghella
1997	*Titanic*	James Cameron
1998	*Shakespeare in Love*	John Madden
1999	*American Beauty*	Sam Mendes
2000	*Gladiator*	Ridley Scott
2001	*A Beautiful Mind*	Ron Howard
2002	*Chicago*	Rob Marshall
2003	*The Lord of the Rings: The Return of the King*	Peter Jackson
2004	*Million Dollar Baby*	Clint Eastwood
2005	*Crash*	Paul Haggis

Source: Academy of Motion Picture Arts and Sciences, <http://awardsdatabase.oscars.org> (accessed April 17, 2006).

Sight & Sound: Top Ten Best Movies of All Time

Every ten years since 1952, the editors of *Sight & Sound*—the official publication of the British Film Institute—have asked some two hundred film critics and directors from around the world to choose the top ten feature films made anytime, anywhere in the world. The results are separated into two lists—one derived from the responses by film critics, and one from the responses by directors. The following are the results from the most recent poll, published in 2002.

Rank	Year of Release	Title	Director(s)
		THE CRITICS' CHOICES	
1	1941	*Citizen Kane*	Orson Welles
2	1958	*Vertigo*	Alfred Hitchcock
3	1939	*The Rules of the Game*	Jean Renoir
4	1972, 1974	*The Godfather* and *The Godfather: Part II*	Francis Ford Coppola
5	1953	*Tokyo Story*	Yasujiro Ozu
6	1968	*2001: A Space Odyssey*	Stanley Kubrick
7	1925	*Battleship Potemkin*	Sergei M. Eisenstein
8	1927	*Sunrise: A Song of Two Humans*	F. W. Murnau
9	1963	*$8\frac{1}{2}$*	Federico Fellini
10	1952	*Singin' in the Rain*	Gene Kelly and Stanley Donen
		THE DIRECTORS' CHOICES	
1	1941	*Citizen Kane*	Orson Welles
2	1972, 1974	*The Godfather* and *The Godfather: Part II*	Francis Ford Coppola
3	1963	*81/2*	Federico Fellini
4	1962	*Lawrence of Arabia*	David Lean
5	1964	*Dr. Strangelove*	Stanley Kubrick
6	1948	*Bicycle Thieves*	Vittorio De Sica
7	1980	*Raging Bull*	Martin Scorsese
8	1958	*Vertigo*	Alfred Hitchcock
9	1950	*Rashomon*	Akira Kurosawa
10	1939	*The Rules of the Game*	Jean Renoir

Source: British Film Institute, <www.bfi.org.uk/sightandsound> (accessed April 17, 2006).

American Film Institute:
One Hundred Greatest American Movies of All Time

The following list was created by a panel of over fifteen hundred screenwriters, directors, actors, producers, cinematographers, editors, executives, film historians, and critics assembled by the American Film Institute (AFI) in 1996 in honor of cinema's first one hundred years. The panel was given a list of four hundred films nominated by the AFI, and asked to select and rank the one hundred best American films from that list. All of these films were made during the first hundred years of cinema (1896–1996), so no films made after 1996 are included.

Rank	Year of Release	Title	Director(s)
1	1941	*Citizen Kane*	Orson Welles
2	1942	*Casablanca*	Michael Curtiz
3	1972	*The Godfather*	Francis Ford Coppola
4	1939	*Gone With the Wind*	Victor Fleming
5	1962	*Lawrence of Arabia*	David Lean
6	1939	*The Wizard of Oz*	Victor Fleming
7	1967	*The Graduate*	Mike Nichols
8	1954	*On the Waterfront*	Elia Kazan
9	1993	*Schindler's List*	Steven Spielberg
10	1952	*Singin' in the Rain*	Gene Kelly and Stanley Donen
11	1946	*It's a Wonderful Life*	Frank Capra
12	1950	*Sunset Blvd.*	Billy Wilder
13	1957	*The Bridge on the River Kwai*	David Lean
14	1959	*Some Like It Hot*	Billy Wilder
15	1977	*Star Wars*	George Lucas
16	1950	*All About Eve*	Joseph L. Mankiewicz
17	1951	*The African Queen*	John Huston
18	1960	*Psycho*	Alfred Hitchcock
19	1974	*Chinatown*	Roman Polanski
20	1975	*One Flew Over the Cuckoo's Nest*	Milos Forman
21	1940	*The Grapes of Wrath*	John Ford
22	1968	*2001: A Space Odyssey*	Stanley Kubrick
23	1941	*The Maltese Falcon*	John Huston
24	1980	*Raging Bull*	Martin Scorsese
25	1982	*E.T. the Extra-Terrestrial*	Steven Spielberg
26	1964	*Dr. Strangelove*	Stanley Kubrick
27	1967	*Bonnie and Clyde*	Arthur Penn
28	1979	*Apocalypse Now*	Francis Ford Coppola
29	1939	*Mr. Smith Goes to Washington*	Frank Capra
30	1948	*The Treasure of the Sierra Madre*	John Huston

Rank	Year of Release	Title	Director(s)
31	1977	*Annie Hall*	Woody Allen
32	1974	*The Godfather: Part II*	Francis Ford Coppola
33	1952	*High Noon*	Fred Zinnemann
34	1962	*To Kill a Mockingbird*	Robert Mulligan
35	1934	*It Happened One Night*	Frank Capra
36	1969	*Midnight Cowboy*	John Schlesinger
37	1946	*The Best Years of Our Lives*	William Wyler
38	1944	*Double Indemnity*	Billy Wilder
39	1965	*Doctor Zhivago*	David Lean
40	1959	*North by Northwest*	Alfred Hitchcock
41	1961	*West Side Story*	Robert Wise and Jerome Robbins
42	1954	*Rear Window*	Alfred Hitchcock
43	1933	*King Kong*	Ernest B. Schoedsack and Merian C. Cooper
44	1915	*The Birth of a Nation*	D. W. Griffith
45	1951	*A Streetcar Named Desire*	Elia Kazan
46	1971	*A Clockwork Orange*	Stanley Kubrick
47	1976	*Taxi Driver*	Martin Scorsese
48	1975	*Jaws*	Steven Spielberg
49	1937	*Snow White and the Seven Dwarfs*	(no director credited)
50	1969	*Butch Cassidy and the Sundance Kid*	George Roy Hill
51	1940	*The Philadelphia Story*	George Cukor
52	1953	*From Here to Eternity*	Fred Zinnemann
53	1984	*Amadeus*	Milos Forman
54	1930	*All Quiet on the Western Front*	Lewis Milestone
55	1965	*The Sound of Music*	Robert Wise
56	1970	*M*A*S*H*	Robert Altman
57	1949	*The Third Man*	Carol Reed
58	1940	*Fantasia*	James Algar et al.
59	1955	*Rebel Without a Cause*	Nicholas Ray
60	1981	*Raiders of the Lost Ark*	Steven Spielberg
61	1958	*Vertigo*	Alfred Hitchcock
62	1982	*Tootsie*	Sydney Pollack
63	1939	*Stagecoach*	John Ford
64	1977	*Close Encounters of the Third Kind*	Steven Spielberg
65	1991	*The Silence of the Lambs*	Jonathan Demme
66	1976	*Network*	Sidney Lumet
67	1962	*The Manchurian Candidate*	John Frankenheimer
68	1951	*An American in Paris*	Vincente Minnelli
69	1953	*Shane*	George Stevens

Rank	Year of Release	Title	Director(s)
70	1971	*The French Connection*	William Friedkin
71	1994	*Forrest Gump*	Robert Zemeckis
72	1959	*Ben-Hur*	William Wyler
73	1939	*Wuthering Heights*	William Wyler
74	1925	*The Gold Rush*	Charles Chaplin
75	1990	*Dances With Wolves*	Kevin Costner
76	1931	*City Lights*	Charles Chaplin
77	1973	*American Graffiti*	George Lucas
78	1976	*Rocky*	John G. Avildsen
79	1978	*The Deer Hunter*	Michael Cimino
80	1969	*The Wild Bunch*	Sam Peckinpah
81	1936	*Modern Times*	Charles Chaplin
82	1956	*Giant*	George Stevens
83	1986	*Platoon*	Oliver Stone
84	1996	*Fargo*	Joel Coen
85	1933	*Duck Soup*	Leo McCarey
86	1935	*Mutiny on the Bounty*	Frank Lloyd
87	1931	*Frankenstein*	James Whale
88	1969	*Easy Rider*	Dennis Hopper
89	1970	*Patton*	Franklin J. Schaffner
90	1927	*The Jazz Singer*	Alan Crosland
91	1964	*My Fair Lady*	George Cukor
92	1951	*A Place in the Sun*	George Stevens
93	1960	*The Apartment*	Billy Wilder
94	1990	*Goodfellas*	Martin Scorsese
95	1994	*Pulp Fiction*	Quentin Tarantino
96	1956	*The Searchers*	John Ford
97	1938	*Bringing Up Baby*	Howard Hawks
98	1992	*Unforgiven*	Clint Eastwood
99	1967	*Guess Who's Coming to Dinner*	Stanley Kramer
100	1942	*Yankee Doodle Dandy*	Michael Curtiz

Source: American Film Institute <www.afi.com/tvevents> (accessed April 17, 2006).

Entertainment Weekly:
One Hundred Greatest Movies of All Time

Following publication of the American Film Institute's list, many critics and pundits criticized it for its omissions and the order of its rankings. Among the alternative lists that were published soon after the AFI's was *Entertainment Weekly*'s *100 Greatest Movies of All Time*, published in book form in 1999. The list was selected from five hundred choices nominated by *Entertainment Weekly*'s editors. In addition to correcting whatever omissions the *Entertainment Weekly* editors perceived in AFI's listing of top American movies, the list also included movies made outside the United States.

Rank	Year of Release	Title	Director(s)
1	1972	*The Godfather*	Francis Ford Coppola
2	1941	*Citizen Kane*	Orson Welles
3	1942	*Casablanca*	Michael Curtiz
4	1974	*Chinatown*	Roman Polanski
5	1980	*Raging Bull*	Martin Scorsese
6	1960	*La dolce vita*	Federico Fellini
7	1974	*The Godfather: Part II*	Francis Ford Coppola
8	1939	*Gone With the Wind*	Victor Fleming
9	1959	*Some Like It Hot*	Billy Wilder
10	1952	*Singin' in the Rain*	Gene Kelly and Stanley Donen
11	1960	*Psycho*	Alfred Hitchcock
12	1954	*The Seven Samurai*	Akira Kurosawa
13	1956	*The Searchers*	John Ford
14	1964	*Dr. Strangelove*	Stanley Kubrick
15	1925	*The Gold Rush*	Charles Chaplin
16	1977	*Star Wars*	George Lucas
17	1954	*On the Waterfront*	Elia Kazan
18	1962	*Lawrence of Arabia*	David Lean
19	1958	*Vertigo*	Alfred Hitchcock
20	1982	*E.T. the Extra-Terrestrial*	Steven Spielberg
21	1950	*All About Eve*	Joseph L. Mankiewicz
22	1948	*Bicycle Thieves*	Vittorio De Sica
23	1937	*Snow White and the Seven Dwarfs*	(no director credited)
24	1938	*Bringing Up Baby*	Howard Hawks
25	1916	*Intolerance*	D. W. Griffith
26	1968	*2001: A Space Odyssey*	Stanley Kubrick
27	1940	*The Grapes of Wrath*	John Ford
28	1950	*Sunset Blvd.*	Billy Wilder
29	1994	*Pulp Fiction*	Quentin Tarantino
30	1939	*Mr. Smith Goes to Washington*	Frank Capra

Rank	Year of Release	Title	Director(s)
31	1941	*The Maltese Falcon*	John Huston
32	1939	*The Wizard of Oz*	Victor Fleming
33	1962	*Jules and Jim*	François Truffaut
34	1924	*Sherlock, Jr.*	Buster Keaton
35	1940	*The Philadelphia Story*	George Cukor
36	1963	*$8\frac{1}{2}$*	Federico Fellini
37	1986	*Blue Velvet*	David Lynch
38	1975	*Nashville*	Robert Altman
39	1936	*Swing Time*	George Stevens
40	1993	*Schindler's List*	Steven Spielberg
41	1976	*Taxi Driver*	Martin Scorsese
42	1986	*Aliens*	James Cameron
43	1933	*Duck Soup*	Leo McCarey
44	1959	*North by Northwest*	Alfred Hitchcock
45	1957	*The Seventh Seal*	Ingmar Bergman
46	1957	*The Bridge on the River Kwai*	David Lean
47	1933	*King Kong*	Ernest B. Schoedsack and Merian C. Cooper
48	1967	*Bonnie and Clyde*	Arthur Penn
49	1957	*The Sweet Smell of Success*	Alexander Mackendrick
50	1944	*Double Indemnity*	Billy Wilder
51	1945	*Children of Paradise*	Marcel Carné
52	1975	*Jaws*	Steven Spielberg
53	1956	*Invasion of the Body Snatchers*	Don Siegel
54	1958	*Touch of Evil*	Orson Welles
55	1967	*The Graduate*	Mike Nichols
56	1946	*It's a Wonderful Life*	Frank Capra
57	1969	*The Wild Bunch*	Sam Peckinpah
58	1939	*The Rules of the Game*	Jean Renoir
59	1941	*The Lady Eve*	Preston Sturges
60	1977	*Annie Hall*	Woody Allen
61	1938	*The Adventures of Robin Hood*	William Keighley and Michael Curtiz
62	1944	*Henry V*	Laurence Olivier
63	1960	*Breathless*	Jean-Luc Godard
64	1973	*Mean Streets*	Martin Scorsese
65	1949	*The Third Man*	Carol Reed
66	1946	*Notorious*	Alfred Hitchcock
67	1980	*Airplane!*	David Zucker, Jerry Zucker, and Jim Abrahams
68	1935	*Bride of Frankenstein*	James Whale

Rank	Year of Release	Title	Director(s)
69	1970	*The Conformist*	Bernardo Bertolucci
70	1991	*Beauty and the Beast*	Gary Trousdale and Kirk Wise
71	1942	*To Be or Not to Be*	Ernst Lubitsch
72	1931	*M*	Fritz Lang
73	1946	*Great Expectations*	David Lean
74	1957	*Funny Face*	Stanley Donen
75	1982	*Tootsie*	Sydney Pollack
76	1962	*The Manchurian Candidate*	John Frankenheimer
77	1925	*Battleship Potemkin*	Sergei Eisenstein
78	1949	*White Heat*	Raoul Walsh
79	1934	*It's a Gift*	Norman Z. McLeod
80	1922	*Nosferatu*	F. W. Murnau
81	1989	*Do the Right Thing*	Spike Lee
82	1955	*Diabolique*	Henri-Georges Clouzot
83	1946	*The Best Years of Our Lives*	William Wyler
84	1966	*Blow-Up*	Michelangelo Antonioni
85	1962	*To Kill a Mockingbird*	Robert Mulligan
86	1955	*Rebel Without a Cause*	Nicholas Ray
87	1930	*L'âge d'or*	Luis Buñuel
88	1968	*The Producers*	Mel Brooks
89	1987	*Wings of Desire*	Wim Wenders
90	1953	*Pickup on South Street*	Samuel Fuller
91	1945	*Mildred Pierce*	Michael Curtiz
92	1927	*Sunrise: A Song of Two Humans*	F. W. Murnau
93	1981	*The Road Warrior*	George Miller
94	1940	*The Shop Around the Corner*	Ernst Lubitsch
95	1953	*Tokyo Story*	Yasujiro Ozu
96	1992	*The Last of the Mohicans*	Michael Mann
97	1993	*The Piano*	Jane Campion
98	1991	*The Silence of the Lambs*	Jonathan Demme
99	1974	*Swept Away*	Lina Wertmüller
100	1974	*Celine and Julie Go Boating*	Jacques Rivette

Source: Entertainment Weekly's 100 Greatest Movies of All Time, <www.filmsite.org/ew100.html> (accessed April 17, 2006).

The Village Voice:
One Hundred Best Films of the Twentieth Century

The following list was published in the January 4, 2000, issue of *The Village Voice*, a free weekly newspaper based in New York City. The list was compiled from the results of a poll administered by the editors of the *Voice* in which fifty of the best-known film critics at the time were asked to list their top ten movies of all time. Individual responses were collated, and the following list of one hundred films is the result.

Rank	Year of Release	Title	Director(s)
1	1941	*Citizen Kane*	Orson Welles
2	1939	*The Rules of the Game*	Jean Renoir
3	1958	*Vertigo*	Alfred Hitchcock
4	1956	*The Searchers*	John Ford
5	1929	*The Man With a Movie Camera*	Dziga Vertov
6	1927	*Sunrise: A Song of Two Humans*	F. W. Murnau
7	1934	*L'Atalante*	Jean Vigo
8	1928	*The Passion of Joan of Arc*	Carl Theodor Dreyer
9	1966	*Au hasard Balthazar*	Robert Bresson
10	1950	*Rashomon*	Akira Kurosawa
11	1968	*2001: A Space Odyssey*	Stanley Kubrick
12	1972	*The Godfather*	Francis Ford Coppola
13	1955	*Pather Panchali*	Satyajit Ray
14	1915	*The Birth of a Nation*	D. W. Griffith
15	1939	*The Wizard of Oz*	Victor Fleming
16	1946	*It's a Wonderful Life*	Frank Capra
17	1943	*Ordet*	Gustaf Molander
18	1916	*Intolerance*	D. W. Griffith
19	1976	*Jeanne Dielman, 23 Quai du Commerce, 1080 Bruxelles*	Chantal Akerman
20	1960	*Psycho*	Alfred Hitchcock
21	1974	*Chinatown*	Roman Polanski
22	1931	*M*	Fritz Lang
23	1954	*The Seven Samurai*	Akira Kurosawa
24	1953	*The Earrings of Madame de...*	Max Ophüls
25	1942	*The Magnificent Ambersons*	Orson Welles
26	1956	*A Man Escaped*	Robert Bresson
27	1919	*Broken Blossoms*	D. W. Griffith
28	1924	*Greed*	Erich von Stroheim
29	1953	*Ugetsu monogatari*	Kenji Mizoguchi
30	1949	*The Third Man*	Carol Reed
31	1974	*The Godfather: Part II*	Francis Ford Coppola

Rank	Year of Release	Title	Director(s)
32	1927	*The General*	Buster Keaton and Clyde Bruckman
33	1957	*The Seventh Seal*	Ingmar Bergman
34	1976	*Taxi Driver*	Martin Scorsese
35	1955	*The Night of the Hunter*	Charles Laughton
36	1953	*Tokyo Story*	Yasujiro Ozu
37	1948	*Bicycle Thieves*	Vittorio De Sica
38	1931	*City Lights*	Charles Chaplin
39	1933	*King Kong*	Ernest B. Schoedsack and Merian C. Cooper
40	1927	*Metropolis*	Fritz Lang
41	1962	*My Life to Live*	Jean-Luc Godard
42	1924	*Sherlock, Jr.*	Buster Keaton
43	1972	*Aguirre: The Wrath of God*	Werner Herzog
44	1933	*Duck Soup*	Leo McCarey
45	1950	*Sunset Blvd.*	Billy Wilder
46	1975	*Barry Lyndon*	Stanley Kubrick
47	1959	*The 400 Blows*	François Truffaut
48	1928	*Steamboat Bill, Jr.*	Charles F. Reisner
49	1963	*Contempt*	Jean-Luc Godard
50	1925	*The Gold Rush*	Charles Chaplin
51	1959	*North by Northwest*	Alfred Hitchcock
52	1966	*Hold Me While I'm Naked*	George Kuchar
53	1966	*The Rise of Louis XIV*	Roberto Rossellini
54	1955, 1957, 1958	The Apu trilogy (*Pather Panchali*, *The Unvanquished*, and *The World of Apu*)	Satyajit Ray
55	1958	*Touch of Evil*	Orson Welles
56	1974	*A Woman Under the Influence*	John Cassavetes
57	1941	*The Lady Eve*	Preston Sturges
58	1970	*The Conformist*	Bernardo Bertolucci
59	1942	*The Palm Beach Story*	Preston Sturges
60	1962	*The Man Who Shot Liberty Valance*	John Ford
61	1959	*Pickpocket*	Robert Bresson
62	1963	*An Actor's Revenge*	Kon Ichikawa
63	1980	*Berlin Alexanderplatz*	Rainer Werner Fassbinder
64	1990	*Close Up*	Abbas Kiarostami
65	1964	*The Gospel According to St. Matthew*	Pier Paolo Pasolini
66	1962	*La jetée*	Chris Marker
67	1936	*Modern Times*	Charles Chaplin
68	1927	*October*	Grigori Aleksandrov and Sergei Eisenstein

Rank	Year of Release	Title	Director(s)
69	1950	*Los Olvidados*	Luis Buñuel
70	1946	*Paisan*	Roberto Rossellini
71	1970	*Performance*	Nicolas Roeg and Donald Cammell
72	1985	*Shoah*	Claude Lanzmann
73	1952	*Singin' in the Rain*	Gene Kelly and Stanley Donen
74	1967	*Two or Three Things I Know About Her*	Jean-Luc Godard
75	1952	*Umberto D*	Vittorio De Sica
76	1915	*Les vampires*	Louis Feuillade
77	1950	*All About Eve*	Joseph L. Mankiewicz
78	1955	*All That Heaven Allows*	Douglas Sirk
79	1925	*Battleship Potemkin*	Sergei Eisenstein
80	1946	*Notorious*	Alfred Hitchcock
81	1965	*Pierrot le fou*	Jean-Luc Godard
82	1975	*Fox and His Friends*	Rainer Werner Fassbinder
83	1974	*The Texas Chainsaw Massacre*	Tobe Hooper
84	1902	*A Trip to the Moon*	Georges Méliès
85	1967	*Wavelength*	Michael Snow
86	1958	*Ashes and Diamonds*	Andrzej Wajda
87	1970	*Beyond the Valley of the Dolls*	Russ Meyer
88	1953	*The Golden Coach*	Jean Renoir
89	1975	*Salo*	Pier Paolo Pasolini
90	1974	*Celine and Julie Go Boating*	Jacques Rivette
91	1966	*Masculine-Feminine*	Jean-Luc Godard
92	1922	*Nosferatu*	F. W. Murnau
93	1977	*Star Wars*	George Lucas
94	1982	*Blade Runner*	Ridley Scott
95	1935	*Bride of Frankenstein*	James Whale
96	1962	*Jules and Jim*	François Truffaut
97	1988	*Landscape in the Mist*	Theo Angelopoulos
98	1973	*Mean Streets*	Martin Scorsese
99	1943	*Shadow of a Doubt*	Alfred Hitchcock
100	1977	*Suspiria*	Dario Argento

Source: Village Voice Media, <www.filmsite.org/villvoice.htm> (accessed April 17, 2006).

Further Reading

Chapter 1: What Is a Movie?

Allen, Richard. *Projecting Illusion: Film Spectatorship and the Impression of Reality*. New York: Cambridge University Press, 1997.

Altman, Rick. *The American Film Musical*. Bloomington: Indiana University Press, 1987.

———. *Film/Genre*. London: British Film Institute Press, 1999.

Andrew, J. Dudley. *The Major Film Theories: An Introduction*. New York: Oxford University Press, 1976.

Armstrong, Richard. *Understanding Realism*. London: British Film Institute Press, 2005.

Arnheim, Rudolf. *Art and Visual Perception: A Psychology of the Creative Eye*. Rev. ed. Berkeley: University of California Press, 1974.

———. *Film as Art*. Berkeley: University of California Press, 1957.

Balio, Tino. *Grand Design: Hollywood as a Modern Business Enterprise, 1930–1939*. History of the American Cinema, vol. 5. Berkeley: University of California Press, 1995.

Barsam, Richard. *Nonfiction Film: A Critical History*. Rev., exp. ed. Bloomington: Indiana University Press, 1992.

Bazin, André. *What Is Cinema? Essays Selected and Translated by Hugh Gray*. 2 vols. Berkeley: University of California Press, 1967–71.

Benjamin, Walter. "The Work of Art in the Age of Mechanical Reproduction," in *Film Theory and Criticism: Introductory Readings*, 5th ed., edited by Leo Braudy and Marshall Cohen, 731–51. New York: Oxford University Press, 1999.

Bordwell, David. *On the History of Film Style*. Cambridge, Mass.: Harvard University Press, 1997.

Bordwell, David, Janet Staiger, and Kristin Thompson. *The Classical Hollywood Cinema: Film Style and Mode of Production to 1960*. New York: Columbia University Press, 1985.

Bowser, Eileen. *The Transformation of Cinema: 1907–1915*. History of the American Cinema, vol. 2. New York: Scribner, 1990.

Braudy, Leo, and Marshall Cohen, eds. *Film Theory and Criticism: Introductory Readings*. 5th ed. New York: Oxford University Press, 1999.

Browne, Nick. *Refiguring American Film Genres: History and Theory*. Berkeley: University of California Press, 1998.

Burch, Nöel. *Life to Those Shadows*. Berkeley: University of California Press, 1990.

———. *Theory of Film Practice*. Princeton, N.J.: Princeton University Press, 1981.

Carroll, Noël. *Interpreting the Moving Image*. New York: Cambridge University Press, 1998.

———. *Theorizing the Moving Image*. New York: Cambridge University Press, 1996.

Cohan, Steven, ed. *Hollywood Musicals, the Film Reader*. New York: Routledge, 2002.

Cook, David A. *A History of Narrative Film*. 4th ed. New York: Norton, 2004.

———. *Lost Illusions: American Cinema in the Shadow of Watergate and Vietnam, 1970–1979*. History of American Cinema, vol. 9. New York: Scribner, 2000.

Crafton, Donald. *The Talkies: American Cinema's Transition to Sound, 1926–1931*. History of American Cinema, vol. 4. New York: Scribner, 1997.

Dixon, Wheeler Winston. *The Exploding Eye: A Re-Visionary History of 1960's American Experimental Cinema*. Albany: State University of New York Press, 1997.

Dixon, Wheeler Winston, and Gwendolyn Audrey Foster, eds. *Experimental Cinema: The Film Reader*. New York: Routledge, 2002.

Dondis, Donis A. *A Primer of Visual Literacy*. Cambridge, Mass.: MIT Press, 1973.

Feuer, Jane. *The Hollywood Musical*. Bloomington: Indiana University Press, 1999.

Fielding, Raymond. *A Technological History of Motion Pictures and Television*. Berkeley: University of California Press, 1967.

Freeland, Cynthia A. *The Naked and the Undead: Evil and the Appeal of Horror*. Boulder, Colo.: Westview, 2000.

Furniss, Maureen. *Art in Motion: Animation Aesthetics*. Bloomington: Indiana University Press, 1998.

Gehring, Wes D., ed. *Handbook of American Film Genres*. New York: Greenwood, 1988.

Grant, Barry Keith, ed. *Film Genre Reader II*. Austin: University of Texas Press, 1995.

Hardy, Phil. *The Western*. London: Aurum, 1991.

Hardy, Phil, Tom Milne, Kim Newman, and Paul Willemen, eds. *Horror*. London: Aurum, 1996.

Hark, Ina Rae, ed. *Exhibition, the Film Reader*. New York: Routledge, 2002.

Henderson, Brian. *A Critique of Film Theory*. New York: Dutton, 1980.

Hollows, Joanne, Peter Hutchings, and Mark Jan-covich, eds. *The Film Studies Reader*. New York: Oxford University Press, 2000.

Jancovich, Mark, ed. *Horror, the Film Reader*. New York: Routledge, 2002.

Kawin, Bruce F. *How Movies Work*. Berkeley: University of California Press, 1992.

Konigsberg, Ira. *The Complete Film Dictionary*. 2nd ed. New York: Penguin, 1997.

Kozarski, Richard. *An Evening's Entertainment: The Age of the Silent Feature Picture, 1915–1928*. History of American Cinema, vol. 3. New York: Scribner, 1994.

Kracauer, Siegfried. *Theory of Film: The Redemption of Physical Reality*. New York: Oxford University Press, 1960.

Le Grice, Malcolm. *Experimental Cinema in the Digital Age*. London: BFI Publishing, 2001.

Lehman, Peter, ed. *Defining Cinema*. New Brunswick, N.J.: Rutgers University Press, 1997.

Lewis, Jon, ed. *The New American Cinema*. (Durham, NC: Duke University Press, 1998).

Mast, Gerald. *Film/Cinema/Movie: A Theory of Experience*. New York: Harper & Row, 1977.

Metz, Christian. *Film Language: A Semiotics of the Cinema*. Translated by Michael Taylor. New York: Oxford University Press, 1974.

Monaco, Paul. *The Sixties: 1960–1969*. History of American Cinema, vol. 8. New York: Scribner, 2001.

Musser, Charles. *The Emergence of Cinema: The American Screen to 1907*. History of the American Cinema, vol. 1. New York: Scribner, 1990.

Neale, Steve, ed. *Cinema and Technology: Image, Sound, Colour*. Bloomington: Indiana University Press, 1985.

———. *Genre and Contemporary Hollywood*. London: British Film Institute, 2002.

Panofsky, Erwin. "Style and Medium in the Motion Pictures," in *Film Theory and Criticism: Introductory Readings*, 5th ed., edited by Leo Braudy and Marshall Cohen, 281–83. New York: Oxford University Press, 1999.

Perkins, V. F. *Film as Film: Understanding and Judging Movies*. Baltimore: Penguin, 1972.

Pilling, Jayne, ed. *A Reader in Animation Studies*. Bloomington: Indiana University Press, 1998.

Plantinga, Carl R. *Rhetoric and Representation in*

Nonfiction Film. New York: Cambridge University Press, 1997.

Prince, Stephen. *A New Pot of Gold: Hollywood Under the Electronic Rainbow, 1980–1989.* History of American Cinema, vol. 10. New York: Scribner, 2000.

Rothman, William. *Documentary Film Classics.* New York: Cambridge University Press, 1997.

Schatz, Thomas. *Boom and Bust: American Cinema in the 1940s.* History of the American Cinema, vol. 6. New York: Scribner, 1997.

———. *Hollywood Genres: Formulas, Filmmaking, and the Studio System.* New York: Random House, 1981.

Smith, Barbara Herrnstein. *Poetic Closure: A Study of How Poems End.* Chicago: University of Chicago Press, 1968.

Solomon, Stanley J. *Beyond Formula: American Film Genres.* New York: Harcourt Brace Jovanovich, 1976.

Thomson, David. *The New Biographical Dictionary of Film.* New York: Knopf, 2002.

Truffaut, François. *Hitchcock.* Rev. ed. New York: Simon and Schuster, 1985.

Tudor, Andrew. *Monsters and Mad Scientists: A Cultural History of the Horror Movie.* Oxford, England: Blackwell, 1989.

Utterson, Andrew. *Technology and Culture, the Film Reader.* New York: Routledge, 2005.

Williams, Christopher. *Realism and the Cinema: A Reader.* London: Routledge & Kegan Paul, 1980.

Wollen, Peter. *Signs and Meanings in the Cinema.* London: Secker & Warburg, 1972.

Youngblood, Gene. *Expanded Cinema.* New York: Dutton, 1970.

Chapter 2: Narrative

Bazin, André. "Evolution of the Western," in *What Is Cinema? Essays Selected and Translated by Hugh Gray*, Vol. 2, 149–57. Berkeley: University of California Press, 1971.

Beardsley, Monroe C. *Aesthetics: Problems in the Philosophy of Criticism.* New York: Harcourt, Brace, 1958.

Black, Gregory D. *Hollywood Censored: Morality Codes, Catholics, and the Movies.* Cambridge, England: Cambridge University Press, 1994.

Bordwell, David. *Making Meaning: Inference and Rhetoric in the Interpretation of Cinema.* Cambridge, Mass.: Harvard University Press, 1989.

———. *Narration in the Fiction Film.* Madison: University of Wisconsin Press, 1985.

———. *The Way Hollywood Tells It: Story and Style in Modern Movies.* Berkeley: University of California Press, 2006.

Branigan, Edward. *Narrative Comprehension and Film.* New York: Routledge, 1992.

———. *Point of View in the Cinema: A Theory of Narration and Subjectivity in Classical Film.* New York: Mouton, 1984.

Buscombe, Edward. *Stagecoach.* London: British Film Institute, 1992.

Chatham, Seymour. *Coming to Terms: The Rhetoric of Narrative in Fiction and Film.* Ithaca, N.Y.: Cornell University Press, 1990.

———. *Story and Discourse: Narrative Structure in Fiction and Film.* Ithaca, N.Y.: Cornell University Press, 1978.

Desmond, John, and Peter Hawkes. *Adaptation: Studying Film and Literature.* New York: McGraw-Hill, 2006.

Fell, John. *Film and the Narrative Tradition.* Norman: University of Oklahoma Press, 1974.

Forster, E. M. *Aspects of the Novel.* New York: Harcourt, Brace, and World, 1927.

Jacobs, Lea. *The Wages of Sin: Censorship and the Fallen Woman Film.* Madison: University of Wisconsin, 1991.

Kozloff, Sarah. *Overhearing Film Dialogue.* Berkeley: University of California Press, 2000.

Martin, Olga J. *Hollywood Movie Commandments: A Handbook for Motion Picture Writers and Reviewers.* New York: Wilson, 1937.

Mercer, John, and Martin Shingler. *Melodrama: Genre, Style and Sensibility.* New York: Columbia University Press, 2004.

Moley, Raymond. "The Birth of the Motion Picture Code," in *The Movies in Our Midst: Documents in the Cultural History of Film in America*, edited by Gerald Mast, 317–21. Chicago: University of Chicago Press, 1982.

———. "The Motion Picture Production Code of 1930," in *The Movies in Our Midst: Documents in* the Cultural History of Film in America, edited by Gerald Mast, 321–33. Chicago: University of Chicago Press.

Neale, Stephen, and Murray Smith, eds. *Contemporary Hollywood Cinema*. New York: Routledge, 1998.

Nichols, Dudley. *Stagecoach: A Film by John Ford and Dudley Nichols*. New York: Simon and Schuster, 1971.

Schumach, Murray. *The Face on the Cutting Room Floor: The Story of Movie and Television Censorship*. New York: Morrow, 1964.

Thompson, Kristin. *Storytelling in the New Hollywood: Understanding Classical Narrative Technique*. Cambridge, Mass.: Harvard University Press, 1999.

Chapter 3: Mise-en-Scène

Affron, Charles, and Mirella Jona. *Sets in Motion: Art Direction and Film Narrative*. New Brunswick, N.J.: Rutgers University Press, 1995.

Albrecht, Donald. *Designing Dreams: Modern Architecture in the Movies*. New York: Harper & Row, 1986.

"American Widescreen" [Special issue]. *Velvet Light Trap*, no. 21 (Summer 1985).

Andrew, James Dudley, ed. *The Image in Dispute: Art and Cinema in the Age of Photography*. Austin: University of Texas Press, 1997.

Annas, Alicia. "The Photogenic Formula: Hairstyles and Makeup in Historical Films," in *Hollywood and History: Costume Design in Film*, edited by Edward Maeder, 52–77. New York: Thames and Hudson, 1987.

Arnheim, Rudolf. *Art and Visual Perception: A Psychology of the Creative Eye*. Rev. ed. Berkeley: University of California Press, 1974.

———. *The Power of the Center: A Study of Composition in the Visual Arts*. Berkeley: University of California Press, 1988.

Barr, Charles. "CinemaScope: Before and After," in *Film Theory and Criticism: Introductory Readings*, 2nd ed., edited by Gerald Mast and Marshall Cohen, 140–168 New York: Oxford University Press, 1979.

———. "A Letter From Charles Barr." *Velvet Light Trap*, no. 21 (Summer 1985): 5–7.

Barsacq, Léon, and Elliot Stein. *Caligari's Cabinet and Other Grand Illusions: A History of Film Design*. New York: New American Library, 1976.

Bazin, André. "Three Essays on Widescreen Film." *Velvet Light Trap*, no. 21 (Summer 1985): 8–18.

Belton, John. "CinemaScope: The Economics of Ideology." *Velvet Light Trap*, no. 21 (Summer 1985): 35–43.

Bordwell, David. *Figures Traced in Light: On Cinematic Staging*. Berkeley: University of California Press, 2005.

———. *On the History of Film Style*. Cambridge, Mass.: Harvard University Press, 1997.

———. "Widescreen Aesthetics and Mise en Scene Criticism." *Velvet Light Trap*, no. 21 (Summer 1985): 118–25.

Braudy, Leo. *The World in a Frame: What We See in Films*. New York: Doubleday, 1976.

Brewster, Ben, and Lea Jacobs. *Theatre to Cinema: Stage Pictorialism and the Early Feature Film*. New York: Oxford University Press, 1997.

Burch, Nöel. *Theory of Film Practice*. Translated by Helen R. Lane. Princeton, N.J.: Princeton University Press, 1981.

Carr, Robert E., and R. M. Hayes. *Wide Screen Movies: A History and Filmography of Wide Gauge Filmmaking*. Jefferson, N.C.: McFarland, 1988.

Carrick, Edward. *Designing for Films*. London: Studio Publications, 1949.

Carringer, Robert L. *The Making of Citizen Kane*. Rev. and updated ed. Berkeley: University of California Press, 1996.

Chisholm, Brad. "Widescreen Technologies." *Velvet Light Trap*, no. 21 (Summer 1985): 67–74.

Corliss, Mary, and Carlos Clarens. "Designed for Film: The Hollywood Art Director." *Film Comment* 14 (May/June 1978): 26–60.

Dalle Vacche, Angela. *Cinema and Painting: How Art Is Used in Film*. Austin: University of Texas Press, 1996.

DeCordova, Richard. "The Emergence of the Star System in America," *Wide Angle* 6, no. 4 (1985): 4–13.

Dunning, William V. *Changing Images of Pictorial Space: A History of Spatial Illusion in Painting*. Syracuse, N.Y.: Syracuse University Press, 1991.

Dyer, Richard. *Heavenly Bodies: Film Stars and Society*. New York: St. Martin's Press, 1986.

———. *Stars*. New ed. London: British Film Institute, 1998.

Eisner, Lotte H. *The Haunted Screen: Expressionism in the German Cinema and the Influence of Max Reinhardt*. Translated by Roger Greaves. Berkeley: University of California Press, 1969.

Gibbons, Cedric. "The Art Director," in *Behind the Screen: How Films Are Made*, edited by Stephen Watts, 41–50. New York: Dodge, 1938.

Harpole, Charles H. *Gradients of Depth in the Cinema Image*. New York: Arno, 1978.

Head, Edith, and Jane Kesner Ardmore. *The Dress Doctor*. Boston: Little, Brown, 1959.

Head, Edith, and Paddy Calistro. *Edith Head's Hollywood*. New York: Dutton, 1983.

Heisner, Beverly. *Hollywood Art: Art Direction in the Days of the Great Studios*. Jefferson, N.C.: McFarland, 1990.

———. *Production Design in the Contemporary American Film: A Critical Study of 23 Movies and Their Designers*. Jefferson, N.C.: McFarland, 1997.

Henderson, Brian. "Notes on Set Design and Cinema." *Film Quarterly* 42 (Fall 1988): 17–28.

Higham, Charles. "Stanley Cortez," in *Hollywood Cameramen: Sources of Light*, 99. London: Thames and Hudson, 1970.

Hincha, Richard. "Selling CinemaScope: 1953–1956." *Velvet Light Trap*, no. 21 (Summer 1985): 44–53.

Hochberg, Julian. "The Representation of Things and People," in *Art, Perception, and Reality*, edited by E. H. Gombrich, 47–94. Baltimore: Johns Hopkins University Press, 1972.

Horner, Harry. "The Production Designer," in *Filmmakers on Filmmaking*, edited by Joseph McBride, 149–61. Los Angeles: Tarcher, 1983.

Hudson, Roger. "Three Designers." *Sight & Sound* 34, no. 1 (Winter 1964–65): 26–31.

Katz, David. "A Widescreen Chronology." *Velvet Light Trap*, no. 21 (Summer 1985): 62–64.

Kehoe, Vincent J.-R. *The Technique of the Professional Make-up Artist for Film, Television, and Stage*. rev. ed. Boston: Focal Press, 1995.

Leese, Elizabeth. *Costume Design in the Movies*. New York: Frederick Ungar, 1976.

LoBrutto, Vincent. *By Design: Interviews With Film Production Designers*. Westport, Conn.: Praeger, 1992.

Lourié, Eugene. *My Work in Films*. San Diego, Calif.: Harcourt Brace Jovanovich, 1985.

Maeder, Edward. *Hollywood and History: Costume Design in Film*. New York: Thames and Hudson, 1987.

Mandelbaum, Howard, and Eric Myers. *Forties Screen Style: A Celebration of High Pastiche in Hollywood*. New York: St. Martin's, 1989.

Marner, Terence St. John, and Michael Stringer. *Film Design*. Screen Textbooks. London: Tantivy, 1974.

McNamara, Brooks. "The Scenography of Popular Entertainment." *Drama Review* 18, no. 1 (March 1974): 16–24.

Meisel, Martin. *Realizations: Narrative, Pictorial, and Theatrical Arts in Nineteenth-Century England*. Princeton, N.J.: Princeton University Press, 1983.

Mills, Bart. "The Brave New Worlds of Production Design." *American Film* 7, no. 4 (February 1982): 40–46.

Moseley, Rachel, ed. *Fashioning Film Stars: Dress, Culture, Identity*. London: British Film Institute, 2005.

Neumann, Dietrich, ed. *Film Architecture: Set Designs From Metropolis to Blade Runner*. Munich: Prestel, 1999.

Nizhny, Vladmir. *Lessons With Eisenstein*. New York: Hill & Wang, 1962.

Olson, Robert L. *Art Direction for Film and Video*. Boston: Focal Press, 1999.

Perkins, V. F. *Film as Film: Understanding and Judging Movies*. Harmondsworth, England: Penguin, 1972.

Pidduck, Julianne. *Contemporary Costume Film: Space, Place and the Past*. London: British Film Institute, 2004.

Preston, Ward. *What an Art Director Does: An Introduction to Motion Picture Production Design*. Los Angeles: Silman-James, 1994.

Sennett, Robert S. *Setting the Scene: The Great Hollywood Art Directors*. New York: Abrams, 1994.

Solso, Robert L. *Cognition and the Visual Arts*. Cambridge, Mass.: MIT Press, 1994.

Spellerberg, James. "CinemaScope and Ideology." *Velvet Light Trap*, no. 21 (Summer 1985): 26–34.

Surowiec, Catherine A. *Accent on Design: Four European Art Directors*. London: British Film Institute, 1992.

Tashiro, C. S. *Pretty Pictures: Production Design and the History Film*. Austin: University of Texas Press, 1998.

Taylor, John Russell. "Satyajit Ray," in *Cinema: A Critical Dictionary*, Vol. 2, edited by Richard Roud, 813–31. New York: Viking, 1980.

Turim, Maureen. "Symmetry/Asymmetry and Visual Fascination." *Wide Angle* 4, no. 3 (1980): 38–47.

Vardac, A. Nicholas. *Stage to Screen: Theatrical Method From Garrick to Griffith*. Cambridge, Mass.: Harvard University Press, 1949.

Vinther, Janus. *Special Effects Make-up*. New York: Routledge, 2003.

Weismann, Donald L. *The Visual Arts as Human Experience*. Englewood Cliffs, N.J.: Prentice-Hall, 1974.

White, John. *The Birth and Rebirth of Pictorial Space*. New York: Harper & Row, 1972.

Wright, Lawrence. *Perspective in Perspective*. London: Routledge and Kegan Paul, 1983.

Chapter 4: Cinematography

Almendros, Néstor. *A Man With a Camera*. Translated by Rachel Phillips Belash. New York: Farrar, Straus, and Giroux, 1984.

Alton, John. *Painting With Light*. Berkeley: University of California Press, 1995.

Andrew, Dudley, ed. *The Image in Dispute: Art and Cinema in the Age of Photography*. Austin: University of Texas Press, 1997.

Astruc, Alexandre. "The Birth of a New Avant-Garde: Le Caméra Stylo," in *The New Wave: Critical Landmarks*, edited by Peter Graham, 7–18. Garden City, N.Y.: Doubleday, 1968.

Barr, Charles. "CinemaScope: Before and After," in *Film Theory and Criticism: Introductory Readings*, 2nd ed., edited by Gerald Mast and Marshall Cohen, 140–68. New York: Oxford University Press, 1979.

Basten, Fred. *Glorious Technicolor: The Movies' Magic Rainbow*. Cranbury, N.J.: Barnes, 1980.

Bazin, André. "The Evolution of the Language of Cinema," in *What Is Cinema? Essays Selected and Translated by Hugh Gray*, Vol. 1, 23–40. Berkeley: University of California Press, 1967.

Beacham, Frank. *American Cinematographer Video Manual*. 2nd ed. Hollywood, Calif.: ASC Press, 1994.

Bordwell, David, Janet Staiger, and Kristin Thompson. *The Classical Hollywood Cinema: Film Style and Mode of Production to 1960*. New York: Columbia University Press, 1985.

Brakhage, Stan. *Metaphors on Vision*. Edited by P. Adams Sitney. New York: Film Culture, 1963.

———. "A Moving Picture Giving and Taking Book," in *Brakhage Scrapbook: Collected Writings, 1964–1980*, edited by Robert A. Haller, 53–77. New Paltz, N.Y.: Documentext, 1982.

Branigan, Edward. "Color and Cinema: Problems in the Writing of History." *Film Reader* 4 (1979): 16–34.

———. *Point of View in the Cinema: A Theory of Narration and Subjectivity in Classical Film*. Berlin: Mouton, 1984.

Brockett, Oscar G., and Robert R. Findlay. *Century of Innovation: A History of European and American Theatre and Drama Since 1870*. Englewood Cliffs, N.J.: Prentice-Hall, 1973.

Brodbeck, Emil E. *Movie and Videotape Special Effects*. Philadelphia: Chilton, 1968.

Bukatman, Scott. *Matters of Gravity: Special Effects and Supermen in the 20th Century*. Durham, N.C.: Duke University Press, 2003.

Campbell, Russell, ed. *Practical Motion Picture Photography*. London: Zwemmer, 1970.

Carr, Robert E., and R. M. Hayes. *Wide Screen Movies: A History and Filmography of Wide Gauge Filmmaking*. Jefferson, N.C.: McFarland, 1988.

Case, Dominic. *Motion Picture Film Processing*. London: Focal Press, 1985.

Chell, David. *Moviemakers at Work: Interviews*. Redmond, Wash.: Microsoft Press, 1987.

Cheshire, David F. *The Book of Movie Photography: The Complete Guide to Better Moviemaking*. New York: Knopf, 1979.

Coe, Brian. *The History of Movie Photography*. London: Ash and Grant, 1981.

Culhane, John. *Special Effects in the Movies: How They Do It*. New York: Ballantine, 1981.

Dalle Vacche, Angela, and Brian Price, eds. *Color: The Film Reader*. New York: Routledge, 2006.

De Grandis, Luigina. *Theory and Use of Color*. Translated by John Gilbert. New York: Abrams, 1986.

Deren, Maya. *An Anagram of Ideas on Art, Form, and Film*. Yonkers, N.Y.: Alicat Book Shop Press, 1946. Reprinted in *The Art of Cinema: Selected Essays*, edited by George Amberg. New York: Arno, 1972.

———. "Cinematography: The Creative Use of Reality," in *Film Theory and Criticism: Introductory Readings*, 5th ed., edited by Leo Braudy and Marshall Cohen, 216–27. New York: Oxford University Press, 1999.

Dreyer, Carl. "Color Film and Colored Films," in *Dreyer in Double Reflection*, edited by Donald Skoller, 168–73. New York: Dutton, 1973.

Dubery, Fred, and John Willats. *Perspective and Other Drawing Systems*. New York: Van Nostrand Reinhold, 1983.

Duncan, Jody. "The Beauty in the Beasts." *Cinefex* 55 (August 1993): 44–95.

———. "A Once and Future War." *Cinefex* 47 (August 1991): 4–59.

Dunn, Linwood G., and George E. Turner. *The ASC Treasury of Visual Effects*. Hollywood: American Society of Cinematographers, 1983.

Durgnat, Raymond. "Colours and Contrasts." *Films and Filming* 15, no. 2 (November 1968): 58–62.

Eisenstein, Sergei. *The Film Sense*. Translated and edited by Jay Leyda. New York: Harcourt Brace, 1947.

Ettedgui, Peter. *Cinematography*. Woburn, Mass.: Focal Press, 1998.

Fielding, Raymond, comp. *A Technological History of Motion Pictures and Television: An Anthology From the Pages of the Journal of the Society of Motion Picture and Television Engineers*. Berkeley: University of California Press, 1967.

Finch, Christopher. *Special Effects: Creating Movie Magic*. New York: Abbeville, 1984.

Graham, Arthur. "Zoom Lens Techniques." *American Cinematographer* 44, no. 1 (January 1963): 28–29.

Guerin, Frances. *A Culture of Light: Cinema and Technology in 1920s Germany*. Minneapolis: University of Minnesota Press, 2005.

Halas, John, and Roger Manvell. *The Technique of Film Animation*. 2nd ed. New York: Hastings House, 1968.

Hamilton, Jake. *Special Effects: In Film and Television*. New York: DK Publishing, 1998.

Harpole, Charles Henry. *Gradients of Depth in the Cinema Image*. New York: Arno, 1978.

Harryhausen, Ray. *Film Fantasy Scrapbook*. South Brunswick, N.J.: Barnes, 1972.

Henderson, Brian. "The Long Take," in *A Critique of Film Theory*, 48–61. New York: Dutton, 1980.

Herdeg, Walter, and John Halas. *Film and TV Graphics: An International Survey of Film and Television Graphics*. Zurich: Graphis, 1967.

Hertogs, Daan, and Nico de Klerk, eds. *Disorderly Order: Colours in Silent Film*. Amsterdam: Stichting Nederlands Filmmuseum, 1996.

Higham, Charles. *Hollywood Cameramen: Sources of Light*. Bloomington: Indiana University Press, 1970.

Joannides, Paul. "The Aesthetics of the Zoom Lens." *Sight & Sound* 40, no. 1 (Winter 1972): 40–42.

Johnson, William. "Coming to Terms With Color." *Film Quarterly* 20, no. 1 (Fall 1966): 2–22.

Kaminsky, Stuart M. "The Use and Abuse of the Zoom Lens." *Filmmakers Newsletter* 5, no. 12 (October 1972): 20–23.

Kawin, Bruce F. *How Movies Work*. Berkeley: University of California Press, 1992.

Krasilovsky, Alexis. *Women Behind the Camera: Conversations With Camerawomen*. Westport, Conn.: Praeger, 1997.

Lightman, Herb A. "The Fluid Camera." *American Cinematographer* 27, no. 3 (March 1946): 82, 102–3.

LoBrutto, Vincent. *Principal Photography: Interviews With Feature Film Cinematographers*. Westport, Conn.: Praeger, 1999.

Malkiewicz, J. Kris. *Cinematography: A Guide for Film Makers and Film Teachers*. 2nd ed. New York: Prentice-Hall, 1989.

———. *Film Lighting: Talks With Hollywood's Cinematographers and Gaffers*. New York: Prentice-Hall, 1986.

Maltin, Leonard. *The Art of the Cinematographer: A*

Survey and Interviews With Five Masters. Rev. ed. New York: Dover, 1978.

Mamer, Bruce. *Film Production Technique: Creating the Accomplished Image.* Belmont, Calif.: Wadsworth, 1995.

Mascelli, Joseph V. *The Five C's of Cinematography: Motion Picture Filming Techniques.* Los Angeles: Silman-James, 1998.

Millerson, Gerald. *The Technique of Lighting for Television and Film.* 3rd ed. Boston: Focal Press, 1991.

Murch, Walter. "Restoring the Touch of Genius to a Classic." *New York Times* 6 (September 1998), sec. 2, pp. 1, 16–17.

Musser, Charles. *The Emergence of Cinema: The American Screen to 1907. History of American Cinema,* vol. 1. New York: Scribner, 1990.

Netzley, Patricia D. *Encyclopedia of Movie Special Effects.* Phoenix, Ariz.: Oryx, 2000.

Ogle, Patrick. "Technological and Aesthetic Influences Upon the Development of Deep-Focus Cinematography in the United States." *Screen* 13 (Spring 1972): 45–72.

Perkins, V. F. "Rope," in *The Movie Reader,* edited by Ian Cameron Alexander, 35–37. New York: Praeger, 1972.

Petrie, Duncan. *The British Cinematographer.* London: British Film Institute, 1996.

Pierson, Michele. *Special Effects: Still in Search of Wonder.* New York: Columbia University Press, 2002.

Ray, Satyajit. *Our Films, Their Films.* New York: Hyperion, 1994.

Rieser, Martin, and Andrea Zapp, eds. *New Screen Media: Cinema/Art/Narrative.* London: British Film Institute, 2001.

Rogers, Pauline B. *Contemporary Cinematographers on Their Art.* Boston: Focal Press, 1998.

Ryan, Roderick T., ed. *The American Cinematographer Manual.* 7th ed. Hollywood, Calif.: American Society of Cinematographers, 1993.

———. *A History of Motion Picture Color Technology.* New York: Focal Press, 1977.

Salt, Barry. "Statistical Style Analysis of Motion Pictures." *Film Quarterly* 28, no. 1 (Fall 1974): 13–22.

Schaefer, Dennis, and Larry Salvato. *Masters of Light: Conversations With Contemporary Cine-matographers.* Berkeley: University of California Press, 1984.

Schechter, Harold, and David Everitt. *Film Tricks: Special Effects in the Movies.* New York: Quist, 1980.

Sharits, Paul. "Red, Blue, Godard." *Film Quarterly* 19, no. 4 (Summer 1966): 24–29.

Society of Motion Picture and Television Engineers. *Elements of Color in Professional Motion Pictures.* New York: Society of Motion Picture and Television Engineers, 1957.

Thomas, David Bowen. *The First Colour Motion Pictures.* London: H.M.S.O., 1969.

Toland, Gregg. "How I Broke the Rules in Citizen Kane," in *Focus on Citizen Kane,* edited by Ronald Gottesman, 73–77. Englewood Cliffs, N.J.: Prentice-Hall, 1971.

Vaz, Mark Cotta, and Patricia Rose Duignan. *Industrial Light and Magic: Into the Digital Realm.* New York: Ballantine, 1996.

Vertov, Dziga. *Kino-Eye: The Writings of Dziga Vertov.* Edited by Annette Michelson, translated by Kevin O'Brien. Berkeley: University of California Press, 1984.

Wees, William C. "Prophecy, Memory, and the Zoom: Michael Snow's Wavelength Re-Viewed." *Ciné-Tracts,* no. 14/15 (Summer/Fall 1981): 78–83.

Weinstock, Neil. *Computer Animation.* Reading, Mass.: Addison-Wesley, 1986.

White, John. *The Birth and Rebirth of Pictorial Space.* 2nd ed. New York: Harper & Row, 1972.

Winston, Brian. *Technologies of Seeing: Photography, Cinematography and Television.* London: British Film Institute, 1996.

Wright, Lawrence. *Perspective in Perspective.* London: Routledge and Kegan Paul, 1983.

Youngblood, Gene. *Expanded Cinema.* New York: Dutton, 1970.

Zelanski, Paul, and Mary Pat Fisher. *Colour for Designers and Artists.* London: Herbert, 1989.

Chapter 5: Acting

Affron, Charles. *Lillian Gish: Her Legendary Life.* New York: Scribner, 2001.

———. *Star Acting: Gish, Garbo, Davis.* New York: Dutton, 1977.

Allen, Robert C. "The Role of the Star in Film History [Joan Crawford]," in *Film Theory and Criticism: Introductory Readings*, 5th ed., edited by Leo Braudy and Marshall Cohen, 547–61. New York: Oxford University Press, 1999.

Allen, Robert C., and Douglas Gomery. *Film History: Theory and Practice*. New York: Knopf, 1985.

Ankerich, Michael G. *Broken Silence: Conversations With Twenty-Three Silent Film Stars*. Jefferson, N.C.: McFarland, 1993.

Antonioni, Michelangelo. "Reflections on the Film Actor." *Film Culture* 22/23 (Summer 1961): 66–67.

Balász, Béla. "The Close-Up," in *Film Theory and Criticism: Introductory Readings*, 5th ed., edited by Leo Braudy and Marshall Cohen, 304–11. New York: Oxford University Press, 1999.

Balio, Tino. *Grand Design: Hollywood as a Modern Business Enterprise, 1930–1939*. History of the American Cinema, vol. 5. Berkeley: University of California Press, 1995.

Barr, Tony. *Acting for the Camera*. Boston: Allyn & Bacon, 1982.

Barthes, Roland. "The Face of Garbo," in *Film Theory and Criticism: Introductory Readings*, 5th ed., edited by Leo Braudy and Marshall Cohen, 536–38. New York: Oxford University Press, 1999.

Basinger, Jeanine. *Silent Stars*. New York: Knopf, 1999.

Bazin, André. "The Myth of Total Cinema," in *What Is Cinema? Essays Selected and Translated by Hugh Gray*, Vol. l, 17–22. Berkeley: University of California Press, 1967.

Blum, Richard A. *American Film Acting: The Stanislavski Heritage*. Ann Arbor, MI: UMI Research Press, 1984.

Brandes, D. "Roman Polanski on Acting." *Cinema Papers*, no. 11 (January 1977): 226–29.

Braudy, Leo. "Film Acting: Some Critical Problems and Proposals." *Quarterly Review of Film Studies* 1, no. 1 (February 1976): 1–18.

Budd, Michael. "Genre, Director and Stars in John Ford's Westerns: Fonda, Wayne, Stewart and Widmark." *Wide Angle* 2, no. 4 (1978): 52–61.

Caine, Michael. *Acting in Film: An Actor's Take on Movie Making*. New York: Applause Theatre Book Publishers, 1990.

Callow, Simon. *Being an Actor*. New York: Grove, 1988.

———. *Orson Welles: The Road to Xanadu*. New York: Viking, 1995.

Campbell, Russell, ed. "The Actor." *Velvet Light Trap*, no. 7 (Winter 1972/73): 1–60.

Cardullo, Bert, Harry Geduld, Ronald Gottesman, and Leigh Woods, eds. *Playing to the Camera: Film Actors Discuss Their Craft*. New Haven, Conn.: Yale University Press, 1998.

Chaplin, Charles. *My Autobiography*. New York: Simon and Schuster, 1964.

Cole, Toby, and Helen Krich Chinoy, eds. *Actors on Acting*. New York: Crown, 1964.

Coleman, Terry. *Olivier*. New York: Holt, 2005.

Crafton, Donald. *The Talkies: American Cinema's Transition to Sound, 1926–1931*. New York: Scribner, 1997.

Cukor, George. "Dialogue on Film: George Cukor." *American Film* 3, no. 4 (February 1978): 33–48.

Dmytryk, Edward, and Jean Porter Dmytryk. *On Screen Acting: An Introduction to the Art of Acting for the Screen*. Boston: Focal Press, 1984.

Dyer, Richard. *Heavenly Bodies: Film Stars and Society*. New York: St. Martin's, 1986.

Eisenstein, Sergei. *Film Form and The Film Sense: Two Complete and Unabridged Works*. Edited by Jay Leyda. New York: Meridian Books, 1957.

Funke, Lewis, and John E. Booth, eds. *Actors Talking About Acting*. New York: Random House, 1961.

Gardner, P. "Bette Davis: A Star Views Directors." *Action*, no. 5 (October 1974): 10–17.

Gish, Lillian, with Ann Pinchot. *The Movies, Mr. Griffith, and Me*. Englewood Cliffs, N.J.: Prentice-Hall, 1969.

Gledhill, Christine. *Stardom: Industry of Desire*. New York: Routledge, 1991.

Higson, Andrew. "Film Acting and Independent Cinema." *Screen* 27, no. 3/4 (1986): 110–32.

Hirsch, Foster. *Acting Hollywood Style*. New York: Abrams, 1991.

———. *A Method to Their Madness: The History of the Actors Studio*. New York: Norton, 1984.

Kael, Pauline. "The Man From Dream City (Cary Grant)." *New Yorker* 51 (July 14, 1975): 40–42ff.

Kaplan, E. Ann. "The Case of the Missing Mother:

Maternal Issues in Vidor's Stella Dallas," in *Feminism and Film*, edited by E. Ann Kaplan, 466–79. New York: Oxford University Press, 2000.

Keane, Marian. "Dyer Straits: Theoretical Issues in Studies of Film Acting." *Post Script: Essays in Film and the Humanities* 12, no. 2 (Winter 1993): 29–39.

Kuleshov, Lev. *Kuleshov on Film: Writings*. Edited by Ronald Levaco. Berkeley: University of California Press, 1974.

Landy, Marcia, and Lucy Fischer, eds. *Stars: The Film Reader*. New York: Routledge, 2004.

McBride, Joseph. *Searching for John Ford: A Life*. New York: St. Martin's, 2001.

McDonald, Paul. *The Star System: Hollywood's Production of Popular Identities*. New York: Columbia University Press, 2001.

McVay, Douglas. "The Art of the Actor." *Films and Filming* 12, no. 10 (July 1966): 19–25.

———. "The Art of the Actor." *Films and Filming* 12, no. 11 (August 1966): 36–42.

———. "The Art of the Actor." *Films and Filming* 12, no. 12 (September 1966): 44–50.

———. "The Art of the Actor." *Films and Filming* 13, no. 1 (October 1966): 27–33.

———. "The Art of the Actor." *Films and Filming* 13, no. 2 (November 1966): 26–33.

Merritt, Russell. "The Griffith-Gish Collaboration: A Tangled Affair." *Griffithiana* 14, no. 40/42 (October 1991): 101–3.

Meyerson, Harold. "The Case of the Vanishing Character Actor." *Film Comment* 13, no. 6 (November–December 1977): 6–15.

Milne, Tom. *Rouben Mamoulian*. Bloomington: Indiana University Press, 1969.

Morin, Edgar. *The Stars*. Translated by Richard Howard. Minneapolis: University of Minnesota, 2005.

Munk, Erika, ed. *Stanislavski and America*. New York: Hill and Wang, 1966.

Naremore, James. *Acting in the Cinema*. Berkeley: University of California Press, 1988.

Olivier, Laurence. *Confessions of an Actor: An Autobiography*. New York: Simon and Schuster, 1982. Reprint, New York: Penguin, 1984.

———. *On Acting*. New York: Simon and Schuster, 1986.

Prouse, Derek. "Notes on Film Acting." *Sight & Sound* 24, no. 4 (Spring 1955): 174–80.

Quart, Leonard. "I Still Love Going to Movies: An Interview With Pauline Kael," *Cineaste* 25, no. 2 (2002), 8–13.

Pudovkin, V. I. *Film Technique and Film Acting*. Edited by Ivor Montagu. New York: Bonanza, 1949.

Rogosin, Lionel. "Interpreting Reality: Notes on the Esthetics and Practices of Improvisational Acting." *Film Culture* no. 21 (Summer 1960): 20–29.

Rosenbaum, Jonathan. "Improvisations and Interactions in Altmanville." *Sight & Sound* 44, no. 2 (Spring 1975): 90–95.

Ross, Lillian, and Helen Ross. *The Player: A Profile of an Art*. New York: Simon and Schuster, 1962.

Smith, Ella. *Starring Miss Barbara Stanwyck*. New York: Crown, 1974.

Stanislavksi, Constantin. *An Actor Prepares*. Translated by Elizabeth Reynolds Hapgood. New York: Theatre Arts Books, 1936.

———. *Building a Character*. Translated by Elizabeth Reynolds Hapgood. New York: Theatre Arts Books, 1949.

Strasberg, Lee. *Strasberg at the Actors Studio*. Edited by Robert H. Hethmon. New York: Viking, 1965.

Tomlinson, Doug, ed. *Actors on Acting for the Screen: Roles and Collaborations*. New York: Garland, 1994.

Tucker, Patrick. *Secrets of Screen Acting*. New York: Routledge, 1994.

Vineberg, Steven. *Method Actors: Three Generations of an American Acting Style*. New York: Schirmer, 1991.

Walker, Alexander. *Stardom: The Hollywood Phenomenon*. New York: Stein and Day, 1970.

Weis, Elisabeth, ed. *National Society of Film Critics on the Movie Star*. New York: Viking, 1981.

Welles, Orson, and Peter Bogdanovich. *This Is Orson Welles*. Edited by Jonathan Rosenbaum. New York: Harper Collins, 1992.

Wexman, Virginia Wright. "Kinesics and Film Acting: Humphrey Bogart in *The Maltese Falcon* and *The Big Sleep*." *Journal of Popular Film and Television* 1 (1978): 42–55.

———. "The Rhetoric of Cinematic Improvisation," *Cinema Journal* 20, no. 1 (Fall 1980): 29–41.

——, ed. "Special Issue on Film Acting." *Cinema Journal* 1 (1980).

Williams, Linda. "'Something Else Besides a Mother': Stella Dallas and the Maternal Melodrama," in *Feminism and Film*, edited by E. Ann Kaplan, 480–504. New York: Oxford University Press, 2000.

Wojcik, Pamela Robertson, ed. *Movie Acting, the Film Reader*. New York: Routledge, 2004.

Wood, Robin. "Acting Up." *Film Comment* 12, no. 2 (April 1976): 20–25.

Yacowar, Maurice. "Actors as Conventions in the Films of Robert Altman." *Cinema Journal* 20, no. 1 (Fall 1980): 14–28.

——. "An Aesthetic Defense of the Star System in Films," *Quarterly Review of Film Studies* 4, no. 1 (Winter 1979): 48–50.

Zucker, Carole. "The Concept of 'Excess' in Film Acting: Notes Toward an Understanding of Non-Naturalistic Performance." *Post Script: Essays in Film and the Humanities* 11, no. 2 (Spring 1993): 20–26.

——. "An Interview With Lindsay Crouse," *Post Script: Essays in Film and the Humanities* 12, no. 2 (Winter 1993): 5–28.

——, ed. *Making Visible the Invisible: An Anthology of Original Essays on Film Acting*. Metuchen, N.J.: Scarecrow, 1990.

——, ed. "Special Issue on Film Acting." *Post Script: Essays in Film and the Humanities* 12, no. 2 (Winter 1993).

Chapter 6: Editing

Balmuth, Bernard. *Introduction to Film Editing*. Boston: Focal Press, 1989.

Barsam, Richard. "Discover and Disclose: Helen Van Dongen and Louisiana Story," in *Filming Robert Flaherty's Louisiana Story: The Helen Van Dongen Diary*, edited by Eva Orbanz, 75–89. New York: Museum of Modern Art, 1998.

Bayes, Steve. *The Avid Handbook*. Boston: Focal Press, 1998.

Bouzereau, Laurent. *The Cutting Room Floor*. New York: Carol, 1994.

Browne, Steven E. *Nonlinear Editing Basics: Electronic Film and Video Editing*. Boston: Focal Press, 1998.

Case, Dominic. *Film Technology in Post Production*. Media Manuals. Jordan Hill, England: Focal Press, 1997.

Dancyger, Ken. *The Technique of Film and Video Editing: Theory and Practice*. 4th ed. Boston: Focal Press, 2006.

Hollyn, Norman. *The Film Editing Room Handbook*. Beverly Hills, CA: Lone Eagle, 1990.

Kerner, Marvin M. *The Art of the Sound Effects Editor*. Boston: Focal Press, 1989.

LoBrutto, Vincent. *Selected Takes: Film Editors on Editing*. New York: Praeger, 1991.

Lustig, Milton. *Music Editing for Motion Pictures*. Communication Arts Books. New York: Hastings House, 1980.

Murch, Walter. *In the Blink of an Eye: A Perspective on Film Editing*. Los Angeles: Silman-James, 1995.

Ohanian, Thomas A. *Digital Nonlinear Editing: Editing Film and Video on the Desktop*. Boston: Focal Press, 1998.

Ondaatje, Michael. *The Conversations: Walter Murch and the Art of Editing*. Knopf, 2002.

Rubin, Michael. *Nonlinear: A Guide to Electronic Film and Video Editing*. Gainesville, Fla.: Triad, 1992.

Schneider, Arthur. *Jump Cut!: Memoirs of a Pioneer Television Editor*. Jefferson, N.C.: McFarland, 1997.

Stafford, Roy. *Nonlinear Editing and Visual Literacy*. London: British Film Institute, 1995.

Thompson, Roy. *Grammar of the Edit*. Boston: Focal Press, 1993.

Walter, Ernest. *The Technique of the Film Cutting Room*. 2nd ed. The Library of Communication Techniques. London: Focal Press, 1973.

Chapter 7: Sound

Amyes, Tim. *The Technique of Audio Post-Production in Video and Film*. The Library of Communication Techniques. London: Focal Press, 1990.

Belton, John. "Technology and Aesthetics of Film Sound," in *Film Sound: Theory and Practice*, edited by Elisabeth Weis and John Belton,

63–72. New York: Columbia University Press, 1985.

Brophy, Philip. *100 Modern Soundtracks*. BFI Screen Guides. London: British Film Institute, 2004.

Brown, Royal S. *Overtones and Undertones: Reading Film Music*. Berkeley: University of California Press, 1994.

Burt, George. *The Art of Film Music*. Boston: Northeastern University Press, 1994.

Chion, Michel. *Audio-Vision: Sound on Screen*. Edited and translated by Claudia Gorbman. New York: Columbia University Press, 1994.

Coyle, Rebecca, ed. *Reel Tracks: Australian Feature Film Music and Cultural Identities*. London: John Libbey, 2005.

Crafton, Donald. *The Talkies: American Cinema's Transition to Sound, 1926–1931*. History of the American Cinema, vol. 4. New York: Scribner, 1997.

Dickinson, Kay. *Movie Music: The Film Reader*. New York: Routledge, 2003.

Donnelly, Kevin. *Film and Television Music: The Spectre of Sound*. London: British Film Institute, 2005.

Eyman, Scott. *The Speed of Sound: Hollywood and the Talkie Revolution, 1926–1930*. New York: Simon and Schuster, 1997.

Geduld, Harry M. *The Birth of the Talkies: From Edison to Jolson*. Bloomington: Indiana University Press, 1975.

Goldmark, Daniel. *Tunes for 'Toons*. Berkeley: University of California Press, 2005.

Gomery, Douglas. *The Coming of Sound*. New York: Routledge, 2004.

Gorbman, Claudia. "Annotated Bibliography on Film Sound (Excluding Music)," in *Film Sound: Theory and Practice*, eds. Elisabeth Weis and John Belton, 426–45. New York: Columbia University Press, 1985.

———. *Unheard Melodies: Narrative Film Music*. Bloomington: Indiana University Press, 1987.

Hickman, Roger. *Reel Music: Exploring 100 Years of Film Music*. New York: Norton, 2006.

Holman, Tomlinson. *Sound for Film and Television*. Boston: Focal Press, 1997.

Kalinak, Kathryn. *Settling the Score: Music and the Classical Hollywood Film*. Madison: University of Wisconsin Press, 1992.

Karlin, Fred. *Listening to Movies: The Film Lover's Guide to Film Music*. New York: Schirmer, 1994.

LoBrutto, Vincent. *Sound-on-Film: Interviews With Creators of Film Sound*. Westport, Conn.: Praeger, 1994.

Lyman, Rick. "A Director's Journey Into a Darkness of a Heart," *New York Times*, June 24, 2001, sec. 2, p. 24.

MacDonald, Laurence E. *The Invisible Art of Film Music: A Comprehensive History*. New York: Ardsley House, 1998.

Marmorstein, Gary. *Hollywood Rhapsody: Movie Music and Its Makers, 1900 to 1975*. New York: Schirmer, 1997.

Pasquariello, Nicholas. *Sounds of Movies: Interviews With the Creators of Feature Sound Tracks*. San Francisco, Calif.: Port Bridge Books, 1996.

Prendergast, Roy. *Film Music: A Neglected Art*. 2nd ed. New York: Norton, 1992.

Sider, Larry, ed. *Soundscape: The School of Sound Lectures, 1998–2001*. London: Wallflower, 2003.

Sonnenschein, David. *Sound Design: The Expressive Power of Music, Voice, and Sound Effects in Cinema*. Seattle, Wash.: Wiese, 2001.

Thom, Randy. "Designing a Movie for Sound," March 13, 1999, <www.filmsound.org/randy thom> (accessed March 2005).

Thomas, Tony. *Music for the Movies*. 2nd ed. Los Angeles: Silman-James, 1997.

Timm, Larry. *The Soul of Cinema: An Appreciation of Film Music*. New York: Simon and Schuster, 1998.

Weis, Elisabeth. *The Silent Scream: Alfred Hitchcock's Sound Track*. Rutherford, N.J.: Fairleigh Dickinson University Press, 1982.

Chapter 8: Thinking About Movies, Theory, and Meaning

Aaron, Michele. *New Queer Cinema: A Critical Reader*. New Brunswick, N.J.: Rutgers University Press, 2004.

Aitken, Ian. *European Film Theory and Cinema: A Critical Introduction*. Bloomington: Indiana University Press, 2001.

Allen, Robert C., and Douglas Gomery. *Film History: Theory and Practice*. New York: Knopf, 1985.

Andrew, J. Dudley. *The Major Film Theories: An Introduction.* New York: Oxford University Press, 1976.

Basinger, Jeanine. *A Woman's View: How Hollywood Spoke to Women, 1930–1960.* New York: Knopf, 1993.

Bean, Jennifer M., and Diane Negra, eds. *Early Women Stars.* Durham, N.C.: Duke University Press, 2001.

———, eds. *A Feminist Reader in Early Cinema.* Durham, N.C.: Duke University Press, 2002.

Beauchamp, Cari. *Without Lying Down: Frances Marion and the Powerful Women of Early Hollywood.* New York: Scribner, 1997.

Beckman, Karen. *Vanishing Women: Magic, Film, and Feminism.* Durham, N.C.: Duke University Press, 2003.

Benshoff, Harry M., and Sean Griffin. *A History of Gay and Lesbian Film in America.* Lanham, MD: Rowman and Littlefield, 2005.

———, eds. *Queer Cinema: The Film Reader.* New York: Routledge, 2004.

Bordwell, David. *Making Meaning: Inference and Rhetoric in the Interpretation of Cinema.* Cambridge, Mass.: Harvard University Press, 1989.

Branigan, Edward. *Projecting a Camera: Language-Games in Film Theory.* New York: Routledge, 2005.

Braudy, Leo, and Marshall Cohen, eds. *Film Theory and Criticism: Introductory Readings.* 6th ed. New York: Oxford University Press, 2004.

Carnes, Mark C., ed. *Past Imperfect: History According to the Movies.* New York: Holt, 1995.

Courtney, Susan. *Hollywood Fantasies of Miscegenation: Spectacular Narratives of Gender and Race.* Princeton, N.J.: Princeton University Press, 2005.

Doane, Mary Ann. *The Desire to Desire: The Woman's Film of the 1940s.* Bloomington: Indiana University Press, 1987.

Elliott, Kamilla. *Rethinking the Novel/Film Debate.* New York: Cambridge University Press, 2003.

Fabe, Marilyn. *Closely Watched Films: An Introduction to the Art of Narrative Film Technique.* Berkeley: University of California Press, 2004.

Feng, Peter X. *Identities in Motion: Asian American Film and Video.* Durham, N.C.: Duke University Press, 2002.

Fischer, Lucy. *Designing Women: Cinema, Art Deco, and the Female Form.* New York: Columbia University Press, 2003.

Forrest, Jennifer, and Leonard R. Koos, eds. *Dead Ringers: The Remake in Theory and Practice.* Albany: State University of New York Press, 2002.

Gabbard, Krin. *Black Magic: White Hollywood and African American Culture.* New Brunswick, N.J.: Rutgers University Press, 2004.

Gerstner, David A., and Janet Staiger, eds. *Authorship and Film.* New York: Routledge, 2003.

Gledhill, Christine, ed. *Home Is Where the Heart Is: Studies in Melodrama and the Woman's Film.* London: British Film Institute, 1987.

Gledhill, Christine, and Linda Williams, eds. *Reinventing Film Studies.* New York: Oxford University Press, 2000.

Henderson, Brian. *A Critique of Film Theory.* New York: Dutton, 1980.

Hill, John, and Pamela Church Gibson, eds. *The Oxford Guide to Film Studies.* Oxford, England: Oxford University Press, 1998.

Horton, Andrew, and Stuart McDougal, eds. *Play It Again, Sam: Retakes on Remakes.* Berkeley: University of California Press, 1998.

Kaplan, E. Ann, ed. *Women in Film Noir.* London: British Film Institute, 1998.

Mayne, Judith. *Directed by Dorothy Arzner.* Bloomington: Indiana University Press, 1995.

———. *Framed: Lesbians, Feminists, and Media Culture.* Minneapolis: University of Minnesota Press, 2000.

McCrisken, Trevor, and Andrew Pepper. *American History and Contemporary Hollywood Film.* Piscataway, N.J.: Rutgers University Press, 2005.

Petro, Patrice. *Aftershocks of the New: Feminism and Film History.* New Brunswick, N.J.: Rutgers University Press, 2002.

Ray, Robert B. *How Film Theory Got Lost and Other Mysteries in Cultural Studies.* Bloomington: Indiana University Press, 2001.

Reid, Mark A. *Black Lenses, Black Voices: African American Film Now.* Lanham, MD: Rowman and Littlefield, 2005.

Rich, B. Ruby. *Chick Flicks: Theories and Memories of*

the Feminist Film Movement. Durham, N.C.: Duke University Press, 1998.

Simpson, Philip, Andrew Utterson, and K. J. Shepherdson, eds. *Film Theory: Critical Concepts in Media and Cultural Studies*. New York: Routledge, 2003.

Staiger, Janet. *Perverse Spectators: The Practices of Film Reception*. New York: New York University Press, 2000.

Thornham, Sue, ed. *Feminist Film Theory: A Reader*. New York: New York University Press, 2000.

Villarejo, Amy. *Lesbian Rule: Cultural Criticism and the Value of Desire*. Durham, N.C.: Duke University Press, 2003.

Waugh, Thomas. *The Fruit Machine: Twenty Years of Writing on Queer Cinema*. Durham, N.C.: Duke University Press, 2000.

Wexman, Virginia Wright, ed. *Film and Authorship*. New Brunswick, N.J.: Rutgers University Press, 2003.

Williams, Linda, ed. *Porn Studies*. Durham, N.C.: Duke University Press, 2004.

Appendix: Hollywood Production Systems

Abramovitz, Rachel. *Is That a Gun in Your Pocket? Women's Experience of Power in Hollywood*. New York: Random House, 2000.

Acker, Ally. *Reel Women: Pioneers of the Cinema, 1896 to the Present*. New York: Continuum, 1991.

Balio, Tino, ed. *The American Film Industry*. Rev. ed. Madison: University of Wisconsin Press, 1985.

Basinger, Jeanine. *A Woman's View: How Hollywood Spoke to Women, 1930–1960*. Hanover, Mass.: Wesleyan University Press, 1995.

Beauchamp, Cari. *Without Lying Down: Frances Marion and the Powerful Women of Early Hollywood*. New York: Scribner, 1997.

Behlmer, Rudy, and Tony Thomas. *Hollywood's Hollywood: The Movies About the Movies*. Secaucus, N.J.: Citadel, 1975.

Berg, A. Scott. *Goldwyn: A Biography*. New York: Knopf, 1989.

Bernstein, Matthew. *Walter Wanger, Hollywood Independent*. Minneapolis: University of Minnesota Press, 2000.

Biskind, Peter. *Down and Dirty Pictures: Miramax, Sundance and the Rise of Independent Film*. New York: Simon & Schuster, 2004.

Bordwell, David, Janet Staiger, and Kristin Thompson. *The Classical Hollywood Cinema: Film Style and Mode of Production to 1960*. New York: Columbia University Press, 1985.

Bouzereau, Laurent, and Jody Duncan. *Star Wars: The Making of Episode I, "The Phantom Menace."* London: Ebury, 1999.

Bruck, Connie. *When Hollywood Had a King: The Reign of Lew Wasserman, Who Leveraged Talent Into Power and Influence*. New York: Random House, 2003.

Compaine, Benjamin M., and Douglas Gomery. *Who Owns the Media: Competition and Concentration in the Mass Media Industry*. 3rd ed. Mahwah, N.J.: Erlbaum, 2000.

Cook, David A. *A History of Narrative Film*. 4th ed. New York: Norton, 2004.

Custen, George F. *Twentieth Century's Fox: Darryl F. Zanuck and the Culture of Hollywood*. New York: Basic Books, 1997.

Davis, Ronald L. *The Glamour Factory: Inside Hollywood's Big Studio System*. Dallas, Tex.: Southern Methodist University Press, 1993.

Epstein, Edward Jay. *The Big Picture: The New Logic of Money and Power in Hollywood*. New York: Random House, 2005.

Eyman, Scott. *Lion of Hollywood: The Life and Legend of Louis B. Mayer*. New York: Simon & Schuster, 2005.

Finler, Joel W. *The Hollywood Story: Everything You Ever Wanted to Know About the American Movie Business But Didn't Know Where to Look*. Rev. ed. New York: Columbia University Press, 2003.

Fitzgerald, F. Scott. *The Last Tycoon: An Unfinished Novel*. New York: Scribner's, 1941.

Fuchs, Daniel. *The Golden West: Hollywood Stories*. Boston: Black Sparrow Books, 2005.

Goldner, Orville, and George E. Turner. *The Making of King Kong: The Story Behind a Film Classic*. New York: Ballantine, 1976.

Goldsmith, Ben, and Tom O'Regan. *The Film Studio: Film Production in the Global Economy*. Lanham, MD: Rowman and Littlefield, 2005.

Gomery, Douglas. *The Hollywood Studio System: A History*. London: British Film Institute, 2005.

Hark, Ina Rae, ed. *Exhibition, the Film Reader*. New York: Routledge, 2002.

Harmetz, Aljean. *The Making of the Wizard of Oz: Movie Magic and Studio Power in the Prime of MGM and the Miracle of Production #1060*. New York: Limelight, 1984.

——. *On the Road to Tara: The Making of Gone With the Wind*. New York: Abrams, 1996.

——. *Round Up the Usual Suspects: The Making of Casablanca, Bogart, Bergman, and World War II*. New York: Hyperion, 1992.

Hayes, Dade, and Jonathan Bing. *Open Wide: How Hollywood Box Office Became a National Obsession*. New York: Miramax, 2004.

Hoberman, J., and Jeffrey Shandler. *Entertaining America: Jews, Movies, and Broadcasting*. Princeton, N.J.: Princeton University Press, 2003.

Kawin, Bruce F. *How Movies Work*. Berkeley: University of California Press, 1992.

Kindem, Gorham, ed. *The American Movie Industry: The Business of Motion Pictures*. Carbondale: Southern Illinois University Press, 1982.

King, Geoff. *New Hollywood Cinema: An Introduction*. New York: Columbia University Press, 2002.

Klinger, Barbara. *Beyond the Multiplex: Cinema, New Technologies, and the Home*. Berkeley: University of California Press, 2006.

Levitan, Eli L. *An Alphabetical Guide to Motion Picture, Television and Videotape Production*. New York: McGraw-Hill, 1970.

Lewis, Jon, ed. *The End of Cinema as We Know It: American Film in the Nineties*. New York: New York University Press, 2003.

——. *Whom God Wishes to Destroy: Francis Ford Coppola and the New Hollywood*. Durham, N.C.: Duke University Press, 1995.

Litman, Barry R. *The Motion Picture Mega-Industry*. Boston: Allyn and Bacon, 1998.

Lumet, Sidney. *Making Movies*. New York: Vintage, 1996.

McClelland, Doug. *Down the Yellow Brick Road: The Making of the Wizard of Oz*. New York: Pyramid, 1976.

Mann, William J. *Behind the Screen: How Gays and Lesbians Shaped Hollywood, 1910–1969*. New York: Penguin, 2001.

Mordden, Ethan. *The Hollywood Studio: House Style in the Golden Age of the Movies*. New York: Knopf, 1988.

Morey, Anne. *Hollywood Outsiders: The Adaptation of the Film Industry, 1913–1934*. Minneapolis: University of Minnesota Press, 2004.

Powdermaker, Hortense. *Hollywood, the Dream Factory: An Anthropologist Looks at the Movie-Makers*. Boston: Little, Brown, 1950.

Ross, Lillian. *Picture*. New York: Avon, 1969.

Ross, Murray. *Stars and Strikes: The Unionization of Hollywood*. New York: Columbia University Press, 1941.

Salt, Barry. *Film Style and Technology: History and Analysis*. London: Starword, 1983.

Schatz, Thomas, ed. *Critical Concepts in Media and Cultural Studies*. New York: Routledge, 2003.

——. *The Genius of the System: Hollywood Filmmaking in the Studio Era*. New York: Holt, 1996.

Scott, Allen J. *On Hollywood: The Place, The Industry*. Princeton, N.J.: Princeton University Press, 2004.

Sedgwick, John, and Michael Pokorny, eds. *An Economic History of Film*. New York: Routledge, 2004.

Selznick, David O. *Memo From David O. Selznick*. Selected and edited by Rudy Behlmer. New York: Viking, 1972.

Simon, Deke, and Michael Wiese. *Film and Video Budgets*. 3rd ed. Studio City, Calif.: Wiese, 2001.

Sklar, Robert. *Movie-Made America: A Cultural History of American Movies*. Rev. and updated ed. New York: Vintage, 1994.

Stringer, Julian, ed. *Movie Blockbusters*. New York: Routledge, 2003.

Thomson, David. *The Whole Equation: A History of Hollywood*. New York: Knopf, 2004.

von Sternberg, Josef. *Fun in a Chinese Laundry*. New York: Macmillan, 1965.

Weinraub, Bernard. "What Makes Boys Laugh: A Philosophy Major Finds the Golden Touch," New York Times, July 23, 1998, sec. E, p. 5.

Glossary

Words set in **boldface** within definitions are also defined in the glossary.

A

AC   See **assistant cameraperson**.

ADR   See **automatic dialogue replacement**.

aerial-view shot   Also known as *bird's-eye-view shot*. An **omniscient-point-of-view shot** that is taken from an aircraft or extremely high crane and implies that the observer can see all.

alienation effect   Also known as *distancing effect*. A psychological distance between audience and stage for which, according to German playwright Bertolt Brecht, every aspect of a theatrical production should strive by limiting the audience's identification with **characters** and events.

ambient sound   Sound that emanates from the ambience (background) of the **setting** or environment being filmed, either recorded during **production** or added during **postproduction**. Although it may incorporate other types of film sound—**dialogue, narration, sound effects, Foley sounds,** and music—ambient sound does not include any unintentionally recorded noise made during production.

amplitude   The degree of motion of air (or other medium) within a sound wave. The greater the amplitude of the sound wave, the harder it strikes the eardrum, and thus the louder the sound. Compare **loudness**.

animated film   Also known as *cartoon*. Drawings or other graphical images placed in a **series photography**—like sequence to portray movement. Before computer graphics technology, the basic type of animated film was created through drawing.

antagonist   The **major character** whose values or behavior are in conflict with those of the **protagonist**.

antirealism   A **treatment** that is against or the opposite of **realism**. However, realism and antirealism (like realism and fantasy) are not strict polarities.

aperture   Also known as *gate*. The camera opening that defines the area of each **frame** of film exposed.

apparent motion   The movie projector's tricking us into perceiving separate images as one continuous image rather than a series of jerky movements. Apparent motion is the result of such factors as the **phi phenomenon** and **critical flicker fusion**.

art director   The person responsible for transforming the **production designer**'s vision into a reality on the screen, assessing the staging requirements for a production, and arranging for and supervising the work of the members of the art department.

aspect ratio   The relationship between the **frame**'s two dimensions: the width of the image related to its height.

assistant cameraperson (AC)   Member of the **camera crew** who assists the **camera operator**. The *first AC* oversees everything having to do with the camera, **lenses**, supporting equipment, and the material on which the movie is being shot. The *second AC* prepares the **slate** that is used to identify each **scene** as it is being filmed, files camera reports, and feeds **film stock** into magazines to be loaded into the camera.

associate (or **assistant) producer**   Person charged with carrying out specific responsibilities assigned by the **producer, executive producer,** or **line producer.**

asynchronous sound   Sound that comes from a source apparent in the image but is not precisely matched temporally with the actions occurring in that image.

auteurism   A **film theory** based on the idea that the **director** is the sole "author" of a movie. The application of auteurism frequently takes two forms: a judgment of the whole body of a film director's work (not individual films) based on style, and a classification of great directors based on a hierarchy of directorial styles.

automatic dialogue replacement (**ADR**)   **Rerecording** done via computer—a faster, less expensive, and more technically sophisticated process than rerecording that is done with actors.

avant-garde film   See **experimental film.**

axis of action   See **180-degree system.**

B

backlight   Lighting, usually positioned behind and in line with the subject and the camera, used to create highlights on the subject as a means of separating it from the background and increasing its appearance of three-dimensionality.

backstory   A fictional history behind the situation extant at the start of the main **story.**

best boy   First assistant electrician to the **gaffer** on a movie **production set.**

bird's-eye-view shot   See **aerial-view shot.**

bit player   An actor who holds a small speaking part.

Black Maria   The first movie studio—a crude, hot, cramped shack in which Thomas Edison and his staff began making movies.

blimp   A soundproofed enclosure somewhat larger than a camera, in which the camera may be mounted to prevent its sounds from reaching the microphone.

blocking   Actual physical relationships among **figures** and **settings.**

boom   A polelike mechanical device for holding the microphone in the air, out of camera range, that can be moved in almost any direction.

C

cameo   A small but significant role often played by a famous actor.

camera crew   Technicians that make up two separate groups—one concerned with the camera, the other concerned with electricity and lighting.

camera obscura   Literally, "dark chamber." A box (or a room in which a viewer stands); light entering (originally through a tiny hole, later through a **lens**) on one side of the box (or room) projects an image from the outside onto the opposite side or wall.

camera operator   The member of the **camera crew** who does the actual **shooting.**

cartoon   See **animated film.**

casting   The process of choosing and hiring actors for a movie.

cel   A transparent sheet of celluloid or similar plastic on which drawings or lettering may be made for use in animation or titles.

celluloid roll film   Also known as *motion picture film* or *raw film stock.* A material for filming that consists of long strips of perforated cellulose acetate on which a rapid succession of **frames** can be recorded. One side of the strip is layered with an emulsion consisting of light-sensitive crystals and dyes; the other side is covered with a backing that reduces reflections. Each side of the strip is perforated with sprocket holes that facilitate the movement of the stock through the sprocket wheels of the camera, the processor, and the projector.

CGI   Computer-generated imagery. Compare **in-camera effect** and **laboratory effect.**

character   An essential element of film **narrative**; any of the beings who play functional roles within the **plot**, either acting or being acted on. Characters can be **flat** or **round; major, minor,** or **marginal; protagonists** or **antagonists.**

characterization   The process of the actor's interpreting a **character** in a movie. Characterization differs according to the actor, the character, the screenplay, and the **director.**

character role   An actor's part that represents a distinctive **character** type (sometimes a stereotype): society leader, judge, doctor, diplomat, and so on.

chiaroscuro   The use of deep gradations and subtle variations of lights and darks within an image.

chrono-photographic gun   See **revolver photographique.**

cinematic conventions   Accepted systems, methods, or customs by which movies communicate. Cinematic conventions are flexible; they are not "rules."

cinematic language   The accepted systems, methods, or conventions by which the movies communicate with the viewer.

cinematic time   The imaginary time in which a movie's

images appear or its **narrative** occurs; time that has been manipulated through **editing**. Compare **real time**.

cinematography   The process of capturing moving images on film or some other medium.

climax   The **narrative's** turning point, marking the transition between **rising action** and **falling action**.

closed frame   A **frame** of a motion picture image that, theoretically, neither **characters** nor objects enter or leave. Compare **open frame**.

close-up (**CU**)   A **shot** that often shows a part of the body filling the **frame**—traditionally a face, but possibly a hand, eye, or mouth.

color   As related to sound, see **quality**.

colorization   The use of digital technology, in a process similar to hand-tinting, to "paint" colors on movies meant to be seen in black and white.

composition   The process of visualizing and putting visualization plans into practice; more precisely, the organization, distribution, balance, and general relationship of stationary objects and **figures**, as well as of light, shade, line, and color, within the **frame**.

content   The subject of an artwork. Compare **form**.

content curve   In terms of cinematic **duration**, an arc that measures information in a **shot**; at the curve's peak, the viewer has absorbed the information from a shot and is ready to move on to the next shot.

continuity editing   A style of **editing** (now dominant throughout the world) that seeks to achieve logic, smoothness, sequential flow, and the temporal and spatial orientation of viewers to what they see on the screen. Continuity editing ensures the flow from **shot** to shot; creates a rhythm based on the relationship between cinematic space and **cinematic time**; creates filmic unity (beginning, middle, and end); and establishes and resolves a problem. In short, continuity editing tells a **story** as clearly and coherently as possible. Compare **discontinuity editing**.

costumes   The clothing worn by an actor in a movie (sometimes called *wardrobe*, a term that also designates the department in a studio in which clothing is made and stored).

cover shot   See **master shot**.

crane shot   A **shot** that is created by movement of a camera mounted on an elevating arm (crane) that, in turn, is mounted on a vehicle that, if **shooting** requires it, can move on its own power or be pushed along tracks.

critical flicker fusion   A phenomenon that occurs when a single light flickers on and off with such speed that the individual pulses of light fuse together to give the illusion of continuous light. See also **apparent motion**.

crosscutting   **Editing** that **cuts** between two or more actions occurring at the same time, and usually in the same place. Compare **intercutting** and **parallel editing**.

CU   See **close-up**.

cut   A direct change from one **shot** to another; that is, the precise point at which shot A ends and shot B begins; one result of **cutting**.

cutting   Also known as *splicing*. The actual joining together of two **shots**. The editor must first cut (or splice) each shot from its respective roll of film before gluing or taping all the shots together.

D

dailies   Also known as *rushes*. Usually, synchronized picture/sound work prints of a day's **shooting** that can be studied by the **director**, editor, and other crew members before the next day's shooting begins.

décor   The color and textures of the interior decoration, furniture, draperies, and curtains of a **set**.

deep-focus cinematography   Using the **short-focal-length lens** to capture **deep-space composition** and its illusion of depth.

deep-space composition   A total visual **composition** that occupies all three **planes** of the **frame**, thus creating an illusion of depth, and that is usually reproduced on the screen by **deep-focus cinematography**.

denouement   The resolution or conclusion of the **narrative**.

depth of field   The distance in front of a camera and its **lens** in which objects are in apparent sharp focus.

design   The process by which the *look* of the **settings**, **props**, lighting, and actors is determined. **Set** design, **décor**, prop selection, lighting **setup**, **costuming**, makeup, and hairstyle design all play a role in shaping the overall design.

dialogue   The lip-synchronous speech of **characters** who are either visible onscreen or speaking offscreen, say from another part of the room that is not visible or from an adjacent room.

diegesis (adj. **diegetic**)   The total world of a **story**—the events, **characters**, objects, **settings**, and sounds that form the world in which the story occurs.

diegetic element   An element—event, **character**, object, **setting**, sound—that helps form the world in which the **story** occurs. Compare **nondiegetic element**.

diegetic sound   Sound that originates from a source within a film's world. Compare **nondiegetic sound**.

digital format   A means of storing recorded sound, made possible by computer technology, in which each sound wave is represented by combinations of the numbers 0 and 1.

director The person who (a) determines and realizes on the screen an artistic vision of the screenplay; (b) **casts** the actors and directs their performances; (c) works closely with the production **design** in creating the look of the film, including the choice of locations; (d) oversees the work of the cinematographer and other key **production** personnel; and, (e) in most cases, supervises all **postproduction** activity, especially the **editing**.

discontinuity editing A style of **editing**—less widely used than **continuity editing**, often but not exclusively in **experimental films**—that joins **shots** A and B to produce an effect or meaning not even hinted at by either shot alone.

dissolve Also known as *lap dissolve*. A transitional device in which **shot** B, superimposed, gradually appears over shot A and begins to replace it at midpoint in the transition. Dissolves usually indicate the passing of time. Compare **fade-in/fade-out**.

distancing effect See **alienation effect**.

documentary film A **nonfiction film** originally created to address social injustice. When they are produced by governments and carry government messages, documentary films overlap with **propaganda films**. The term is also used more generally to refer to the entire category of nonfiction films. Compare **factual film** and **instructional film**.

dolly A wheeled support for a camera that permits the cinematographer to make noiseless moving **shots**.

dolly-in Slow movement of the camera toward a subject, making the subject appear larger and more significant. Such gradual intensification is commonly used at moments of a **character**'s realization and/or decision, or as a **point-of-view shot** to indicate the reason for the character's realization. See also **zoom-in**. Compare **dolly-out**.

dolly-out Movement of the camera away from the subject that is often used for *slow disclosure*, which occurs when an edited succession of images leads from A to B to C as they gradually reveal the elements of a **scene**. Each image expands on the one before, thereby changing its significance with new information. Compare **dolly-in**.

dolly shot Also known as *traveling shot*. A **shot** taken by a camera fixed to a wheeled support called a **dolly**. When the dolly runs on tracks (or when the camera is mounted to a crane or an aerial device such as an airplane, a helicopter, or a balloon) the shot is called a *tracking shot*.

double-system recording The standard technique of recording film sound on a medium separate from the picture; this technique allows both for maximum quality control of the medium and for the many aspects of manipulating sound during **postproduction editing**, **mixing**, and synchronization.

down shot See **high-angle shot**.

dubbing See **rerecording**.

duration The time a movie takes to unfold onscreen. For any movie, we can identify three specific kinds of duration: **story duration**, **plot duration**, and **screen duration**. Duration has two related components: **real time** and **cinematic time**.

Dutch-angle shot Also known as *Dutch shot* or *oblique-angle shot*. A **shot** in which the camera is tilted from its normal horizontal and vertical positions so that it is no longer straight, giving the viewer the impression that the world in the **frame** is out of balance.

Dutch shot See **Dutch-angle shot**.

E

ECU See **extreme close-up**.

editing The process by which the editor combines and coordinates individual **shots** into a cinematic whole; the basic creative force of cinema.

ellipsis In filmmaking, generally an omission of time—the time that separates one **shot** from another—to create dramatic or comedic impact.

ELS See **extreme long shot**.

ensemble acting An approach to acting that emphasizes the interaction of actors, not the individual actor. In ensemble acting, a group of actors work together continuously in a single **shot**. Typically experienced in the theater, ensemble acting is used less in the movies because it requires the provision of rehearsal time that is usually denied to screen actors.

establishing shot See **master shot** and **extreme long shot**.

executive producer Person responsible for supervising one or more **producers**, who in turn are responsible for individual movies.

experimental film Also known as *avant-garde film*, a term implying a position in the vanguard, out in front of traditional films. Experimental films are usually about unfamiliar, unorthodox, or obscure subject matter and are ordinarily made by independent (even underground) filmmakers, not studios, often with innovative techniques that call attention to, question, and even challenge their own artifice.

explicit meaning Everything that a movie presents on its surface. Compare **implicit meaning**.

exposition The images, action, and **dialogue** necessary to give the audience the background of the **characters**

and the nature of their situation, laying the foundation for the rest of the **narrative**.

exposure index   See **film stock speed**.

external sound   A form of **diegetic sound** that comes from a place within the world of the **story**, which we and the **characters** in the **scene** hear but do not see. Compare **internal sound**.

extra   An actor who, usually, appears in a nonspeaking or crowd role and receives no screen credit.

extreme close-up (ECU, XCU)   A very close **shot** of a particular detail, such as a person's eye, a ring on a finger, or a watch face.

extreme long shot (ELS, XLS)   A **shot** that is typically photographed far enough away from the subject that the subject is too small to be recognized, except through the context we see, which usually includes a wide view of the location, as well as general background information. When it is used to provide such informative context, the extreme long shot is also referred to as an *establishing shot*.

eye-level shot   A **shot** that is made from the observer's eye level and usually implies that the observer's attitude is neutral toward the subject being photographed.

eyeline match cut   A **match cut** that joins **shot** A (often a **point-of-view** shot of a **character** looking offscreen in one direction) and shot B (the person or object that the character is seeing). Compare **graphic match cut** and **match-on-action cut**.

F

factual film   A **nonfiction film** that, usually, presents people, places, or processes in a straightforward way meant to entertain and instruct without unduly influencing audiences. Compare **documentary film**, **instructional film**, and **propaganda film**.

fade-in/fade-out   Transitional devices in which a **shot** fades in from a black field on black-and-white film or from a color field on color film, or fades out to a black field (or a color field). Compare **dissolve**.

falling action   The events that follow the **climax** and bring the **narrative** to conclusion (**denouement**). Compare **rising action**.

familiar image   Any image that a **director** periodically repeats in a movie (with or without variations) to help stabilize the **narrative**.

fast motion   **Photography** that accelerates action by photographing it at a filming rate less than the normal 24 **frames** per second so that, in **cinematic time**, it takes place at a more rapid rate than the real action took place before the camera. Compare **slow motion**.

featured role   See **major role**.

feed spool   The storage area for unexposed film in the movie camera.

fiction film   See **narrative film**.

fidelity   The faithfulness or unfaithfulness of a sound to its source.

figure   Any significant thing that moves on the screen—person, animal, object.

fill light   Lighting, positioned at the opposite side of the camera from the **key light**, that can fill in the shadows created by the brighter key light. Fill light may also come from a **reflector board**.

film criticism   Evaluating a film's artistic merit and appeal to the public. Film criticism takes two basic forms: reviews written for a general audience and appearing in the popular media, and essays published in academic journals for a scholarly audience. Compare **film theory**.

film speed   See **film stock speed**.

film stock   Celluloid used to record movies. There are two types: one for black-and-white films, the other for color. Each type is manufactured in several standard **formats**.

film stock length   The number of feet (or meters) of **film stock** or the number of reels being used in a particular film.

film stock speed   Also known as *film speed* or *exposure index*. The rate at which film must move through the camera to correctly capture an image; very fast film requires little light to capture and fix the image; very slow film requires a lot of light.

film theory   Evaluating movies from a particular intellectual or ideological perspective. Compare **film criticism**.

first AC   See **assistant cameraperson**.

first-person narration   Narration by an actual **character** in the movie. Compare **voice-over narration**.

flashback   A device for presenting or reawakening the memory of the camera, a **character**, the audience—or all three—in which the action **cuts** from the **narrative** present to a past event, which may or may not have already appeared in the movie either directly or through inference. Compare **flashforward**.

flashforward   A device for presenting the anticipation of the camera, a **character**, the audience—or all three—in which the action **cuts** from the **narrative** present to a future time, one in which, for example, the **omniscient** camera reveals directly or a character imagines, from his or her **point of view**, what is going to happen. Compare **flashback**.

flat character   A **character** that is one-dimensional and easily remembered because his or her motivations and actions are predictable. Flat characters may be **major**, **minor**, or **marginal** characters. Compare **round character**.

floodlight A lamp that produces soft (diffuse) light. Compare **focusable spotlight**.

focal length The distance from the optical center of a **lens** to the focal point (the film **plane** that the camera-person wants to keep in focus) when the lens is focused at infinity.

focusable spotlight A lamp that produces hard, mirrorlike light. Compare **floodlight**.

Foley sound A sound belonging to a special category of **sound effects**, invented in the 1930s by Jack Foley, a sound technician at Universal Studios. Technicians known as Foley artists create these sounds in specially equipped studios, where they use a variety of **props** and other equipment to simulate sounds such as footsteps in the mud, jingling car keys, or cutlery hitting a plate.

form The means by which a subject is expressed. The form for poetry is words; for drama, it is speech and action; for movies, it is pictures and sound; and so on. Compare **content**.

format Also called *gauge*. The dimensions of a **film stock** and its perforations, and the size and shape of the image **frame** as seen on the screen. Formats extend from Super 8mm through 70mm (and beyond into such specialized formats as IMAX), but they are generally limited to three standard gauges: Super 8mm, 16mm, and 35mm.

frame A still photograph that, recorded in rapid succession with other still photographs, creates a motion picture.

framing The process by which the cinematographer determines what will appear within the borders of the moving image (the **frame**) during a **shot**.

freeze-frame Also known as *stop-frame* or *hold-frame*. A still image within a movie, created by repetitive printing in the laboratory of the same **frame** so that it can be seen without movement for whatever length of time the filmmaker desires.

frequency The speed with which a sound is produced (the number of sound waves produced per second). The speed of sound remains fairly constant when it passes through air, but it varies in different media and in the same medium at different temperatures). Compare **pitch**.

full-body shot See **long shot**.

fusil photographique A form of the chrono-photographic gun (see **revolver photographique**)—a single, portable camera capable of taking twelve continuous images.

FX See **special effects**.

G

gaffer The chief electrician on a movie **production set**.

gate See **aperture**.

gauge See **format**.

generic transformation The process by which a particular **genre** is adapted to meet the expectations of a changing society.

genre The categorization of **narrative films** by **form**, **content**, or both. Examples of genres are musical, comedy, biography, western, and so on.

graphic match cut A **match cut** in which the similarity between **shots** A and B is in the shape and form of what we see. The shape, color, or texture of objects matches across the edit, providing continuity. Compare **eyeline match cut** and **match-on-action cut**.

grip All-around handyperson on a movie **production set**, most often working with the **camera crews** and electrical crews.

group point of view A **point of view** captured by a **shot** that shows what a group of **characters** would see, but at the group's level, not from the much higher **omniscient point of view**. Compare **single character's point of view**.

H

harmonic content The wavelengths that make up a sound. Compare **quality**.

high-angle shot Also known as *high shot* or *down shot*. A **shot** that is made with the camera above the action and that typically implies the observer's sense of superiority to the subject being photographed. Compare **low-angle shot**.

high-key lighting Lighting that produces an image with very little contrast between darks and lights. Its even, flat illumination expresses virtually no opinions about the subject being photographed. Compare **low-key lighting**.

high shot See **high-angle shot**.

hold-frame See **freeze-frame**.

hub A major event in a **plot**; a branching point in the plot structure that forces a **character** to choose between or among alternate paths. Compare **satellite**.

I

ideological meaning Meaning expressed by a film that reflects beliefs on the part of filmmakers, **characters**, or the time and place of the movie's **setting**. Ideological meaning is the product of social, political, economic, religious, philosophical, psychological, and sexual forces that shape the filmmakers' perspectives.

imaginary line   See **180-degree system**.

implicit meaning   An association, connection, or inference that a viewer makes on the basis of the given (explicit) **story** and **form** of a film. Lying below the surface of **explicit meaning**, implicit meaning is closest to our everyday sense of the word *meaning*.

improvisation   1. Actors' extemporization—that is, delivering lines based only loosely on the written script or without the preparation that comes with studying a script before rehearsing it. 2. "Playing through" a moment—that is, making up lines to keep **scenes** going when actors forget their written lines, stumble on lines, or have some other mishap.

in-camera effect   A **special effect** that is created in the **production** camera (the regular camera used for **shooting** the rest of the film) on the original **negative**. Examples of in-camera effects include **montage** and **split screen**. Compare **laboratory effect** and CGI.

inciting moment   The event or situation during the **exposition** stage of the **narrative** that sets the rest of the narrative in motion.

instructional film   A **nonfiction film** that seeks to educate viewers about common interests rather than persuading them with particular ideas. Compare **documentary film**, **factual film**, and **propaganda film**.

intercutting   **Editing** of two or more actions taking place at the same time that creates the effect of a single **scene** rather than of two distinct actions. Compare **crosscutting** and **parallel editing**.

interior monologue   One variation on the mental, subjective **point of view of** an individual **character** that allows us to see a character and hear that character's thoughts (in his or her own voice, even though the character's lips don't move).

internal sound   A form of **diegetic sound** in which we hear the thoughts of a **character** we see onscreen and assume that other characters cannot hear them. Compare **external sound**.

iris   1. A circular cutout made with a **mask** that creates a **frame** within a frame. 2. An adjustable diaphragm that limits the amount of light passing through the **lens** of a camera.

iris-in/iris-out   See **iris shot**.

iris shot   Optical **wipe** effect in which the wipe line is a circle; named after the **iris** of a camera. The *iris-in* begins with a small circle, which expands to a partial or full image; the *iris-out* begins with a large circle, which contracts to a smaller circle or total blackness.

J

jump cut   The removal of a portion of a film, resulting in an instantaneous advance in the action—a sudden, perhaps illogical, often disorienting **ellipsis** between two **shots**.

K

key light   Also known as *main light* or *source light*. The brightest light falling on a subject.

kinesis   The aspect of **composition** that takes into account everything that moves on the screen.

kinetograph   The first motion picture camera.

kinetoscope   A peephole viewer, an early motion picture device.

L

laboratory effect   A **special effect** that is created in the laboratory through **processing** and printing. Compare **in-camera effect** and CGI.

lap dissolve   See **dissolve**.

leading role   See **major role**.

lens   The piece of transparent material in a camera that focuses the image on the film being exposed. The four major types of lenses are the **short-focal-length lens**, the **middle-focal-length lens**, the **long-focal-length-lens**, and the **zoom lens**.

lighting ratio   The relationship and balance between illumination and shadow—the balance between **key light** and **fill light**.

line of action   See **180-degree system**.

line producer   The person, usually involved from **preproduction** through **postproduction**, who is responsible for the day-to-day management of the **production** operation.

long-focal-length lens   Also known as *telephoto lens*. A **lens** that flattens the space and depth of an image and thus distorts perspective relations. Compare **middle-focal-length lens**, **short-focal-length lens**, and **zoom lens**.

long shot (LS)   Also known as *full-body shot*. A **shot** that shows the full human body, usually filling the **frame**, and some of its surroundings.

long take   Also known as *sequence shot*. A **shot** that can last anywhere from one minute to ten minutes. (Between 1930 and 1960, the average length of a shot was 8–11 seconds; today it's 6–7 seconds, signifying that directors are telling their stories with a tighter pace.)

looping   See **rerecording**.

loudness   The volume or intensity of a sound, which is defined by its **amplitude**. Loudness is described as either *loud* or *soft*.

low-angle shot   Also known as *low shot*. A **shot** that is made with the camera below the action and that typically places the observer in a position of inferiority. Compare **high-angle shot**.

low-key lighting   Lighting that creates strong contrasts; sharp, dark shadows; and an overall gloomy atmosphere. Its contrasts between light and dark often imply ethical judgments. Compare **high-key lighting**.

low shot   See **low-angle shot**.

LS   See **long shot**.

M

magic lantern   An early movie projector.

main light   See **key light**.

main role   See **major role**.

major character   One of the main **characters** in a movie. Major characters make the most things happen or have the most things happen to them. Compare **minor character** and **marginal character**.

major role   Also known as *main role*, *featured role*, or *leading role*. A role that is a principal agent in helping move the **plot** forward. Whether **movie stars** or newcomers, actors playing major roles appear in many **scenes** and—ordinarily, but not always—receive screen credit preceding the title. Compare **minor role**.

marginal character   A **minor character** that lacks both definition and screen time.

mask   An opaque sheet of metal, paper, or plastic (with, for example, a circular cutout, known as an **iris**) that is placed in front of the camera and admits light through that circle to a specific area of the **frame**—to create a frame within a frame.

master shot   Also known as *establishing shot* or *cover shot*. A **shot** that ordinarily serves as a foundation for (and usually begins) a **sequence** by showing the location of ensuing action. Although usually a **long shot** or **extreme long shot**, a master shot may also be a **medium shot** or **close-up** that includes a sign or other cue to identify the location. Master shots are also called *cover shots* because the editor can repeat them later in the film to remind the audience of the location, thus "covering" the **director** by avoiding the need to **reshoot**.

match cut   A **cut** that preserves continuity between two **shots**. Several kinds of match cuts exist, including the **eyeline match cut**, the **graphic match cut**, and the **match-on-action cut**.

match-on-action cut   A **match cut** in which the action continues seamlessly from one **shot** to the next or from one camera angle to the next. Compare **eyeline match cut** and **graphic match cut**.

MCU   See **medium close-up**.

mechanical effect   A **special effect** created by an object or event mechanically on the **set** and in front of the camera.

mediation   An agent, structure, or other formal element, whether human or technological, that transfers something, such as information in the case of movies, from one place to another.

medium close-up (MCU)   A **shot** that shows a **character** from the middle of the chest to the top of the head. A medium close-up provides a view of the face that catches minor changes in expression, as well as some detail about the character's posture.

medium long shot (MLS)   Also known as *plan américain* or American shot. A **shot** that shows a **character** from the knees up and includes most of a person's body.

medium shot (MS)   A **shot** showing the human body, usually from the waist up.

method acting   Also known as simply *the method*. A naturalistic acting style, loosely adapted from the ideas of Russian **director** Konstantin Stanislavsky by American directors Elia Kazan and Lee Strasberg, that encourages actors to speak, move, and gesture not in a traditional stage manner, but in the same way they would in their own lives. An ideal technique for representing convincing human behavior, method acting is used more frequently on the stage than on the screen.

middle-focal-length lens   Also known as *normal lens*. A **lens** that does not distort perspectival relations. Compare **long-focal-length lens**, **short-focal-length lens**, and **zoom lens**.

minor character   A supporting **character** in a movie. Minor characters have fewer traits than **major characters**, so we know less about them. They may also be so lacking in definition and screen time that we can consider them **marginal characters**.

minor role   Also known as *supporting role*. A role that helps move the **plot** forward (and thus may be as important as a **major role**), but that is played by an actor who does not appear in as many **scenes** as the featured players do.

mise-en-scène   Also known as *staging*. The overall look and feel of a movie—the sum of everything the audience sees, hears, and experiences while viewing it.

mixing   The process of combining different **sound tracks** onto one composite sound track that is synchronous with the picture.

MLS   See **medium long shot**.

montage   1. In France, the word for **editing**, from the verb *monter*, "to assemble or put together." 2. In the former Soviet Union in the 1920s, the various forms of editing that expressed ideas developed by theorists and filmmakers such as Sergei Eisenstein. 3. In Hollywood, beginning in the 1930s, a **sequence** of **shots**, often with superimpositions and optical effects, showing a condensed series of events.

motion picture film   See **celluloid roll film**.

movie star   A phenomenon, generally associated with Hollywood, comprising the actor and the **characters** played by that actor, an image created by the studio to coincide with the kind of roles associated with the actor, and a reflection of the social and cultural history of the period in which that image was created.

moving frame   The result of the dynamic functions of the **frame** around a motion picture image, which can contain moving action but can also move and thus change its viewpoint.

MS   See **medium shot**.

N

narration   The commentary spoken by either offscreen or onscreen voices, frequently used in **narrative films**, where it may emanate from an **omniscient** voice (and thus not one of the **characters**) or from a character in the movie. There are two main types of narration: **first-person narration** and **voice-over narration**.

narrative   The overall connection of events within the world of a movie, consisting of **exposition, rising action, climax, falling action**, and **denouement**. Compare **story** and **plot**.

narrative film   Also known as *fiction film*. A movie that tells a **story**—with **characters**, places, and events—that is conceived in the mind of the film's creator. Stories in narrative films may be wholly imaginary or based on true occurrences, and they may be realistic, unrealistic, or both. Compare **nonfiction film**.

narrator   A voice that helps tell the **story**. The narrator may be either a **character** in the movie or a person who is not a character.

negative   A negative **photographic** image on transparent material that makes possible the reproduction of the image.

nondiegetic element   Something that we see and hear on the screen that comes from outside the world of the **story** (including background music, titles and credits, and **voice-over narration**). Compare **diegetic element**.

nondiegetic sound   Sound that originates from a source outside a film's world. Compare **diegetic sound**.

nonfiction film   Factual, **instructional, documentary**, or **propaganda film** traditionally produced by a government, foundation, charity organization, or independent filmmaker. The terms *nonfiction film* and *documentary film* are often used synonymously, but although all documentaries are nonfiction films, not all nonfiction films are documentaries. Compare **narrative film**.

nonsimultaneous sound   Sound that has previously been established in the movie and occurs when a **character** has a mental **flashback** to an earlier voice that recalls a conversation or a sound that identifies a place. Compare **simultaneous sound**.

normal lens   See **middle-focal-length lens**.

O

oblique-angle shot   See **Dutch-angle shot**.

offscreen sound   A form of sound, either **diegetic** or **nondiegetic**, that derives from a source we do not see. When diegetic, it consists of **sound effects**, music, or vocals that emanate from the world of the **story**. When nondiegetic, it takes the form of a musical score or **narration** by someone who is not a **character** in the story. Compare **onscreen sound**.

offscreen space   Cinematic space that exists outside the **frame**. Compare **onscreen space**.

omniscient   Providing a third-person view of all aspects of a movie's action or **characters**. Compare **restricted**.

omniscient point of view   The most basic and most common **point of view**. *Omniscient* means that the camera has complete or unlimited perception of what the cinematographer *chooses* for it to see and hear; this point of view shows what that camera sees, typically from a high angle. Compare **single character's point of view** and **group point of view**.

on location   Shooting in an actual interior or exterior location away from the studio. Compare **set**.

180-degree rule   See **180-degree system**.

180-degree system   Also known as *axis of action, imaginary line, line of action,* or *180-degree rule*. The fundamental means by which filmmakers maintain consistent **screen direction**, orienting the viewer and ensuring a sense of the cinematic space in which the action occurs. The system assumes three things: (a) the action within a **scene** will always advance along a straight line, either from left to right or from right to left of the **frame**; (b) the camera will remain consistently on one side of that action; and (c) everyone on the **production set** will understand and adhere to this system.

onscreen sound   A form of **diegetic sound** that emanates from a source that we both see and hear. Onscreen sound may be **internal sound** or **external sound**. Compare **offscreen sound**.

onscreen space   Cinematic space that exists inside the **frame**. Compare **offscreen space**.

open frame   A **frame** around a motion picture image that, theoretically, **characters** and objects can enter and leave. Compare **closed frame**.

option contract   During the classical Hollywood era, an actor's standard seven-year contract, reviewed every six months: if the actor had made progress in being assigned roles and demonstrating box-office appeal, the studio picked up the option to employ that actor for the next six months and gave the actor a raise; if not, the studio dropped the option and the actor was out of a job.

order   The arrangement of **plot** events into a logical sequence or hierarchy. Across an entire **narrative** or in a brief section of it, any film can use one or more methods to arrange its plot: chronological order, cause-and-effect order, logical order, and so on.

outtake   Material that is not used in either the rough cut or the final cut, but is cataloged and saved.

overlapping sound   Sound that carries over from one **shot** to the next before the sound of the second shot begins.

P

pan shot   The horizontal movement of a camera mounted on the gyroscopic head of a stationary tripod; like the **tilt shot**, the pan shot is a simple movement with dynamic possibilities for creating meaning.

parallel editing   Also called *crosscutting* and *intercutting*, although the three terms have slightly different meanings. The intercutting of two or more lines of action that occur simultaneously, a very familiar convention in chase or rescue **sequences**. See also **crosscutting** and **intercutting**. Compare **split screen**.

persistence of vision   The process by which the human brain retains an image for a fraction of a second longer than the eye records it.

phi phenomenon   The illusion of movement created by events that succeed each other rapidly, as when two adjacent lights flash on and off alternately and we seem to see a single light shifting back and forth. See also **apparent motion**.

photography   Literally, "writing with light"; technically, the recording of static images through a chemical interaction caused by light rays striking a sensitized surface.

pitch   The level of a sound, which is defined by its **frequency**. Pitch is described as either *high* or *low*.

plan américain   See **medium long shot**.

plane   Any of three theoretical areas—foreground, middle ground, and background—within the **frame**. See also **rule of thirds**.

plot   A structure for presenting everything that we see and hear in a film, with an emphasis on causality, consisting of two factors: (a) the arrangement of the diegetic events in a certain **order** or structure and (b) added nondiegetic material. See **diegesis** and **nondiegetic elements**. Compare **narrative** and **story**.

plot duration   The elapsed time of the events within a **story** that a film chooses to tell. Compare **screen duration** and **story duration**.

point of view (**POV**)   The position from which a film presents the actions of the **story**; not only the relation of the **narrator**(s) to the story but also the camera's act of seeing and hearing. The two fundamental types of cinematic point of view are **omniscient** and **restricted**.

point-of-view editing   The joining together of a **point-of-view shot** with a **match cut** (specifically, a **match-on-action cut**) to show, in the first shot, a **character** looking and, in the second, what that character is looking at.

postproduction   The third stage of the production process, consisting of **editing**, preparing the final print, and bringing the film to the public (marketing and distribution). Postproduction is preceded by **preproduction** and **production**.

POV   See **point of view**.

preproduction   The initial, planning-and-preparation stage of the production process. Preproduction is followed by **production** and **postproduction**.

prime lens   A lens that has a fixed **focal length**. The **short-focal-length**, **middle-focal-length**, and **long-focal-length lenses** are all prime lenses; the **zoom lens** is in its own category.

processing   The second stage of creating motion pictures, in which a laboratory technician washes exposed film (which contains a **negative** image) with processing chemicals. Processing is preceded by **shooting** and followed by **projecting**.

process shot   Live **shooting** against a background that is front- or rear-projected on a translucent screen.

producer   The person who guides the entire process of making the movie from its initial planning to its release and is chiefly responsible for the organizational and financial aspects of the **production**, from arranging the financing to deciding how the money is spent.

production   The second stage of the production process, the actual **shooting**. Production is preceded by **preproduction** and followed by **postproduction**.

production designer   A person who works closely with the **director**, **art director**, and director of **photography**, in visualizing the movie that will appear on the screen. The production designer is both an artist and an executive, responsible for the overall **design** concept, the *look* of the movie—as well as individual **sets**, locations, furnishings, **props**, and **costumes**—and for supervising the heads of the many departments (art, costume design and construction, hairstyling, makeup, wardrobe, location, etc.) that create that look.

production value   The amount of human and physical resources devoted to the image, including the style of its lighting. Production value helps determine the overall style of a film.

projecting   The third stage of creating motion pictures, in which edited film is run through a projector, which shoots through the film a beam of light intense enough to project a large image on the movie theater screen. Projecting is preceded by **shooting** and **processing**.

propaganda film   A **nonfiction film** that systematically disseminates deceptive or distorted information. Compare **documentary film**, **factual film**, and **instructional film**.

properties   Also known as simply *props*. Objects such as paintings, vases, flowers, silver tea sets, guns, or fishing rods that help us understand the **characters** by showing us their preferences in such things.

props   See **properties**.

protagonist   The **major character** who serves as the "hero" and who "wins" the conflict. Compare **antagonist**.

pull-down claw   Within the movie camera and projector, the mechanism that controls the intermittent cycle of **shooting** and **projecting** individual **frames** and advances the film frame by frame.

pull focus   See **rack focus**.

Q

quality   Also known as *timbre*, *texture*, or *color*. The complexity of a sound, which is defined by its **harmonic content**. Described as *simple* or *complex*, quality is the characteristic that distinguishes a sound from others of the same **pitch** and **loudness**.

R

rack focus   Also known as *select focus*, *shift focus*, or *pull focus*. A change of the point of focus from one subject to another within the same **shot**. Rack focus guides our attention to a new clearly focused point of interest while blurring the previous subject in the shot.

raw film stock   See **celluloid roll film**.

realism   An interest in or concern for the actual or real; a tendency to view or represent things as they really are. Compare **antirealism**.

real time   The actual time during which something takes place. In real time, **screen duration** and **plot duration** are exactly the same. Many **directors** use real time within films to create uninterrupted "reality" on the screen, but they rarely use it for entire films. Compare **cinematic time**, **stretch relationship**, and **summary relationship**.

reflector board   A piece of lighting equipment, but not really a lighting instrument, because it does not rely on bulbs to produce illumination. Essentially, a reflector board is a double-sided board that pivots in a *U*-shaped holder. One side is a hard, smooth surface that reflects hard light; the other is a soft, textured surface that reflects softer **fill light**.

reframing   A movement of the camera that adjusts or alters the **composition** or **point of view** of a **shot**.

repetition   The number of times that a **story** element recurs in a **plot**. Repetition signals that a particular event has noteworthy meaning or significance.

rerecording   Also known as *looping* or *dubbing*. The replacing of **dialogue**, which can be done manually (that is, with the actors watching the footage, synchronizing their lips with it, and rereading the lines) or, more likely today, through computerized **automatic dialogue replacement** (ADR). (*Dubbing* also refers to the process of replacing dialogue in a foreign language with English, or the reverse, throughout a film.)

reshoot   To make additional **takes** of a **shot** in order to meet the **director**'s standards or as supplemental material for **production** photography.

restricted   Providing a view from the perspective of a single **character**. For example, restricted **narration** reveals information to the audience only as a specific character learns of it. Compare **omniscient**.

reverse-angle shot   A **shot** in which the angle of **shooting** is opposite to that of the preceding shot.

revolver photographique   Also known as *chrono-photographic gun*. A cylinder-shaped camera that creates exposures automatically, at short intervals, on different segments of a revolving plate.

rising action   The development of the action of the **narrative** toward a **climax**. Compare **falling action**.

rough-draft screenplay   Also known as *scenario*. The next step after a **treatment**, the rough-draft screenplay results from discussions, development, and transformation of an outline in sessions known as **story conferences**.

round character A **character** that is three-dimensional, unpredictable, complex, and capable of surprising us in a convincing way. Round characters may be **major** or **minor** characters. Compare **flat character**.

rule of thirds A principle of **composition** that enables filmmakers to maximize the potential of the image, balance its elements, and create the illusion of depth. A grid pattern, when superimposed on the image, divides the image into horizontal thirds representing the foreground, middle ground, and background **planes** and into vertical thirds that break up those planes into additional elements.

rushes See **dailies**.

S

satellite A minor **plot** event in the **diegesis**, or world, of the **narrative** but detachable from it (although removing a satellite may affect the overall texture of the narrative). Compare **hub**.

scale The size and placement of a particular object or a part of a **scene** in relation to the rest—a relationship determined by the type of **shot** used and the placement of the camera.

scenario See **rough-draft screenplay**.

scene A complete unit of **plot** action incorporating one or more **shots**; the **setting** of that action.

scope The overall range of a **story**.

screen direction The direction of a **figure**'s or object's movement on the screen.

screen duration A film's running time. Compare **plot duration** and **story duration**.

screen test A filming undertaken by an actor to audition for a particular role.

script supervisor The member of the crew who is responsible for ensuring continuity throughout the filming of a movie. Although script supervisors once had to maintain detailed logs to accomplish this task, today they generally rely on the **video assist camera** for this purpose.

second AC See **assistant cameraperson**.

select focus See **rack focus**.

sequence A series of edited **shots** characterized by inherent unity of **theme** and purpose.

sequence shot See **long take**.

series photography The use of a series of still photographs to record the phases of an action, although the actions within the images do not move.

set Not reality, but a fragment of reality created as the setting for a particular **shot** in a movie. Sets must be constructed both to look authentic and to photograph well. Compare **on location**.

setting The time and space in which a **story** takes place.

setup One camera position and everything associated with it. Whereas the **shot** is the basic building block of the film, the setup is the basic component of the film's **production**.

shift focus See **rack focus**.

shooting The first stage of creating motion pictures, in which images are recorded on previously unexposed film as it moves through the camera. Shooting is followed by **processing** and **projecting**.

shooting angle The level and height of the camera in relation to the subject being photographed. The five basic camera angles produce **eye-level shots**, **high-angle shots**, **low-angle shots**, **Dutch-angle shots**, and **aerial-view shots**.

shooting script A guide and reference point for all members of the **production** unit, in which the details of each **shot** are listed and can thus be followed during filming.

short-focal-length lens Also known as *wide-angle lens*. A **lens** that creates the illusion of depth within a **frame**, albeit with some distortion at the edges of the frame. Compare **long-focal-length lens**, **middle-focal-length lens**, and **zoom lens**.

shot One *uninterrupted* run of the camera. A shot can be as short or as long as the **director** wants, but it cannot exceed the length of the **film stock** in the camera. Compare **setup**.

shot/reverse shot One of the most prevalent and familiar of all **editing** patterns, consisting of **parallel editing** (**crosscutting**) between **shots** of different **characters**, usually in a conversation or confrontation. When used in **continuity editing**, the shots are typically **framed** over each character's shoulder to preserve **screen direction**.

shutter A camera device that shields the film from light at the **aperture** during the film-movement portion of the intermittent cycle of **shooting**.

simultaneous sound Sound that is **diegetic** and occurs onscreen. Compare **nonsimultaneous sound**.

single character's point of view A **point of view** that is captured by a **shot** made with the camera close to the line of sight of one **character** (or animal or surveillance camera), showing what that person would be seeing of the action. Compare **omniscient point of view** and **group point of view**.

slate The board or other device that is used to identify each **scene** during **shooting**.

slow motion **Photography** that decelerates action by photographing it at a filming rate greater than the normal 24 **frames** per second so that, in **cinematic time**, it takes place at a slower rate than the real action took place before the camera. Compare **fast motion**.

sound crew The group that generates and controls a movie's sound physically, manipulating its properties to produce the effects that the **director** desires.

sound design A state-of-the-art concept, pioneered by director Francis Ford Coppola and film editor Walter Murch, combining the crafts of **editing** and **mixing** and, like them, involving both theoretical and practical issues. In essence, sound design represents advocacy for movie sound (to counter some people's tendency to favor the movie image).

sound effect A sound artificially created for the **sound track** that has a definite function in telling the **story**.

soundstage A windowless, soundproofed, professional **shooting** environment that is usually several stories high and can cover an acre or more of floor space.

sound track A separate recording tape occupied by one specific type of sound recorded for a movie (one track for vocals, one for **sound effects**, one for music, etc.).

source light See **key light**.

special effects (**SPFX, FX**) Technology for creating images that would be too dangerous, too expensive, or, in some cases, simply impossible to achieve with traditional cinematographic materials. The goal of special-effects **cinematography** is generally to create **verisimilitude** within the imaginative world of even the most fanciful movie.

SPFX See **special effects**.

splicing See **cutting**.

split screen A method, created either in the camera or during the **editing** process, of telling two **stories** at the same time by dividing the screen into different parts. Unlike **parallel editing**, which **cuts** back and forth between **shots** for contrast, the split screen can tell multiple stories within the same **frame**.

sprocketed rollers Devices that control the speed of unexposed film as it moves through the camera, printer, or projector.

staging See **mise-en-scène**.

stand-in An actor who looks reasonably like a particular **movie star** (or at least an actor playing a **major role**) in height, weight, coloring, and so on, and who substitutes for that actor during the tedious process of preparing **setups** or taking light readings.

Stanislavsky system A system of acting, developed by Russian theater **director** Konstantin Stanislavsky in the late nineteenth century, that encourages students to strive for **realism**, both social and psychological, and to bring their past experiences and emotions to their roles. This system influenced the development of **method acting** in the United States.

Steadicam A camera suspended from an articulated arm that is attached to a vest strapped to the camera-person's body, permitting the operator to remain steady during "handheld" shots. The Steadicam removes jumpiness and is now often used for smooth, fast, and intimate camera movement.

stock See **film stock**.

stop-frame See **freeze-frame**.

story In a movie, all the events we see or hear on the screen, and all the events that are implicit or that we infer to have happened but that are not explicitly presented. Compare **diegesis**, **narrative**, and **plot**.

storyboard A **scene**-by-scene (sometimes **shot**-by-shot) breakdown that combines sketches or photographs of how each shot is to look and written descriptions of the other elements that are to go with each shot, including **dialogue**, sound, and music.

story conference One of any number of sessions during which the **treatment** is discussed, developed, and transformed from an outline into a **rough-draft screenplay**.

story duration The amount of time that the implied **story** takes to occur. Compare **plot duration** and **screen duration**.

stream of consciousness A literary style that gained prominence in the 1920s in the hands of such writers as Marcel Proust, Virginia Woolf, James Joyce, and Dorothy Richardson and that attempted to capture the unedited flow of experience through the mind.

stretch relationship A time relationship in which **screen duration** is longer than **plot duration**. Compare **real time** and **summary relationship**.

stuntperson A performer who doubles for another actor in **scenes** requiring special skills or involving hazardous actions, such as crashing cars, jumping from high places, swimming, or riding (or falling off of) horses.

summary relationship A time relationship in which **screen duration** is shorter than **plot duration**. Compare **real time** and **stretch relationship**.

supporting role See **minor role**.

surprise A taking unawares that is potentially shocking. Compare **suspense**.

suspense The anxiety brought on by partial uncertainty: the end is certain, but the means are not. Compare **surprise**.

synopsis See **treatment**.

T

take   An indication of the number of times a particular **shot** is taken (e.g., shot 14, take 7).

take-up spool   A device that winds the film inside the movie camera after it has been exposed.

telephoto lens   See **long-focal-length lens**.

texture   As related to sound, see **quality**.

theme   A shared, public idea, such as a metaphor, an adage, a myth, or a familiar conflict or personality type.

three-point system   Perhaps the best-known lighting convention in feature filmmaking, a system that employs three sources of light—**key light**, **fill light**, and **backlight**—each aimed from a different direction and position in relation to the subject.

tilt shot   The vertical movement of a camera mounted on the gyroscopic head of a stationary tripod. Like the **pan shot**, the tilt shot is a simple movement with dynamic possibilities for creating meaning.

timbre   See **quality**.

tracking shot   See **dolly shot**.

traveling shot   See **dolly shot**.

treatment   Also known as *synopsis*. An outline of the action that briefly describes the essential ideas and structure for a film.

two-shot   A **shot** in which two **characters** appear; ordinarily a **medium shot** or **medium long shot**.

typecasting   The **casting** of actors because of their looks or "type" rather than for their acting talent or experience.

V

variable-focal-length lens   See **zoom lens**.

verisimilitude   A convincing appearance of truth; movies are verisimilar when they convince you that the things on the screen—people, places, and so on, no matter how fantastic or **antirealistic**—are "really there."

video assist camera   A tiny device, mounted in the viewing system of the film camera, that enables a **script supervisor** to view a **scene** on a video monitor (and thus compare its details with those of surrounding scenes, to ensure visual continuity) before the film is sent to the laboratory for **processing**.

viewfinder   On a camera, the little window that the cameraperson looks through when taking a picture; the viewfinder's frame indicates the boundaries of the camera's **point of view**.

voice-over narration   **Narration** heard concurrently and over a **scene** but not synchronized to any **character** who may be talking on the screen. It can come from many sources, including an objective **narrator** (who is not a character) bringing us up-to-date, a first-person narrator commenting on the action, or, in a **nonfiction film**, a commentator. Compare **first-person narration**.

W

walk-on   A role even smaller than a **cameo**, reserved for a highly recognizable actor or personality.

wardrobe   See **costumes**.

wide-angle lens   See **short-focal-length lens**.

wipe   A transitional device between **shots** in which shot B wipes across shot A, either vertically or horizontally, to replace it. Although (or because) the device reminds us of early eras in filmmaking, **directors** continue to use it.

X

XCU   See **extreme close-up**.

XLS   See **extreme long shot**.

Z

zoom-in   A **shot** in which the image is magnified by movement of the camera's **lens** only, without the camera itself moving. This magnification is the essential difference between the zoom-in and the **dolly-in**.

zoom lens   Also known as *variable-focal-length lens*. A **lens** that is moved toward and away from the subject being photographed, has a continuously variable **focal length**, and helps **reframe** a **shot** within the **take**. A zoom lens permits the **camera operator** during **shooting** to shift between wide-angle and telephoto lenses without changing the focus or **aperture** settings. Compare **long-focal-length lens**, **middle-focal-length lens**, and **short-focal-length lens**. See also **prime lens**.

zoopraxiscope   An early device for exhibiting moving pictures—a revolving disk with photographs arranged around the center.

Permissions Acknowledgments

Chapter One

Still from Victor Fleming's *The Wizard of Oz*. Courtesy of Photofest.

Praxiteles's Hermes with infant Dionysos on his arm. The Archeological Museum, Olympia, Greece. Photo © Erich Lessing/ Art Resource, NY.

Alberto Giacometti's Walking Man. Photo © The Burnstein Collection/Corbis.

Keith Haring's Self Portrait 1989. In the outdoor exhibition L'Homme qui Marche at the Gardens of Le Palais Royal, Paris, March 23–June 18, 2000. Photo © Bernard Annebicque/Corbis.

A staging of Shakespeare's *Henry V*. Courtesy of the Alabama Shakespeare Festival, Montgomery, Alabama.

Edward Muybridge's horses. Photo © Corbis.

Thomas Edison's Black Maria. Courtesy of the Museum of Modern Art/Film Stills Archive, New York.

Interior view of Thomas Edison's Black Maria. Courtesy of the Museum of Modern Art/Film Stills Archive, New York.

Standard motion picture film gauges. Filmstrips courtesy of Photofest.

The Hon. Frances Duncombe by Thomas Gainsborough. © Geoffrey Clements/Corbis.

Marcel Duchamp's *Nude Descending a Staircase, No. 2*. Courtesy of the Philadelphia Museum of Art; The Louise and Walter Arensberg Collection.

Still from the Lumiére brothers' *Workers Leaving the Lumière factory*. Courtesy of the Museum of Modern Art/Film Stills Archive, New York.

Still from Georges Méliès's *A Trip to the Moon*. Courtesy of the Museum of Modern Art/Film Stills Archive, New York.

Still from Robert Flaherty's *Nanook of the North*. Courtesy of the Museum of Modern Art/Film Stills Archive, New York.

Still from Leni Riefenstahl's *Triumph of the Will*. Courtesy of the Museum of Modern Art/Film Stills Archive, New York.

Stills from Fernand Léger's *Ballet Mecanique*. Courtesy of the Museum of Modern Art/Film Stills Archive, New York.

Chapter Two

Still from Joe Wright's *Pride and Prejudice*. Courtesy of Photofest.

Storyboard from Alfred Hitchcock's *The Birds*. Courtesy of Photofest.

Posters for Robert Z. Leonard's *The Divorcee* and Howard Hawk's *Scarface*. Courtesy of Photofest.

Still from David Lean's *Great Expectations*. Courtesy of the Museum of Modern Art/Film Stills Archive, New York.

Chapter Three

Still from Peter Weir's *Master and Commander*. Courtesy of Photofest.

Still from W.S. Van Dyke's *Marie Antoinette*. Courtesy of the Museum of Modern Art/Film Stills Archive, New York.

Still from Robert Wiene's *The Cabinet of Dr. Caligari*. Courtesy of the Museum of Modern Art/Film Stills Archive, New York.

Still from Vittorio De Sica's *Bicycle Thieves*. Courtesy of the Museum of Modern Art/Film Stills Archive, New York.

Still from Yasujiro Ozu's *Late Spring*. Courtesy of the Museum of Modern Art/Film Stills Archive, New York.

Chapter Four

Still from Bernardo Bertolucci's *The Last Emperor*. Courtesy of Photofest.

Tracking shot for Victor Fleming's *Gone With the Wind*. Courtesy of Photofest.

Steadicam used on the set of James Cameron's *Titanic*. Courtesy of Photofest.

Still from Fritz Lang's *Metropolis*. Courtesy of the Museum of Modern Art/Film Stills Archive, New York.

Chapter Five

Still from Clint Eastwood's *Million Dollar Baby*. Courtesy of Photofest.

Photo of cinematographer Lee Grames and producer William Goetz on the set of Alexander

Korda's *Lilies of the Field*. Courtesy of the Museum of Modern Art/Film Stills Archive, New York.

Chapter Six

Still from Christopher Nolan's *Memento*. Courtesy of Photofest.

Chapter Seven

Still from Taylor Hackford's *Ray*. Courtesy of Photofest.

Still from Laurence Olivier's *Hamlet*. Courtesy of the Museum of Modern Art/Film Stills Archive, New York.

Stills from Alfred Hitchcock's *The 39 Steps*. Courtesy of the Museum of Modern Art/Film Stills Archive, New York.

Chapter Eight

Still from Curtis Hanson's *Wonder Boys*. Courtesy of Photofest.

Frame Illustrations by Chapter

Chapter One

Heist, © 2001 Warner Bros. Pictures; *Black Hawk Down*, © 2001 Sony Pictures Entertainment; *Bonnie and Clyde*, © 1967 Warner Bros. Pictures; *Silence of the Lambs*, © 1991 Orion Pictures Corporation; *Battleship Potemkin*, © 1925 Goskino; *Gold Rush*, © 1925 Charles Chaplin Productions; *The Grapes of Wrath*, © 1940 20th Century Fox; Donnie Darko, © 2001 Pandora Cinema and Newmarket Films; *Kill Bill*, © 2003 Miramax Films; *Kinsey*, © 2004 American Zoetrope and Fox Searchlight Pictures; *There's Something About Mary*, © 1998 20th Century Fox; The Warriors, © 1979 Paramount Pictures; *Far From Heaven*, © 2002 Focus Features; *LA Confidential*, © 1997 Warner Bros. Pictures; *Kissing Jessica Stein*, © 2001 20th Century Fox; *The Thin

Red Line, © 1998 20th Century Fox; *Red River*, © 1948 United Artists; *The Fog of War*, © 2003 Sony Pictures Classics; *Super Size Me*, © 2004 The Con.

Chapter Two

Frances, © 1982 Universal Pictures; Aguirre: *Wrath of God*, © 1972 Werner Herzog Filmproduktion; *Casablanca*, © 1942 Warner Bros. Pictures; *Memento*, © 2000 Newmarket Films; *Gladiator*, © 2000 Dreamworks Pictures and Universal Studios; *Raging Bull*, © 1980 United Artists; *Time Code*, © 2000 Red Mullet Productions; *The Crying Game*, © 1992 Miramax Films; *Lost in Translation*, © 2003 American Zoetrope and Focus Features; *Fellowship of the Ring*, © 2001 NewLine Cinema; *Breaking the Waves*, © 1996 Zentropa Entertainments, Canal +, and Pandora Film; *Blue Velvet*, © 1986 DeLaurentiis Entertainment Group; *Blade Runner*, © 1982 Warner Bros. Pictures; *The Last Emperor*, © 1987 Columbia Pictures; *Clueless*, © 1995 Paramount Pictures Inc; *Fight Club*, © 1999 20th Century Fox; *Stagecoach*, © 1939 Walter Wanger Productions, Inc., and United Artists.

Chapter Three

Moulin Rouge, © 2001 20th Century Fox; *Leopard*, © 1963 20th Century Fox; *Eyes Wide Shut*, © 1999 Warner Bros. Pictures; *Portrait of a Lady*, © 1996 Gramercy Pictures; *Gosford Park*, © 2001 USA Films Inc.; *Cabiria*, © 1957 Paramount Pictures and Rialto Pictures, Inc; City of God, © 2002 Miramax Films; *Hoffa*, © 1992 20th Century Fox; *Wolf*, © 1994 Columbia Pictures Corp.; *Something's Gotta Give*, © 2003 Columbia Pictures Corp., and Warner Bros Pictures.; *Edward Scissorhands*, © 1990 20th Century Fox; *The Elephant Man*, © 1980 Brooksfilms Ltd. and Paramount Pictures; *Batman*, © 1989 Warner Bros. Pictures; *The Court Jester*, © 1956 Paramount Pictures; *The Last Laugh*, © 1924 Universum Film A. G. (UFA); *The Third Man*, © 1949 British Lion Film Corporation; *The Best Years of Our Lives*, © 1946 Samuel Goldwyn Company; *China-*

town, © 1974 Paramount Pictures; *Cast Away*, © 2000 20th Century Fox and DreamWorks SKG; *Crouching Tiger, Hidden Dragon*, © 2000 Sony Pictures Classics; *Royal Wedding*, © 1958 Metro-Goldwyn-Mayer; *Forrest Gump*, © 1994 Paramount Pictures; *Sleepy Hollow*, © 1999 Paramount Pictures; *American Beauty*, © 1999 DreamWorks SKG; *Hamlet*, © 1948 Universal Pictures.

Chapter Four

The Last Emperor, © 1987 Columbia Pictures; *The Searchers*, © 1956 Warner Bros. Pictures; *High Noon*, © 1952 United Artists; *The Sweet Smell of Success*, © 1957 United Artists; *Gone with the Wind*, © 1939 Metro-Goldwyn-Mayer; *Barry Lyndon*, © 1975 Warner Bros. Pictures; *Juliet of the Spirits*, © 1965 Rizzoli Film S.P.A.; *My Darling Clementine*, © 1946 20th Century Fox; *Some Like it Hot*, © 1959 United Artists; *Titanic*, © 1997 Paramount Pictures and 20th Century Fox; *Manhattan*, © 1979 United Artists; *The Scarlet Empress*, © 1934 Paramount Pictures; *THX 1138*, © 1970 Warner Bros.; *Bride of Frankenstein*, © 1935 Universal Pictures; *The Godfather*, © 1972 Paramount Pictures; *T-Men*, © 1947 Eagle-Lion Films; *Dogville*, © 2003 Zentropa Entertainments and Lions Gate Films; *Dr. Strangelove*, © 1963 Columbia Pictures; *Sunset Boulevard*, © 1950, Paramount Pictures; *Boyz N the Hood*, © 1990 Columbia Pictures; Philadelphia, © 1993 TriStar Pictures; *The Graduate*, © 1967 Embassy Pictures Corporation; *The Great Dictator*, © 1940 Charles Chaplin Productions and United Artists; *Singin' in the Rain*, © 1952 Metro-Goldwyn-Mayer; *Taxi Driver*, © 1976 Columbia Pictures; The Quiet Man, © 1952 Republic Pictures Corporation; *Love Me Tonight*, © 1932 Paramount Pictures; *Elephant*, © 2003 Home Box Office Inc.; *Jules et Jim*, © 1962 Les Films du Carosse, SEDIF; *Gold Diggers of 1933*, © 1933 Warner Bros. Pictures; *Applause*, © 1930 Paramount Pictures; *Trouble in Paradise*, © 1932 Paramount Pictures; *Notorious*, © 1946 RKO Radio Pictures, Inc.; *The Little Foxes*, © 1941 Samuel Goldwyn Company and RKO Radio

Chapter Five

Chapter Six

Chapter Seven

Index

Page numbers in *italics* refer to illustrations and captions; those in **boldface** refer to main discussions of topics.

mechanical, in-camera, and laboratory effects, **188–89**
mediation, 14, 25
medium long shot, 163
medium shot, 162–63, *163*
Meek, Donald, *80*, 81
Meet John Doe (Capra), 37
Meet the Fockers (Roach), 288, 368
Meirelles, Fernando, 101, *102*, 252
Méliès, Georges, 25, *27*, 31, 42, 108, 146, 189
melodrama genre, 32, *33*
Memento (Nolan), 34, 64, 65, *65*, 237, 243
Mendes, Sam, 6, 103, 123, 127–32, 304
Menjou, Adolphe, 228
Menke, Sally, 243, 269
Menzel, Adolf von, 147
Menzies, William Cameron, 34, 97*n*, 105, 111
Mercanton, Louis, 201, *202*
Mercer, David, 285
Merry Widow (Stroheim), 146
Mescall, John, 152, *174*
Meshes of the Afternoon (Deren), 47
Messmer, Otto, 42
method acting, 200, **208–10**, *209*
Metro-Goldwyn-Mayer, *see* MGM
Metropolis (Lang), 109, 189, *189*, **333–34**, *333*
Metty, Russell, *169*, 180
Metz, Christian, 317
Meyer, Emile, *150*
Meyers, Nancy, 103, *103*
MGM (Metro-Goldwyn-Mayer), 97*n*, *105*, 153, 207, *207*, 350, 352, 354–55, 357, 365*n*
Micheaux, Oscar, 215
Mickey Mouse, 42
middle-focal-length lens, 156, *156*
Midler, Bette, *232*
Midnight Cowboy (Schlesinger), *282*
Mifune, Toshiro, 215, 223, 229, *229*
Mighty Joe Young (Schoedsack), 43
Mildred Pierce (Curtiz), 93, *207*, 208
Milestone, Lewis, 35, 169, *170*, 338
Milky Way, The (Buñuel), 47
Millan, Victor, 180
Miller, Arthur, 11*n*
Miller, Bennett, 230, 365
Miller, David, 208
Miller, Frank, 72, 306, 370
Miller, Henry, 284
Miller, Michael R., *242*, 259
Million Dollar Baby (Eastwood), *195*, 217, 231, **233–35**, *234*

Mills, Charles, *157*
Mills, John, *63*
Milner, Victor, *163*, *166*, 169, 171
Milton, Franklin, 282
mimesis and catharsis, **321–22**
   in *Die Hard*, **328–29**
Minghella, Anthony, 21, 105
Minnelli, Vincente, 33, 354
minor characters, 72, 74, 84–85
Minority Report (Spielberg), 359
minor roles, 217, *217*
Miramax, 363, 365*n*
Mirren, Helen, *99*
Mirrione, Stephen, 243
mise-en-scène, **92–137**, *93*, *94*, 223
   audio/sound, 278, 307, *307*
   composition and, 92, **113–22**, *114*
   costume, makeup, and hairstyle and, mise-en-scène, design and, 92, **96–113**
   defined, **92–137**, *93*, *94*, 95
   framing and, **113–19**, *116*, *118*, *119*
   kinesis and, **120–22**, *121*
   Miss Congeniality 2: Armed and Fabulous (Pasquin), 62
   movement of figures and, **121–22**, *122*
   production designer and, **96–97**
   staging as, 92, 95
Mission, The (Joffé), 290
Mitchell, John, 284
Mitchell, Thomas, *80*, 81
Mitchum, Robert, 101, 160, *161*, *261*, 298, 304
mixing sound, **278**
Miyazaki, Hayao, 44–45, *44*, 277
Mizoguchi, Kenji, 96, 111, 188
Mizrahi, Isaac, 199
Modern Times (Chaplin), 162
Moggach, Deborah, 53
"moguls," 350
Molina, Alfred, 215
Monogram Productions, 353
monologue, interior, 284
Monroe, Marilyn, *149*, 354
Monster (Jenkins), 73, 198
Monster-in-Law (Luketic), *213*
Monster's Ball (Forster), *215*
montage:
   sound, 302
   visual, 67, **245–47**, *246*
Montalban, Ricardo, 215
Móntez, Maria, 215
Moody, Rick, 113
Moore, Julianne, *33*, 93, *93*, 211, 292
Moore, Michael, 38, 39, 41

Moorehead, Agnes, 224–26, *224*
Moreau, Jeanne, *164*, 165
Moreno, Rita, 215
Morgan, Helen, 205
Morgan, Ira H., 162
Morgan, Lois, *232*
Moriarty, Cathy, 69, 186
Moritz, David, 245
Morocco (Sternberg), 227, *227*
Morosco, Walter, *205*
Morricone, Ennio, *275*, 288, 299
Morris, Errol, 38, 39, *40*
Morris, Michael, *106*
Morrison, Phil, 21, 120
Morrissey, Paul, 269
Moscow Art Theater, 208, 209
Mothersbaugh, Mark, 288
Mother's Day (Broughton), 48
Motion Picture Association of America (MPAA), 58, 364, *364*
motion picture film, 19
Motion Picture Patents Company, 350
motion picture photography, **18–22**, *20*
Motion Picture Production Code, 58
motivation, character, 74, *75*
Motorcycle Diaries, The (Salles), 77
Moulin Rouge! (Luhrmann), 33, 93, *94*
movement:
   blocking and, 121
   bullet time and, 24
   of figures, **121–22**, *122*
   illusion in movies of, **22–23**, *24*
moves, experimental, **45–48**, *45*, *46*
movie rating system, *364*
movies, **1–51**
   animated films as, **42–45**, *43*, *44*
   apparent motion in, 23
   attendance, 365
   cinematic language in, **27–29**
   cost to produce, 345
   as dependent on light, **14–21**, *16*
   development of photography in, **16–18**
   film form principles in, **11–23**
   form and content in, **2–6**
   form and expectations in, **6–7**
   genre in, **29–42**
   illusion of movement in, **22–23**, *24*
   illusion of succession in, 23
   labor and unions and, 346, **355**
   the making of, **347–50**
   meaning and, 316, **318–20**
   as motion picture photography, **18–22**
   movement in, *24*
   narrative in, 6, 21, **29–38**, **53–89**